# POPULATION

# POPULATION

## SECOND EDITION

# BY WILLIAM PETERSEN

ROBERT LAZARUS PROFESSOR OF SOCIAL DEMOGRAPHY

THE OHIO STATE UNIVERSITY

## THE MACMILLAN COMPANY
## COLLIER-MACMILLAN LIMITED, LONDON

Library of Congress catalog card number: 69–10542

THE MACMILLAN COMPANY
COLLIER-MACMILLAN CANADA, LTD., TORONTO, ONTARIO

Printed in the United States of America

# PREFACE TO
# THE SECOND
# EDITION

This edition, like the first one, is intended mainly for undergraduate sociology courses. Most students who enroll in a first course in demography see it as part of their liberal education, and this work stresses the links between population phenomena and their sociological, economic, historical, and biological contexts. The book is not an almanac: many up-to-date figures are given but primarily to illustrate theses with numerical examples. Nor is it a professional manual; the tools of the discipline are taught not to train the technician but to inform the layman or beginner. For although population data are generally the most accurate and complete of any in the social sciences, they are also far less so than is generally supposed; a person totally ignorant of how a census is taken, for example, or of the effect of age structure on crime rates, is bound to misunderstand much in the world around him.

Any author of a book in sociology with some pretense to generality faces a dilemma. To write, without close attention to culture-bound specifics, about other social systems, markets, family structures, and so on could easily become an exercise in half-disguised ethnocentrism. But to analyze in full even some of the social-cultural data relevant to so broad a subject as population could swamp the reader in minutiae. A compromise is difficult to realize, especially so in a volume that assumes no prior knowledge of the field. Whether I have succeeded in maintaining a balance between broad theory and topical exemplification, using each to reinforce the other, the reader will judge better than I; but it may help to elucidate how I have tried to resolve this dilemma.

The book is divided into two parts, the first on the general determinants of population processes and the second on how these operate in primitive, preindustrial, and modern societies. To some degree, the division is thus between the two main theories generally used to analyze population trends, the culture-free Malthusian opposition between people and resources and, on the other hand, the culture-bound theory of the demographic transition. Compared with the first edition, this one includes far more on the main non-Western nations, especially India, China, and Latin America; and somewhat more on industrial countries other than the United States. In line with the great activity of demographers over the past decade, the analysis of all basic topics has been extended to include works published up through late 1968. To balance this expansion, some contraction was required, and I have cut large sections of parochial or even personal interest (such as the chapter on how immigration restrictions came to be imposed in the United States) whenever they seemed to lack wider relevance.

I received welcome help from a number of persons during the extended period I spent in rewriting the book. The Macmillan Company distributed a questionnaire about the first edition to professors who teach demography, many of whom were kind enough to respond (sometimes anonymously) with detailed comments. Some of their suggestions were most valuable; in other instances, the features of the first edition that some found to be, for example, a digression, others especially commended. There was no consensus, as another example, on whether to develop the book from the specific to the general (as in the first edition) or from the general to the specific (as in this one). I decided on this change nevertheless partly because reordering the chapters made necessary the basic and complete revision that I wanted to effect.

In the preface to the first edition I listed a number of colleagues and specialists who had read portions of that manuscript. Their collective wisdom has, I hope, been retained in this revision, and I renew my appreciation of their assistance. Portions of the new manuscript were reviewed by Judith Blake, of the University of California at Berkeley; Ashley Montagu, of Princeton; and Brewton Berry, of Ohio State University. Comments on the entire book were given me by David Heer, of Harvard University; Frits Kool, of the *International Review of Social History*, Amsterdam; and John D. Moore, at that time an editor at The Macmillan Company. I thank all most gratefully.

WILLIAM PETERSEN

*Columbus, Ohio*

# PREFACE TO THE FIRST EDITION

During the several years that I have worked on this book, I have submitted drafts of chapters for criticism to a number of colleagues and specialists. This was particularly important since some sections of the manuscript presume a greater competence in history, anthropology, and economics than I, as a sociologist and demographer, can pretend to from my own background. Those from whom I requested assistance responded with detailed and often extremely helpful comments. While they cannot of course be held responsible for the final product, they did help to improve it considerably. I offer my sincere appreciation to the following, listed in noninvidious alphabetical order:

Reinhard Bendix, Department of Sociology, University of California, Berkeley

William S. Bernard, Co-Director, American Council for Nationalities Service, New York

Otis Dudley Duncan, Department of Sociology, University of Chicago

Ronald Freedman, Department of Sociology, University of Michigan

D. V. Glass, London School of Economics and Political Science

Gregory Grossman, Department of Economics, University of California, Berkeley

Philip M. Hauser, Department of Sociology, University of Chicago

Gordon Hewes, Department of Anthropology, University of Colorado

John T. Krause, Department of History, Ohio State University

David S. Landes, Departments of Economics and History, University of California, Berkeley

Josiah Cox Russell, Department of History, University of New Mexico

Neil J. Smelser, Department of Sociology, University of California, Berkeley

Mortimer Spiegelman, Associate Statistician, Metropolitan Life Insurance Company, New York

P. K. Whelpton, Scripps Foundation for Research in Population Problems, Oxford, Ohio.

I would like to thank especially three fellow demographers—

Robert Gutman, Department of Sociology, Rutgers University

Kurt B. Mayer, Department of Sociology, Brown University

Vincent H. Whitney, then associated with the Population Council, New York.

They were kind enough to read the whole of an earlier draft carefully, sympathetically, and critically, and to give me both guidance and encouragement.

W. P.

*Berkeley, Calif.*

# CONTENTS

### PART I  THE UNIVERSAL ELEMENTS OF POPULATION ANALYSIS

ix

PART II    FACTORS IN THE POPULATION OF
VARIOUS TYPES OF SOCIETY

# 1 POPULATION AS A FIELD OF STUDY

Demography, or the systematic analysis of population phenomena, denotes a subject matter that impinges on our everyday life in a variety of ways, but that most persons are ill equipped to understand. We read that in underdeveloped areas the increase in numbers is outstripping the food supply; is this a correct appraisal, and are there means available to cope with the problem? We are told that "the marriage rate" has gone up; what is a marriage rate, and how adequate a measure is it of the formation of new families? The United States is becoming increasingly "urban"; what size of population is defined as an urban settlement, and what difference does living in towns make in the way that people behave? Our insurance broker informs us that the cost of insuring our life is not the same as it would have been a year before; what is a "life table," which gives the probability that a person of one or another age will die during the next year? The decision of our church to erect a new building across town from our home was based on an expert's prognosis that the population of that presently barren area would grow very fast and would moreover include a large proportion of the social class from which our church membership is drawn; how accurate are such forecasts likely to be?

The first reason, then, for studying demography is to attain an appreciably better understanding of the world in which we live. Just as a person who spends much of his life putting electric plugs into sockets might do well to know something about electricity though he will never become a physicist, an electrician, or even a do-it-yourself repairman, so an educated person also ought to be aware of the fundaments of his own culture. This one essential part of a liberal education can conveniently be attained by focusing one's attention on what are very aptly termed the vital processes.

Supplementing this most general reason for studying population is a second, more specific one that applies to those particularly interested in the analysis of society. One cannot put a society under a microscope; one cannot take an institution into a laboratory; one cannot photograph a social class. Some of the important techniques that have made possible the rapid advance in physical and natural sciences [1] are largely ruled out of sociology, and many of the central issues in methodology relate to the dilemmas that this contrast poses. How is it possible to structure social data so that the analyst can try to use the same procedures as other sciences; or, in a more specific version of this question, how can one quantify social findings without falsifying them?

In demography this dilemma is not so persistent a problem. Its data, unlike most that the sociologist analyzes, are assembled by the government, and at least in the Western world this means that they constitute the most complete and the longest series available on almost any subject. It also means that the collection of the data has the authority of the state behind it; and, although no questionnaire is ever answered completely accurately by all respondents, where vital statistics and the census have been in existence for a long time and have thus attained an almost automatic acceptance, this established legitimacy is as good a guarantee of reliability as one can hope for. Moreover, these excellent data pertain to the most significant happenings—literally life-and-death—and to events that often constitute natural units. It is not necessary to convert births or deaths into a form amenable to mathematical analysis; one begins by counting them and proceeds by comparing the fertility or mortality of various sectors of the population. On the other hand the difficulties encountered in classifying a population by social class, urban-rural residence, or ethnic group are much closer to the usual methodological problems in the social sciences. There is no single entity that defines itself, as it were, to be "middle class," or a "city," or even "American Indians." Because all definitions of such

---

[1] This statement does not imply that we in the social disciplines should accept a naive view of how natural sciences advance. For a fascinating analysis specifically aimed at positivist sociologists, see Thomas S. Kuhn, "The Function of Measurement in Modern Physical Science," in *Quantification: A History of the Meaning of Measurement in the Natural and Social Sciences*, edited by Harry Woolf, Bobbs-Merrill, New York, 1961, pp. 31–63.

categories are somewhat arbitrary, an analysis based on them varies according to how each is delimited. A beginning student in the field must thus learn to take full advantage of the unique quality of basic demographic data and to avoid a facile acceptance of any classificatory principle.

Demography, essentially a social science, in some respects borders on disciplines as diverse as biology, mathematics, and ethics. In order to demarcate this area of study, therefore, we must note its boundaries along several dimensions, and in doing so we will also indicate more fully than in the table of contents how the theme of the book is developed.

## Formal Demography vs. Population Analysis

Population growth can be analyzed with three different models:

**1.** It is a self-contained process; for example, a high (or low) fertility tends to generate an age structure with a large (or small) proportion of potential parents in the following generation.

**2.** Such self-propelled population processes, however, are controlled in their rate and especially in their ultimate limit by such other factors as natural resources, economic growth, social mobility, and family norms, all of which can be taken as independent variables that together determine the population.

**3.** On the other hand, population growth acts also as an independent variable, as a cause of change in the economy or in society—for instance, as a stimulus to business activity or as an impediment to development.

There is an important difference between the first model and the other two. Population growth as a self-contained process can be analyzed apart from the muddying influences of its social context and thus with greater precision and depth. The analysis of population trends in their total setting, on the other hand, involves every element of a culture or a social structure that may have a significant effect on population trends and, vice versa, every such element that may be influenced by a change in population size or composition. Thus, greater breadth is achieved by sacrificing narrow precision. It is convenient to label these two emphases in demography: **formal demography,** the gathering, collating, statistical analysis, and technical presentation of population data, and **population analysis,** the systematic study of population trends and phenomena in relation to their social setting. The distinction relates in part to training: Formal demography demands mathematical skills, sometimes of a high order; population analysis is tied to the data and concepts of sociology, economics, or another of the social disciplines. The differentiation exists also in the fields for which these two types of training prepare one. Most of the professional practitioners of formal demography are employees of government bureaus or insurance companies, and the pressure (indeed, sometimes resisted) from such official or commercial positions is to avoid broad interpretations of the figures they compile. On the other hand, social scientists who recognize the importance of population trends and therefore include them among the social, economic, and historical processes they study typically do this without first acquiring the skills of an actuary. There is a legitimate division of labor here but also the necessity for communication. For example, a census director must be able to judge which of several possible questions would ultimately yield the most significant results in subsequent analyses, and a sociologist must know something of how population data are collected and compiled if he is to use them well.

This introduction to demography, it is hoped, will of itself make each person who uses it into an intelligent consumer of population analysis. This ability demands a limited competence, but a rare one; for just as a person barely able to read accepts as gospel anything in print, so the average product of the American school system, only just literate in mathematics, tends to be insufficiently critical of any numerical datum. A large portion of this book—all of Chapter 2 and sections of other chapters—is designed to instill both discrimination and appreciation of demographic statistics and techniques, the ability to see them for what they are, neither more nor less. Technical details and demographic tools are discussed when they are deemed useful in the skillful *interpretation* of population trends. For instance, the full description of the life table in Chapter 7 is designed to teach the minimum function of this indispensable tool, but anyone who wants to understand the full range of uses that actuaries make of it must seek guidance from other works. Or, as another example, the analysis of forecasts in Chapter 17, although it does not equip the reader to calculate projections himself, should enable him to understand better the meaning and probable accuracy of those prepared by others. In short, some of the techniques that a student would learn in a more advanced course are passed over in order to lay heavier stress on the significance of such techniques in the various social disciplines.

## Biology vs. Culture

Man is born, he lives, and he dies. These are the natural dimensions of human life, as they are of all life. The immutable facts of birth and death designate man as part of nature, one animal species among the others. Like all other living things, man must meet certain physical needs to live, and he must reproduce his kind if the species is not to die out.

But while man is a part of the biological world, he is also set off from other species by a fundamental difference. The relation of all other living things to their physical environment is mainly passive. When it changes, they adapt to it principally at the ponderous rate of evolutionary change; once such an adaptation has been completed, the new body-form that has evolved may prove to be overspecialized, leading to a limited life-sphere or even to the extinction of the species, as of the great reptiles of an earlier geologic era. Man on the contrary takes a more active part than any other species in shaping his environment to suit his needs. Instead of growing hooves for walking, he has made shoes of animal hides or of synthetics that did not exist in nature; instead of talons for grasping, he has iron pliers. Instead of the specialized parts of the body evolved by other animals for certain narrow functions, man has developed tools. In contradistinction to all other living beings, mankind has a full culture.

Defining the boundary line between man as an animal and man as a member of a social group—that is to say, between the influence of biology and that of culture—has been a recurrent and vexatious problem in all of the social sciences. For example, psychologists who use the results of experiments on lower animals to increase our knowledge of "human nature" can be contrasted with social psychologists who study "personality" as it has developed in various specific cultural settings. Similarly, the sharpest split in anthropology, "the study of man and his works," has always been between the two terms of this definition, between the physical anthropologists who study man as an animal and the cultural or social anthropologists who study him in the context of his works. Analysts of population have also had to cope with this distinction. The birth and death of an individual are biological events, but they take place in a social milieu. Population processes are the consequence of both natural laws and cultural conditions, but where does one leave off and the other begin?

Consider, for example, nineteenth-century birth rates, which in one Western country after another underwent a long-term decline. The many analysts who attempted to explain this new trend can be divided into two broad schools—those who held that the *physiological* ability of women to bear children was being impaired by the urban-industrial way of life, and those who held that this new *cultural* setting was creating the desire for smaller families and the means to satisfy it. Decades passed before this dispute was settled to the satisfaction of all leading demographers.

The two elements of population phenomena, factors general to all of mankind and those specific to one type of society, are analyzed respectively in the two parts of this work. The contrast is not always sharp, particularly when, as in many instances in the book, general theses are exemplified with data drawn from one or another particular culture. Yet without such a distinction to structure our thinking we can hardly escape the most common failing of social scientists—confusing the characteristic features of *our own* society with the necessary components of *every* society. All humans irrespective of their specific cultural setting are born both as a consequence of sexual intercourse and also into a family, a social unit of adults that cares for and protects the helpless infant and trains the child, but the norms by which families are formed vary greatly. All humans are subject to death from the same general causes—lack of food, disease, injury, and old age, but the average expectation of life differs over a considerable range from one societal type to another. Men are distinguished from women both by physiology and by cultural roles, which differ according to sex in various societies. Any population larger than a primitive band of food-gatherers is structured into subpopulations according to some principle of internal classification, but how this differentiation is established depends very often on criteria specific to each culture.

Man's culture alters the biological balance with his environment. Land is reclaimed from the sea, in Holland (*Netherlands Information Service*), . . .

The framework in which universal factors are usually assembled is "the" Malthusian theory that populations everywhere tend to grow faster than the resources on which they subsist.[2] The thesis would be more aptly formulated if for the ambiguous term "tend" one substituted "have the potential." If any population were to breed up to its biological limit, it would indeed outpace its food supply. Sometimes this happens, and many die from starvation; sometimes, on the contrary, the level of fertility is kept well below the maximum possible. Which type of accommodation between

[2] The ascription of this point of view to Malthus is correct but incomplete. As we shall see, he anticipated both Darwin's theory of natural selection and the Dumont-Banks model of social mobility (see pp. 155–156), so that in an important sense he is the progenitor of both the Malthusian theory as this is popularly understood and of the theory of the demographic transition.

. . . and from the desert, in Israel (*Jerry Cooke*).

man and his habitat predominates varies from one societal type to another. Part II of this book traces this demographic transition, or, in other words, the cultural evolution of mankind as it pertains to population trends.

As the very words "cultural evolution," however, still constitute almost an invitation to misunderstanding, it is important to distinguish the classical definition of this term from what it is intended to convey here. Anthropology in the middle of the nineteenth century was passing from an emphasis on the collection of data to their systematization. Partly as a result of the intellectual furor aroused by Darwin's *Origin of Species*, partly as a parallel expression of the Zeitgeist of progress, this systematization usually took the form of a theory of cultural evolution. According to Edward B. Tylor, Lewis Henry Morgan, Herbert Spencer, and dozens of lesser figures, mankind evolved through a series of cultural stages, each one well defined by its technical culture, family type, social organization, religion, art, and so on. Morgan, for example, divided all of human history and prehistory into three main stages, which he termed Savagery, Barbarism, and Civilization (as we shall see, there is a partial parallel with the three stages of the demographic transition). The data he collated on peoples as widely separated as ancient Greeks and Romans, the natives of Australia and America, were structured largely in terms of the Iroquois, whom he knew by personal study. Thus, because the relatively advanced Polynesians lacked the bow and arrow, they were placed in the middle status of Savagery, or below the level of all North American tribes.[3] This example is typical of the most egregious error of the nineteenth-century evolutionary theorists—their assumption that the level of technology determined directly and without exception all other cultural and social forms. The family, thus, was postulated to have begun with indiscriminate mating in a food-gathering horde, developed through matriarchy to polygyny in agricultural societies, and reached its moral apex in the monogamy of industrial Europe. Today no Western anthropologist would support either the substance or the ethical overtones of this "history" of the family, and as more and better ethnographic data were collected from various parts of the world, it became clear that the evolutionary schema was no more adequate in many of its other details.

By the beginning of the twentieth century anthropologists were attacking the doctrine of cultural evolution itself. It was necessary to start fresh, to clean out all these fanciful theories and concentrate on building a solid empirical base. The most influential person in this movement, at least in the United States, was Franz Boas, who taught a whole generation of anthropologists and stamped them with his methodological and conceptual predilections.[4] Boas had important limitations, however, as well as great merit. The "Boas school," although performing a very necessary pruning

[3] For a convenient summary and commentary, see Robert H. Lowie, *The History of Ethnological Theory*, Rinehart, New York, 1937, Chapter 6.

[4] Representative statements on evolutionary theory include Franz Boas, *The Mind of Primitive Man*, Macmillan, New York, 1929, Chapter 7 and *passim;* Robert H. Lowie, *Primitive Society*, Liveright, New York, 1947; and Alexander A. Goldenweiser, *Early Civilization: An Introduction to Anthropology*, Knopf, New York, 1922. For a sympathetic appreciation of Boas, see Melville J. Herskovits, *Franz Boas: The Science of Man in the Making*, Scribner, New York, 1953.

job, ended by chopping at the very tree of the theory of culture change.

During the past several decades interest in the concept of cultural evolution has undergone a marked revival. The **unilinear** evolutionary scheme developed by Tylor, Morgan, and others was clearly wrong in many respects, but its essential outline is beyond question. The culture of the human species has indeed developed through a number of broad stages. No one doubts that hunting and gathering preceded the domestication of plants and animals, and that agriculture was a prerequisite to urban civilization wherever this developed. All of mankind, that is, has participated in **universal** evolution, but as a concept this is highly abstract and difficult to relate to actual cultures, rather than "culture." A third schema, **multilinear** evolution, is more empirical than deductive, and variation within societal types is no less emphasized than their general features.[5] By such an approach, an attempt is made to overcome the conceptual limitations both of unilinear evolutionists (culture stages relatively bare of empirical data) and of anti-evolutionists (a large number of ethnographic studies with no over-all theory in which their interrelations can be indicated).

Multilinear evolution is a theoretical framework especially appropriate to a work on population. Whether the art or the religion or the language of advanced civilizations is "higher" than that of primitives is a moot, if not indeed a meaningless, question. That there is an enormous difference in population, however, is indisputable; and with respect to this variable, apart from short-term fluctuations, the change has been all in one direction. Even to term this consistent increase "progress" is not ethnocentric, for the death control that has been attained by modern Western society, and to a lesser degree by other high civilizations, is a universal value.

## The Theory of the Demographic Transition

As we can see from the rate of increase in the human species over the whole of the time that man has inhabited the earth, our present era is a demographic anomaly. The first higher primates evolved from an apelike predecessor some 2 or 2.5 million years ago, and the first specimens of *Homo sapiens* appeared about 100,000 years ago. Whether we discuss the human genus, which includes such extinct varieties as Neanderthal man, or the human species in its present form, is of no importance here. In either case, we can postulate that the number started from a single pair and that it grew more or less steadily up to the date for which we have the earliest reliable estimate of the population of the world. That date is 1650, and at that time mankind totaled about 500 million. Three hundred years later, in 1950, the figure was more than 2,500 million, and in 1960 it was close

[5] See Julian H. Steward, *Theory of Culture Change: The Methodology of Multilinear Evolution,* University of Illinois Press, Urbana, 1955, Chapter 1.

to 3,000 million. In the year 2000, according to a United Nations estimate, the world's population will be between a "low" of 5,300 million and a "high" of 6,800 million. These figures, enormous though they are, are based on an assumption that the world's present fertility will decline somewhat, but if the birth rates of each age group remain constant the world at the end of the century will have 7,400 million people, growing at an accelerating rate (United Nations, 1966b).[6]

The significance of these data can be seen more easily in Figure 1-1. It must be emphasized that this is a *schematic* representation; what little

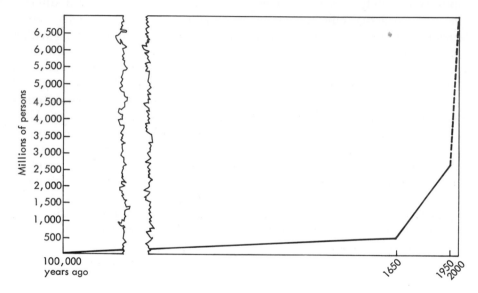

**Figure 1-1.** A schematic representation of the increase in numbers of the human species.

we know about the growth of particular areas before the modern era suggests an irregular alternation of periods of rapid increase with stagnation or decline. We have good reason to believe that the population of the world in 1650 was about 500 million and that it had never been larger than that at any earlier date, but there are no data to round out these statements. For well over 99 per cent of the time since the human species first evolved, it grew slowly, fitfully. Then, during the remaining fraction of one per cent, it increased fivefold, and the rate of increase is continuing to rise. In the physical sciences such a sudden acceleration is called an explosion, and demographers have adopted this metaphor to describe what is happening during our era—a population explosion.

[6] Abbreviated citations refer to the "Suggestions for Further Reading" appended to each chapter.

The reason that the population of the world is increasing at an unprecedentedly high rate to unprecedented totals is no mystery; mortality has fallen sharply, and fertility has not. As originally formulated a generation ago, this demographic transition was conceived as taking place in three broad stages: (1) preindustrial societies, with high fertility and mortality and a consequent low natural increase; (2) societies in transition, with continuing high fertility but declining mortality and a consequent rapid natural increase; and (3) modern societies, with both fertility and mortality stabilized at a low level and a consequent more or less static population.[7] Although some of its details have proved to be false and some of its implications misleading, in its simplest form the theory of the demographic transition is nevertheless one of the best documented generalizations in the social sciences. Duly amended and supplemented, it is one useful framework within which to organize an analysis of population.

The types of society that form the units of the demographic transition are not simple reflections of the real world, but rather what are termed "ideal" or "constructed" types. They are deliberate deviations from empirical reality, abstractions formed by accentuating those elements that are relevant to a particular research purpose. They are *ideal* types in the sense of being mental constructs, logical expedients, tools to be used in the analysis of the *real* world.

### PREINDUSTRIAL SOCIETIES

In this type are included all cultures with little or no contact with modern Western technology and science, i.e., all cultures before that great transformation that we call the Industrial Revolution as well as those contemporary nonindustrial societies that have not been significantly influenced by the West. Seemingly, this is a catch-all category, with subclasses as diverse as prehistoric peoples, contemporary primitives, and twenty of the twenty-one civilizations that Arnold Toynbee demarcated in his *Study of History*. But, however varied in other respects, these cultures are similar at least in those features that shape their populations. In all of them people live no more than thirty-five or forty years on the average, for as many, or almost as many, die in infancy and childhood as grow to maturity.

---

[7] Though it derives in part from earlier theories, of course, the hypothesis of the demographic transition was first specifically formulated in 1929 (Thompson, 1929). Its subsequent refinement to what can be termed its classic form took place over the following decade, when it was thought that the generally low fertility of Western countries would decline further still. Based on this perspective, the population of Western societies was seen as "stationary" (Thompson, 1948) or more typically as in "incipient decline" (Notestein, 1945 and 1950), only occasionally as "rationally balanced" (Reed, 1949). After the implications of the postwar "baby boom" were absorbed, the theory was criticized for this false prognosis concerning Western population trends (e.g., Hatt *et al.*, 1955; Van Nort and Karon, 1955).

Cultural values typically favor a high birth rate, without which the continuing existence of the society would be threatened.

In this book the population of preindustrial societies is analyzed in the two opening chapters of Part II, one on primitive societies and one on preindustrial civilizations.

### EARLY WESTERN SOCIETIES

The contrast between preindustrial and modern societies is one of the most familiar conceptual frameworks in sociology. It has become customary to use Ferdinand Tönnies's terms, **Gemeinschaft** and **Gesellschaft** (sometimes translated as Community and Society) to designate the two culture types not only as defined by him but also, more generally and approximately, as drawn by other social analysts. For, though the variety of terminology reflects some differences in meaning and especially in emphasis, there is also a large overlap among all of the pairs,[8] as well as with the dichotomies rural versus urban and developed versus underdeveloped in their most general senses.

In a population analysis perhaps the most pertinent element of the polarity is that discussed in detail by Max Weber in his contrast between traditionalist and rational. In his words, **traditionalism** is "the belief in the everyday routine as an inviolable norm of conduct." "Domination that rests upon this basis, that is, upon piety for what actually, allegedly, or presumably has always existed," he termed "traditionalist authority." A **rational** pattern, on the other hand, denotes "the methodical attainment of a definitely given and practical end by means of an increasingly precise calculation of adequate means," or, on an abstract level, the "increasing theoretical mastery of reality by means of increasingly precise and abstract concepts."[9] The rational sector of culture, in short, includes any area of social life in which a realizable end is consciously sought by nonmystical means.[10] The development of advanced civilizations from primitive societies has in large measure

---

[8] A list of only some of the most important examples in addition to Tönnies would include Henry Maine's society of status vs. society of contract, Max Weber's traditional vs. rational authority, Emile Durkheim's mechanical vs. organic solidarity, Robert Mac-Iver's culture vs. civilization, Howard Becker's sacred vs. secular society, Robert Redfield's folk vs. urban society, David Riesman's tradition-directed vs. other-directed character.

[9] Max Weber, *Essays in Sociology*, edited and translated by H. H. Gerth and C. Wright Mills, Oxford University Press, New York, 1946, pp. 296, 293.

[10] In Tylor's classical definition of culture—"that complex whole which includes knowledge, belief, art, morals, law, customs, and any other capabilities and habits acquired by man as a member of society"—even knowledge and capabilities, which can be taken as the rational elements, are often also in part nonrational. Belief, art, morals, custom, and habits are mainly nonrational in Weber's sense: these have functions but not purposes; they are not adaptations consciously contrived in order to meet definite needs. Edward B. Tylor, *Primitive Culture*, 6th Ed., Murray, London, 1920, 1, 1.

consisted in the extension of the area of rational action.[11] In the modern West in particular, the calculated choice between alternative acts on the basis of their probable consequences is a usual behavior pattern. In technology and commerce, two broad areas of life whose rational element is strong in many cultures, Western man has reached the ultimate point, scientific method and bookkeeping. And, what is more important in this context, rationality has spread from these to such other institutions as childbearing, which in other cultures are typically regulated mainly or exclusively by traditionalist norms.

Until a situation is seen in rational (i.e., instrumental) terms, no instrument is revelant, however effective it may be. The point can be illustrated by citing a health survey of an Iraqi village made by the inhabitants themselves. According to this self-estimate the state of health in the village was good: the incidence of many diseases was so high that they were not seen as abnormalities. All persons have two eyes, and most of them have trachoma; the difference was seen as one in degree, not in kind. Both two-eyedness and trachoma are part of "nature," and a person who knows this would not attempt either to create a third eye or to remove the inflammation from the two that are there. That such a community lacks scientific medicine is obvious, but this cannot be supplied in the portable form of Western know-how. For, as the villagers define their situation, there is no problem to be solved, no sickness to be cured.

This distinction between the efficiency of an instrument and its relevance pertains more often to the control of fertility than of mortality. To analyze the causes of the secular decline in Western birth rates, it is necessary to consider not only the instrument (the invention of effective contraceptives) and the social environment (the conversion of an agrarian civilization into an urban-industrial one), but also the shift in typical attitudes that made these other factors operative. Children were no longer seen as facts of nature, as gifts of God, but rather as the consequence of acts that could be regulated, within limits, in order to bring about families of a larger or a smaller size. Once childbearing came to be so defined, in rational rather than natural terms, other circumstances could vary without affecting the fertility trend decisively.

In this book the principal analysis of the population transition is presented in two chapters, one mainly historical and the other mainly theoretical. The first concerns England in the late eighteenth and early nineteenth centuries, the birthplace of modern industry and the earliest and

---

11 This is not meant to imply that there has been no change from more to less rational. In many preindustrial cultures marriages are arranged according to a careful reckoning of which potential mate would best serve family interests rather than by the more erratic dictates of romantic love, and a religious *quid pro quo* of so much sacrifice for so much benefit is less mystical than present-day Christianity.

perhaps most thoroughly studied example of population change during such a social transformation. The second chapter, concerning the cities of industrial and underdeveloped societies, poses the question whether urbanization, the prime medium of modernization, has been essentially the same in the Western nations that achieved industrialization in the past and those of Asia, Africa, and Latin America that are going through a somewhat similar process today.

When the theoretical reconstruction of history into three population types was first proposed, it was assumed that the demographic transition of the West would be followed in its essentials by the countries of the world currently undergoing industrialization. And indeed, one might ask, are not India and Egypt experiencing the same process that began in the English Midlands some two centuries ago? Is it not true that industrialism implies a high incidence of several important characteristics—not only nonagricultural employment but also, for instance, urban residence, literacy, and secularization—and that these will presumably also evolve in any developing society today? But the social change is so much faster than in the past, and the contrast between the traditional style of life and the one that is replacing it is so much sharper, that it is misleading to perceive the process today as merely a continuation of nineteenth-century Western history. In Europe some of the features of modern society unfolded over a period of centuries. For example, the most specific element of industrialism, the introduction of technical innovations, is in part an expression of scientific method, that is, of a way of perceiving and understanding the world that was already well advanced at the time of the grand synthesis in Isaac Newton's *Principia* (1687). Because today's underdeveloped countries lack this long preparation for modernization, any attempt to predict the non-Western future from the Western past, as in the first statement of the demographic transition, is likely to be quite unsuccessful.[12] Indeed, the shift in thinking from unilinear to multilinear evolution as a theoretical framework means precisely that to postulate a single type of transition, leading to a single type of modern society, is far too simplistic.

## MODERN WESTERN SOCIETIES

Analysis of the transitional type, designated as Early Western, is followed by one of populations in the modern Western world, that is, the countries

---

[12] A second focus of criticism of the transition theory (see footnote 7, p. 11) is on this weakness. Recent declines in the mortality of underdeveloped areas are so much faster than earlier in the West as to constitute, in effect, a new phenomenon (Taeuber, 1952; Davis, 1956). Nor is the analysis of the supposed transition in fertility much better (Ryder, 1957; Van Nort, 1956; Meier, 1958). Migration is ignored in the theory (Hillery, 1966), as well as any but the barest allusion to urbanization (Abu-Lughod, 1964). In some recent reformulations, an effort is made to give the essence of the theory while taking such criticisms into account (Cowgill, 1963; Davis, 1963).

of Western Europe and some of its principal overseas extensions. They are mostly industrial; or, if their economies are based on agriculture, like those of Denmark or New Zealand, it is a rationalized agronomy rather than traditional peasant practice. They are mostly democratic or, at least, lack the full development of a totalitarian state. Rational—in Weber's sense of the word—death control was followed, after a considerable interim, by rational birth control, so that as a goal if not yet in actuality, babies are born only to parents who want them, and persons die, at least in peacetime, only of old age or accidents. These populations naturally comprise a major element of any general work on demography, because the countries are important and because the data available are excellent.

### UNDERDEVELOPED SOCIETIES

The outline of Part II up to this point has both followed the essentials of the transition theory and noted the criticisms that various demographers have made of it. These criticisms can be summarized in the valid allegation that theory distorts reality by oversimplifying it. An appropriate response, therefore, is to acknowledge a greater complexity than in the earliest formulations. Instead of the one transitional type, we posit two: the historical past in the West and the present underdeveloped world.

Even to lump together countries as diverse as those in Latin America, Central Africa, the Near East, and Asia, passing over the great variety in historical and cultural background, is permissible only because of two overriding characteristics—the lack of modern industry and the endeavor to achieve parity with the Western nations. As the very designation "underdeveloped" suggests, today's nonindustrial societies take the "developed" countries as one of their standards. "Underdeveloped," like the analogous "underprivileged" as applied to individuals, implies an egalitarian norm; it includes both the fact of difference and the no less important fact that it is seen as unjust and remediable. It is generally not true of today's nonindustrial peoples, as it used to be true of their preindustrial partial counterparts, that most persons accept their lower level of life as their inevitable, immutable fate.

Whether the efforts to achieve parity with the industrial nations will succeed depends in part on the indigenous society and culture, but exactly what their influence is we do not know. Is it more relevant that India has an old and complex civilization, comparable in these respects with that of the West, or that one important element of this civilization is the pervasive caste system, which impedes any shift in the social structure? Modernization means a greater transformation in Negro Africa than in India; but as the traditional society there, just because of the lower cultural level, is weaker, is it not therefore perhaps less resistant to change? Can underdeveloped areas that have acquired a European language and religion, as in Latin America, be regarded as half-way toward full modernization? To all such questions we have no firm answers. Paradoxically, the more unprepared a country is, the more likely it is to be interested in rapid development; an area that has had least association with the West and thus perhaps the smallest benefit from its more efficient institutions may for that very reason be most strongly motivated to seek immediate and direct contact with industrial society. The relation then is in the form of a fantastic jump, with the most backward areas absorbing the most advanced elements of modern urban culture. Eskimos who have never seen a bicycle or automobile are quite familiar with airplanes. The potions of witch-doctors are replaced by the latest antibiotic. "It is quite common to see Papuans walking along jungle trails listening to transistor radios." [13] One of the largest steel plants in the world is in India. Countries like Russia and China, less developed economically and thus with a smaller proportion of industrial workers, have undergone the "proletarian" revolution that Marx predicted for the West. In short, the urban-industrial civilization, the most dynamic force in the world today, does not gradually seep into other societies but often splits their traditional forms asunder.

To analyze specifically the population trends that accompany modernization demands a certain simplification. But it is also true that population is a key question: the success of developmental programs depends on very many factors, but none is more crucial than whether the increased production leads to improved living or only to an increased number of persons existing at the same substandard level. Typically the measures to reduce mortality, introduced on a mass scale, resulted in precipitous falls in the death rates. But efforts to cut fertility, although partially successful in a few areas, have lagged far behind. The growth of numbers has been on a scale new in human history.

### TOTALITARIAN SOCIETIES

Just as it is useful to divide the transitional type into Early Western and Underdeveloped, so it adds considerably to our understanding if economically advanced societies are classified according to their style of government. In contrast to the laissez-faire West of the nineteenth century, states today intervene in various ways in trying to achieve demographic goals with respect to fertility (family subsidies, state birth-control or abortion centers); with respect to mortality (state support of medical and agricultural research, health insurance, genocide); with respect to migration (immigration or emigration restrictions or subsidies; forced migration). Simply to relate population to the natural resources and unplanned economy is no longer adequate.

[13] *The New York Times,* June 3, 1960.

This is particularly so in totalitarian societies, where the processes of fertility, mortality, and migration are significantly different from those typical in the West, because all institutions are essentially subordinated to the state and its ideological guide, the party. That such states constitute a different species of society is a commonplace among political scientists, but in most demographic analyses the differentiation is ignored. If totalitarian practices intrude too obviously on the demographers' consciousness, they sometimes define population phenomena so as to leave them out. For example, a high proportion of those who migrate today, especially within or from totalitarian countries, do so under one degree or another of coercion, but standard works usually omit all such migration from the concept. A generation that has witnessed the willful slaughter of millions of Jews is informed even in a work relating demography to politics that "the adoption of a policy to increase mortality, or to diminish efforts to increase longevity, is unthinkable" (Hauser, 1960). Ethnocentrism, which used to create a view of the analysts' own society as supreme in all respects, now more often blinds them to those systematic differences that, in terms of our values, indicate the unique virtues of Western society.

In this book one chapter relates to the populations of totalitarian societies, the Soviet Union and Nazi Germany, as well as Communist China, which is an example of a combined underdeveloped-totalitarian type.

## Summary

Whether there are theories appropriate to demographic analysis is a moot question (Vance, 1952; Gutman, 1960). In fact, such conceptual models as exist are of two kinds. Some apply to populations anywhere, because of the transcultural qualities of the age structure, for instance, or of the interaction between humans and the plant and animal life on which they must subsist. Such theories are expounded and exemplified in Part I. But other population theories are specific to a particular time and place (Van Nort, 1960). Part II of the book is arranged according to an amended version of the theory of the demographic transition, which is a useful framework in spite of the valid criticism that can be made of the early formulations. The five societal types to be analyzed are summarized in Table 1-1.

The purpose of this text is to introduce students to the subject of demography. Some undoubtedly will go on with further study in the field, and a few may eventually become professional demographers. Even those who stop with this work will have been trained, it is hoped, as intelligent and discriminating consumers of population figures. The extended discussion of demographic concepts, data, and techniques is structured, first of all, to facilitate the correct *interpretation* of population trends, a quality useful both in itself and as preparation for more advanced work.

Table 1-1. Demographic and Social Characteristics of Five Conceptual Types of Society

| TYPE | ECONOMY | FERTILITY | MORTALITY | POPULATION GROWTH |
|---|---|---|---|---|
| I. Preindustrial | Primitive or agrarian | High | Fluctuating and high | Static to low |
| II. Early Western | Mixed | High | Falling | High |
| III. Modern Western | Urban-industrial | Controlled | Low | Indeterminate; often low |
| IV. Underdeveloped | Mixed | High | Falling rapidly to low | Very high |
| V. Totalitarian | Urban-industrial | Controlled | Controlled | Indeterminate; often fluctuates widely |

## Suggestions for Further Reading

A number of general works at more or less the introductory level are worth noting. Thompson and Lewis (1965) is the fifth edition of a standard text whose senior author was one of the most important demographers of the past generation. Thomlinson (1965) attempts more fully than Thompson-Lewis to assimilate demographic analysis with sociological themes. Carr-Saunders (1964), an unchanged reprint of a work originally published in 1936, is obviously out of date in both its statistics and its obsessive concern with depopulation, but it remains a useful and interesting work. Perhaps the best short introduction to demography is the paperback by Wrong (1967). The pamphlet summarizing the 1965 world population conference, United Nations, 1966a, is a useful supplement to any earlier work.

Among multi-authored works, the best known is *The Determinants and Consequences of Population Trends* (United Nations, 1953); though now out of date (a new edition has been in process for several years), it still represents a significant effort to bring together all that was known or surmised on the subject, with the virtues but also the faults of an anonymous work by an international agency. The collection of articles edited by Hauser and Duncan (1959) suffers from undue repetition and certain gaps, yet constitutes one important inventory of demographic knowledge. That edited by Freedman (1964) is more popular but no less authoritative. Two recent anthologies (Nam, 1968; Heer, 1968) have been compiled with discernment.

Most of the books here listed include bibliographies of varying completeness and usefulness; an especially long list in several languages is given in United Nations (1953). The best annotated bibliography up to the date of its publication is Eldridge (1959). It can be supplemented by *Population Index,* a bibliographic quarterly published by the Office of Population Research, Princeton University, and by Fuguitt (1964) for references to dissertations.

In the following lists, starred items are especially recommended.

* ABU-LUGHOD, JANET. 1964. "Urban-Rural Differences as a Function of the Demographic Transition: Egyptian Data and an Analytical Model," *American Journal of Sociology,* **69,** 476–490.

CARR-SAUNDERS, A. M. 1964. *World Population: Past Growth and Present Trends.* Cass, London.

COWGILL, DONALD O. 1963. "Transition Theory as General Population Theory," *Social Forces,* **41,** 270–274.

DAVIS, KINGSLEY. 1956. "The Unpredicted Pattern of Population Change," *Annals of the American Academy of Political and Social Science,* **305,** 53–50.

————. 1963. "The Theory of Change and Response in Modern Demographic History," *Population Index,* **29,** 345–366.

* ELDRIDGE, HOPE T. 1959. *The Materials of Demography: A Selected and Annotated Bibliography.* International Union for the Scientific Study of Population and Population Association of America. Columbia University Press, New York.

FREEDMAN, RONALD, editor. 1964. *Population: The Vital Revolution.* Doubleday-Anchor, Garden City, N.Y.

FUGUITT, GLENN V. 1964. "Dissertations in Demography, 1933–1963." Department of Rural Sociology, College of Agriculture, University of Wisconsin, Madison. Mimeographed.

GUTMAN, ROBERT. 1960. "In Defense of Population Theory," *American Sociological Review,* **25,** 325–333.

HATT, PAUL K., NELLIE LOUISE FARR, and EUGENE WEINSTEIN. 1955. "Types of Population Balance," *American Sociological Review,* **20,** 14–21.

HAUSER, PHILIP M. 1960. "Demographic Dimensions of World Politics," *Science,* **131,** 1641–1647.

————, and OTIS DUDLEY DUNCAN, editors. 1959. *The Study of Population: An Inventory and Appraisal.* University of Chicago Press, Chicago.

HEER, DAVID M., editor. 1968. *Readings on Population.* Prentice-Hall, Englewood Cliffs, N.J.

HILLERY, GEORGE A., JR. 1966. "Navajos and Eastern Kentuckians: A Comparative Study in the Cultural Consequences of the Demographic Transition," *American Anthropologist,* **68,** 52–70.

MEIER, RICHARD L. 1958. "Concerning Equilibrium in Human Population," *Social Problems,* **6,** 163–175.

NAM, CHARLES B., editor. 1968. *Population and Society: A Textbook of Readings.* Houghton Mifflin, Boston.

NOTESTEIN, FRANK W. 1945. "Population—The Long View," in *Food for the World,* edited by Theodore W. Schultz. University of Chicago Press, pp. 35–57.

————. 1950. "The Population of the World in the Year 2000," *Journal of the American Statistical Association,* **45,** 335–349.

REED, STEPHEN W. 1949. "World Population Trends," in *Most of the World: The Peoples of Africa, Latin America, and the East Today,* edited by Ralph Linton. Columbia University Press, New York, pp. 94–155.

RYDER, NORMAN B. 1957. "The Conceptualization of the Transition in Fertility," *Cold Spring Harbor Symposium on Quantitative Biology*, **22**, 91–96.

TAEUBER, IRENE B. 1952. "The Future of Transitional Areas," in *World Population and Future Resources*, edited by Paul K. Hatt. American Book Company, New York, pp. 25–38.

THOMLINSON, RALPH. 1965. *Population Dynamics: Causes and Consequences of World Demographic Change*. Random House, New York.

THOMPSON, WARREN S. 1929. "Population," *American Journal of Sociology*, **34**, 959–975.

————. 1948. *Plenty of People*. Revised Ed. Ronald, New York.

————, and DAVID T. LEWIS. 1965. *Population Problems*, 5th Ed. McGraw-Hill, New York.

UNITED NATIONS. 1953. *The Determinants and Consequences of Population Trends*. Population Studies, No. 17. New York.

* ————. 1966a. *World Population: Challenge to Development*. Summary of the Highlights of the World Population Conference, Belgrade, Yugoslavia, 1965. New York.

————. 1966b. *World Population Prospects, as Assessed in 1963*. New York.

VAN NORT, LEIGHTON. 1956. "Biology, Rationality, and Fertility: A Footnote to Transition Theory," *Eugenics Quarterly*, **3**, 157–160.

* ————. 1960. "On Values in Population Theory," *Milbank Memorial Fund Quarterly*, **38**, 387–395.

————, and BERTRAM P. KARON. 1955. "Demographic Transition Re-Examined," *American Sociological Review*, **20**, 523–527.

VANCE, RUPERT B. 1952. "Is Theory for Demographers?" *Social Forces*, **31**, 9–13.

* WRONG, DENNIS H. 1967. *Population and Society*, 3rd Ed. Random House, New York.

# PART I

# THE UNIVERSAL ELEMENTS OF POPULATION ANALYSIS

# 2
## BASIC DEMOGRAPHIC CONCEPTS AND DATA

Each of the societal types specified in the last chapter has a different range and quality of population data. Primitive societies, which by definition lack any written records of their own, begin to acquire accurate measurements only as they lose their isolation. And although virtually every civilization of the past compiled records on certain portions of its population, for demographic analysis such counts have two important flaws. (1) Because their usual purpose was to impose taxation, military duty, or some other onerous service upon those eligible, some—the proportion varied with the regime's efficiency—always succeeded in evading enumeration; thus, (2) once one has evaluated the accuracy of the figures themselves, one must still extrapolate from this part to the whole population.

Demographic statistics *per se* are a product of modern societies. The first complete enumeration was of the population of New France (present-day Quebec) in 1665, and in all sixteen counts were taken there over the next century. Like the several early censuses in England's American colonies, these may be viewed as an extension of mercantilist bookkeeping.[1]

[1] The word *statistics* (brought into English from the French *statistique*, which derived from the German *Statistik*) is related to the word *state*, and the connotation from

The earliest accurate counts that any country made of its own population were in Scandinavia,[2] largely for the same kind of reasons. Like the clergy elsewhere, the Lutheran ministers of Sweden had long been keeping records of their parishioners, and at five-year intervals from 1749 on the government required all clergy to submit data from which population totals could be calculated. The system applied also in Finland as long as it was joined to Sweden, and a similar gradual secularization of ecclesiastical records took place in Denmark and Iceland.

In the United States, the institution of the census was related to efforts to establish the national government. One of the principal impediments to a federal system was the jealousy between large states and small ones. Power was balanced between them by establishing a bicameral Congress: in the Senate, with equal representation from each member of the Union, the less populous states had relatively greater power; and in the House, with representation proportionate to the population, the larger ones dominated. To maintain this balance, the number in the lower house had to be adjusted periodically to population growth; the Constitution itself provided for a decennial count. The first American census, in 1790, was thus not the first in the world, but because of this political context, it set an important precedent.

Until the nineteenth century the statistical data gathered by countries of continental Europe were usually treated as secrets of state. The modern census began in the United States in close association with democratic forms of government, and even at the start the results were immediately made public. . . . There can be no doubt that the periodic censuses of the United States have been preeminently responsible for introducing the practice into other countries (Willcox, 1930).

From these various beginnings, a system for the regular collection of population statistics was gradually established. By modern standards most of the earliest data are quite poor. The total head count was not accurate, and consistent classification into even the most basic categories developed only slowly. Yet by the end of the nineteenth century the compilation of population statistics was well established in Western Europe and its over-

---

this etymology is that statistics constitute a kind of national accounting. The word *statist*, now rare in any sense, can mean either statesman or statistician.

[2] It may be, however, that a seventeenth-century census was taken in France. In 1694 a head count was ordered, a questionnaire was distributed, and returns from three districts are extant; but whether the forms were completed throughout the country and have since been lost is not clear; see Edmond Esmonin, *Études sur la France des XVIIe et XVIIIe siècles*, Presses Universitaires de France, Paris, 1964. The many partial and unreliable data for France of the seventeenth and eighteenth centuries generally do not afford more than a shaky base from which to estimate total population figures (see pp. 638–639).

seas extensions, and more erratic, generally less satisfactory efforts had been made in some countries of Eastern Europe and Latin America. In the rest of the world, more or less adequate population statistics exist for the period before 1900, or even 1945, only when a European power instituted them in a colony: thus, England in India and the British West Indies, France in Algeria and (as we have noted) Canada, the Netherlands in the Dutch East Indies. Before today's underdeveloped nations began to collect population data systematically, techniques had developed greatly from these beginnings in the West European nucleus.

## International Statistics

Enumerating the inhabitants of a designated area and registering its vital events [3] are such straightforward procedures that, in the early days of population statistics, no conceptual framework was deemed to be necessary. It became evident, however, that the understanding of "obvious" terms and "simple" procedures varied greatly from one person to another even within a single country. Each statistical office undertook to standardize its own terminology and to issue increasingly detailed instructions to those charged with the collection and presentation of its data, and this effort to establish professional norms started to become meaningful once the compilation of statistics was made the responsibility of a separate agency.

A greater impetus toward standardization came with the development of international statistical organizations (United Nations, 1955, pp. 9–11). Even before the Statistical Society of London grew into the Royal Statistical Society, it was the cradle of international cooperation. Two men played an especially significant role: Adolphe Quetelet, the Belgian astronomer and social statistician,[4] and that indefatigable patron of all scientific progress, Prince Albert of Saxe-Coberg-Gotha, later the husband of Queen Victoria. In 1853, at an international statistical congress they helped to organize, representatives of twenty-six countries met in Brussels and recommended that all nations adopt uniform bases for their statistics, which only then would be internationally comparable. The permanent commission that eventually developed out of the congress often could get no more than partial and reluctant cooperation from the various national governments; Imperial Germany objected regularly even to the convention that proceedings were published in French, at the time still the standard language of diplomacy. The effective life of the commission came to an end after the Franco-Prussian War, and its successor, which met at irregular intervals between

---

[3] Note how the two processes of collection are differentiated in conventional terminology: **enumeration,** the periodic count of the whole population and its characteristics made in a census, is contrasted with **registration,** a continuous notation of vital events recorded usually right after their occurrence.

[4] For an interesting appreciation of Quetelet's work, see Lazarsfeld, 1961.

1878 and 1912, almost foundered during the First World War (Willcox, 1949). As these dates suggest, the difficulties derived mainly from the basic contradiction of international statistics: the cold quantitative record of nations' achievements and failures—for scholars the neutral subject matter of their discipline—by some interpretations of national interest may not be fully divulged.

Nevertheless the International Institute of Statistics survived World War I, and, during the following years, three periodical publications gave population figures for the world and its major components: the Institute's *Aperçu de la démographie des divers pays du monde;* the *Statistical Year-Book,* published by the League of Nations; and the *International Year-Book of Agricultural Statistics,* published by the International Institute of Agriculture. In 1930 the difference between the highest and the lowest estimates of the world's population given in these three works was only 40 million, or less than 2 per cent of their average. The reason for this seeming agreement, however, was that the three estimates were in fact not wholly independent, particularly with respect to countries with the least reliable statistics.[5]

These series have now been superseded by the various publications of the United Nations, which reflect both the continuing inherent difficulties of an international organization and the substantial improvement in professional demographic standards during the past quarter century. The Population Commission, established only two years after the founding of the United Nations itself with representatives from twelve (later eighteen) nations, guides the demographic activities of the organization's various units, especially but not exclusively through the Population Division. However, the Commission has been divided between a Catholic-Communist coalition, strangely allied on population matters, and what might be termed "neo-Malthusians" or, perhaps more accurately, the professional demographers of Western nations, so that any work related to policy questions has been seriously hampered (Cook, 1955; *cf.* Pressat and Sauvy, 1959). Changes in Communist and Catholic thinking on population matters had to be brought into U.N. documentation by other channels.[6]

In spite of the reluctance of the Population Commission to move on policy matters, the U.N. Population Division has realized other goals on its remarkably small budget. In the *U.N. Demographic Yearbook* are compiled the latest data from all countries, with a valuable introduction each

[5] A. M. Carr-Saunders, *World Population: Past Growth and Present Trends,* Cass, London, 1964, pp. 17–18.

[6] In December 1966, thus, the heads of twelve states (including Catholic Colombia and Communist Yugoslavia) sent the Secretary-General a strong statement supporting family planning, and during the same month the General Assembly passed without opposition a resolution that in effect endorsed such population programs of U.N. agencies. The texts of both statements are reproduced in *Population Bulletin,* Vol. 23, February 1967. See also below, pp. 635–637.

year to a particular range of data. Several international population congresses under U.N. auspices have afforded excellent opportunities for exchange of ideas across geographical and ideological lines. In the context of this chapter, perhaps the most significant work of the United Nations has been to initiate censuses and vital statistics in countries or whole regions where they hardly existed before. From these post-1945 efforts to develop population statistics in underdeveloped countries it became even more apparent that, in demography no less than in other disciplines, before we start counting we must designate our units.

## Definition of Concepts

It is now universally recognized that a precise definition of concepts is the prerequisite to the collection of data. Nothing can be taken for granted. The meanings that have been given to even the most basic terms—*family* or *live birth,* for example—have varied from one time or place to another, and such concepts as the *cause of death* or *international migration* can be delineated only by accepting one convention or another as a compromise. These terms will be discussed as we come to them in the following chapters; here we shall restrict ourselves to a general introduction to the problem they exemplify.

Take so simple a question, one so fundamental to population analysis, as "How many persons inhabited Country *A* on such and such a date?" This would seem to be so straightforward as to admit, apart from errors, of only one answer. In fact, neither "inhabitant" nor "country" is free from ambiguity.

By the standards of the U.S. Department of State, the number of independent states in the world increased from 71 on the eve of World War II to 125 in 1965. (Of the total in 1965, only 112 were members of the United Nations, not including Byelorussia, Mongolia, and the Ukraine, which are component elements of the Soviet Union.) Ten areas were classified as quasi-independent, meaning usually that self-rule was combined with lack of control over foreign affairs, and almost as many were said to "defy classification." As any day's newspaper informs us, national independence has typically been realized by such protracted processes as war, revolution, and persistent nonviolent pressure. To decide on the moment when a state comes into being or ceases to exist must often be arbitrary. For instance, the forcible Anschluss of Estonia, Latvia, and Lithuania into the Soviet Union has not been recognized by the United States; yet even a publication of the U.S. Department of State no longer defines them as independent. Many other ambiguities exist that can confound the uninitiated (U.S. Department of State, 1965). The political boundaries of national states and their subdivisions, moreover, often define units quite inappropriate for social or economic analysis, and to set more suitable boundaries usually requires a more or less arbitrary judgment. What are the precise limits of "Western Europe," "Southeast Asia," "the Arab World," "Latin America," and all the other designations that we accept in the context of a historical or political analysis? Are the new African states the best units of a particular analysis, or rather the tribal areas that in many cases overlap their boundaries? If, in a country like the United States, counties and most states do not constitute meaningful social-economic units, how shall we fashion these?

Once the geographical boundaries of an area have been designated, it is necessary to define what is meant by an "inhabitant." The United States uses a so-called *de jure* enumeration, meaning that persons are listed under their "usual place of residence." In Australia, as an example of a *de facto* enumeration, persons are classified according to where they happen to be on the day of the census count.[7] In England, the two are combined: for persons enumerated elsewhere than at their usual place of residence, this is also given. The difference between *de facto* and *de jure* enumeration, moreover, is only the most important of the variations in how "inhabitant" is understood. Consider American students who leave their state of residence to spend a protracted, but presumably temporary, period at a college in another state; when the U.S. Census Bureau changed its definition of "usual place of residence" to include such institutions, the population of college towns and even of some states increased appreciably. The estimated population of the United States on March 1, 1968, was 197,015,000 or 199,253,000 or 200,507,000, depending on whether armed forces were included, and if so whether also troops overseas.[8] In an extreme case, the population statistics of Finland provided four different totals for Finnish nationals, with a difference of some 8 per cent between the maximum and the minimum at any one date (Kirk, 1949). Of course, anyone who uses the original documents or authoritative compilations and reads all the introductory definitions and the explanatory footnotes knows what is intended by each such figure; but that is the point: "What was the population of Country A in 19___?" is not so simple a question as it seems.

The **classification** of a population into groups and subgroups must also often seem arbitrary. Any population is what is known as a discontinuous variable; that is, it changes only by whole units. A hamlet with 100 inhabi-

---

[7] For a discussion of the relative advantages and disadvantages of *de jure* and *de facto* enumerations, see Spiegelman, 1955, pp. 9–10. In societies with cultures markedly different from those of Western countries, the classification of residences can be yet more complicated. Fischer (1958) gives some examples of the problems that one encounters in enumerating primitive peoples and offers some partial solutions.

[8] In 1960 there were an estimated 1.4 million American civilians resident abroad for six months or more, but data on this sizable category are admittedly incomplete or nonexistent. They are not included in the census by enumeration but are asked to return questionnaires distributed through United States consular offices, so that any analysis of the characteristics of this population cannot provide more than probable guesses (Rubin, 1966).

tants can increase to 101 or decrease to 99, but it cannot change to an intermediate figure. Many characteristics of a population, however, are continuous variables, changes in which cannot be measured precisely by even the smallest unit. The measurement of age, for instance, whether counted in years, as is usual, or by the smallest unit conceivable, say milliseconds, transforms the continuous process of aging into a more or less jerky counterpart. The classification of any population according to its characteristics, thus, often means that one must group variables more or less arbitrarily into precise class intervals.

The pattern of distribution of some data suggests a dividing point or occasionally forces it (as between male and female), but the statistical expression of most demographic concepts forms a continuum, with or without recognizable clusters. There is, for instance, one segment of the population of the United States that can incontrovertibly be defined as Negro, in contrast to another segment no less clearly white; and, as this differentiation marks a distinction in educational and employment opportunities and achievements, in family structure and fertility, in health and mortality, it is a useful datum for a social analyst. Yet because the boundary is not sharp, because by reasonable criteria one could classify certain individuals as in one race or the other, a considerable sentiment has arisen to delete the category from all public documents. The dilemma, however, is much broader than this single instance. The real and significant differences, to take two other examples, between rural and urban or between those engaged and not engaged in a gainful occupation make some classification appropriate. But one must accept relatively arbitrary standards to decide whether these simple dichotomies are fine enough, whether division along one dimension or a more complex classification is called for. And the problem always remains of what is to be done with the intermediate cases.

Dividing a continuum into class intervals can be exemplified in terms of age: (1) Women are physiologically able to reproduce between puberty and menopause or, roughly, between the ages of 15 and 45; and the general fertility rate, defined as the number of births per 1,000 females in the fecund age group, varies widely according to where the age limits of fecundity are put (see p. 81). (2) In 1940 the U.S. Census Bureau revised the concept of the working population, which from that date on was understood to be part of the age group 14 years and over, rather than 10 years and over. Certainly the age at which persons ordinarily begin to work had risen: was this new definition the best possible reflection of the actual trend? (3) The author of one work on aging set 60 years as the lower limit of future research, in spite of the fact that in the United States 65 is the usual point to mark retirement, social-security benefits, and so on. In setting such dividing points, there is no one correct decision even at any particular time in a given culture. In most cases any of several more or less arbitrary classifications is equally acceptable.

In sum, "measurement presupposes a bounded network of shared meanings, i.e., a theory of culture" (Cicourel, 1964, p. 14). This completely valid statement is unfortunately no truism. The naiveté of laymen has combined with the positivist orientation of some demographers to obscure the fact that to some degree population data, like those in all other social disciplines, are culturally defined. Analytic rigor is sacrificed when we postulate a firmer and more universal base to our discipline than in fact exists.

## Population Registers

Population data are available primarily from three sources: the census, which corresponds in business practice to a periodic inventory of stock; vital statistics, which are like a record of inputs and outputs; and migration statistics, which are comparable to domestic and foreign purchases and sales.

In most advanced firms these three kinds of accounts are in fact part of a permanent inventory, which gives the businessman a precise overview of his stock on hand at any time and of the production and sales during a specified period. The counterpart in demography is a continuous **population register**, such as is maintained in the Netherlands, Belgium, Finland, and the three Scandinavian countries.[9] In each of these European nations, local registration bureaus maintain a separate card for each individual from the time of his birth (or immigration) to his death (or emigration), and on this are entered such changes in his civil status as marriage and divorce and other demographic data. With a population register, it is thus possible at any time to have the information ordinarily derived from both vital statistics and the census and, in addition, to know what part migration has played in bringing about population changes. Disadvantages are that it is quite expensive to set up and maintain, that to work properly it requires a high cultural level in the general population,[10] and that conceivably so complete a record might constitute an infringement on individual liberty.

## The Census

In the United Nations manual on the subject, a **census** is defined as "the simultaneous recording of demographic data by the government, at a particular time, pertaining to all the persons who live in a particular terri-

---

[9] In the United States a population register is maintained of certain Indian tribes (*cf.* Johnston, 1966, p. 11), and the establishment of an integrated Federal Statistical Data Center has been proposed (*cf.* Glaser *et al.*, 1967; Dunn, 1967). Thomas (1938) has given an interesting account of the establishment of the system in Europe.

[10] As well, one might add, as a strong motivation. When I was last in the Netherlands, living in an outlying district of Amsterdam for a year, I went downtown to register my arrival. But as I did not repeat the trolley trip of almost an hour to inform the bureau of my imminent departure, I was responsible for the fact that, until the next census, the recorded population of the country was too large by one!

tory" (United Nations, 1954, p. 1). Indeed, the term is often used to denote population counts of all kinds, and even other enumerations by a government (like the U.S. Census of Manufactures), but it is preferable to restrict its meaning to those that more or less comply with this United Nation definition, whose terms are elucidated in the following paragraphs:

1. A census is **made by the government.** No other institution can provide the legitimate authority and thus the presumption of objectivity, or the elaborate and expensive organization required to make a full and accurate enumeration.

2. A census is of **the population of a strictly defined territory,** a criterion we have already noted. One major difficulty in using the so-called censuses of ancient China, for example, is that "China" varied considerably from one period to another, depending on the military successes of the central government, and it is often not clear how much of the outlying regions was included in population counts.

3. The census enumeration is in principle **universal,** including every person in the designated area without omission or duplication. However, as we shall note shortly, this inclusion can be merely implicit, through the enumeration only of a properly drawn sample of the total population.

4. Ideally, a census consists of a **personal enumeration** of each individual in the area covered. In the usual practice of Western nations, enumerators try to reach at least one adult in each household or, if he proves to be repeatedly unavailable, a neighbor. In some population counts a personal enumeration is not attempted. Colonial censuses of Negro Africa, for example, have often consisted of compilations of data furnished by village chieftains; and the so-called censuses of religious bodies in the United States, similarly, were based on information given by the various denominations.

5. The enumeration of the entire population should be **simultaneous,** made on a single day, and in the small nations of the Western world this ideal is approached. In so large a country as the United States the census ordinarily takes three or four weeks, and in more primitive areas it may take months or even years. One day is nevertheless set as the date of the census, and demographic events occuring after this are in principle excluded from the count.

6. Censuses furnish not only information about the population at a given time but, in combination, no less significant data about its development over a period. Censuses are most useful if a **regular interval** is maintained between them. The director of a census, moreover, must weigh the advantages to be derived from any new procedure that is proposed against the disadvantage that comparability with previous data will be lost.

A long period of preparatory work must precede the actual enumeration. The legal and financial foundations must be assured, the census organization instituted if it does not already exist, and the general program laid out.

Geographers mark the census areas on large-scale maps, others design the questionnaire and preferably test it in a trial census. Particularly in countries without a census tradition, the bureau must try to allay possible suspicion of the enumerators by full and repeated publicity on the benefits to be derived from a formal count of the population. After enumeration, the

U.S. Census Bureau cartographers laying out block-identification maps in preparation for a census (*Remington Rand—Curt Gunther*).

data are checked for accuracy and consistency, compiled and tabulated, and published, often first in a preliminary version and then in final form. In some countries the questions raised by the data are regularly followed by special research, with consequent postcensal reports.

Even in their original form, **census schedules** (as the questionnaires are called) have generally included more questions than required for their stipulated purpose, and over the decades, in response to the needs of increasingly complex civilizations and sometimes anticipating these needs, new questions were added to the various countries' schedules. In the United States, for instance, the regularity of the decennial count is in contrast with a great diversity in the information collected (Table 2-1). The unit for

Table 2-1. Subjects of Inquiries Included in the U.S. Population Censuses, 1790–1960

| | 1790 | 1800 | 1810 | 1820 | 1830 | 1840 | 1850 | 1860 | 1870 | 1880 | 1890 | 1900 | 1910 | 1920 | 1930 | 1940 | 1950 | 1960 |
|---|---|---|---|---|---|---|---|---|---|---|---|---|---|---|---|---|---|---|
| Address | x | x | x | x | x | x | x | x | x | x | x | x | x | x | x | x | x | x |
| Farm residence | | | | | | | | | | | | | | | x | x | x | x |
| Families, persons, per house | | | | | | | | | | | x | | | | | | | |
| Name | P[a] | P | P | P | P | P | P | x | x | x | x | x | x | x | x | x | x | x |
| Relationship to family head | | | | | | | | | | x | x | x | x | x | x | x | x | x |
| Sex | P | P | P | P | P | P | x | x | x | x | x | x | x | x | x | x | x | x |
| Age | P | P | P | P | P | P | x | x | x | x | x | x | x | x | x | x | x | x |
| Marital status | | | | | | | | | | x | x | x | x | x | x | x | x | x |
| Free whites | x | x | x | x | x | x | | | | | | | | | | | | |
| Free nonwhites | P | P | P | P | P | P | | | | | | | | | | | | |
| Slaves | x | x | x | x | x | x | | | | | | | | | | | | |
| Color | | | | | | | P | P | x | | | | | | | | | |
| Race | | | | | | | | | | x | x | x | x | x | x | x | x | x |
| Year of immigration | | | | | | | | | | | x | x | x | x | x | | | |
| Unnaturalized aliens | | | | x | x | | | | | | x | x | x | x | x | | x | |
| Naturalization papers taken out | | | | | | | | | | | x | | | | | | | |
| Year of naturalization | | | | | | | | | | | | | | x | | | | |
| Speak English | | | | | | | | | | | x | x | x | x | x | | | |
| Native language | | | | | | | | | | | x | | x | x | x | x | | x |
| Place of birth | | | | | | | x | x | x | x | x | x | x | x | x | x | x | x |
| Places of parents' birth | | | | | | | | | | P | x | x | x | x | x | x | x | x |
| Parents' native languages | | | | | | | | | | | | | | x | | | | |
| Citizenship | | | | | | | | | | | x | | | | x | | | |
| Residence one (five) year(s) earlier | | | | | | | | | | | | | | | | x | x | x |
| How long at present address | | | | | | | | | | | | | | | | | | x |
| Profession, occupation, or trade | | | | x | | | x | x | x | x | x | x | x | x | x | x | x | x |
| Unemployed | | | | | | | | | | x | x | x | x | | S[b] | S | x | x |
| How long unemployed | | | | | | | | | | | | | | | | | x | x |
| Hours worked | | | | | | | | | | | | | | | | x | x | x |
| Place of work | | | | | | | | | | | | | | | | | | x |

Table 2-1. Subjects of Inquiries Included in the U.S. Population Censuses, 1790–1960 (*Continued*)

| | 1790 | 1800 | 1810 | 1820 | 1830 | 1840 | 1850 | 1860 | 1870 | 1880 | 1890 | 1900 | 1910 | 1920 | 1930 | 1940 | 1950 | 1960 |
|---|---|---|---|---|---|---|---|---|---|---|---|---|---|---|---|---|---|---|
| Means of transportation | | | | | | | | | | | | | | | | | | x |
| Income | | | | | | | | | | | | | | | | x | x | x |
| Value of real (and personal) estate | | | | | | | x | x | x | | | | | | | x | x | |
| Home (farm) rented or owned, mortgaged | | | | | | | | | | | x | x | x | x | x | x | | |
| Radio set | | | | | | | | | | | | | | | x | x | | |
| Whether attending school | | | | | | | x | x | x | x | x | | x | x | x | x | x | x |
| Public or private school | | | | | | | | | | | | | | | | | | x |
| Educational attainment | | | | | | | | | | | | | | | | x | x | x |
| Whether literate | | | | | | | x | x | x | x | x | x | x | x | x | | | |
| Deaf or dumb | | | | | x | x | x | x | x | x | x | | x | | | | | |
| Blind | | | | | x | x | x | x | x | x | x | | x | | | | | |
| Sick or disabled | | | | | | | | | | x | x | | | | | | | |
| Insane or idiotic | | | | | | x | x | x | x | x | x | | | | | | | |
| Acute or chronic disease | | | | | | | | | | x | x | | | | | | | |
| Military pensioner or veteran | | | | | | x | | | | | P | | P | | x | x | x | x |
| Pauper or convict | | | | | | | x | x | | | x | | | | | | | |
| Social-security or retirement status | | | | | | | | | | | | | | | | | x | x |
| Born within year | | | | | | | | x | x | | | | | | | | | |
| Death in the family | | | | | | | x | x | x | x | x | | | | | | | |
| Age at first marriage | | | | | | | | | | | | | | | x | x | | x |
| When, how often, married | | | | | | | P | P | P | P | P | x | | | | x | x | x |
| How long married | | | | | | | | | | | | | x | | | x | | |
| How many (living) children | | | | | | | | | | | x | x | x | | | x | x | x |
| Persons in family | | | | | | | | | | | x | | | | | | | |

*a* P—partial data.
*b* S—special report or details.

most of the data, which until 1850 was the family, was changed in that year's count to the individual, and in Willcox's opinion (1930) this revision in procedure was "perhaps the most important in the history of the census." The effort to measure America's ethnic patterns, exerted in various ways, was boiled down eventually to four questions: race, citizenship, birthplace, and parents' birthplaces. The measurement of physical disabilities during the latter half of the nineteenth century was largely abandoned. And so on. According to the policy agreed on by most of the top Bureau officials, the schedule designed for the 1970 census will differ very little from that used in 1960. The major innovation will probably be that data on small areas will be more readily available (Miller, 1967).

In England, as another instance, the large in-migration to the new industrial towns brought a question on birthplace in 1841 and more detailed ones on the job structure in 1851. From 1901 on, the effort to cope with Britain's housing problem was reflected in new queries.

The items recommended by international agencies have also varied, though the minimum is fairly well established at something like the following list for the total population: sex, age, marital status, place of birth, citizenship (or nationality) and language, educational characteristics (including literacy), fertility, urban and rural residence, size of household, economically active and inactive population, occupation and industry, industrial status (class of worker), population dependent on agriculture.[11]

"The quality of the census results is wholly dependent on the enumeration, and no country can afford to have a poor enumeration in the hope that office work will subsequently improve it" (United Nations, 1954, p. 21). For the United States census of 1960, for instance, some 160,000 enumerators were hired and trained, or approximately one per 1,100 persons to be counted (the world average is about one per 500 persons). Most of the enumerators were women, who are more often able and willing to take on a full-time job for two weeks or so. They were given nine hours of classroom training designed to explain both the specific duties and the importance of taking an accurate census and then had to pass an examination. Paid on a piece-work basis, they received about $13 a day (in many countries enumerators get only a token remuneration or even no payment at all), and about 2,000 were fired for inefficiency. Work in the field was directly controlled by about 10,000 crew leaders and, at a greater distance, by about 400 district supervisors. The census was taken in two stages, the first covering the items asked of all households and the second a more detailed schedule asked of only a sample of the population. Only about a third of the enumerators were retained for stage two, and the possibility of this additional income provided another incentive to careful and accurate work.

The difficulties of enumeration in a country like the United States are as nothing compared to those in some territories. Each of the approximately 18,500 enumerators who counted Australia's population in 1966 took along

[11] This was the "Inter-American Minimum" schedule recommended in 1950 by the Coordinating Board of the Committee on the 1950 Census of the Americas (United Nations, 1954, p. 35). Subsequent lists differ only in detail.

A Japanese enumerator counting a few of the thousands who live on boats and barges on Tokyo's canals (*Wide World Photos*).

not only the schedule but a guide to eight languages and instructions on how to communicate with the aborigines in sign language. They moved about Australia's vast spaces by plane and jeep, on horseback and skis, by motor launch. From Humbug Scrub to Boologooroo, census takers sought out opal gougers, oil drillers, boundary riders, and wandering rabbit hunters. A truck driver induced to help returned from No Tree Plain with two hundred completed questionnaires and five tons of rabbits.[12]

Nor was it an easy task to administer the 1962 census of Nigeria, the first since that country's independence. The central government undertook a massive propaganda effort: radio singers gave daily census chants, school children marched for the census, placards covered the towns and villages. According to reports reaching the capital, enumerators were nonetheless beaten and kidnapped, for they were taken to be tax collectors in disguise. Census officials discovered whole areas—for example, a cluster of fishing villages with a total population of some 20,000—that had been overlooked

[12] *Time,* July 22, 1966.

An operator and a controller at the console of a UNIVAC 1107 computer in use at the U.S. Census Bureau as of March 1967. In the background containers hold reels of magnetic tape (*U.S. Bureau of the Census*).

in the 1952 count, the last taken under British auspices. On the other hand, administrators worked to inflate the count in their constituencies, in order to get a larger share of development and welfare funds.[13]

The technical skill and equipment in compiling the data collected have improved greatly. As long ago as 1890, American census results were entered on Hollerith punch cards, with which it is possible by a simple adjustment to sum up involved cross tabulations (for example, the income of college-educated Negroes, married or single, north or south of the Mason-Dixon line). In 1960 the enumeration books were assembled at the Jeffersonville office of the Bureau of the Census, counted, classified by district, provided with numbers, and microfilmed. Then the data went through the FOSDAC (Film Optical Sensing Device and Computer), which translated the enumerators' entries into pulses on magnetic tape. The electronic computer performed the following tasks with great accuracy: editing and control of records, evaluation of their quality, determination of sample weights,

[13] *The New York Times,* May 27, 1962.

and tabulation. The population could be divided into some 5,000 categories at the rate of 3,000 persons a minute. As a final step, the computer presented a completed table, ready for photo-offset reproduction. In short, the principle of the electronic computer is the same as that of Hollerith cards, but the new machine's speed, accuracy, and efficiency began a new era in data analysis (Brunsman, 1963).

### SAMPLING

In principle, as we have noted, a census is universal, but in practice this universality can be approximated by getting information only from a **survey population,** a fraction which is related to the aggregate population in a known and regular way. The ideal relation is what one author terms Epsem (equal probability of selection method) Sampling, by which each element in the population has the same chance of being represented in the sample (Kish, 1965, p. 21). This results in the smallest **sampling error,** or the difference in the count that could result from using a sample rather than a full enumeration.

A sample can have a number of advantages over a complete census: (1) economy; (2) speed, and therefore timeliness when this is relevant; (3) quality and accuracy, for it is often difficult to obtain enough trained personnel for even a large sample; and (4) reduced bulk of completed records. Among the advantages of complete enumeration or registration, as opposed to a sample survey, are: (1) data are provided for small geographical units, small classes of the population, and, in particular, individuals; and (2) the public is less likely to understand the limitations of a sample survey and is thus more apt to misinterpret the data.[14]

In the United States sampling was first used in the 1940 census, when one person out of twenty was asked questions in addition to those on the regular schedule, and this procedure set a precedent for the subsequent censuses. A recurrent survey that the Works Progress Administration (WPA) had initiated during the 1930s to chart the trend in unemployment was later transferred to the Census Bureau, which converted it into a monthly **Current Population Survey** (Hansen *et al.,* 1955; U.S. Bureau of the Census, 1963). Intercensal sample surveys have been used both to check the accuracy of the census itself and to obtain population estimates for the intervening years (Zitter and Shryock, 1964). In Britain a one-in-ten sample filled in a complete census schedule in 1966, thus reducing the period between censuses from ten to five years. The cost was less than half that of a census of the 1961 type, with basic information from the whole popula-

---

[14] Much of the journalistic commentary on unemployment statistics, for example, ignores the fact that most of the month-to-month change may be sampling error. *Cf.* Raymond T. Bowman and Margaret E. Martin, "Special Report on Unemployment Statistics: Meaning and Measurement," *American Statistician,* **16** (1962), 14–22.

tion and more elaborate data from a sample of ten per cent, and only a small fraction of one of the 1951 type, when all respondents answered all questions. These several examples indicate the wide use of sample surveys in a number of countries and suggest the range of future possibilities.

## Vital Statistics

Vital statistics are defined as those pertaining to each person's birth, change in his civil status throughout his lifetime, and his death. In almost every culture there is associated with each such event a religious ritual to mark it: birth and baptism, marriage and wedding, death and burial service, and so on. The use of church records for demographic analysis, however, is hampered by the fact that there has seldom really been a one-to-one ratio between event and ceremony. Secularization, therefore, has brought an important progress in recording vital events. Apart from the ancient Inca empire in Peru, seventeenth-century Massachusetts was the first state to record the occurrence and date of the actual events rather than of the subsequent ecclesiastical ceremonies, and the first to shift the responsibility for this registration from the clergy to civil authorities.

In spite of this early beginning, the development of vital statistics in the United States has been slow. In contrast to most West European countries, in the United States vital statistics are still collected by local authorities, so that their completeness and reliability have varied greatly from one region to another. In several nineteenth-century censuses, attempts were made to find a substitute for national vital statistics by asking how many births or deaths had taken place during a designated period before the enumeration date (see Table 2-1). The responses were quite inadequate, however; the census reports themselves estimated that perhaps as many as half the deaths were omitted.

Following such fiascos, the federal government undertook to guide the procedures of local authorities. Model registration laws were written, and the states were urged to enact them. States in which it was judged on the basis of sample counts that the registration was at least 90 per cent complete were gradually included in a Death-Registration Area (established in 1880) and a Birth-Registration Area (established in 1915). In 1933, with the admission of Texas to the Death-Registration Area, they both became coextensive with the continental United States, and American birth and death statistics first came into being on a national scale. Even today the accuracy and completeness of registration still varies from one state to another, though now ordinarily above the minimum set as the national norm (see pp. 51–52).

Indeed, the fairly common contrast between relatively advanced and backward regions of a country is typically reflected in the quality of the vital statistics collected. In India, as another example, the parts known before 1947 as the British Provinces are now denoted the "registration area," for which a more elaborate statistical coverage is attempted than for the rest of the country. However difficult it may be for an underdeveloped nation to set up a national census, to institute the collection and compilation of vital statistics imposes even greater problems. The best of a country's technical and administrative skills are ordinarily congregated at the capital and can be mustered for the periodic census. But the regular registration of vital events must depend on local talents. In Kenya, as one example, births and deaths are in principle registered by the attendant physician (usually there is none); or as a second alternative by the headmen, parents, or other relatives (most are illiterate); or, in fact in most cases, by school registrars or district clerks (Huxtable, 1967).

A count of births and deaths constitutes, of course, only the beginning of the data needed to analyze fertility and mortality. If persons differ in one or the other according to their occupation, ethnic group, urban or rural residence, or whatever, we can draw conclusions from such patterns only if the accuracy of registration can be assumed to be the same in all the groups being compared. The reasonable assumption from the regional differences we have noted, however, is the contrary—that with improvements, e.g., in controlling early death there go improvements in registering those deaths that do occur. Epidemiological research is based fundamentally on an analysis of deaths classified by cause and contributing factors, but the cause of death can generally be established only by a physician, whose very availability means that sickness is under control. Thus, some 60 per cent of the deaths registered in British India up to 1945 (which had better demographic statistics than most other underdeveloped countries) were ascribed simply to "fever" and over 25 per cent to a catch-all category of "other causes." In all countries infant mortality is generally less accurately registered than the deaths of adults, and records of fetal mortality are usually so poor that one can hardly base any conclusions on them at all.

Data on changes in civil status are inherently more difficult to collect than those on births or deaths. In the United States registration areas have been established with respect to marriage and divorce statistics, and various federal agencies have been endeavoring to improve the still quite inadequate national records (e.g., U.S. Public Health Service, 1966).[15] Consensual unions, often termed common-law marriages, are almost the standard lower-class pattern in much of Latin America; yet some of the countries do not recognize it in their statistics (Dedrick, 1949). More generally, until the

[15] One important impediment is that states that have made a business of marriage and divorce are reluctant to cooperate in the compilation of complete and accurate statistics on their activities. Since all divorces handed down in Nevada, for example, are to persons legally defined as residents of that state, migratory divorce is not a fact that the Nevada administrators will officially acknowledge. Cf. William Petersen and Lionel L. Lewis, *Nevada's Changing Population*, State Printing Office, Carson City, Nevada, 1963, pp. 34–39.

family, that universal but highly variable institution, is everywhere analyzed according to international standards, we shall not have wholly comparable data.

## Migration Statistics

If we define **migration** as the permanent movement of persons or groups over a significant distance, some of the key terms of this definition ("permanent," "significant") are ambiguous and in practice have to be delimited by an arbitrary criterion. We know whether someone has been born or has died, but who shall say whether a person has migrated? A farmer who goes to the nearest town on a Saturday to buy a suit, we feel, is not a migrant. A person who leaves his home and goes to another country and settles there for the rest of his life, on the other hand, is a migrant. But between these two extremes lies a bewildering array of intermediate instances; and such criteria as distance, duration of stay, and importance of purpose do not clarify the concept entirely. "No objective, natural criterion exists on the basis of which migrants distinguish themselves from travelers, . . . [and] one should not expect to arrive at a unique criterion or definition of migration" (Lacroix, 1949).

The basic distinction in migration statistics is that between **international migration,** in which the migrant crosses the boundary between one country and another, and **internal migration,** in which he does not. A difference is made also in the terms designating the two types of persons: international migrants are called **emigrants** when they leave and **immigrants** when they arrive, while internal migrants are called **out-migrants** when they leave and **in-migrants** when they arrive.

The distinction between internal and international migration is not always clear-cut, for as we have noted territories often have some but not all of the characteristics of independent states. Thus, according to the purpose for which the statistics are gathered, one might designate as either internal or international the movement among the occupied zones of postwar Germany; or between Puerto Rico and the United States; or between Britain and the British dominions, colonies, or mandated territories; and so on through scores of examples of ambiguous sovereignty. Each such case is decided on the basis of particular circumstances, and there are many strange anomalies. To cite but one: in the migration statistics of the United Kingdom, citizens of the Republic of Ireland are treated throughout as British subjects!

Another limitation to the internal-international dichotomy is that it tends to obscure processes that cut across it. We usually think of labor mobility or of urbanization, for example, as intranational phenomena, forgetting that much of the movement of workers to cities has been across national boundaries. We speak of the assimilation of immigrants, but usually not of in-migrants. The implication that the difference between national cultures is *always* greater than that between rural and urban is certainly not in accord with the facts: a native of Toronto who moves to Detroit would ordinarily be, in any but a legal sense, less of an alien than an in-migrant from rural Alabama; and this contrast might also hold, for example, in the cases of a Viennese citizen and a French peasant who go to live in Paris. These comments are not meant to imply, of course, that whether or not a migrant crosses an international border is not important with respect to any demographic study. The point is rather that, even when an analyst deems this distinction to be irrelevant to the problem with which he is concerned, he must use the two sets of statistics as they have been separately collected; to combine data on international and internal migration is seldom feasible.

### INTERNATIONAL MIGRATION

The statistics of international migration, as collected by the various national governments, are not ordinarily accurate, complete, or comparable. There are three main reasons for this:

**1.** The statistics collected are an adjunct to a border patrol that many try to evade. The neutral character of modern Western censuses and vital statistics—the fact that they are data collected for their own sake rather than as a step preparatory to unpopular state controls—is thus lacking in the statistics of international migration. Distinctions made for legal or political reasons, moreover, are seldom relevant to a demographic study; for example, the difference in the United States between quota and nonquota immigrants relates only to American law and has no counterpart in the statistics of other countries. Each such specific regulation reduces the international comparability of the statistics based on it.

**2.** Even apart from variations in migration law, migrants are not classified by a uniform system in different countries. Among the totals entering and leaving a country, designated as **arrivals** and **departures,** the first subclassification is usually between **nationals** and **aliens,** who are both further subdivided between **visitors** and **permanent migrants.** All of these terms are ambiguous to some degree. Between "national" and "alien" there are persons of dual nationality, permanent stateless residents, and others who exemplify the complexities of international law. The distinction between "visitor" and "migrant," similarly, is hard to draw precisely. The criterion recommended by the United Nations, to define removal for one year or more as "permanent," does not satisfactorily classify persons who remain abroad for more than a year but who intend to return. In the United States, for example, travelers in transit, tourists, businessmen, students, and others may get a visa for a year's stay and still remain "nonimmigrant aliens." It might be better to distinguish between **permanent migrants,** who intend to settle in a new country for the rest of their lives, and **quasipermanent migrants,** who intend to leave for a year or more but to return at some time after that. In any case, the "permanence" is based on the migrants' stated intentions at the time of their removal, and some may not tell the truth and others may change their minds.

Several classes of international migrants do not fit into this scheme. Refugees, deportees, displaced persons, transferred populations, etc., are often, but not always, admitted under special conditions and outside the legal and statistical framework of "normal" movements. Also, persons who live on one side of an international border and work or shop or perform similar routine activities on the other side ordinarily carry frontier cards, with which they can short-circuit the usual control of passports and visas, and their movement back and forth is usually also segregated in the statistics.

3. The relevance of the data available varies with the problem being studied. An analysis of a country's labor force would obviously have to include seasonal workers and daily commuters, though the latter would not have to be included in a study, e.g., of housing. For an analysis of future population growth, including the children to be born to immigrants, age would be more relevant than citizenship. And for some purposes the total *de facto* population, including even one-day tourists, would be the most useful figure. But migration statistics are not ordinarily compiled so that one can take out just those data that are pertinent.

### INTERNAL MIGRATION

Statistics on internal migration are quite limited in most countries. If there are no direct data, it is possible to calculate internal migration as a residue. The difference between births and deaths gives one the natural increase, which, when compared with the total intercensal increase, yields the presumed net movement into or out of the area. Symbolically this can be represented for the simplest case by the following equation:

$$M = P_1 - P_0 - B + D$$

With this method, however, it can happen that the errors in all the other data are added up as part of the assumed migration (Hamilton, 1966).

Beginning with the 1850 census, native-born Americans have been asked to name their state of birth. This information, when compared with their state of residence at the time of the census, is a gauge of internal migration, but only a rough one, for the migration could have taken place at any time during the respondent's whole life, and intermediate stopovers, if any, are not given. Even so, the data are sufficient to indicate both the tremendous magnitude of the movement (according to each of the censuses, only about three persons out of four lived in their native state) and the general direction of the streams (that is, East to West, South to North), with sometimes strong presumptive evidence of the country-to-town movement. Place of birth has been recorded also in almost every European census and the indicated movement is usually to the national center—in England to London, in Sweden to Stockholm, in Denmark to Copenhagen, in France to Paris— or in such multilingual countries as Switzerland, Belgium, and Spain, or such large countries as Germany, to the regional center (Kirk, 1946, Chapter 7).

Beginning with the 1940 census, Americans have been asked where they were living five years, or one year, earlier; and from 1945 on, questions of this kind were introduced into the Current Population Survey. The **mobile population,** defined as those who were living in different houses within the United States on the two dates, is divided first of all into **intracounty movers** and **intercounty migrants.** The latter category is further divided according to whether the migration was within the same state, to a contiguous state, or to a noncontiguous state. Migrants to the United States from another country are separately classified (e.g., U.S. Bureau of the Census, 1968). This differentiation between "mover" and "migrant" is intended to distinguish changes in residence that are and are not accompanied by concomitant changes in job, school, type of neighborhood, etc., but it is not possible to mark this social-economic boundary clearly by a geographical index. Persons who leave a farm and move to a town, who are classified as migrants by rural sociologists, may or may not fall into the category so defined. A move from a city center to a suburb often crosses a county line; social theory is not clear on whether this should rate as "migration" (Shryock, 1964, Chapters 2–3).

According to the data from the census and sample surveys, one American out of five moves each year to another house. The annual growth of the country's population from both natural increase and net international migration has amounted to about three million persons in recent years. Annual migration across county lines is more than three times this figure and that between states more than one and a half times. In many parts of the country, therefore, particularly in the West, internal migration is by far the most important determinant of population size and composition, but it is still the demographic factor we know least about.

## Errors in Demographic Data

Modern demographic data are no closer to perfection than any other creation of fallible humans, though in the context of social disciplines they constitute a unique reservoir of reliable statistical information. Indeed, it is a measure of the discipline's maturity that today few in it attempt to realize the unattainable. As any count approaches the theoretical total (termed the **universe,** as distinguished from the empirical total, the **population**), each additional reduction in error is bought at a higher cost in effort and money. With respect to sample surveys, the textbook admonition is to obtain only the maximum precision obtainable at the permitted expenditure (e.g., Kish, 1965, p. 25).

The objective of "optimum design" in sampling is coming to be the objective [also] in census taking. Instead of striving for perfection, we view the task as that of balancing the costs of producing statistics against the losses from errors in the statistics (Hansen et al., 1953; cf. Bogue, 1965; Taeuber and Hansen, 1966).

Of course, a count of the whole population and a sample survey are not wholly comparable. The **precision** of a sample survey can be calculated from probability theory alone; given the size and nature of the sample, we know what the sampling error is likely to be. The **accuracy** of a survey, whether sample or complete, is the inverse of the total error, including biases. And there is no simple, efficient mode of measuring accuracy, for the unknown biases present in the original count may be retained in any subsequent check (Kish, 1965, pp. 12–13). Even so, inasmuch as accuracy, especially extreme accuracy, is expensive, administrators may decide to aim at no more than "reasonable" completeness and correctness and to use the funds so saved to obtain additional data.

### SOURCES OF ERROR

Demographic data, as has been noted with respect to censuses, ought to be universal; that is, every instance of the phenomenon being measured ought to be counted once and only once. **Errors in coverage** can mean, thus, either that a person (or a population characteristic) is omitted or that he (or it) is counted twice. Duplicate registration of vital events is negligible. Duplicate counts in a census, although they exist, ordinarily cause far less error than passing over some of those who should have been counted. In migration statistics too high a count is sometimes made as a result of careless classification, as when a native returning from abroad is treated in the statistics as an immigrant. With respect to all types of population data, however, an undercount is more frequent and larger than an overcount.

Either over- or undercounts can be significant even if not very large, for they are typically concentrated in particular sectors of the population, particular areas, or particular time periods. It is not merely that, for instance, at one time every tenth birth in the United States as a whole escaped registration, but rather, to take an extreme hypothetical example, every second birth to a Negro in the rural South. An interregional or interracial comparison of fertility would be seriously off if this differential pattern in under-registration were not corrected. As another example, the census of 1870 (the first after the Civil War) was marked by an especially large under-

★ **UNITED STATES OF AMERICA** ★
1960 Census of Population

# WERE YOU COUNTED?

The enumeration of Americans in the 1960 Census is now almost finished. As you know, it is very important that the Census be complete and correct. If you believe that you were **not** counted, please fill out the form below and mail it **immediately** to:➡ U.S. Census District Office

(Insert address)

---

● I have checked with the members of my household, and I believe that one (or more) of us was NOT counted, here or anywhere else, in the 1960 Census.

● On April 1, 1960, I lived at _____
(House Number)          (Street or Road)                    (City)                      (State)              (Apartment Number or Location)

● This address is located between _____ and _____
(Name of Street or Road)                                          (Name of Street or Road)

● I am listing below the name and required information for myself and each member of my household.

**PLEASE LIST:**

1. Everyone who usually lives in this household, whether related to you or not.

2. All persons staying here who have no other home.

**PLEASE BE SURE TO LIST—**
● All members of your family living with you, including babies.
● All other relatives living here.
● Lodgers and boarders living here.
● Servants, hired hands, others not related to you who are living here.
● Anyone else staying here but who has no other home.

**ALSO LIST—**
Persons who usually live here but who are away temporarily on business, on vacation, or in a general hospital.

**DO NOT LIST—**
● College students who are away at college (or who are here only on vacation).
● Persons stationed away from here in the Armed Forces.
● Persons away in institutions, such as a sanitarium, nursing home, home for the aged, mental hospital.

*They will be counted there.*

| NAMES OF PERSONS LIVING IN THIS HOUSEHOLD ON APRIL 1, 1960, AND THOSE STAYING HERE WHO HAVE NO OTHER HOME | | | What is the relationship of each person to the head of this household? (For example, wife, son, daughter, grandson, mother-in-law, lodger, lodger's wife) | Male or Female (M or F) | Is this person— White Negro American Indian Japanese Chinese Filipino Hawaiian Part Hawaiian Aleut Eskimo (etc.)? | When was this person born? | | Is this person— Married Widowed Divorced Separated Single (never married)? (Leave blank for children born after March 31, 1946) |
|---|---|---|---|---|---|---|---|---|
| Write names in this order: Head of household on first line / Wife of head / Unmarried children, oldest first / Married children and their families / Other relatives / Others not related to head of household (If you list more than 6 persons, use an additional sheet) (P2) | | | | | | | | |
| Last name | First name | Middle initial | (P3) | (P4) | (P5) | Month | Year | (P7) |
| | | | Head | | | (P6) | | |
| | | | | | | | | |
| | | | | | | | | |
| | | | | | | | | |
| | | | | | | | | |
| | | | | | | | | |
| | | | | | | | | |

● Name of person who filled this form: _____

Form 60PH-16   Budget Bureau No. 41-6002.
Approval expires 12-31-60.

In an effort to correct underenumeration in the 1960 count, the Census Bureau placed this form in newspapers throughout the country (*U.S. Bureau of the Census*).

enumeration in the South; if not corrected, this nonrandom error would seriously affect any analysis of the pattern of national growth during the nineteenth century. Similarly, there is no reason to suppose that immigrants from various European countries were randomly distributed between steerage, where they were counted, and first and second class, where for most of the period of heavy immigration they were not.

Best statistical results are to be expected, to repeat, when data are gathered for their own sake, rather than as an appendage to some other administrative procedure. One might say *a priori* that in a totalitarian state there would be more reasons than in the democratic West for evading a population count of any type and less opportunity to do so, but there is little evidence to substantiate such a judgment. In the comparative works of international bodies like the United Nations, which include member-nations of every political type, the contrast itself is of course never made. In the United States census information is completely private, carefully guarded against even other government bureaus, and never published in a form that would make the identification of individuals possible. The protection of a person against the use of census data to his detriment, according to a 1929 decision in one of the few cases challenging the Census Bureau's defense of this position, "is akin to the protection afforded by the prohibitions against the evidential use of communication between attorney and client, priest and penitent, and physician and patient." [16] Insofar as certainty is possible, Americans know that others will not be permitted to use, against the respondents' interests, any information they submit to the Census Bureau.

The enumerator (or, more generally, the person who solicits and records any type of data) should exude an air of sympathetic objectivity, neither resisting nor overstressing the import of any question (e.g., Hanson and Marks, 1958; Powell and Pritzker, 1965). One can reasonably assume that **rapport** with the respondent, though it can be improved by training, is more fundamentally a function of whether the communication is across the ethnic, regional, class, and other structural lines of a society. In the 1960 census of the United States, the problem was in part circumvented by instituting a new procedure: forms were mailed to respondents, filled out without the promptings, but also without the assistance, of an enumerator, returned by mail, and then followed up with a personal contact only when the response was unacceptable. Whether the change effected an over-all improvement in the quality of the data is a polemical question (Bogue, 1965; Taeuber and Hansen, 1966), though we can say that the gains outweighed the losses if we take into account the fact that the new procedure cost much less.

**Errors of classification** should be suspected whenever a reply can give the respondent a lower or a higher social standing. Questions on such matters as income, occupation, and education might be regarded as almost an invitation to boost one's self-esteem by stretching the truth a bit. Paradoxically, the same factor plays some part in misreporting of age (see pp. 61–

---

[16] Brauner *v.* Mutual Life Insurance Co. of N.Y., 4 D & C 2d 106 (1929); see Petersen, 1964, pp. 226–267, for further details. During a period of not quite a year there was a partial break in this confidentiality. On December 11, 1961, the Supreme Court ruled in the case of St. Regis Paper Co. *v.* United States that government agencies could subpoena not the reports a company made to the Census Bureau, but the copies of such reports it retained for its own files. Public Law 87–813, signed on October 15, 1962, extended the confidentiality of reports to copies (Corcoran, 1963; Rubin, 1962; Taeuber, 1967).

62). The distortion can be particularly significant when a difference in group norms effects a different mode of response. For instance, the growing influence of sadhus, or holy men, on India's politics and society is in contrast to their number, which has fallen off from 5 million in pre-independence India to less than half a million today. (But the vaguely defined category of sadhus was expanded in the censuses of British India—"the British were eager to swell the figure in order to prove the Indians' reluctance to work" —and contracted in the counts since independence—in an effort "to destroy the image of India as a *yogi*-land." [17]) In one of the classics of sociology, Durkheim noted that the suicide rate was consistently lower for Catholics than for Protestants, and he explained the difference by the stronger social cohesion of Catholics, and thus the greater insulation of each individual Catholic from suicide-generating factors.[18] (Another likely—more likely?—interpretation is that because suicide denotes a greater sin for Catholics, they take greater care than Protestants, Jews, or atheists to disguise it as a normal death.)

The misclassification of the "insane" in the 1840 census of the United States is an example of official prejudice so gross that it is difficult to believe. At the time the American Statistical Association and a number of other organizations and individuals criticized the returns for their patent deficiencies. According to one of the memorials submitted to Congress, "In many towns all the colored population are stated to be insane; in very many others, two-thirds, one-third, one-quarter, or one-tenth of this ill-starred race are reported to be thus afflicted." The congressional committee to which these criticisms were referred admitted that this and a number of similar errors had been made, but took no steps to correct them or to remove the official sanction from the published census volumes (Wright, 1900, p. 38).

Errors of all kinds can be illustrated from the records of immigration to the United States. Surreptitious crossings take place along the borders of every country, of course, and the number entering the United States without benefit of an official welcome has in some periods been quite large. The past movement from Canada, both of Canadians and of transmigrant aliens, is largely unrecorded; according to the author of one study of the subject, his reconstruction of it "has a status intermediate between pure fact and pure speculation" (Keyfitz, 1950). As late as the mid-1950s the estimated number of Mexicans entering the United States illegally by its southern border was more than a million a year (Hadley, 1956).

And to say merely that there were errors in classifying the nationalities of European immigrants is hardly to characterize the record compiled by unbelievably harried officials. According to the Commissioner of Immigration in New York during the 1890s:

---

[17] Khushwant Singh, "Holy Men of India: In Search of the Seekers of Truth," *New York Times Magazine,* January 8, 1967.

[18] Emile Durkheim, *Suicide,* Free Press, Glencoe, Ill., 1951, pp. 152–170.

The few registry clerks in the office were supposed . . . to take a statement from the immigrants about their nationality, destination and ages, [but] as a matter of fact whole pages did not contain any reply to any of these points. They were nothing more than an index of names of people arriving at the port. It was, as a matter of fact, physically impossible for . . . the port officers to do more. There were but a few of them who had to register sometimes 4,000 or 5,000 in a day. Now, under no circumstances could it be expected from them that they could examine the immigrants as to all these specific points, and put them down, and then expect that when through with the day's work they would make up the statistics.[19]

Apparently immigrants were often listed as natives of the country from which they had sailed, though many more than English left from Liverpool, or Germans from Hamburg. This confusion was particularly likely when the language spoken by the immigrants was not the one associated with their native country; thus, Flemish-speaking Belgians arriving on Dutch boats were often counted as Dutch. And what the immigration officers did with the complex ethnic structures of the empires of Austria-Hungary and Russia, no one really knows. Certainly there is no consistency in the records: Ukrainian immigrants, for instance, were sometimes so listed, and sometimes as Russians, Austrians, Galicians, and Ruthenians; eventually each of these several categories was solemnly totaled.[20]

Enumerators in countries otherwise as different as Malaya and the United States have made the same **error in recording**. When a woman who was asked how many children had been born to her answered "None," enumerators noted this reply in a manner that coders later repeatedly interpreted to mean "No answer." The number of childless couples, a most important datum for any analysis of fertility, was thus misstated (El-Badry, 1961).

Generally speaking, the greatest improvements in demographic data have come with the reduction of errors in processing. The importance of improved administration can be illustrated negatively with respect to the agency responsible for collecting immigration data in the United States. This has been shifted a number of times—from the Department of State (1820–74) to the Bureau of Statistics of the Treasury Department (1867–95), to the Bureau of Immigration (1892–1932), to the Immigration and

[19] *Reports of the Industrial Commission*, **15**, Washington, D.C., 1901, p. 179; quoted in Brinley Thomas, *Migration and Economic Growth: A Study of Great Britain and the Atlantic Economy*, Cambridge University Press, Cambridge, 1954, p. 45.

[20] This ignorance is not limited to Eastern Europe or to the past. In 1958 the Passport Office of the U.S. Department of State issued some statistics on the number of American tourists that had visited various European countries during the first three quarters of that year. "Holland," with 17,621 visitors, was eighth on the list, and "Netherlands" was eighteenth with 5,110. A few weeks later, the somewhat embarrassed passport authorities issued a revised list, pointing out that these two countries were, of course, the same (*Nieuwe Rotterdamse Courant*, November 1, 1958).

Naturalization Service, first in the Department of Labor (1933–40) and then in the Department of Justice (1940 to date). For some periods, it will be noted, duplicate sets of statistics were taken, but until the 1920s none was satisfactory. A law passed in 1819 required masters of arriving ships to declare the number of their passengers, as well as their age, sex, occupation, and the country "of which it is their intention to become inhabitants." Had these manifests been filled in accurately, they would have furnished a reasonable source of immigration statistics, but actually the records are neither complete nor consistent. In particular, immigrants were not distinguished from visitors in the annual totals, and naturalized citizens returning from abroad were not differentiated from aliens (Hutchinson, 1958). When the current series of statistics began in 1892 with the establishment of the Bureau of Immigration, the quality of the data did not improve markedly. For a number of years, as we have noted, the officials excluded cabin passengers from the list of immigrants, and included steerage passengers regardless of the duration of their intended stay in the United States. Until 1903, when this arbitrary definition was abolished, immigrants could evade the legal restrictions on entry that existed simply by paying the difference in the cost of passage! It was not until 1908 that the present distinction was made between "immigrant alien," or one intending (and permitted) to remain permanently, and "nonimmigrant alien," meaning either a visitor or a prior immigrant alien returning from a trip abroad. In the first decade of the twentieth century registration at points of entry along the land borders was introduced and a number of other improvements was made, so that by 1914 essentially the same system of controls as presently exists was instituted. That is to say, reasonably accurate and complete statistics were begun about the same time that restrictive legislation cut down immigration to a fraction of the pre-1914 flow.

Some of the complexity of immigration statistics is the result of the frequent change in the responsible agency, and of the patent fact that the purposes these records were supposed to serve were neither clear nor constant. Similarly, the first nine United States censuses were supervised by federal marshals as a relatively unimportant portion of their regular duties. Full-time supervisors were appointed for the first time in 1880, and a permanent Bureau of the Census was established only in 1902. This permanent institution had a salutary effect on professional standards, both in the census itself and in the collection of vital statistics. Several technical inventions, particularly the Hollerith card and its various analogues, have made it possible virtually to eliminate some types of errors.[21] It is the stage

---

[21] Errors are never totally absent even from data processed with the best equipment and greatest care. To take one example, the 1950 United States census showed an improbably high number of Indians in certain age groups and of widowed teen-agers. The reason for the disparities was that on a few of the cards some punches were made one column to the right of the correct position, and the errors were never picked up in subsequent checks (Coale and Stephan, 1962).

of the process that cannot be mechanized, the original collection of the data, where most errors occur.

## CORRECTION OF ERRORS

Any single set of data can be checked for its internal consistency. There cannot be, as an extreme example, more mothers or more housewives than there are women. In recent American censuses, the first check of this kind is made right in the field. Crew leaders look for contradictory statements in the schedule (for example, a respondent reported as born in the United States and also as naturalized) and for incomplete answers (for example, a person born in "Ireland" rather than Eire or Northern Ireland); and when they find one, the enumerator asks the original respondent to complete the form correctly.

There must also be a temporal consistency in any statistical series. Some characteristics, once acquired, are permanent—for example, literacy or legal majority; and a decline in the proportion able to read or to vote, if not due to emigration or a change in age structure or whatever, would make one suspect the accuracy of the data. Age does not remain constant but changes at a regular rate, and an unexplained variation from this pattern would also make one check the figures again.

It is often possible to compare data collected in different ways on the same facts, such as country-of-birth returns in the census with immigration records. Or the latter can be contrasted with the statistics maintained by some emigration countries.[22] As a particular kind of such comparisons, it is always possible to check a census against birth or death registrations. In the 1940 census of the United States an especially careful cross-check of this kind was made. Enumerators filled in a separate card for each infant under four months old on April 1, the official date of the census, and these cards were compared with the registrations of births and infant deaths in each area. The results were appalling. For the entire country only 92.5 per cent of births had been registered. In sixteen states the complete figure was below 90 per cent, the standard that had been used to admit them to the Birth-Registration Area; in six states it was under 85 per cent; in South Carolina and Arkansas hardly more than three births in every four were

---

[22] In general, the records of the receiving countries are better. For the entire period from the first colonization to the present, overseas emigration totaled over 60 million by the statistics of the receiving countries but about 10 per cent less by those of the sending countries (Kirk, 1946, pp. 72–73). For specific countries or periods, however, the discrepancy is much greater. For example, "for the years 1916 to 1920, Italian passport statistics indicate 633,000 emigrants to the United States; but the statistics of that country registered only 171,000 Italian immigrants" (Lacroix, 1949). Similarly, Dutch statistics show a total of 130,222 departures to *all* countries during 1882–1924, while for this period American statistics alone record 179,258 arrivals from the Netherlands (Willcox and Ferenczi, 1931, 2, 125, 737–746).

registered. Partly as a consequence of renewed efforts to improve registration procedures, and partly because of the larger proportion of hospital confinements, a similar check ten years later showed that there had been a considerable increase in the proportion of births registered. In 1950 this was almost 98 per cent over the whole nation, and for the South it was 96 per cent. Only two states still remained below the standard of 90 per cent (Shapiro, 1954). Similarly, in 1958 the Census Bureau and the National Office of Vital Statistics conducted a joint study in Memphis, matching the data on death certificates with those listed in the 1950 census and a special questionnaire. Among the 83 per cent of the cases that could be matched, only 85.6 per cent were identical on the birthplace of the decedent, and only 78.4 per cent were within five years of the same age (Guralnick and Nam, 1959). When one imperfect instrument is used to gauge the accuracy of another, the over-all improvement attained can be great, even though it is not possible by such a comparison to detect parallel errors.

It is also possible to correct errors by an especially scrupulous recount of a small sample of the population (e.g., Lahiri, 1958). For example, after the 1950 United States census a **Post-Enumeration Survey** was made using scrupulously selected and specially trained interviewers. About 3,500 small areas were recanvassed in order to gauge the number of households omitted in the original census, and 22,000 households were revisited in order to see how many persons had been miscounted. On this basis, it was estimated that there had been an underenumeration of 3,400,000 persons and an over-enumeration of 1,309,000 in the census, or a net undercount equal to 1.4 per cent of the total enumerated population. Errors were relatively more frequent in the South, in rural areas, and among nonwhites. Following the 1960 census, a check through a general sample of the population was supplemented with samples of three particular groups—social-security pensioners, selective-service registrants, and college students.

A final method of correcting errors in data and particularly of filling in gaps is by the construction of a mathematical model. Fertility, mortality, and the age structure are related to each other in such a way that if any two of these are known the range of the third can be determined. The curve of each of the major demographic variables can be smoothed by techniques that for many countries yield not precise data but probably more accurate figures than any alternative method. But "mathematical models in demography . . . can be but a rough approximation to reality and do no harm so long as they are not taken too seriously" (Carrier and Farrag, 1959).

## Summary

Population data are of four main types: the census, vital statistics, international migration records, and those on internal migration. Although partial precursors were found in previous historical eras, in a strict sense all four types are a product of modern Western culture. It was almost inevitable, therefore, that population theory tended to be ethnocentric, for even after World War II "the good population data on which demographic generalizations are based almost entirely relate to populations of European race" (Kirk, 1949). The most important example of this bias was noted in the previous chapter, the supposition—almost universally accepted in the 1930s—that the demographic transition in Europe would be followed with no essential change in all underdeveloped areas.

The censuses of the Western world, held every ten years or so with few or no interruptions since some date in the nineteenth century, have gradually become more accurate and broader in the range of questions covered. Today they are an indispensable tool for, among others, statesmen, social scientists, and businessmen. Vital statistics, because of the historical accident that usually they are gathered by local authorities rather than by national governments, have developed more slowly. International migration records, inadequate in a number of ways during the nineteenth century, were brought up to a reasonable standard of accuracy and completeness by about 1914 in the United States, the prime country of destination in the prior period. The statistics of many demographic phenomena, for example, marriage and divorce, morbidity, and internal migration, are still quite poor in many economically advanced countries and practically nonexistent in underdeveloped areas.

During the past century, originally as an extension of the national statistics of Western Europe, several international congresses and organizations have tried in various ways to establish worldwide statistical standards. These efforts are wholly laudable, and it is particularly useful that the underdeveloped countries presently beginning their statistical records will be able, at least in some respects, to start from the highest level of the procedures so painfully worked out in Western countries. It must be emphasized, however, that variation in statistical methods is in part accidental —and with sufficient effort and good will this can be reduced—and in part a reflection of differences in national culture. International migration statistics, for example, so long as they are collected as an adjunct to the political control of national borders, will be noncomparable mainly because of the great differences in various countries' migration laws. Or, as another example, what are termed common-law marriages in the United States are very frequent in Latin America, where, however, they are often not recognized either in law or in the statistics, so that thousands of mothers or even grandmothers are classified as single. In short, some standardization of population data is both possible and desirable, but so long as national cultures are not homogenized into a worldwide uniformity, the international comparability of statistics will not be fully achieved.

To avoid errors in demographic statistics, the following conditions must be met: (1) All categories to be measured must be precisely defined. (2)

French-speaking team at the Census Training Center for Asia and the Far East, Tokyo. A peasant is watching the instructor point out a farm household near the city (*United Nations*).

Each instance of the phenomenon being measured must be counted once, and only once. (3) Respondents must be induced to answer truthfully the questions put to them. (4) Answers must be classified in the appropriate categories and subcategories. (5) Errors must not be introduced in the compiling, processing, and publication of the data.

As even this list suggests, perfect accuracy is not attainable. Indeed, it is not sought. The aim in modern demographic statistics is to reduce the error to a small proportion of known range rather than to try to eliminate it altogether. The errors that are made can be detected and in part corrected by checking: (1) any form for collecting information, such as a census schedule or a birth certificate, for internal consistency; (2) data of the same series, such as successive censuses, for serial consistency; (3) data of different types, such as vital statistics and the census, or the census and immigration records, for external consistency; (4) the grosser count with an especially carefully drawn sample; and (5) the components of the population for consistency with a mathematical model.

## Suggestions for Further Reading

The best introductory works are probably the three manuals issued by the United Nations (1949, 1954, 1955); all three contrast recommended procedures with actual practices. Of considerably greater interest and no less importance is Milbank Memorial Fund, 1949, a series of essays on how various demographic concepts are interpreted in various countries. Techniques of population analysis are expounded in Barclay, 1958; Smith, 1948; McArthur, 1961; and, at a more advanced level, Spiegelman, 1955 (1968).

U.S. Bureau of the Census, 1957, a short pamphlet that describes the Bureau's operations in popular terms, can best be supplemented by various articles written by Bureau personnel, e.g., Hanson and Marks, 1958; Powell and Pritzker, 1965; Taeuber and Hansen, 1966. The history of the early censuses, given in full and sometimes fascinating detail in Wright, 1900, is summarized, as it were, in U.S. Bureau of the Census, 1960.

Gutman, 1959 is the definitive study of America's earliest registration system. Various articles on registration, e.g., Shapiro, 1954, indicate both the problems that persist and methods of coping with them.

In spite of its date, Willcox and Ferenczi, 1929–31 is still the best work on historical migration statistics. See, for example, the essay by Marian Rubins Davis, "Critique of Official United States Immigration Statistics" (2, 645–658), which is brought up to date in Hutchinson, 1958. Comparable analyses of American data on internal migration are given in Lee and Lee, 1960 and in the early chapters of Shryock, 1964.

Uses of demographic data in sociological research are discussed in Glick, 1962, 1965.

*BARCLAY, GEORGE W. 1958. *Techniques of Population Analysis*. Wiley, New York.

BOGUE, DONALD J. 1965. "The Pros and Cons of 'Self-Enumeration,'" *Demography*, **2**, 600–626.

*BRUNSMAN, HOWARD G. 1963. "Significance of Electronic Computers for Users of Census Data," in Milbank Memorial Fund, *Emerging Techniques in Population Research*. New York, pp. 269–277.

CARRIER, N. H., and A. M. FARRAG. 1959. "The Reduction of Errors in Census Populations for Statistically Underdeveloped Countries," *Population Studies*, **12**, 240–285.

CICOUREL, AARON V. 1964. *Method and Measurement in Sociology*. Free Press of Glencoe, New York.

COALE, ANSLEY J., and FREDERICK F. STEPHAN. 1962. "The Case of the Indians and the Teen-Age Widows," *Journal of the American Statistical Association*, **57**, 338–347.

COOK, ROBERT C. 1955. "Population in the United Nations," *Population Bulletin*, **11**, 93–107.

CORCORAN, THOMAS F. 1963. "On the Confidential Status of Census Reports," *American Statistician*, **17**, 33–40.

DEDRICK, CALVERT L. 1949. "Cultural Differences and Census Concepts," in Milbank Memorial Fund, 1949,[23] pp. 65–70.

*DUNN, EDGAR S., JR. 1967. "The Idea of a National Data Center and the Issue of Personal Privacy," *American Statistician,* **21**, 21–27.

EL-BADRY, M. A. 1961. "Failure of Enumerators to Make Entries of Zero: Errors in Recording Childless Cases in Population Censuses," *Journal of the American Statistical Association,* **56**, 909–924.

FISCHER, J. L. 1958. "The Classification of Residence in Censuses," *American Anthropologist,* **60**, 508–517.

GLASER, E., D. ROSENBLATT, and M. K. WOOD. 1967. "The Design of a Federal Statistical Data Center," *American Statistician,* **21**, 12–20.

GLICK, PAUL C. 1962. "The 1960 Census as a Source for Social Research," *American Sociological Review,* **27**, 581–590.

———. 1965. "Census Data as a Source for Theses and Dissertations in the Field of Sociology," *Milbank Memorial Fund Quarterly,* **43**, 17–30.

GURALNICK, LILLIAN, and CHARLES B. NAM. 1959. "Census-NOVS Study of Death Certificates Matched to Census Records," *Milbank Memorial Fund Quarterly,* **37**, 144–151.

GUTMAN, ROBERT. 1959. *Birth and Death Registration in Massachusetts, 1639–1900.* Milbank Memorial Fund, New York.

HADLEY, ELEANOR M. 1956. "A Critical Analysis of the Wetback Problem," *Law and Contemporary Problems,* **21**, 334–357.

HAMILTON, C. HORACE. 1966. "Effect of Census Errors on the Measurement of Net Migration," *Demography,* **3**, 393–415.

HANSEN, MORRIS H., WILLIAM N. HURWITZ, and LEON PRITZKER. 1953. "The Accuracy of Census Results," *American Sociological Review,* **18**, 416–423.

HANSEN, MORRIS H., WILLIAM N. HURWITZ, HAROLD NISSELSON, and JOSEPH STEINBERG. 1955. "The Redesign of the Census Current Population Survey," *Journal of the American Statistical Association,* **50**, 701–719.

* HANSON, ROBERT H., and ELI S. MARKS. 1958. "Influence of the Interviewer on the Accuracy of Survey Results," *Journal of the American Statistical Association,* **53**, 635–655.

HUTCHINSON, E. P. 1958. "Notes on Immigration Statistics of the United States," *Journal of the American Statistical Association,* **53**, 963–1025.

HUXTABLE, DEANE L. 1967. "Vital Statistics Aid in Developing Nations," *American Journal of Public Health,* **57**, 504–508.

JOHNSTON, DENIS FOSTER. 1966. *An Analysis of Sources of Information on the Population of the Navaho.* Bureau of American Ethnology, Bulletin 197. Washington, D.C.

KAPLAN, DAVID L. 1967. "Plans for the 1970 Census of Population and Housing," *Statistical Reporter,* No. 68–5, pp. 73–79.

KEYFITZ, NATHAN. 1950. "The Growth of Canadian Population," *Population Studies,* **4**, 47–63.

KIRK, DUDLEY. 1946. *Europe's Population in the Interwar Years.* League of Nations. Princeton University Press, Princeton, N.J.

---

[23] In the lists of references appended to the chapters of this book, a short citation directs the reader to the full reference given in the same list.

————. 1949. "Problems of Collection and Comparability of International Population Statistics," in Milbank Memorial Fund, 1949, pp. 20–39.

KISH, LESLIE. 1965. *Survey Sampling.* Wiley, New York.

* LACROIX, MAX. 1949. "Problems of Collection and Comparison of Migration Statistics," in Milbank Memorial Fund, 1949, pp. 71–105.

LAHIRI, D. B. 1958. "Recent Developments in the Use of Techniques for Assessment of Errors in Nation-Wide Surveys of India," *Bulletin de l'Institut International de Statistique,* **36,** 71–93.

LAZARSFELD, PAUL F. 1961. "Notes on the History of Quantification in Sociology —Trends, Sources and Problems," in *Quantification: A History of the Meaning of Measurement in the Natural and Social Sciences,* edited by Harry Woolf. Bobbs Merrill, Indianapolis, pp. 147–203.

LEE, EVERETT S., and ANNE S. LEE. 1960. "Internal Migration Statistics for the United States," *Journal of the American Statistical Association,* **55,** 664–697.

McARTHUR, NORMA. 1961. *Introducing Population Statistics.* Oxford University Press, Melbourne.

* MILBANK MEMORIAL FUND. 1949. *Problems in the Collection and Comparability of International Statistics.* New York.

MILLER, HERMAN P. 1967. "Considerations in Determining the Content of the 1970 Census," *Demography,* **4,** 744–752.

PETERSEN, WILLIAM. 1964. *The Politics of Population.* Doubleday, Garden City, N.Y.

* POWELL, BARBARA A., and LEON PRITZKER. 1965. "Effects of Variation in Field Personnel on Census Results," *Demography,* **2,** 8–32.

PRESSAT, ROLAND, and ALFRED SAUVY. 1959. "L'activité des Nations-Unies pour les questions de population," *Population,* **14,** 535–550.

RUBIN, ERNEST. 1962. "Government Statistics and Confidentiality of Response," *American Statistician,* **16,** 27–30.

* ————. 1966. "A Statistical Overview of Americans Abroad," *Annals of the American Academy of Political and Social Science,* **368,** 1–10.

SHAPIRO, SAM. 1954. "Recent Testing of Birth Registration Completeness in the United States," *Population Studies,* **8,** 3–21.

SHRYOCK, HENRY S., JR. 1964. *Population Mobility Within the United States.* Community and Family Study Center. University of Chicago, Chicago.

SMITH, T. LYNN. 1948. *Population Analysis.* McGraw-Hill, New York.

SPIEGELMAN, MORTIMER. 1955 (1968). *Introduction to Demography.* Society of Actuaries, Chicago (Revised ed.; Harvard University Press, Cambridge, Mass.).

TAEUBER, CONRAD. 1967. "Invasion of Privacy," *Eugenics Quarterly,* **14,** 243–246.

* ————, and MORRIS H. HANSEN. 1966. "Self-Enumeration as a Census Method," *Demography,* **3,** 289–295.

THOMAS, DOROTHY SWAINE. 1938. "The Continuous Register System of Population Accounting," in National Resources Committee, Committee on Population Problems, *The Problems of a Changing Population.* U.S. Government Printing Office, Washington, D.C., Appendix C.

* UNITED NATIONS, DEPARTMENT OF SOCIAL AFFAIRS. 1949. *Problems of Migration Statistics.* Population Studies, No. 5. New York.

* ————, DEPARTMENT OF ECONOMIC AFFAIRS, STATISTICAL OFFICE. 1954. *Hand-*

*book of Population Census Methods.* Studies in Methods, Series F, No. 5. New York.

\* ———, DEPARTMENT OF ECONOMIC AND SOCIAL AFFAIRS, STATISTICAL OFFICE. 1955. *Handbook of Vital Statistics Methods.* Studies in Methods, Series F, No. 7. New York.

U.S. BUREAU OF THE CENSUS. 1957. *Fact Finder for the Nation.* Washington, D.C.

\* ———. 1960. *Historical Statistics of the United States, Colonial Times to 1957.* Washington, D.C.

\* ———. 1963. "The Current Population Survey: A Report on Methodology." Technical Paper No. 7.

———. 1968. "Mobility of the Population of the United States, March 1966 to March 1967," *Current Population Reports,* Series P–20, No. 171.

U.S. DEPARTMENT OF STATE. 1965. *Status of the World's Nations.* Bureau of Intelligence and Research, Geographic Bulletin No. 2. Washington, D.C.

U.S. PUBLIC HEALTH SERVICE. 1966. *Report of the Fifteenth Anniversary Conference of the United States National Committee on Vital Health Statistics.* Washington, D.C.

\* WILLCOX, WALTER F. 1930. "Census," *Encyclopedia of the Social Sciences,* **3,** 295–300. Macmillan, New York.

———. 1949. "Development of International Statistics," in Milbank Memorial Fund, 1949, pp. 9–19.

\* ———, and IMRE FERENCZI, editors. 1929, 1931. *International Migrations.* Vol. **1,** *Statistics;* Vol. **2,** *Interpretations.* Publications 14 and 18. National Bureau of Economic Research, New York.

\* WRIGHT, CARROLL D. 1900. *The History and Growth of the United States Censuses, Prepared for the Senate Committee on the Censuses.* Government Printing Office, Washington, D.C.

ZITTER, MEYER, and HENRY S. SHRYOCK, JR. 1964. "Accuracy and Methods of Preparing Postcensal Population Estimates for States and Local Areas," *Demography,* **1,** 227–241.

# 3 AGE AND SEX STRUCTURE AND SOME BASIC DEMOGRAPHIC TECHNIQUES

It is convenient to distinguish **population structure,** or the distribution by sex and age, from **population composition,** or the distribution by other attributes; for the former is in several respects more basic to demography.

1. Sex and age are **universal.** Indeed, some types of occupational pattern and class structure, of religion, of ethnic differentiation, are also to be found in virtually every society, but the effect of such factors on the population varies greatly. If the god of the ancient Aztecs demanded enormous human sacrifices and Roman Catholicism has inhibited the spread of contraception, one cannot therefore speak of *the* influence of religion on mortality and fertility.

2. Sex and age are **always relevant** and always in roughly the same way. Some religions, to continue with the same example, have no effect on population phenomena, but in every culture throughout the world children are borne only by females in the fecund age group, and the probability of dying is greater among infants and the aged than among young adults. One of the principal modes of refining demographic rates, therefore, is to relate the incidence of such demographic events as births or deaths to a population delimited by its age and sex characteristics.

**59**

3. The population structure is the **basis of a population model,** which is the principal subject matter of formal demography (see pp. 3–4). The processes of fertility, migration, and mortality together determine not only the current size of the population of any area but also its structure; and, conversely, to the degree that other factors remain unchanged, the population structure sets the future rates of fertility, migration, and mortality. What is termed a **young population**—that is, one in which young persons are relatively more numerous—is more fecund, less susceptible to many causes of death, and usually more migratory than an **old population.**

## Quality of the Data

Statistics on sex are generally the best in any demographic record. There is no ambiguity about the meaning of *male* and *female* and seldom any motivation for misrepresentation. In the United States the historical record has only two significant gaps: the sex of Negroes before 1820 and the sex of immigrants before about 1850. The data on sex listed for the whole population, however, may be a good deal more accurate than figures for the various subgroups. Among foreign-born, for instance, females are less likely to list themselves as natives than males, whose occupation outside the home affords both a stronger motive and a more rapid acculturation. Most casual and migrant laborers, who are likely to be passed over in any population count, are male adults, and although their omission affects over-all totals only insignificantly, this might not be the case for such smaller groups as, for example, the Negroes in particular localities (Smith, 1948, Chapter 5).

Data on age, available in almost all types of population records, are also relatively accurate and complete, though far less so than the uninitiated would suppose. Although all peoples have roles specific to infants, children, youth, adults, and the aged, many are alien to a more precise designation of age. In the first population counts undertaken by the European administrators of the various Pacific islands, for example, the only age differentiation attempted was to distinguish children from adults. Then the populations were divided by social-status groups, roughly associated with particular age ranges. "Even now, relatively few are conscious of age as the number of years which have elapsed since their birth; if asked their age, many will reply with a number, but often the answer is quite meaningless" (McArthur, 1961, p. 24).

Present-day recapitulations of the population growth of Western countries are often broken down by age, but in many of the earliest censuses these data were in fact not collected. Thus in England no question was asked about age in 1801; in 1821 the question was included in the schedule, but persons were required to answer it only "if not inconvenient"; in 1831 the only return concerning age was an estimate of the number of males over twenty. Respondents had to state their age only from 1841 on. The age statistics collected in the United States, as another instance, varied even more during the first decades of the national census (Wright, 1900, p. 91):

Free Whites:
  1790: Males divided into two age groups only—under 16 years, and 16 years and over; females not classified by age.
  1800–1820: Males and females each classified as follows: under 10, 10–16, 16–26, 26–45, 45 and over.
  1830–1840: Males and females each classified as follows: under 5, 5–10, 10–15, 15–20, 20–30, 30–40, 40–50, 50–60, 60–70, 70–80, 80–90, 90–100, 100 and over.
Colored (except Indians not taxed):
  1790–1810: Divided into slave and free; not classified by sex or age.
  1820: Divided into slave and free and by sex, and each subgroup classified by age as follows: under 14, 14–26, 26–45, 45 and over.
  1830–1840: Divided into slave and free by sex, and each subgroup classified by age as follows: under 10, 10–24, 24–36, 36–55, 55–100, 100 and over.

Beginning in 1850, enumerators were instructed to ask for the exact age. Since that date, this has been defined as the age on the last birthday except in 1890, when the question called for age at the nearest birthday, and in 1960, when each person was asked the month and year of his birth.

Age, in short, can be defined in grosser units than single years. If in years, it can be measured to the last birthday or to the nearest one. Or, most precisely, the date of birth can be asked for. Practice varies considerably from one country to another, and in any country from one type of demographic data to another.[1]

Once persons in a Western society have been asked for their age, it might be supposed that most respondents both could furnish this datum and would be willing to do so. However, even in a country like the United States some report that they do not know their age. Others give it only approximately, either because they do not know it precisely or because they do not recognize the importance of accuracy. They "heap" their stated age at an even number, a number ending in five, or particularly one ending in zero (Myers, 1940; Bachi, 1954; Zelnik, 1961, 1964). How old a person is might be regarded as a relatively neutral characteristic, but the prestige associated with a particular age is likely to be reflected in the record. Thus, respondents often overstate the correct figure to heap ages at the 21 years marking majority. The age of infants and young children is often overstated,

---

[1] In the United States, the standard certificate of live birth, in the form recommended by the National Center for Health Statistics, calls only for the mother's and the father's "age (at time of birth)" (U.S. National Center for Health Statistics, 1968, p. 6; cf. Lunde and Grove, 1966). Not only is this somewhat ambiguous, but it is a less precise designation particularly of the mother's age than would be useful in analyzing fertility.

and that is one reason for their usual underenumeration. The very old also often exaggerate their longevity; the number of American centenarians was probably closer to 3,700 than the 10,326 reported in the 1960 census (Myers, 1966). At least by popular legend, although this has seldom been validated in an empirical study,[2] middle-aged persons and particularly women often understate their age or refuse to reveal it.

The problems in interpreting the age data of non-Western population records are similar, though with some interesting differences. In Japan, inasmuch as respondents are asked for their date of birth, there is no tendency to heap replies on ages ending in two, five, or zero (this is thus an important additional advantage to phrasing the question in the most precise form). Even so, when data were compared from the same persons in a census and in a sample survey, discrepancies were found in 17 per cent of the returns, partly because of errors, partly because of the exaggeration of advanced ages (Morita, 1958). In Ghana, similarly, the dates of registered birth of one thousand children aged up to eight years were compared with their ages as given in the 1960 census. Of the 608 cases for which two designations of age were obtained, 35 per cent were different. Misstatements of age were due in part to digital preference, in part to raising the age to the next birthday (Caldwell, 1966).

Among Chinese a special problem is created by the traditional mode of calculating the age of infants. A child is reckoned to be one year old at birth, and two years old at the subsequent Chinese New Year (which usually comes in February), so that in an extreme case an infant born one week before the New Year would be two years old by the Chinese system when he is one week old by the Western one. Correcting for the difference in Singapore, for example, is complicated by the fact that the proportion of Chinese who use each system is not known. When enumerators were instructed to ask for the age "according to the English reckoning"—thus in effect asking the more traditional respondents to calculate their age before replying—it was impossible to know how many in fact complied. The solution is to ask for the totemic animal of each person. For persons born in the Chinese years falling mainly in 1920, 1932, 1944, 1956, 1968, etc., for instance, this is the monkey, and if a person so identified gives his age in 1957 as 14, we know that by the Western system it is 13 (You, 1959; cf. Saw, 1967).

Errors in reported ages can generally be adjusted by either of two principles, which are termed the cohort method and the smoothing method.

A **cohort** constitutes all persons born during the same year (or some other unit of time), who are analyzed as a unit throughout their lifetime.[3]

---

[2] But see T. Lynn Smith and Homer L. Hitt, "The Misstatement of Women's Ages and the Vital Indexes," *Metron*, **13** (1939), 95–108; cited in Smith, 1948, p. 116.

[3] More precisely, this is a birth cohort. One can also designate marriage cohorts (all persons married during a given year), cohorts of college graduates, and so on.

Apart from such factors as, for instance, a migration into or out of the area under study, each cohort changes from one year to the next only by the proportion of persons who die off at that age—a figure that one can derive from the life table for the population (see pp. 209–213). Whether there is heaping at age 25, for example, could be shown by a sample survey the following year, when the age of this cohort would be 26.

For any one census, similarly, one can assume that under normal conditions there will have been a gradual reduction in the size of cohorts of successive ages. Thus, the number aged 26 should be only slightly less than that aged 25; and if it is not, the age curve can be smoothed by the calculation of **age ratios,** or the number of persons at each age divided by the average of the number at the adjacent five older and five younger ages (Zelnik, 1961). In many cases, however, it is impossible to be sure whether deviations from a smooth curve are the consequence of spurious reporting or actual differences in the size of certain cohorts. For instance, take the age structure of Indonesia in 1961, which showed a very large proportion aged 5 to 9, an extraordinarily small proportion aged 10 to 24, and again a larger proportion aged 25 to 44. If one accepts the figures as reported, the plausible reason is that during the Japanese occupation and the subsequent revolution the birth rate was lower and the infant death rate higher (Keyfitz, 1965). However, it may be that in Indonesia, as in a number of African countries, young persons on the verge of adult roles tend to understate their ages, and then to overstate them once social adulthood has been achieved (Van de Walle, 1966, with a reply by Keyfitz). Abstract models may be useful, in short, but any "post-census adjustment should be carried out by reference to the factors underlying the various biases rather than by cut-and-dried mathematical formulae" (You, 1959).

## The Sex Ratio

The simplest measure of population structure is the **sex ratio,** defined as the number of males per 100 females.[4] For the estimated population of the United States including all armed forces, the sex ratio on July 1, 1966, was:

$$\text{Sex ratio} = \frac{\text{Number of males}}{\text{Number of females}} \times 100$$

$$= \frac{96,900,000}{99,942,000} \times 100 = 97.0$$

This figure of 97.0, unchanged from 1960, is the lowest in American history (Figure 3-1). The deficit in males, slightly over 3 million in 1966, will in-

---

[4] Some authorities define it as the number of males per *1,000* females, thus eliminating the decimal from the form used by the U.S. Census Bureau. In Europe the conventional form is the number of females per 100 (or 1,000) males.

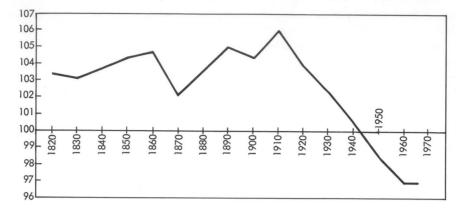

**Figure 3-1.** Sex ratio of the population of the United States, 1820–1966. [Sources: U.S. Bureau of the Census, *Historical Statistics of the United States, Colonial Times to 1957* (1960), Series A 34–35; *Census of the Population, 1960*, Vol. 1, Part 1, Table 42; *Current Population Reports*, Series P-25, No. 352, November 18, 1966].

crease to more than 4 million by 1985 according to Census Bureau projections (Siegel and Akers, 1964).

The sex ratio of any population is affected by past fertility, mortality, and migration. The evidence available indicates that many more males than females are conceived, and that the proportion of males among fetal deaths is also high. According to a recent study, the reported sex ratio at birth ranged in various territories from a high of 116.2 (Gambia, 1951–57) to a low of 90.2 (Montserrat), with a usual worldwide average of between 104 and 107 (Visaria, 1967; *cf.* Rubin, 1967). The higher mortality of males continues throughout most of life, for not only are they generally more susceptible to disease but—apart from childbearing under primitive conditions—their vocations are typically more dangerous. The American sex ratio of 102.2 in 1870, the lowest up to that point, was partly the consequence of the heavy male losses in the Civil War,[5] probably aggravated by a greater underenumeration of males. As males and females are seldom balanced in migration, whether internal or international, this also can have an important effect on the sex ratios of both the sending and the receiving areas. In the United States, thus, the highest sex ratio was 106.0, recorded in 1910 after a quarter century of very large male-dominated immigration. In the most recent period, almost all factors have helped lower the sex

---

[5] There is a persistent allegation, supported by some seemingly solid evidence, that military losses are usually balanced by a larger proportion of males born during wartime. The most reasonable among several hypotheses offered to explain this phenomenon is that the prolonged absence of males from their wives increases the interval between births and thus reduces the proportion of conceptions ending in fetal deaths (Panunzio, 1943).

ratio: immigration was sharply curtailed and shifted in large part to the family movement of refugees; there were sizable male losses in World War II; some of the most significant medical advances—in particular in the control of cancers—have been more successful in reducing the number of female deaths.

One reason for studying the sex ratio is its relevance to family formation. The number of marriages possible in monogamous countries and thus also the number of legitimate births depend in part on whether there are as many men as women. A marked and growing disparity has often been viewed as a threat to family stability. Following World War II, when Australia was endeavoring to increase its population through subsidized immigration, the strong male predominance among the immigrants was reinforced by the emigration of Australian females who had married Allied servicemen temporarily stationed in Australia. With such a pattern of net immigration, a country committed to doubling its population was forgoing many of the immigrants' potential progeny.[6]

The sex ratio of the entire population, however, hardly indicates the number of potential new families. The pertinent figure is rather the sex ratio of that portion able to wed. This class is delimited, first of all, by age (it is conventional in the United States to include that sector of the population aged 14 and over) and, secondly, by marital status (in a monogamous society, those with one spouse may not take another). If marriageable persons are defined as those denoted as "single" in the U.S. census classification—that is, those aged 14 years or over and never married [7]—for the United States in 1960 their sex ratio was 123.4 (Table 3-1). Thus, in spite of the slight female surplus in the population as a whole, among single adults there were almost five males to every four females. During the 1960s, as a consequence of this skewed sex ratio, American men have been marrying at an increasing rate but females at a decreasing rate (Akers, 1967).

This marriageable class, moreover, is not homogeneous (Rubin, 1962). One of the prerequisites to romantic love is that most prosaic characteristic, spatial propinquity, and the availability of partners varies widely from one section of the country to another, as the figures in Table 3-1 roughly indicate.[8] Intermarriage is atypical also across lines set by race, religion, and social class—to name only the most important—and the sex

[6] W. D. Borrie, *Immigration, Australia's Problems and Prospects,* Angus and Robertson, Sydney, 1949, pp. 93–95.

[7] Whether to include widowed and divorced persons is a moot point. Legally they are marriageable, but actually in the United States a large proportion of the persons so designated in any census will never remarry; and of those that do, many will be too old to bear children. Note that more females than males report themselves as married (Table 3-1).

[8] The relevant distance is actually measured not in thousands of miles but in tens of city blocks; see James H. S. Bossard, "Residential Propinquity as a Factor in Marriage

Table 3-1. Sex Ratio of Persons 14 Years and Over, by Marital Status and Region, United States, 1960

| REGION | SINGLE | MARRIED | SEPARATED | WIDOWED | DIVORCED |
|--------|--------|---------|-----------|---------|----------|
| | | | MARITAL STATUS | | |
| Northeast | 109.9 | 98.7 | 63.8 | 29.3 | 64.1 |
| North Central | 122.7 | 99.6 | 82.3 | 29.5 | 74.6 |
| South | 124.5 | 90.9 | 70.7 | 25.5 | 67.5 |
| West | 149.1 | 100.5 | 80.9 | 26.6 | 79.0 |
| United States | 123.4 | 96.8 | 71.7 | 27.9 | 70.9 |

SOURCE: Ernest Rubin, "Aspects of Statistical Aggregate Measures: I. The Sex Ratio," *American Statistician*, 16 (1962), 37–39.

ratio of each one of the essentially endogamous subgroups formed by the composite effect of all of these factors is thus the most relevant to the probability of family formation. Particularly among the smaller nonwhite races in the United States, the large surplus of males combined with the small chance of intermarriage has made a normal family life something of a rarity.[9] In a more detailed analysis, it would be necessary to study the effect of all of the relevant variables simultaneously; for, say, a white Catholic physician, aged 32, living in New York City, is more likely to marry if he finds a woman aged, say, 29 whose social background is similar to his in every respect.

## The Three Main Age Groups

The most useful single figure summarizing a population's age structure is its **median age,** which divides the population into two equal parts, half older and half younger. In the United States, with the gradual decline in fertility and rise in life expectancy, the median age rose steadily from the

Selection," *American Journal of Sociology*, 38 (1932), 219–224, and the many subsequent studies that have validated the findings of this pioneer work.

[9] In 1880, when the number of Chinese males in the United States first exceeded 100,000, Chinese females numbered fewer than 5,000. Among Japanese the ratio in 1900 was even more than twenty to one, still more than seven to one in 1910. In 1960, the sex ratio of Chinese in the United States was 133.2, and that of Filipinos was 175.4 (U.S. Bureau of the Census, *Historical Statistics of the United States, Colonial Times to 1957*, Washington, D.C., 1960; *U.S. Census of Population, 1960*, Vol. I: *Characteristics of the Population*, Part 1: *United States Summary*, Washington, D.C., 1964).

first censuses, when half the white population was under 16 years, to 1950, when the median was almost double that (Table 3-2). During the next decade it fell slightly, reflecting the postwar revival in the birth rate. This historical record of one Western country is similar to the worldwide range

Table 3-2. Median Age of the Population, by Sex, United
States, 1790–1960

|  | MALE | FEMALE | TOTAL |
|---|---|---|---|
| 1790 [a] | 15.9 | — | — |
| 1800 [a] | 15.7 | 16.3 | 16.0 |
| 1810 [a] | 15.9 | 16.1 | 16.0 |
| 1820 | 16.6 | 16.7 | 16.7 |
| 1830 | 17.1 | 17.3 | 17.2 |
| 1840 | 17.8 | 17.7 | 17.8 |
| 1850 | 19.2 | 18.6 | 18.9 |
| 1860 | 19.8 | 19.1 | 19.4 |
| 1870 | 20.2 | 20.1 | 20.2 |
| 1880 | 21.2 | 20.7 | 20.9 |
| 1890 | 22.3 | 21.6 | 22.0 |
| 1900 | 23.3 | 22.4 | 22.9 |
| 1910 | 24.6 | 23.5 | 24.1 |
| 1920 | 25.8 | 24.7 | 25.3 |
| 1930 | 26.7 | 26.2 | 26.5 |
| 1940 | 29.1 | 29.0 | 29.0 |
| 1950 | 29.9 | 30.5 | 30.2 |
| 1960 | 28.7 | 30.3 | 29.5 |

SOURCES: U.S. Bureau of the Census, *Historical Statistics of the United States, Colonial Times to 1957*, Washington, D.C., 1960, Series A 96–91; *Census of Population, 1960*, Vol. I, *Characteristics of the Population*, Part 1, *United States Summary*, Washington, D.C., 1964, Table 60.
[a] White population only.

around 1960, when for various countries the median age fell between 17.7 (Taiwan) and 36.2 (Sweden). Only 26 per cent of the Swedish population was under the Taiwanese median, and only 23 per cent of Taiwan's population was older than the Swedish median.[10]

A more detailed representation of a society's age structure can be based

[10] Warren S. Thompson and David T. Lewis, *Population Problems*, 5th Ed., McGraw-Hill, New York, 1965, p. 90.

on a division of its population into three main age groups: dependent children, aged 14 years and under; the active population, 15 to 64 years; and dependent aged, 65 years and over. This distribution is shown in Table 3-3

Table 3-3. Percentage Distribution Among Three Main Age Groups, United States, 1880–1966

| YEAR | DEPENDENT CHILDREN (14 YEARS AND UNDER) | ACTIVE POPULATION (15–64 YEARS) | DEPENDENT AGED (65 YEARS AND OVER) | INDEX OF AGING $\frac{(4)}{(2)} \times 100$ | DEPENDENCY RATIO $\frac{(2)+(4)}{(3)} \times 100$ |
|---|---|---|---|---|---|
| (1) | (2) | (3) | (4) | (5) | (6) |
| 1880 | 38.1 | 58.5 | 3.4 | 8.9 | 70.9 |
| 1890 | 35.5 | 60.4 | 3.9 | 11.0 | 65.2 |
| 1900 | 34.4 | 61.3 | 4.1 | 11.9 | 62.8 |
| 1910 | 32.1 | 63.4 | 4.3 | 13.4 | 57.4 |
| 1920 | 31.7 | 63.4 | 4.7 | 14.8 | 57.4 |
| 1930 | 29.3 | 65.1 | 5.4 | 18.4 | 53.3 |
| 1940 | 25.0 | 68.1 | 6.8 | 27.2 | 46.6 |
| 1950 | 26.8 | 65.3 | 8.2 | 30.6 | 53.5 |
| 1960 | 31.0 | 59.8 | 9.2 | 29.7 | 67.2 |
| 1966 | 30.5 | 60.1 | 9.4 | 30.8 | 66.4 |

SOURCES: Conrad Taeuber and Irene B. Taeuber, *The Changing Population of the United States*, Wiley, New York, 1958, p. 31; U.S. Bureau of the Census, *Current Population Reports*, series P-25, No. 352, November 18, 1966.

for the United States since 1880, the date at which America's transformation from an agrarian to an industrial society passed its preliminary stage.

**DEPENDENT CHILDREN**

From the first three censuses of the United States until 1940, the proportion of children steadily fell, at first slowly and then more rapidly. In 1850 two-fifths of the population was under 15 years, in 1910 almost one-third, and after the depression of the 1930s one-fourth. The most obvious reason for these changes in the percentage under 15, of course, was the long-term fall in fertility, its revival after World War II, and its subsequent decline. The secular fall in the death rate, since it was concentrated in infant and child mortality, was equivalent to a rise in the birth rate. The effect of immigration was complex; most immigrants were young adults, and the immediate consequence of their entry was to decrease the proportion of children in the population, but in the somewhat longer run this was countered by their higher than average fertility.

As with the change in median age so also with that in the proportion of children, the progression over time in the United States can be matched with today's range among countries of the world. The poorest countries, like the poorest families, generally have the most children, and in both cases that is an important reason why they are poor (Davis, 1965). The future of any country lies with its children, and if their excess numbers make it impossible to afford them adequate care, the prognosis for social progress is likely to be bleak.

#### DEPENDENT AGED

The percentage of the United States population aged 65 and over rose from 3.4 in 1880 to 9.4 in 1966. Over the same period, while the population as a whole increased 3.9 times, the aged increased 10.7 times. What caused this rise in the proportion of the aged in the United States, as in all Western countries? The common-sense reply to this question might be that it was the combined effect of falling mortality and falling fertility, but such an answer would be misleading. The increase in the *number* of old people was indeed the consequence of improvements in death control. However, because declines in mortality have been greatest among infants and children, the larger proportion who remained alive *retarded* the aging of the population. "In most Western countries the fraction over 65 would be *larger* than it is if mortality rates had remained at their 1900 level. The average age of the population would be *greater* if [control over] mortality had *not* improved" (Coale, 1956; *cf*. Valaoras, 1950; Sauvy, 1954).

The two influences can be combined into a single figure,[11] as follows:

$$\text{Index of aging} = \frac{\text{Persons 65 years and over}}{\text{Children 14 years and under}} \times 100$$

The long-term rise in this index, shown in Column 5 of Table 3-3, not only slowed down but was actually reversed from 1950 to 1960. Even with the renewed increase in the most recent period (mainly the consequence of the decline in fertility), this retardation in the aging of the American population should be emphasized, for it contradicts so much that is written on the subject. That in Western societies both the proportion of elderly persons and their absolute number have been increasing has received wider public attention than most demographic developments. Writings on **gerontology,** the study of the aged, and **geriatrics,** the healing of the aged, however, have often been distinguished more by the authors' noble senti-

---

[11] This index is suggested by Valaoras (1950), except that he defines the aged as those 60 years and over.

ments, not to say sentimentality, than by their knowledge and acuity. In response, one demographer observed: "Viewed as a whole the 'problem of aging' is no problem at all. It is only the pessimistic way of looking at a great triumph of civilization" (Notestein, 1954).

In a preindustrial familistic culture, like America of circa 1800 or traditional China, the old were no "problem."

The social status given them was of the best. They did not fear to grow old; for the old were not pitied or shoved aside, and were not treated as objects of charity and special worry. This situation (ideal from the standpoint of the aged) was made possible by the social and economic structure of the society in two ways. First, the structure was of the static, agricultural, and familistic type in which the old could perform useful functions. Second, it produced such high mortality that there were relatively few old people in the population (Davis and Combs, 1950).

In a dynamic industrial society, the aged can play fewer useful roles. Generally the family ties of young adults are to their children more than to their parents; and the more extended kin, who have an important place in traditional rural cultures, in an urban society are often less meaningful than friends. Even if the proportion of aged had remained constant, it would have been more difficult to accommodate them in the city apartments, say, of their married children; and the actual much larger proportion could have been given the same deference as once had been standard only by sacrificing some other significant values.

The problems associated with the physiological concomitants of aging are often exaggerated (cf. p. 205). The life span beyond 65 years in fact comprises two phases, the first beginning when a sizable proportion retire from full participation in the labor force and the second when a sizable proportion need constant aid merely to carry on as retired pensioners. According to medical evidence this second phase, what may be designated as the passage into true old age, starts in Western countries when persons approach their mid-seventies (LeGros Clark, 1966, p. 16). In the United States, substantial numbers of retired persons who have not yet become physically dependent have moved to states with a pleasant climate, particularly Florida and California, and there begun a new life (Hitt, 1954, 1956).

With the aged there live on the ideas, limitations, and surviving hopes of the past. For example, when today's very old were children, about a quarter of the population of the United States were given no more than four years of schooling, an education now considered so inadequate that it is used to define the upper limit of the "functionally illiterate." Similarly, since immigration was sharply curtailed after 1914, the proportion of aged among foreign-born is much higher than in the native population. The out-migration of young adults left disproportionate numbers of older persons on the farms, and in eastern cities the earlier decline in fertility also resulted in a more rapid aging of the population.

All those who will pass into the aged category over the next decades have already been born, and we can therefore project its dimensions without having to forecast the future trend in fertility. For example, if there is no revolutionary change in mortality, the proportion of older voters, which in Western countries has been rising rapidly in this century, will reach a peak in the next decades and then decline; and it is reasonable to suppose that such a "younging" population will probably be less interested in security than in other, quite different social and political questions (Dickinson, 1958).

### THE ACTIVE POPULATION

The definition of adulthood, although it has a biological base, varies greatly from one culture to another. Children on a farm are assigned their chores; in today's cities child labor is prohibited. Any delimitation of active adulthood in terms of chronological ages rather than functions, therefore, must be approximate and to some degree arbitrary. The definition used here, those aged 15 to 64, conforms with some statistical and legal conventions, but in several respects it overstates the actual size of the active population in a typical Western country. Few outside this age group perform adult roles, and many in it do not, especially married women, those in school beyond age 14, and those who have retired before age 65. In the United States, not only are rather high percentages at either end of the so-called active age range typically not in the labor force, but significant percentages have never worked at all (Table 3-4).[12]

To define this middle group as the society's producers means, therefore, that for Western countries we are in effect estimating the **labor potential**, the figure to which the labor force might expand in a period of national emergency. If we measure the burden carried by the economically active by calculating the ratio between the age groups,[13] therefore, this under-

---

[12] If we define the active population by noneconomic roles, the same deviations can be noted. The median age at marriage, though it has been going down, is still nearer 20 than 15; and women's childbearing period ends between 45 and 50. The age at which young men are conscripted has usually been around 18; and meaningful military service ends long before 65. In most states, legal maturity is set at 18 or 21 years. Voting usually begins at 21 and gradually sloughs off in the advanced ages.

[13] The dependency ratio, shown in Column 6 of Table 3-3, is defined as the number of dependent children and aged per hundred persons in the economically active range, whether or not they are actually in the labor force. In a book on the populations of the Pacific islands, the dependency ratio is defined as the number of children aged 14 or under per thousand *males* aged 20 to 64 (McArthur, 1961, p. 12), and for some purposes this may be the better measure. One may also want to calculate the youth-dependency and aged-dependency ratios separately from the total-dependency ratio. Or, more precisely, one can calculate the average number of dependents carried by those actually working, as in Table 3-5. For a discussion of this problem, see Kleiman, 1967.

Table 3-4. Labor Force Participation of Designated Age Groups, by Sex, United States, 1960

| AGE GROUP | TOTAL IN AGE GROUP (–000) | NOT IN LABOR FORCE (PER CENT) | NEVER WORKED (PER CENT) |
|---|---|---|---|
| Male: | | | |
| 15–19 | 6,684 | 56.8 | 35.5 |
| 20–24 | 5,276 | 13.8 | 2.8 |
| 25–29 | 5,339 | 6.1 | 1.0 |
| 55–59 | 4,195 | 12.3 | 0.5 |
| 60–64 | 3,385 | 22.3 | 0.6 |
| Female: | | | |
| 15–19 | 6,589 | 72.4 | 50.7 |
| 20–24 | 5,506 | 55.1 | 14.3 |
| 25–29 | 5,537 | 65.0 | 12.1 |
| 55–59 | 4,406 | 60.3 | 20.4 |
| 60–64 | 3,719 | 70.6 | 25.9 |

SOURCE: U.S. Bureau of the Census, *U.S. Census of Population, 1960*, "Labor Reserve," Final Report PC (2)-6C, Washington, D.C., 1966, calculated from Table 1.

states the number of persons that the average worker must support. Even with this conservative index, the ratio has risen by approximately twenty percentage points during the past quarter century, after a prior continuous fall to the minimum in 1940. As one can see from inspection of its component elements, the ratio has varied mainly with changes in the proportion of dependent children.

Leridon (1962) has combined recent estimates and projections of the economically active population from three international agencies. Whether we measure the dependency ratio by age group or by economically active and inactive categories, it is clear that the rise in the dependency burden will generally be greatest in the poorest areas of the world (Table 3-5).

### YOUTH

Especially for an analysis focused on social rather than economic roles, it is useful to separate out the youngest sector of the adult group, the youth of any population. To define this in terms of its age limits is notoriously difficult. And if we designate it by its "youthful" behavior, we find

Table 3-5. Dependency Ratios by Demographic and Economic Categories, Major World Areas, 1950, 1960, 1975

| | $\dfrac{\text{POPULATION AGED } 0\text{–}14,\ 65+}{\text{POPULATION AGED } 15\text{–}64} \times 100$ | | | $\dfrac{\text{ECONOMICALLY INACTIVE POPULATION}}{\text{ECONOMICALLY ACTIVE POPULATION}} \times 100$ | | | PERCENTAGE INCREASE, 1960–75 | |
|---|---|---|---|---|---|---|---|---|
| | 1950 | 1960 | 1975 (PROJECTED) | 1950 | 1960 | 1975 (PROJECTED) | TOTAL POPU-LATION | ECONOMICALLY ACTIVE POPULATION |
| Africa | 75 | 79 | 84 | 125 | 130 | 135 | 30 | 27 |
| Northern America | 55 | 67 | 63 | 137 | 146 | 140 | 27 | 30 |
| Latin America | 74 | 80 | 86 | 171 | 181 | 190 | 51 | 47 |
| Asia | 74 | 76 | 79 | 160 | 161 | 166 | 37 | 35 |
| Europe | 50 | 54 | 59 | 120 | 126 | 133 | 14 | 11 |
| Oceania | 62 | 66 | 66 | 160 | 167 | 162 | 31 | 33 |
| U.S.S.R. | 59 | 58 | 64 | 123 | 122 | 129 | 28 | 24 |
| World | 67.5 | 70 | 75 | 146 | 150 | 156 | 33 | 30 |

SOURCE: Françoise Leridon, "Prévisions de population active: Trois publications internationales," *Population*, 17 (1962), 97–120.

73

many roles tailored to fit adults who have never fully matured (Berger, 1963). Perhaps the least arbitrary definition of **youth** is those in the age range 15 to 24, thus including adolescents or teenagers as well as the first years of legal maturity. Together with children aged 5–14, youth constitute almost the entire enrollment of educational institutions (*cf.* U.S. Bureau of the Census, 1967). Most who enter the labor force for the first time are in this age range, and in the United States by far the highest proportion of unemployment is usually among teenagers (Silberman, 1965; Korbel, 1966).

In the 1960s a fascinating manifestation of youth has been the so-called generational revolt. A symposium entitled "Youth in Flux" included German feuilletons on young Chinese Communists and on "beats" wandering over Europe; a query from an English playwright on whether this phenomenon is not "simple hooliganism"; articles on delinquency in Israel and "dropouts on the run in the Soviet Union"; and, as an intimation of a possible new reversal, the rising "Concrete Generation" in France.[14] In all these places— except perhaps China—the percentage of youth in revolt was very small; in the United States, for instance, the adolescents in the Boy Scouts and the 4-H clubs always far outnumbered those participating in demonstrations. Some have on this account called the youth revolt a "myth,"[15] but revolts and even revolutions are typically generated by a small minority.

A demographer can more reasonably make two other points that usefully supplement cultural-political analyses of youth rebellions:

1. The proportion of youth has grown enormously, as a consequence in Western countries of the baby boom and in underdeveloped countries of the precipitous decline in infant mortality after the end of World War II. In the United States, for instance, the birth rate rose immediately after the war and remained about 24 from 1946 to 1960. The persons born in these years will be aged 15–24 over the years 1961 through 1984, and the cohort born in the peak birth year of 1947 will reach these ages in 1962 through 1971. The postwar baby boom was shorter in some countries and in others the decline in infant mortality has continued, but in most of the world's nations during the 1960s and 1970s youth will be attaining a new numerical importance. From infancy on, these cohorts burst the bounds of institutions built to accommodate more modest numbers, and as adolescents they saw ahead of them adult societies with too few jobs, swollen and yet inadequate universities, and in general a world seemingly ill prepared

---

[14] "Youth in Flux," *Atlas*, March, 1966, pp. 146–162. An especially interesting account of the "nihilists" and "anarchists" in the Soviet Union is given in Darrell P. Hammer, "Among Students in Moscow: An Outsider's Report," *Problems of Communism*, 13 (1964), 11–18. The whole of the Fall, 1968 issue of *Public Interest* is devoted to generally excellent analyses of student movements.

[15] For example, Robert C. Bealer, Fern K. Willits, and Peter R. Maida, "The Rebellious Youth Subculture—A Myth," *Children*, 11 (1964), 43–48.

to absorb its progeny. In Indonesia, to take a non-Western example, annual entry into the labor force will increase from 1.5 million in the mid-1960s to more than double that in the early 1970s. "Each entrant will literally bring his brother along, and the brother will want a job as well" (Keyfitz, 1965). Indeed, such a stupendous rise constitutes the stimulus to change that some analysts have termed it, but it is less apparent whether a country like Indonesia can respond to the stimulus by developing its economy sufficiently fast.

2. An analysis in terms of cohorts combines the *general* determinants of behavior associated with certain ages with the *specific* determinants set by each cohort's past history. To take a purely demographic example, women aged 40–44, who are close to the end of their fecund period, generally have few children; but the American cohorts born in 1911–15, many of whom postponed getting married—or, if married, having children—during the depression of the 1930s, showed a high fertility late in their reproductive life (see pp. 528, 532). Similarly, one can come to a limited understanding of youthful revolts merely by noting that those tied to their parents as children break away during adolescence in order to achieve adult independence.[16] But however much credence one gives this maxim, it hardly helps in explaining the differential incidence of youthful revolt. For example, during the 1920s and again during the 1950s young Americans generally accepted the society that their parents had built, and in the 1930s and 1960s many rebelled against it. This cyclical pattern suggests that what is seen as revolt may in many cases be the contrary, a docile acceptance of one's parents' ideas: the children of the "Babbitts" became the "quiet generation," and the children of CCNY radicals invented the academic sit-in. The background of Columbia University's radical students, according to surveys by *The New York Times*, is "strikingly similar to the pattern across the nation . . . at a dozen other campuses."

The activists are typically very bright and predominantly Jewish, usually reared in affluent or financially comfortable families in the big cities and suburbs of the Eastern Seaboard. They are students of the humanities rather than the sciences. Their fathers came of age during the Great Depression of the 1930s and were often insecure about money and jobs, if not downright needy. Many of them are now successful in the professions or creative fields. They are permissive parents, politically oriented toward liberalism and the left.

[16] The literature on this theme is enormous even if the sizable Freudian or general psychological components are passed over. Among the best known sociological analyses are Kingsley Davis, "The Sociology of Parent-Youth Conflict," *American Sociological Review*, 5 (1940), 523–535; Talcott Parsons, "Age and Sex in the Social Structure of the United States," in *Essays in Sociological Theory, Pure and Applied*, Free Press, Glencoe, Ill., 1949, pp. 218–232. For a more recent bibliography, see David Gottlieb and Jon Reeves, *Adolescent Behavior in Urban Areas*, Free Press of Glencoe, New York, 1963, with a supplement by Gottlieb, "American Adolescents in the Mid-Sixties," *Journal of Marriage and the Family*, 27 (1965), 285–287.

The overwhelming majority of the radical leaders at Columbia said their parents had been sympathetic to their protests, more loving than judging. The proud "my son, the revolutionary" response of Mrs. Jacob Rudd, mother of Mark [leader of the extremist Students for a Democratic Society on campus] was absolutely typical.[17]

Such an example suggests that the concept of cohort, or what some analysts term a "political generation" (Rintala, 1963), can be useful not only in demography but in almost any social, political, or economic analysis of age differentiation.

## The Population Pyramid

The distribution of a population by age and sex together is usually represented by a special type of bar graph, called a population pyramid. Figure 3-2 is a population pyramid for the United States in 1966. The various bars represent successive age groups, from the lowest age at the bottom to the highest at the top, each divided between the males at the left and the females at the right. The length of all the bars together represents, according to the scale along the horizontal axis, the total population either in absolute figures or as a percentage. Each bar thus designates what proportion that age group is of the total.

The reason for the basic shape of the pyramid is that among those born, e.g., in 1875, some have died in each year since then, gradually reducing the length of the bars representing successively higher ages. The shape is not ordinarily a perfect pyramid, however, because mortality varies from year to year, and because fertility and migration also affect the population structure. Whether recent fertility has been high or low is shown by the relative length of the bottom bar. The depletion caused by a past famine, epidemic, or war, or by a period of particularly low fertility or large emigration, is represented by an indentation from a smooth pyramid; and, on the contrary, a past period of high fertility or of large immigration is represented by a corresponding protuberance. These irregularities remain on population pyramids of successive dates, gradually moving up to the top of the graph and disappearing only when the cohorts finally die off.

Usually the population represented in a pyramid is broken down into five-year age groups, into which the typical misreporting of age is largely absorbed. Very often, also, one population pyramid is superimposed on another, in order to illustrate the contrast between two populations or between the structures of one population at different times. Figure 3-3,

---

[17] *The New York Times*, June 10, 1968. At the Berkeley campus of the University of California, I termed this the Aptheker Syndrome. Bettina Aptheker, one of the student radicals and an avowed Communist, in her revolt religiously followed the line of Herbert Aptheker, her father and a leading member of the American Communist Party.

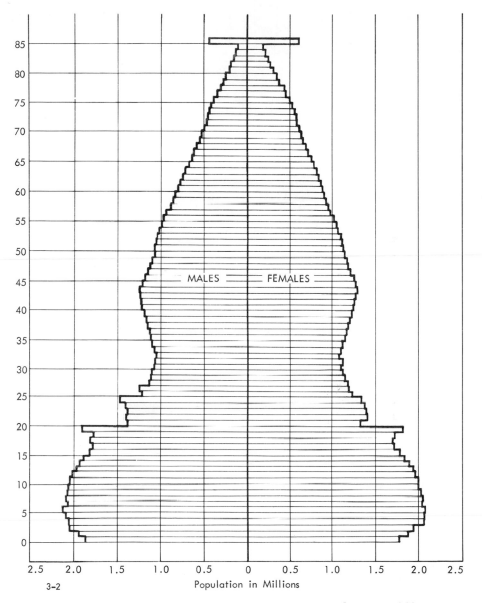

**Figure 3-2.** Population by single years of age and sex, United States, 1960.

thus, represents the population of the United States at two dates. For 1900 there is a regular progression of age groups in an almost completely regular pyramid, whereas for 1960 the extremely low birth rates in the 1930s are reflected in a pinched waist, which is reinforced by the larger proportions at higher ages.

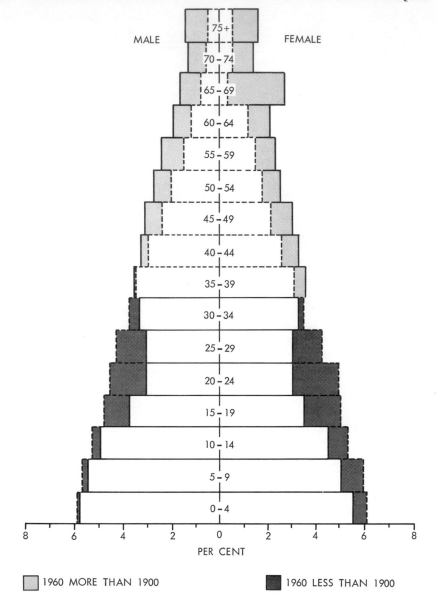

**Figure 3-3.** Population by age and sex, United States, 1900 and 1960. (Source: U.S. Bureau of the Census, *U.S. Census of Population, 1960,* Vol. I, *Characteristics of the Population,* Part 1, *United States Summary,* Washington, D.C., 1964, Figure 49).

## Ratios and Rates

The calculations made in analyzing population data depend, of course, mainly on the information available and the analyst's purpose. But very often the tools thus fashioned are closely related to the age and sex structure. Indeed, a gross figure is sometimes more appropriate than any alternative. The datum that the Chinese are increasing by 15 million a year, or that over a particular holiday weekend there were 325 deaths in automobile accidents, could hardly be put more forcibly than as these simple statements. Usually, however, a ratio or a proportion or a rate tells us more.

A **ratio** is of the form $\frac{a}{b}$ $k$, where $a$ and $b$ denote sectors of a population and $k$ any convenient constant. One example has already been cited in the text—the sex ratio (males per 100 females). The child-woman ratio (sometimes called the fertility ratio) is the number of children under five per 1,000 women in the fecund ages. In one of these cases the value assigned to $k$ is 100 and in the other 1,000. More generally, in both ratios and other types of calculations, $k$ is conventionally fixed according to the relative frequency of the phenomenon, in order to avoid cumbersome decimals. Thus, occupational rates are ordinarily expressed as percentages (Latin for "per 100"), whereas suicide rates are usually given per 100,000. Note that the two components of the sex ratio together make up the whole of any population (males plus females) but that this is not a necessary condition for a ratio (young children plus fecund women leaves men, older children, etc.).

A **proportion** is of the form $\frac{a}{a+b}$ $k$, that is, a relation between a total and one of its parts. For example, one can express a sex ratio of 100 as the statement that 50 per cent of the population is male.

### CRUDE RATES

A **crude rate** is of the form $\frac{m}{P}$ $k$, where $P$ is the total midyear population and $m$ the number of births, or deaths, or marriages, or other demographic events during that year. Note that $m$ and $P$ are not from the same set of statistical records; in the birth rate, for example, the numerator comes from vital statistics, and the denominator from the census. The two universes, thus, do not refer to quite the same population: that enumerated in the census, or estimated from the successive censuses, is fixed at one particular time; that included in the vital registration fluctuates throughout the year. For this reason, among others, this rate is indeed "crude."

A more serious question is whether the total population is the most apposite base. Ideally, a rate should express the relation between the actual and the potential. Suppose we want to compare the military forces of two countries. A direct comparison—Country A has 2 million men under arms as against 4 million in Country B—might for some purposes be the most relevant one. But if we want to judge the relative drain on the population, and thus the relative possibility of expanding the size of the armed forces, the 2 or 4 million can be compared with the respective total population or, better, with the number of men of military age (or men and women, if the latter are to be drafted; or healthy men only, for a further refinement; and so on). In this example, if the proportion of young men of military age is the same in both populations, then it is a matter of indifference whether a rate is calculated with this reservoir or the whole population as the denominator. Or, more generally, if the age and sex structure of two populations being compared are identical, then the crude rates need no refinement. As this relation often obtains more or less, the easily calculated, readily understood crude rate may be more appropriate than a complex substitute, particularly if the basic data are not thoroughly accurate (see p. 84).

If the structures of the populations differ greatly, however, then crude or insufficiently refined rates can be grossly misleading, as in the following historic examples:

1. In a special Massachusetts state census in 1905 it was pointed out that the average number of children ever born to mothers then living was only 2.77. This figure was compared with that in the previous generation by asking the respondents how many children *their* mothers had borne— namely, 6.47 on the average. The contrast was interpreted as evidence of a very sharp decline in average family size. Actually, of course, the number of children to the respondent mothers—some of whom were still in their teens, others in their twenties, and so on—was compared with the *completed* fertility of a group virtually all of whom had reached the end of their fecund years (Chaddock, 1936).

2. During the Spanish-American War there was great public concern over the large number of soldiers dying in the Philippines. In his annual report for 1899 the Secretary of War replied to the criticism by pointing out that the death rate among the troops was almost identical with that of the civilian population of Washington or Boston. In making a polemical point, he overlooked the fact that soldiers are all young adults while the general population includes infants and old persons, who generally have a higher death rate (Chaddock, 1936).

3. The national-quota system underlying American immigration policy for some four decades was based to an important degree on the analysis of Dr. Harry H. Laughlin, associated with the Eugenics Record Office of the Carnegie Institution of Washington. As "expert eugenics agent" to the House Committee on Immigration and Naturalization, he submitted a report entitled "Expert Analysis of the Metal and the Dross in America's Modern Melting Pot." [18] In order to show that social ills are not randomly

18 U.S. House of Representatives, *Hearings before the Committee on Immigration and Naturalization, November 21, 1922,* 67th Congress, 3rd Session, Serial 7-C; Washington, D.C., 1923. According to one authority, this report "is often considered the

distributed among the various nationalities in the United States, Laughlin compared for each ethnic group its proportion in the total population with that in prisons, asylums, and similar institutions. For example, in 1910 persons of Italian birth made up 1.46 per cent of the total population, and if proportionally represented in the ninety-three insane asylums that Laughlin surveyed, they would have constituted 1.46 per cent of the total number of inmates, or 1,228. Since there were actually 1,938 Italian-born persons in these institutions, the incidence of insanity among Italians was concluded to be more than one and a half times higher than that of the general population.

Among many other flaws in Laughlin's influential analysis, the fundamental ones in this context are that he made no allowance for the regional variation in communal care (institutions were scarce in the immigrant-free South and much more numerous in northern cities, where most of the immigrants lived) and that he ignored the difference in structure of the populations he compared (immigrants were concentrated in the middle male age groups, which typically show the highest incidence of many social ills).[19]

## MEASURES OF FERTILITY

One important method of refinement that such examples suggest is the one we have indicated—to substitute a sector of the population for the whole as the denominator. This principle can be exemplified by several measures of fertility used to supplement, or to replace, the crude birth rate. The simplest of these is the **general fertility rate,** or the number of births per 1,000 women in the fecund ages. Here we have, it would seem, a direct relation of actual procreation to potential procreators, but in fact the difficulty of defining the "potential" has not been overcome entirely. Female fecundity develops gradually during adolescence, slowly declines from age 30 or 35 on, and disappears between the ages, approximately, of 45 and 50 (see pp. 175–176). Demographers are not agreed on a conventional definition of the "childbearing ages." In the United Nations *Demographic Yearbooks*, which include data from all societies for which figures are available, the fecund period is taken to begin at age 10, which makes little sense for many populations. In the West a now generally insignificant but once larger proportion of all births have been to women aged 45 to 49, who typically constitute much more than this percentage of the total fecund age group. Whether or not these ages are included, a decision difficult to make on

---

principal basis of the Act of 1924"—Roy L. Garis, *Immigration Restriction: A Study of the Opposition to and Regulation of Immigration into the United States,* Macmillan, New York, 1927, pp. 239–240.

   [19] *Cf.* William Petersen, *The Politics of Population,* Doubleday, Garden City, N.Y., 1964, pp. 195–215.

principle (*cf.* Kuczynski, 1928, pp. 102–103), thus effects a considerable difference in the rate.

The basic pattern of relating births to women in the fecund period can be varied as widely as the data permit and the analyst's purpose demands. For example, *legitimate* births per 1,000 *married* women aged 15 to 44 define the **marital fertility rate.** Children ever born to women aged 45 and over define the **completed family size.** If no vital statistics are available for the country or period being analyzed, data wholly from the census can be substituted to calculate the **child-woman ratio,** already defined as the number of children under five years per 1,000 women in the fecund period.

Inasmuch as even within the fecund period the ability to have children varies according to age, a more precise measure is to calculate an **age-specific fertility rate,** defined as the number of births to a specified age group per 1,000 women in that group. Usually the division is made by five-year periods, as in the illustrative data shown in Table 3-6. The figures

Table 3-6. Age-Specific Fertility Rates, United States, 1950

| AGE GROUP | NUMBER OF FEMALES | BIRTHS TO WOMEN OF SPECIFIED AGE GROUP | AGE-SPECIFIC FERTILITY RATES |
|---|---|---|---|
| (1) | (2) | (3) | (3)/(2) × 1,000 |
| 15–19 | 5,305,256 | 424,556 [a] | 80.0 |
| 20–24 | 5,875,535 | 1,131,234 | 192.5 |
| 25–29 | 6,270,182 | 1,021,902 | 163.0 |
| 30–34 | 5,892,284 | 597,821 | 101.5 |
| 35–39 | 5,728,842 | 293,440 | 51.2 |
| 40–44 | 5,133,704 | 74,804 | 14.6 |
| 45–49 | 4,544,099 | 4,830 [a] | 1.1 |

603.9 × 5

SOURCE: U.S. National Office of Vital Statistics, *Vital Statistics of the United States, 1950,* Washington, D.C., 1954, **2,** 198.

[a] Births to mothers aged under fifteen and over forty-nine are included, respectively, in the first and last rows.

in the last column of this table, for greater convenience of presentation, can be added up to one figure, which is multiplied by five in order to relate it to the age of mothers by single years. The resultant figure, called the **total fertility rate,** is in this case 603.9 × 5, or 3,019.5. It tells us how many children on the average each 1,000 women have while passing through their childbearing period.

Sometimes this rate is calculated as in Table 3-7, to show rather how many daughters—that is, future mothers—they would have. With a sex ratio at birth of 1,054 in 1950, it is necessary to reduce the total fertility

Table 3-7. Calculation of Reproduction Rates from Age-Specific Fertility Rates and Life-Table Survival Rates, White Females, United States, 1950

| AGE GROUP | AGE-SPECIFIC FERTILITY RATES | PROPORTION SURVIVING FROM BIRTH TO MID-POINT OF AGE GROUP | COLUMNS $(2) \times (3)$ |
|---|---|---|---|
| (1) | (2) | (3) | (4) |
| 15–19 | 80.0 | 0.96683 | 77.3 |
| 20–24 | 192.5 | 0.96338 | 185.4 |
| 25–29 | 163.0 | 0.95915 | 156.3 |
| 30–34 | 101.5 | 0.95387 | 96.8 |
| 35–39 | 51.2 | 0.94658 | 48.5 |
| 40–44 | 14.6 | 0.93569 | 13.7 |
| 45–49 | 1.1 | 0.91912 | 1.0 |
| | 603.9 | | 579.0 |

Gross Reproduction Rate $= 603.9 \times 5 \times 0.487 \times 0.001 = 1.47$
Net Reproduction Rate $= 579.0 \times 5 \times 0.487 \times 0.001 = 1.41$

rate by slightly more than half (multiplying by 0.487); and it is the convention to give the resultant figure, called the **gross reproduction rate,** per woman rather than per 1,000 women. In this case, it is 1.47. In order to include also the effect of mortality, each age-specific fertility rate is reduced by the proportion that would not survive, on the basis of current age-specific death rates, from birth to the midpoint of each age group (Column 3). The sum of Column 4 is then multiplied by the same series of figures, for the same reasons, to get the **net reproduction rate** (Kuczynski, 1932). This rate, in this case 1.41, is of course always smaller than the gross reproduction rate, although when female mortality is as low as in the United States in 1950, the difference is not very great.

If the age-specific fertility and death rates of a population with no migration remained constant for a century or more, then the population structure would also eventually become fixed. Such a **stable population,** in which the proportion in each age group remains constant, is a useful model for various demographic purposes. It must be emphasized that a stable population is not necessarily one of constant size, but one whose growth is at a constant rate (which can be negative or zero as well as positive).[20] The vital rates of a stable population, called its "true" or

[20] It is thus to be distinguished from a stationary population; see pp. 87–88, 210–212.

**intrinsic birth** and **death rates,** reflect the fertility and mortality apart from the effect of the population structure on them. The difference between them, the "true" or **intrinsic rate of natural increase,** thus, is similar to the net reproduction rate except that it is calculated on an annual rather than a generational basis (Dublin *et al.,* 1949, Chapter 12; Coale, 1968).

How useful are these more elaborate measures of fertility? They are a significant improvement over the crude rate, to repeat, only when the proportion of fecund women in the total population varies greatly, and in any particular society during a period of uniform demographic change, this proportion is likely to be more or less fixed. Even Kuczynski, who did more than any other individual to popularize reproduction rates, pointed out that the percentage of women of childbearing ages was virtually constant between 1860 and 1910 in the countries of Northwest Europe. It rose by several points after World War I, when fertility and therefore the relative number of minors declined faster (Kuczynski, 1928, pp. 17–19). The issue that this datum suggests was developed by Stolnitz in an interesting paper. He compiled all the reproduction rates available for the period up to the late 1940s, and in each case matched the gross reproduction rate with the birth rate (the obvious analogue among crude vital measures) and the net reproduction rate with the crude rate of natural increase. For example, for France the gross reproduction rate fell from 1.31 in 1904–07 to 1.23 in 1908–13, or by about 6.1 per cent, while over the same period the birth rate fell from 20.4 to 19.3, or by 5.4 per cent. As in this example, the trend of the reproduction rate was in general not markedly different from that of the crude birth rate.

Among the eleven countries with 20 or more values on record, the coefficient of linear correlation between the two measures was .93 in one instance, .98 to .99 in four cases, and .99 or over in the remaining six. The implications of these results for purposes of estimation are obvious. Perhaps equally interesting is their bearing on traditional methodology. Judging from the past at least, our substantive knowledge of movements in the gross reproduction rate would have been very nearly the same, had it been necessary to rely on the birth rate alone (Stolnitz, 1955).

The correlation, though not quite so high, was also sizable between net reproduction rates and crude rates of natural increase. Some of these divergencies, moreover, were due to the lesser precision of the reproduction rates, when these had been computed on the basis of life tables some years out of date.

These comparisons do not condemn the reproduction rates altogether, of course, but they do challenge the widespread notion that the more work that goes into a computation, the more precisely its end product reflects reality. The limitations of a crude rate must be pointed out, but in some discussions perhaps they have been stressed too much.

## STANDARDIZATION

When the total population is used as the base in calculating a crude birth rate, the "potential" parents include some who can never become actual. The crude death rate is not illogical in the same sense: all persons are mortal. But the probability of dying within a year varies greatly according to age and sex, and in practice the two crude rates have the same virtues and limitations. They are simple to calculate from data often available, and if the effect of the population structures on fertility or mortality does not differ greatly in several populations, they give a good basis for comparison. When a Western and a non-Western country are contrasted, however, or a recent period with the past, then the difference in age structure is likely to be so large that a measure of mortality that takes it into account may be preferable. Apart from infant and other age-specific rates, and life expectation from various ages as derived in life tables (see pp. 209–213), the principal tool in refining measures of mortality is **standardization.** This means, simply, "holding constant" the age structure (or other variable) while comparing the differential effect of other factors.

Suppose, for example, that in order to compare the relative efficiency of social welfare in the various states of the United States, we use as one index their crude death rates. Some of the differences among these rates, however, will be due to the extraneous fact that there are proportionately more elderly people, or more infants, in some states than in others. The usual way to remove this effect is to calculate the specific death rates of convenient age groups for each of the states, multiply these by the number of persons in the same age groups of the United States (the so-called standard population), thus deriving the number of deaths in each age group that would have obtained if the age structure had been uniform throughout the country. For each state the total of such deaths per thousand is its **standardized death rate.**[21]

The one problem more complex than simple arithmetic relates to the choice of the standard population. For years the population of England and Wales in 1901 was used as a worldwide standard, but its structure was so different from that of non-Western populations that this was eventually deemed to be a poor choice. A standard population can be any, either actual or constructed, that is similar in structure to the populations whose rates are being standardized. When two populations are being com-

---

[21] This is the so-called direct method of standardization. If the data needed for it are not available, it is possible to achieve a similar result by multiplying the age-specific rates of the standard population by each age group for the various states (the so-called indirect method). A more detailed discussion of standardization is included in almost any elementary work on statistics. See, for example, Barclay, 1958, pp. 161–166, 175–177; Jaffe, 1951, Chapter 3; Linder and Grove, 1963, Chapter 4.

pared, either can be designated as the standard, or, alternatively, a composite containing both, as in the example cited above. No absolute rule applies, but as the standardized rates can differ widely according to the selection of the standard, this cannot be made randomly.

The value of standardization is merely suggested by this discussion. It can be used to "hold constant" any variable while comparing the effect of any other, so long as these are expressed in figures and the data are available. Suppose, as another example, that we wanted to study the effect of occupations on marital status. It would be appropriate to standardize not only for age, but also for sex ratio, ethnic and religious homogeneity, and any other possibly relevant demographic characteristic (Kitagawa, 1964).

## Summary

The structure of a population, or the distribution by age and sex, can be analyzed with a number of tools—among others, the sex ratio, median age, and the population pyramid. For some purposes, it is useful to compare the three main age groups of dependent children, the active population, and the dependent aged, and to construct from them indices of aging and of dependency.

The increment to the population of any area can be measured simply by noting the natural increase (births less deaths) and the net migration (immigration less emigration). In such a preliminary analysis, however, the interdependence of fertility, migration, and mortality has yet to be included. Population structure is relevant to every demographic study because birth, death, and migration rates affect the proportions of the various ages and the two sexes, and in turn are affected by them.

For one who has accustomed himself to think in terms of population structure, many of the generalizations made about all kinds of social behavior are incomplete, if not actually false. Supposing we read, for instance, that in Detroit during the past ten years proportionately three times as many Negroes as whites were convicted of robbery. If we are satisfied that the statistics are accurate and that they do not reflect a bias in the rates of arrest and conviction, the implications of the datum may still be false. Robbery is a behavior pattern predominantly of young males; and many Negroes in Detroit, recent in-migrants from other areas, are young adults. Thus, the rate of the whites—but not so much of the Negroes—is calculated as a proportion of a population that includes the usual number of infants and grandmothers, who seldom commit robbery no matter what their color. Such examples, both hypothetical and actual, could easily be multiplied; but the point rather is that all social statistics, no matter what their specific subject matter, must be interpreted with the possible relevance of population structure in mind.

The principal limitations of the simple ratios and crude rates conventional in demographic analysis, similarly, is that the population structure is ignored in them. They are useful, therefore, only when the distribution by sex and age in the populations being studied is either the same, or is not pertinent to the question being analyzed. In other cases, some degree of refinement is called for, and this generally means specifying the elements of the population structure sufficiently to compare demographic events independently of its influence.

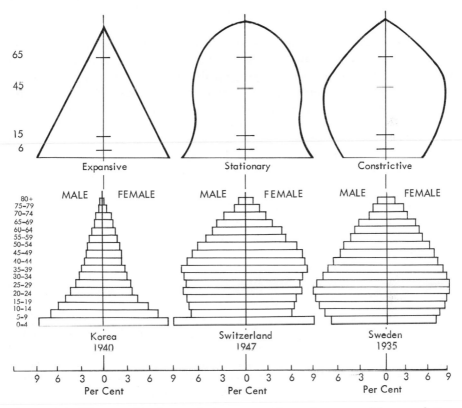

**Figure 3-4.** Three stylized population pyramids and comparable population structures.

It is useful to distinguish three fixed patterns of interaction between population structure and fertility plus mortality. These three stable populations are: (1) **expansive,** with a broad base to the population pyramid, indicating a high proportion of children and a rapid rate of population growth; (2) **stationary,** with a narrower base to the population pyramid, indicating a moderate proportion of children and a slow or zero rate of growth; and (3) **constrictive,** with a base narrower than the middle of the pyramid, indicating a proportion of children insufficient to maintain the population. In Figure 3-4 three stylized pyramids are compared with three actual population structures that approximate their shape. The expansive type could have been exemplified as well by the structure of almost any other Asian or Latin American population. By 1947 Switzerland had already experienced a considerable increase in fertility, so that the bottom bar is longer than it ought to be to represent exactly the stationary type. Any one of several West European countries in the mid-1930s—France, Germany, or England, for example, as well as Sweden—approximate the constrictive type fairly closely. The postwar revival of fertility in all of these countries has changed the shape of their population pyramids radically.

The three types of population structure also approximate three stages in the demographic transition of Western countries, corresponding to periods of actual or potential rapid growth, little or no growth, and actual or potential decline in numbers. One reason that demographers in the 1930s generally spoke of an "incipient decline" even of those Western countries— like the United States—whose population was still growing, was that they knew this increase was more the consequence of the population structure than of the average family size. Once the large proportion of young adults— the temporary heritage of the high birth rates several decades earlier— was reduced, then the "true" vital rates would become actual. The analysis represented a considerable improvement in method; it failed only because the assumption that fertility would remain constant, or continue to decline, proved to be unrealistic.

## Suggestions for Further Reading

Every general work on population includes an analysis of structure, and many specific topics (e.g., labor force, fertility measures) relate to it very directly. A full bibliography on population structure, therefore, could be almost as long as one on the topic of the whole book, and the following list is highly restricted. Elementary discussions are available in Barclay, 1958; Smith, 1948 (which introduces "index numbers of age"); and Coale, 1964. More advanced general analyses are given in Coale, 1956; Valaoras, 1950. Errors in age reporting are discussed in Zelnik, 1961, 1964, and with elements of special interest in You, 1959; Myers, 1966; and the exchange between Keyfitz and Van de Walle.

AKERS, DONALD S. 1967. "On Measuring the Marriage Squeeze," *Demography*, **4**, 907–924.

BACHI, ROBERTO. 1954. "Measurement of the Tendency to Round Off Age Returns," *Bulletin de l'Institut International de Statistique*, **34**, 129–138.

BARCLAY, GEORGE W. 1958. *Techniques of Population Analysis*. Wiley, New York.

BERGER, BENNETT M. 1963. "On the Youthfulness of Youth Cultures," *Social Research*, **30**, 319–342.

CALDWELL, JOHN C. 1966. "Study of Age Misstatement among Young Children in Ghana," *Demography*, **3**, 477–490.

° CHADDOCK, ROBERT E. 1936. "Age and Sex in Population Analysis," *Annals of the American Academy of Political and Social Science*, **188**, 185–193. Reprinted in *Demographic Analysis,* edited by Joseph J. Spengler and Otis Dudley Duncan. Free Press, Glencoe, Ill., 1956, pp. 443–451.

* COALE, ANSLEY J. 1956. "The Effect of Declines in Mortality on Age Distribution," in Milbank Memorial Fund, *Trends and Differentials in Mortality.* New York, pp. 125–132.

* ———. 1964. "How a Population Ages or Grows Younger," in *Population: The Vital Revolution,* edited by Ronald Freedman. Doubleday-Anchor, Garden City, N.Y., pp. 47–58.

———. 1968. "Convergence of a Human Population to a Stable Form," *Journal of the American Statistical Association,* 63, 395–433.

DAVIDSON, MARIA. 1967. "Social and Economic Characteristics of Aged Persons (65 Years Old and Over) in the United States," *Eugenics Quarterly,* 14, 27–44.

DAVIS, KINGSLEY. 1965. "The Population Impact on Children in the World's Agrarian Countries," *Population Review,* 9, 17–31.

———, and J. W. COMBS, JR. 1950. "The Sociology of an Aging Population," in Eastern States Health Education Conference, *The Social and Biological Challenge of Our Aging Population.* Columbia University Press, New York, pp. 146–170.

DICKINSON, FRANK G. 1958. "The 'Younging' of Electorates," *Journal of the American Medical Association,* 166, 1051–1057.

DUBLIN, LOUIS I., ALFRED J. LOTKA, and MORTIMER SPIEGELMAN. 1949. *Length of Life: A Study of the Life Table.* Revised Ed. Ronald, New York.

HITT, HOMER L. 1954. "The Role of Migration in Population Change among the Aged," *American Sociological Review,* 19, 194–200.

———. 1956. "The Demography of America's Aged: A Current Appraisal," in *Aging: A Current Appraisal,* edited by Irving L. Webber, Institute of Gerontology Series, Vol. 6. University of Florida Press, Gainesville, pp. 12–41.

JAFFE, A. J. 1951. *Handbook of Statistical Methods for Demographers: Selected Problems in the Analysis of Census Data.* U.S. Bureau of the Census, Washington, D.C.

KEYFITZ, NATHAN. 1965. "Age Distribution as a Challenge to Development," *American Journal of Sociology,* 70, 659–668.

———. 1966. "Reply" to Van de Walle, *American Journal of Sociology,* 71, 556–557.

KITAGAWA, EVELYN M. 1964. "Standardized Comparisons in Population Research," *Demography,* 1, 296–315.

KLEIMAN, E. 1967. "A Standardized Dependency Ratio," *Demography,* 4, 876–893.

KORBEL, JOHN. 1966. "Labor Force Entry and Attachment of Young People," *Journal of the American Statistical Association,* 61, 117–127.

KUCZYNSKI, ROBERT R. 1928. *The Balance of Births and Deaths.* Brookings Institution. Macmillan, New York.

———. 1932. *Fertility and Reproduction: Methods of Measuring the Balance of Births and Deaths.* Falcon, New York.

LeGROS CLARK, F. 1966. *Work, Age and Leisure: Causes and Consequences of the Shortened Working Life.* Michael Joseph, London.

* LERIDON, FRANÇOISE, 1962. "Prévisions de population active: Trois publications internationales," *Population,* 17, 97–120.

* LINDER, FORREST E., and ROBERT D. GROVE. 1963. *Techniques of Vital Statistics.* National Office of Vital Statistics, Washington, D.C.

LUNDE, ANDERS S., and ROBERT D. GROVE. 1966. "Demographic Implications of the New United States Certificates," *Demography,* 3, 566–573.

McARTHUR, NORMA. 1961. *Introducing Population Statistics.* Oxford University Press, Melbourne.

MORITA, YUZO. 1958. "The Accuracy of Age-Reporting in the Population Census," *Bulletin de l'Institut International de Statistique,* 36, 183–189.

MYERS, ROBERT J. 1940. "Errors and Bias in the Reporting of Ages in Census Data," *Transactions of the Actuarial Society of America,* 41, Part 2, 395–415. Reprinted in Jaffe, 1951, pp. 115–125.

———. 1966. "Validity of Centenary Data in the 1960 Census," *Demography,* 3, 470–476.

NOTESTEIN, FRANK W. 1954. "Some Demographic Aspects of Aging," *Proceedings of the American Philosophical Society,* 98, 38–45. Reprinted in *Demographic Analysis,* edited by Joseph J. Spengler and Otis Dudley Duncan. Free Press, Glencoe, Ill., 1956, pp. 464–470.

PANUNZIO, CONSTANTINE. 1943. "Are More Males Born in Wartime?" *Milbank Memorial Fund Quarterly,* 21, 281–291.

RINTALA, MARVIN. 1963. "A Generation in Politics: A Definition," *Review of Politics,* 25, 509–522.

* RUBIN, ERNEST. 1962. "Aspects of Statistical Aggregate Measures I. The Sex Ratio," *American Statistician,* 16, 37–39.

———. 1967. "The Sex Ratio at Birth," *American Statistician,* 21, 45–48.

SAUVY, ALFRED. 1954. "Le vieillissement des populations et l'allongement de la vie," *Population,* 9, 675–682.

SAW SEE-HOCK. 1967. "Errors in Chinese Age Statistics," *Demography,* 4, 859–875.

SIEGEL, JACOB S., and DONALD S. AKERS. 1964. "Outlook for Population at Mid-Decade," *Proceedings of the American Statistical Association,* Business and Economic Statistics Section, pp. 358–366.

SILBERMAN, CHARLES E. 1965. "What Hit the Teenagers," *Fortune,* April, pp. 130–133 and 228–234.

SMITH, T. LYNN. 1948. *Population Analysis.* McGraw-Hill, New York.

* STOLNITZ, GEORGE J. 1955. "Uses of Crude Vital Rates in the Analysis of Reproductivity," *Journal of the American Statistical Association,* 50, 1215–1234.

U.S. BUREAU OF THE CENSUS. 1967. "School Enrollment: October 1965," *Current Population Reports,* Series P-20, No. 162, March 24.

U.S. NATIONAL CENTER FOR HEALTH STATISTICS. 1968. "The 1968 Revision of the Standard Certificates." Series 4, No. 8. Washington, D.C.

* VALAORAS, VASILIOS G. 1950. "Patterns of Aging of Human Populations," in Eastern States Health Education Conference, *The Social and Biological Challenge of Our Aging Population.* Columbia University Press, New York, pp. 67–85.

———. 1959. "Population Profiles as a Means for Reconstructing Demographic Histories," in International Union for the Scientific Study of Population, *International Population Conference.* Vienna, pp. 62–72.

VAN DE WALLE, ETIENNE. 1966. "Some Characteristic Features of Census Age

Distributions in Illiterate Populations," *American Journal of Sociology*, **71**, 549–555.

VISARIA, PRAVIN M. 1967. "Sex Ratio at Birth in Territories with a Relatively Complete Registration," *Eugenics Quarterly*, **14**, 132–142.

WRIGHT, CARROLL D. 1900. *The History and Growth of the United States Censuses, Prepared for the Senate Committee on the Censuses.* Government Printing Office, Washington, D.C.

* YOU POH-SENG. 1959. "Errors in Age Reporting in Statistically Underdeveloped Countries," *Population Studies*, **13**, 164–182.

ZELNIK, MELVIN. 1961. "Age Heaping in the United States Census: 1880–1950," *Milbank Memorial Fund Quarterly*, **39**, 540–573.

———. 1964. "Errors in the 1960 Census Enumeration of Native Whites," *Journal of the American Statistical Association*, **59**, 437–459.

# 4 SUBNATIONS

What characteristics of a population ought to be included in the demographic records we compile? The number of possible classifications is all but infinite. One might, for example, divide a population into blonds, brunets, and redheads in order to relate hair color to other variables, but the results would not be illuminating, except possibly to a physical anthropologist. On the other hand, it is standard to classify the population by skin color—which intrinsically is no more significant than hair color—because the fertility and mortality of a society's various races are usually different, as well as their distribution by region, occupation, education, and so on. That is to say, a population datum is relevant if either demographic or social rates differ by this variable. On this basis, the fundamental characteristics of any population are its sex and age, which were analyzed in the previous chapter. Classification by residence (rural, urban, metropolitan), together with associated differences in education, occupation, and income, will be discussed in later chapters.

The subject of this chapter is the composition of a population by ethnic or analogous divisions—race, caste, origin, national stock, language, citizenship, religion, region, etc. Some of these have a biological component (race) or a geographical one (region), but basically all denote a differentiation in culturally determined belief systems, behavior patterns, and/or social statuses. Some analysts subsume all or most of these categories under the single one of "ethnic group" (e.g., Francis, 1947) or "minority group" (e.g., Wirth, 1945). A better term might be **subnation,** for apart from their usually smaller size they have some of the characteristics that we associate with nationality—an actual or putative biological link, a common territory, an easier communication inside than outside the group, an emotional identification with the insiders and thus a relative hostility to outsiders, a more or less mandatory norm stipulating marriage within the community, and so on. Subnations are also like nations in that their precise dimensions are difficult to fix, especially when they lack a single formal organization, the counterpart of a state.

## Quality of the Data

According to the first of two international surveys by the United Nations (the second survey was not essentially different), thirty-nine countries classified their populations by nationality or a corresponding geographical unit, ten by race, eight by culture, twenty-two by a combination of race and culture, eleven by a combination of culture and geography, one or two by the original stock as indicated by the language of the respondent's father, and several by the mode of life.

Even where the concept employed in several countries or census operations is apparently the same, . . . the meaning or definition of the concept may have changed and the amount of detail shown in the final tabulations may differ considerably. . . . The adequacy of the response may be seriously affected by the clarity of the question used, [and] . . . there is always a considerable chance of deliberate falsification in connection with questions having to do with matters affecting social prestige (United Nations, 1957, pp. 32–33).

The indices are more or less immutable, some in principle entirely so (place of birth, race, etc.) and others subject to slow and cumbrous change (citizenship, usual language, etc.). But—

Ethnic group . . . relate[s] to a series of categories which are not uniform in concept or terminology. . . . It is impossible to define these concepts precisely (United Nations, 1964, p. 38).

The difficulties in defining subnations are discussed more fully with respect to three typical indices—one biological (race), one cultural (language), and one geographical (region)—chosen out of the dozen or more characteristics that are used to denote the ethnic structure of various countries.

## Race

In the sense that biologists use *population* to mean a breeding group, race is "a population concept"; that is, "races are groups between which restricted gene flow has taken place" (Laughlin, 1966). Or, in the words of another physical anthropologist, a race is "a population which differs significantly from other human populations in regard to the frequency of one or more of the genes it possesses. It is an arbitrary matter which, and how many, gene loci we choose to consider as a significant 'constellation'" (Boyd, 1950, p. 207). Isolation of a minuscule population, either a primitive hunting band or a village cut off from outside contacts, results in what is termed **genetic drift,** or the concentration of a small proportion of the original range of hereditary elements, because the laws of probability are distorted. The principal factor inhibiting interbreeding has always been geographical separation. Thus, what anthropologists term the "major" races —Caucasoid, Mongoloid, Negroid, American Indian, and Australoid—are each associated with one continent. However, groups in physical proximity often retain a degree of racial separation through rules prescribing endogamy or various other boundary-maintaining features of their cultures.[1]

For physical anthropologists the concept of race, while still a matter of dispute,[2] is fairly clear in its broad outline. There are, in the common phrase, no pure races; but in the process of genetic differentiation, characteristics tend to cluster in groups that, as groups, can be distinguished from one another by the relative frequency of specific characteristics. In demography, however (as also in law), the differentiation must be specified in a way that can apply not only to populations but to each individual; therefore, the problem of how to classify intermediate types cannot be evaded. There are five alternative principles by which the race of an individual is established in population counts: (1) genealogy, (2) physical characteristics, (3) reputation, (4) self-identification, and (5) cultural attributes. None of these yields wholly satisfactory results, and in many cases the officials responsible for collecting data have vacillated among several criteria.

**1. Genealogy.** To denote a person as in a particular race if no less than one-half, or one-quarter, or some other fraction of his forebears were

---

[1] A particularly interesting example is the two clans of the Menabe, a primitive tribe in Madagascar. In skin color, one is Negroid, the other similar to Mediterranean Europeans, and this difference was maintained not only by selective mating but also by killing off all infants of deviant color. In the dark clan it was held that a light child would grow into a malevolent sorcerer, leper, or thief, and the light clan had similar beliefs concerning dark children.

[2] From the series of articles and forums on the subject in *Current Anthropology* during the early 1960s, it is clear that differences on many issues (including whether the word *race* is a useful term) have not been resolved.

in·that race is, in itself, a procedure in some accord with the notion of race as a breeding group. But there are several problems:

**a.** Genealogies are typically not available over a sufficient period and, if they are, may not be accurate concerning the forebears' races.

**b.** The definition of the races is a function of how officials designate the distinguishing fraction, which typically varies from one jurisdiction or time period to another. Consider, as one example, the official definitions of *mulatto* in the United States. The enumerators' instructions for the 1890 census included the following:

Be particularly careful to distinguish between blacks, mulattoes, quadroons, and octoroons. The word "black" should be used to describe those persons who have three-quarters or more black blood; "mulatto," those persons who have from three-eighths to five-eighths black blood; "quadroon," those persons who have one-quarter black blood; and "octoroon," those persons who have one-eighth or any trace of black blood (quoted in Carroll D. Wright, 1900, p. 187).

The census volume, however, after listing the figures by this elaborate breakdown, commented as follows:

These figures are of little value. Indeed, as an indication of the extent to which the races have mingled, they are misleading (*ibid.*).[3]

In most of the previous censuses *mulatto* had been defined generically to include all persons but full Negroes "having any perceptible trace of African blood," and enumerators were warned that "important scientific results depend on the correct determination of this class" (*ibid.*, p. 171). That "mulattoes" increased from 11.2 per cent of all Negroes in 1850 to 20.9 per cent in 1910 was due in part to such variations in the definition of the term (Cummings, 1918, p. 208).

**c.** When the designated fraction is very small, the definition based on genealogy contradicts the evidence of one's senses. For example, the Five Civilized Tribes in Oklahoma include on the tribal rolls persons who are 1/256 Indian (Beale, 1958).[4]

**2. The physical characteristics** used to distinguish races can be any that are known to be hereditary. Those used in traditional nineteenth-

---

[3] Throughout this book, "*ibid.*" in the text refers to the work last cited in the text, and "*ibid.*" in a footnote to the last one cited in a footnote.

[4] In an appeal before a South Carolina judge in 1835, the issue was whether witnesses permitted to testify in the original trial had been white, as they had to be under the law, or in fact Negro. The appellate judge held that "not every admixture of negro blood, however slight and remote, will make a person of color within the meaning of the law," and that even to raise the question does "unnecessary violence to the feelings of persons, who in this instance are admitted to be of much worth and respectability." State *v.* Cantey, 2 Hill, *South Carolina Reports* (1835), 613–618; reprinted in Thompson and Hughes, 1958, pp. 22–24.

century anthropology were height, and sometimes sitting height; cephalic index, or the ratio of the breadth to the length of the head, together with other skull and face measurements; color of skin, eyes, and hair; texture of hair and degree of the body's hairiness; and such special features as the epicanthic fold, which gives Mongoloids the appearance of slant eyes, or steatopygia, the heavy deposit of fat on the buttocks of some African peoples. Such somatic characteristics generally depend on the interaction of a large number of genes, so that each person falls somewhere along a continuum from short to tall, for example, or from light to dark. More recently anthropologists have classified races also according to traits that are known to be determined by the action of a single gene, of which the best known are the four blood groups (A, B, AB, and O), the three blood types (M, N, and MN), and the eight Rhesus blood types. With such serological criteria, *each individual* can be placed into all-or-none categories, but classifying *populations* incurs the same kind of difficulties as with the traditional somatic traits.

**a.** The principal objection to these indices is that they are not, as hypothesized, wholly determined by heredity but also, in some cases at least, markedly affected by environment. Americans of European origin, for example, are generally about two inches taller than their parents, and as Boas demonstrated in a classic study, a new environment can effect within a single generation great changes even in the shape of the skull, which used to be the major criterion of racial differentiation (Boas, 1911). For a while it was believed that serological traits are neutral with respect to human survival, but this is certainly not the case for at least some of them, which in this respect are little better than somatic traits as classificatory criteria of presumed biological groupings.

**b.** These various physical indices of race are not highly correlated with each other in a population of widespread miscegenation, so that the lines of division differ according to which characteristic is used. In Brazil, for example, "the social handicap of a dark skin may be alleviated by straight hair; a lighter skin may be handicapped by Negroid facial features; Negroid facial features may be partially compensated by straight hair and a light skin" (Bertram Hutchinson, 1959).

**3. The reputation** of a person in the local community has often been used to resolve such dilemmas. For instance, instructions to enumerators of the United States census in 1900, contrary to earlier censuses, did not define race, and according to a subsequent census monograph, the enumerators' "answers reflect local opinion, and that opinion probably is based more on social position and manner of life than upon relative amounts of blood" (U.S. Bureau of the Census, 1906, p. 177). Such a dependence on popular definition may not be haphazard, as in this case, but called for in the census instructions. For example, in 1951 the Union of South Africa redefined a "white" as follows:

A white person is now defined as a person who in appearance obviously is, or who is generally accepted as, a white person, but does not include a person who, although in appearance obviously a white person, is generally accepted as a colored person. This means that the appearance and associations of a person are the main consideration in determining whether he is white or not, rather than the parentage, as in the past (United Nations, 1956, p. 5).

Similarly, enumerators of the 1950 Guatemala census were told to distinguish between Indians and Ladinos (originally, of mixed Indian-white stock) as follows:

In deciding whether a person is Indian or Ladino, the enumerator must use as a base the social esteem in which the person is held in the place being enumerated. In small villages, there is a certain local feeling which classifies persons as Indian or Ladino. . . . Negroes and Chinese are regarded as Ladinos (*ibid.*, p. 7).

4. **Self-identification** by each respondent is not an unambiguous guide to classification. In Latin America during the colonial period, "whereas the Indian might wish to pass for a mestizo in order to escape paying tribute, the mestizo might find it convenient to present himself as an Indian to escape the jurisdiction of the Inquisition" (Moerner, 1966). Today, similarly, any marginal type often finds it expedient to stress one or another element of his dual background.

Self-identification depends on self-perception, which changes with new ideological fashions.[5] There has been a certain change in the attitude toward color in the United States and in Brazil, two countries that now use self-identification to designate race. In the United States, at the time the National Association for the Advancement of Colored People was founded in 1909, "negro" was regarded as a term of abuse. Today, while "Negro" with a capital letter is standard in scholarly discourse (except when it is displaced by such euphemisms as "underprivileged"), black nationalists prefer "Afro-American," "African," or "black" (Isaacs, 1963, pp. 62–71).

Brazil adopted self-identification to classify its population in 1950, and this procedure gave "greater precision to the census results" according to

[5] This assertion can be exemplified most pertinently, perhaps, with the doctrine of "négritude." The word was first used in *Cahier d'un retour au pays natal*, written in 1939 by the Martiniquan poet Aimé Césaire—and acclaimed by André Breton as "nothing less than the greatest lyric monument of our time." Recognizing how much of European culture and prejudice he has assimilated, the poet sets out to purge himself of them and to return from white reason and technology to black passion and primitiveness. Negroes around the world, he writes, seek to escape their alienation, try to find their real identity in a common "black soul." While the literary movement that this poem started rose to a flashy zenith and almost as quickly subsided, it is another matter whether the element of racism will disappear so quickly from African nationalism (or from a segment of the new self-consciousness of Negroes in the Americas).

the introduction to the census volume. Bertram Hutchinson (1959) specu-
lates, on the contrary, that in 1950 the definition of race was based more
on social-economic factors than in earlier censuses.[6] When the United States
adopted a similar procedure in the 1960 census, the effects on the count
of various races were no less difficult to determine. One might assume that
some Negroes used the occasion to pass into the white category, while
others reflected their new pride of race, with blackness defined as a
desirable trait. According to the Census Bureau, there was no net difference:
"The distribution by color in 1960 was close to that shown by postcensal
estimates for 1960 based on the 1950 Census counts by color and estimated
population changes during the decade. The increase in the Negro population in particular was consistent with the statistics on its natural increase
during this period" (U.S. Bureau of the Census, 1963, p. xi).

5. **Cultural attributes** sometimes define the supposedly biological category of race not incidentally, as when local reputations or self-identification
are the criteria, but unambiguously and entirely. This is especially so of
American Indians. In the censuses of some countries, they are defined by
their native language; in popular usage, also by their dress. For Mexico,
Moore suggests a range of "Indianness," from 100 per cent for those who
wear Indian clothes and speak only an Indian language, to nil for those who
wear European clothes and speak only Spanish. Thus, the charge that the
Indian is inferior in industrial tasks is not only true but a truism, for when
this inferiority disappears he acquires cultural attributes that redefine him
as a non-Indian.[7]

The Indian minority has also been the race most ambiguously defined
in the United States. The government volume on Federal law pertaining to
Indians has a long section aptly titled "Definitions of 'Indian,' " which opens
with a warning against any simple interpretations:

Legally speaking, an Indian is what the law legislatively defines, or juridically
determines, him to be. General definitions ordinarily do not suffice (U.S. Department of the Interior, 1958, p. 4).

[6] In Brazil the dominant influence in revising self-perception has been Gilberto
Freyre, whose apologetic view of Brazilian slavery in *Masters and Slaves* has become
yet more indulgent with each succeeding volume of his opus. During the years that he
was developing the thesis that for Brazil miscegenation represented not only no defect,
but her great asset, large numbers of Brazilians of mixed stock were rising to higher
status, and their welcome made Freyre "the most influential figure in the last thirty
years of Brazilian intellectual history" (Skidmore, 1964). His views, once highly regarded also in the United States, have recently been subjected to more criticism. Patterson (1966) holds that Freyre's opinions have been responsible for "romantic nonsense,"
and according to Stein (1961), "the perfervid regionalist who exhumed the colonial past
seems now enamored of a corpse."

[7] Wilbert E. Moore, *Industrialization and Labor: Social Aspects of Economic Development,* Cornell University Press, Ithaca, N.Y., 1951, p. 216. But Moore's total
omission of the biological factor may not be realistic; *cf.* Julian Pitt-Rivers, "Who Are
the Indians?" *Encounter,* 25 (1965), 41–49.

"Do you go barefoot, wear sandals, or wear shoes?" asked an enumerator for the 1960 census in a Mexico City slum (*Wide World Photos*).

Each legal definition—enrollment in a tribe, tribal membership, adoption (e.g., of a wholly white person), etc.—has its own background of legislation and court decisions. Each "tribe" (sometimes the status is not clear) may have its own treaty-guaranteed relations with the government. Each individual has the option of maintaining full, partial, or no status in the tribe. Some of the legal disabilities of Indians have been onerous; but sometimes the benefits of government wardship or of membership in a wealthy tribe have been substantial. It is often not only convenient but also possible for a single individual both to be and not to be an Indian, depending on the context. A volume on the Navaho, the largest "tribe," distinguishes three possible counts: the *de jure* population, comprising all who are legally classifiable as Navaho; the administrative population, comprising all who as Navahos use the services or otherwise participate in Navaho affairs; and the core population, comprising those with a primary involvement with traditional Navaho culture (Johnston, 1966, p. 12).

Untaxed Indians—that is, those living in Indian Territories or on reservations—were the only group excluded from the census when it was prescribed in the Constitution. They were not counted until 1890, and in subsequent censuses policy varied on how an "Indian" should be defined.

In 1910, a special effort was made to secure a complete enumeration of persons with any perceptible amount of Indian ancestry. This probably resulted in the enumeration as Indian of a considerable number of persons who would have been reported as white in earlier censuses. There were no special efforts in 1920, and the returns showed a much smaller number of Indians than in 1910. Again in 1930 emphasis was placed on securing a complete count of Indians, with the results that the returns probably overstated the decennial increase in the number of Indians (U.S. Bureau of the Census, 1960, p. 3).

The Indian population fluctuated together with census policy: from 248,000 in 1890 down to 237,000 in 1900, up to 266,000 in 1910, down to 244,000 in 1920, up to 332,000 in 1930 (*ibid.*, Series A-61, 67). The approximately 343,000 Indians enumerated in the 1950 census include neither an estimated 75,000 persons who would normally report themselves as Indians on public documents (of whom about 30,000 hybrids were enumerated as whites), nor an additional 25,000 persons entitled to legal recognition as tribe members who would not usually report themselves as Indians (Hadley, 1957). In 1960, as we have noted, the Census Bureau initiated self-identification as its index of race, and by at least one informed judgment the enumeration off reservations "appears to have been substantially improved by this procedure" (Johnston, 1966, p. 13). However, if the intent was to count Indians as they are designated in the census volumes—including persons of mixed blood "if they are enrolled on an Indian tribal or agency roll or if they are regarded as Indians in their community"—self-identification resulted not in an improved enumeration but in a changed definition.[8]

Partly because *race* is in any case an ambiguous category, partly because of the consequent disarray of public records on race, some liberal groups in the United States have exerted a considerable pressure to delete race from all such schedules. The stand may be based on a failure to make an important distinction. So long as discrimination by race persists, individuals should not be forced to publicize it on such *personal* documents as birth certificates. But only by maintaining (or establishing) the *group* data through such institutions as the census is it possible to document whether inequality and discrimination exist, and whether efforts to reduce them have succeeded (*cf.* Huyck, 1966). Both of these aims are realized in a policy

[8] A special problem relates to "triracial isolates," who by the usual criteria could be classified as white, Negro, or Indian. In Robeson County, N.C., to take a striking instance, the number of persons classified in the census as Indians increased from 174 in 1890 to 16,629 in 1940, the result of neither in-migration nor what would have been a miraculous fertility (Beale, 1958). The number east of the Mississippi who were counted as Indians rose from 50,082 in 1950 to 114,465 in 1960, when self-enumeration facilitated the re-identification of hybrids (Berry, 1965, p. 14).

concerning the birth certificates issued in New York City: beginning in 1961, the designation of race was dropped from the certificates themselves but retained in the confidential files from which group data are compiled.[9]

## Language

The difficulties in classifying languages are analogous to those in classifying races, for in both cases the basic problem is how to distinguish clusters in a continuum from one another.

All languages that are known to be genetically related, i.e., to be divergent forms of a single prototype, may be considered as constituting a "linguistic stock." . . . When we set it up, we merely say, in effect, that thus far we can go and no farther. At any point in the progress of our researches an unexpected ray of light may reveal the "stock" as but a "dialect" of a larger group. The terms dialect, language, branch, stock—it goes without saying—are purely relative terms. They are convertible as our perspective widens or contracts (Sapir, 1921, pp. 163–164).[10]

This is equivalent to the sentence quoted earlier from Boyd—that "it is an arbitrary matter which, and how many, gene loci we choose to consider as a significant 'constellation.'" The analogy between race and language is strengthened when we consider such peoples as Basques or Lapps or Eskimos, who represent enclaves on either a racial or a linguistic map. But generally the confusion of linguistic with racial stocks is an error against which responsible scholars have been struggling for several generations; to use a linguistic term like *Aryan* as a racial designation is the surest sign of an ignoramus.

If the anthropological tradition affords little basis for standardizing the differentiation between *language* and *dialect*, the distinction that linguists make, though embedded in a different professional vocabulary, is not in this respect more helpful.[11] In any case, perhaps linguistic characteristics matter less in determining the designation than the cultural or political status of the group that uses it. For example, Flemish was once the "dialect" of Dutch spoken in Belgium, but now, after the successful effort of Flemish nationalists to establish it as such, it is one of the country's two official "languages."

[9] *The New York Times,* December 27, 1960.

[10] Copyright, 1921, by Harcourt, Brace and Company, Inc.; renewed 1949, by Jean V. Sapir. This quotation reprinted by permission of the publishers.

[11] "A *language* is a collection of more or less similar idiolects [defined earlier as "the totality of speech habits of a single person at a given time"]. A *dialect* is the same thing, with this difference: when both terms are used in a single discussion, the degree of similarity of the idiolects in a single dialect is presumed to be greater than that of all the idiolects in the language." Charles F. Hockett, *A Course in Modern Linguistics,* Macmillan, New York, 1958, pp. 321–322.

The place of local speech forms in the national culture has been a political issue also in such other European nations as Ireland, Scotland, Wales, Norway, Finland, the Netherlands, France, Spain, and Yugoslavia, as well, of course, as in virtually all the countries of European immigration, particularly Canada and South Africa. In India, advocates of English, Hindi, and the regional languages have struggled so vigorously that, in the view of one Indian expert, the country "stands the risk of being split up into a number of totalitarian small nationalities" (quoted in Harrison, 1960, p. 3). In the new states of sub-Saharan Africa at least 800 distinct languages are spoken, none by more than 8 per cent of the total population (Ornstein, 1964). The governments of multilingual countries face demands that are in part irreconcilable: each minority typically wants education, official proceedings, and culture in its own speech, while the continuity of the nation as a whole depends on developing a means of easy communication across the existent, and sometimes growing, language boundaries.

Language statistics of the various countries of the world as compiled by the United Nations refer to three different units: (1) "mother tongue," usually defined as the language spoken in the respondent's home during his early childhood; (2) "usual language," defined as the language(s) currently spoken in his home; and (3) all the languages, or all those in a specified list,[12] that the respondent can speak. Of the thirty-seven countries with data, twelve were based on (1), eleven on (2), eleven on (3), and three on some combination of these. Manifestly such compilations are not comparable, even apart from differences in the designated age range, the manner of recording deaf-mutes, the distinction made between "language" and "dialect," and other details (United Nations, 1964, p. 39; cf. Lieberson, 1966b). According to more complete compilations, there are between 3,000 and 6,000 languages, of which only about 130 are spoken by at least one million persons. The top dozen are the following: [13]

| Chinese-Mandarin | 460 million |
|---|---|
| English | 250 |
| Hindustani | 160 |
| Spanish | 140 |
| Russian | 130 |
| German | 100 |
| Japanese | 95 |

[12] This list sometimes includes only the official languages spoken by core populations. The 1960 data for the Union of South Africa, for instance, include no information on Africans; and whites, colored, and Asians were asked only whether they could speak English, Afrikaans, or both, or neither. Thus, for example, of the 477,125 Asians, 403,868 speak languages listed as "other" (United Nations, 1956).

[13] *Time*, February 24, 1961, reporting research by a team of linguists at George Washington University. A list of all languages spoken by a million persons or more has also been compiled by a professor of psychology at the University of Washington; see *World Almanac, 1968*, Newspaper Enterprises Association, New York, 1968, p. 160.

| Arabic | 80 million |
| Bengali | 75 |
| Portuguese | 75 |
| French | 65 |
| Italian | 55 |

## Region

Odum and Moore began their book on regionalism (1938, p. 2) by quoting twenty-eight different definitions of *region*, to which they added a twenty-ninth of their own. The basic element of most of these definitions (or sometimes, particularly among plant and animal ecologists and some geographers, the only element) is the natural area, or a physiographic unit delineated by its topography, soil type, climate, and similar features.[14] The natural environment formed by a mountain range, or a river valley, or a seacoast, can have a considerable influence on the lives of its inhabitants. For example, an invisible boundary line, running from eastern North Dakota to western Texas divides an area to the east with an annual rainfall of more than twenty inches from one to the west with less than this amount, and to this day the semi-arid Rocky Mountain region between this isogram and the coastal area is the most sparsely populated in the United States. In Dr. C. A. Bentley's 1916 report of the Indian Medical Service, now a classic of epidemiology, he presented a map of Bengal showing the relative incidence of malaria, which depended on the distribution of mosquito-breeding areas. When this map is compared with one showing the relative increase in population from 1901 to 1911 (the two maps are reproduced in Stamp, 1964, pp. 22–23), it is clear that the differential pattern of mortality, supplemented perhaps by migration to more healthful areas, largely set the regional growth pattern. To take a third example, the major epidemic diseases of Europe—smallpox, scarlet fever, the plague, diphtheria, influenza, etc.— either kill or permit a complete recovery, often with immunity to a subsequent attack. The major diseases of Africa, on the other hand—bilharziasis, filariasis, malaria, sleeping sickness, etc.—cause illnesses of indefinite duration, with repeated attacks that confer no immunity and seriously debilitate those they do not kill. Some portion of the contrast between European and native African cultures can plausibly be related to this difference in the natural environment (Browne, 1953).

A second meaning of region, the **culture area,** was developed by anthropologists, in particular Wissler and Kroeber. They divided the pre-Colum-

[14] Unfortunately, human ecologists have also used the term *natural area* to designate a homogeneous neighborhood of a city, even though most of its characteristics, of course, are culturally determined. In this usage, "natural" means developing outside of policy decisions rather than from the forces of nature. This confusing double meaning of a key term is probably too well established to be eliminated, but it will not be used in this book.

bian population of North America into groups of contiguous tribes with similar patterns of life:

> A culture area is delineated by listing the tribes with similar cultures and plotting their habitats on a map. The geographical shapes of the culture areas appear to vary according to the topography and other physical features that enter into the environmental complex.[15]

From the substantial overlap between physical and cultural elements, it could be assumed that the history of each culture area has been essentially self-contained and more or less determined by the natural environment. There was not, however, a perfect correlation between natural and culture areas; eastern tribes living in the same type of habitat were sometimes not at all alike, and the Navaho and Hopi, although occupying the same natural area in the Southwest, had markedly different native cultures.

Geography, in other words, determines the limits of a group's development, but within these limits a considerable variation in culture is possible. In the words of Vidal de la Blache, "Nature is never more than an advisor." Some degree of identity between natural and culture areas is thus usual, particularly among primitive peoples, but the greater the control over its natural environment a society has, the smaller this correlation will generally be, and the less can one regard it as an inescapable cause-effect relation. A reasonable stance can be based neither on geographic determinism nor on the denial that geographic factors are sometimes decisive, particularly in the past (and on occasion the quite recent past), in underdeveloped countries, and in those regions of advanced economies subject to extremes of climate or topography.

That the correlation between natural and cultural region depends on how much technical skill has been exercised to free the culture from geographic limitations means that time is also a relevant factor. Historical areas retain their local character until the unifying effect of the national culture permeates every corner of a country. Thus, the regional boundaries drawn today, whether by geographical or cultural criteria, may be obsolete tomorrow, when the topography has been conquered and the frontier between contiguous cultures has disappeared.

In the United States few concepts of social history have generated more interest, and less agreement, than "the frontier." "The West" began to evolve as a self-conscious section when it was still to the east of the Appalachians. By the first quarter of the nineteenth century, the frontier was at the Mississippi; by the middle of the century, at the Missouri and in California; and by the end of the century, in the Rocky Mountains. This

---

[15] Clark Wissler, *The American Indian,* p. 346; quoted in Odum and Moore, 1938, p. 308. See also Kroeber, 1939.

east-to-west social evolution, according to Turner,[16] "worked a political transformation." The frontier "promoted the formation of a composite nationality," in part by decreasing America's dependence on England. He saw this fusion as the dominant theme of nineteenth-century American history, compared with which "the slavery question is an incident." The Middle West was "the typically American region," "democratic and non-sectional," where frontier individualism has most successfully developed into American democracy (Turner, 1949).

Beginning in the 1930s Turner and his thesis began to be challenged and rejected, and defended anew. The main criticisms were the following: (1) Turner's key concept is so loosely defined that it is difficult to test his assertions. The frontier "is defined and used as area, as population, as process, . . . at times everything Western or pre-industrial or non-European" (Pierson, 1949). (2) The European element of American culture, as transmitted by the East, is persistently minimized. The state universities of the Middle West, said to derive from frontier conditions, are in their essentials replicas of their European and eastern predecessors; the provisions of state constitutions vary but little from one region of the country to the other (Benjamin F. Wright, 1949). (3) The availability of free land in other parts of the world had no appreciable effect on social institutions there, nor did it necessarily even in the Americas. "Did the Mississippi Valley make [the Spaniards] democratic, prosperous, and numerous?" (Pierson, 1949). (4) Turner's praise of the composite American, "English in neither nationality nor characteristics," was, paradoxically, part of an attack on immigrants of other nationalities. Turner joined with the older historians in propounding such dubious theses as that immigrants from southern Italy were "of doubtful value judged from the ethical point of view," that Jews were a "people of exceptionally stunted stature and of deficient lung capacity" (quoted in Saveth, 1948, p. 129). (5) Turner's "safety-valve"—the proposition that the availability of free land on the frontier cut down economic discontent in eastern cities by drawing off the surplus urban population to the farm— was no more effective than "a whistle on a peanut roaster," for class conflict was actually extremely sharp just during the decades that free land was available. The dominant migration was in the wrong direction: for each industrial laborer who moved to the land, at least twenty farmers moved to the city. In fact, the free land did not even absorb the rural natural increase:

[16] In 1893 Frederick Jackson Turner, then a young historian recently out of graduate school, read a paper before his colleagues entitled "The Significance of the Frontier in American History." Over the rest of his lifetime, he developed its thesis in two dozen essays, which combined careful historical analysis with exuberant poetic vision into an extraordinarily convincing argument. According to the testimony of his students, he was one of the most effective teachers in the country's universities; and for a period his students, grand-students, associates, and followers all but monopolized the historical scholarship of the United States (Taylor, 1949, pp. v–vii).

for each farmer's son who became the owner of a new farm other than his father's, ten moved to the city (Shannon, 1949).

Each step taken so far in the formulation of *region* has increased the complexity of defining this ambivalent concept. A natural region is not typically sharply bounded; its overlap with a cultural region is usually only partial; and the frontier, the border between a developed and an undeveloped region, remains a subject of scholarly dispute. The demographer's concept of a region combines these three compromises with yet one more, which can be illustrated with the "regions" of the United States. The question whether *New England, the South, the Great Plains,* and so on denote regional subcultures can be answered empirically, but the answer will vary greatly according to where the boundaries between them are drawn. Regions, however defined, merge into one another, but for a statistical analysis the lines between them must be sharp. And if the regional division is to have the greatest practical use, the boundaries must correspond to those of the administrative units by which census data are segregated, that is, states or counties.[17]

The presentation of United States census data by region developed gradually (Mood, 1965). The ordering of data in the 1790 census—a list of states from north to south, followed by the western territories—was maintained with appropriate additions in the next two censuses. From 1820 to 1840 the list went from north to south along the Atlantic seaboard and then from south to north for the "Western states," thus keeping the latter together as a section. In a work based on the censuses, *Progress of the United States in Population and Wealth* (1843), George Tucker held that the states and territories "naturally arranged themselves" into five divisions, based both on this "geographical position" and "modes of industry and commercial interest," or into only four when the east-west contrast was crossed with one between slaveholding and non-slaveholding states. J. D. B. DeBow, the superintendent of the 1850 census, followed Tucker's schema in part, especially in a subsequent monograph, *Statistical Views of the United States* (1854), but his precedent was not to take hold. The 1870 census, prepared under Francis A. Walker as superintendent, introduced two innovations. State data were presented alphabetically, thus abandoning any concept of regionalism; and for the first time the census statistics were illustrated with maps, which clearly showed the regional distribution of many variables. Walker assigned one of his staff, Henry Gannett, to work out a new basis for a regional system, and his schema was adopted and maintained, with minor variations, to the present day. Gannett divided the country into three topographical units—the Atlantic region, the Mississippi valley, and the

---

[17] The distortion is less, of course, if we combine not states, but counties. The Census Bureau has divided the country into 501 **State Economic Areas,** each consisting of one or more whole counties, and these are more homogeneous in their economic and social characteristics than either states or regions. See Bogue, 1951.

West—and subdivided the first two along the Mason-Dixon line (with an approximate westward extension) into two units differing mainly in history and social structure.

The four regions presently used by the Bureau of the Census are shown in Figure 4-1. On the whole, this breakdown represents accurately the major geographic areas in American history: the Northeast (equivalent to "the North" of the nineteenth century), the South, the North Central region (equivalent to "the Middle West"), and the West. Each region is broken down further into **divisions:** the Northeast between the two historic areas of New England and the Middle Atlantic states, the North Central region between an eastern division of five industrial-agricultural states and a western one of seven grain-producing states, and the West between the five Pacific states and the semiarid Mountain states.[18] So long as this official pattern lasts, it determines the presentation of regional data and thus our perception of this country's regions. One should not assume, however, that the Census Bureau's present schema is necessarily fixed. For example, the prestigeful Committee for Economic Development published a work that both departs from the Census Bureau denotation of regions in a number of important respects (Perloff, 1963, p. 15) and better represents the present distribution of at least some important variables.

To sum up: Out of the dozen or so ethnic indicators used by various countries, three—race, language, and region—have been examined in some detail in order to see how the objective reality, as seen by specialized scholars, is translated into demographic data. In all three cases (and this is generally true of ethnic indicators), the demographer is faced with the same paradox: the incidence of the variable tends to cluster, indicating that a significant group difference exists; but the clusters are not sharply bounded, and the assignment of intermediate units therefore must be more or less arbitrary.

## Ethnic Variables and Social Structure

One of the world's best examples of ethnic "stability in diversity" is the linguistic and religious structure of Switzerland (Mayer, 1952, Chapter 8; 1957). The renowned amity among the Swiss subnations was not the nat-

[18] The breakdown of the South, however, is less satisfactory. The subculture areas defined by most indexes would seem to be the intermediate region between the South and the Southwest, which is adequately represented by the West South Central division; the Deep South, from the Carolinas west to Mississippi or farther; and the border states, from Delaware west to Missouri. Odum and Moore, following some earlier precedents, even assign Delaware, Maryland, West Virginia, and the District of Columbia to the North. The line between the South Atlantic and the East South Central divisions, on the contrary, groups these states with the Carolinas and Georgia, and Kentucky with Mississippi and Alabama.

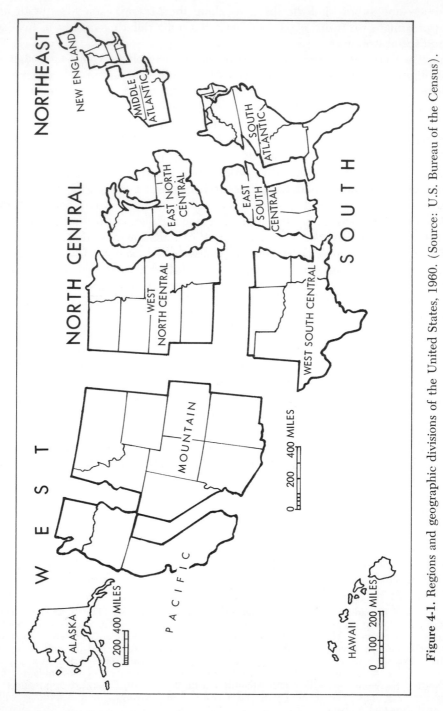

**Figure 4-1.** Regions and geographic divisions of the United States, 1960. (Source: U.S. Bureau of the Census).

ural consequence of their history: "the religious rivalry had been of the utmost intensity imaginable and had lasted for years." That statesmanlike political measures were successful in reducing the hostility between religions and between language groups was due in part to several fortuitous demographic factors. Since both German Swiss and French Swiss adhere to both Catholicism and Calvinism, the antipathy along one dimension is mitigated rather than reinforced by that along the other. Moreover, the different rates of natural increase have been almost canceled by opposite differences in migration rates. Thus, the proportion of German Swiss, almost three-quarters of the total population, has been slowly increasing since 1910; but the disparity between it and other sectors is less than it might have been because the lower fertility of the French Swiss has been partly balanced by the net migration of German Swiss into the French region, where they (or, at latest, their children) learn to speak French as their first language. Similarly, the lower rate of increase of Italian Swiss has been offset by the sizable immigration from Italy. Something of the same process can be seen in the recent development of Catholics in the United States. As they spread from concentrations in eastern cities throughout the country and moved into middle-class status, even seeing one of their number elected President of the United States, some of the social ramifications from their religious separation were weakened.

More typically, perhaps, a subnation defined by one criterion comes to be differentiated also by others. French Canadians, for example, differ from English Canadians not only in language but also in dominant religion, region, traditional occupations, degree of urban concentration, and general way of life. American Negroes are distinguished from whites not only by genetic characteristics but also by most social-economic indices. The effect of such a pattern on a nation's social structure can be illustrated conveniently by examining an extreme case, the caste system of Hindu India.

*Caste,* it is true, is sometimes used as a generic concept to denote any subnation separated by a considerable number of ethnic indicators, but most Indologists agree that "the only genuine parallels to Hindu caste are to be found in communities which, though professing other faiths, live with or near Hindu communities" (Srinivas, 1959, p. 149). The English word *caste* is used to translate two Hindi words, *varna* and *jati*, which must be differentiated. The literal meaning of *varna* is "color," [19] and although there is no absolute color line along any dimension, color is a significant differentiation. The population of the North is generally fairer than that of the South, and the highest castes are generally lighter than the Untouchables.

---

[19] According to some interpretations the system originated in an attempt to distinguish the prehistoric fair invaders from the darker peoples they conquered. This theory was propounded by Sir Herbert Risley, the director of the 1901 census, who made the first systematic attempt to classify the Indian population by races. Today his conclusions are more or less accepted by some (e.g., Ghurye, 1961) and rejected by others (e.g., B. S. Guha, cited in Béteille, 1967).

A light skin color is valued almost universally. . . . In many Indian languages the words *fair* and *beautiful* are often used synonymously. . . . Virginity and a light skin color are among the most desirable qualities in a bride (Béteille, 1967).

There are four varnas: in hierarchical order, *Brahmin,* the priest or scholar; *Kshatriya,* the warrior-ruler; *Vaishya,* the merchant; and *Sudra,* the peasant or craftsman. This four-level hierarchy makes the caste system of one region of India intelligible in another, though usually with some oversimplification or distortion. In fact, the more significant broad classification divides Hindu India into only three parts: the "twice-born," who undergo a *rite de passage* that makes them full members of society (the first three varnas); the "once-born" *Sudras;* and the Untouchables (or Avarnas, "noncaste persons"), who are below the varna system altogether.

However, "it is necessary for the sociologist to free himself from the hold of the varna-model if he wishes to understand the caste system" (Srinivas, 1962, p. 66). Hinduism divides Indian society not into three to five broad orders but into perhaps 3,000 castes and subcastes—some subunits of varnas, some associated with particular territories or traditional occupations, some the consequence of the spread of Hinduism to tribal peoples, and so on (Hutton, 1963, p. 2). These smaller units are the *jatis,* the breeding units of the Indian population. The word derives from *jan,* "to give birth to," and jati "comes closer to the meaning of 'race' than perhaps any other word in popular usage" (Béteille, 1967). As caste defines the units of endogamy, one should not be surprised that both of the words to denote it reflect a concern with genetic purity.

Ghurye (1961, Chapter 1) has defined six main features of Hindu society before it was markedly affected by Western ideas, as follows:

1. Endogamy. Each subcaste restricts marriage to within its own group, and so famous an anthropologist as Westermarck termed this endogamy "the essence of the caste system." The one important traditional exception is that in some areas a man may take a wife of lower caste; but, apart from this hypergamy, intercaste marriage is condemned more strongly than almost any other transgression of Hindu tradition. All castes of good position, moreover, are bound by its *sapinda* rule, which prohibits the union of any two persons with a common ancestor not more than six degrees removed on the male side, or four degrees on the female side. Thus, some 2,121 kinds of relatives are excluded, as compared with 30 by the relatively rigid rules (for the West) of the Anglican Church. In part as a consequence of these restrictions, the lack of suitable mates compels even rigid high castes to take lower-caste women as wives. "But in such cases both the husband and his caste connive at their own deception and, if they are willing to ignore custom, are very unwilling that the fact should be generally known" (Blunt, 1931, pp. 48, 60).

**2.** Caste segments society into distinct units, each governed by a caste council (or panchayat), which has the power to impose strong sanctions on those members who break its rules. To the extent that their lives are so governed, thus, caste members are not members of a general society. There is no over-all moral norm in Hinduism, no revealed divine laws, no equivalent to sin, hardly even a universal deity. All the rules and the ritual depend on the individual's subcaste, each of which is analogous to an extended family. Beyond this the individual in practice recognizes no society or community; "the Hindu has become an abstraction, a sociological fiction" (Panikkar, 1933, p. 17).

**3.** Not only the varnas but also the subcastes are ranked in a hierarchy down through a varying, often disputed, ordering to the lowest of several categories of Untouchables at the bottom. The widely divergent rules cover every facet of life—the length of twig with which one brushes one's teeth, the size of wheel a potter must use, the color of the flower one may wear, the type of house that may be built, the clothing that may be worn, the punishment to be meted out for identical misdeeds, and so on and on through a catalog that includes both life's fundamentals and its minutiae. The rigidity with which such rules were enforced in British India "would put to shame even the Great Inquisition" (*ibid.*, p. 9).

**4.** The ranking of castes is denoted by restrictions on social intercourse. Members of higher castes are polluted by the touch of a lower-caste person (a modern Brahmin physician attending a Sudra wraps his patient's wrist in a piece of silk before taking his pulse), by his shadow, or even by his presence closer than a specified number of paces. The most important indicator of rank is the transfer of water: one takes water from one's equals or superiors, not from one's inferiors. Food is divided into two types: *kachcha*, cooked with water and therefore subject to the strictest rules, and *pakka*, cooked with ghee (or clarified buffalo butter) and thus subject to less stringent restrictions. The most familiar sanction that panchayats use to force members to adhere to the infinity of commandments, to forbid a fellow member from giving them water or receiving it from them, in effect excommunicates the delinquents from the caste system. Yet, more generally, the values that define the hierarchy are not imposed from the top but permeate all levels, even in modern times. When Nehru tried to bring up an Untouchable girl together with his daughter, the parents were delighted until they heard that she ate with Brahmins; then they withdrew her in horror.

**5.** Since defilement can be by any member of specified groups, efforts to avoid it go beyond setting up institutions that regulate the relations among individuals. Untouchables typically live in segregated areas at the outskirt of the village and sometimes, particularly in the South, various other castes also have their own segregated quarters or streets, to which in extreme cases they are restricted. Brahmins, the traditional priests of Hinduism, administer two types of ritual—the very holy Vedic for themselves and other "twice-born," and the Puranic, of lesser sanctity, for such as Sudras—whereas to Untouchables no Brahmin would minister at all.

**6.** Castes are sometimes associated with a traditional occupation, in which case many in the caste, perhaps between half and three-quarters, make their living in it (Davis, 1951, p. 168; *cf.* Driver, 1962). Beyond this, the choice of occupation is restricted at both ends, with the priesthood excluded to all but Brahmins and all caste members forbidden to do work defined as degrading or polluting.

In principle, the caste system is fixed: every person is born into the status that he will retain throughout his life, and the social structure summing up this complete lack of social mobility is also stable. In fact, the structure has never been immutable, in part because it is both one system and many systems. The key concept is "pollution," but who or what pollutes and under which circumstances varies widely and inconsistently. As with modern totalitarianism, which has undergone certain revisions in its original structure, one must try to distinguish within-system changes from changes in the system.

Apart from the kind of excommunication already mentioned, most social mobility in caste society is of groups rather than of individuals. It is convenient to classify changes in the social structure and resistance to them into several types:

**1.** Over a generation or two, lower castes (thus, not Untouchables) have always been able to rise by what Srinivas terms Sanskritization, that is, the conscious adoption of certain of the customs, rites, and beliefs of the Brahmins (Srinivas, 1962, pp. 42–62). Moreover, "a caste which owned land exercised an effective dominance regardless of its ritual status" (Srinivas, 1959, p. 140). This means that at any particular time the precise order of local subcastes may be in dispute; in one village of highland Orissa, the third rank, immediately under Brahmins and Warriors, was held jointly by Herdsmen, Distillers, Writers, and Oriya (Bailey, 1957, p. 8). A *jati* that succeeds in rising typically acquires "all the intolerance of the parvenu" (Blunt, 1931, p. 103), so that whatever social mobility takes place by this route tends to strengthen adherence to the system rather than to disrupt it.

**2.** Individuals, or occasionally whole subcastes, have attempted to rise in Indian society by joining one of the non-Hindu religions. The principal result of this process, however, has been to recreate the caste system among Muslims, Christians, Buddhists, and Jews. Four centuries after their conversion, Goan Catholics until recently sought mates for their children from the appropriate caste (Zinkin, 1962, p. 2). Through an analogous process the primitive tribal peoples of central India assimilate to Hinduism by becoming another *jati*, usually at the bottom of the caste ordering but above the line of pollution (*cf.* Srivastava, 1966).

3. "The village communities," Sir Charles Metcalfe wrote in 1832, "are little republics, almost independent of any foreign relations." The intrusion of British influence on this Hindu world was of several kinds. The principle of equality before the law undercut "the whole basis of Hindu justice," by which "punishment or penalties did not merely depend upon the nature of the crime committed but also on the caste of the criminal and that of the victim" (Sinha, 1965). Political democratization, started in British India and greatly accelerated since independence, has in many respects undercut the caste hierarchy, but at least one analyst holds that "the power and activity of caste have increased in proportion as political power passed increasingly to the people from the rulers" (Srinivas, 1962, p. 23). For what seem to be disputes between political parties or language or regional groups are often, a half-inch below the surface, manifestations of persistent caste hostilities.

4. Industrialization and urbanization also attacked the village-based social structure. New occupations did not fit into the traditional ranking; greater migration afforded more opportunities to escape from local hierarchies; in the crowded city the rules concerning touchability are unenforceable among an anonymous population; the main criterion of pollution, accepting water from an inferior, is all but impossible to apply to municipal water that comes through a tap.

5. The greatest change relates to the 65 million ex-Untouchables, as Isaacs terms Indians below the line of pollution.[20] The "Scheduled Castes" are now favored by special provisions in the Indian Constitution, the Untouchability (Offenses) Act of 1955, and quotas in colleges and in civil-service jobs. Important advances have been made in some respects, but hardly in all. One response to the ambiguity is "semi-passing"—"passing in public while not passing in private" (Isaacs, 1965, p. 147)—which permits a person to take advantage of new opportunities, but does not cut him off completely from his caste community, through which such crucial affairs as marriage typically must still be arranged.

"Shall we have democracy or shall we have caste? . . . That we cannot have both of them at the same time is certain" (Panikkar, 1933, p. 37). On balance, there has been a decline in the importance of caste except in the barrier against intermarriage, which remains almost unbreached. Yet the caste system—ancient, ingrained, not disturbed by flagrant inconsistencies— has also retained a degree of invulnerability. Some caste organizations have responded to the challenge of modernization not with passivity or retreat

[20] As with so many of the world's depressed classes, the name used to refer to them is not neutral. "Untouchables" is wholly accurate only for the past; "Exterior" or "Scheduled" castes are officialese at its most pompous; "*Harijans*," the term bestowed by Gandhi, means "children of God"—that is, persons conceived illegitimately (Isaacs, 1965, Chapter 2). According to the 1961 census, there were 64.4 million in Scheduled Castes plus 30.1 million in Scheduled Tribes. Together they made up 21.5 per cent of India's population (India, 1965, p. 347).

A village of Untouchables, Tondiarpet, India (*Camera Press—PIX*).

but with educational institutions, fraternal orders, social agencies, and other means of helping good caste members solve, within the framework of the caste, the problems that urban-industrial society poses. In the view of perhaps the foremost scholar of the subject, "Caste is so tacitly and so completely accepted by all, including those who are most vocal in condemning it, that it is everywhere the unit of social action" (Srinivas, 1962, p. 41).

## Assimilation Processes

The Hindu social structure, particularly in its classical, pre-British form, represents an extreme type, with the maximum overlap of the social-economic statuses that are defined by various ethnic indices. A person's position in society, and also that of his subcaste, are in theory fixed; the assimilation of minorities into the broader society is in principle impossible. In contrast, this section discusses the various types of assimilation as these take place in an open society like the United States. In both cases, of course, the model has been less than fully realized: just as the caste system was never as rigid as it was supposed to be, so the equal opportunity guaranteed in the American creed has been unequally available.

The interaction of ethnic minorities and the larger society has been known by a number of terms—among others, "assimilation," "acculturation," "integration," "adjustment," in addition to such nationally specific ones as "Americanization," "Australization," etc. Sometimes these have a loose association with academic disciplines (sociologists—assimilation, anthropologists—acculturation, etc.), sometimes with a more or less invidious tone. But generally they are used without clear distinctions (*cf.* Gordon, 1964, Chapter 3).

It is convenient to retain **assimilation** as the generic term denoting the entire process by which nations and the subnations comprising them penetrate each other and become more similar. During the first decades of the twentieth century, when the large numbers of immigrants entering the United States made it a subject of great interest, assimilation was usually seen as an all-or-none process. America was a "melting pot." [21] Native Americans urged immigrants to be "hundred per cent" Americans, not Swedish-Americans or Italian-Americans or other "hyphenated" Americans. Even sociologists generally interpreted assimilation in this total sense. Perhaps the most important theorist of ethnic relations, Robert Park of the University of Chicago, saw the ethnic partition of nations as only a temporary phase of national histories.

If it is true that races are the products of isolation and inbreeding, it is just as certain that civilization, on the other hand, is a consequence of contact and communication. . . . Changes in race . . . inevitably follow, at some distance, changes in culture. . . .

When migration leads to conquest, either economic or political, assimilation is inevitable. The conquering peoples impose their culture and their standards upon the conquered, and there follows a period of endosmosis [or osmosis toward the core].[22]

Similarly, we are told in a later work that "assimilation . . . goes on wherever contact and communication exist between groups. . . . It is as

---

[21] The phrase comes from the title of a play by Israel Zangwill, himself an immigrant. The message of the play is that all the European strains would disappear entirely, blending into a nobler American compound. Its hero, a Russian Jewish immigrant, marries the immigrant daughter of the tsarist official responsible for the pogrom in which his own parents were killed. See Israel Zangwill, *The Melting Pot,* Revised Ed., Macmillan, New York, 1920.

[22] "Human Migration and the Marginal Man" (1928), in Park, 1950, pp. 345–356. This article introduced the terms *marginal man* and *marginality,* which were to generate a sizable literature around the question of whether a person sharing two cultures is psychologically handicapped (e.g., Stonequist, 1937) or intellectually stimulated (e.g., Seeman, 1956); Dickie-Clark (1966) gives a critical review of many of the works on the subject. For a discerning critique of Park's theory, see Lyman, 1968.

inevitable as it is desirable. The process may be hastened or delayed; it cannot be stopped" (Davie, 1949, pp. 498–499). If assimilation is hindered only by the accidental impediments consequent from mutual misunderstanding or feelings of strangeness, then over a sufficient period of time it is indeed likely that two or more culture groups in continuous contact will merge. But to apply words like "inevitable" to this process is manifestly incorrect; in some instances of culture contact a pattern of limited interaction has remained stable for centuries.

To analyze the process of assimilation more adequately, it is useful to divide it into several parts, as follows (*cf.* Roy, 1962): (1) **Acculturation** is the process of interpenetration of two cultures by the continuous personal contact of their representatives and the consequent adoption by one or both groups of alien culture traits. (2) **Political integration** is the process by which ethnic minorities acquire equal civil rights and lose any tendency to identify themselves as political blocs. (3) **Economic integration** is the process by which ethnically disparate elements of the labor force penetrate a whole economy; it is thus essentially synonymous with the "social mobility" of ethnic groups. (4) **Institutional integration** is the process of interpenetration of two institutional structures, by which persons of different subnations come to be identified with the same schools, social clubs, formal organizations, etc. (5) **Amalgamation** is the process by which genetically different subnations become more similar through miscegenation. These types of assimilation are discussed in turn.

### ACCULTURATION VS. NATIVISM

In the United States, European additions to the Anglo-Saxon base have melted down into a relatively homogeneous people. Neither the dichotomy between Old and New Immigrants (that is, those from Northwestern Europe and those from Southern and Eastern Europe) nor that between natives and aliens retain nearly so much salience as they had a half-century ago. It is possible with census data to differentiate the foreign-born and their native-born offspring (who together are termed the **foreign stock**), but native-born of native-born parents merge into the general population. For the third and higher generations, since no reliable data on European background are available, theories about whether European identities are retained necessarily are impressionistic.[23]

[23] Nevertheless the immigration quotas set in the 1920s were based on the "national origins" of the American population. It was necessary to calculate "the number of inhabitants in continental United States in 1920 whose origin by birth or ancestry is attributable to [each] geographical area" designated in the immigration statistics as a separate country, and this task was undertaken by the Bureau of the Census, assisted by two experts paid by the American Council of Learned Societies. The frequent and untraceable marriages across ethnic lines, however, made it impossible to divide the 1920

The proportion of foreign-born whites has fallen off rapidly since the restrictionist laws of the 1920s. Native-born increased from 85 per cent of the population in 1920 to almost 95 per cent in 1960, and those with native-born parents from slightly over 60 to about 80 per cent. The foreign stock, a small proportion already, is rapidly getting smaller still, both because it includes relatively few new arrivals and because its age structure results in a greater mortality. At the height of the immigration the newcomers were mostly young adults: they were born into American society, so to speak, at the age of twenty and ranged upward from this figure. This age structure (as well as old-country family patterns) brought about many children in the average family; and in 1890 the country's youngest ethnic group was native-born of foreign-born or mixed parentage. But today the typical foreign-born American is near the age of retirement, and his older sons are middle-aged.

That the foreign stock has declined in size and importance is of less significance than that no European nationality has impelled its American-born descendants to resist significantly the drift toward the dominant culture. Among the descendants of Europeans, in other words, there has been a relative lack of **nativism,** or the conscious, organized effort on the part of a society's members to perpetuate selected aspects of its subculture (Linton, 1943). The usual passive, unorganized attempt by the members of any group to resist the disappearance of their own culture, it should be noted, is not included in this definition, whose crux is the phrase "conscious, organized effort." Nativism includes both attempts by the dominant group to maintain its culture pure, undefiled by immigrant infiltration (such as the Know-Nothing movement in nineteenth-century United States), and a minority's resistance to its disappearance into the dominant culture (as with the Ghost Dance of the Paiute Indians or, among literate peoples, the revival of Celtic as an element of Irish nationalism). A nativist movement may seek to perpetuate elements of its culture or to revive extinct or moribund or mythical elements. Almost all nativism is unrealistic to one degree or an-

---

population itself into distinct ethnic groups, and the committee undertook instead to find the proportionate contribution of various national stocks to the total white American gene pool. It began by dividing the country's original white population by national origin, principally from the family names as enumerated in the 1790 census. As the committee itself pointed out, however, there was a "considerable element of uncertainty" in such a classification, and even small discrepancies in 1790, when increased geometrically from that date until 1920, made a substantial difference in the size of the quota each country was allowed. To this base were added immigration figures, such as they were, and—for lack of a breakdown by ethnic groups—an over-all rate of natural increase (U.S. Senate, 1928). In short, the paucity and the poor quality of the available statistics made it impossible to carry out the committee's assignment, yet until 1965 American immigration law was based on the results of this calculation. See William Petersen, *The Politics of Population*, Doubleday, Garden City, N.Y., 1964, pp. 195–215, for a fuller discussion.

other, but it includes wholly irrational flights from reality as well as movements that at least by contrast can be termed rational.

Under what conditions is nativism, the conscious, deliberate attempt to frustrate acculturation, likely to arise? How the two groups define their comparative cultural level, to the degree that this can be separated out, is probably the most important determinant of nativist tendencies. If both immigrants and natives, for instance, regard the culture of the receiving country as superior to that of the sending country, then the immigrants' effort to move "up" into the former pays the natives implicit deference; and all can be happy. However, when one group is dominant in numbers or power and the other regards itself, in spite of its minority status, as superior in cultural level, then acculturation is impeded. The point can be illustrated by an interesting study of acculturation of British migrants to Canada (Reynolds, 1935), which challenges the implicit, and certainly often valid, assumption in the immigration laws of both Canada and the United States that newcomers will be most fully assimilated if they are from the most similar countries. But even though one could characterize the movement almost as an internal migration, few Britons ever became completely Canadian in their habits and outlook. For them Canada was only a place of residence, inferior to England, which always remained home. With such attitudes, Britons also failed to be economically integrated even by the grossest of indices: during the depression of the 1930s a disproportionately large number was unable to hold their jobs and thus became dependent on public support.

The perception of one culture as "superior" and the other as "inferior" need not be, of course, a realistic view of the actual relation between the interacting groups (*cf.* Van Baal, 1960). As by definition acculturation involves contact with cultures of which all concerned are more or less ignorant, it is typically an interrelation between groups in terms of two stereotypes:

For the most part we do not first see, and then define, we define first and then see. . . . Americanization, for example, is superficially at least the substitution of American for European stereotypes.[24]

The picture that the typical immigrant had of America was a composite of the fables circulating in his home country with generalizations drawn from an extremely limited experience after he had arrived. And, on the other side, even American immigration officials were puzzled by the complex multiplicity of European peoples, as we have seen from the records that they collected. The mass of the American public, which was certainly no less

---

[24] Walter Lippmann, *Public Opinion*, Macmillan, New York, 1947, pp. 81, 85. *Stereotype* in this sense was introduced into the language in 1922 by the first printing of Lippmann's book.

ignorant, simplified matters by classifying newcomers into a small number of easy categories, and very often the first stage of acculturation was an immigrant's redefinition of himself in accordance with this classification. In the nineteenth century, the Germans and Irish came from self-conscious groups that had not yet achieved legal unity; they were nations but not yet states. The Norwegians and Swedes, on the contrary, came from states that were not yet nations; only the upper classes were self-conscious bearers of the national culture (cf. Glazer, 1953). This variation was to be found also among the later immigrants. An East European, for example, as he saw himself when he first arrived in the United States, had four identities. He was a subject of a particular state, for example, Russia; he spoke a particular language, for example, Lithuanian; he was an adherent of one or another religion; and he regarded a certain village or province as "home." Typically the peasant emigrants had no special feeling of identification with Russia or "Lithuania." This was often true even of emigrants from a nation that had achieved political unity: an "Italian," for instance, was much more likely to look on himself as a Sicilian or Calabrian. (Similarly, for a Navaho or a Hopi today to redefine himself as an "Indian" is to accept the perception of the broader society.)

In many cases it was only after they had left it that migrants learned to identify themselves with "their" country. They were taught this first of all by the native Americans, who demanded a simple, understandable answer to the question, "What are you?" Having learned that they belonged to a nation, some of the immigrants became nationalists. They submerged their provincialisms into a broader patriotism, their local dialects into languages. The first Lithuanian newspaper was published in the United States; the Erse revival began in Boston; the Czechoslovak nation was launched at a meeting in Pittsburgh; the very name of Pakistan was coined by students in London. The nativism of such groups would often be one facet of their acculturation, paradoxical as this may seem.

The paradox is even more striking in the phenomenon known as third-generation nativism, which is based on the psychological certainty that in all essential respects one's integration into American society has been completed. While immigrants to the United States were linked to their native countries by childhood memories and nostalgia, as well as by immigrant-aid societies, national churches, and other ethnic organizations, their acculturation was not ordinarily impeded by a conscious reluctance to give up these old-country remnants. On the contrary, most immigrants tried to be more American than a Mayflower descendant, and this aspiration was taken over, a little more realistically, by the second generation, which typically attempted to learn nothing of the language and other culture traits of its European forebears. It has been suggested (e.g., Handlin, 1951) that some of the characteristics specific to the American family derive from the fact that the immigrant father has an ambivalent authority over his native-born son, who speaks English without a foreign accent and also in other respects is likely to be more successful in American society. The third generation, however, has often tried to organize a revival of old-country culture. Thus, the procession of ethnic groups that came to the United States in some instances at least was followed two generations later by a succession of amateur historical societies, folklore associations, and other organized efforts to keep alive specific elements of the various overseas cultures. In short, it is an "almost universal phenomenon that what the son wishes to forget the grandson wishes to remember" (Hansen, 1938; but see also Appel, 1960, 1961).

To sum up, we know rather little about what factors tend to generate a nativist movement. "The most that we can say is that nativistic movements are unlikely to arise in situations where both societies are satisfied with their current relationship, or where societies which find themselves at a disadvantage can see that their condition is improving" (Linton, 1943). It is at least suggestive that nativism is typically the reaction of upper or lower extremes rather than the middle social class. Great insecurity, whether economic or psychological, or, on the contrary, an unusual degree of security, has sometimes resulted in nativism, but not inevitably. Often the decisive factor seems to have been the presence of a charismatic leader who galvanized vague sentiments into a social movement.

### POLITICAL INTEGRATION

Every nation-state, virtually by definition, expects its ethnic groups to be loyal to itself. But these subnations often have some ties to other nations, and the issue of divided loyalty arises frequently. Not only in colonial days but also in the nineteenth century, some immigrants to America believed that they were carrying the superior culture of the Old World to a benighted backwoods area (and, indeed, there was sometimes substance to this sentiment). The Germans who settled in Missouri or Wisconsin, the Scandinavians who settled in Minnesota, did not come with the idea of giving up their native language and way of life. From its side, the American government did little more to foster the assimilation of early immigrants than to prohibit their formal segregation by nationalities. In 1818, when Irish immigrant-aid societies petitioned Congress for a land grant on which to settle some of the charitable cases they were attempting to help, this request was denied on the ground that it would be undesirable to concentrate alien peoples geographically. "Probably no decision in the history of American immigration policy possesses more profound significance" (Hansen, 1948, p. 132). By the natural cohesion of their common background, the immigrants from each country tended in any case to congregate in the same region of the Middle West, or later in the same quarters of eastern cities; but the fact that there was no formal boundary greatly facilitated contacts with the native culture.

Integration did not proceed, however, in an altogether laissez-faire framework. Policy decisions on other matters often resulted in the dissemination of the native culture. The public school system, gradually set up during the first half of the nineteenth century, was based on the general principle that democracy, to be viable, must rest on a literate electorate. But the influence of public schools was also decisive in establishing English as the native language of all immigrant groups, at the latest among the second generation. Foreign-language publications, which numbered 1,350 in thirty-six different languages at the time of World War I, declined sharply from this high point (Taft and Robbins, 1955, pp. 532–535). The principal function of these newspapers and magazines has not been to retain foreign languages—they all but disappear anyway among the native-born—but to facilitate acculturation. In their political ideas, their advertising of American goods, and their use of cartoons and similar features, these newspapers and magazines often imitated their larger English-language counterparts. Now that the issue is dead and we know that the nativist fear of a polyglot America had no substance, we can wonder whether the victory of English was not too great. The national interest of the United States is not served by the fact that so few Americans can speak even one other language.

The rate of naturalization of a national group, another common index of acculturation, is also ambiguous. Although the proportion naturalized has varied greatly from one nationality to another, the seeming relation often is spurious. Especially in the past, when farmers were isolated from national or state politics, many Old Immigrants were slower in becoming citizens than New Immigrants, who were often accused around the turn of the century of feeding their votes too quickly to the political machines of the eastern cities. In any case, acquiring citizenship may mean that the shift in allegiance has been completed, or that the allegiance is a critical public issue. Around the time of World War II, German and Italian immigrants found it expedient to declare themselves American, and the same is true today of those of Russian birth.

Another indication of political integration is the voting record of the various ethnic groups. This is a subject that still retains emotional overtones from the beginning of the century, when the New Immigrants were accused of being hyphenated Americans if they permitted their vote to be influenced by their national origin. At that time they were too insecure to reply with anything except a resounding denial of the charge, and it became a prime shibboleth of liberal politics that a person's ethnic or religious affiliation has no possible effect on the way he votes. A contrary point of view has been presented most provocatively in Samuel Lubell's *Future of American Politics* (1956), which offers not only an analysis of public-opinion polls and elections but also a reinterpretation of much of American history. As the successive waves of immigrants arrived in the United States, fitting in at the bottom of the economic scale, they were opposed in social-class terms to their Anglo-American employers. Whenever social conflict was expressed in political terms, thus, it tended also to result in a confrontation of ethnic groups (*cf*. Holden, 1966). For example, in the middle of the nineteenth century most of the eastern cities were governed by Republican machines led by men of English stock. The Irish immigrants joined the Democratic opposition, and by their success built a link between Catholic and Democratic that to a large degree persists to the present day. In national politics, by Lubell's analysis, the vestigial link of the various ethnic groups to Europe has had an important influence on American foreign policy. The isolationism before World War II, for instance, he interprets as not a withdrawal from European politics but the contrary. The descendants of German and Scandinavian immigrants tended to be pro-German, and the Irish to be anti-English; but as it was patently impossible to involve the United States on the side of Germany, this sympathy was expressed by the demand that America remain at home minding its own business. Even the Yankee descendants of the original settlers voted to assist England when her need was great enough (*cf*. Lubell, 1956, p. 141).

Every group is required, however, to rationalize its demands in terms of the national interest of the United States. English, Polish, or Jewish interventionists, German or Irish isolationists, debated America's attitude toward what was to become World War II in the name of multinational parties or other similarly broad institutions. The Irish associate anonymously, as it were, in the Roman Catholic Church, in the Democratic Party, in trade unions and professional societies, but specifically as Irish only in an organization like the Ancient Order of Hibernians, and the same is true of every other national group. Moreover, Lubell's analysis is far from universally accepted. In a posthumously published work by V. O. Key, one of America's foremost political scientists, the theory of bloc-voting developed mainly by sociologists was rejected in favor of a classical defense of "the responsible electorate." Concerning the election that Lubell stressed most, he wrote that "foreign policy seemed to have far less bearing on the vote [in 1940] than did questions of domestic policy. . . . The data indicate a comparatively mild relation between attitudes on foreign policy and vote shifting" (Key, 1966, p. 50).

## ECONOMIC INTEGRATION

No other type of human intercourse, perhaps, is so likely to remain partial as one based on economic relations. The interdependence of different peoples through trade, an example of the type of adaptation human ecologists term *symbiosis*, can remain absolutely stable in this truncated form, particularly if the effort to keep the groups separate in other respects acquires ideological legitimacy and institutional form. An obvious example is the Jewish minority in Gentile societies. Ever since the diaspora, Jews have generally been in continuous commercial relations with the peoples among whom they lived; the degree of integration varied considerably from one country or era to another, but Jews were seldom completely assimilated. Their merging with the broader society was generally prevented by the anti-Semitism of Gentiles and the pro-Semitism of Jews, as well as the ghettos and similar institutions that both reflected these attitudes and helped perpetuate them. Or, to cite another instance, over many generations four adjacent native tribes of India exchanged the products of their specialized skills—buffalo rearing, agriculture, metalwork, and sorcery. But this continuous contact did not blur the linguistic and other cultural differences among them. "Social intercourse was confined to a fixed number of narrowly defined activities. Any intimate contact, of a kind which would allow members of one group to mingle freely with another, was stringently tabooed" (Mandelbaum, 1941).

In the modern West, and particularly in the United States, economic integration has been more closely linked with other types of assimilation. To Europeans of every nationality, the democratic system of the overseas Republic was an attraction of enormous strength, and particularly the fact that the democracy extended also to social and economic relations. It was necessary to work hard in the new country, but what a man produced was his own to enjoy.

The per-capita expense of government was only one fourth of the Netherlands and less than a tenth that of England. No percentage was deducted as tithes for the clergy or as rates for the poor. Though the United States had about the same population as Prussia, the standing army of the latter was fifty times as large. It was amazing that a farm that kept eight horses paid a tax in America of only twelve dollars (Hansen, 1951, p. 158).

Immigrants themselves strongly reinforced this established trend toward egalitarian social relations. Of humble birth in overwhelming majority, ignorant of one another's background, they were impatient with class distinctions that rested on family pedigree or even on "the natural aristocracy of knowledge and virtue" (Tocqueville, 1947, p. 44). There was a country to be built, and when it was built it would be theirs. This sense of participation in a joint venture, founded in American law and tradition but more subtle than either, is the key to the successful assimilation of millions of Europeans of such diverse backgrounds.

The part that each immigrant group played in building the American economy, however, was specific to it, so far as inadequate sources permit us to judge. In a few cases apart from agriculture, skills developed in

Europe were transferred to the United States (Jewish furriers and tailors, as an example), but in general the young immigrants, including most Jews, found work in occupations that were new to them. Employment opportunities in the United States varied considerably from one period or region to another, and each nationality tended to be shunted into a particular type of occupation. There was a good deal of overlap in occupation among nationalities arriving during the same decades, but sometimes also marked differences. The Irish, for instance, who immigrated in great numbers from the 1840s on, did not become farm laborers or farmers but stayed in the towns in spite of their peasant background. Such a trend, once started, tended to continue. Each immigrant found work alongside men who could speak his language, drawn there both by that fact and by directives from immigrant-aid groups, clergymen, or employment agents of his nationality. Thus, for example, a National Society for German Emigration was in operation by the early 1850s; and "after his arrival the [German] immigrant could proceed from city to city, receiving advice at each stage" from compatriots who had already established themselves (Hansen, 1951, p. 302). A similar network, either formally organized or not, existed for each of the immigrant nationalities.

The resultant differences are suggested in Table 4-1, in which only Scots and Irish are compared for only two years and a few occupations. The index numbers for each nationality express the proportion engaged in the given occupation as a percentage of the proportion of all native whites

**Table 4-1. Index Numbers of Relative Participation of Scots and Irish Males in Certain Occupations, United States, 1890–1900**

| | | SCOTS | | | IRISH | | |
|---|---|---|---|---|---|---|---|
| | TOTAL NATIVE WHITE | 1890 | 1900 | NATIVE-BORN OF SCOTS PARENTS, 1900 | 1890 | 1900 | NATIVE-BORN OF IRISH PARENTS, 1900 |
| Miners | 100 | 739 | 441 | 329 | 232 | 188 | 153 |
| Cotton-mill workers | 100 | 417 | 140 | 80 | 263 | 140 | 100 |
| Servants | 100 | 212 | 200 | 120 | 358 | 340 | 180 |
| Clerks | 100 | 92 | 105 | 155 | 44 | 55 | 160 |
| Teachers | 100 | 27 | 33 | 83 | 17 | 17 | 50 |
| Physicians | 100 | 53 | 86 | 114 | 19 | 29 | 57 |

SOURCE: Brinley Thomas, *Migration and Economic Growth: A Study of Great Britain and the Atlantic Economy,* Cambridge University Press, Cambridge, 1954, p. 145; data from U.S. censuses.

in that occupation. Thus, in 1890 there were relatively 7.39 times as many miners among those born in Scotland as among native white males, but only 2.32 times as many among the Irish-born. Among those born in Scotland, work in the mines or cotton mills was relatively most frequent, but the highest proportion among the Irish-born was servants. From 1890 to 1900 the relative proportion of Scots working as miners fell by almost half, and those working in cotton mills by two-thirds. The miners were replaced by Central Europeans and the textile workers by Jews or Italians, while the Scots were becoming clerks or even physicians. In 1900 there were proportionately more doctors among sons of Scots immigrants than in the native white population generally. The Irish moved up too, by a different route: here the next higher rung for most of the second generation was a job as a clerk.

In the more general analysis summarized in Table 4-2, the median occupational rank (according to the Alba Edwards scale) was computed for ten nationalities, each divided by generation and standardized for age and

Table 4-2. Median Occupational Rank of Selected European Nationalities, by Generation, United States, 1950

| FOREIGN-BORN | | SECOND GENERATION | |
|---|---|---|---|
| | | Russians | 4.87 |
| Russians | 4.47 | | |
| | | Swedes | 3.97 |
| English and Welsh | 3.92 | English and Welsh | 3.92 |
| | | Norwegians } | |
| | | Irish } | 3.91 |
| | | Germans | 3.78 |
| Germans | 3.75 | | |
| 3.72 | | | |
| | | Austrians | 3.70 |
| Austrians | 3.55 | | |
| Swedes | 3.50 | | |
| Norwegians | 3.43 | | |
| | | Czechs | 3.41 |
| | | Italians | 3.39 |
| | | Poles | 3.24 |
| Czechs | 3.08 | | |
| Italians | 3.04 | | |
| Irish | 2.99 | | |
| Poles | 2.97 | | |

SOURCE: Charles B. Nam, "Nationality Groups and Social Stratification in America," *Social Forces,* 34 (1959), 328–333.

residence (Nam, 1959). The highest possible rank, for a group of which all were professional and technical workers, would be 6.00; the median for native-born workers of native parents was 3.72. Among the foreign-born, three nationalities ranked higher, and among the second generation five out of the ten. The data do not permit a cross-classification by religion, but one can presume that many of the Russians and some of the Germans and Austrians were Jewish.

If such tables could be expanded to include all of the major nationalities and occupations and the whole of the past century and a half, then we would have a good picture of the interrelation between country of birth and occupation in the United States. Lack of data precludes so complete a study, but Hutchinson has squeezed all that could be gotten out of the record. He sums up his work on this subject as follows:

> In 1919 the foreign-born white male workers were most heavily concentrated in some branches of the clothing industry, . . . among bakers, and in several semiskilled or unskilled employments. . . . Relatively few were found in clerical work and the learned professions; but they were well represented in the artistic professions and among welfare and religious workers. In 1950 they are much less identified with unskilled labor, and more concentrated than formerly in the clothing industry . . . and have become relatively numerous in a wider variety of occupations than before. . . . Although still underrepresented in the learned professions and clerical work as a whole they have made considerable progress in the fields of employment (E. P. Hutchinson, 1956, p. 216).

More generally put, all white immigrants were congregated at the bottom of the social scale on their arrival, but in different occupations. And all of them, or their children, moved up from these several starting points, but along different routes. This hypothesis—which the data available merely suggest—marks one important limitation to the melting-pot thesis. Total assimilation by ethnic background is possibly only if nationalities are randomly distributed among all occupations; for to the degree that the contrary is the case, variation by ethnic background tends to persist in the form of class differences.

#### INSTITUTIONAL INTEGRATION

Although the distinction between Old and New Immigrants as such has lost much of its earlier significance, some of this has remained in the differentiation among Protestants, Catholics, and Jews. It is appropriate, therefore, to exemplify the institutional integration of the American population by concentrating the analysis on the churches.

There are no satisfactory data on the religious distribution of the American population.[25] Table 4-3 lists the number of members claimed by the

---

[25] For annotated bibliographies on the sources available, see Good, 1959; Landis, 1959. For some of the census years during the second half of the nineteenth century,

Table 4-3. Distribution of the Population by Claimed Church Membership, United States, c. 1965

| | NUMBER OF BODIES REPORTING | CHURCH MEMBERS (THOUSANDS) | PERCENTAGE OF TOTAL POPULATION |
|---|---|---|---|
| Protestants | 141 | 69,657 | 35.8 |
|   Baptist | 27 | 23,812 | 12.2 |
|   Methodist | 19 | 13,287 | 6.8 |
|   Lutheran | 9 | 9,024 | 4.6 |
|   Presbyterian | 9 | 4,421 | 2.3 |
|   Episcopal | 1 | 3,644 | 1.9 |
|   Churches of Christ | 1 | 2,600 | 1.3 |
|   United Church of Christ | 1 | 2,071 | 1.1 |
|   Latter-Day Saints | 3 | 1,963 | 1.0 |
|   Christian Churches (Disciples of Christ) | 1 | 1,918 | 1.0 |
|   All other [a] | 70 | 6,917 | 3.6 |
| Catholics | 27 | 50,201 | 25.8 |
|   Roman | 1 | 46,246 | 23.8 |
|   Eastern Orthodox | 18 | 3,172 | 1.6 |
|   All other | 8 | 783 | 0.4 |
| Jews | 3 | 5,600 | 2.9 |
| Buddhists | 1 | 100 | — |
| Not members of any church [b] | | 69,014 | 35.5 |
| | 172 | 194,572 [c] | 100.0 |

SOURCE: Calculated from *World Almanac and Book of Facts 1967*, pp. 148–149.

[a] Includes all non-Catholic Christian sects with less than a million members, whether or not these are ordinarily termed "Protestant"; does not include Church of Christ Scientist and American Evangelical Christian Churches, for which there are no data.

[b] Calculated as the difference between the estimated population and the total membership of all churches.

[c] Official estimate as of July 1, 1965; see U.S. Bureau of the Census, *Current Population Reports*, Series P-25, No. 366, March 15, 1967.

"social statistics" were collected from county officials, including detailed data on church membership. In this century four "censuses of religious bodies" were taken each ten years from 1906 to 1936; it had been planned to continue these, but in 1946 and 1956 Congress failed to appropriate the necessary funds. See William Petersen, *The Politics of Population*, Doubleday, Garden City, N.Y., 1964, pp. 248–270.

various denominations as of about 1965. One can reasonably assume that the figures represent maxima, and even in that sense they are not wholly comparable. The Roman Catholic Church reports as members all persons who have been baptized, including infants and those who have drifted away. Most Protestant churches report only those who have been confirmed, thus omitting infants and children under 14 years.

In addition to the membership claimed by various denominations, partial data are available on individuals' stated religious preference from two other sources—public-opinion research firms and institutes, which have included questions on religion in national polls several dozen times, and the one nationwide sample survey the Census Bureau ever made, in March 1957.[26] There are typically considerable differences among the three sources mainly because the church membership claimed by ecclesiastical officials is not the same as the religious preferences reported by individuals. The figures needed for social analysis—the proportion of each denomination living in cities and in the countryside; with large, medium, and small incomes; and so on—are even less precise than the totals. Yet it is only with such data that one could give an empirical reply to the basic question of the sociology of religion: what are the social effects of religious faith?

One official doctrine in the United States is that a faith has no social consequences of any importance, so that immigrants urged to acculturate in every other sense were guaranteed the right to religious freedom by the Constitution itself. On the other hand, it would not be accurate to describe the separation of church and state in the United States as absolute. Americans now pledge allegiance to one nation "under God," [27] and it is taken for granted that churches are partly supported out of public funds: the institutions themselves pay no taxes even on their nonecclesiastical property, and individuals may deduct donations from their taxable income.

Undoubtedly the ambiguity surrounding the social effects of religious faith, and thus the definition of religious freedom, has encouraged some zealots to go beyond the legitimate limits of politics under the guise of religion. During the nineteenth century Protestant ministers often confused orthodoxy with persistence of the old-country language, and among Lutherans the dispute between proponents of English and German "provoked riots and bloodshed" (Hansen, 1951, p. 75). About the time of the First World War, the Calvinist ministers of the Michigan Dutch community attempted to establish what they termed a "Christian society," with

[26] U.S. Bureau of the Census, *Current Population Reports*, Series P-20, No. 79, February 2, 1958. For data from the National Opinion Research Center, see Donald J. Bogue, *The Population of the United States*, Free Press of Glencoe, New York, 1959, pp. 697ff.

[27] Congress added the words "under God" to the Pledge of Allegiance in 1954. In 1960 a unanimous decision of the Appellate Division of the New York State Supreme Court, affirming the ruling by a lower court, refused to order the State Educational Department to delete the phrase. See *The New York Times*, December 3, 1960.

a Calvinist political party, a Calvinist newspaper, Calvinist trade unions, a Calvinist school system of which Calvin College still exists (Petersen, 1955, p. 49). The Irish Catholic Benevolent Society had even broader plans: separate banks, steamship companies, hotels, labor unions—"in fact almost a complete Irish Catholic economic system," but these fanciful aspirations were never realized (Kane, 1951). Much of whatever interreligious hostility exists is the consequence of the Catholic Church's effort to have the entire population—rather than only its own constituents—governed in accordance with its specific norms governing birth control, divorce, and censorship; of the Fundamentalist Protestants' attempt to make Prohibition the law of the land or forbid public schools to teach evolution; of the Zionists' endeavor to influence American foreign policy in the Middle East. In short, prejudice exists against "Wasps" or Catholics or Jews as such, but what is termed religious bias is often due rather to the overlap of religion with other dimensions of American subnations.

An analysis of the social correlates of religion cannot be satisfactory if it is made in terms of denominations, as some of these comprise as many as twenty-five subdenominations. The divisions are based first of all on differences in doctrine important enough to have caused schisms. Partly because of the persistence of old-country languages, differences in national origin affect social attitudes even within the same church (e.g., Abramson and Noll, 1966). For most denominations, there is also a heavy concentration in particular regions, as can be most clearly seen from maps representing their distribution (Zelinsky, 1961). Members of the religions established in this country for a longer period are more likely to be in the upper middle class, though with important exceptions. According to the composite findings of three surveys in 1957–58, the major religions could be ranked in education, occupation, and income as follows (Lazerwitz, 1961):

| Top | Middle | Bottom |
|---|---|---|
| Episcopalians | Methodists | White Baptists |
| Jews | Lutherans | Negro Baptists |
| Presbyterians | Roman Catholics | |

However, even if those in any religious faith are divided by occupation, income, region, and so on, those in the subcategories are likely to vary greatly. A "Jew" may be an atheist, and a "Protestant" or "Catholic" may subscribe to a faith too nominal to affect his behavior.

Not surprisingly, social analysts have not agreed on whether in the United States religion indeed has a significant effect on behavior patterns. To do so, one would have to isolate this often vague adherence to ill defined faiths from the social variables correlated with it, and then determine how the secular behavior of those of various religions (and of none) differs independently. Perhaps the most notable effort to isolate this "religious factor" is Lenski's work (1961), but even he has failed to convince some that in the United States today religion in itself is an important determinant of social behavior (e.g., Babbie, 1965; Winter, 1967).

### AMALGAMATION

The ultimate assimilation, according to many analysts, is achieved when the diverse physical types merge into a new one through successive generations of intermarriage. This was the original meaning of "melting pot" in Zangwill's play: "Celt and Latin, Slav and Teuton, Greek and Syrian— black and yellow. . . . East and West, and North and South . . . how the great Alchemist melts and fuses them with his purging flame!" In this physiological sense the melting pot has been quite inefficient. Marriage is still atypical across lines set by racial, religious, nationality, or class differentiation. Indeed, one might say that intermarriage is atypical by definition, for if an initial hostility no longer persists toward a marriage between blonds and brunettes, for instance, then one no longer characteristizes such a union as intermarriage.

Much has been written on intermarriage, but so little of quality that the basic theory is still to be worked out. Is it true even that intermarriage breaks down structural lines (e.g., Price, 1966, pp. A22 ff.)? Sometimes the person who converts to Catholicism in order to marry a Catholic becomes the most doctrinaire member of the Church. Even a person with "a trace of Negro blood" is typically classified as a Negro in the United States, and sometimes the light-skinned Negro is more antiwhite than darker Negroes (cf. Richardson, 1962). What is the effect of intermarriage on the social structure when there is a sort of exchange of values along two structural dimensions—when, for example, a Negro professional marries a lower-class white woman (e.g., Davis, 1941; Bertram Hutchinson, 1957; Merton, 1941)? [28]

Most American marriages are class-endogamous, and in the interclass marriages that do occur, the man usually marries down and the woman up. Interclass marriage is so little analyzed, probably because statistics are even poorer than for other kinds of intermarriage, that such broad generalizations sum up most of our knowledge. In particular it is all but impossible to judge to what degree the opposition to interracial, interreligious, or internationality marriage is specific, and to what degree rather it is an index of an all but unexpressed opposition to interclass marriage.

---

[28] The empirical data with which to answer such questions are often lacking, and when data are available the rates to measure intermarriage are sometimes inappropriate. The most obvious confusion in measurement is between rates based on the number of persons who intermarry and those based on the number of marriages (Rodman, 1965; Besanceney, 1965). It is also not clear how such factors as the subnations' age structure and sex ratio should be reflected in rates (Price and Zubrzycki, 1962a, 1962b; Lieberson, 1966a).

Marriages across nationality lines used also to be atypical. According to an early study, three out of four marriages were within the same group, and the fourth between two of closely related cultures (Bossard, 1939). But in one city in-group marriages among Italians fell from 71 per cent in 1930 to 27 per cent in 1960, and among Poles from 79 per cent to 33 per cent over the same period (Bugelski, 1961). According to another study, intermarriage across nationality lines is becoming relatively common, so long as both partners are Protestant or Catholic or Jewish (Kennedy, 1944, 1952; cf. Herberg, 1955), but this much cited finding may be out of date.

Marriage across religious lines is generally opposed by clergymen of all denominations, and this attitude is often reflected also in the advice given by secular marriage counselors. Yet some local studies have indicated that interfaith marriages are far more numerous than is generally recognized (e.g., Thomas 1951; Chancellor and Monahan, 1955; Chancellor and Burchinal, 1962); and in Canada—a somewhat similar culture with better data—the trend in interfaith marriages has been upward (Heer, 1962). The serious concern that has been expressed about the out-marriage of Jews (e.g., Cahnman, 1963) is not based on reliable evidence. The only national datum available is the Census Bureau's 1957 survey, according to which only 3.6 per cent of those who identified themselves as Jews had non-Jewish spouses. The rate seems to be higher in some cities, for example Washington, but not in others, for example Providence (Goldstein and Goldscheider, 1966). There would appear to be little warrant in writing about "The Vanishing Jews," Professor Erich Rosenthal's article in the 1964 *American Jewish Year Book*.

Interracial marriages are apparently at the lowest rate of all types of intermarriage. Until recently they were forbidden by law in the South, the border states, and most of the West. In 1967, when this prohibition remained in force in sixteen states, it was abolished by a sweeping, unanimous decision of the U.S. Supreme Court.[29] Even where legal, marriages across racial lines offer the greatest affront to conventional norms, which generally are strong enough to be effective without a legal reinforcement. Thus, it was surmised several decades ago that Negroes in particular, far from merging physiologically into the general population, are becoming more sharply distinguished. Extramarital relations between white males and Negro females, probably less common than they had once been, at any rate result less often in conception. Persons who range in physical type between Negro and white are more likely than some decades earlier to move into one group or the other, rather than building a bridge between them (Rose, 1948, pp. 47–48). More recently there has been some speculation that Negro-white marriages have become more numerous, based on the only five states that have data on their incidence. Except for Hawaii, where the 1964 rate at which

[29] *The New York Times*, June 13, 1967.

Negroes married whites was the highest ever recorded in the United States, the incidence was both very low and apparently rising slowly. If the present trend is projected into the future, it would take, depending on various assumptions, between 351 and 27,000 years for amalgamation to be completed (Heer, 1966).

Interracial marriage of Asians is also uncommon on the mainland and remarkably frequent in Hawaii. The general miscegenation in Hawaii suggests that much of the opposition to marriage across racial lines is mitigated when members of the various races move into equivalent social classes.[30] In recent years, one marriage out of three has been across racial lines. The most striking evidence of the degree of racial admixture is in a recent study by three geneticists at the University of Hawaii. With thirty possible racial identifications for each parent,[31] there were 900 possible crossings, of which 524 were included in the record. According to the serological evidence, "Hawaiians" have an 8.5 per cent Caucasian mixture and a 13.7 per cent Chinese mixture, and the other presumably pure racial groups include a smaller but usually also significant element from other components of the Islands' population (Morton et al., 1967; cf. Taeuber, 1962; Lind, 1967). Hawaii, in short, represents the amalgamation that is likely in a mixed population when the typical link between race and social-economic status begins to disappear.

## Summary

The composition of a population pertains to its *subnations,* or the groups defined by such characteristics as race, national origin, language, religion, and region. The distribution by any of these indices typically shows a decided clustering, indicating that subnations are significantly different from

[30] The sugar companies in Hawaii successively imported field laborers from China, Japan, Portugal, the Philippines, and Puerto Rico. Initially no different from coolies in any plantation system, they developed from this status by an all but unique process. This transformation began, but did not end, with a rise in economic level. As plantation agriculture became mechanized, its labor requirements gradually changed from a host of unskilled to a much smaller number of skilled and semi-skilled, with a rise in income and status available to many. In spite of the continued commercial importance of sugar and pineapples, Hawaii today is highly urbanized, with almost half of the total population living in Honolulu. Many more work in servicing tourists or the armed forces than in agriculture. This shift in the social structure was made possible first of all by the free public school system, which furnished the initial step of each generation in rising out of their parents' occupation. The social mobility was facilitated by the complexity of the population's ethnic composition. Whites from mainland United States have always constituted a relatively small proportion, and there was no poor white class that sought to maintain its higher status in terms of color (cf. Schmitt, 1968).

[31] The racial identification of parents listed on the birth certificates of 179,327 babies born from 1948 to 1958 was adjudged substantially reliable when checked against evidence based on samples from the Hawaii Blood Clinic. Each father and each mother were placed in one of the following races: Caucasian, Hawaiian, Chinese, Filipino, Japanese, Puerto Rican, and Korean, plus combinations of each of these primary categories with each of the other six.

the general population, but also a tendency for these clusters to be linked by intermediate instances. In a literary analysis one can concentrate on the clusters and ignore the others. But when a population count is made, each individual person must be categorized according to each of the classifications being used, so that demographers are forced to define sub-nations, however arbitrarily, with precise boundaries. No resolution of this dilemma can be wholly satisfactory, and time series of ethnic data often reflect changes in the units' definitions.

The social structure associated with a population composition depends in part on whether the various types of ethnic differentiation overlap or, on the contrary, cut across one another. The greatest inequality is realized in a caste system, which can conveniently be analyzed in terms of the Hindu tradition. The assimilation of subnations into the broader society can be along several routes, ranging from the adoption of culture traits to inter-marriage. Assimilation, thus, is not an all-or-none process, but rather a continuum from total assimilation to total nonassimilation, with various degrees and types of adaptation in between.

Assimilation can be facilitated by a number of factors, of which the most important seem to be the following: (1) A relatively small difference between the interacting cultures, either actual or as defined by the partic-ipants: in particular, if differences are defined as immutable, then assimila-tion is ruled out as impossible. (2) Agreement between the interacting groups that one of the cultures, the same one, is superior: a minority finds it rankling to be dominated by a group whose culture it sees as inferior to its own. (3) The relative size of the minority: for maximum acculturation, it should be large enough to furnish psychological security to its members, but small enough to be integrated without difficulty. (4) A long period of interaction between the groups: the generalization that the longer the con-tact, the more acculturation, is not, however, invariably true, for some pat-terns of partial interrelation have remained constant over centuries.

If these generalizations about assimilation are tested against trends in the United States, they prove to be tentative with respect to whites and often completely invalid when applied to nonwhites. Negroes have been in America longer even than most of the Old Immigrants; whereas among whites Daughters of the American Revolution are a rare phenomenon, a probable majority of Negroes are descended from the Africans brought here during the eighteenth century. More significantly still, American Negroes have no vestigial tie to their "homeland"; apart from ideological sympathies with new African states, their world is defined almost wholly in American terms. Asians and the other smaller minorities are so tiny that one might have expected them to sink into the white sea. Obviously neither the size of a minority, nor its period of residence, nor the strength of its ties to other cultures, determines its relative integration in American society—if the minority is not white.

That such minorities have not been assimilated in American culture is sometimes explained by their greater "visibility." One suspects, however, that the visibility of an ethnic group is less a cause than a symptom of its nonassimilation. It is easy to distinguish a Jew, for example, by his "hooked nose, oily skin, thick lips"; the only difficulty is that these features typify not real Jews but the abstraction attacked by anti-Semites. And to recognize as Negro such a man, for example, as Walter White, a blue-eyed blond who for many years was a leader of the National Association for the Advancement of Colored People, was something of a feat. On the other hand, an American is quite likely not to recall, say, the color of the eyes of a person he met casually a week or so ago. Skin color is more "visible" than eye color because one is, and the other is not, a symbol of social differentiation.

Racial minorities remain separate groups in American society mainly because of the laws, behavior patterns, and attitudes that force them to be so. Any analysis of these minority races must consist in large part of an examination of the special means by which their differences from the white population are maintained and accentuated. The purpose of such laws and institutions is usually to discriminate against the minority, but sometimes (for example, Indian reservations or Negro colleges) it is the opposite. In either case, the distinctive behavior due to these special institutions is often confused with biological variation.

## Suggestions for Further Reading

The analysis of population composition overlaps with a number of other disciplines, and several of the topics briefly discussed here—caste or intermarriage, for instance—each have enormous bibliographies. This list consists only of the works cited in this chapter. Starred items are recommended, either because they constitute a better-than-average presentation of the topic in general or because they are especially relevant to a demographic analysis of subnations.

ABRAMSON, HAROLD J., and C. EDWARD NOLL. 1966. "Religion, Ethnicity, and Social Change," *Review of Religious Research*, **8**, 11–26.

APPEL, J. J. 1960. "New England Origins of the American Irish Historical Society," *New England Quarterly*, **33**, 462–475.

————. 1961. "Hansen's Third Generation 'Law' and the Origins of the American Jewish Historical Society," *Jewish Social Studies*, **23**, 3–20.

BABBIE, EARL R. 1965. "The Religious Factor—Looking Forward," *Review of Religious Research*, **7**, 42–53.

BAILEY, F. G. 1957. *Caste and the Economic Frontier: A Village in Highland Orissa*. Manchester University Press, Manchester.

BEALE, CALVIN L. 1958. "Census Problems of Racial Enumeration," in Thompson and Hughes, 1958, pp. 537–543.

* BERRY, BREWTON. 1965. *Almost White*. Macmillan, New York.

BESANCENEY, PAUL H. 1965. "On Reporting Rates of Intermarriage," *American Journal of Sociology*, **70**, 717–721.

\* BÉTEILLE, ANDRÉ. 1967. "Race and Descent as Social Categories in India," *Daedalus*, **96**, 444–463.

BLUNT, E. A. H. 1931. *The Caste System of Northern India, with Special Reference to the United Provinces of Agra and Oudh*. Humphrey Milford-Oxford University Press, London.

BOAS, FRANZ. 1911. "Changes in Bodily Form of Descendants of Immigrants," in U.S. Senate Immigration Commission, *Report*, Vol. 38. Washington, D.C.

BOGUE, DONALD J. 1951. *State Economic Areas*. U.S. Bureau of the Census, Washington, D.C.

BOSSARD, JAMES H. S. 1939. "Nationality and Nativity as Factors in Marriage," *American Sociological Review*, **4**, 792–798.

\* BOYD, WILLIAM C. 1950. *Genetics and the Races of Man: An Introduction to Modern Physical Anthropology*. Heath, Boston.

BROWNE, WILLIAM J. 1953. "Health as a Factor in African Development," *Phylon*, **13**, 148–156.

BUGELSKI, B. R. 1961. "Assimilation through Intermarriage," *Social Forces*, **40**, 148–154.

CAHNMAN, WERNER J., editor. 1963. *Intermarriage and Jewish Life: A Symposium*. Herzl Press, New York.

CHANCELLOR, LOREN E., and LEE G. BURCHINAL. 1962. "Relations among Inter-Religious Marriages, Migratory Marriages and Civil Weddings in Iowa," *Eugenics Quarterly*, **9**, 75–83.

———, and THOMAS R. MONAHAN. 1955. "Religious Preference and Interreligious Mixtures in Marriages and Divorces in Iowa," *American Journal of Sociology*, **61**, 233–239.

CUMMINGS, JOHN. 1918. *Negro Population, 1790–1915*. U.S. Bureau of the Census, Washington, D.C.

DAVIE, MAURICE R. 1949. *World Immigration, with Special Reference to the United States*. Macmillan, New York.

DAVIS, KINGSLEY. 1941. "Intermarriage in Caste Societies," *American Anthropologist*, **43**, 376–395.

———. 1951. *The Population of India and Pakistan*. Princeton University Press, Princeton, N.J.

DICKIE-CLARK, H. F. 1966. "The Marginal Situation: A Contribution to Marginality Theory," *Social Forces*, **44**, 363–370.

DRIVER, EDWIN D. 1962. "Caste and Occupational Structure in Central India," *Social Forces*, **41**, 26–31.

FRANCIS, E. K. 1947. "The Nature of the Ethnic Group," *American Journal of Sociology*, **52**, 393–400.

GHURYE, G. S. 1961. *Caste, Class and Occupation*. Popular Book Depot, Bombay.

GLAZER, NATHAN. 1953. "America's Ethnic Pattern," *Commentary*, April, pp. 401–408.

GLOCK, CHARLES Y., and RODNEY STARK. 1965. *Religion and Society in Tension*. Rand McNally, Chicago.

\* GOLDSTEIN, SIDNEY, and CALVIN GOLDSCHEIDER. 1966. "Social and Demographic Aspects of Jewish Intermarriage," *Social Problems*, **13**, 386–399.

GOOD, DOROTHY. 1959. "Questions on Religion in the United States Census," *Population Index*, **25**, 3–16.

* GORDON, MILTON M. 1964. *Assimilation in American Life: The Role of Race, Religion, and National Origins*. Oxford University Press, New York.

* HADLEY, J. NIXON. 1957. "The Demography of the American Indians," *Annals of the American Academy of Political and Social Science*, **311**, 23–30.

HANDLIN, OSCAR. 1951. *The Uprooted: The Epic Story of the Great Migration that Made the American People*. Grosset & Dunlap, New York.

* HANSEN, MARCUS LEE. 1938. *The Problem of the Third Generation Immigrant*. Augustana Historical Society, Rock Island, Ill. Reprinted in *Commentary*, November 1952, pp. 492–500.

————. 1948. *The Immigrant in American History*. Harvard University Press, Cambridge, Mass.

————. 1951. *The Atlantic Migration 1607–1860: A History of the Continuing Settlement of the United States*. Harvard University Press, Cambridge, Mass.

* HARRISON, SELIG S. 1960. *India: The Most Dangerous Decades*. Princeton University Press, Princeton, N.J.

HEER, DAVID M. 1962. "The Trend of Interfaith Marriages in Canada, 1922–1957," *American Sociological Review*, **27**, 245–250.

* ————. 1966. "Negro-White Marriage in the United States," *Journal of Marriage and the Family*, **28**, 262–276.

HERBERG, WILL. 1955. *Protestant, Catholic, Jew: An Essay in American Religious Sociology*. Doubleday, New York.

HOLDEN, MATTHEW, JR. 1966. "Ethnic Accommodation in a Historical Case," *Comparative Studies in Society and History*, **8**, 168–180.

HUTCHINSON, BERTRAM. 1957. "Some Evidence Related to Matrimonial Selection and Immigrant Assimilation in Brazil," *Population Studies*, **11**, 149–156.

————. 1959. "Race Differences in Fertility: A Note on their Estimation in Brazil," *Population Studies*, **13**, 151–156.

* HUTCHINSON, E. P. 1956. *Immigrants and Their Children, 1850–1950*. Wiley, New York.

HUTTON, J. H. 1963. *Caste in India: Its Nature, Function, and Origin*. 4th Ed. Oxford University Press, Bombay.

HUYCK, EARL E. 1966. "White-Nonwhite Differentials: Overview and Implications," *Demography*, **3**, 548–565.

INDIA. MINISTRY OF INFORMATION AND BROADCASTING. 1965. *The Gazetteer of India*, Vol. 1: *Country and People*. Nasik.

ISAACS, HAROLD R. 1963. *The New World of Negro Americans*. Viking-Compass, New York.

* ————. 1965. *India's Ex-Untouchables*. Asia Publishing House, Bombay.

JOHNSTON, DENIS FOSTER. 1966. *An Analysis of Sources of Information on the Population of the Navaho*. Bureau of American Ethnology, Smithsonian Institution, Bulletin 197. Washington, D.C.

KANE, JOHN J. 1951. "Protestant-Catholic Tensions," *American Sociological Review*, **16**, 663–672.

KENNEDY, RUBY JO REEVES. 1944. "Single or Triple Melting Pot? Intermarriage Trends in New Haven, 1870–1940," *American Journal of Sociology*, **49**, 331–339.

————. 1952. "Single or Triple Melting Pot? Intermarriage Trends in New Haven, 1870–1950," *American Journal of Sociology*, **58**, 56–59.

KEY, V. O., JR. 1966. *The Responsible Electorate: Rationality in Presidential Voting, 1936–1960.* Belknap Press of Harvard University Press, Cambridge, Mass.

KROEBER, A. L. 1939. *Cultural and Natural Areas of Native North America.* University of California Press, Berkeley.

LANDIS, BENSON Y. 1959. "A Guide to the Literature on Statistics of Religious Affiliation with Reference to Related Social Studies," *Journal of the American Statistical Association,* **54,** 335–357.

LAUGHLIN, WILLIAM S. 1966. "Race: A Population Concept," *Eugenics Quarterly,* **13,** 326–340.

LAZERWITZ, BERNARD. 1961. "A Comparison of Major United States Religious Groups," *Journal of the American Statistical Association,* **56,** 568–579.

LENSKI, GERHARD. 1961. *The Religious Factor.* Doubleday, New York.

* LIEBERSON, STANLEY. 1966a. "The Price-Zubrzycki Measure of Ethnic Intermarriage," *Eugenics Quarterly,* **13,** 92–100.

———. 1966b. "Language Questions in Censuses," *Sociological Inquiry,* **36,** 262–279.

LIND, ANDREW W. 1967. *Hawaii's People,* 3rd Ed. University of Hawaii Press, Honolulu.

* LINTON, RALPH. 1943. "Nativistic Movements," *American Anthropologist,* **45,** 230–240.

LUBELL, SAMUEL. 1956. *The Future of American Politics.* 2nd Revised Ed. Doubleday-Anchor, New York.

LYMAN, STANFORD M. 1968. "The Race Relations Cycle of Robert E. Park," *Pacific Sociological Review,* **11,** 16–22.

MANDELBAUM, DAVID G. 1941. "Culture Change among the Nilgiri Tribes," *American Anthropologist,* **43,** 19–26.

MAYER, KURT B. 1952. *The Population of Switzerland.* Columbia University Press, New York.

———. 1957. "Recent Demographic Developments in Switzerland," *Social Research,* **24,** 331–353.

MERTON, ROBERT K. 1941. "Intermarriage and the Social Structure: Fact and Theory," *Psychiatry,* **4,** 361–374.

MOERNER, MAGNUS. 1966. "The History of Race Relations in Latin America: Some Comments on the State of Research," *Latin American Research Review,* **1,** 17–44.

* MOOD, FULMER. 1965. "The Origin, Evolution, and Application of the Sectional Concept, 1750–1900," in *Regionalism in America,* edited by Merrill Jensen. University of Wisconsin Press, Madison, pp. 5–98.

MORTON, NEWTON E., CHIN S. CHUNG, and MING-PI MI. 1967. *Genetics of Interracial Crosses in Hawaii.* S. Karger, New York and Basel.

NAM, CHARLES B. 1959. "Nationality Groups and Social Stratification in America," *Social Forces,* **34,** 328–333.

ODUM, HOWARD W., and HARRY ESTILL MOORE. 1938. *American Regionalism: A Cultural-Historical Approach to National Integration.* Holt, New York.

ORNSTEIN, JACOB. 1964. "Patterns of Language Planning in the New States," *World Politics,* **17,** 40–49.

* PANIKKAR, K. M. 1933. *Caste and Democracy.* Hogarth Press, London.

PARK, ROBERT EZRA. 1950. *Race and Culture*. Free Press, Glencoe, Ill.

PATTERSON, H. O. L. 1966. "Slavery, Acculturation, and Social Change: The Jamaican Case," *British Journal of Sociology*, 17, 151–164.

PERLOFF, HARVEY S. 1963. *How a Region Grows: Area Development in the U.S. Economy*. Committee for Economic Development, New York.

PETERSEN, WILLIAM. 1955. *Planned Migrations: The Social Determinants of the Dutch-Canadian Movement*. University of California Press, Berkeley.

PIERSON, GEORGE WILSON. 1949. "The Frontier and American Institutions: A Criticism of the Turner Theory," in Taylor, 1949, pp. 65–83.

* PRICE, CHARLES A. 1966. *Australian Immigration: A Bibliography and Digest*. Australian National University, Canberra.

———, and JERZY ZUBRZYCKI. 1962a. "The Use of Inter-marriage Statistics as an Index of Assimilation," *Population Studies*, 16, 58–69.

——— and ———. 1962b. "Immigrant Marriage Patterns in Australia," *Population Studies*, 16, 123–133.

REYNOLDS, LLOYD G. 1935. *The British Immigrant: His Social and Economic Adjustment in Canada*. Oxford University Press, Toronto.

RICHARDSON, ALAN. 1962. "A Note on Mixed Marriage as a Factor in Assimilation," Research Group for European Migration Problems *Bulletin*, 10, 115–119.

RODMAN, HYMAN. 1965. "Technical Note on Two Rates of Mixed Marriage," *American Sociological Review*, 30, 776–778.

ROSE, ARNOLD. 1948. *The Negro in America*. Beacon, Boston.

ROY, PRODIPTO. 1962. "The Measurement of Assimilation: The Spokane Indians," *American Journal of Sociology*, 67, 541–551.

SAPIR, EDWARD. 1921. *Language: An Introduction to the Study of Speech*. Harcourt, Brace, New York.

SAVETH, EDWARD N. 1948. *American Historians and European Immigrants, 1875–1925*. Columbia University Press, New York.

* SCHMITT, ROBERT C. 1968. *Demographic Statistics of Hawaii: 1778–1965*. University of Hawaii Press, Honolulu.

SEEMAN, MELVIN. 1956. "Intellectual Perspective and Adjustment to Minority Status," *Social Problems*, 3, 142–153.

* SHANNON, FRED A. 1949. "A Post Mortem on the Labor-Safety-Valve Theory," in Taylor, 1949, pp. 51–60.

SINHA, V. K. 1965. "Secularism and Indian Democracy," in *Studies in Indian Democracy*, edited by S. P. Aiyar and R. Srinivasan. Allied Publishers, Bombay, pp. 59–96.

* SKIDMORE, THOMAS. 1964. "Gilberto Freyre and the Early Brazilian Republic: Some Notes on Methodology," *Comparative Studies in Society and History*, 6, 490–505.

* SRINIVAS, M. N. 1962. *Caste in Modern India and Other Essays*. Asia Publishing House, Bombay.

——— et al. 1959. "Caste: A Trend Report and Bibliography," *Current Sociology*, 8, 135–183.

SRIVASTAVA, RAM P. 1966. "Tribe-caste Mobility in India and the Case of Kumaon Bhotias," in *Caste and Kin in Nepal, India, and Ceylon*, edited by Christoph von Fuerer-Haimendorf. Asia Publishing House, Bombay, pp. 161–212.

STAMP, L. DUDLEY. 1964. *The Geography of Life and Death*. Fontana, London.

STEIN, STANLEY J. 1961. "Freyre's Brazil Revisited: A Review of *New World in the Tropics: The Culture of Modern Brazil*," *Hispanic American Historical Review*, **41**, 111–113.

STONEQUIST, EVERETT V. 1937. *The Marginal Man: A Study in Personality and Culture Conflict*. Scribner's, New York.

TAEUBER, IRENE B. 1962. "Hawaii," *Population Index*, **28**, 97–126.

TAFT, DONALD R., and RICHARD ROBBINS. 1955. *International Migrations: The Immigrant in the Modern World*. Ronald, New York.

* TAYLOR, GEORGE ROGERS, editor. 1949. *The Turner Thesis Concerning the Role of the Frontier in American History*. Heath, Boston.

THOMAS, JOHN L. 1951. "The Factor of Religion in the Selection of Marriage Mates," *American Sociological Review*, **16**, 487–491.

THOMPSON, EDGAR T., and EVERETT C. HUGHES, editors. 1958. *Race: Individual and Collective Behavior*. Free Press, Glencoe, Ill.

TOCQUEVILLE, ALEXIS DE. 1947. *Democracy in America*, edited by Henry Steele Commager. Oxford University Press, New York.

TURNER, FREDERICK JACKSON. 1949. "The Significance of the Frontier in American History," in Taylor, 1949, pp. 1–18.

UNITED NATIONS. STATISTICAL OFFICE. 1956. "1960 World Population Census Programme: 1945–1954 Experience—Ethnic Characteristics and Native Customs." Mimeographed.

———. 1957. *Demographic Yearbook, 1956*. New York.

———. 1964. *Demographic Yearbook, 1963*. New York

U.S. BUREAU OF THE CENSUS. 1906. "Special Reports. Supplementary Analysis and Derivative Data." *Census of Population, 1900*. Washington, D.C.

———. 1960. *Historical Statistics of the United States, Colonial Times to 1957*. Washington, D.C.

* ———. 1963. *U.S. Census of Population: 1960. Subject Reports. Nonwhite Population by Race: Social and Economic Statistics for Negroes, Indians, Japanese, Chinese, and Filipinos*. Final Report PC(2)-1C. Washington, D.C.

U.S. DEPARTMENT OF THE INTERIOR. 1958. *Federal Indian Law*. Washington, D.C.

U.S. SENATE. 1928. "Immigration Quotas on the Basis of National Origin," *Miscellaneous Documents 8870*, Vol. 1, No. 65. 70th Congress, 1st Session. Washington, D.C.

VAN BAAL, J. 1960. "Erring Acculturation," *American Anthropologist*, **62**, 108–121.

WINTER, GIBSON. 1967. "Methodological Reflections on 'The Religious Factor,'" in *The Sociology of Religion: An Anthology*, edited by Richard D. Knudten. Appleton-Century-Crofts, New York, pp. 46–56.

WIRTH, LOUIS. 1945. "The Problem of Minority Groups," in *The Science of Man in the World Crisis*, edited by Ralph Linton. Columbia University Press, New York, pp. 347–372.

WRIGHT, BENJAMIN F., JR. 1949. "Political Institutions and the Frontier," in Taylor, 1949, pp. 42–50.

WRIGHT, CARROLL D. 1900. *The History and Growth of the United States Censuses, Prepared for the Senate Committee on the Censuses*. Washington, D.C.

ZELINSKY, WILBUR. 1961. "An Approach to the Religious Geography of the United States: Patterns of Church Membership in 1952," *Annals of the Association of American Geographers*, **51**, 139–193.

\* ZINKIN, TAYA. 1962. *Caste Today*. Institute of Race Relations. Oxford University Press, London.

# 5 MALTHUSIAN THEORY AND ITS DEVELOPMENT

"The" population problem as most persons define it has little to do with the topics discussed so far. It pertains rather to the world's explosive growth, the dearth of food, the means by which the disparity between numbers and resources can be reduced and, one hopes, eventually eliminated. Although the struggle to survive has always been the fundament of human existence, the serious analysis of this effort did not begin until modern times. It started in England of the early nineteenth century, the birthplace of the Industrial Revolution, and from the name of the principal theorist the designation of the problem became "the Malthusian dilemma."

Malthus has the faults of a pioneer, but his *Essay on the Principle of Population* is more directly relevant today than the works of any predecessor, and even of many successors. He saw the potential for the rapid growth that has indeed taken place since he wrote, and for the deterioration in human welfare that this increase in numbers can effect. He saw also how control over such multiplication could be established—by the gradual inculcation in each person of a higher aspiration, which would induce him to forgo a numerous progeny in exchange for other values. Malthus's work is important also for a significant line of development from it, the theory of population optimum. The question, what size of population is best suited to a given environment, is hardly more than a modern paraphrase of the issue that Malthus analyzed.

Malthus's relevance to the world today will be apparent in subsequent chapters on specific countries or elements of demographic analysis. Here we shall look at the theory as he developed it and the more general developments from it.

## Malthus

Thomas Robert Malthus (from childhood on he was known as "Robert") was born in 1766, one of eight children of a country gentleman. He was educated privately and at Jesus College, Cambridge, where he read English and French literature and ancient history, won prizes in Latin and English declamation, and was graduated with honors in mathematics. At the age of twenty-two he took orders so as to realize, he wrote, "the utmost of my wishes, a retired living in the country." For a short period he was curate at Okewood, Surrey, a village "truly remarkable throughout the eighteenth century for its enormous number of baptisms and its small number of burials" (James, 1966, p. 7). From 1793 until he forfeited it by his marriage in 1804, he held a fellowship at Jesus College. In the latter year he became Professor of History and Political Economy in the newly founded East India College, soon to be domiciled at Haileybury. This was the first professorship in political economy established in Britain, and he filled the post with distinction until his death in 1834.

Malthus was one of the founders of nineteenth-century economics, a direct successor of Adam Smith,[1] a good personal friend of David Ricardo, and a telling influence on neoclassicists. Ricardo incorporated Malthus's principle of population virtually intact into economic theory and, indeed, carried it even farther than the author himself. In one respect, however, Malthus stood outside the main line of development of classical theory: in the 1930s, when Keynes started a new trend in economics by emphasizing "effective demand," this concept was revived from an insight of Malthus's that had been neglected for more than a century.

Malthus's most important work in the context of this book, and also the one for which he is most honored and maligned, is his *Essay on the Principle of Population*. It was first published anonymously in 1798, when the author was 32 years old. This short work was written with an aggressive confidence, a dashing style that passed over exceptions, anomalies, and

---

[1] Before Malthus traveled to Scandinavia, he jotted down the topics he was interested in under the heading "Smith's Questions": "Interest of money. Corn laws. Inland merchants & at the Ports. Recompence of Laborer. Relative prices of provisions & manufactures at different times. Bills & Bankers. Religious establishments & sects" (James, 1966, p. 24).

minor points, and swept on to the main conclusion with youthful confidence. It brought the author immediate fame and notoriety, but if he had been content to let it rest with this version, his name would not be known to every educated person today. Malthus spent a good portion of the rest of his life collecting data on the relation between population and environment in various cultures, bringing his theory in accord with these facts, and adjusting it to criticism. (There were seven editions of the *Essay* in all, the last published posthumously in 1872.) Since most countries of the Western world were just beginning to compile reliable demographic statistics, this empirical orientation required an extraordinary effort.[2] The second edition of the *Essay*, issued after five years of travel and study, was four times as long as the first. The style is much more sober: "If I had confined myself to general views, I could have entrenched myself in an impregnable fortress," Malthus wrote in the preface. "I was willing to sacrifice all pretensions to merit of composition to the chance of making an impression on a larger class of readers."

### BACKGROUND TO THE THEORY

As his critics have often pointed out, Malthus's ideas were not wholly original with him. According to the author of the *Essay* himself, before he wrote the first edition he had read the works of only four writers on population—David Hume, Adam Smith, Robert Wallace, and Richard Price—and of these only Wallace is really relevant to Malthus's specific theory. For Hume and Smith population was a relatively subordinate subject, and Price was convinced that England's depopulation was proceeding apace. Although in his later study Malthus found a much longer list of men who had anticipated him, the *Essay* was original in an important sense. By putting these ideas that other men had expressed into a larger framework and examining in detail the relation of population growth to economic and political development, Malthus did more than any of his predecessors or all of them together. He wrote a book that, whether as guide or as target, has become for all the beginning of modern population theory. And although in certain respects the *Essay* was derivative, in more important ways it opposed two strong schools of thought, mercantilism and revolutionary utopianism.

**Mercantilism** marks the transition between the medieval and the modern, a phase in the history of economic policy "compounded of elements that were bureaucratic and modern and others that were feudal and patrimonial" (Dorn, 1963, p. 18). The universalist elements of the Middle Ages, the Church and the Empire, had lost their ability to hold society together,

---

[2] James has printed on facing pages the chapter "On the Checks to Population in Norway" and the travel notes on which this was based. It is a fascinating exposition of Malthus's method of work (James, 1966, Appendix 1).

and their place was taken by highly centralized nation states. Political and economic institutions were closely intertwined. Very often state officials planned, initiated, developed, and regulated economic enterprises;[3] and the trading companies they formed had powers so broad that within their territories they were equivalent to sovereign states.[4] Moreover,

The building of dams, reservoirs, canals, roads, bridges, drainage projects, the rebuilding of towns, the altering of rivers to make them navigable demanded a new type of engineering official; new government departments were created for registration, land, mortgages, postal service, forests, agriculture, stud farms and stock raising, internal colonization and a score of pressing problems (Dorn, 1963, p. 17).

According to a prime tenet of mercantilist theory, any nation could benefit only at the cost of others. A great London merchant, speaking of France in Parliament, proclaimed the doctrine at its barest: "Our trade will improve by the total extinction of theirs" (*ibid.*, p. 9). The major aim of political-economic policy was to prepare for war, which came frequently. A wise state produced goods cheaply and exported them in exchange not for other commodities but for the maximum amount of gold.

And just as it hoarded bullion, so also the state hoarded people, and for the same reason, to increase its economic, political, and military prowess. The trade in slaves was seen as indispensable (*ibid.*, pp. 261–262). Armies were amalgams of native and foreign riffraff.

Many of [the mercenaries] had been kidnapped, forcibly dragged from taverns, swept up from the streets or released from the prisons. It was the pinch of poverty, however, that drove the great mass of mercenary soldiers into enlistment (*ibid.*, p. 83).

The function of the mass of the population was to produce for the greater power of the state, and to this end no child was too young to begin working.

Whereas from the beginning of the nineteenth century onwards, after tentative beginnings, stronger and stronger measures were taken to limit child labor by law, under mercantilism the power of the state was exerted in precisely the

---

[3] When the French East India Company was about to be formed, Colbert had Louis XIV write a letter to various financiers "to the effect that he did not doubt their willingness to take so favorable an opportunity of placing themselves at the service of God, himself and the community by subscribing shares" (Heckscher, 1935, 1, 346).

[4] "The companies had the right to administer newly discovered or appropriated territories, set up law courts there, make local laws, grant titles, build fortresses, mobilize troops, wage war and conclude peace with non-Christian princes and nations, ruthlessly crush whatever threatened their privileges and arrest and deport anybody trading in their territory without permission, in certain cases even the right to have coinage struck for local currency. . . . [Disobedience was described] as an offense against 'God and the company' " (*ibid.*, 1, 451).

opposite direction. . . . In a decree of 1668 affecting the lace-making industry in Auxerre, . . . [Colbert] commanded . . . that all the inhabitants of the town should send their children into this industry at the age of six, on pain of a penalty of 30 *sous* per child (Heckscher, 1935, 2, 155).

Wages should be at subsistence but never higher. A worker, in the words of Sir William Petty, should be able only to "live, labor, and generate," and "if you double wages, then he works but half so much as he could, or otherwise would." [5]

The population theories and policies of the mercantilist period, though they varied from one nation or time to another, were remarkably consistent. "An almost fanatical desire to increase population prevailed in all countries" (Heckscher, 1935, 2, 158). France under Colbert in particular attempted to stimulate fertility and to proscribe emigration.[6] The most important of the pronatalist measures (1666) exempted those who married early from certain taxes and granted pensions to the fathers of ten or more living legitimate children. These stimulants had little or no effect and were revoked in 1683, but the idea behind them survived in a considerable "repopulationist" literature during the eighteenth century (Spengler, 1942, pp. 24–26, Chapter 3).

In spite of the axiom that a large population is good and a larger one better, mercantilist writers continually noted the "overcrowding" evidenced by a high incidence of vagrancy and crime. Anxious about both the insufficiency of people and their unemployment, they never reconciled these two positions. "French writers failed to recognize, explicitly and completely, the dependence of the population upon the food supply" (*ibid.*, p. 19). The way to solve overcrowding in the mercantilist framework was to ship the surplus to colonies, where they could aggrandize the state's power in another quarter of the globe. And here the same cycle was started again, with renewed efforts to increase the overseas population as rapidly as possible. Whole boatloads of women, usually corralled from houses of correction but sometimes also young country girls, were sent to the French colonies, where soldiers who refused to marry them were punished. In the innumerable letters back and forth, these females were quite clearly seen simply as breeders. "In the same breath mention is made of shiploads of women, mares, and sheep, the methods of propagating human beings and cattle being regarded as roughly on the same plane" (Heckscher, 1935, 2, 300).

[5] Quoted in Eduard Heimann, *History of Economic Doctrines: An Introduction to Economic Theory*, Oxford University Press, New York, 1945, p. 36.

[6] Indeed, the revocation of the Edict of Nantes in 1685 resulted, on the contrary, in an emigration of 500,000 to 1,000,000 Huguenots and Jews, but this represented a different policy that reached its fruition after Colbert's death. The asylum that the refugees found in England and Holland, however, was not merely a reflection of the greater tolerance in these Protestant countries, but also of a competition for foreign workers, particularly skilled craftsmen.

**Revolutionary Utopianism,** a new conception of humanity, gradually evolved during the eighteenth century, particularly in the writings of the French political philosophers. With respect to demographic theory and policy, however, there was neither a clear line of development nor a clean break with mercantilism (Spengler, 1942, Chapter 6). One recurrent theme was the strong probability, or even inevitability, of human betterment, and those who believed this also generally held that growth in numbers was a social good, a clear index of the nation's health. Convinced on the contrary that the population of France, and indeed of the whole world, had diminished because of "interior vice and bad government," Montesquieu also advocated that Colbert's laws, which rewarded only the prodigiously fertile, be broadened into a more general pronatalist policy. According to Voltaire, a nation was fortunate if its population increased by so much as 5 per cent a century. Saint-Just, later one of the instigators of the Jacobin Terror, proclaimed that misery could never follow from overpopulation, but only from social institutions. One can usually depend on nature "never to have more children than teats," but to keep the balance in the other direction nature needs the state's assistance. His notion of a just family law, inspired by Rousseau, was that marriage should be encouraged by state loans, and a couple still childless after seven years ought to be forcibly separated (Fage, 1953).[7]

In the context of a discussion of Malthus, two revolutionary ideologues are especially relevant, Condorcet and Godwin. The first edition of Malthus's *Essay,* as its very title indicated, was intended to reply to "the speculations of Mr. Godwin, M. Condorcet, and other writers."

Marie-Jean-Antoine-Nicolas Caritat, Marquis de Condorcet, was an ardent revolutionary, a prominent member of the moderate Girondin faction. In 1793, after the more radical Jacobins had gained full control, Condorcet was tried *in absentia* and sentenced to death. He remained in Paris, hiding in a students' boarding house, and over the next six months, while the tumbrils were rolling by almost under his window, he wrote his famous *Esquisse d'un tableau historique des progrès de l'esprit humain,* a history of human progress from its earliest beginnings to its imminent culmination in human perfection. According to Condorcet, all inequalities of wealth, of education, of opportunity, of sex, would soon disappear. Animosities between nations and races would be no more. All persons would speak the same language. The earth would be bountiful without stint. All diseases would be conquered, and if man did not become immortal, the span of his life would have no assignable upper limit. The question of whether production would always suffice to satisfy the people's wants could not be answered, for the problem would not have to be faced for ages to come,

---

[7] This list, one should note, does not reflect all of the diversity of eighteenth-century thought on population. For example, Quesnay, a physician as well as an eminent economist, was in some of his precepts closer to Malthus than to his French contemporaries.

by which time man would have acquired new types of now still unimagined knowledge. In this rational age to come, men would recognize their obligation to those not yet born and to the general well-being both of their society and of all humanity, and "not to the puerile idea of filling the earth with useless and unhappy beings." At that time a limit could be set to population other than by the premature death of a portion of those born. "Thus we find in Condorcet the entire genesis [though indeed no more than this hint] of the Malthusian population law, but in France these ideas remained unnoticed" (Fage, 1953; *cf.* McCleary, 1953, pp. 86–88).

In the same year in which Condorcet went into hiding, a book was published across the channel by William Godwin, *Enquiry Concerning*

William Godwin, 1756–1836 (*N.Y. Public Library, Victorian Collection*).

*Political Justice.* It looked forward to the early establishment of a similarly perfect society, in which a half hour's work a day would amply supply the wants of all.

There will be no war, no crimes, no administration of justice, as it is called, and no government. Besides this, there will be neither disease, anguish, melancholy, nor resentment. Every man will seek, with ineffable ardor, the good of all.

There is little in this book about population, and Godwin's ideas on this subject are better represented in a later work, written specifically in reply to Malthus's *Essay*. This is altogether a curious document. Its factual base is suggested by the statement that "the Chinese and the people of Industan carry back their chronology through millions of years" (Godwin, 1820, p. 14). Its logic is suggested by the author's belief that with his contention that half of those born die before maturity he was refuting Malthus's principle of population (*ibid.*, p. 28). Its style is suggested by the allegation that because of Malthus "a woman walking the streets in a state of pregnancy was an unavoidable subject of alarm" (*ibid.*, p. 110). In short, its message is that "the numbers of mankind have no permanent tendency to increase. . . . In some countries [the population] is certainly diminished; and we have, I believe, no sound reason to think that in any [except North America] it has increased" (*ibid.*, p. 502).

France's Revolutionary Assembly, like the earlier philosophers, was in the main pronatalist. The principal instrument used by the republican government to stimulate population growth was the same as Colbert's, differential taxation; single persons thirty years old and over paid a surtax of 25 per cent. As defined in the new constitution itself, "No one can be a good citizen who is not a good son, a good father, a good brother, a good husband" (Reinhard, 1946). Membership in the *Conseil des Anciens* was constitutionally restricted to married men. A national celebration to honor Husbands and Wives provoked a deluge of sentimental panegyrics. A campaign against celibates was reflected both in legislation and in crackpot ideas of fanatics—for example, that all celibates be required to wear clothing of a specific color, so that they might not escape the just ridicule of the people; or the petition to the Convention that celibacy be made a capital offense (Fage, 1953; Glass, 1940, p. 146).

The population policy under Napoleon represented a compromise. Pronatalist decrees continued; in 1813, though the need for soldiers was great, married men were exempted from military service. Under the Civil Code, marriage remained a civil contract and divorce was possible, though difficult. The authority of the father was strengthened, both over his children and over his wife. As under the Republic, primogeniture was supplanted by a law requiring each owner of property to divide the bulk of it equally among all his children; and at one time some analysts believed that this clause had effected a decline in French fertility, particularly among the peasants, for whom a numerous progeny would mean a rapid subdivision of the farm into uneconomic plots. Actually, however, even before the Revolution equal division of property had been the usual practice except among the nobility, so that the decline in family size cannot be ascribed to the law, and certainly not to its purpose (Blacker, 1957).

These two schools of thought, mercantilism and revolutionary utopianism, dominated European thinking on population in the eighteenth century. It was to comment on the first that Adam Smith had written *Wealth of Nations,* and Malthus followed in that new path with his *Essay.*

### THE PRINCIPLE OF POPULATION

"In an inquiry concerning the improvement of society," Malthus begins the final edition of the *Essay*, the natural procedure is to investigate past impediments to "the progress of mankind towards happiness" and the probability that these would be totally or partially removed in the future (Malthus, 1872, Book 1, Chapters 1–2). He does not pretend to be able to discuss so large a subject in its entirety, but "one great cause" is "the constant tendency in all animated life to increase beyond the nourishment prepared for it."

Population, "when unchecked," doubles once every generation. Among plants and "irrational animals," the potential increase is actual, and its "superabundant effects are repressed afterwards by want of room or nourishment." The matter is "more complicated" in the human species, for man, a rational being, can consider the effects of his potential fertility and curb his natural instinct. With man there are two types of controls of population growth, which Malthus terms the **preventive** and the **positive checks.** "In no state that we have yet known, has the power of population been left to exert itself with perfect freedom."

The principal preventive check is "moral restraint," or the postponement of marriage with no extramarital sexual gratification. Other types of preventive checks he terms "vice," namely, "promiscuous intercourse, unnatural passions, violations of the marriage bed, and improper arts to conceal the consequences of irregular connections"—or, in modern terminology, promiscuity, homosexuality, adultery, and birth control (or abortion) applied either within or outside marriage.

Positive checks include "wars, excesses, and many others which it would be in our power to avoid"; but in a country already fairly densely populated (Malthus used Great Britain as an example, and specifically excluded the America of his day), lack of food is the decisive factor. If the average produce from the land were doubled over one generation, or about 25 years, this would be "a greater increase than could with reason be expected." A second doubling in the following 25 years "would be contrary to all our knowledge of the properties of land." That is to say, the "tendency" or "power" of every species, including the human one, is to increase at a geometric rate, while under the most favorable circumstances usually to be found, its subsistence increases at an arithmetic rate. Thus, "the human species would increase as the numbers, 1, 2, 4, 8, 16, 32, 64, 128, 256; and the subsistence as 1, 2, 3, 4, 5, 6, 7, 8, 9. In two centuries the population would be to the means of subsistence as 256 to 9; in three centuries as 4,096 to 13, and in two thousand years the difference would be almost incalculable." Lack of food, then, is the principal ultimate check to population growth but "never the immediate check, except in cases of actual famine."

Apart from migration, the population growth of any area depends on the preventive and positive checks taken together, or, in modern terminology, on practices affecting fertility and those affecting mortality. Moreover,

The preventive and the positive checks must vary inversely as each other; that is, in countries either naturally unhealthy, or subject to a great mortality, from whatever cause it may arise, the preventive check will prevail very little. In those countries, on the contrary, which are naturally healthy, and where the preventive check is found to prevail with considerable force, the positive check will prevail very little, or the mortality be very small.

Or, as we would say today, fertility and mortality, apart from transitional periods, are generally either both high or both low.

Population tends to oscillate around its means of subsistence. If a country with a population of 11 million, say, has food adequate for this number, then in most cases the population would increase sooner than the subsistence, which eventually would have to be divided among perhaps 11.5 million. Because of the consequent distress among the poor, more would put off getting married (the high negative correlation between the price of wheat and the marriage rate that Malthus noted has been repeatedly confirmed in subsequent studies). With a fall in the wage rate, farmers would be encouraged to hire more hands to "turn up fresh soil and to manure and improve more completely what is already in tillage," until the food supply was again on a par with the population, and the cycle began again. In primitive societies, where there is no market system, the same kind of oscillation takes place more directly. "When population has increased nearly to the utmost limits of the food, all the preventive and the positive checks will naturally operate with increased force . . . till the population is sunk below the level of the food; and then the return to comparative plenty will again produce an increase, and, after a certain period, its further progress will again be checked by the same causes" (*cf.* pp. 344–345).

The tension between population and subsistence, which Malthus saw as the major cause of misery and vice, could also have a beneficial effect. A man who postpones marriage until he is able to support his family is driven by his sexual urge to work hard. Malthus was therefore opposed to contraceptives, for their use permits sexual gratification free, as it were, and does not generate the same drive to work as would either a chaste postponement of marriage or children to care for. If a misunderstanding of Malthus's meaning was possible in the first edition, this should have been removed by a very specific denunciation of birth control that he made in the appendix to the 1817 edition, answering one James Grahame:

I should always particularly reprobate any artificial and unnatural modes of checking population, both on account of their immorality and their tendency to remove a necessary stimulus to industry. If it were possible for each married couple to limit by a wish the number of their children, there is certainly reason to fear that the indolence of the human race would be very greatly increased, and that neither the population of individual countries nor of the whole earth would ever reach its natural and proper extent. But the restraints which I have recommended are quite of a different character. They are not only pointed out by reason and sanctioned by religion, but tend in the most marked manner to stimulate industry (Malthus, 1872, p. 512).

A considerable difference in average family size was already discernible in Malthus's day, and the lower fertility of the upper classes was effected, at least in large part, by the postponement of marriage that he considered desirable. If prudence is exercised at the top, "the obvious mode" of extending this practice to the lower classes is "to infuse into them a portion of that knowledge and foresight which so much facilitates the attainment of this object in the educated part of the community" (*ibid.*, p. 437). The way to do this, Malthus continued, would be to set up a universal educational system, as had been proposed by Adam Smith. Educating the mass would afford everyone the possibility of improving his situation, and this was, in Malthus's view, a strong counter force to the principle of population. "The desire of bettering our condition, and the fear of making it worse, has been constantly in action and has been constantly directing people into the right road" (*ibid.*, p. 477).

Once the people have been educated to regard prudential restraint as both feasible and good, this mode of checking the growth of population can be spread through society by raising the people's aspirations. This argument, which is merely suggested in the last chapters of the *Essay*, Malthus developed more fully in his *Principles of Political Economy* (Malthus, 1951; *cf.* Spengler, 1945). The lowest level to which wages can fall, in his theory as in classical economics generally, is the cost of bringing another generation of laborers into the world at the subsistence level. Malthus believed, however, that wages can be forced up from this minimum by an increase in "the amount of those necessaries and conveniences without which [the workers] would not consent to keep up their numbers to the required point" (*cf.* pp. 158–159, 501).

### CRITICISM AND ANALYSIS

It is standard that important books are more often cited than read, but in the whole development of the social sciences, there has probably never been anyone attacked and defended with so little regard for what he had written as Malthus. The errors and misrepresentations have been so general and so persistent that an account of his theory cannot be considered complete until some attention has been paid them. Accounts in responsible works are sometimes mistaken even on matters of simple, easily ascertainable facts—when Malthus was born,[8] where he was educated and in what,[9] what his profession was,[10] whether he was married,[11] how many children he had,[12] how many editions there were of the *Essay*,[13] and so on. Those most interested in Malthus, whether to praise or to damn him, have often started out with a misconception so fundamental that it enveloped the whole man. The "Malthusian" (later "Neo-Malthusian") Leagues sometimes took several generations to discover that the person whose name they used had been opposed in principle to the birth control they advocated. And the opponents of Malthus have often propagated the myth that he was a reactionary, that "the *Essay on Population* chimed with a growing tendency to repress—discussion, association, political organization were becoming less free, as the wars became more exacting and more intense" (Beales, 1953). A widely used text denounces Malthus as "an apologist for feudalism on a capitalist and utilitarian basis"—feudalism in England of 1800! Malthus, we are told, was "probably thinking in terms of a permanent social structure having the qualities of the transitional phase of the eighteenth century." [14]

These arguments, one might say, have a certain relevance to the highly simplified version of Malthus's theory that appeared in the first edition of the *Essay*, or that his avid supporters later bandied about in his name. Anyone in favor of absolute laissez faire found in Malthus's principle of population, as later in Darwin's principle of natural selection, a doctrine that seemed to give his political views scientific backing. The main impact on contemporary social and political events was not made by the *Essay* or the *Origin of Species*, but by vulgarized caricatures of these works, which generally had, it is true, a pernicious influence on British social policy. Malthus has been criticized for ignoring the many distortions of his theory that appeared during his lifetime; he might have answered that to refute all of them he would have had to devote full time to the task, and that in the

---

[8] His date of birth, often given as February 14, 1766 (one recent work even makes a point that this is St. Valentine's Day), was in fact February 13 (James, 1966, p. 1).

[9] It is a rare account that mentions that he left Cambridge as a 9th Wrangler, that is, with honors in mathematics.

[10] See McCleary, 1953, pp. 94–95. The major complaint here is the constant emphasis on his term as a curate, with no mention of his major adult role as a professor.

[11] Marx was apparently responsible for spreading the legend that Malthus "had taken the monastic vow of celibacy" (Karl Marx, *Capital*, Kerr, Chicago, 1906, 1, 675–677, footnote 1).

[12] A myth arose somehow about eleven daughters, and it "persists to this day in the introduction to a recent edition of the *Essay* (Himmelfarb, 1960, p. xxv). In fact, Malthus had two daughters and one son, all of whom died without issue.

[13] We are told, for example, that there were five during his lifetime in Beales, 1953.

[14] Erich Roll, *A History of Economic Thought*, Revised Ed., Faber & Faber, London, 1954, pp. 211, 205.

prefaces to successive editions of the *Essay* he did try to correct the most important errors. Yet while subsequent generations have managed to distinguish Darwin from Social Darwinism,[15] Malthus is still usually pictured as a cartoon figure, Good or Evil incarnate, depending on one's politics.

Malthus was no revolutionary. His sensibilities were revolted by the Terror in Paris, and his solid English empiricism by such utopian extrava-

Thomas Robert Malthus, 1766–1834.

gances as that man can become immortal by establishing a new form of government. But neither was he a reactionary. He is vilified for having denounced the Speenhamland system (see pp. 418–419), but he is less well known as the advocate of free universal education, free medical care for

[15] Even Jacques Barzun, who has written what is undoubtedly the least sympathetic recent account of Darwin, distinguishes "The Newton of Biology" from "The Uses of Darwinism"; see *Darwin, Marx, Wagner: Critique of a Heritage*, Doubleday-Anchor, New York, 1958, Chapters 4 and 5.

the poor, state assistance to emigrants, and even direct relief to casual laborers or families with more than six children; or as the opponent of child labor in factories and of free trade when it benefited the traders but not the public.[16] More fundamentally, these policy recommendations derived from Malthus's underlying principles. That his sympathies lay with the upper classes is true, but these sympathies were weakened by the fact that they were divided between the gentry and the urban middle class. Brought up the son of a country gentleman, he ended his life as a staunch Whig. Appreciative of certain elements of country life ("feudalism"), he was nevertheless for parliamentary reforms that would shift the political power to the cities. When he termed "most" men lazy, who would "sink to the level of brutes" if permitted to remain idle, he certainly had some basis for this judgment among the declassed peasants of his day. The key to his social philosophy is not his unflattering appraisal of the illiterate mass, but his conviction that their state was not ingrained, that social classes are *not,* as Edmund Burke wrote, "as it were, different species of animals." Following the example of Adam Smith in *The Wealth of Nations,* Malthus proclaimed the right of each individual to seek happiness rather than serve the state, and to do this by following his own conscience rather than traditional usages. A full break with mercantilism—and with its paternalistic obverse, represented in Speenhamland—was a necessary prerequisite to the development of modern democracy. However, unlike some proponents of laissez-faire liberalism, who demanded of each man only that he seek his own interest, Malthus did not see the upper classes as automatically right by reason of their social position. If they failed to assist the lower classes in becoming self-reliant, they were thereby censurable.

To reject the frequent errors and misrepresentations in discussions of Malthus's work does not mean that we must accept it as gospel. He is still worth studying today because he forcefully posed a few very important questions, but his answers to them are inadequate by modern standards. These deficiences derive in large part from three contradictions in his work that were never wholly resolved.

**1. Moralist vs. Scientist.**   To this day, social theorists find it difficult to separate an analysis of what is from what, in their opinion, ought to be. Malthus wrote at a time when such subjects as population were ordinarily discussed in the context of "moral philosophy"; he himself was a trained mathematician who helped found the Royal Statistical Society and, as mentioned above, was England's first professor of political economy. The pages of his books, reflecting this transition from a moralist to a scientific frame of reference, are sprinkled with allusions to "the Creator" and what He would prefer. The modern reader, even a pious one, finds such stylistic mannerisms inappropriate to a work in social science.

---

[16] *Cf.* Bonar, 1924, p. 343, where citations are given to the passages in Malthus's work expressing these opinions.

Sometimes the competition between the two analytical systems comes to the surface. Consider the proposition that "vice" leads to "misery." This might be the topic of a sermon, and Malthus the moralist would be pleased with the formulation. Malthus the scientist could hardly be. The main impetus to rapid population growth and thus, in his system, to misery, came from early marriage. Although he strongly advocated "moral restraint," he never quite designated the failure to exercise it—getting married—as "vice." And, on the other hand, as he pointed out in an interesting footnote, some vice—for example, extramarital intercourse—may "have added to the happiness of both parties and have injured no one."

These individual actions, therefore, cannot come under the head of misery. But they are still evidently vicious, because an action is so denominated which violates an express precept, founded upon its general tendency to produce misery, whatever may be its individual effect; and no person can doubt the general tendency of an illicit intercourse between the sexes to injure the happiness of society (Malthus, 1872, p. 9).

Or, as a present-day sociologist would put it, no society can be viable if it lacks so fundamental an institution as the family, which, to persist, must be protected by a principle of legitimacy and moral injunctions against extramarital relations. In the *Essay* a hint of such a functional analysis is sometimes perceptible, intertwined with "moral philosophy."

As one other example, compare his opposition to birth control with that in Catholic dogma. When contraceptives are denounced as "unnatural," there is no way of translating this moral judgment into scientific language. Malthus disapproved of them "both on account of their immorality and their tendency to remove a necessary stimulus to industry," and of the two reasons he stressed the second. Birth control was what modern sociologists would term "dysfunctional." Malthus was partly wrong on this point, of course: man's ambition can be excited by other stimulants than his sexuality. But the interesting point is that Malthus was not satisfied with labeling birth control as "immoral"; he tried to state his opposition also in an empirical context, in which he *could* be proved wrong.

Although Marx and others habitually referred to him as "Parson Malthus," many clergymen found his interpretation of Providence not to their liking, and one went so far as to charge the author of the *Essay* with atheism (Bonar, 1924, p. 365). The population theory appropriate to a "parson," they felt, was something along the lines of Luther's adage, *"Gott macht Kinder, der wird sie auch ernähren"*—God makes children, and He will also nourish them.[17] The principle of population, on the contrary, brought man fully into nature, one species among others. As Darwin himself re-

[17] It is remarkable how close this truly pious sentiment is to the adage of the revolutionary Saint-Just about teats; *cf.* p. 146. Godwin held that "Mr. Malthus's is not the religion of the Bible" but "in diametrical opposition to it" (Godwin, 1820, p. 623).

marked, his casual reading of the *Essay*, "for amusement," furnished the first clue out of which the theory of evolution developed. Thus, in the dispute between evolutionists and traditional theologians, a momentous struggle that set the tone of intellectual life during the whole second half of the nineteenth century, the role of Malthus was not that of a theologian but rather a forerunner of scientific biology.

**2. Deductive vs. Inductive System.** The principle of population, as enunciated in the first edition of the *Essay*, was wholly deductive. It started with axioms and proceeded to conclusions drawn from them. Subsequent editions, as we have seen, were based also on a mass of empirical data, gathered to check and support the original thesis. In its final statement, Malthus's theory is not clearly either deductive or inductive, but a sometimes confusing mixture of the two (Davis, 1955). But this is very often true of scientific discourse, particularly in the social disciplines. One reason that Malthus continued to express his thoughts in deductive terms was his training as a mathematician, and many passages in the *Essay* are verbalizations of general mathematical formulas (Rubin, 1960).

Nevertheless, the shuttling back and forth between empirical data and axiomatic theses muddled the theory, so that the meaning of a number of key terms is ambiguous. In the phrase, "the ultimate check to population appears to be a want of food," what is the meaning of "ultimate"? Sometimes it seems to mean "in the long run" (if the potential population increase is realized, then ultimately the lack of food will become the most important check), but Malthus emphasized that the potential had never been fully realized and, if moral restraint became general, the population need never press on the means of subsistence. Sometimes "ultimate" seems to mean "fundamental, underlying all other checks" (for both vices and moral restraint were often the consequence of hunger, or of the fear of it), yet Malthus also emphasized that the standard of living could rise above the subsistence level, so that hunger would be completely irrelevant to actual population trends, as indeed it has become in the countries of the West since his day.

A more important symptom of the confusion between Malthus's deductive and inductive systems is the ambiguity of the concept "tendency." [18] In the sentence, apart from "extreme cases, . . . population always increases where the means of subsistence increase," the tendency seems to be a summary of empirical data. In other contexts, however, the "tendency" of population to increase up to the means of subsistence means its "power . . . when unchecked."

**3. Biological Determinist vs. Sociologist.** Sometimes Malthus's emphasis on the fact that man is an animal, with sexual passions and the need

---

[18] See the interesting exchange between Malthus and Nassau Senior, reprinted in McCleary, 1953, pp. 114–128.

for food, has been taken as the sum of his theory, so that he is attacked as a biological determinist. This is a reasonable interpretation of the first edition of the *Essay*, and Malthus's lifelong effort to improve the initial statement of his theory has failed to impress many analysts, who note the revisions only to point out the inconsistencies. Malthus's emphasis on man's biological nature, which today often sounds like an insistence on the obvious, was not so pointless in his day. Many then believed that the fecundity of the human species was being reduced by its urban setting or by the food it was then eating. Sadler, for instance, was not the first to contend that "the fecundity of human beings under similar circumstances varies inversely as their numbers on a given space"; or Doubleday, that abundant food destroys the physiological ability to reproduce, so that "in a nation highly and generally affluent and luxurious, population will [necessarily] decrease and decay." [19] And according to Godwin, if sexual intercourse were stripped of "all its attendant circumstances, . . . it would be generally despised" (quoted in Malthus, 1872, p. 392). Against such adversaries, it was relevant to stress man's physiological drives and needs.

By a widely prevalent carelessness, even persons who certainly know better present the biological element in Malthus as the whole of his population theory.[20] For example, what Malthus called "positive checks" to population (thus, one of two types, the other being "preventive checks") are commonly termed simply "Malthusian checks." [21] According to what one economist denotes "the Malthusian population theory," "population growth at any one time tends to be the maximum consistent with the level of per capita income," and he contrasts this with what he calls "the Neo-Malthusian theory" (Demeny, 1965). "Conditions somewhat similar to those Malthus envisioned" are said to be high birth and death rates and a low average income equilibrium (Leibenstein, 1954, p. 8). In fact, one might better term this the model of classical nineteenth-century economics, from which Malthus notably dissented. For most members of this school, the problem to be analyzed was production, and consumption was viewed rather mechanically in terms of a reified Economic Man. For Malthus, the

---

[19] Michael Thomas Sadler, *Ireland, Its Evils and Their Remedies*, Murray, London, 1829, p. xxviii; Thomas Doubleday, *The True Law of Population Shewn to be Connected with the Food of the People*, Simpkin, Marshall, London, 1842, p. 7.

[20] One critic tells us that "the clear alternative" to Malthus's biological theory is "the hypothesis that economic as well as social conditions affect the growth and size of populations, and that sexual passions operate only within the restrictions or stimuli imposed by these conditions." And yet two pages earlier he had informed the reader that Malthus had "emphasized the dependence of the actual level of population upon the laws, institutions and habits of each society" (Ian Bowen, *Population*, Nisbet, London, 1954, pp. 109, 111).

[21] Sometimes Malthus is even pictured as the advocate of the vice and misery he discussed. McCleary cites a passage to this effect from an introductory text "emanating from a famous American seat of learning, Dartmouth College," and published in 1941 (McCleary, 1953, p. 96).

standard of living was not simply a biological factor, but also a cultural one. It is worth recalling again the debt Keynes acknowledged to Malthus on this point:

> The idea that we can safely neglect the aggregate demand function is funda-mental to Ricardian economics, which underlie what we have been taught for more than a century. Malthus, indeed, vehemently opposed Ricardo's doctrine that it was impossible for effective demand to be deficient; but . . . Ricardo conquered England as completely as the Holy Inquisition conquered Spain. . . . [Malthus was one of] the brave army of heretics, . . . who, following their intuitions, have preferred to see the truth obscurely and imperfectly rather than to maintain error, reached indeed with clearness and consistency and by easy logic, but on hypotheses inappropriate to the facts (Keynes, 1935, pp. 32, 371).

If it is true that the principle of population and the principle of effective demand were competitive in Malthus's mind and works, it is also true that the trend over his life was from the former to the latter. The whole of the first edition of the *Essay* is concerned with man's prodigious capacity to reproduce himself and his more modest power to produce food, but in the successive revisions this biological view was tempered more and more by a vision of a new social structure.

> I have not considered the evils of vice and misery arising from a redundant population [Malthus wrote] as unavoidable and incapable of being diminished. On the contrary, I have pointed out a mode by which these evils may be re-moved or mitigated by removing or mitigating their cause (Malthus, 1872, p. 511).

The final chapter of the *Essay*'s last edition, titled "Of Our Rational Ex-pectations Respecting the Future Improvement of Society," draws up a balance that is far from the gloom of the first edition.

> The prudential check to marriage has increased in Europe; and it cannot be unreasonable to conclude that it will still make further advances. . . . Norway, Switzerland, England, and Scotland are above all the rest in the prevalence of the preventive check; and . . . from the little that I know of the continent, I should have been inclined to select them . . . as rather above than below their neighbors in the chastity of their women, and consequently in the virtuous habits of their men. Experience therefore seems to teach us that it is possible for moral and physical causes to counteract the effects that might at first be expected from an increase of the check to marriage. . . .
>
> From a review of the state of society in former periods compared with the present, I should certainly say that the evils resulting from the principle of popu-lation have rather diminished than increased, even under the disadvantage of an almost total ignorance of the real cause (*ibid.*, pp. 477, 480).

It may be well to amplify this quotation with a passage from Sidney and Beatrice Webb, who probably had a juster appreciation of his social philosophy than any other socialist writer, or than many a more recent commentator.

No argument could . . . be founded on the "principle of population" against Trade Union efforts to improve the conditions of sanitation and safety, or to protect the Normal Day. And the economists quickly found reason to doubt whether there was any greater cogency in the argument with regard to wages. . . . From the Malthusian point of view, the presumption was, as regards the artisans and factory operatives, always in favor of a rise in wages. For [as Malthus had written in the *Principles*] "in the vast majority of instances, before a rise of wages can be counteracted by the increased number of laborers it may be supposed to be the means of bringing into the market, time is afforded for the formation of . . . new and improved tastes and habits. . . . After the laborers have once acquired these tastes, population will advance in a slower ratio, as compared with capital, than formerly." . . . The ordinary middle-class view that the "principle of population" rendered nugatory all attempts to raise wages, otherwise than in the slow course of generations, was, in fact, based on sheer ignorance, not only of the facts of working-class life, but even of the opinions of the very economists from whom it was supposed to be derived.[22]

Whether Malthus was correct about the pressure of population on resources can still be a polemical issue, since resources as well as numbers of people have grown. But his vision that the lower classes might acquire a taste for middle-class life, and thus the self-restraint to work for it, is incontrovertible.

If Malthus had to abandon [the principle of population] (at least implicitly), he was more than recompensed by . . . the *embourgeoisement* of the lower classes, [which] did prove to be, as he hoped, both their deliverance and society's salvation. In this, even more than his predictions about population, he was truly the prophet of our times (Himmelfarb, 1960, p. xxxii).

## Population Optima

If the term "Neo-Malthusian" had not been appropriated by the advocates of birth control, it would be an apt designation for the economists who developed the concept of population optimum.[23] In this sense, as in the usual one, "Neo-Malthusianism" would mean not merely a continuation of Malthus's ideas but their projection to a new level. The mathematical formulation of Malthus's principle could be called no more than a first approximation: population tends to increase by a geometrical ratio and food by an arithmetical ratio; therefore, population tends to press against

[22] Sidney and Beatrice Webb, *Industrial Democracy,* New Ed., Longmans, Green, London, 1902, pp. 632–635.

[23] For accounts of the development of the optimum theory, see Robbins, 1927; Buquet, 1956; Sauvy, 1960.

the means of subsistence. These two progressions can be reformulated in terms of the **law of diminishing returns,** as follows: To produce food, two factors are required—land and labor. If to a fixed amount of land more and more labor is added, the result will generally be a declining per capita return. For while the two factors are interchangeable to some degree (as can be seen in the difference between extensive and intensive agriculture), eventually increasing the workers per acre by $x$ per cent will result in a rise of production by less than $x$ per cent. The first statement of population optimum was essentially a development from such a simple model.

In his discussion of a newly settled area like America, Malthus some-times half-intimated that population increase there was not only no problem but an actual benefit. If he meant to say this, he certainly did not say it clearly, and the first improvement on his theory is to posit **underpopulation** as well as **overpopulation** as a possible relation between people and land.

Overpopulation. An engraving by George Cruikshank, 1792–1878 (*The Bettmann Archive, Inc.*).

Or, to continue with the same simple model, if to a fixed number of acres, more and more laborers are added, the first result may be a greater than proportionate increase in per capita production, then a proportionate increase, and only finally a decreasing return. As Cannan put it, "If we want to preserve the phrase 'diminishing returns' we must take the point of maximum return as the starting point, and say that returns diminish in either direction, all commodities or industries being always and everywhere subject to this 'Law of diminishing returns'" (Cannan, 1928, p. 59).

Cannan's second emendation of Malthus's theory is no less important: the correction of his almost exclusive concern with food. Even the simplest list of economic factors includes land, labor, and also capital, and of the three the last is crucial in many circumstances. And if we analyze not only agriculture but also industry, then land is only one of the relevant natural resources that can be exhausted by growing numbers (Harold Wright, 1923; Day and Day, 1965).

The optimum population of any country, as defined in terms of these criticisms of Malthus, is the number of people that produces the highest per capita economic return. In the writings of various analysts, this "return" has been specified as total production per head, or real income per head, or the point at which the marginal and the average product per laborer are equal. Which criterion is used is less important than the idea that it should be an exact measure of specifically economic welfare. Such a definition of a population optimum, however, has been challenged on a number of grounds.

### ACTUAL OR OPTIMUM INSTITUTIONAL FRAMEWORK?

The issue between Godwin and Malthus, or between Malthusians and Marxists (cf. pp. 634–637), is relevant also to the definition of optimum population. The famous dispute in the 1920s between Keynes and Beveridge about whether England was overpopulated, as another example, was largely terminological. As Warren Thompson later summarized it:

If we are thinking of overpopulation as a condition which cannot arise so long as there are conceivable ways in which more people can be employed so as to produce larger real incomes, then apparently Sir William [Beveridge] was right, and there is no overpopulation in England or in Europe. . . . On the other hand, if we think of overpopulation as a condition in which there are too many people to be employed at good real wages under the conditions which actually exist and which appear likely to exist for some time to come, it would seem that Professor Keynes was fully justified in saying that England and Europe are overpopulated.[24]

In more recent years, the issue has often arisen with respect to the new nations of Asia and Africa, whose present population pressure is ascribed

[24] Warren S. Thompson, *Population Problems,* 2nd Ed., McGraw-Hill, New York, 1935, p. 436. *Cf.* Dalton, 1928.

to the imperial powers' maladministration during the earlier colonial period. By such an analysis, even Egypt is not overpopulated (Nassif, 1950). As we will see, Soviet spokesmen generalized this kind of argumentation in preposterously utopian terms.

In order to discuss the concept of optimum at all, one must first agree, then: (1) that population *is* a factor in economic welfare, no matter what the social organization, and (2) that it is the present institution, with whatever changes may be reasonably expected, that are relevant—not those of the past ("imperialism") or of the supposed future ("socialism").

### ECONOMIC OR GENERAL WELFARE?

As the separate discipline of demography developed, population theorists began to wonder whether the economists had not delimited the optimum too narrowly. Attempts were made to restate it in terms of general welfare rather than income or production per head. Sometimes the new measure chosen was a demographic one, such as expectation of life (Mukerjee, 1930), but once a reasonably precise economic standard was abandoned as too narrow, the tendency was toward broader, vaguer criteria. By one definition, for example, the optimum population is "the numbers socially desirable" (Penrose, 1934, p. 90). The income and welfare concepts of optimum population are identical, in this view, "on the assumption that this income is spent in the consumption of the kinds and amounts of goods and services that make the maximum contribution to welfare." For example, all the money for food should be spent in accord with a consensus among biochemists on the kind and amount needed for optimum physiological welfare, and similarly for other products (*ibid.*, pp. 74–83). There is, of course, no such consensus, even within any one culture. The concept of a general-welfare optimum, more broadly, "does not give sufficient weight to the influence of culture-patterns upon *how* given needs are satisfied, [and] it ignores the influence of the culture-pattern upon the *number* of needs that must be satisfied" (Spengler, 1938, pp. 274–275).

One of the cultural elements that are relevant is the level of aspiration. Quite often, as the real income of a country (or of one social class) goes up, the people see their situation as deteriorating, for their expectations rise still faster. Thus, in the words of a League of Nations study committee, "Overpopulation may be said to exist, not so much in actual figures as in the consciousness of the country concerned" (quoted in Fergus C. Wright, 1939, p. 80). With such a definition, *the* optimum is indeterminate. As Adolphe Landry put it, "A country is overpopulated in relation to another country when its standard of living is lower than in the latter. Thus country A, though underpopulated with reference to an absolute optimum, may consider itself overpopulated in relation to its neighbor *B*" (International Studies Conference, 1938, p. 122).

An economic measure and a more general one are both indexes of the same variable, the first more reliable and the second more valid. But is the people's welfare the only objective that a nation seeks with its population policy? In particular, is the number of people that produces the maximum income per capita necessarily the same as the one best able to defend the country at war? Obviously not, yet these are only two out of several possible goals of policy. Sauvy has listed a number of such different national objectives, each of which would have a different optimum population associated with it. Rather than maximum wealth, a country may seek a maximum rate of increase in wealth, or the conservation of its natural resources for future generations, or power, whether military or other, or full employment, or the maximum distribution of knowledge and culture among its people, or general well-being, as measured by health or longevity or otherwise. He concludes:

> The optimum population is that which insures the realization of a given objective in the most satisfactory manner. . . . The concept is nothing more than a convenience at the present time. The demographer may use it as an intermediary tool in the same way that the mathematician uses imaginary numbers (Sauvy, 1952, pp. 50–53).

Over two or three decades, thus, the concept of optimum population became so rarefied as to lose all real meaning; and the various attempts to coalesce these diverse goals into a single definition of optimum cannot be regarded as very successful (Ferenczi, 1938). Perhaps the very word "optimum" was too moralistic to serve aptly as a scientific term. Originally it meant the number of people that would make best use of a given economy, but it gradually came to mean simply "the best population," with each analyst furnishing his own yardstick of what is "good." An optimist might hold that there is an inherent tendency in every population to move toward the optimum, which therefore could differ only slightly from the actual number (Carr-Saunders, 1922, Chapter 9). A nature enthusiast might call for more and larger national parks, with the optimum over large areas set at zero. A nationalist might be affronted at the very notion that there could be too many natives of his country. A utopian derides the proposition that population size has any economic or other effect at all in an optimum social environment. It cannot be the function of one definition to decide such questions, or even to take sides on them.

## THE ECONOMIC OPTIMUM

The **optimum population** of any area is the number of people which, in the given natural, cultural, and social environment, produces the maximum economic return. The definition does not imply that this environment ought, or ought not, to be changed. Nor does it state that the maximum economic return is the only legitimate goal of a nation's population policy. These are different questions, and specifying the economic effects of population size is in itself a difficult enough problem.

The *size* of a population, first of all, is a very gross measure of its economic relevance. Among purely demographic characteristics, the rate of growth is of almost equal significance, not to mention health, literacy, skill, and especially age structure. Western Europe is too populous, let us suppose, in the sense that a smaller number of people would enjoy a higher average real income, and it is agreed that an attempt should therefore be made to reduce the rate of growth. This can be done in only three ways: by increasing mortality (which is, of course, ruled out as a policy in non-totalitarian countries), decreasing fertility, and increasing net emigration. But either a decline in births or a rise in emigration cuts down the proportion of young people, and thus aggravates Europe's other demographic problem—the large proportion of dependent aged. "These conditions pose a dilemma—to grow or to age—a conflict between population structure and population size." [25]

Moreover, the relation between population and resources in "Malthusian" terms, and that between population and economic growth in Keynesian terms, are quite different. Ultimately, the former model is still relevant even in wealthy countries; in the long run, maximum numbers are indeed set by the total resources available and the skill in exploiting them. However, in the long run, as Keynes once remarked, we are all dead. Within any one industrial country with a capitalist or mixed economy, over a period of, say, one generation, rapid growth not only uses up some of the resources but—and this is often the more important point—keeps the economy going.

In classical economic theory, just as every feasible demand elicits a supply, so supply creates its own demand; for in a free economy the production of goods in itself gives the eventual consumers the power to purchase them. True, the commodities produced may not wholly coincide in kind with those in demand; that is, local, specific crises are possible, but these are checked by the automatic adjustment between supply and demand. But a *general* economic crisis—a general fall of prices to below cost, general overproduction, general unemployment—is impossible by the very nature of the economic system. This doctrine, usually termed Say's Law, after Jean-Baptiste Say, who gave it its most precise formulation, had been challenged by Malthus and, in different terms, by Marx, but among orthodox economists it held its own until Keynes upset it by reviving the Malthusian concept of effective demand.

According to Keynes, the automatic circuit posited by classical theory is completed only in the special case when planned savings and planned

---

[25] Alfred Sauvy, *L'Europe et sa population*, Éditions Internationales, Paris, 1953, p. 119.

investment are equal; in all other cases, a part of the potential purchasing power is siphoned off into idle savings, or "hoards." It is particularly in wealthy countries (that is, also those whose populations were presumed to be in "incipient decline") that investment tends to be inadequate, for two reasons: because a smaller share of the national income is consumed and thus a larger share is left to be invested, and because the larger capital stock means that new investment opportunities are more difficult to find. Thus, as the stock of capital grows in any one country, the possibilities for new investment are less; or, in Keynesian terms, other things being equal, the marginal efficiency of capital is the lower, the greater the existing amount of capital. Why should this long-term decline in the marginal efficiency of capital not have been operative during the nineteenth century? Because, as Keynes put it, "the growth of population and of invention, the opening-up of new lands, the state of confidence and the frequency of war over the average of (say) each decade seem to have been sufficient" (Keynes, 1935, p. 307).

Keynes's primary concern was with another problem; but his few *obiter dicta* on population encouraged other economists to formulate a tentative theory of demographic-economic development. "With increasing population, investment can go roaring ahead, even if invention is rather stupid; increasing population is therefore actually favorable to employment. It is actually easier to employ an expanding population than a contracting one, whatever arithmetic would suggest." [26] It may even be that the economic progress of the modern era had been based principally or largely on its population growth.

One is tempted to a "population interpretation" of modern capitalism. Professor Cannan sensed it. Professor J. R. Hicks now toys with it as he wonders in a footnote at the end of his *Value and Capital* whether the "whole industrial revolution of the last two centuries has been nothing else but a vast secular boom, largely induced by the unparalleled rise in population". . . . Perhaps the long cycle (1787–1929) was mainly conditioned by population growth. . . . Modern capitalist free enterprise may prove to have been a boom system, and the modern trend to something like the old mercantilism may be a trend toward institutions appropriate to an era of stationary population.[27]

Thus, on the one hand, an increasing population requires a larger investment in capital equipment; but, on the other hand, in a capitalist country with a developed economy, this very demand keeps investment "roaring ahead" and the economy healthy. That is to say, if the number of a country's inhabitants is at its optimum point by one economic criterion, by

---

[26] J. R. Hicks, "Mr. Keynes' Theory of Employment," *Economic Journal,* 46 (1936), 238–253.

[27] V. W. Bladen, "Population Problems and Policies," in *Canada in Peace and War,* edited by Chester Martin, Oxford University Press, Toronto, 1941, pp. 86–119.

another it may be too small, or, better, its rate of growth may be too low. There are at least two economic optima, a population-resources one and a Keynesian one. The first is the population that, in terms of present or prospective technology and institutions, affords the highest per capita standard of living; the second is the population growing at the rate that, in terms of . . . etc. Though it is obvious that these are not the same concept, they are often treated as though they were. Thus, as one example out of many, the argument of the 1930s against immigration to Australia (that its empty land was largely uninhabitable desert) has been answered by postwar proponents of immigration in part within the same framework (by pointing out the potentialities of irrigation), but principally in Keynesian terms (a rapidly growing population is beneficial to the economy). A Keynesian analysis, however, is appropriate only when "Malthusian" pressure is not acute. On a true Sahara, more people bring no benefits.

The ambiguity between population-resources and Keynesian economics has been aggravated by the tendency of economic thought to follow not the specifics of a case so much as the fashion of the day. Malthus's principle of population, once established as part of economic theory, went virtually unchallenged among professional economists for some fifty years, then after the turn of the century was subjected to greater and more sweeping criticism. In the 1920s Keynes was among those who led an international Malthusian revival, which was dissipated a decade later in the widespread fear of Western depopulation. In the most recent period, apart from an occasional echo of Communist or Catholic points of view, Western social scientists generally have come again to perceive overpopulation as a serious threat. The revival of the more pessimistic element of Malthusian thought is based, moreover, not merely on population projections but also on actualities. Malthus is relevant whether we observe underdeveloped countries, with their critical and sometimes growing shortage of food (see pp. 216–218); or industrial nations, whose superior economies use up irreplaceable resources at prodigious rates and substitute for them a vast pollution; or the world as a whole, with its population demanding more and more *Lebensraum.*

## Summary

Malthus's *Essay on the Principle of Population,* in spite of its faults and limitations, marks the beginning of scientific demographic theory. His main ideas in present-day terms are the following: Man's physiological ability to reproduce is great enough to permit any population to double each generation (true). Actual fertility was never so high as this fecundity (probably true). In most cases, however, the checks on population growth imposed by reduced fertility were less important than those effected by heavy mortality (generally true of Malthus's day and of prior periods, though the postponement of marriage had also been a significant factor). The most important reason for late marriage, and for high death rates, was usually an actual or threatened shortage of food (the postponement of marriage had been enforced by institutionalized regulations, and, at least in Europe, disease was more significant than hunger as the cause of early death).

Malthus's population theory is neither wholly acceptable nor wholly defective. It suffers from inconsistencies and ambiguities. Yet Malthus's work helped establish two valid theses: (1) Contrary to beliefs widely held in his day, the population was growing rapidly. Wise social policy consisted in the opposite of pronatalist decrees, an effort to substitute the control of fertility for high death rates. (2) Contrary to utopian dogmas, man is not only a social being but also a biological one. The population of even a perfect society depends on births and deaths, and thus on the sexual drive and food.

The difficulty that Malthus had in separating scientific from ethical canons has persisted in various formulations of the optimum, a development from the population-resources dilemma that he analyzed. It is certainly correct that any conceivable index of the population optimum could not be "of very great precision." "We could hardly hope to determine the optimum, for any given area at any given time, more closely than within a range of, say, five per cent on either side" (Dalton, 1928). Even the restrained optimism of this "hope" is not warranted in many cases. For example, Spengler wrote that France's population of 42 million (in 1938) ought to be cut down by a quarter to maximize the per capita income (Spengler, 1938, p. 273), while Sauvy set the optimum in the postwar period at somewhere between 50 and 75 million (Sauvy, 1952, p. 186). When two men so eminently qualified to discuss the population of France differ to this degree, others may wonder whether the concept has any utility. Myrdal, for instance, terms the theory of optimum population "one of the most sterile ideas" ever developed in economics. "Its elaboration has not increased its scientific significance or practical applicability. The theory stands mainly as an excuse for, and also as an actual inhibition of, the proper posing of the problem of the economic effects of population changes." [28]

Yet the idea underlying the concept, that national income can sometimes be increased by adjusting the population to the economy, should not be abandoned. It is the rationale behind many specific policies, including, for example, the pronatalist program that Myrdal helped work out in Sweden. If the theory of population optimum is to be at all useful, however, it is necessary first of all to set aside, at least in this context, both the heavy ideological luggage and the legitimate scientific questions to which we can as yet give no definite answers. Secondly, we must recognize that any

[28] Gunnar Myrdal, *Population: A Problem for Democracy,* Harvard University Press, Cambridge, Mass., 1940, pp. 26–27. *Cf.* T. Lynn Smith, *Population Analysis,* McGraw-Hill, New York, 1948, pp. 388–389.

measure of the optimum must be crude: to say that India is overpopulated is meaningful and correct, but with respect to a country like France it is perhaps pointless to ask whether it is under- or overpopulated.

## Suggestions for Further Reading

In order to know what Malthus said, it is necessary to read him. The first edition of the *Essay* is readily available in an Ann Arbor Paperback and, together with an abridged version of the seventh edition, in a volume of the Modern Library. The seventh edition, which in this chapter is cited from the original 1872 printing, is also available in a recent Everyman reprint. An appreciation of Malthus's method of work can be had from his superbly edited travel diaries (James, 1966), and for a full understanding, one must know also his *Principles of Political Economy* (see also Spengler, 1945). A delightful biographical sketch of Malthus is given in Keynes, 1933; more detailed accounts, together with sympathetic analyses of his theory, are given in Bonar, 1924 and McCleary, 1953. The short biography in James, 1966 corrects several widespread errors.

The literature on the Malthusian debate is enormous. Spengler, 1942 is a conscientious summary of French eighteenth-century thought; for a comparable analysis of Malthus's English predecessors, see Hutchinson, 1967.[29] A bibliography "intended to cover the genesis and course of the Malthusian controversy in Britain" from Godwin to only 1880 takes more than thirty pages (Glass, 1953, pp. 79–112); for analyses of the controversy see Eversley, 1959; Coontz, 1957; Hutchinson, 1967. I have written earlier on Marx vs. Malthus and on Keynes's theories of population.[30]

Robbins, 1927; Wolfe, 1926; and Day and Day, 1965 are among the better discussions of population optimum. Malthus-Huxley-Osborn, 1960 and Francis, 1958 are two interesting collections of articles on Malthusian themes. The best book-length modern economic analysis of the theories examined in this chapter is Leibenstein, 1954, which can be usefully supplemented by Peacock, 1952 and 1954; Spengler, 1956, 1966.

BEALES, H. L. 1953. "The Historical Context of the *Essay on Population*," in Glass, 1953, pp. 1–24.

BLACKER, J. G. C. 1957. "Social Ambitions of the Bourgeoisie in 18th Century France, and their Relation to Family Limitation," *Population Studies*, 11, 46–63.

\* BONAR, JAMES. 1924. *Malthus and his Work*. Macmillan, New York.

BUQUET, LÉON. 1956. *L'optimum de population*. Presses Universitaires de France, Paris.

---

[29] Raymond A. Preston, the editor of a modern edition of Godwin's *Enquiry Concerning Political Justice,* Knopf, New York, 1926, omitted Chapter VII, "Of the Objection to This System from the Principle of Population," as "more than ordinarily conjectural, and . . . altogether superseded by the more careful considerations of the subject made later by Malthus, his followers, and his refuters, including Godwin himself" (p. 280).

[30] William Petersen, *The Politics of Population*, Doubleday, Garden City, N.Y., 1964, pp. 46–89.

CANNAN, EDWIN. 1928. *Wealth: A Brief Explanation of the Causes of Economic Welfare.* 3rd Ed. King, London.

CARR-SAUNDERS, A. M. 1922. *The Population Problem: A Study in Human Evolution.* Clarendon, Oxford.

COONTZ, SYDNEY H. 1957. *Population Theories and the Economic Interpretation.* Routledge & Kegan Paul, London.

DALTON, HUGH. 1928. "The Theory of Population," *Economica*, 8, 28–50.

* DAVIS, KINGSLEY. 1955. "Malthus and the Theory of Population," in *The Language of Social Research: A Reader in the Methodology of Social Research*, edited by Paul F. Lazarsfeld and Morris Rosenberg. Free Press, Glencoe, Ill., pp. 430–553.

DAY, LINCOLN H., and ALICE TAYLOR DAY. 1965. *Too Many Americans.* Delta, New York.

DEMENY, PAUL. 1965. "Investment Allocation and Population Growth," *Demography*, 2, 203–232.

DORN, WALTER L. 1963. *Competition for Empire, 1740–1763.* Harper Torchbooks, New York.

* EVERSLEY, D. E. C. 1959. *Social Theories of Fertility and the Malthusian Debate.* Clarendon, Oxford.

* FAGE, ANITA. 1953. "La révolution française et la population," *Population*, 8, 311–338.

FERENCZI, IMRE. 1938. *The Synthetic Optimum of Population: An Outline of an International Demographic Policy.* League of Nations. International Institute of Intellectual Co-operation, Paris.

FRANCIS, ROY G., editor. 1958. *The Population Ahead.* University of Minnesota Press, Minneapolis.

GLASS, D. V. 1940. *Population Policies and Movements in Europe.* Clarendon, Oxford.

———, editor. 1953. *Introduction to Malthus.* Wiley, New York.

GODWIN, WILLIAM. 1793. *An Enquiry Concerning Political Justice.* London.

———. 1820. *Of Population: An Enquiry Concerning the Power of Increase in the Numbers of Mankind, Being an Answer to Mr. Malthus's Essay on That Subject.* Longman, Hurst, Rees, Orme, and Brown, London.

HECKSCHER, ELI F. 1935. *Mercantilism.* 2 Vols. Allen & Unwin, London.

HIMMELFARB, GERTRUDE. 1960. "Introduction," in Malthus, 1960, pp. xiii–xxxvi.

HUTCHINSON, E. P. 1967. *The Population Debate: The Development of Conflicting Theories up to 1900.* Houghton Mifflin, Boston.

INTERNATIONAL STUDIES CONFERENCE. 1938. *Peaceful Change: Procedures, Population, Raw Materials, Colonies.* League of Nations. International Institute of Intellectual Co-operation, Paris.

* JAMES, PATRICIA, editor. 1966. *The Travel Diaries of Thomas Robert Malthus.* Cambridge University Press, New York.

KEYNES, JOHN MAYNARD. 1933. *Essays in Biography.* Harcourt, Brace, New York.

———. 1935. *The General Theory of Employment, Interest, and Money.* Harcourt, Brace, New York.

LEIBENSTEIN, HARVEY. 1954. *A Theory of Economic-Demographic Development.* Princeton University Press, Princeton, N.J.

\* McCLEARY, G. F. 1953. *The Malthusian Population Theory.* Faber & Faber, London.

MALTHUS, T. R. 1872. *An Essay on the Principle of Population.* 7th Ed. Reeves and Turner, London.

——. 1951. *Principles of Political Economy Considered with a View to their Practical Application.* 2nd Ed. Kelley, New York.

——. 1959. *Population: The First Essay.* University of Michigan Press-Ann Arbor Paperbacks, Ann Arbor, Mich.

——. 1960. *On Population.* Gertrude Himmelfarb, editor. Modern Library, New York.

——, JULIAN HUXLEY, and FREDERICK OSBORN. 1960. *On Population: Three Essays.* New American Library-Mentor, New York.

MUKERJEE, RADHA KAMAL. 1930. "Optimum and Over-Population," *Indian Journal of Economics,* 10, 407–421.

NASSIF, E. 1950. "L'Égypte est-elle surpeuplée?" *Population,* 5, 513–522.

PEACOCK, ALAN T. 1952 and 1954. "Theory of Population and Modern Economic Analysis," *Population Studies,* 6, 114–122, and 7, 227–234. Reprinted in Joseph J. Spengler and Otis Dudley Duncan, editors. *Population Theory and Policy.* Free Press, Glencoe, Ill., 1956, pp. 190–206.

PENROSE, E. F. 1934. *Population Theories and Their Application with Special Reference to Japan.* Food Research Institute, Stanford, Calif.

REINHARD, MARCEL. 1946. "La révolution française et le problème de la population," *Population,* 1, 419–427.

\* ROBBINS, LIONEL. 1927. "The Optimum Theory of Population," in *London Essays in Economics in Honour of Edwin Cannan,* edited by T. E. Gregory and Hugh Dalton. Routledge, London, pp. 103–134.

RUBIN, ERNEST. 1960. "The Quantitative Data and Methods of the Rev. T. R. Malthus," *American Statistician,* 14, 28–31.

SAUVY, ALFRED. 1952 and 1954. *Théorie générale de la population.* 1: *Économie et population.* 2: *Biologie sociale.* Presses Universitaires de France, Paris.

——. 1960. "Évolution récente des idées sur le surpeuplement," *Population,* 15, 467–484.

SPENGLER, JOSEPH J. 1938. *France Faces Depopulation.* Duke University Press, Durham, N.C.

——. 1942. *French Predecessors of Malthus: A Study in Eighteenth-Century Wage and Population Theory.* Duke University Press, Durham, N.C.

\* ——. 1945. "Malthus's Total Population Theory: A Restatement and Reappraisal," *Canadian Journal of Economics and Political Science,* 11, 83–110, 234–264.

——. 1955. "Marshall on the Population Question," *Population Studies,* 8, 264–287, and 9, 56–66.

——. 1956. "Population Threatens Prosperity," *Harvard Business Review,* 34, 85–94.

——. 1966. "The Economist and the Population Question," *American Economic Review,* 56, 1–24.

WOLFE, A. B. 1926. "The Optimum Size of Population," in *Population Problems in the United States and Canada,* edited by Louis I. Dublin, Houghton Mifflin, New York, pp. 63–76.

WRIGHT, FERGUS CHALMERS. 1939. *Population and Peace: A Survey of International Opinion on Claims for Relief from Population Pressure.* League of Nations. International Studies Conference. International Institute of Intellectual Co-operation, Paris.

WRIGHT, HAROLD. 1923. *Population.* Harcourt, Brace, New York.

# 6 THE GENERAL DETERMINANTS OF FERTILITY

"General" determinants of fertility are those not specific to any particular culture. The ones most clearly general in this sense are the biological characteristics of the human species relevant to conception and childbearing, and these are discussed in the first section of this chapter.

It is atypical in almost any society, however, to realize the physiologically maximum family size. The actual number of children is reduced both by birth control and by value systems and institutional patterns that influence fertility even though this is not their purpose. As these social usages are manifestly part of what we mean by a culture, one might discuss them as part of the analyses of particular societies, rather than in a chapter on the general determinants of fertility. However, some of these culture traits are universal. For instance, most anthropologists agree, even if with some haggling, that the nuclear family exists in all societies and that all of its varieties are similar in a number of basic respects. And it is convenient in this preliminary look at fertility to consider the range of such variables as the age at marriage, which exemplifies a social pattern with a wide variation from one society to another, similar "in classification, not in content." [1]

---

[1] George Peter Murdock, "The Common Denominator of Cultures," in *The Science of Man in the World Crisis*, edited by Ralph Linton, Columbia University Press, New York, 1945, pp. 123–142.

## Biological Determinants of Fecundity

The analysis of fertility trends, especially though not exclusively by nineteenth-century theorists, has been an egregious example of the common confusion between biological and cultural determinants of human behavior (e.g., Reynolds and Macomber, 1924, Chapter 2). Did the smaller families in cities, for instance, result from an impairment of the physiological ability to bear children or from the desire for fewer children that the urban setting stimulated? The facts available to the earliest investigators, mainly that the urban middle classes were leading the trend toward lower fertility, could be used to support either theory, and indeed the two were often not sharply distinguished.

The terms *fecundity* and *fertility*, originally used synonymously, were differentiated from one another only gradually. In 1934 the Population Association of America officially endorsed the distinction between **fecundity,** the physiological ability to reproduce; and **fertility,** the realization of this potential, the actual birth performance as measured by the number of offspring.[2] Now that the distinction is made conceptually, it is still difficult to apply it in practice. For at the present level of medical knowledge, the only absolute evidence that a person is fecund is the production of an offspring, in which case fecundity and fertility are operationally identical. The successful fertilization of a human egg, in one sense the beginning of a new life, is also the climax of a process complex enough to make the number of elements in an analysis of fecundity extremely large. Moreover, with rapid advances in obstetrics, the dominion of "the natural" has constantly given way to medical controls.[3] The available evidence suggests

[2] This distinction is not always made in nonprofessional writings, but it is now fairly consistently maintained in demographic works in English. However, "in many Latin languages, the etymological equivalents of fertility and fecundity are used in a sense diametrically opposite to that in English. Thus, the French *fécondité* or the Spanish *fecondidad* are properly translated by fertility, and *fertilité* or *fertilidad* by fecundity. [Some French writers, however, use *fécondité biologique* to mean "fecundity"; *cf.* Vincent, 1961.] It should also be noted that although the conventions outlined above are generally followed by demographers, the terms fertility and fecundity are used much more loosely in medical literature, where they are sometimes treated as being almost synonymous" (United Nations, Department of Economic and Social Affairs, *Multilingual Demographic Dictionary: English Section,* Population Studies, No. 29, New York, 1958, p. 38). The definitions in Norman L. Hoerr and Arthur Osol, eds., *Blakiston's New Gould Medical Dictionary* (2nd Ed., McGraw-Hill, New York, 1956), pp. 440, 443, agree with demographers' usage; but in *Stedman's Medical Dictionary* (17th Revised Ed., Williams & Wilkins, Baltimore, 1957), pp. 514, 517, the meanings are not distinguished.

[3] Some of those working in the new discipline of molecular biology predict a revolution in biology with incalculable effects on some of the topics examined in this chapter. As recently as 1953, it was discovered that one substance, the DNA (*for* deoxyribonucleic acid) molecule, controlled the germ plasm of all living things, and in 1961 its structure

that the fecundity of each of the partners can be affected by several physical factors, of which the most important are discussed briefly in the following paragraphs.

### HEREDITY

Although the evidence is not clear-cut, it seems that one factor influencing the innate ability to reproduce is the relative fecundity of one's forebears. Such a physiological determinant is often very difficult to estimate, of course, for whenever children remain in the same social-economic situation as their parents—which is the typical case—a similar size in the two generations may be due merely to the continuous pressure of this unchanged environment. It is only at the two extremes of the fecundity range that hereditary influence is definitely perceptible. On the one hand, fecundity can be impaired by any one of a number of defects in the sexual organs; and a predisposition toward such constitutional impediments can be inherited. Certain of such hereditary defects inhibit reproduction altogether, and with others offspring die before they in turn can procreate. The inheritance of a high level of fecundity, on the other hand, is sugggested by the fact that the proportion of multiple births, which seems to be correlated with general fertility, differs significantly both from one family line to another and from one race to another. In one notable case, when one of a set of quadruplets married one of a pair of twins, they had thirty-two children in eleven pregnancies (Pearl, 1939, pp. 34–36, 58–65).

### HEALTH

Like any other animal, a human being with a certain innate reproductive capacity has the highest possible fecundity when he or she is in a state of vigorous health. Certain infections, such as syphilis, gonorrhea, or tuberculosis of the genital tract, impede or prevent procreation directly. And if a person's health is impaired by any other causes—such as, among others, a nonvenereal disease (e.g., Ballew and Masters, 1954), nutritional deficiency (Hulme, 1951; Williams, 1962, Chapters 5 and 6), or psychoneurosis (Marsh and Vollmer, 1951; Bos and Gleghorn, 1958)—this also affects his reproductive capacity adversely.[4]

---

was determined. If it becomes possible to adjust genetic factors to human desires, then the meaning of "hereditary" will be altered immeasurably. For an account of this fascinating research that is intelligible to a nonbiologist, see Lessing, 1966.

[4] According to some studies with rats, mice, woodchucks, hare, and deer, an excessive crowding effects a disturbance in the glandular system, so that fecundity is reduced when the species is pushing too hard against the resources of its environment. Some researchers reject this thesis even as applied to lower animals, and no one has attempted to analyze its relevance to humans.

The seemingly obvious statement that good health is correlated with fecundity does not follow, however, simply and directly from the empirical evidence. On the contrary, human misery and high fertility are very frequently associated, and some analysts have interpreted this correlation to mean that the relatively healthful and comfortable life of the middle class in Western countries has reduced the average fecundity. Thus, Charles suggested that the decline in the size of the Western family was due to factors like "the widespread habit of excessive washing"; Castro that it was due to the high-protein diet of well-to-do classes and nations.[5] Contrary to such interpretations, most demographers today would agree that cleanliness and good food, together with all other conditions conducive to good health, increase reproductive capacity to the degree that they affect it at all, but that these physical factors have often been negated in industrial societies by the higher social valuation put on small families.

### AGE

Procreation is a function primarily of young adults. The capacity to reproduce, entirely lacking in childhood, begins to appear at puberty, develops gradually during adolescence, and reaches a high point at maturity. There follows a decline in middle age, relatively rapid and complete in females, slow and apparently sometimes only partial in males (*cf.* Vincent, 1958). Individual cases vary widely: children have been born to a mother of 6.5 years, at one extreme, and to one of 59 or possibly even 63 years, at the other (Pearl, 1939, pp. 57–58; Kuczynski, 1935, pp. 106–110). The narrower range between the averages of social groups suggests that some of the seemingly physiological variation is related to differences in their social environment.

In the female the **menarche,** or first menstruation, is usually taken to define puberty. The many studies analyzing the age at menarche (Pearl, 1939; Kumar, 1967) clearly indicate several patterns: (1) The better the food, the lower the age; e.g., among a sample of urban Yugoslav girls, it was 14.10 years ±0.111 among those subsisting mostly on carbohydrates and 12.65 ±0.133 among those fed ample proteins. (2) Certain diseases apparently delay the onset of menstruation. (3) Because of these two factors, there is a difference in the average age according to the country's social development. In the United States and Europe it is below 14 years, in African countries above 14 years, and in Asian countries between the two. (4) In advanced countries, similarly, the gradual improvement in the level of living has resulted in a decline in the average age at menarche. In Norway, the country with the longest record, it fell from above 17 years

---

[5] Enid Charles, *The Menace of Under-Population*, Watts, London, 1936, pp. 182–183; Josué de Castro, *Geography of Hunger*, Gollancz, London, 1952, *Cf.* p. 157.

in 1844 to about 13.2 in the early 1950s. On a world scale (omitting a Bantu sample because of their especially poor diet), during the past three decades the average age fell by 1.5 years to about 13.66 years. This suggests that the earlier interest in sex so much discussed in Western countries may have a physiological basis.

The menarche is only one step, the most clearly marked one, in a long process, and the regular development of healthy ova usually begins later. For several years, during a period of **adolescent subfecundity,**[6] the female is able to produce a child, but the probability that she will do so with a given amount of exposure is less than at maturity. Apparently the earlier the menarche, the longer the adolescent subfecundity lasts, so that regardless of the age at menarche, full sexual maturity of females is reached roughly between the ages of 16.5 and 18.25 years.

Corresponding to the gradual rise of fecundity during adolescence, there is from early adulthood on a gradual decline, which in females is termed the climacteric. **Menopause,** or the cessation of menstruation, is the sharpest manifestation of this process and is therefore typically used to mark, though only approximately, the end of a woman's fecund period. According to various studies the age at natural menopause varied only slightly among a number of populations (MacMahon and Worcester, 1966):

|  | Mean Age |
|---|---|
| United States (1966; median) | 49.8 years |
| Israel (1963) | 49.5 |
| Finland (1961) | 49.8 |
| Basel, Switzerland (1961) | 49.8 |
| South Africa—Zulu (1960) | 49.2 |
| South Africa—white (1960) | 48.7 |
| Denmark (1942) | 48.0 |
| Great Britain (1933) | 47.5 |
| Pittsburgh, Pa. (1918) | 47.1 |

### OVULATION CYCLE

The human female, like all other female mammals, produces ova periodically rather than continuously. In most subprimate species, the same hormone that controls this ovulation cycle also regulates the female's sexual desire. When the egg is ready to be fertilized, the female animal is "in heat" (**estrus**) and accepts, or seeks, the male's advances; and at all other times (during **anestrus**) she rejects them. Sexual union in such species is, in two senses, narrowly physiological: its timing is determined by the animal's

---

[6] To term it "adolescent sterility" (Montagu, 1957) adds an unnecessary confusion; it is better to restrict the meaning of the word *sterility* to total physiological inability to procreate.

glandular flow, and the union has the single function of physical reproduction.

In most primate species the female exhibits this estrus-anestrus cycle in a vestigial form. The vaginal skin of the female chimpanzee, for example, tightens and reddens at the time of ovulation, and the greater prominence of the sexual organ stimulates the male to more frequent copulation. In most respects, however, the sexual behavior of monkeys and apes resembles that of humans rather than that of mammals lower on the evolutionary scale. As with humans, there is a menstrual cycle, overlapping with the ovulation cycle. And, as with humans, the female is accessible to the male at any time, not only when she is estrous. Among primates, that is to say, the sex drive serves two functions: to reproduce the species, and to induce a mating couple to form a permanent union.[7]

In the normal cycle of the human female, during the years of sexual maturity, one or more ova are released from each ovary once every twenty-eight days. Each month, while they are developing, the wall of the uterus swells, preparatory to receiving a fertilized ovum. Unless a successful copulation takes place during the several days (or, according to some authorities, the several hours) that fertilization is possible (Tietze, 1960; Potter, 1961), the female is then sterile until the following cycle. In that case the ova and the wall of the uterus disintegrate, discharging blood through the vagina. There is thus also a menstrual cycle of twenty-eight days, with each menstruation spaced about half-way between two ovulations. Human females, however, have no remnant of the estrus-anestrus cycle. On the contrary, if women experience a cyclical variation in sex drive, they are likely to feel the strongest desire just before and just after menstruation, when fertile copulation is normally impossible, and the weakest desire just at the time of ovulation (Katharine Davis, 1929, Chapters 8–9; Pearl, 1939, pp. 32–34).

### LACTATION AND THE INTERVAL BETWEEN PREGNANCIES

The median time required by a large sample of American women to become pregnant, according to one study, is only 2.3 months. About 30 per cent do so within a month, 60 per cent within three months, and more than 90 per cent by the end of a year (Tietze *et al.*, 1950).

After a woman has given birth, if she does not breast-feed the child, the menstrual cycle normally begins again in about two months and the ovulation cycle two months later still. The recurrence of regular ovulation, and thus the probability of another pregnancy, are usually impeded so

[7] For an interesting if somewhat dated elaboration of this thesis, see S. Zuckerman, *The Social Life of Monkeys and Apes,* Kegan Paul, Trench, Trubner, London, 1932. A short work summarizing more recent field work is S. L. Washburn and Irven DeVore, "The Social Life of Baboons," *Scientific American* (June 1961), reprint No. 614.

long as the mammary glands remain active, though the evidence on this relation is not firmly established (e.g., Ford and Beach, 1951, pp. 217–220). According to one authoritative review, breast-feeding "offers better protection than 'ineffective' contraception up to about ten months after confinement, but not beyond that point. 'Effective' contraception offers better protection than nursing at all intervals" (Tietze, 1961; cf. Potter, 1963b; Potter et al., 1965).

### SEX DRIVE

The social dominance of the male in most cultures means that his sexuality is more likely than the female's to determine coital incidence. According to nine American and European studies, the average frequency of marital coitus is very slightly more than ten times per month (Pearl, 1939, p. 69). Kinsey gives a much lower over-all figure, 1.06 times per week (Kinsey et al., 1948, p. 568). If what anthropologists are told on this matter can be accepted, the frequency is considerably higher among nonindustrial peoples. "In most of the [primitive] societies on which information is available, every adult normally engages in heterosexual intercourse once daily or nightly during the periods when coitus is permitted" (Ford and Beach, 1951, p. 78). In all cultures the range of individual differentiation is wide. And whether any of these data are trustworthy may be questioned, for they are distorted both by the inclination everywhere to preserve the privacy of the sexual act and the tendency, probably no less universal, of at least the male to exaggerate his prowess.[8]

### PREGNANCY WASTAGE

Out of every hundred pregnancies in the West, two result in stillbirths, between ten and twenty in spontaneous abortions, and between seventy-eight and eighty-eight in live births. The lower of the two figures reflects the number of miscarriages typically recorded, but many are not reported and some occur even before the woman is aware that she is carrying a child (Potter, 1963b). Pregnancy wastage increases with age, perhaps doubling from 20–24 to 35–39 years. As any pregnancy is followed by a temporary cessation of menstruation and probably of ovulation, a miscarriage or stillbirth constitutes a longer interruption in reproduction potential than the period of the pregnancy itself.

[8] The comment of a physician in Central Africa may well be relevant generally: "We have interrogated a small proportion of our patients about the frequency of intercourse in young married couples, but do not wish to publish the results of the poll taken, because the answers, usually given rapidly, tend to cluster around two standards which are maybe in the mind of the people as much as in their practice; these two standards are three intercourses per week and three intercourses per day, the latter being much rarer" (Barlovatz, 1955).

## THE FECUNDITY OF COUPLES

With the development of diagnostic skill, it should become possible to devise a reasonably accurate criterion of fecundity by combining measures of the various relevant physical characteristics of the two partners. Indeed, an attempt to construct such an index was made in one study of a sample of subfecund couples. They had all tried unsuccessfully to conceive for a year or more, and none had had any children. Males were divided into two fecundity classes, "good" and "poor," on the basis of a sperm count and several other measurable characteristics of the spermatozoa. Females were divided into two age groups and, within each, into the same two classes according to such characteristics as the regularity of the menses and ovulation, the state of the Fallopian tubes, etc. As can be seen from Table 6-1, on the basis of this diagnostic differentiation in fecundity, the authors

Table 6-1. Percentage of Pregnancies Within One Year of Exposure, by Diagnosed Fecundity of the Marriage Partners and Age of Wife

|  | WIFE UNDER 30 YEARS | | WIFE 30 YEARS AND OVER | |
|---|---|---|---|---|
|  | WIFE'S FECUNDITY "GOOD" | WIFE'S FECUNDITY "POOR" | WIFE'S FECUNDITY "GOOD" | WIFE'S FECUNDITY "POOR" |
| Husband's Fecundity "Good" | 40 | 23 | 18 | 8 |
| Husband's Fecundity "Poor" | 25 | 3 | 16 | 4 |

SOURCE: John MacLeod *et al.*, "Correlation of the Male and Female Factors in Human Infertility," *Fertility and Sterility*, 6 (1955), 112–143. Copyright, American Society for the Study of Sterility.

were able to predict to some degree the actual birth performance of various couples. That the age of the wife is a most important factor is evident from these data. When the wife was under 30, the rate of pregnancy was markedly low only when the fecundity of *both* partners was rated as "poor." But if a wife of 30 years or over had "poor" fecundity, the "good" fecundity of her husband did not much increase the probability of pregnancy. The highest figure, 40 per cent, would be low for normal couples, but for these it is an impressive performance. By such a test, the differentiation between fecundity and fertility is expressed in operational terms; that is, the potential ability to bear children can be measured, however imperfectly, by an index other than the actual bearing of children.

## THE FECUNDITY OF POPULATIONS

A reproductive potential can be assigned to individuals, somewhat more realistically to couples, or, at least in theory, to populations. As it is possible to designate each couple's approximate fecundity, one could add up these figures for any population and get a measure of the group's biological potential; but this has never been done. Two approximations are commonly used, the incidence of sterility and, sometimes, of subfecundity, and the recorded fertility of populations that are presumed not to practice contraception.

According to nineteenth-century records of an isolated Swedish population, among married women aged 15 to 39 years 12 per cent had no children, and in this population they (or their husbands) were therefore deemed to be sterile. The proportion varied from 2 per cent of women who had married at ages 15–19 to 20 per cent of those who had married at ages 30–39 (Hyrenius, 1958). According to the reconstructed family histories of a Normandy village from 1674 to 1742, the interval between pregnancies in this population varied from about fifteen to about thirty-nine months, depending especially on the mother's age (Henry, 1958; cf. Dandekar, 1959). According to a sample survey of wives aged 18 through 39, the white population of the United States is divided as follows: (1) Approximately 10 per cent of all couples are completely sterile, including 9 per cent with one partner who has been sterilized, either as therapy or for contraception. (2) Approximately 7 per cent of couples are probably sterile, and 12 per cent are subfecund. The incidence of subfecundity is greater among older women, among those who have borne more children, and possibly (though on this point the evidence is not clear) among lower-class women. (3) The fecundity of 5 per cent of the couples is indeterminate. (4) The remaining 66 per cent are fecund (Freedman et al., 1959, Chapter 2). In an earlier survey in Indianapolis, the respondents were classified into only two categories: 73 per cent "relatively fecund" and 27 per cent "relatively sterile" (ibid., p. 407).

Completed family size in a number of underdeveloped countries has ranged from 5.1 to 6.2 children per woman, 5.9 to 6.6 per wife, and 6.5 to 7.3 per mother (ibid., p. 412). In the Cocos-Keeling Islands, girls usually married before age twenty, and those who survived through the childbearing period bore an average of eight to nine children. Among a population of Mexican Mennonites, the mean age at which females marry is 20.9 years and the gross reproduction rate in 1966 was 5.258 (Allen and Redekop, 1967). The maximum family size possible in the West, where fecundity is improved by modern health measures, is suggested by the fertility of the Hutterites, a fundamentalist sect whose members practice no birth control. They average 10.4 births per couple (Eaton and Mayer, 1954, p. 20; Tietze, 1957).

A Dutch couple and their children (*Copyright Anfoto, Amsterdam*).

These are minimum estimates of fecundity, for the age range of the women studied was generally under the outside limit of the childbearing period, some births were probably not reported, and in the underdeveloped countries, as we have noted, the lower level of health reduced the physiological ability to reproduce. The assumption is often made that deliberate contraception is more or less restricted to modern Western societies, so that among either primitives or isolated rural populations of the early modern era, the fertility recorded can be equated with the fecundity obtaining under the conditions of that society. For example, Hyrenius's study (1958) of one Swedish locality was titled a population "without family limitation." It is possible to test this thesis with more complete data from Sweden. Of the almost 300 judiciary districts (*harad*) in the country, seventy-three were overwhelmingly agrarian and nonurban still in 1930. As far back as 1860, there was a considerable variation among these in marital fertility, based not on different degrees of urban influence but on quite stable parochial patterns of family formation. "This preindustrial variation strongly suggests that fertility was in fact controlled long before 1880, [and] not only among urban middle-class families" (Carlsson, 1966).

The rather frightening number of children actually born to some populations, thus, cannot be taken as the maximum achievable. Guttmacher has deduced from a number of American and English studies that on the average a woman in these countries who nurses all her children can give birth each twenty-four months, and one who does not each nineteen months. According to this timetable, if a girl marries at age sixteen, if the couple remains married and fecund for thirty years, if there are no fetal deaths, and if all babies are breast-fed, the average completed family size resulting from uncontrolled normal intercourse would be fifteen children (Guttmacher, 1952; but cf. Henry, 1961; Vincent, 1961; James, 1963).

## Social Determinants of Fertility

Fertility is often perceived as the resultant of fecundity and birth control: biology sets a maximum number of possible births, and man contrives by one means or another to reduce it. But such purposive action on the part of the parents, or, in an attempt to work through parents, of churches or governments, is only one subclass of a broader category, **fertility determinants,** which include any of a society's policies, laws, institutions, styles of living, and so on that influence the average family size, whether or not this is their conscious purpose or generally known effect. A number of analysts have suggested, for instance, that one reason for the lower fertility in cities is the less frequent marital coitus because of the competitive diversions of urban life. In such a case the persons involved may be completely unaware of the cause-effect relation. Another example would be the factors, whatever they may be, that determine the "proper" age at which to marry. In this case, while the effect on fertility is patent, this is not necessarily the purpose of the behavior pattern.

### DEVIANT SEXUAL PRACTICES

The "total sexual outlet," to use Kinsey's term, includes intercourse with objects unlikely or unable to conceive—a prostitute, a person of the same sex, an animal, an imagined partner. Although such relations absorb in the aggregate a large portion of the total sexual energy expended in virtually any society, presumably they have little effect on fertility. Some or all are everywhere defined as vice, and the moral pressure of the community induces most persons to conform most of the time. These deviant practices, then, are concentrated among a minority of "perverts," experimenting adolescents (masturbation, homosexuality in the United States),[9] and

[9] Kinsey et al., 1948, Chapter 21. Of Kinsey's male sample, 37 per cent had had some homosexual experience to the point of orgasm, usually during their adolescence, but only

adults lacking a marital outlet (nocturnal emissions, intercourse with prostitutes) or seeking a supplement to such an outlet (intercourse with prostitutes, homosexuality in the Levant). In short, the usual pattern is that these practices represent an addition to marital intercourse rather than a substitute for it, and thus probably do not affect fertility significantly.

Religiously inspired celibacy is a deviancy of a different kind, but also with little effect on population growth. In 1966, the Roman Catholic Church claimed a total membership in the United States of 46.2 million, of whom only 253,111, or 0.5 per cent, were celibates.[10] The proportion is probably larger in some other countries, but nowhere does Roman Catholicism draw off into celibacy a significant segment of the fertility potential. In Tibet, where the tradition used to be that one male child in three was assigned to the clerical order, celibacy probably did reduce the country's fertility considerably, though even in this extreme case the allegation cannot be demonstrated.[11]

## FAMILY FORMATION

The sex drive is sufficient to induce copulation and thus reproduction, but this biological link between man and woman is almost everywhere reinforced by ethical norms. A society's demographic and cultural persistence depends on the fact that the physical care, socialization, and social placement of its young are not left to the sometimes haphazard dictates of sexuality alone. The family, in short, is not merely a biological group but one held together also by complementary economic needs, moral codes, and the integrative force of the whole social structure. In particular, the bond between father and offspring, which physiologically is the weakest in the nuclear family, is culturally reinforced by what Malinowski termed "the principle of legitimacy," which designates one man (usually though not necessarily the biological father) as responsible for each infant born into the society. Illegitimacy is relatively common in some societies or subcul-

---

4 per cent were exclusively homosexual throughout their lives. Probably no section of Kinsey's work has excited more adverse comment than the one on homosexuality; for a balanced criticism see William G. Cochran et al., *Statistical Problems of the Kinsey Report on Sexual Behavior in the Human Male*, American Statistical Association, Washington, D.C., 1954, pp. 142 ff. and *passim*.

10 John F. Broderick, S.J., "Roman Catholic Church," *Americana Annual, 1967*, Americana Corporation, New York, 1967, p. 592. For a general comment on religious statistics, see pp. 126–128.

11 The gross effect of celibacy on Tibet's population growth would have to be distinguished from that of the widespread polyandry, the high incidence of venereal diseases, and the possibility that fecundity is impaired by the country's extreme altitude. Population estimates before 1950 were most approximate, usually ranging between 1.0 and 1.5 million, and figures released since the Chinese conquest of 1953, though expressed more precisely, are not necessarily more accurate. *Cf.* Leo A. Orleans, "A Note on Tibet's Population," *China Quarterly*, 27 (1966), 120–122.

tures (e.g., portions of Latin America, lower-class Negroes in the United States), but with this lack of a two-adult team working in the interest of their offspring, socialization is markedly less efficient.

While the conjugal family is designated as the basic social unit in all cultures, the wider structures built from this base vary considerably. Incest taboos, universal within the nuclear family, are extended to include cousins and other relatives of second and higher degree according to a number of different patterns; and these various limitations on the choice of a marriage partner reinforce the societal type from which they derive.[12] Family types and the kind of social structure with which they are generally associated, moreover, tend together to encourage different levels of fertility (Kingsley Davis and Blake, 1956). A priori, one can assume, for instance, that the relative importance of the family in any society strongly influences its fertility. Although the marital state is the norm everywhere, the pressure to follow it differs according to the social structure. Since in a traditional agrarian setting many wants can be satisfied only through the family, persons are induced to form one early; in an industrial urban complex, on the contrary, since the many other institutions make the family relatively less important, there is less pressure on any individual to marry, or to marry early. In the abstract, then, the average age at marriage, to the degree that it is rationally determined, would seem to depend primarily on two factors: how much preparation the two partners need in order to take over adult roles, and how much assistance they can expect.

It is not easy, however, to spell out these plausible generalizations with empirical data from various societies. The few works on the joint family, for instance, do not altogether support the thesis, derived deductively from reasonable postulates, that this type of institution encourages a large progeny (see pp. 381–383). Similarly, the notion that the precarious condition of life among primitive peoples necessitates a compensating high fertility, and thus an early age at marriage, is not wholly validated by ethnographic data (Nag, 1962). The shift from tradition that accompanies industrialization is not consistent: India and Ireland, two countries noted for their very low and very high ages at marriage and, related to these, their low and high proportions who never marry, are both in their different ways traditionalist (see pp. 514–517). And the effect on fertility of such a family type as polygamy is also difficult to measure empirically, in part because one cannot judge whether such marriages include a high proportion of exceptionally virile men and of barren women. According to the best study, the main raison d'être of polygyny, to afford the man a greater number of offspring, is realized, but each wife has fewer children on the average than one in a monogamous union (Muhsam, 1956).

More generally, a cross-cultural analysis must be based on data that

[12] Cf. George Peter Murdock, Social Structure, Macmillan, New York, 1949. Cf. pp. 620–622.

are neither complete nor wholly comparable. Only eighty-one geographic units (including some nonsovereign districts) provide data on marriages by the ages of bride and groom. These sparse data, moreover, are based on the various definitions of "marriage" in different cultures and on systematically misstated ages, it would seem, in at least some instances. For example, "in some countries there appears to be an abnormal concentration of marriages at the minimum marriageable age and at the age at which valid marriage may be contracted without parental consent, indicating perhaps an overstatement in some cases to comply with the law. Factors which may influence age reporting, particularly at older ages, include an inclination to understate the bride's age in order that it may be equal to or less than that of the groom" (United Nations, 1966, pp. 4–14).

### BEHAVIOR PATTERNS WITHIN MARRIAGE

The ethical norm by which the family is maintained—for example, the prescription of absolute filial obedience in traditional China or India—may strongly influence attitudes toward family size. The discussion here is restricted to a more direct determinant of fertility, sexual continence other than that intended as a means of birth control.

Virtually all societies impose periods of sexual abstinence within marriage. Many of these are set by female physiology: intercourse is often banned during menstruation, during the gestation period, or at least the last portion of it, and for some time after the birth of a child. These taboos generally have little effect on fertility, except perhaps indirectly through promoting the health of the woman or increasing coital incidence when conception is possible. Other prescriptions of periodic abstinence may represent a denial of pleasurable experience, analogous to fasting, during a time when solemnity or mourning is appropriate. Or they may be determined by occasions when the man's virility is deemed to be particularly important (thus, among many primitives during a war, and, in our own culture, during the training period of a professional athlete). As many of these miscellaneous bans are enforced by a religious sanction, they may be more important in agrarian than in industrial societies.

It is convenient to exemplify such impositions of sexual abstinence with the traditional practices of China, for in most Western texts the Chinese family is cited as an institution adapted to virtually unlimited procreation. In fact, marital coitus is inauspicious or even dangerous on the first, seventh, fifteenth, twenty-first, twenty-eighth, and twenty-ninth days of each lunar month; on the sixteenth day of the fifth month; during solar or lunar eclipses, the days of equinoxes and solstices; when there is an earthquake, rain, thunder and lightning, great heat or great cold; after washing the hair, a long trip, heavy drinking or eating; when the man is tired, very excited, too old; during the woman's menstruation, for one month following the birth of a child, and after the woman has reached 40; during twenty-seven months following the death of a parent; permanently after the birth of a grandchild. In various texts only some of these rules are stressed, but books and astrological calendars denoting the auspicious and inauspicious days still circulate today in Taiwan (and, one presumes, possibly they are still extant also in Mainland China). If all the basic rules are observed, only about a hundred days per year are auspicious for intercourse. In addition, the traditional Chinese family typically uses *coitus interruptus* and an inaccurately based "safe period" deliberately to control conception. Even the enormous stress in Confucian teaching on the overriding importance of male progeny should not lead one to pass over these other determinants of family size (Eberhard and Eberhard, 1967).

## Methods of Birth Control

One of the most important social determinants of fertility is **birth control,** or the conscious use of any practice permitting heterosexual intercourse while reducing the likelihood of conception. The term thus includes "not only the use of mechanical or chemical contraceptives, but also such other practices as 'withdrawal' and 'safe period,'"[13] for the important factor is not the means used but the intention to control conception.

The commonest method of birth control throughout the world is the simplest, **coitus interruptus,** or male withdrawal just before ejaculation. This is "the most popular, widely diffused method of contraception, . . . probably nearly as old as the group life of man" (Himes, 1936, pp. 183–184). It requires no preparations or appliances, costs nothing, is available at all times. It has, however, the disadvantage that it requires that the male be strongly motivated enough to frustrate his desire at the moment of highest excitation. We should expect to find, therefore, that *coitus interruptus* is less frequently practiced in societies or societal sectors where the economic and social responsibility for the child is borne by the mother or the broader kin group, rather than mainly or entirely by the father.

The postnatal mode of "birth control," **infanticide,** however barbarous by modern Western standards, also goes back immemorially. Moral considerations aside, infanticide has the disadvantage of exposing the mother to pain and risk to no purpose, but it is also the only method of birth control that permits a selection among offspring. Wherever infanticide is practiced, female infanticide is the rule, supplemented by the elimination of defective and unhealthy offspring and those undesirable by reason of some magical (e.g., multiple births) or social (e.g., illegitimacy) factor. Infanticide is thus associated with the higher valuation of males, as in a hunting society, in which they lead an especially dangerous life (Eskimos); among certain

[13] United Nations, Department of Social Affairs, *The Determinants and Consequences of Population Trends,* Population Studies, No. 17, New York, 1953, p. 74, footnote 37.

polyandrous peoples (the Toda, a primitive people of southern India); and in many of the great agrarian civilizations (traditional China and India and even Japan well into the twentieth century, as well as medieval and early modern Europe). In contemporary Western societies infanticide is a rarity not only because of strong moral and legal sanctions, but also because other methods of birth control reduce the number of unwanted children born, and when, in spite of contraceptives and abortions, these do arrive, they can be disposed of by offering them for adoption.

**Abortion,** also an old means of controlling family size, "may be the most widely used single method in the world today" (Freedman, 1965). Its analysis, however, is manifestly difficult. Even in advanced countries the statistics are scanty and not based on random samples, and the meaning of basic terms is indefinite and in flux. The dictionary definition of *abort* is "to give birth prematurely" or "to cause to be delivered prematurely," whereas *abortionist* means "one who practices the producing of criminal abortions." The word *abortion* takes on both colorations: as used by physicians it refers to the physiological process, and as used by lawyers it refers to the law prohibiting persons from inducing premature birth; the usage in vital statistics recommended by the World Health Organization is to avoid the word altogether (United Nations, 1954, p. 4).

Underdeveloped societies, as they are unable to develop effective contraceptive means, very often sanction birth control by some crude form of abortion. In industrial societies, with some exceptions (the Soviet Union and its European satellites, Japan after World War II), the law generally permits induced abortions only when the mother's life is endangered or under other special circumstances. This does not mean, of course, that no other operations are performed. The record of incidence is not accurate, because induced abortions are often illegal or, if legal, nevertheless secret, and because they are often difficult to distinguish from spontaneous fetal deaths, of which the count is also quite inadequate. According to a summary of several studies in the 1960s, "about one out of every five pregnancies in the United States terminates in illegal abortion" (Bates and Zawadzki, 1964, p. 3; *cf.* Calderone, 1958, pp. 50–59; Lader, 1966).

**Sponges and tampons** placed in the vagina go back to before the Christian era. They are still used throughout the world, mainly as improvised contraceptives among the poor. **Douches** are also a frequent household contraceptive.

The **condom,** made of intestines of sheep or other animals, first appeared in eighteenth-century England. Today's product is of rubber. Since 1938, when the Food and Drug Administration began to control their quality, an estimated 997 out of every 1,000 rubber sheaths sold in the United States are free from defects. American production totals between 720 million and 864 million units per year, of which perhaps a fifth are exported (Tietze, 1963).

An important new factor in Western fertility during the second half of the nineteenth century was the development of improved contraceptive devices. In the 1880s, the **diaphragm** (also called pessary or cervical cap) was invented by Dr. W. P. J. Mensinga, later a professor of anatomy at Breslau. In the following decades a considerable improvement in **chemical spermicides** took place. A diaphragm used with spermicidal jelly or cream was the means that most American physicians and clinics recommended until very recently. Mechanical and chemical contraceptives were novel in several senses. (1) With their use, the control is put at the beginning of the procreative process, so that the woman's health and life are not endangered by repeated unwanted pregnancies, and Western ethical injunctions against abortion and infanticide can be obeyed. (2) On the other hand, in contrast to continence and *coitus interruptus,* contraceptives permit full expression to one of man's strongest natural drives. The link between the sexual instinct and reproduction, absolute in lower animals and mitigated in primates, is made subject to man's will. (3) These contraceptives, however, have been more or less restricted to industrial societies, for agrarian countries are generally unable or unwilling to either manufacture or import them in sufficient quantities.

The most popular middle-class contraceptive in the United States today is "the pill," a steroid tablet that when taken orally prevents ovulation. **Oral contraceptives** have the prime advantage of convenience and efficiency, as well as some disadvantages. Some users report nausea and other side-effects. From the considerable research under way, improved types may become available (Pincus, 1965, Chapter 8; Nelson, 1965; Sobrero and Lewit, 1964).

**Intra-uterine devices** (or IUD's) were first developed in the 1920s by a Berlin physician named Ernst Gräfenberg. They consist of a small ring, loop, Y-shape, or other compressible device, made of metal, silk-worm gut, or plastic, which when inserted into the uterus expands to its original shape and holds in place. How it prevents conception is not known precisely, possibly by impeding the ovum's implantation on the wall of the uterus. A small proportion of users, differing according to the device used, have reported bleeding or other side-effects, and others have ejected the device, sometimes without knowing it. For many it is a quite effective contraceptive, remarkably cheap and not at all troublesome. It is widely used in some underdeveloped countries and in Japan and Israel, but still relatively infrequently in the United States (Tietze, 1965*b*; Tietze and Lewit, 1964; Population Council, 1967).

**Sterilization** in females is ordinarily accomplished by salpingectomy, or the cutting or tying of the Fallopian tubes through which ova pass from the ovary. Ordinarily, this is a major operation, but at the time of childbirth it can be performed with minimal added discomfort and danger. Male sterilization, or vasectomy, can be performed expeditiously with only local anesthesia; risk to life is practically nil. In a very small proportion of cases contraception is not achieved, but more generally either type of steriliza-

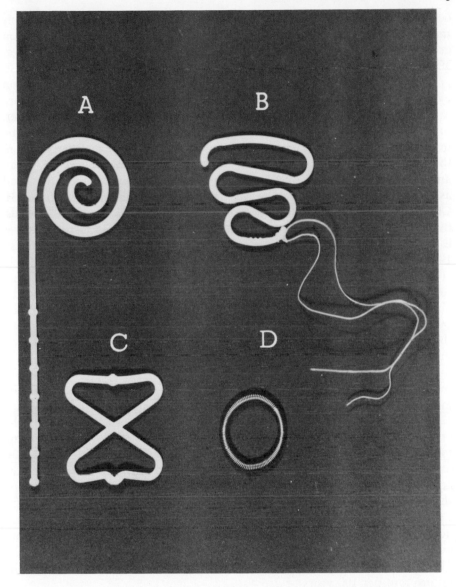

An intra-uterine contraceptive device can be of various shapes. Four in use in various countries (actual size) are: Margulies (A), Lippes (B), Birnberg (C), and Ball Ring (D) (*Planned Parenthood/World Population*).

tion is wholly effective (Tietze, 1965a). In many societies the operation is hedged in by magical fears and legal restrictions, but in Puerto Rico it is one of the most popular methods of birth control, and it is becoming more prevalent in such other countries as India and, seemingly, the mainland of the United States. The principal advantages of sterilization are simplicity, economy, and permanence. These characteristics can appeal to under-developed countries seeking a means of controlling their population growth, or to individuals with low or moderate incomes (*cf.* Poffenberger, 1963; Wood, 1967).

The **rhythm** method, or periodic continence, is based on the ovulation cycle. If coitus is avoided during the short period each month that mature ova are in place, in theory conception can be completely avoided. However, to determine this period precisely is not easy. As used for centuries, the method was based on fallacious physiology; the present system derives from the almost simultaneous work of two physicians, Kyusaku Ogino in Japan and Hermann Knaus in Austria, who correctly placed the fecund period as roughly "fourteen days *before* the onset of menstruation" (Knaus, 1964, Chapter 6). For women with any but absolutely regular menstrual periods, this is not a precise specification, and research is in process to use changes in body temperature and blood enzymes as a more accurate index (Pincus, 1965, pp. 206 ff.). As rhythm is now used, the couple must be completely continent for a number of months while a trained worker determines how regular the menstruation and ovulation cycles are, and thereafter periodic abstention must be practiced not only during the assumed ovulation phase but also for several days before and after it. Under such circumstances, the method "offers a satisfactory degree of protection against unwanted pregnancy to rigorously selected and carefully instructed wives who, with their husbands, are intelligent and strongly motivated. For others and for those to whom pregnancy would be dangerous, the effectiveness of the method in preventing conception is not considered adequate" (Tietze *et al.*, 1951). Many American Catholics begin with rhythm and then, after the birth of several unwanted children, shift to more efficient means. According to a 1965 survey, more than half of the Catholic couples in the United States use methods condemned by the Church.[14] Some countries of Latin America honor Dr. Ogino by calling the children inadvertently born to parents using rhythm "oginitos."

The effectiveness of contraceptives, as this is ordinarily measured, means not their theoretical efficacy under ideal conditions but how they work when used by a sample of fallible humans (Tietze, 1962; Seklani, 1963). The usual index until recently, sometimes called "Pearl's formula," is the failure rate per 100 years of use:

$$R = \frac{\text{Number of accidental pregnancies} \times 1200}{\text{Total months of use}}$$

The rate of accidental pregnancies, so calculated, varies greatly for different contraceptive methods (Table 6-2). With this formula, however,

---

[14] *The New York Times,* December 3, 1966. Compare earlier data in Freedman *et al.*, 1959, pp. 182–183.

Table 6-2. Accidental Pregnancy Rates, per 100 Years of Exposure, by Method of Contraception

|  | VARIOUS STUDIES | METROPOLITAN AMERICAN FAMILIES | COMPOSITE FROM SIX STUDIES |
|---|---|---|---|
| Oral progestin-estrogen | 0.1–1.1 | — | — |
| Intra-uterine devices | 0.9–8.5 | — | — |
| Condom |  | 13.8 | 14 |
| Diaphragm and spermicide |  | 14.4 | 12 |
| Withdrawal |  | 16.8 | 18 |
| Spermicide alone |  | — | 20 |
| Rhythm |  | 38.5 | 24 |
| Douche |  | 40.5 | 31 |
| Others |  | 30.3 | — |
| No contraception, with lactation | 50 |  |  |
| No contraception, no lactation | 63 |  |  |

SOURCES: Gregory Pincus, *The Control of Fertility,* Academic Press, New York, 1965, pp. 297–299; Alan F. Guttmacher, "Fertility of Man," *Fertility and Sterility,* 3 (1952), 281–289.

one gets merely an approximation of the actual proportion of failures. Among any group of women that start to control births, those that discontinue over the following period are not representative of the whole. Those who find the particular method objectionable shift to another. Those that have an accidental pregnancy are presumably less conscientious or less skillful users, possibly more fecund. Month by month, the original mixed population is reduced to a more and more homogeneous residue of satisfied, highly motivated users, including all of the sterile and most of the subfecund. Thus, the rates of accidental pregnancies calculated at intervals of several months start higher than $R$ and gradually decline to a figure lower than $R$ (Table 6-3, observed rates). To correct this, one can adapt the life-table model to the risk of pregnancy, obtaining the adjusted rates in Table 6-3 (Potter, 1963a, 1967).

Moreover, the efficiency of a contraceptive cannot be equated with the reduction in fertility of the population that uses it. One with an 80 per cent efficacy, for instance, reduces fertility by about half. A single failure may result in conception, but a contraceptive success must be repeated at each new ovulation. "A little contraception is a nugatory thing" (Ryder, 1965).

Table 6-3. A Comparison of Observed and Adjusted Pregnancy Rates

| MONTH OF EXPOSURE | PREGNANCIES PER 100 YEARS OF EXPOSURE | |
| --- | --- | --- |
| | OBSERVED | ADJUSTED |
| 1–3 | 29.1 | 28.8 |
| 4–6 | 11.5 | 11.6 |
| 7–9 | 5.7 | 5.7 |
| 10–12 | 3.5 | 3.5 |
| 13–20 | 1.3 | 1.5 |
| 1–20 | 10.4 | 8.3 |

SOURCE: Robert G. Potter, Jr., "Additional Measures of Use-Effectiveness of Contraception," *Milbank Memorial Fund Quarterly,* **41** (1963), 400–418.

## Summary

Fecundity, the physiological ability to procreate, varies with a number of physical characteristics, of which the most important are heredity, health, age, the ovulation cycle, lactation, and sex drive. The distribution of these characteristics, particularly age, determine the relative ability of populations to reproduce themselves.

Determinants of fertility include both the deliberate control of births and social usages or institutions that influence birth rates, even with no such purpose and sometimes without a general awareness of this relation. In a traditional society many social wants can be satisfied only through the family, and persons are thereby induced to form one early, while in the institutional complex of an industrial urban society, on the contrary, the family is relatively less important, and there may be less pressure on any individual to marry, or to marry early. Thus, although the marital state is the norm everywhere, the age at marriage and the proportion married may depend on how important the family is in the social structure.

In Table 6-4 fertility determinants have been divided into four broad types according to the point in the physiology of reproduction they affect: continence, contraception, fetal mortality, and infant mortality (Kingsley Davis and Blake, 1956). For each type the relative importance of deliberate and nondeliberate regulation is indicated. The overriding differentiation that this table suggests is that between industrial and nonindustrial societies. An industrial society, first of all, is one with more knowledge of the natural world and better techniques to control it. Infant mortality and, to a smaller degree, fetal mortality are reduced, and effective contraceptives obviate the need for clumsier, more dangerous methods of birth control later in the physiological process. This improved control of both fertility and

## Table 6-4. Types of Fertility Determinants

| | CONSCIOUS MEANS OF BIRTH CONTROL | SIGNIFICANT EFFECT ON FERTILITY |
|---|---|---|
| **CONTINENCE** | | |
| Permanent celibacy | No | Generally not, except possibly Tibet |
| Premarital | Generally not; yes in Ireland | Yes in Western societies |
| Intermarital | Generally not | Often |
| Intermittent | No, except "rhythm" | "Rhythm" and magical rules |
| **CONTRACEPTION** | | |
| Vices | No | Generally not |
| Coitus interruptus | Yes | Yes |
| Chemical, mechanical | Yes | Yes in industrial societies |
| Sterilization | Generally yes | Not usually; yes in Puerto Rico, portions of India, etc. |
| Oral | Yes | Yes, especially in wealthy societies |
| Intra-uterine devices | Yes | Yes, especially in a few underdeveloped countries |
| **FETAL MORTALITY** | | |
| Spontaneous miscarriage | No | Yes |
| Induced abortion | Yes | Yes, especially in nonindustrial countries, France, and Japan |
| **INFANT MORTALITY** | | |
| Unintended | No | Yes in nonindustrial societies, though less than before 1945 |
| Infanticide | Yes | Yes in nonindustrial societies |

School for young Tibetan lamas, Delhousie, India. They will remain celibate all their lives (*T. S. Satyan, Camera Press—PIX*).

mortality means that institutional patterns have a less significant influence on the birth rate. Industrialization loosens the social structure of an agrarian society: the sharp increase in both geographical and social mobility means that more and more persons are removed from the influence and control of the extended kin group to the relatively anonymous life of the large city. The normative system of the agrarian society (religious values, family sentiments, etc.) may also be weakened by this loss of its institutional base, which is challenged as well by the higher valuation of rationality in an industrial urban setting. Fertility, in brief, tends to be associated with social structure, technological standards, and specific prescriptions or taboos; and all three of these determinants have been markedly changed by industrialization.

However, the theory that associates industrial societies and low fertility, while valid up to a point, has important flaws. As we shall note in subsequent chapters, such exceptions as the low fertility of Tokugawa Japan and the unanticipated rise of Western birth rates after World War II have never really been fitted into the general analysis. More pertinently, the assertion that industrialization results in a small-family system, even if absolutely valid, is of little practical value. For in much of the underdeveloped world, the large-family system is efficiently blocking efforts to create an industrial economy.

# Suggestions for Further Reading

Excellent guidance through the enormous literature on fertility, including elements not covered in this chapter, is provided in Freedman, 1961–62; Liu, 1968. Many of the other works cited here have more specialized bibliographies.

One type of analysis of fecundity, by physicians or physiologists, is peripheral to the subject matter of this book. A layman can derive greater understanding from, e.g., MacLeod, 1955 and a work marginal to biological sciences and out of date in some respects, Pearl, 1939. Good analyses by those in social disciplines include Kumar, 1967; Eaton and Mayer, 1954.

Recent summaries of advances in contraception range from the thoroughly professional Pincus, 1965 to the excellent popularization in Guttmacher, 1962; more detailed information can best be sought in the many articles of Tietze and Potter.

There are remarkably few works on the general sociology of fertility. Meier, 1959 and Goode, 1963 are interesing; among the best efforts to break new ground are Kingsley Davis and Blake, 1956; Stycos, 1962; Blake, 1965; and Carlsson, 1966.

ALLEN, GORDON, and CALVIN REDEKOP. 1967. "Individual Differences in Survival and Reproduction among Old Colony Mennonites in Mexico: Progress to October 1966," *Eugenics Quarterly*, **14**, 103–111.

* AMERICAN MEDICAL ASSOCIATION. COMMITTEE ON HUMAN REPRODUCTION. 1967. "Evaluation of Intrauterine Contraceptive Devices," *Journal of the American Medical Association*, **199**, 141–143.

* ———, COUNCIL ON DRUGS. 1967. "Evaluation of Oral Contraceptives," *Journal of the American Medical Association*, **199**, 144–147.

BALLEW, JOHN W., and WILLIAM H. MASTERS. 1954. "Mumps: A Cause of Infertility," *Fertility and Sterility*, **5**, 536–543.

BARLOVATZ, A. 1955. "Sterility in Central Africa," *Fertility and Sterility*, **6**, 363–364.

BATES, JEROME E., and EDWARD S. ZAWADZKI. 1964. *Criminal Abortion: A Study in Medical Sociology*. Thomas, Springfield, Ill.

* BLAKE, JUDITH. 1965. "Demographic Science and the Redirection of Population Policy," in Sheps and Ridley, 1965, pp. 41–69.

BOS, CARLO, and R. A. GLEGHORN. 1958. "Psychogenic Sterility," *Fertility and Sterility*, **9**, 84–98.

CALDERONE, MARY STEICHEN, editor. 1958. *Abortion in the United States*. Hoeber-Harper, New York.

* CARLSSON, GÖSTA. 1966. "The Decline of Fertility: Innovation or Adjustment Process," *Population Studies*, **20**, 149–174.

DANDEKAR, KUMUDINI. 1959. "Intervals between Confinements," *Eugenics Quarterly*, **6**, 180–186.

DAVIS, KATHARINE BEMENT. 1929. *Factors in the Sex Life of Twenty-Two Hundred Women*. Harper, New York.

* DAVIS, KINGSLEY, and JUDITH BLAKE. 1956. "Social Structure and Fertility: An Analytical Framework," *Economic Development and Cultural Change*, **4**, 211–235.

° EATON, JOSEPH W., and ALBERT J. MAYER. 1954. *Man's Capacity to Reproduce: The Demography of a Unique Population.* Free Press, Glencoe, Ill.

EBERHARD, WOLFRAM, and ALIDE EBERHARD. 1967. "Family Planning in a Taiwanese Town," in Wolfram Eberhard. *Settlement and Social Change in Asia.* Hong Kong University Press, Hong Kong.

FORD, CLELLAN S., and FRANK A. BEACH. 1951. *Patterns of Sexual Behavior.* Harper, New York.

° FREEDMAN, RONALD. 1961–62. "The Sociology of Human Fertility: A Trend Report and Bibliography," *Current Sociology,* Vol. 10–11, No. 2.

————. 1965. "Family Planning Programs Today: Major Themes of the Geneva Conference," *Studies in Family Planning,* No. 8 (supplement), pp. 1–7.

° ————, PASCAL K. WHELPTON, and ARTHUR A. CAMPBELL. 1959. *Family Planning, Sterility, and Population Growth.* McGraw-Hill, New York.

GOODE, WILLIAM J. 1963. *World Revolution and Family Patterns.* Free Press of Glencoe, New York.

GUTTMACHER, ALAN F. 1952. "Fertility of Man," *Fertility and Sterility,* 3, 281–289.

° ————, and EDITORS OF CONSUMER REPORTS. 1962. *The Consumers Union Report on Family Planning.* Consumers Union, Mt. Vernon, N.Y.

HENRY, LOUIS. 1958. "Intervals between Confinements in the Absence of Birth Control," *Eugenics Quarterly,* 5, 200–211.

————. 1961. "Some Data on Natural Fertility," *Eugenics Quarterly,* 8, 81–91.

HIMES, NORMAN E. 1936. *Medical History of Contraception.* Williams & Wilkins, Baltimore.

HULME, HAROLD B. 1951. "Effect of Semistarvation on Human Semen," *Fertility and Sterility,* 2, 319–331.

HYRENIUS, HANNES. 1958. "Fertility and Reproduction in a Swedish Population Group without Family Limitation," *Population Studies,* 12, 121–130.

JAMES, W. H. 1963. "Estimates of Fecundability," *Population Studies,* 17, 57–65.

KINSEY, ALFRED C., WARDELL B. POMEROY, and CLYDE E. MARTIN. 1948. *Sexual Behavior in the Human Male.* Saunders, Philadelphia.

KISER, CLYDE V., editor. 1962. *Research in Family Planning.* Princeton University Press, Princeton, N.J.

KNAUS, HERMANN H. 1964. *Human Procreation and its Natural Regulation.* Obolensky, New York.

KUCZYNSKI, ROBERT R. 1935. *The Measurement of Population Growth: Methods and Results.* Sidgwick & Jackson, London.

° KUMAR, JOGINDER. 1967. "Age at Menarche: A Comparative Study," paper presented at the 1967 Annual Meeting of the Population Association of America.

LACHENBRUCH, PETER A. 1967. "Frequency and Timing of Intercourse: Its Relation to the Probability of Conception," *Population Studies,* 21, 23–31.

LADER, LAWRENCE. 1966. *Abortion.* Bobbs-Merrill, Indianapolis, Ind.

LESSING, LAWRENCE. 1966. "Into the Core of Life Itself," *Fortune,* March, pp. 146–151, 174–176.

LIU, WILLIAM T. 1968. "Selected Works on Fertility and Family-Planning Studies in the United States, 1960–1967," *Journal of Marriage and the Family,* 30, 346–366.

* MACLEOD, JOHN, *et al.* 1955. "Correlation of the Male and Female Factors in Human Infertility," *Fertility and Sterility,* 6, 112–143.

MACMAHON, BRIAN, and JANE WORCESTER. 1966. *Age at Menopause, United States, 1960–1962.* National Center for Health Statistics, Series 11, No. 19. Washington, D.C.

MARSH, EARLE M., and ALBERT M. VOLLMER. 1951. "Possible Psychogenic Aspects of Infertility," *Fertility and Sterility,* 2, 70–79.

MEIER, RICHARD L. 1959. *Modern Science and the Human Fertility Problem.* Wiley, New York.

MONTAGU, ASHLEY. 1957. *The Reproductive Development of the Female, with Especial Reference to the Period of Adolescent Sterility: A Study in the Comparative Physiology of the Infecundity of the Adolescent Organism.* Julian, New York

MUHSAM, H. V. 1956. "Fertility of Polygamous Marriages," *Population Studies,* 10, 3–16.

NAG, MONI, 1962. *Factors Affecting Human Fertility in Nonindustrial Societies: A Cross-Cultural Study.* Department of Anthropology, Yale University, New Haven.

NELSON, WARREN O. 1965. "Current Research on New Contraceptive Methods," in Sheps and Ridley, 1965, pp. 481–486.

PEARL, RAYMOND. 1939. *The Natural History of Population.* Oxford University Press, New York.

* PINCUS, GREGORY. 1965. *The Control of Fertility.* Academic Press, New York.

POFFENBERGER, THOMAS. 1963. "Two Thousand Voluntary Vasectomies Performed in California: Background Factors and Comments," *Marriage and Family Living,* 25, 469–474.

POPULATION COUNCIL. 1967. "Retention of IUD's: An International Comparison," *Studies in Family Planning,* No. 18, pp. 1–12.

POTTER, ROBERT G., JR. 1961. "Length of the Fertile Period," *Milbank Memorial Fund Quarterly,* 39, 132–162.

———. 1963a. "Additional Measures of Use-Effectiveness of Contraception," *Milbank Memorial Fund Quarterly,* 41, 400–418.

———. 1963b. "Birth Intervals: Structure and Change," *Population Studies,* 17, 155–166.

* ———. 1967. "The Multiple Decrement Life Table as an Approach to the Measurement of Use Effectiveness and Demographic Effectiveness of Contraception," in International Union for the Scientific Study of Population, *Proceedings, 1967,* Sydney, pp. 869–883.

——— *et al.* 1965. "Applications of Field Studies to Research on the Physiology of Human Reproduction: Lactation and Its Effects upon Birth Intervals in Eleven Punjab Villages, India," in Sheps and Ridley, 1965, pp. 377–399.

REYNOLDS, EDWARD, and DONALD MACOMBER. 1924. *Fertility and Sterility in Human Marriages.* Saunders, Philadelphia.

RYDER, NORMAN B. 1965. "The Measurement of Fertility Patterns," in Sheps and Ridley, 1965, pp. 287–306.

SEKLANI, MAHMOUD. 1963. "Efficacité de la contraception: Méthodes et résultats," *Population,* 18, 329–348.

* SHEPS, MINDEL C., and JEANNE CLARE RIDLEY, editors. 1965. *Public Health and Population Change: Current Research Issues.* University of Pittsburgh Press, Pittsburgh.

SMITH, T. E. 1960. "The Cocos-Keeling Islands: A Demographic Laboratory," *Population Studies,* 14, 94–130.

SOBRERO, AQUILES J., and SARAH LEWIT, editors. 1965. *Advances in Planned Parenthood.* Proceedings of the Annual Meeting of the American Association of Planned Parenthood Physicians. Schenkman, Cambridge, Mass.

* STYCOS, J. MAYONE. 1962. "A Critique of the Traditional Planned Parenthood Approach in Underdeveloped Areas," in Kiser, 1962, pp. 477–501.

TIETZE, CHRISTOPHER. 1957. "Reproductive Span and Rate of Reproduction among Hutterite Women," *Fertility and Sterility,* 8, 89–97.

* ———. 1960. "Probability of Pregnancy Resulting from a Single Unprotected Coitus," *Fertility and Sterility,* 11, 485–488.

———. 1961. "The Effect of Breastfeeding on the Rate of Conception," *Proceedings of the International Population Conference,* New York, 2, 129–136.

———. 1962. "The Use-Effectiveness of Contraceptive Methods," in Kiser, 1962, pp. 357–369.

———. 1963. "The Condom as a Contraceptive," in Society for the Scientific Study of Sex, *Advances in Sex Research.* Harper & Row-Hoeber, New York, pp. 88–102.

———. 1965a. "Induced Abortion and Sterilization as Methods of Fertility Control," *Journal of Chronic Diseases,* 18, 1161–1171.

———. 1965b. "History and Statistical Evaluation of Intrauterine Contraceptive Devices," in Sheps and Ridley, 1965, pp. 432–449.

———, and SARAH LEWIT. 1964. "Intra-Uterine Contraception: Effectiveness and Acceptability," *Excerpta Medica,* International Congress Series, No. 86, New York.

——— et al. 1950. "Time Required for Conception in 1727 Planned Pregnancies," *Fertility and Sterility,* 1, 338–346.

——— et al. 1951. "Clinical Effectiveness of the Rhythm Method of Contraception," *Fertility and Sterility,* 2, 444–450.

UNITED NATIONS. DEPARTMENT OF SOCIAL AFFAIRS. POPULATION DIVISION. 1954. *Foetal, Infant and Early Childhood Mortality. 1: The Statistics.* Population Studies No. 13, New York.

———. 1966. *Demographic Yearbook, 1965,* New York.

U.S. DEPARTMENT OF HEALTH, EDUCATION, AND WELFARE. 1966. *Report on Family Planning,* Washington, D.C.

* VINCENT, PAUL E. 1958. "Variations de la fertilité selon l'âge: Méthode de recherche: Aperçu de quelques résultats d'enquête," *Bulletin de l'Institut International de Statistique,* 36, 218–226.

———. 1961. "Recherches sur la fécondité biologique: Étude d'un groupe de familles nombreuses," *Population,* 16, 105–112.

WILLIAMS, ROGER J. 1962. *Nutrition in a Nutshell.* Doubleday-Dolphin, Garden City, N.Y.

WOOD, H. CURTIS, JR. 1967. *Sex Without Babies: A Comprehensive Review of Voluntary Sterilization as a Method of Birth Control.* Whitmore, Philadelphia.

# 7 THE GENERAL DETERMINANTS OF MORTALITY

Though there are no terms analogous to *fecundity* and *fertility*, the determinants of mortality are also biological and social. As with birth so also with death, the ultimate factor is physiology; no matter how much the expectation of life is increased, man remains mortal. And the *social* determinants of mortality, as of fertility, can also be classified into two types. "Accidents," "acts of God," and similar concepts are in part cultural artifacts, for each society defines the area that is beyond human control. When a consensus reigns that man can do nothing to mitigate it, such a condition or mishap is part of "nature." When this consensus breaks down, the evil is redefined as a "social problem"; antagonistic interest groups polemicize first over whether there can, or may, be a solution, and only then over what it is. Once a new consensus develops that one type of mortality is *not* part of nature, it becomes subject to a process analogous to birth control, comprising all the efforts deliberately to reduce mortality. This death control is thus one variable species of the larger genus, the social determinants of mortality, which include also all the social customs and structural elements that affect the death rate, even though this is not their purpose or, in some instances, their known effect.

Like all other forms of life, human beings must have a regular supply of food, and they have a better chance of surviving when living in an environment relatively free of their natural enemies, especially the microscopic organisms that cause various diseases. Each of these truisms, on closer examination, turns out to be less simple than this first statement would indicate. Man's ability to resist infection, or to remain healthy with less than the optimum amount of food, differs greatly from one individual to another; and this variation depends on both biological and social factors. And concerning the less direct influences on the death rate, it is often still more problematic where physiology ends and the culture begins.

## Individual Factors in Mortality

The organism that dies is the individual. A social analysis of mortality, thus, is an attempt to relate general determinants to the distribution in the particular population of the several personal characteristics that, to one degree or another, set each individual's relative chance of dying within a certain period. The most important are reviewed here.

### INHERITED LONGEVITY

Long life seems to depend to some degree on an inherited capacity, but whenever children remain in essentially the same social and economic situation as their parents, a similar average length of life in the two generations may be due either to a genetic proclivity or to the continued influence of the unchanged environment, or to both. What is inherited, moreover, is not a trait but a predisposition to react in certain ways to various environments, so that if these change, the significance of the inheritance may change with them. Notwithstanding these methodological difficulties—the same that were met in analyzing the heredity of fecundity—the genetic factor in mortality can be indicated in a number of ways.

Several investigators have studied the average length of life in successive generations of various families in order to see whether a trend is discernible. According to the combined results of a number of such studies, two decades ago in the United States a favorable ancestry would have added two to four years to one's expectation of life from age 25 (Dublin et al., 1949, p. 117). In contrast, all males' expectation of life from age 20 increased from 42.19 years in 1900–02 to 50.1 years in 1963. The relative insignificance of the hereditary element, however, is largely due to quite recent advances in medicine. In 1915, having long-lived parents supposedly added seven more years to one's expectation of life than the utmost that medical science could then achieve (Pearl, 1922, p. 165).[1]

---

[1] A later monograph by Pearl and his wife (1934), although now out of date, is still worth reviewing in its own terms. Nonagenarians were shown to have a significantly

Fugen, a Japanese Buddhist god, patron of those who practice "ecstatic contempla-
tion" in order to increase their length of life. Guimet Museum, Paris (*The Bettmann
Archive, Inc.*).

It is known that the incidence of some diseases varies markedly from
one race to another. Although this datum suggests that susceptibility to
them may be inherited, here again the evidence is muddied by the difficulty
of distinguishing biological from environmental factors. The first meeting
of two peoples previously isolated from one another frequently marks in
a dramatic way the effect of such race differences. For example, when the
whites took measles with them to the South Seas, it was transformed from
a relatively minor illness to a raging epidemic; and when Columbus's men
brought syphilis to Europe from the West Indies, its virulence was also
much greater among this fresh population. Such events may indicate a
genetic factor: if the constitutional immunity to any disease originally varies

---

higher percentage of longevous parents than the general population. However, the study
hardly attempted to differentiate between biological and cultural influences: in the four-
page questionnaire on which the study was based, only two questions related to social
variables. More generally, Pearl and other early investigators have been criticized for
their methodological flaws; according to a study under way in the mid-1960s at Johns
Hopkins University, the hereditary element in longevity and mortality seems to be more
questionable than Pearl asserted (Cohen, 1965).

in a population, an epidemic kills off the more susceptible, and the survivors pass on to their progeny their greater inherent resistance. It may be, however, that sometimes the relative immunity to an endemic disease is acquired not genetically but by a mild, perhaps unrecognized, case of it in infancy or childhood.

A more specific racial comparison, that between whites and Negroes in the United States, shows wide differences in both the incidence of various diseases and mortality from them. Some, but not all, of this contrast is due to the generally lower economic level of Negroes. The clearest example of a disease that is genetic in origin, sickle-cell anemia, is virtually confined to Negroes, perhaps wholly so. Kroeber, after compiling the list of such race-related diseases given here in Table 7-1, warns the reader that care is

### Table 7-1. Comparative Pathology of Negroes and Whites in the U.S., 1940.

| | DISEASES WITH HIGHER INCIDENCE | |
| --- | --- | --- |
| | AMONG NEGROES | AMONG WHITES |
| Difference definite and marked, almost certainly racial | Sickle-cell anemia Whooping cough Fibroids in womb Keloid tumors Nephritis | Diphtheria Yellow fever Hemophilia Peptic ulcer Psoriasis Lupus Trachoma Surgical suppuration |
| Difference perceptible, possibly racial | Lobar pneumonia Hypertension Cerebral hemorrhage Syphilitic heart disease Cancer of female genitalia | Scarlet fever Measles Infantile paralysis Angina pectoris Arteriosclerosis Coronary occlusion Gallstones Urinary stones Most cancers |
| Fact or cause of difference in dispute | Tuberculosis Syphilis Typhoid fever Malaria | Pernicious anemia Diabetes |

SOURCE: A. L. Kroeber, *Anthropology*, New Ed., Revised, copyright, 1923, 1948, by Harcourt, Brace and Company, Inc.; renewed 1951, by A. L. Kroeber. Reprinted by permission of the publishers.

necessary in interpreting these data. "While it is as good as certain that races differ genetically in their pathology, as in other traits, the problem is beset by so many contingencies and pitfalls that exact proof can be brought only rarely, and in general we are lucky if reasonable probabilities can be determined." As with the inheritance of longevity, the data concerning race differences indicate that genetic influences are operative but not precisely how important they are.

## SEX DIFFERENCES

Except during their childbearing years, females generally have lower age-specific death rates than males; and in modern Western societies the rule holds without this exception. The higher the age group, the higher the proportion of females usually is. For example, in the United States in 1964 the estimated sex ratio ranged from 103.6 for those aged 14 and under to 78.4 for those 65 and over. This contrast, moreover, has been increasing over the past half-century: among the white population, the female expectation of life at birth was 2.9 years greater in 1900, 3.6 in 1930, and 6.9 in 1963.

One reason for this differentiation is that as mortality declined and the relative importance of various causes of death changed, those affecting females fell off more. The bearing of children, for example, used to be a great hazard. During the 1920s, 66 women died from causes related to maternity per 10,000 live births in the U.S. Death-Registration Area. This rate was almost stable, lower than during the influenza epidemic of 1918 but slightly higher than in 1915. About one generation later, in 1957, the rate was 4.3! In other terms, there was one maternal death for every 165 births in 1915, and one per 2,300 births in 1957. This was indeed "one of the most significant achievements of modern medical science," [2] and the progress has continued since that date.

The relative decline of infectious diseases as a cause of death has also meant a marked change in sex differentials. In the mid-1950s, nearly 40 per cent of all deaths were ascribed to heart disease, and for every 100 females 178 males died from this cause. The reasons for the disparity are not well understood; it has been suggested that one factor may be the greater tension associated with male occupations, particularly as contrasted with the lack of it in a housewife's life. In the early 1920s, however, deaths from arteriosclerosis increased for both sexes but more for females, whereas deaths from hypertensive heart disease decreased for both sexes but less for females (Klebba, 1966, p. 16). In cancers, the other cause of death that has become more important in recent years, the age-adjusted death rate for the white

[2] "Advances in Maternal Health," *Progress in Health Services*, Vol. 7, No. 9, November, 1958.

population was 65 per cent higher for females in 1900, about equal for the two sexes in 1947, and 21 per cent higher for males in 1963. One reason for this reversal, presumably, is that the diagnosis and cure of the cancers most frequent among females, breast and uterus, improved faster than of those most frequent among males, digestive system and lungs (Dorn, 1956a; cf. Enterline, 1961).

Some of the sex difference in mortality, however, is almost certainly innate. The much larger proportion of males who die in infancy (and presumably also in the uterus, though here the evidence is not firm) cannot be explained by any systematic variation in the environment. Although for most adults it is difficult to distinguish biological from environmental influences, such a differentiation was made by comparing the mortality of Catholic monks and nuns engaged principally in teaching. The life patterns of these two groups were very similar, especially in the absence of sex-linked activities most relevant to mortality, namely, childbearing for females and dangerous occupations and strains for males. In these culturally standardized groups the divergence in expectation of life by sex was greater than in the population as a whole, and it had also been increasing over the past decades, suggesting that biological factors are more important than sociocultural ones in effecting the differentiation in death rates by sex. The author proposes as a hypothesis—

*Under conditions of equal stress* women may be no more resistant to the *infectious* and *contagious* diseases than men—perhaps even less so—and . . . the gains which women have been making over men in this century may be chiefly bound up with a greater constitutional resistance to the *degenerative* diseases. . . . The growing advantage of American women over men is a function of the transition from conditions when infectious and contagious diseases were the main causes of death to conditions wherein the degenerative diseases play this role (Madigan, 1957).

### SENESCENCE

The most important characteristic related to innate susceptibility to death is age. The power of self-renewal and the ability to reproduce the species, the principal features that distinguish living beings from inert matter, both decline with advancing age. We tend to think that "aging" begins some time after full adulthood, and in some contexts this is a useful interpretation of the term. Actually, physiological senescence begins before birth and continues throughout life. One index of this process is the rate at which body lesions heal. If persons of various ages sustain a wound of 20 square centimeters, under otherwise identical conditions this will heal in 20 days on the body of a child of ten, in 31 with a man of twenty, in 41 with one aged thirty, in 78 with one aged fifty, and in 100 with one aged sixty (DuNoüy, 1936, pp. 154–155). A child of ten thus typically cicatrizes a wound at five times the rate of a man of sixty.

However, the rate at which one ages, whether by this or any other index, varies widely according to life conditions. A person of any particular age combines the effects of physiological senescence, which we may take as the same for the whole of the species, with those of his particular life experience. It would be useful to separate these two elements into what has ben termed "chronologic age," or the number of years lived, and "biologic age," or the person's relative functioning capacity as determined by the sum of genetic and environmental factors, including his chronologic age (Benjamin, 1947; cf. Bain, 1945; Cowdry, 1940). Although this distinction cannot yet be finely drawn, an approximation is sometimes attempted. Whether or not a life insurance company grants a policy to any applicant, for instance, depends not only on the probability that someone of his chronologic age will die but also on such rough indications of his biologic age as his parents' longevity, his personal and medical history, his present state of health, and his occupation.

It is now possible to retard senescence to some degree, and this control may improve during the coming decades. In that case, as the proportion of aged in the population increases, the physiological and psychological characteristics typical of elderly persons might also change. We still know rather little about how much the biological process of senescence can be altered by a favorable medical, social, and psychological environment.

A priori, it is often assumed that aging is accompanied by measurable and meaningful mental deterioration,  and this negative assumption is the starting point for much of the research in gerontology. An examination of the literature reveals that most information has been obtained from senile inmates of mental institutions and homes for the aged and that the findings from such studies have been generalized to the aged at large. . . . [There has been a general] failure to control pertinent variables which may have far more influence on the experimental findings than age per se (Arnhoff, 1955).

How far can the conquest of nature go? When will the remarkable advances in medical science reach the impassable barrier? The utopian vision of Condorcet and his contemporaries—an era free from disease, in which old age and death could be postponed indefinitely—has in this century attained a certain respectability when well known personages extrapolated the growing number of actual achievements. In the words of M. G. Candau, then Director General of the World Health Organization—

If the great advances gained in science and technology are put at the service of all the people of the world, our children will live in an age from which most of the diseases our grandparents and parents took for granted will be banished. It may no longer be utopian to envisage a new chapter in the history of medicine (quoted in Dubos, 1959).

Opposed to this rosy perspective is one that emphasizes the rise of new ailments associated, actually or supposedly, with modern Western civilization—cancers from smoking and x-rays, ailments from polluted air and water, allergies from detergents and synthetics, alcoholism, and so on. Some responsible physicians, moreover, have begun to express concern about the "medicated survival" of the infirm, the mentally ill, the socially and financially dependent.

More suffering and helpless people are kept alive whom it would be kinder to allow to die. . . . Not long ago I heard a minister talk on the various freedoms he would like to see available to all mankind. After reviewing the more familiar ones, he added a new one: Freedom to die (Clark, 1958).

## Differentials in Mortality by Age

In any society a person's age and sex are important factors in the probability that he will die within that year; and with the convergence of other differentials, these physiological determinants have become relatively more significant in recent years. The **crude death rate,** or the number of deaths in a year per 1,000 persons in the midyear population, thus has the same virtues and limitations as the crude birth rate (see pp. 79–84): it is easy to calculate from data often available, but it blurs the effects of age and sex distribution on the level of over-all mortality. For a more refined analysis, age- and sex-specific rates can be calculated, and in a number of particular instances this is usual.

The shape of the curves in Figure 7-1, showing the age-specific death rates for males and females, is characteristic. Wherever modern death control has not been fully established, infancy and early childhood are dangerous periods; but for those who survive them the death rate is relatively low until senescence becomes a significant factor, at the age of forty or fifty. As the greatest advance has been in the control of infectious diseases, the sharpest drop was in the mortality of infants and young children. Even so, the probability of dying during infancy is still greater than during childhood or early adulthood. That is to say, some sort of U-shape or J-shape describes the age-specific death rates of all cultures, no matter how primitive or advanced. If one imagines superimposed on such a curve another one representing age-specific fecundity—that is, inverted to ∩—one can see why age structure can have so great an effect on population growth; the young adults who are most likely to have children are also the persons least likely to die within a given year.

**Infant and Fetal Mortality.** In any analysis of general mortality, it obviously makes good statistical sense to segregate so important a class of deaths as those of the very young and consider it separately. This is done in the **infant mortality rate,** or the number of deaths between birth and

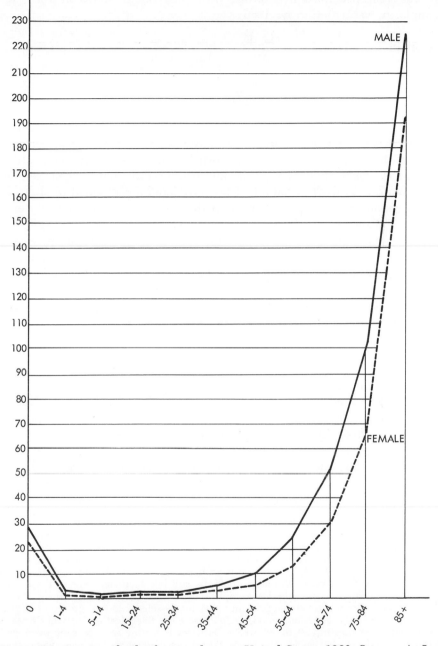

**Figure 7-1.** Age-specific death rates, by sex, United States, 1963. Source: A. Joan Klebba, *Mortality Trends in the United States, 1954–1963*, National Center for Health Statistics, Series 20, No. 2, U.S. Public Health Service, Washington, D.C., 1966, p. 8.

age one year per 1,000 live births.[3] For the United States in 1963, for example, it was (McCarthy, 1966):

$$\text{Infant mortality rate} = \frac{\text{Deaths at age one year or under}}{\text{Live births}} \times 1,000$$

$$= \frac{103,390}{41,028,000} \times 1,000 = 25.2$$

Infant mortality is high relative to that at other ages for two reasons—because a baby, if barely born alive, may not be able to remain so very long, and because any baby, even if born healthy, is especially susceptible to disease. These two causes of infant mortality have been termed **endogenous,** referring to what might be considered a postponed fetal death, and **exogenous,** referring to a death that differs from general mortality only in the age of the person affected (Bourgeois-Pichat, 1946–51). The differentiation is important in that it separates causes of death difficult or impossible to control at the present level of medical knowledge (inherent weakness of the mother or fetus, extraordinary difficulty in delivery, etc.) from those that can be prevented by modern medicine and public-health measures. The same distinction can be made in statistical terms, though only approximately, by separating deaths during the first twenty-eight days from those during the rest of the first year. The first class, **neonatal mortality,** represents that part of infants' deaths that until a few years ago was regarded as the irreducible minimum. More recently, marked improvements in obstetrics have cut down the critical period to the seven days after birth.

According to the definition recommended by the World Health Organization (WHO), **fetal mortality** is "death prior to the complete expulsion or extraction from its mother of a product of conception, irrespective of the duration of pregnancy; the death is indicated by the fact that after such separation the fetus does not breathe or show any other evidence of life." [4]

---

[3] Since both the numerator and the denominator designate these groups during any one calendar year, the ratio does not really indicate the risk of dying before one's first birthday, for some of the children born in any calendar year die the following year but still before they are one year old. That is to say, the infant mortality rate assumes a constant fertility, and a large and rapid change in the number born will introduce a significant error (see Moriyama and Greville, 1944). In most cases, however, the rate as conventionally calculated is satisfactory without adjustment. An age-specific death rate for those aged one year and under would be still less accurate, because the census count of young babies is generally less complete than the registration of births.

[4] The WHO also suggested that fetal mortality be classified into four groups according to the duration of the gestation period, as follows: early fetal deaths, 20 weeks or less; intermediate fetal deaths, 20 to 28 weeks; late fetal deaths, 28 weeks or over; and gestation period not classifiable. The term *stillbirth,* according to this recommendation, would be abandoned, and stillbirths would be classified either as late fetal deaths or neonatal deaths, according to whether any sign of life was evident after the complete expulsion of the fetus.

As is implied in the distinction between endogenous and exogenous infant mortality, deaths shortly before and shortly after birth may not be different in principle. The two types are grouped together as **perinatal mortality,** meaning deaths between the time when the fetus becomes viable to the time after birth when prenatal causes of death are no longer operative. Although usage differs, it may be that the most useful definition of perinatal mortality includes that between the twentieth week of gestation and the first week after birth.[5]

As the reader may have found this multiplicity of definitions confusing, it will be well to review the principles underlying them, for on these there is more agreement. An effort is being made to refine the natural notion, which has been the basis of most demographic rates, that human life begins with birth. In one sense, life begins with conception, and from that point on one can designate several stages of development: (1) a viable fetus, (2) birth, and (3) a time after birth when endogenous causes of death are no longer significant. The precise designation of these three stages must be somewhat arbitrary, and conventions have not yet been universally accepted. Even "birth," which is less vague than the other two, must be very precisely defined to avoid confusion; the variation at one time in the meaning of "stillbirth" used to make international comparisons somewhat dubious.

Another reason for the differences noted in definitions is that all these rates represent something of a compromise between an abstract ideal and the measure most useful with the data actually available. If five out of six fetal deaths still remain unreported, it can be questioned whether it is worth while using a refined rate incorporating such incomplete data, but some analysts nevertheless prefer to do so.

### THE LIFE TABLE

A **life table** (or, as it is sometimes called, a mortality table) shows what the probability is of surviving from any age to any subsequent age, according to the age-specific death rates prevailing at a particular time and place. This information is the basis of life-insurance rates, and the life table also has a much wider range of uses. It is assumed, as a convention, that 100,000 babies are all born on the same day, and the experience of this cohort is followed until its last surviving member finally dies. The life table does not

---

[5] Unfortunately, there are two ways of calculating the perinatal mortality *rate* (*cf.* Dorn, 1956*b*). The usual method is to relate the appropriate sum of prenatal and postnatal deaths to the number of live births, as in calculating the infant mortality rate. It makes better sense, however, to calculate perinatal mortality as a proportion of the total number of viable fetuses conceived, whether or not they survive till after the birth. The best analysis of perinatal mortality may be one based on the data available through Britain's National Health Service (Butler and Bonham, 1963).

show what will happen, but what *would* happen if the age-specific death rates remained constant. When the control of death is rapidly improving, as generally in the modern period, life tables have to be revised frequently. Sometimes they are calculated for a period of several years in order to eliminate the effect of short-term fluctuations.

A full life table, by single years of age, gives more detail than is needed for most purposes. It is often abridged as in Table 7-2, which will be used in a brief explanation of each of the columns.

The figures in column 1, the year of age, are precise; that is, 0 is the date of birth, 1 is the date of the first birthday, and so on. The first of the two figures (which sometimes is the only one given) is denoted in subsequent column headings by $x$.

The figures given in column 2 ($_nq_x$) are *not* the usual age-specific death rates but the probability of not surviving from one birthday to the next one given in column 1. (The highest probability, absolute certainty, is conventionally denoted by unity; but in order to avoid a long series of decimals, the figures in column 2 are sometimes, though not in this example, multiplied by 1,000.) Thus, of those born 2.36 per cent do not survive to age one; of those alive on their first birthday, 0.37 per cent die before they reach precise age five; and so on.

Column 3 ($l_x$) is the number surviving at precise age $x$ given in column 1. The convention, as we have noted, is to begin with a cohort, called a **radix**, of 100,000. From this figure, each successive one is obtained by subtracting the number who died in the previous interval, obtained from column 4 ($_nd_x$). Thus:

$$100,000 - 2,361 = 97,639$$
$$97,639 - 363 = 97,276$$
$$97,276 - 213 = 97,963$$

and so on.

Column 4, the number dying, is calculated for each row by multiplying the number that survived (column 3, $l_x$) by the proportion that die during the interval (column 2, $_nq_x$). Thus—

$$0.0236 \times 100,000 = 2,361$$
$$0.0037 \times 97,639 = 363$$
$$0.0022 \times 97,276 = 213$$

and so on.

Columns 5 and 6 both refer to what is called a **stationary** (or life-table) **population**, i.e., one that does not change in either its age composition or its size. While the assumptions underlying a life table are unrealistic (no immigration or emigration, the birth each year of a new cohort of 100,000, and no change in the age-specific death rates), the concept of a stationary population is often useful as a model. Much can be learned by comparing

**Table 7-2.** Abridged Life Table for the Total Population, United States, 1966

| AGE INTERVAL | PROPORTION DYING | OF 100,000 BORN ALIVE | | STATIONARY POPULATION | | AVERAGE REMAINING LIFETIME |
|---|---|---|---|---|---|---|
| PERIOD OF LIFE BETWEEN TWO EXACT AGES STATED IN YEARS (1) | PROPORTION OF PERSONS ALIVE AT BEGINNING OF AGE INTERVAL DYING DURING INTERVAL (2) | NUMBER LIVING AT BEGINNING OF AGE INTERVAL (3) | NUMBER DYING DURING AGE INTERVAL (4) | IN THE AGE INTERVAL (5) | IN THIS AND ALL SUBSEQUENT AGE INTERVALS (6) | AVERAGE NUMBER OF YEARS OF LIFE REMAINING AT BEGINNING OF AGE INTERVALS (7) |
| $x$ to $x + n$ | $nq_x$ | $l_x$ | $nd_x$ | $nL_x$ | $T_x$ | $°e_x$ |
| 0–1 | 0.0236 | 100,000 | 2,361 | 97,918 | 7,012,760 | 70.1 |
| 1–5 | .0037 | 97,639 | 363 | 389,687 | 6,914,842 | 70.8 |
| 5–10 | .0022 | 97,276 | 213 | 485,805 | 6,525,155 | 67.1 |
| 10–15 | .0021 | 97,063 | 200 | 484,864 | 6,039,350 | 62.2 |
| 15–20 | .0051 | 96,863 | 495 | 483,179 | 5,554,486 | 57.3 |
| 20–25 | .0067 | 96,368 | 641 | 480,267 | 5,071,307 | 52.6 |
| 25–30 | .0068 | 95,727 | 655 | 477,021 | 4,591,040 | 48.0 |
| 30–35 | .0086 | 95,072 | 814 | 473,419 | 4,114,019 | 43.3 |
| 35–40 | .0121 | 94,258 | 1,140 | 468,629 | 3,640,600 | 38.6 |
| 40–45 | .0186 | 93,118 | 1,728 | 461,579 | 3,171,971 | 34.1 |
| 45–50 | .0289 | 91,390 | 2,637 | 450,838 | 2,710,392 | 29.7 |
| 50–55 | .0448 | 88,753 | 3,974 | 434,417 | 2,259,554 | 25.5 |
| 55–60 | .0678 | 84,779 | 5,750 | 410,313 | 1,825,137 | 21.5 |
| 60–65 | .0978 | 79,029 | 7,731 | 376,748 | 1,414,824 | 17.9 |
| 65–70 | .1475 | 71,298 | 10,517 | 331,195 | 1,038,076 | 14.6 |
| 70–75 | .2090 | 60,781 | 12,703 | 273,065 | 706,881 | 11.6 |
| 75–80 | .2920 | 48,078 | 14,038 | 205,892 | 433,816 | 9.0 |
| 80–85 | .4167 | 34,040 | 14,185 | 134,018 | 227,924 | 6.7 |
| 85 and over | 1.0000 | 19,855 | 19,855 | 93,906 | 93,906 | 4.7 |

SOURCE: U.S. Public Health Service, *Vital Statistics of the United States, 1966*, Vol. 2, Section 5: *Life Tables*, Washington, D.C., 1962, Table 5-1.

this hypothetical population with a real one that shares some of its characteristics.[6]

Column 5 ($_nL_x$) gives the number of persons in the stationary population in the age interval indicated in column 1. A census taken of a population based on the assumptions of the life table—100,000 births annually and age-specific deaths in accordance with column 2, would on any date show, say, 480,267 persons aged 20–25.

Column 6 ($T_x$) gives the total number of years lived by the survivors in the year $x$ and all subsequent years. It is derived from column 5 by calculating a cumulative total, beginning with the highest age. For age 85 and over, thus, the two columns have the same figure, and successive figures are calculated as follows:

$$93,906 + 134,018 = 227,924$$
$$227,924 + 205,892 = 433,816$$
$$433,816 + 273,065 = 706,881$$

and so on.

Column 7 ($^0e_x$) gives the average number of years of life remaining at the beginning of the age interval or, in the usual phrase, the average life expectancy from age $x$. Column 6 ($T_x$) gives the *total* number of years to be lived by all the survivors in the cohort, and column 3 ($l_x$) gives the number of survivors in the cohort at each age; the average is calculated by dividing the total years by the number of persons. Thus,

$$7,012,760 \div 100,000 = 70.1$$
$$6,914,842 \div \phantom{0}97,639 = 70.8$$
$$6,525,155 \div \phantom{0}97,276 = 67.1$$

and so on. This, for our purposes the most important column in the life table, measures mortality conditions independent of the effect of age structure. The first figure in the column, the expectation of life at birth (70.1 years in this case), is usually the best index of mortality whenever a crude death rate is not sufficiently accurate.

Since the average life expectancy at birth is based in part on the considerable number who die during the first year, it indicates an expected life shorter than at any subsequent age. Indeed, some of the figures given in column 7 are smaller, but they indicate the expectation of life from year $x$, which increases for each row. Obviously, the total years lived is the sum of each figure in column 7 and the appropriate value for $x$. Thus—

$$70.1 + 0 = 70.1 \text{ total years lived}$$
$$70.8 + 1 = 71.8$$
$$67.1 + 5 = 72.1,$$

[6] Compare the definition of stable population, pp. 83–84. Note also the discussion of the net reproduction rate at the same place.

and so on. The **median expectation of life** (or what is sometimes called the "probable lifetime") is always greater than the average. It is the age to which a person has a 50–50 chance of living or, from birth, the age at which the original cohort of 100,000 will be reduced to 50,000. In this example, then, at age 70 (the *average* life expectation) 60.8 per cent of the original cohort is still alive (column 3); the median expectation is close to 77 or 78 years.[7]

The life table given in Table 7-2 is for the total population of the United States in 1966. Since there are appreciable differences in mortality by sex, race, occupation, and other structural dimensions, it is usual to calculate separate life tables for the appropriate segments of the population when this additional information is needed. For the same date, thus, the average life expectancy from birth (corresponding to 70.1 in Table 7-2) was as follows for the designated subpopulations of the United States (U.S. Public Health Service, 1966):

| | |
|---|---|
| Males | 66.7 |
| Females | 73.8 |
| Whites | |
|    Total | 71.0 |
|    Male | 67.6 |
|    Female | 74.7 |
| Nonwhites | |
|    Total | 64.0 |
|    Male | 60.7 |
|    Female | 67.4 |

From birth, thus, females have an average life expectation 7.1 years greater than males, and this advantage holds to some degree also from any other age in the schedule. Since women not only can expect to live longer than males of equal age but also generally marry men a few years older than they are, there are many more widows than widowers in the United States, as in most countries.

---

[7] With the life table the risks of dying at various ages are calculated in terms of a model that can be adapted to much wider applications than its original use. For example, any marriage runs the risk of dissolution either by death of one of the partners or by divorce, and as these risks can be expressed numerically they can be analyzed with a life table to give useful new data. Thus, in the United States in 1955 a marriage's average life expectancy from the date of the wedding (or the average number of years remaining until dissolution by either divorce or death) was 31.5 years; see Paul H. Jacobson, *American Marriage and Divorce*, Rinehart, New York, 1959, p. 145. The tool can be adapted to the risks of orphanhood (Gregory, 1965), the risks of pregnancy using different methods of contraception (Potter, 1966), the risks of failure in business, the risks of hospitalization (Little, 1965), and any one of dozens of other situations, whether or not these are related to demography narrowly conceived, in which rates can be calculated according to a schedule of ages or elapsed time.

## Food Requirements and Supplies

Perhaps the simplest extension from a purely demographic model to the social-economic environment relates to man's need of nutrients. In order to estimate whether there is enough food in the world, presumably one would ask for only three figures—the minimum requirements per person, the population of the world, and the total production of all types of food. None of these can be given precisely, of course, and when one links data from various disciplines—nutrition, demography, agronomy, economics— the resultant calculation must do justice to all of them. Except in the grossest terms, in fact, the equation cannot be written.

### THE INDIVIDUAL'S FOOD REQUIREMENTS

Food nourishes man in two ways, by supplying fuel for energy and warmth, and by providing the material with which the body is built, maintained, and regulated. Food requirements, thus, include both a certain amount and a certain balance among various types of nutrients. Either a deficiency in quantity or an imbalance has as its successive consequences a less than optimum well-being, sickness, and ultimately death.

An individual's calorie requirements depend on a large number of variables, among others, his age, sex, basal metabolism rate, body type, occupation and avocation, the climate he lives in, and the type of clothing he wears. In a sizable population, of course, most of these factors balance out. The Committee on Calorie Requirements of the Food and Agriculture Organization (FAO) used an arbitrarily defined "Reference Man," 25 years old, healthy and moderately active, weighing 65 kilograms (or about 144 pounds), and living in a moderate climate. This man requires 3,200 calories per day. The Committee that came to this conclusion, according to one of its members, had no disagreements among its fourteen members. "The report is, in fact, orthodox. It is unlikely that substantial changes in its recommendations will be necessary—at least in this century" (Passmore, 1963). There are, unfortunately, other orthodoxies. A moderately active, mature person, living in a temperate climate, requires, according to the Food and Nutrition Board of the U.S. National Research Council, 3,000 calories per day for a 154-pound man (thus, 200 calories less for a man weighing ten pounds more) and 2,400 per day for a 123-pound woman (MacLeod and Sherman, 1951). One cannot extend these "recommended allowances" (*not* "standards") to other countries without considering temperature and other factors, and whether they should be accepted even for the United States is disputed. A different authority recommends 18 calories per pound of ideal body weight for the average woman (or 2,214 calories per day for the 123-pound woman, rather than 2,400) and 21 calories per pound for the man (or 3,234 per day for the 154-pound man rather than 3,000) (Goodhart, 1964). According to still another authority, "the orienting philosophy behind [the National Research Council's recommendations] has been to emphasize the frequency and danger of undernutrition and to promote an abundance of food supplies" (Keys, 1951*b*). Actually, in Keys's view, caloric inadequacy is a far less significant cause of ill health in Western countries, even in times of economic depression, than overeating and obesity, and various surveys indicate that eating less than the recommended allowance is not only not detrimental but, within limits, beneficial to health.

Energy requirements are ordinarily provided mainly out of carbohydrate staples, which in wealthy countries are strongly reinforced by fats and proteins. These latter are also essential nutrients, though in what amount is not known. "It is not yet possible to state definitely a reasonable allowance for fat in the diet" (Goodhart, 1964). "The minimum daily protein requirement . . . can be approximated only crudely" (Albanese and Orto, 1964).

The optimum ingestion of other nutrients is no more determinate. The etiology of the major food-deficiency maladies (scurvy, pellagra, goiter, beriberi, and others) was established before the end of the nineteenth century, but only in the sense that certain rough dietary rules were stipulated. Scurvy, for example, was clearly described in the Ebers papyrus, which dates from about 1500 B.C. Its cause was established by Dr. James Lind of the British navy in an experiment that he later described in *Treatise on Scurvy* (1757): out of a dozen equally scorbutic members of one ship's crew, he subjected two to each of the six cures then in vogue, and the pair who were given oranges and lemons made a dramatic recovery. The active ingredient of citrus fruits was identified as vitamin C, or ascorbic acid, only in the 1920s, and about five years later it was synthesized. Scurvy is now a rare disease in developed countries, but it is probable that much subclinical ascorbic-acid deficiency exists.

The term *vitamin* was coined by Casimir Funck, a Polish chemist, in 1912. As they were isolated one after the other, vitamins were labeled with successive letters; but with the rapid expansion of knowledge only a few of these original names have remained an adequate denotation. "Vitamin B," for example, turned out to be a complex of several substances.[8] These and a number of minerals are essential elements of human diet in small amounts. With some of them, for example, calcium and vitamins A and C, the consumption of larger amounts than the minimum required seems to confer corresponding increases in well-being, while with others this apparently is not the case. Moreover, the interaction among food ele-

---

[8] The chapter on vitamins in a recent manual lists them as follows: vitamins A, C, D, E, and K, thiamine, riboflavin, niacin, pantothenic acid, the vitamin $B_6$ group, folic acid, vitamin $B_{12}$, bioflavonoids, choline, inositol, biotin, carnitine (Wohl and Goodhart, 1964, Chapter 11; *cf.* Williams, 1962).

ments means that the correct amount of any one varies also according to the amounts of others consumed (Harte and Chow, 1964).

Whether malnutrition short of starvation contributes substantially to mortality is not entirely clear. One view, to which the FAO holds in most of its publications, is that "the inadequacy of food in poor countries has always contributed directly to a high death rate." [9] But apart from infancy and childhood, when the continued growth of the body depends on good nutrition, and from certain ailments, the most important of which is tuberculosis, whether the susceptibility to disease is *directly* affected by malnutrition remains an open question. "Definitive statements on the relationship of specific dietary components to resistance to infection are difficult to make (Axelrod, 1964). On a mass scale, the effects of famine can seldom be distinguished from those of social disorder. In Nazi-occupied Holland and Greece, where the mass starvation was not accompanied by a general breakdown of society, the typical association of famine and epidemic was lacking, whereas the 1946 diphtheria epidemic in Germany, on the other hand, seemed to affect the well nourished American occupation troops as severely as the underfed German population (Keys, 1951a).

## THE WORLD'S FOOD PRODUCTION

Though it is impossible to state with great precision either the amount or the range of nutrients that the "average" person requires for maximum well-being, the rough estimates that nutritionists agree on are sufficiently accurate to fit into any equation we might construct, for all of the other terms are also most approximate. Within the framework of existent institutions and production methods, the Malthusian thesis is being validated on a world scale: population *is* tending to increase faster than the means of subsistence. If the world's numbers continue to increase at the 1965 rate, the caloric requirements will grow by more than half in 1985. If one optimistically assumes an over-all decline of 30 per cent in the fertility rate, caloric requirements will still increase by 43 per cent at that date (President's Science Advisory Committee, 1967, 1, 12). According to FAO's estimates, the total food production of the world remained static during the 1965–66 harvest year, while its population increased by some 70 million. Such global averages give only a first indication of how serious the shortages are, for the differences are enormous between rich and poor nations and, within each of them, between regions and social classes. In most underdeveloped countries improvements in agriculture have failed to keep pace with the growth in numbers. Over the period 1939 to 1965, according to FAO estimates, per capita food production declined by 2.8 per cent in the Far East (excluding Communist China, for which data are lacking; but

[9] Warren S. Thompson and David T. Lewis, *Population Problems,* 5th Ed., McGraw-Hill, New York, 1965, pp. 388–389.

Harvesting a bumper wheat crop, Washington State (*Bill Lilley*).

Hens laying eggs on production line, Georgia. They eat and drink from troughs
that refill automatically, while another conveyor belt takes away the droppings.
One man can care for 7,000 chickens with a daily production of 4,000 eggs (*Burk
Uzzle, Leviton-Atlanta*).

see pp. 674–676), by 4 per cent in Africa, and by 5.7 per cent in Latin
America. Widespread hunger would have deteriorated into gigantic famines
in the major agricultural countries except for massive shipments of food-

stuffs from such urbanized societies as the United States, Canada, and Australia. The barometer of the FAO annual reports, which on occasion has reflected an almost sanguine expectation of progress, turned gloomy again. "The world food situation," the 1966 report declared, "is now more precarious than at any time since the period of acute shortage immediately after the Second World War." The following year, it is true, the FAO asserted that "the world food and agricultural situation is now in a state of transition and hope," for by its calculation world food production per capita had increased by 0.5 per cent during 1967. Two favorable factors suggest the possibility of continuing improvement: new high-yield varieties of rice and other grains have been developed and introduced into a number of countries with startling results, and some governments are taking advantage of high agricultural prices and beginning to invest more in food production (Brown, 1968).

The enormus gap in agricultural productivity between developed and underdeveloped areas is not due merely to differences in soil or climate. Demonstration farms in various peasant countries, when cultivated under the guidance of technicians sent by such international agencies as FAO, frequently produce as much food per acre as in technically advanced countries. That is, if the best farming practices were adopted throughout the world, its present population could probably be fed at an adequate level of subsistence. But using traditional techniques, countries with three-quarters of their populations engaged in agriculture cannot feed themselves and, to one degree or another, must depend on imports from industrial nations. At the other extreme, the United States, where under a tenth of the labor force produces all of the country's food, built up a curious "farm problem"—a government subsidy to limit agricultural production in order to reduce the accelerating growth of agricultural stockpiles. These surpluses, which for several decades provided a cushion against crop failures anywhere in the world, were seriously depleted in the mid-1960s by the especially large grants and sales to agricultural countries. Some publicists started, therefore, to call for a change in American farm policy: "With surpluses dwindling and a hungry world to be fed, there's no longer any justification for a policy that restricts production and burdens taxpayers. It's time to turn the farmers loose" (Myers, 1966).

It is a paradox that industrial nations have helped feed agricultural countries, and this anomaly suggests why it is so difficult to overcome the world's food shortage. Raising the level of agricultural production is not, as it is often pictured, simpler and easier than industrialization and over-all modernization. Indeed, the two are in large part the very same process.

To analyze potential sources of a future food supply, one can divide possible developments into several types (Pirie, 1963; cf. Sukhatme, 1961):

1. Conventional approaches begin with **irrigation**, which was the basis of large population concentrations in the preindustrial era (see pp. 372–

A thoroughly eroded terrain, since reclaimed by the Tennessee Valley Authority, 1930s (*U.S. Information Agency—National Archives*).

376). To provide water for today's much larger numbers, however, is a task for an industrial society, for projects on the scale required involve much more than control of agricultural water. The World Health Organization (WHO), in commenting on the deleterious effects of African irrigation projects, referred to bilharziasis as a "man-made sickness." *A fortiori,* the large-scale **desalination** of sea water, a recourse of nations with an ample supply of cheap power, probably must wait for the development of commercial atomic energy.

**2. Fertilizers** were once provided through the "night-soil" (or human feces) collector, whose function it was to return nutrients to the farm. And in the early modern agriculture of Europe, crops were carefully balanced with livestock, whose main product was manure. But on today's scale, fertilizers in sufficient quantity must be synthesized—which implies, once again, an industrial economy.

The general distribution of fertilizers would be the quickest way to increase food production in the hungry parts of the world. . . . Except in acute emergencies, therefore, it would seem preferable to send fertilizers rather than food to areas of need, for they not only give a better return on the costs of transport but also start a useful cycle of technical development and objective thinking about the processes of agriculture (Pirie, 1963).

When land is plowed along the contour lines, each furrow catches the runoff. A correctly plowed field, Clayton County, Iowa (*Soil Conservation Service—U.S.D.A.*).

3. The traditional mode of coping with **pests and diseases** is to suffer enormous losses. For each dollar spent on the pesticides and medicines that an industrial economy can furnish and trained agronomists can administer, the return in increased production is four or five times as much.

4. **Transportation** is one of the main controls of famines, which can often be kept to local dimensions if food is shipped in promptly from more productive areas or central storehouses. The traditional famines of India, thus, were successfully combated with the railroads that the English built, and without today's imports of staples, India's ever present food shortages would indeed develop into mass starvation. To build and maintain transportation facilities adequate to the task of distributing food throughout the world is, again, a problem only an industrial society can cope with. And this is even more true concerning such subsidiary processes as canning, refrigerating, dehydrating, freezing, and so on.

5. **Ocean farming**, the **synthesis of foodstuffs** and various other unexploited or underexploited modes of producing nutrients are sufficient in combination, it has sometimes been argued, to feed not only the present world population but its projected increase for an extended period. Apart from the technical problems involved, however, one must consider the conservatism with which peoples, particularly in agrarian societies, adhere to their traditional diets. One might as well try to change the diet of

Americans, who depend on beef, pork, and fish as their main sources of essential amino acids, by pointing out that other good sources of high-quality protein, consumed with relish by some peoples, include horsemeat, dogs, rats, locusts, and snakes (Goodhart, 1964). A generation ago, at a less utopian level, a number of American enthusiasts for the soybean tried to popularize this excellent and inexpensive source of vegetable protein, but to little effect. Yet the United States, with its affluent cosmopolitan population, is probably less tied to dietary tradition than any other culture. To achieve an adequate subsistence in many countries, it would be necessary not only to furnish more food but to develop an acceptance of better food. For example,

> The Africans in general are very conservative in their habits, . . . [and they] have never achieved a satisfactory diet. Almost all those examined are short of fats, vitamins, and mineral substances, and all except those of pastoral tribes, of protein also. . . . Ignorance and social custom often operate badly; eggs and mutton are taboo for women, especially pregnant women, among some tribes in Uganda; milk is not taken by the men. . . .
> This vicious circle, malnutrition and ignorance preventing improvement, and lack of improvement increasing poverty, could never be broken without help from outside (Russell, 1954, pp. 234–236).

**6.** The improvement of peasant agriculture is impeded not only by traditional cultures but also, and perhaps even more, by the traditional **institutional structure.** The low productivity and high population density of a subsistence economy are closely interrelated. Significant proportions of the agrarian populations of many underdeveloped countries are economically surplus—in the specific sense that if these workers left the land, the amount of food produced would not be less. This "hidden unemployment," as it is sometimes called, is not corrected in a family enterprise: a peasant does not "fire" a kinsman who is not needed to work the family plot. Because of the very fact that the relation is not merely contractual, it continues even when it is no longer economically efficient. Under such circumstances, increasing labor productivity may not be a meaningful improvement; heavy population density can best be eased by building up industry and thus furnishing an alternative occupation to those willing to accept it.

In short, a certain increase in food production is possible within the framework of traditional peasant agriculture, and in some areas a portion of this has been realized. Most of the enormous improvement in Western agriculture, however, derives from its close association with an industrial economy, and in the programs suggested to raise productive standards in underdeveloped countries, it is sometimes tacitly assumed that the commodities, personnel, institutions, and even the individual drive of industrial nations are available, or can be made to appear at little or no cost.

## Disease vs. Health

That infectious diseases are the consequence of an invasion of the body by micro-organisms has been a secure datum of medical science only for a bit over a century, since the epoch-making experiments of Louis Pasteur in the 1860s. Once the cause of these ailments was known, much more effective ways were devised to control their transmission. Simply the rigorous segregation of sewage from drinking water, for example, broke the usual path of infection of such water–borne plagues as cholera, and spraying with DDT brought under control malaria and other insect-transmitted diseases. The Western pharmacopoeia now includes not only specific medicaments against a large number of germs but also antibiotics and other general anti-infection preparations. Moreover, these death-control measures, unlike Western agriculture, can be successfully exported even to primitive populations.

### DISEASES, INFECTIOUS AND OTHER

If a germ is not prevented from entering the body by public-health measures, and if it is not destroyed in the body by medicaments, will the germ cause an infection, and if so how virulent will it be?

Every infectious disease is the result of a struggle between two variables—the pathogenic powers of the bacteria on the one hand, and the resistance of the subject on the other—each of these again modified by variations in the conditions under which the struggle takes place. . . . The concepts "resistance," "immunity," and "susceptibility" are relative terms which can never be properly discussed without consideration of all modifying conditions (Zinsser *et al.*, 1940, p. 106).

These modifying conditions may include an inherited resistance to the particular disease, whether on the part of the race or of the particular individual. They may include an acquired immunity, the consequence of either an inoculation or an earlier case of the same disease. The will to live may be relevant. Variations in the environment, as in the temperature, may reduce the body's resistance. The virulence of the germ itself may be markedly increased or weakened by, for example, passage through the body of an animal of a different species.

These changes in the relation between germs and their human hosts have resulted occasionally in the disappearance of diseases, and in the appearance of new ones. Bubonic plague, which devastated Europe in the fourteenth century and struck again in the seventeenth, has not occurred in epidemic proportions anywhere in the Western world for more than a hundred years. Leprosy, similarly, was all but unknown in Europe by the seventeenth century. On the other hand, the first reliable evidence of infantile paralysis in epidemic form dates from 1840, and there are other examples of new maladies. Sometimes a terrifying plague appears briefly and then completely and inexplicably vanishes. The most remarkable example is the so-called English sweating disease, of which there is no mention either before 1485 or after 1552, but which during that short period disorganized English society (Zinsser, 1935, Chapter 5; cf. Shrewsbury, 1964).

In spite of the puzzles that such instances pose, it has been possible, especially but no longer exclusively in advanced countries, to reduce the incidence of mortality from many infectious diseases, in some cases almost to nil. As a consequence, noncommunicable causes of death (heart diseases, cancers, and "stroke," as well as accidents) have become much more significant. This change is illustrated in Table 7-3, which lists the top ten causes of death in the United States in 1900 and in 1963.

Table 7-3. Death Rates by Selected Causes, Death-Registration Area of the United States, 1900 and 1963

|  | RANK OF CAUSE | | DEATHS PER 100,000 POPULATION | |
|---|---|---|---|---|
|  | 1900 | 1963 | 1900 | 1963 |
| Influenza and pneumonia, except pneumonia of newborn | 1 | 5 | 202.2 | 37.5 |
| Tuberculosis, all forms | 2 | < 10 | 194.4 | 4.9 |
| Gastroenteritis | 3 | < 10 | 142.7 | 4.4 |
| Diseases of the heart | 4 | 1 | 137.4 | 375.4 |
| Vascular lesions affecting central nervous system ("stroke") | 5 | 3 | 106.9 | 106.7 |
| Chronic nephritis | 6 | b | 81.0 | b |
| All accidents | 7 | 4 | 72.3 | 53.4 |
| Malignant neoplasms ("cancer") | 8 | 2 | 64.0 | 151.4 |
| Certain diseases of early infancy a | 9 | 6 | 62.6 | 33.3 |
| Diphtheria | 10 | — | 40.3 | 0.0 |
| General arteriosclerosis | < 10 | 7 | — | 19.9 |
| Diabetes mellitus | b | 8 | b | 17.2 |
| Other diseases of the circulatory system | < 10 | 9 | 12.0 | 12.9 |
| Other bronchopulmonic diseases | < 10 | 10 | 12.5 | 12.3 |
| All causes |  |  | 1,719.1 | 961.9 |

SOURCE: U.S. Public Health Service, The Facts of Life and Death, Washington, D.C., 1965, Tables 14 and 15.

a Birth injuries, asphyxia, infections of newborn, ill defined diseases, immaturity, etc.

b Not comparable because of change in classification.

Today important frontiers of medical science lie somewhere beyond infections, in the difficult terrain of "morbid conditions," psychosomatic ailments, allergies, and "positive health." That in advanced countries morbid conditions now cause more deaths than infectious diseases can be interpreted in two ways. In one sense, the statement is simply a tautology, meaning no more than that with medical science we can control what we understand. At one time, for instance, the condition of the body called "fever" was regarded as the cause of much mortality; today it is interpreted as a symptom associated with the action of many different germs. What we term "heart disease" is a current example of such a composite term, and, similarly, "cancer is not a single clear-cut disease entity" but "a group of diseases, involving a multitude of possible causative factors" (U.S. Public Health Service, 1955, p. 17). That is to say, some morbid conditions are simply those diseases about which we know too little either to effect cures or to classify, except in such a composite grouping.

Or, to make the same point in a different way, the category of diseases known as "chronic" is usually defined operationally simply in terms of their duration, either as a morbid condition lasting for three months or more (U.S. National Health Survey) or as one that is permanent, non-reversible, or requiring a long period of care (Commission on Chronic Illness). Once it is known what causes a morbid condition, however, in many cases it is no longer chronic in this sense; and this can be so whether the cause is genetic (hyperthyroidism) or environmental (pellagra). In the recent past a considerable number of both types of chronic diseases have become subject to therapy, either wholly or in part (Seegal, 1950).

The greater importance of morbid conditions as causes of death may be due, however, not merely to ignorance but to inherent, irremovable weaknesses in the human body. As more and more of the controllable causes of death are brought under control, the residual group acquires a greater and greater relative importance. Cures for infectious diseases effected a sharp reduction in infant and child mortality, and an increase in life expectancy to ages when organic senescence is significant. Thus, although heart diseases have caused fewer deaths at younger ages, at ages 35 and over (males) or 75 and over (females) there was no improvement in specific death rates (Figure 7-2).

The trend in the death rates from cancers (Figure 7-3), however, has been generally upward for all age groups (males) or decreasing very slowly for some age groups (females). (The sudden jump in the rates for those aged 1–24 years in Figure 7-3 is spurious, the consequence of a new classification of malignant neoplasms in 1949.) There has been a substantial increase in deaths from cancers in many countries, particularly among males aged over 45 years (Table 7-4). Even for this especially susceptible category, however, the incidence and trend varied considerably according to site: in every country the very high rates of death from lung cancer increased, but

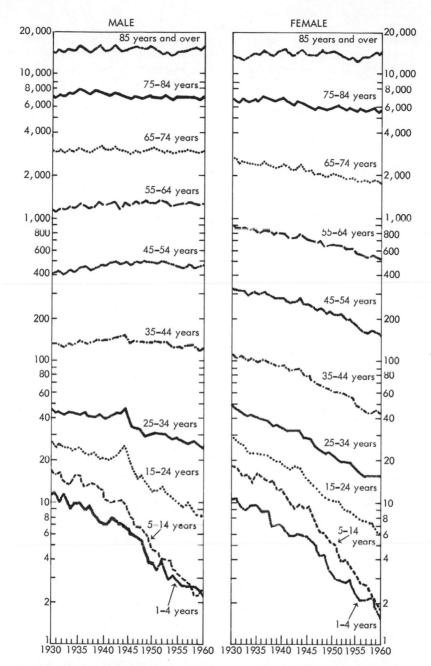

**Figure 7-2.** Rates per 100,000 population of deaths from major cardiovascular-renal diseases, by age and sex, white population of the United States, 1930–1960. Source: U.S. National Center for Health Statistics, *The Change in Mortality Trend in the United States,* Vital and Health Statistics, Series 3, No. 1, U.S. Public Health Service, Washington, D.C., 1964, Figure 10A.

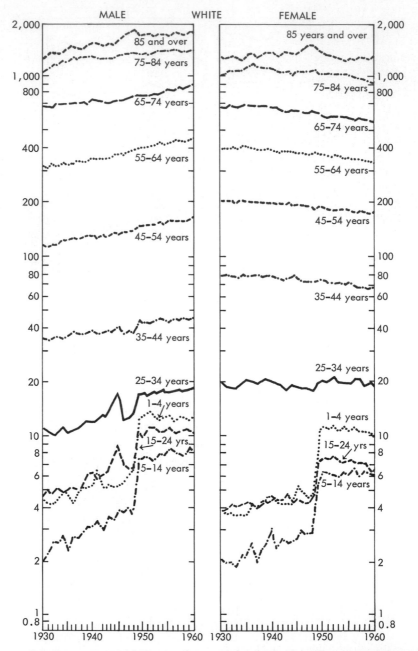

**Figure 7-3.** Rates per 100,000 population of deaths from malignant neoplasms, by age and sex, white population of the United States, 1930–1960. Source: U.S. National Center for Health Statistics, *The Change in Mortality Trend in the United States*, Vital and Health Statistics, Series 3, No. 1, U.S. Public Health Service, Washington, D.C., 1964, Figure 11A.

Table 7-4. Rates [a] per 100,000 Population of Deaths from Malignant Neoplasms Among Males Aged 45–64, Selected Countries, 1960–61 and Per Cent Change from 1952–53

| | ALL SITES | | LUNG AND BRONCHUS | | LEUKEMIA | | PANCREAS | | STOMACH | |
|---|---|---|---|---|---|---|---|---|---|---|
| | RATE 1960–61 | CHANGE FROM 1952–53 | RATE 1960–61 | CHANGE FROM 1952–53 | RATE 1960–61 | CHANGE FROM 1952–53 | RATE 1960–61 | CHANGE FROM 1952–53 | RATE 1960–61 | CHANGE FROM 1952–53 |
| Canada [b] | 251.1 | +4 | 66.1 | +38 | 7.7 | −7 | 15.3 | +15 | 33.8 | −29 |
| Denmark | 272.3 | +6 | 79.8 | +33 | 10.9 | +16 | 14.3 | +31 | 39.0 | −27 |
| England and Wales | 362.6 | +5 | 169.5 | +22 | 7.5 | +10 | 13.5 | +9 | 51.3 | −15 |
| France | 336.2 | +13 | 62.6 | +56 | 8.9 | +22 | N.A. | N.A. | 43.3 | −18 |
| Germany, Federal Republic | 308.8 | +8 | 96.9 | +34 | 9.1 | +18 | 11.2 | +33 | 67.3 | −17 |
| Israel (Jewish population) | 209.4 | +7 | 42.6 | +59 | 14.0 | +77 | 18.0 | +35 | 36.5 | −20 |
| Italy | 300.7 | +16 | 71.2 | +74 | 9.0 | +30 | 7.8 | +30 | 69.4 | −13 |
| Japan | 295.2 | +6 | 22.5 | +139 | 4.4 | +76 | 8.3 | +98 | 157.0 | −6 |
| Norway | 212.7 | −2 | 36.9 | +54 | 8.6 | −23 | 10.8 | −8 | 48.9 | −35 |
| Portugal [c] | 223.2 | +16 | 23.3 | +23 | 6.0 | +22 | N.A. | N.A. | 73.3 | +12 |
| Sweden | 205.8 | >0.5 | 36.6 | +22 | 10.2 | +2 | 14.2 | +15 | 39.4 | −26 |
| United States, White | 278.0 | +5 | 86.4 | +34 | 7.9 | +33 | 16.6 | +11 | 19.3 | −32 |
| Nonwhite | 369.9 | +12 | 96.3 | +59 | 5.1 | +51 | 23.3 | +26 | 45.6 | −22 |

SOURCE: Metropolitan Life Insurance Company, *Statistical Bulletin*, 47 (1966), 1–13.
[a] Age-adjusted to United States census population, 1940.
[b] The 1960–61 data include Yukon and Northwest Territories, and the 1952–53 data do not.
[c] The change is from base year of 1955.

in every country except one the generally lower rates for stomach cancer decreased. Some of the variation among countries may be due to differences in reporting and classifying deaths, but the over-all similarity is noteworthy.

### DEFINITIONS OF DISEASE

The biological view of disease is manifestly incomplete. Sometimes the infection or physiological state listed on a death certificate brings an end to life only because of a particular social setting. Medicine is not merely an applied physical science but also a service distributed, like any other, in accordance with the contours of a country's social structure. Its efficacy depends in part on a number of nonmedical factors, of which one is how the culture defines disease.

Among many primitive peoples the cause of death, as of illness or misfortune, is sorcery. When a sample of Zulu under forty-five were asked whether they had ever been bewitched, a sizable number replied in the affirmative, especially those who scored low on tests of general, cardio-vascular, and psychological health (Scotch and Geiger, 1963–64). Concepts of health and therapy are based on the physiology accepted in a culture (Polgar, 1962; Opler, 1963). Since among the Yap Islanders intestinal worms are thought to be a necessary element of the digestive process, Yap parents are not disturbed if their children have worms (most do) but only if they do not. Among Spanish Americans in the United States, diseases are de-fined according to an amalgam of medieval Spanish lore, Indian and Anglo folk beliefs, and modern medicine. An illness may be the work of a "witch," and particularly chronic ailments are likely to be seen as "punishment" for sin (Saunders, 1954; Samora, 1961). In "Regionville," the disguised name of a town in the United States, a persistent cough, swollen ankles, a chest or back pain, are often perceived simply as nuisances. A low-income house-wife felt she would look "silly" seeing a physician about a backache. "My mother always had a backache, as long as I can remember, and didn't do anything about it. It didn't kill her either. . . . That's just something you have, I guess" (Koos, 1954, p. 34).

Belief systems that compete with modern medicine are not necessarily dissipated in a middle-class environment of an industrial country. Most Christian Scientists, who hold that all disease is "error," are moderately well educated, as well, it would seem, as many of the patients of chiro-practors and naturopaths; and certainly those who spend months or years in psychoanalysis have sizable incomes. As not even the most efficient medicine can eliminate illness and death, competing faiths will never lack clients.[10] Yet it may be true that "superstitions" of this type are more com-mon among primitives and, in advanced societies, among the lower classes;

[10] Cf. Kingsley Davis, *Human Society*, Macmillan, New York, 1950, pp. 564–586.

thus, a *portion* of the social-economic differences in mortality probably derives from the greater readiness of the better educated to accept soundly based medical advice. "Medicine is part of the value system of the higher social classes" (Watts, 1966).

## HEALTH AND MORBIDITY

With the reduction in early death has come a tendency to conceptualize "health" not merely in negative terms, as the physical condition that inhibits mortality, but also positively. WHO has made the distinction explicit: "Health is a state of complete physical, mental, and social well-being, and not merely the absence of disease or infirmity." Such a positive definition, however attractive it may be as an ethical norm, involves logical and statistical puzzles that are yet to be solved.

The death rate and the average life expectancy, certainly meaningful indexes of a population's level of health, were almost the only ones ever used until the 1930s. It is true, of course, that there can be a wide discrepancy between either of these and morbidity. Some diseases with virtually no effect on mortality may bring about a considerable decline in efficiency, a high degree of discomfort, or other impairments of well-being. The common cold, for instance, is not a direct cause of death, but it is a leading reason for absenteeism among school children and industrial workers. Trachoma, an infection of the eye prevalent in the Near East, is another example; those afflicted with it and not treated eventually become blind, but they do not die appreciably earlier than their uninfected neighbors. Blindness is one example of what is called a "permanent total disability"; the very term emphasizes that life can continue for a period with well-being markedly below the optimum level. It would be useful, then, to devise other measures of health, in order to supplement mortality statistics. Any such alternative would be difficult to apply with the grossly inadequate morbidity data presently available, but this deficiency could be remedied in the future. A more significant obstacle is to define "health" in terms that make it possible to collect meaningful statistics. Death is a precise event, occurring only once for each person and at a time that can be specified fairly exactly. It is hard, on the other hand, even for the person affected or for a physician always to distinguish a morbid condition precisely from acceptable good health.

Cross-cultural comparisons in level of health are still more precarious. Illness or disability is typically penalized by the loss of one's function, income, prestige, and so on, but the severity of the penalty varies greatly from one society to another. Moreover, each individual's state of health depends in part on his personality; he may imagine he has diseases and produce real symptoms, or he may ignore actual impairments and function efficiently in spite of them.

It is possible to compile morbidity data from existent medical records, as collected by physicians, clinics and hospitals, or health-insurance plans of one type or another. However, any such data have an obvious flaw. The incidence of disease as measured in medical records depends on the existence of the physicians who compiled them; and in this sense the more medical facilities that are available, the higher is the incidence and thus the lower the apparent level of health. (This is one example of the recurrent difficulty in interpreting the historical record of any social deficiency: typically measures taken to control it and the quality of the data improve together, so that we are likely to interpret the trend as a decline from an idyllic past when everything was perfect—in the sense that nothing imperfect was recorded.)

If the state of health is to be measured independently of the differential access to medical care, the index cannot be a byproduct of existent records. It was not until very recently, however, that special health surveys were made. In 1949, in an effort to improve the morbidity statistics then available in the United States, a National Committee on Vital and Health Statistics was established, and a number of important local studies of health conditions followed. In 1956 Congress passed an act under which the U.S. Surgeon General is authorized to gather data regularly on the health of the whole country's population. In this continuing Health Household-Interview Survey, the concept of morbidity is defined as "a departure from a state of physical or mental well-being, resulting from disease or injury, of which the affected individual is aware." Similarly, "illness" is defined as a period when a person considers himself to be "sick" or "injured." [11] However inaccurate these subjective reports may be in one sense, they undoubtedly reflect fairly precisely the behavior of the respondents. A man must be quite sick or disabled before he is deprived completely of choice of action, and, short of that state, the way he himself defines his health is an important determinant of what he does.

These subjective reports are supplemented, moreover, by a periodic Health Examination Survey made by physicians of a sample of the population. Its purpose is not to prescribe therapy, but only to provide comparable national estimates of the incidence of important diseases for which accurate and simple diagnostic criteria exist. Because of its high cost, it must be limited to a relatively small sample, which is further restricted by the fairly large number of persons who refuse to be examined.

During the few years that the National Health Survey has been in existence, it has only begun to grapple with the difficult conceptual and methodological problems inherent in its work. As the third element of its function, the service conducts its own methodological studies (Nisselson

[11] U.S. Public Health Service, *Origin and Program of the U.S. National Health Survey* and *Concepts and Definitions in the Health Household-Interview Survey*, Series A-1 and A-3, Health Statistics from the U.S. National Health Survey, Publications 584-A1 and 584-A3, Washington, D.C., 1958.

and Woolsey, 1959; Cartwright, 1959, 1963). To measure precisely and for the whole country the economic cost of illness and disability, for instance, requires a new combination of several types of noncomparable data—gross national product, attitude surveys, physicians' diagnoses, census classifications, and concepts specific to the survey itself.

Another measurement of health, both mental and physical, is made by the U.S. Army when it checks whether those drafted are suited for combat duty—thus, for a function considerably more demanding than many civilian occupations. The population so tested, moreover, is not wholly representative of young American males, because it excludes those who volunteered and were accepted (who are qualified by definition) and those deferred on grounds other than health (who may be qualified in higher proportion), but the results were disturbing nonetheless (Table 7-5).

Table 7-5. Percentage Distribution of Combined Results of Pre-induction and Induction Examinations of Draftees, by Army Area, United States, 1965

| ARMY AREA | QUALI-FIED | DISQUALIFIED | | | | |
|---|---|---|---|---|---|---|
| | | TOTAL | ADMIN-ISTRATIVE REASONS | MENTALLY DISQUAL-IFIED[a] | MEDI-CALLY DISQUAL-IFIED | MENTALLY AND MEDI-CALLY DIS-QUALIFIED |
| First [b] | 48.9 | 51.1 | 1.7 | 16.4 | 30.5 | 2.5 |
| Second [c] | 51.8 | 48.2 | 1.4 | 16.5 | 26.8 | 3.5 |
| Third [d] | 40.4 | 59.6 | 0.9 | 33.9 | 21.5 | 3.3 |
| Fourth [e] | 47.3 | 52.7 | 1.2 | 23.5 | 25.4 | 2.6 |
| Fifth [f] | 58.0 | 42.0 | 1.7 | 12.0 | 27.4 | 0.9 |
| Sixth [g] | 51.4 | 48.6 | 3.3 | 12.1 | 31.8 | 1.4 |
| Outside Zone of Interior [h] | 34.1 | 65.9 | 1.8 | 46.8 | 12.8 | 4.5 |

SOURCE: U.S. Army, Office of the Surgeon General, *Supplement to Health of the Army,* "Results of the Examination of Youths for Military Service, 1965," 21 (July 1966), 25.

[a] Includes both those who failed the Armed Forces Qualification Test (or its Spanish equivalent), a mental test, and those classified in an aptitude test as "Trainability Limited."

[b] Connecticut, Maine, Massachusetts, New Hampshire, New Jersey, New York, Rhode Island, Vermont.

[c] Delaware, District of Columbia, Kentucky, Maryland, Ohio, Pennsylvania, Virginia, West Virginia.

[d] Alabama, Florida, Georgia, Mississippi, North Carolina, South Carolina, Tennessee.

[e] Arkansas, Louisiana, New Mexico, Oklahoma, Texas.

[f] Colorado, Illinois, Indiana, Iowa, Kansas, Michigan, Minnesota, Missouri, Nebraska, North Dakota, South Dakota, Wisconsin, Wyoming.

[g] Arizona, California, Idaho, Montana, Nevada, Oregon, Utah, Washington.

[h] Alaska, Hawaii, Guam, Mariana Islands, Puerto Rico, Panama Canal Zone, and Virgin Islands.

Since data on health are by their very nature inferior to those on mortality or fertility, some demographers have been reluctant to extend the domain of their discipline to include this new territory. Others have argued persuasively that the study of such qualitative characteristics of populations is just as important as the analysis of quantitative data (Linder, 1967; Lindhardt, 1959; Feldman, 1958). Indeed, as deaths become concentrated in the older ages, the illnesses of a nation's workers constitute in one sense a more important datum than mortality.

## Accidents, Crime, and War

The men who compile statistics on mortality classify some deaths into a strange-sounding category called "nonbiological." If a man who is run over by a car or shot by a rifle dies, it is obviously because some essential portion of his body no longer functions, but this failure was effected *directly* neither by lack of nutrients nor by a disease. Thus, deaths from this third broad class of causes may depend less on the efficiency of medical facilities than on social and political controls. And at a deeper level such controls depend in part on how accidents, crime, and war are perceived—whether as part of nature or to some extent subject to man's will.

### ACCIDENTS

What is perceived as an accident, the reaction of a society to it, and the types of record kept vary considerably from one culture to another; it is convenient to restrict the discussion to one. In the United States some 50 million persons, or over a quarter of the population, were injured in accidents in each year of the mid-1960s. The death rate was lower than at the beginning of the century (see Table 7-3, p. 223), but rising fairly rapidly. In 1966, an estimated 112,000 persons lost their lives; the rate per unit of population had increased by 4 per cent from the year before and by 13 per cent from five years earlier.

Of the three broad types of accidents, those occurring at the place of work account for only some 15 per cent of the total injuries. Industrial mishaps were halved during a third of a century, in part because of the sizable shift to less dangerous office work, but in part also because public controls forced factory owners to set appropriate safety standards.

Deaths and injuries from accidents in the home have increased, but analysis is hampered by the absence of pertinent data. Regulations exist for the construction of new buildings, the maintainence of tenant-occupied residences, the manufacture of electrical and some other household equipment, and so on, but in general the privacy of the home guarantees each adult the right to determine the safety of the enviroment in which he and his children live.

The principal rise was in deaths from automobile and motorcycle accidents. Facilities of all types—roads, signal systems, traffic police, driver training, etc.—have not kept pace with motor vehicles, whose number rose some 27 million in 1930 to 86 million in 1964, plus the 985,000 motorcycles registered at the latter date. In the 1960s the accident rate went up faster than the vehicle-miles traveled. A popular exposé of automobile manufacturers' evident indifference to safety features, Ralph Nader's *Unsafe at Any Speed,* helped induce Congress to move toward government controls. Indeed, since juries had proved willing to hold the manufacturers liable for deaths in unsafe cars, the industry needed federal regulation for its own protection. Before this policy can have much effect, however, the almost total lack of data, apart from the number of deaths, will have to be repaired.

It is hardly a complicated matter to conceive what basic national data ought to be collected: rates for deaths, injuries, and accidents; geographical and temporal distribution of such; types of vehicles involved; types of drivers involved; types of roadway and environmental failures. That would be a beginning. Most of the data could be gathered by standard sampling techniques (Moynihan, 1966).

### MURDER AND SUICIDE

Crime statistics are notoriously inadequate, and this is especially so when an analysis is attempted across cultural lines. In a society lacking efficient law enforcement, the record of crimes committed, not to say data on arrests and imprisonment, will give no clue to the state of civil order. The American West at its most rambunctious can be exemplified by Nevada, an area with few natural attractions to in-migrants apart from the gold and silver booms. The men attracted to raw mining towns were not by and large what one would term responsible citizens; the state's newspapers carried almost daily accounts of murder on the streets. And yet, according to the census of 1870, during the year ending on June 1 of that year, only 132 persons had been convicted of any crime, and on that date only 99 were in prison—figures that, compared with a population of more than 40,000, might suggest a thoroughly law-abiding state. The truth was, of course, that law-enforcement agents were too few, often too weak, and sometimes too dishonest to protect citizens even against murder.

Homicide is a subject, moreover, that social scientists have found remarkably unsusceptible to analysis. A generally law-abiding person who commits murder under emotional stress, a psychopath, a professional killer for organized crime—these are not individuals who can easily be fitted into the social categories with which a sociologist works. Each year in the mid-1960s there were some 8,500 reported murders in the United States, or only slightly fewer than the deaths from all forms of tuberculosis. The number has been rising.

Even in countries with a good registration system, the accuracy of suicide data varies widely. Religious and other cultural inhibitions induce an indeterminate, but sometimes probably sizable, amount of underreporting.[12] According to figures assembled by WHO on the thirteen countries with 1,000 or more reported suicides in 1963–64, suicide rates showed an increase in many countries (Table 7-6). In only four of the thirteen, Austria, Hun-

Table 7-6. Reported Suicide Rates, Selected Countries, 1962–63 and Change from 1952–53

| | RATE PER 100,000 POPULATION, 1962–63 | | PER CENT CHANGE FROM 1952–53 | |
|---|---|---|---|---|
| | MALES | FEMALES | MALES | FEMALES |
| Hungary | 35.5 | 14.1 | +34[a] | −24[a] |
| Austria | 29.5 | 11.1 | +3 | −19 |
| Sweden | 24.0 | 8.8 | >0.5 | +21 |
| Germany (West) | 23.1 | 10.4 | 0[b] | +3[b] |
| Japan | 21.3 | 14.3 | −22 | −19 |
| France | 20.8 | 6.2 | 0 | +9 |
| Australia | 20.7 | 9.9 | +33 | +80 |
| United States | | | | |
| White | 18.0[c] | 6.7[c] | +10 | +49 |
| Nonwhite | 9.6[c] | 2.7[c] | +33 | +80 |
| Poland | 16.6 | 3.5 | +58[d] | +46[d] |
| Belgium | 16.2 | 6.4 | −1[a] | +14[a] |
| England and Wales | 12.7 | 7.9 | +8 | +39 |
| Canada | 12.6 | 3.9 | +9[e] | +11[e] |
| Italy | 7.1 | 2.9 | −25[f] | −17[f] |

SOURCE: Metropolitan Life Insurance Company, "International Rise in Suicide," *Statistical Bulletin,* 48 (1967), 4–7.

[a] Change from 1954–55.
[b] Excludes Saarland for 1952–53.
[c] Excludes New Jersey for 1962–63.
[d] Change from 1955–56.
[e] Excludes Yukon and Northwest Territories for 1952–53.
[f] Change from 1952.

gary, Italy, and Japan, was there a decline from the 1952–53 rates for males or females. The highest rate in 1963–64, 35.5 per 100,000 population recorded for Hungarian males, was up more than a third over the earlier

[12] "For some time, some reasonable men have rejected the use of 'public,' or even any form of statistical, data for the study of suicide" (Wilkins, 1967). Those who use the figures recorded typically offer no defense for them except that nothing better exists.

date. In most of the countries with an increase, it was especially great among youth; in the United States suicide has alternated with homicide as the third-ranking cause of death (with accidents first and cancer second) in the 15–24 age group. A sharp increase occurred among nonwhite Americans between the two dates, but their death rate from this cause still remained only half that among whites.

## WAR

Over the centuries the deadliness of weapons has increased considerably, and to the extent that this is the decisive factor, the number of casualties should have gone up proportionately. According to one reckoning, thus, the proportion of the armed forces of four major European powers that were killed or wounded increased from less than 5 per cent in the thirteenth and fourteenth centuries to more than 16 per cent in the nineteenth (Sorokin, 1937, p. 337). By another estimate, on the contrary, military casualties decreased from about 30–50 per cent of the armed forces in the Middle Ages to about 6 per cent in World War I (Wright, 1942, 1, 242). One reason for such divergencies, obviously, is that military data are not only sparse but systematically falsified. An account deserving no credence at all was, in Napoleon's phrase, "false as a bulletin," and his own reports fit the pattern (Dumas and Vedel-Petersen, 1923, p. 22).

Although the data are too poor to make precise comparisons over several centuries, one can reasonably assert that there has been a downward trend in the human cost of war if we include in this class also deaths from war-related disease. Before the development of modern surgery, a serious wound was more or less equivalent to death, and in the past the epidemics that wars stimulated were deadlier than battles. Zinsser (1935) has a chapter entitled, "On the influence of epidemic diseases on political and military history, and on the relative unimportance of generals." Disease was the decisive factor in many of the wars of the preindustrial world  in the Crusades, in the struggle between Catholics and Protestants during the Reformation, in the wars of the Napoleonic period (particularly the disastrous retreat from Moscow), in colonial wars (independent Haiti was established mainly because 22,000 of the 25,000 invading French troops died of yellow fever).

Sorokin's main thesis, that war is especially characteristic of modern, rationalized, so-called "sensate" societies, is questionable. Industrialism spread from England during the nineteenth century, and its rise coincided with a phenomenon unheard of in the annals of Western civilization—a century of peace in Europe. From 1815, the end of the Napoleonic wars, to 1914, the beginning of World War I, "apart from the Crimean war— a more or less colonial event—England, France, Prussia, Austria, Italy, and Russia were engaged in war among each other for altogether only

Assembling place for wounded, Savage Station, Virginia, June 27, 1862 (*The Bettmann Archive, Inc.*).

eighteen months. A computation of comparable figures for the two preceding centuries gives an average of sixty to seventy years of major wars in each." [13] To equate industrialism with belligerence is obviously inadequate.

One can distinguish three types of military conflict—absolute war, in which the annihilation of the enemy is sought without rules; instrumental war, in which the cost of gaining access to values that the enemy controls is calculated against possible benefits; and agonistic fighting, which is very closely regulated by strict observance of rules (Speier, 1952, pp. 223–229). Such a social definition of the purpose of a war—annihilation of the enemy, relative advantage (economic or other), or glory—has a much greater effect on mortality than the efficacy of the weapons used.

Absolute war is waged at all levels of society—among certain primitive peoples, for whom this is a way of life (Wright, 1942, Vol. 1, Appendixes 9, 10, and 13); among advanced civilizations, particularly against enemies defined as "savages" or "infidels"; and among present-day totalitarian powers. By the twelfth century, when Sorokin's figures begin, the social controls of feudal society had been established in Europe; wars were fought for limited aims and, when Christians opposed other Christians according to the code of chivalry. With the breakdown of feudalism, this chivalric norm disappeared, and the religious and civil conflict of the following cen-

[13] Karl Polanyi, *The Great Transformation*, Rinehart, New York, 1944, p. 5.

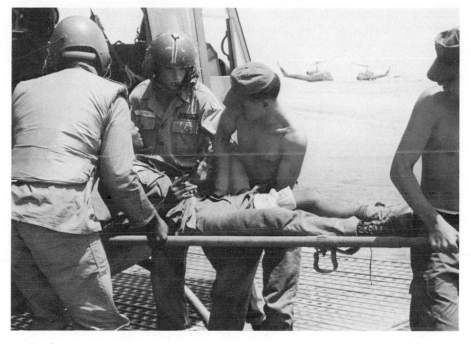

Medical care in the Vietnam War: a wounded man is being evacuated by helicopter to a field hospital (*U.S. Army Photograph*).

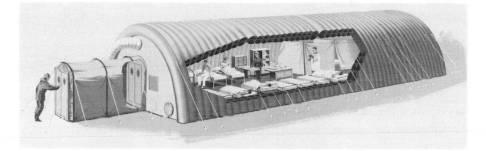

A MUST (Medical Unit Self-Contained Transportable) Unit comprises three compact elements. The shipping container, when unfolded, serves as a modern facility for surgery; the inflatable shelter, with all basic hospital ward equipment, can accommodate twenty combat casualties; the self-contained utility system provides electric power, air-conditioning, heating, hot and cold running water, and waste-water disposal (*U.S. Army Photograph*).

turies took a much greater toll. In the nineteenth century, with bourgeois industrial society well established in Europe, a new code—the balance-of-power system—effectively limited warfare and mortality from it.

The military conflicts since 1914 have been more devastating principally because the international structure of the nineteenth century has broken down. In the two world wars, regulations of various kinds have successively been abrogated—concerning places (open cities, etc.), concerning weapons (tanks, poison gas, atomic bombs), concerning forms (declaration of war, treatment of prisoners), and concerning values (setting limits to the spoliation of property or of persons, etc.).

Comparing the total (military and civilian) casualties in the two world wars, we find that the estimated number of dead increased from 9.7 to 54.8 million and of wounded from 21.1 to 35.0 million.[14] This greater mortality was concentrated among the nationals of only a few countries, particularly Germany, Poland, and the Soviet Union, whereas for the other European belligerents World War II proved to be considerably less deadly than World War I. In the case of France, for example, military casualties amounted to about 200,000, or about one-seventh of those in 1914–18 (Vincent, 1946); France's total loss of life due to World War II, including both direct and indirect mortality, amounted to about 1,130,000, which was made up in a few years by the unusually high postwar fertility. This decline in casualties was due in part to the improvement in military technology, with which the Nazi armies were really able to conduct a "lightning war."

In Germany, from one world war to the next, the number of military dead increased by about half (from 2,037,000 to 3,050,000), but the number of civilian dead by more than four times (from 500,000 to 2,050,000). Of the approximately 25 million adults killed in the Soviet Union during the war of 1941–45, more were civilians (some 15 million) than soldiers (see pp. 663–665). These figures illustrate what is perhaps the most important change that total war has effected with respect to mortality—the all but complete disappearance of the prior distinction between military and civilians as legitimate targets. Indeed, with the most devastating of modern weapons, the hydrogen bomb, such a distinction is hardly possible.

What would be the effects on the American population of a nuclear attack? No one knows, of course, but it is possible to speculate against a background of relevant knowledge. Two of the patterns of bombing analyzed by defense experts, depending on whether the raids were primarily at military targets or at both military and industrial targets, might result in an over-all fatality ranging from 18 to 30 per cent of the population. Since either kind of attack would be directed mainly at urban centers, the sectors of the population concentrated there—Catholics, Negroes, highly educated, and so on—would presumably suffer even greater losses than these figures. American institutions would be transformed by the post-attack manpower shortages. Greater public controls would have to be substituted, at least for a period, for the free market in goods and services; larger welfare

14 German Federal Government, Press and Information Office, *Germany Reports* (Wiesbaden, 1953), pp. 101–103. For World War I, *cf.* also Dumas and Vedel-Petersen, 1923.

One of the main squares of Rotterdam, before (above) and after (below) the Germans bombed it in 1940. This was not a military action but rather a punishment of the Dutch for having resisted the Nazis' invasion of their country (*Royal Dutch Airlines—KLM*).

payments would demand heavier taxes to pay for them; with the state responsible both for the care of orphans and for urgent stimulation of greater fertility, the family system would be changed appreciably (Heer, 1965).

## The Etiology of Mortality

In surveying some of the main facts concerning nutrition and food production, diseases and their control, and the incidence of nonbiological mortality, we have been discussing three main categories of the causes of death. Since death is typically the effect of a number of factors, both intrinsic and extrinsic, whether to assign one or another as *the* cause is to some degree an arbitrary decision.

### "THE" CAUSE OF DEATH

As specified by a physician and later included in a nation's vital statistics, each cause of death is ideally in accordance with the International Statistical Classification of Diseases, Injuries, and Causes of Death. This schedule has evolved gradually over the past century—from 1853, when the First Statistical Congress commissioned two of its leading members to work up an improvement in the alphabetical list of causes of death then in general use, to January 1, 1968, when the Eighth Revision went into effect. The categories in the Seventh Revision had included 612 diseases and morbid conditions, 153 types of injury, and 189 types of lesion (WHO, 1957). In 1965, after a good deal of preparatory work (*cf.* U.S. National Center, 1964a), 86 delegates representing 36 member states of WHO met in Geneva to prepare a new edition. The changes incorporated knowledge gained in the interim (for example, concerning viral diseases) and new concepts (for example, a different classification of heart diseases). Several disputes, however, were not resolved. The United States committee hoped to classify congenital defects in a manner that would facilitate the study of human genetics, but its proposal was rejected. The classification of mental illness in the Seventh Revision had not been accepted by the American Psychiatric Association for use in the mental hospitals of the United States, and "irreconcilable differences in concept and diagnostic practices arose in discussions with psychiatrists of other countries" concerning this class of diseases in the Eighth Revision (Moriyama, 1966).

While the International Classification is an enormously valuable instrument, to which some of the best epidemiologists and demographers over the past century have devoted much thought, in analytical terms it remains inelegant. As a practical statistical tool, it reflects compromises made with the current state of medical knowledge, international differences in usage, and the greater or lesser relevance, with respect to any category, of medicine, anatomy, or law. The physician's job is to prevent death, and his attention is therefore typically fixed on the proximate factor involved in it—in the words of a death certificate, the "disease or condition directly leading to death." The standard form specifically instructs him *not* to designate "the mode of dying, e.g. heart failure"; and if he lists as the cause of death simply the breakdown of an organ, without specifying the external agent or the type of malfunctioning responsible, this is only because the limits either of medical knowledge or of his examination do not permit him to do more.

"The" cause of death, so conceived, is what the physician writes on the certificate he signs. It has been generally recognized that this classification is quite inadequate in a number of ways, and some hoped that the Eighth Revision would shift from single diseases to disease-complexes, for example, coronary disease with diabetes rather than either one separately (e.g., Spiegelman *et al.*, 1958). Such a practice would have been an extension of the present one, by which the certifying physician is instructed to report "other significant conditions contributing to the death but not related to the disease or condition causing it." In fact, however, this proposal was rejected "as an arbitrary and inflexible solution to a problem which should be handled by multiple-cause coding" (Moriyama, 1966).

## SOME OTHER CAUSES OF DEATH

How far the introduction of disease-complexes might have led can be cogently suggested by a hypothetical case. Let us suppose that a number of persons were in an accident and sustained identical injuries. Two-thirds recovered after being treated. In most types of analysis this fact alone would make us hesitate in describing the accident as the "cause" of death for the others. Of those that died, let us suppose, one was an elderly man, whose lesions healed too slowly; one had a chronically weak heart; one had had an appendectomy, the scar of which released a thrombus; one, a Negro, was denied admission to the nearest hospital. For all these persons the accident would be listed as "the" cause of death; and of the other circumstances and those like them, some might be included as contributory factors, but many would not be mentioned or even known to the person compiling the statistics.

A child had died of diphtheria. At the clinical pathological conference, the pathologist demonstrated the organs, showed the culture of diphtheria bacilli isolated from the lesions and expressed regret at the relatively uninstructive program of the morning. The case was so straightforward, the cause of death so evident. An elderly physician in the audience then rose to say that he did not believe the real cause of death had been brought out at all; that he had other information. The birth of the child had never been reported to the responsible authority. As a consequence the family was not visited at the child's first birthday, as was the practice of the Health Department, to present to the father and mother the advantages of immunization against diphtheria and the means to obtain that service. The child was not immunized. The cause of death was social, and biological.[15]

In 1958 a British doctor issued a death certificate listing as the cause "carcinoma [cancer] of bronchus due to excessive smoking." The registrar refused to accept so unorthodox a juncture of "natural" and social causes, and there had to be an inquest. The coroner, an unrepentant smoker, declared that the physician had been attempting "to judge the habits of [his] fellow men. That must be the province of the coroner." His verdict was death from natural causes.[16] Two years later an American sued Liggett & Myers Tobacco Company for $1,250,000, charging that from smoking the company's Chesterfield cigarettes he had developed cancer in one lung. As experts did not then agree on the relation between smoking and cancer, the judge directed the jury to return a verdict in favor of the company; [17] but a new suit was filed on essentially similar grounds. With the alarming rise in the incidence of lung cancer, however, public officials have sought other means of carrying out their responsibility to guard the community's health. In Britain, the Royal College of Physicians recommended that cigarette advertising be curbed,[18] and in mid-1965 it was abolished altogether from commercial television in that country. The Danish National Society for the Combating of Cancer recommended that advertising be restricted or abolished and that smoking in public be restricted and forbidden to minors.[19] The U.S. Surgeon General issued reports officially affirming the scientific indictment of cigarettes,[20] and the industry was required to place a label on each package warning against them. Some have called for voluntary curbs on advertising (for example, LeRoy Collins, then president of the National Association of Broadcasters), but most representatives of news media have behaved like "hucksters," as a physician with the Public Health Service put it (Guthrie, 1966). A spokesman for the advertising business termed mandatory health warnings "unthinkable": "a compulsory curb of this kind upon business is inconsistent with the principles of competitive enterprise and individual freedom which are the bedrock of our democratic system." If cigarette advertising were eliminated altogether, there would be $300 million less per year in advertising revenue (Decker, 1966), and the economic effect on tobacco-producing areas might be more

[15] John E. Gordon, "Discussion," in Milbank Memorial Fund, *Trends and Differentials in Mortality*, New York, 1956, pp. 43–47.
[16] *Time*, November 17, 1958.
[17] *The New York Times*, May 5, 1960.
[18] *Ibid.*, March 8, 1962.
[19] *Ibid.*, March 9, 1962.
[20] *Ibid.*, January 12, 1964; August 21, 1967. *Cf.* Brownlee, 1965.

serious. The dilemma of public officials is aggravated by the fact that all the publicity concerning the dangers of smoking has not prevented a rise in the consumption of cigarettes. If the public cannot be educated, can it be coerced? The historic precedent of Prohibition should be in the minds of those who propose more rigorous solutions.

When an inhabitant of Los Angeles with a weak heart died during one of the city's recurrent bouts of smog, the physician called the smog "a significant condition contributing to death." The coroner refused to accept the certificate. "Los Angeles smog is not a disease," he declared, and added: "We would be opening the gates to litigation against the Board of Supervisors if we accepted such a certificate." [21] Air pollution is also a likely cause of lung cancer, and it is generally conceded that in most areas the principal culprit, once again, is the automobile. Frank M. Stead, California's chief of environmental sanitation, has proposed that all gasoline-powered vehicles be banned from the state by 1980; and this is only one of several demands for drastic reform (Lessing, 1967; cf. McDermott, 1961).

Such examples could be multiplied, but these should suffice to indicate the range of difficulties that would ensue if a serious attempt were made to list the main cause, the ancillary causes, and the significant contributing factors leading to each death. The analytic problem can perhaps be clarified by recalling the several types of causation that Aristotle and the medieval schoolmen used. The proximate factor, the **efficient cause** of death, is what physicians have generally concentrated on. Their job is to keep their patient alive, not to understand the whole social context of dying.

Lawyers, on the other hand, are concerned with the **formal cause** of death. From their point of view, all deaths are divided into "violent" and "natural," depending on whether they do or do not involve the law. For some types of death this differentiation is of such practical importance that it is included in the physicians' International Classification.

The **material cause** is the particular susceptibility of the organic system affected. In the same sense that one can say a house burned down because it was built of combustible material, so one can say that a person died of enteritis only because his intestinal tract was too weak to withstand an attack of the germs (cf. Pearl, 1922, Chapter 2). If the building had been made of concrete, or if the man's intestines could be made more resistant to this disease, then neither the arsonist nor the germ could have caused any damage. With the transplantation of organs, a branch of surgery certain to develop greatly in the next decades, this classificatory principle may acquire a new relevance.

The **first cause** of death, on the other hand, is that ultimate beginning of a chain of occurrences that eventually led to the one being analyzed. In

21 *Time*, November 17, 1958.

such a view, any death takes place only because unicellular animals, which in a favorable environment live until they split into two,[22] began to evolve into more complex beings.

The **final cause** of anything is its plan or design. A building has two stories, for example, because it was so drawn in the architect's blueprint. Although it is difficult outside a religious context to discuss such a teleological principle with respect to natural phenomena, one can say that death does have a function in nature. It makes possible the evolution of the species by removing one generation and replacing it with its slightly different successor. Natural selection can operate only because living beings are not immortal.

In the recent period our concept of the cause of death has in some cases been broadened to include much more than the proximate factor. This is particularly manifest when legal responsibility for automobile accidents, e.g., is now shared by the manufacturers of defective vehicles. If Los Angeles indeed were held responsible for deaths resulting from its smog— the legal principle that the city's coroner found abhorrent and ridiculous— this would provide the most efficacious goad imaginable to corrective action by public agencies.

Even physicians are re-examining their conception of "death." A prestigious committee of the Harvard Medical School recently suggested that "responsible medical opinion is ready to adopt a new criterion for death to have occurred in an individual sustaining irreversible coma as a result of permanent brain damage." For with the new techniques available, it is possible in some cases to restore "life," as defined by the present criteria of persistent respiration and continuation of the heart beat, even when there is not the remotest possibility that the individual will ever recover consciousness. As the committee sees it, the problem is a purely medical one, for the legal definition of death, whenever a question arises, depends on the testimony of a physician. The medical question is how to determine whether a brain is *permanently* nonfunctioning even when other organs continue to function; the principal symptom is a flat electro-encephalogram (Beecher *et al.*, 1968).

## Summary

It would be useful to divide mortality into two types analogous to fecundity and fertility, but in practical terms such a division is hampered

----

22 Contrary to what one might suppose, thus, death is not the inevitable concomitant of life, but only of specialized forms of life. In a favorable environment unicellular bodies have been observed to live for millions of generations with no diminution of vitality; and to the degree that the word has any empirical meaning, they can be called "immortal." In the laboratory a portion of a chicken's heart has been kept alive much longer than the natural span of the species. The question arises, then, whether the link between specialization and death is inevitable, or whether a suitable change in environment might alter it.

by the fact that in most deaths biological and environmental influences are too closely interlinked. The physiological causes of death pertain to the individual organism, whereas most measures of death control operate through social institutions. One can pair the findings of nutritionists on the individual's food requirements with economists' data on the world's food production, or the characteristics that influence the individual's susceptibility to disease with the social organization of medical facilities, but at our present level of knowledge these are not equations that yield precise answers. In areas where food production and disease control are efficient, accidents and homicide have been relatively more important causes of death. And if the world should engage in another all-out war, fought with weapons of unique destructive power, the devastation could be greater than at any time in all history. This must be noted as a possibility in spite of the fact that through the war of 1939–45 and beyond improved military (including medical) technology generally was associated with a proportionate decline in casualties.

The progress in medical science that has taken place during the lifetime of today's adults is probably greater than during the previous five thousand years. If *all* mortality before the age of 40 had been eliminated and age-specific death rates for age 41 and over had remained the same as they were in 1948, it was pointed out shortly after that year, the average expectation of life at birth would be 70.7 years for white males and 75.0 years for white females (Dorn, 1952). The actual figures for whites in 1966 were, respectively, 67.6 and 74.7 years. That is to say, any appreciable decline in mortality from its present level will be attained, if at all, less by a simple extension of past improvements than by the introduction of new factors, especially control over senescence.

How much has life expectation increased over the whole of human existence? As indicated by the approximate figures in Table 7-7, the average length of life about doubled from prehistoric times to the Middle Ages, and then remained more or less static until the nineteenth century. During the last 150 years it has doubled again. The increase from roughly eighteen to roughly thirty-five years, which took place before the development of industrial society, was due in the main to social innovations, in particular, the consolidation of large areas over which a powerful state maintained social order. The second doubling, from about thirty-five to about seventy years, can be ascribed in large part to technological improvements in agriculture, medicine, and public health, whose efficacy is so great that they tend to obscure other relevant factors. The successful application in underdeveloped countries of the most recent innovations in death control is almost completely independent, as we shall see in Chapter 15, of whether or not these nations are able to effect concomitant rises in social welfare. It is hardly an exaggeration to say that the social determinants of mortality have been reduced more and more to the single decisive one, whether the fruits of modern Western science are available.

Table 7-7. Expectation of Life at Birth through History

| PERIOD | AREA | AVERAGE LENGTH OF LIFE (YEARS) |
|---|---|---|
| I. Bronze Age | Greece | 18 |
| Beginning of Christian era | Rome | 22 |
| II. Middle Ages | England | 33 |
| 1687–91 | Breslau, Germany | 33.5 |
| Before 1789 | Massachusetts and New Hampshire | 35.5 |
| III. 1838–54 | England and Wales | 40.9 |
| 1900–02 | United States | 49.2 |
| 1966 | United States | 70.1 |
| 1966 | Sweden, females | 76.49 |

SOURCES: Various authors, compiled by Louis I. Dublin, Alfred J. Lotka, and Mortimer Spiegelman, *Length of Life: A Study of the Life Table*, Revised Ed., Ronald, New York, 1949, p. 42. Copyright 1949, The Ronald Press Company. U.S. Public Health Service, *Vital Statistics of the United States, 1966*, Vol. 2, Section 5: *Life Tables*, Washington, D.C., 1966.

## Suggestions for Further Reading

There is so large a bibliography possible on the social-political factors in death control that no works are singled out here, beyond noting that the starred items are especially recommended.

The methods of constructing a life table, a subject beyond the scope of this book, are discussed briefly in Dublin *et al.*, 1949, Chapter 15, more thoroughly in Spiegelman, 1955, Chapter 5, or George W. Barclay, *Techniques of Population Analysis*, Wiley, New York, 1958, Chapter 5 and Appendix. See also U.S. National Center, 1964*b*. Dublin *et al.*, 1949 is still the best book on the use of the life table; a work that includes its more general utility, actual and possible, beyond the analysis of mortality is still to be written. Lerner and Anderson, 1963, offers an excellent summary of the determinants of health in this country.

Few fields are developing more rapidly than nutritional biochemistry. A good introduction is Williams, 1962, written for the lay public by an authority in the discipline. Wohl and Goodhart, 1964 is a thoroughly professional analysis of nutrition. The *Handbook of Nutrition* of the AMA Council on Food and Nutrition is medically authoritative and readable.

Pearl, 1922, though obviously out of date in some respects, is still a stimulating discussion of the general biology of death. Winslow, 1952; Zinsser, 1935; and Shrewsbury, 1964 are works by experts on epidemiology for the general reader;

those who enjoy reading about this type of detection might well supplement those works with the more popular Roueché, 1955.

In addition to the standard professional journals in demography, a number of periodicals devote a good deal of their content to the subject matter of this chapter: *Milbank Memorial Fund Quarterly* (as well as occasional proceedings issued by the Fund); Health Information Foundation, *Progress in Health Services*; Metropolitan Life Insurance Company, *Statistical Bulletin*; *Journal of Gerontology*, which is more likely than other biological serials to include articles of interest to a social scientist; *American Journal of Public Health*, the official organ of the professional society; the several series of *Vital and Health Statistics*, issued by the U.S. National Center for Health Statistics.

ALBANESE, ANTHONY A., and LOUISE A. ORTO. 1964. "The Proteins and Amino Acids," in Wohl and Goodhart, 1964, pp. 125–193.

AMERICAN MEDICAL ASSOCIATION. COUNCIL ON FOODS AND NUTRITION. 1951. *Handbook on Nutrition*. 2nd Ed., New York.

AMERICAN PUBLIC HEALTH ASSOCIATION. 1966. "From Epidemiology to Ecology— Smoking and Health in Transition," *Journal of Public Health*, Vol. **56**, No. 12.

ARNHOFF, FRANKLYN N. 1955. "Research Problems in Gerontology," *Journal of Gerontology*, **10**, 452–456.

AXELROD, A. E. 1964. "Nutrition in Relation to Acquired Immunity," in Wohl and Goodhart, 1964, pp. 646–656.

BAIN, READ. 1945. "The Ages of Man," *American Sociological Review*, **10**, 337–343.

BEECHER, HENRY K., *et al.* 1968. "A Definition of Irreversible Coma: Report of the Ad Hoc Committee of the Harvard Medical School to Examine the Definition of Brain Death," *Journal of the American Medical Association*, **205**, 337–340.

BENJAMIN, HARRY. 1947. "Biologic versus Chronologic Age," *Journal of Gerontology*, **2**, 217–227.

BOURGEOIS-PICHAT, JEAN. 1946–51. "De la mesure de la mortalité infantile," *Population*, **1**, 53–68, and **6**, 233–248, 459–480.

BROWN, LESTER R. 1968. "New Directions in World Agriculture," *Studies in Family Planning*, No. 32, pp. 1–6.

* BROWNLEE, K. A. 1965, "A Review of 'Smoking and Health,'" *Journal of the American Statistical Association*, **60**, 722–739.

BUTLER, NEVILLE R., and DENNIS G. BONHAM. 1963. *Perinatal Mortality: The First Report of the 1958 British Perinatal Mortality Survey*. Livingstone, Edinburgh.

* CARTWRIGHT, ANN. 1959. "Some Problems in the Collection and Analysis of Morbidity Data Obtained from Sample Surveys," *Milbank Memorial Fund Quarterly*, **37**, 33–48.

————. 1963. "Memory Errors in a Morbidity Survey," *Milbank Memorial Fund Quarterly*, **41**, 5–24.

CLARK, DEAN A. 1958. "Where Does the Nation's Health Stand Today?" in Milbank Memorial Fund. *Selected Studies of Migration Since World War II*. New York, pp. 233–242.

* COHEN, BERNICE H. 1965. "Family Patterns of Longevity and Mortality," in *Genetics and the Epidemiology of Chronic Diseases*, edited by James V. Neel,

Margery W. Shaw, and William J. Schull. U.S. Public Health Service, Washington, D.C., pp. 237–263.

COWDRY, E. V. 1940. "We Grow Old," *Scientific Monthly*, **50**, 51–58.

DECKER, FREDERIC. 1966. "The Economic Effect of Reduced Cigarette Consumption on Advertising," in American Public Health Association, 1966, pp. 29–32.

DORN, HAROLD F. 1952. "Prospects of Further Decline in Mortality Rates," *Human Biology*, **24**, 235–261.

———. 1956a. "Ecological Factors in Morbidity and Mortality from Cancer," in Milbank Memorial Fund, 1956, pp. 74–97.

———. 1956b. "Some Problems for Research in Mortality and Morbidity," *Public Health Reports*, **71**, 1–5.

* DUBLIN, LOUIS I., ALFRED J. LOTKA, and MORTIMER SPIEGELMAN. 1949. *Length of Life: A Study of the Life Table*. Revised Ed. Ronald, New York.

DUBOS, RENÉ J. 1959. "Medical Utopias," *Daedalus*, **88**, 410–424.

DUMAS, SAMUEL, and K. O. VEDEL-PETERSEN. 1923. *Losses of Life Caused by War*. Carnegie Endowment for International Peace. Clarendon, Oxford.

DUNOÜY, PIERRE. 1936. *Biological Time*. Methuen, London.

ENTERLINE, PHILIP E. 1961. "Causes of Death Responsible for Recent Increases in Sex Mortality Differentials in the United States," *Milbank Memorial Fund Quarterly*, **39**, 312–328.

FELDMAN, JACOB J. 1958. "Barriers to the Use of Health Survey Data in Demographic Analysis," *Milbank Memorial Fund Quarterly*, **36**, 203–220.

GOODHART, ROBERT S. 1964. "Criteria of an Adequate Diet," in Wohl and Goodhart, 1964, pp. 617–632.

GREGORY, IAN. 1965. "Retrospective Estimates of Orphanhood from Generation Life Tables," *Milbank Memorial Fund Quarterly*, **43**, 323–348.

* GUTHRIE, EUGENE H. 1966. "What's Happened Since the Surgeon General's Report on Smoking and Health?" in American Public Health Association, 1966, pp. 1–6.

HARTE, ROBERT A., and BACON CHOW. 1964. "Dietary Interrelationships," in Wohl and Goodhart, 1964, pp. 534–544.

HEER, DAVID M. 1965. *After Nuclear Attack: A Demographic Inquiry*. Praeger, New York.

* KEYS, ANCEL. 1951a. "Caloric Undernutrition and Starvation, with Notes on Protein Deficiency," in AMA, 1951, pp. 409–444.

———. 1951b. "Energy Requirements of Adults," in AMA, 1951, pp. 259–274.

* KLEBBA, A. JOAN. 1966. *Mortality Trends in the United States, 1954–1963*. National Center for Health Statistics, Series 20, No. 2. U.S. Public Health Service, Washington, D.C.

KOOS, EARL L. 1954. *The Health of Regionville*. Columbia University Press, New York.

* LERNER, MONROE, and ODIN W. ANDERSON. 1963. *Health Progress in the United States, 1900–1963*. University of Chicago Press, Chicago.

LESSING, LAWRENCE. 1967. "The Revolt Against the Internal-Combustion Engine," *Fortune*, July, 78–83, 180–184.

LINDER, FORREST E. 1967. "The Health of the American People," *Statistical Reporter*, **67**, 113–118.

LINDHARDT, MARIE. 1959. "The Danish National Morbidity Survey of 1950: Brief Description of Methods together with Some Numerical Results," in International Union for the Scientific Study of Population. *International Population Conference*, Vienna, pp. 498–512.

LITTLE, ALAN. 1965. "An 'Expectancy' Estimate of Hospitalization Rates for Mental Illness in England and Wales," *British Journal of Sociology*, 16, 221–231.

McCARTHY, MARY A. 1966. *Infant, Fetal, and Maternal Mortality, United States, 1963*. National Center for Health Statistics, Series 20, No. 3. U.S. Public Health Service, Washington, D.C.

McDERMOTT, WALSH. 1961. "Air Pollution and Public Health," *Scientific American*, 205, 49–57.

MACLEOD, GRACE, and HENRY C. SHERMAN. 1951. "Recommended Dietary Allowances," in AMA, 1951, pp. 233–257.

* MADIGAN, FRANCIS C., S.J. 1957. "Are Sex Mortality Differentials Biologically Caused?" *Milbank Memorial Fund Quarterly*, 35, 202–223.

* MILBANK MEMORIAL FUND. 1956. *Trends and Differentials in Mortality*. New York.

MORIYAMA, IWAO M. 1966. "The Eighth Revision of the International Classification of Diseases," *American Journal of Public Health*, 56, 1277–1280.

———, and THOMAS E. N. GREVILLE. 1944. "Effect of Changing Birth Rates upon Infant Mortality Rates," *Vital Statistics—Special Reports*, Vol. 19, No. 21.

MOYNIHAN, DANIEL P. 1966. "The War against the Automobile," *Public Interest*, No. 3, pp. 10–26.

MYERS, ROBERT J. 1966. "The Impact of Medicare on Demography," *Demography*, 3, 545–547.

NISSELSON, HAROLD, and THEODORE D. WOOLSEY. 1959. "Some Problems of the Household Interview Design for the National Health Survey," *Journal of the American Statistical Association*, 54, 69–87.

OPLER, MORRIS E. 1963. "The Cultural Definition of Illness in Village India," *Human Organization*, 22, 32–35.

PASSMORE, R. 1963. "Estimation of Food Requirements," in Royal Statistical Society, 1963, pp. 22–33.

* PEARL, RAYMOND. 1922. *The Biology of Death*. Lippincott, Philadelphia.

———, and RUTH DEWITT PEARL. 1934. *The Ancestry of the Long-Lived*. Johns Hopkins Press, Baltimore.

PIRIE, N. W. 1963. "Future Sources of Food Supply: Scientific Problems," in Royal Statistical Society, 1963, pp. 34–52.

POLGAR, STEVEN. 1962. "Health and Human Behavior: Areas of Interest Common to the Social and Medical Sciences," *Current Anthropology*, 3, 159–205.

POTTER, ROBERT G., JR. 1966. "Application of Life Table Techniques to Measurement of Contraceptive Effectiveness," *Demography*, 3, 297–304.

PRESIDENT'S SCIENCE ADVISORY COMMITTEE. 1967. *The World Food Problem*. 3 Vols. The White House, Washington, D.C.

ROUECHÉ, BERTON. 1955. *Eleven Blue Men and Other Narratives of Medical Detection*. Berkley, New York.

* ROYAL STATISTICAL SOCIETY. 1963. *Food Supplies and Population Growth*. Oliver & Boyd, Edinburgh.

RUSSELL, E. JOHN. 1954. *World Population and World Food Supplies*. Allen & Unwin, London.

SAMORA, JULIAN. 1961. "Conceptions of Health and Disease Among Spanish-Americans," *American Catholic Sociological Review*, **22**, 314–323.

* SAUNDERS, LYLE. 1954. *Cultural Difference and Medical Care: The Case of the Spanish-speaking People of the Southwest*. Russell Sage Foundation, New York.

SCOTCH, NORMAN A., and H. JACK GEIGER. 1963–64. "An Index of Symptom and Disease in Zulu Culture," *Human Organization*, **22**, 304–312.

SEEGAL, DAVID. 1950. "On Longevity and the Control of Chronic Disease," in Eastern States Health Education Conference. *The Social and Biological Challenge of Our Aging Population*. Columbia University Press, New York, pp. 96–111.

SHREWSBURY, J. F. D. 1964. *The Plague of the Philistines and Other Medical-Historical Essays*. Gollancz, London.

SOROKIN, PITIRIM A. 1937. *Social and Cultural Dynamics*. **3**: *Fluctuations of Social Relationships, War, and Revolution*. American Book Company, New York.

SPEIER, HANS. 1952. *Social Order and the Risks of War*. Stewart, New York.

SPIEGELMAN, MORTIMER. 1955. *Introduction to Demography*. Society of Actuaries, Chicago.

* ———. 1965. "Mortality Trends for Causes of Death in Countries of Low Mortality," *Demography*, **2**, 115–125.

———, et al. 1958. "Problems in the Medical Certification of Causes of Death," *American Journal of Public Health*, **48**, 71–80.

SUKHATME, P. V. 1961. "The World's Hunger and Future Needs in Food Supplies," *Journal of the Royal Statistical Society*, **124**, 463–525.

U.S. NATIONAL CENTER FOR HEALTH STATISTICS. 1964a. *The Change in Mortality Trend in the United States*. Vital and Health Statistics, Series 3, No. 1. U.S. Public Health Service, Washington, D.C.

———. 1964b. *Comparison of Two Methods of Constructing Abridged Life Tables by Reference to a "Standard" Table*. Vital and Health Statistics, Series 2, No. 4. U.S. Public Health Service, Washington, D.C.

U.S. PUBLIC HEALTH SERVICE. 1955. *Meeting the Challenge of Cancer*. Washington, D.C.

* ———. 1965. *The Facts of Life and Death: Selected Statistics on the Nation's Health and People*. Washington, D.C.

———. 1966. *Vital Statistics of the United States, 1966*. Vol. 2, Section 5; *Life Tables*. Washington, D.C.

VINCENT, PAUL. 1946. "Conséquences de six années de guerre sur la population française," *Population*, **1**, 429–440.

WATTS, DOROTHY D. 1966. "Factors Related to the Acceptance of Modern Medicine," *American Journal of Public Health*, **56**, 1205–1212.

WEST, HOWARD. 1967. "Health Insurance for the Aged: The Statistical Program," *Social Security Bulletin*, **30**, 3–16.

WILKINS, JAMES. 1967. "Suicidal Behavior," *American Sociological Review*, **32**, 286–298.

* WILLIAMS, ROGER J. 1962. *Nutrition in a Nutshell*. Doubleday-Dolphin, Garden City, N.Y.

WINSLOW, C.-E. A. 1952. *Man and Epidemics*. Princeton University Press, Princeton, N.J.

* WOHL, MICHAEL G., and ROBERT S. GOODHART, editors. 1964. *Modern Nutrition in Health and Disease: Dietotherapy*. 3rd Ed. Lea & Febiger, Philadelphia.

WORLD HEALTH ORGANIZATION. 1957. *Manual of the International Statistical Classification of Diseases, Injuries, and Causes of Death*. 7th Ed. 2 Vols. Geneva.

WRIGHT, QUINCY. 1942. *A Study of War*. University of Chicago Press, Chicago.

* ZINSSER, HANS. 1935. *Rats, Lice and History: . . . The History of Typhus Fever*. Little, Brown, Boston. (Reissued as a Bantam paperback, 1960.)

——, JOHN F. ENDERS, and LeRoy D. FOTHERGILL. 1940. *Immunity: Principles and Application in Medicine and Public Health*. 5th Ed. Macmillan, New York.

# 8 THE GENERAL DETERMINANTS OF MIGRATION

The modern era has seen sizable movements of peoples in various parts of the world—for instance, the migration of Chinese into Southeast Asia, of Indians to Eastern and Southern Africa, or of Africans to the Americas. The most significant in terms of both numbers and the diffusion of culture patterns was the emigration of Europeans. In the great awakening of Western civilization that we term the Renaissance, European man began to explore not only the Greek and Roman foundations of his civilization and the physical and biological laws of nature, but also the world beyond the Mediterranean basin and the eastern Atlantic. The ships of Spain and Portugal, of England and Holland, worked their way down the coast of Africa and, around the middle of the fifteenth century, found a sea route to Asia; at the end of the century, 3,000 miles to the west, they discovered a veritable New World, vast, rich in every natural resource, and virtually unpeopled. During the two centuries following, tiny bands of explorers sought gold, glory, or salvation, establishing dominion over a million square miles by the planting of a flag.

The age of discovery and colonization merged into the Great Migration. The mass movement from Europe in the nineteenth century was on a scale new in human history. Of the 67 million persons who crossed an ocean from 1800 to 1950, some 60 million were Europeans, and of these two out of every three went to the United States. That analysts of migration, and particularly the Americans among them, should derive their precepts entirely from this prototype is perhaps understandable, for the strong ten-

A group of immigrants, segregated by sex, waiting for further processing at Ellis Island, ca. 1910 (*The Bettmann Archive, Inc.*).

dency in all of us toward ethnocentrism is here reinforced by the universal significance of this element of American civilization. Here we shall try to avoid that trap. Migration does not always follow whatever laws can be derived from the trans-Atlantic movement during the nineteenth century; for all its importance, it should be seen as one type among others.

When we speak of the general determinants of migration, we cannot begin with an analogy to fecundity and the biology of mortality. Migration is not universal: we are all born and we all die, but only some of us migrate. Even the strongest motivation results in migration only when it has been translated into action by human will. And the migration that does take place, on the other hand, often completely lacks any biological incentive. As was noted in the earlier discussion of migration statistics (see pp. 41–44, 48–50), the concept is riddled with ambiguity. When one speaks of migratory birds, or migrant laborers, or nomads, the connotation is not of a permanent move from one area to another, but rather of a permanently migratory way of life, which often means a cyclical movement within a more or less restricted area. On the other hand, the sense associated with the word's derivation from the Latin *migrare*, "to change one's residence," is rather to change one's community. A person who moves from one home to another in the same neighborhood and who therefore retains the same social framework is ordinarily not deemed to be a migrant. "Change of community" as an index of migration affords a very rough gauge of the meaning to be assigned to such indeterminate words as "permanent" and "significant" in the usual definition of **migration**—the relatively permanent movement of persons over a significant distance.

## Migration and Population Growth

That individual migrants become permanent residents of the new country does not mean that one can merely add them up to derive the demographic effect of the migration. Common sense tells us that if 1,000 persons migrate from Country A to Country B, the population of Country A is decreased by 1,000 and that of Country B is increased by the same number. However, in all probability the shift will bring about changes in the population structure, economy, and social conditions of both countries, and these changes in turn will influence the population growth of each. If we take these indirect effects into account, the relation between migration and population is a good deal more complex than it would seem at first sight (*cf.* Tabah and Cataldi, 1963).

**1.** Under some circumstances, particularly in large international movements, the effect of migration on the sending country may be nil. As we have seen, one of Malthus's principal theses was that, other things being equal, the population of any area generally tends to increase up to the maximum that the economy can support. Wherever this is indeed the case, the effect of migration on the size of the population of either of the areas involved cannot be very great: emigrants will eventually be replaced through a higher natural increase, and immigrants will merely take the place of natives who would otherwise have been born (or, if born, would have stayed alive).[1] People leaving a country like India or China, thus, have practically no effect on the eventual number remaining.

[1] Under such conditions migration effects a real shift in population only when those who move have special skills, so that there is a concomitant shift in what Benjamin Franklin termed "the state of the arts." In general, emigration was for Malthus "a slight palliative," "a partial and temporary expedient" with "no permanent effect on population." See T. R. Malthus, *An Essay on the Principle of Population*, 7th Ed., Reeves and Turner, London, 1872, Book 3, Chapter 4. It must be noted, however, that with respect to policy Malthus's usual emphasis was not on this presumed absence of long-term effects but on the more immediate, temporary consequences. He considered emigration "well worthy the attention of the government, both as a matter of humanity and policy" (*ibid.*). The evidence that he gave before the Second Select Committee on Emigration in 1827 was based on these considerations rather than on the hypothesis that emigration would have no permanent effect on the size of the Irish population.

[Thompson] made diligent inquiry in China to ascertain whether the migration to Manchuria from Shantung and Hopei had relieved population pressure in those provinces and the answer he received was that it had not. . . . Emigration had reduced the death rate but the birth rate remained high and population soon grew to its former level. . . . Emigration can do little or nothing to mitigate the actual physical poverty of the densely settled lands of Asia.[2]

In one of the first efforts to add up Europe's population, Willcox estimated that it had increased from 130 million in 1750 to 500 million in 1900, and "the persons of European stock living outside of Europe in 1900 were three-fourths as many as the entire number of inhabitants of that continent in 1750" (Willcox, 1906). "Instead of draining off Europe's population, the steady stream of emigrants promoted its unprecedented growth, [for] the removal of the excess population prevented catastrophes such as those which had formerly destroyed peoples and economies" (Kulischer, 1948, p. 28). Or, with respect to a specific country, "it is arguable that the population of Italy is not less than it would have been if emigration had not taken place, and perhaps is greater" (Foerster, 1924, p. 469).

2. However, movement out of an area, particularly one with a small population to begin with, can remove the base from which subsequent recuperation would have taken place. Migrants are characteristically young adults, and their departure typically means a rise in the country's average age and thus an increase in its death rate. And as they take with them, as it were, their future progeny, the birth rate typically falls. Most countries in which either urbanization or emigration from the countryside has been sizable have complained recurrently of rural depopulation, even occasionally in nations that as a whole suffer from agrarian overpopulation. The effects of emigration on certain districts in southern Italy, for example, "have been officially compared with those of a pestilence."

Here are villages all but abandoned, the houses uninhabited and in decay, grass growing in the streets, and in the gardens weeds choking whatever vegetables come up. Far and wide, it is the aged, the women, and the children who constitute the labor force (*ibid.*, p. 449).

In the United States, similarly, the out-migration from New England left behind some half-abandoned villages; Lyme, N.H., having reached a maximum size around 1830, thereafter lost people to the new land in the West

[2] Warren S. Thompson, *Plenty of People: The World's Population Pressures, Problems, and Policies, and How They Concern Us*, Ronald, New York, 1948, pp. 154–155. Once again, this fact does not determine policy. Thompson continues: "Permitting these peoples to migrate even though relatively few could actually move would help greatly in creating a better atmosphere in which to discuss the problems of population pressure and the better distribution of the world's resources. This in itself would be a well worthwhile achievement."

and later to the manufacturing towns (Goldthwait, 1927). Very often the abandoned land is marginal in one sense or another, either because of its low fertility (as in the Southeast of France), or because of particularly oppressive relations with landowners (as sometimes in Italy), or because of the decline of rural industries (as in parts of England; cf. Saville, 1957, pp. 20–30).

Rural depopulation can affect whole districts or even whole countries. The classic examples are Ireland and Scotland, in particular the island of Skye. More recently, an interesting case study was made of the Greek island of Ithaca. In the nineteenth-century tradition, the island's population was supported in large part by seamen, who after long separations came home to settle down with their families. Around 1910 this somewhat precarious balance was disturbed by the new opportunities opening up in the United States and other immigration countries, so that many of the young men who sailed away never returned. With the radically altered sex ratio, marriages were fewer and at a later age, and the strong patrifocal extended family started to fall apart. With the shortage of labor, between 1896 and 1951 the cultivated land declined by more than a quarter and the value of agricultural production by almost half. Over these same years the island's population fell off by more than half, from 11,409 to 5,877 (Lowenthal and Comitas, 1962).

3. The effect of migration to cities on urban populations has been enormous. In the early modern period, when infections spread uninhibited through the dirty congested quarters of the growing towns, these probably had higher death rates than the surrounding countryside. After some control was established over urban mortality, the birth rate of cities still kept the natural increase relatively low. The stupendous rise of urban centers over the past two centuries, thus, has been in large part the consequence of in-migration.

4. The possible effect of immigration on the population of the receiving country can be illustrated with the United States. Immigration to that country from the beginning of the statistical record in 1819 is summarized in Table 8-1. The number arriving rose after 1880 both absolutely and as a proportion of the resident population, fell off during the depression of the 1890s, and after the turn of the century again set new records. In the fiscal year ending June 30, 1907, the high point of 1,285,349 was reached, and in each of five other years up to 1914 more than a million immigrants were recorded. Even at the peak of this wave, however, the proportion of newcomers to the resident population—perhaps a more meaningful index than the absolute number[3]—did not rise much above that in the 1840s and

---

[3] The rates listed in Table 8-1 are inelegant, for they are calculated as a proportion of a population to which the migration itself has contributed. With the data ordinarily available, however, there is no entirely satisfactory migration rate. The numerator, the number who have moved, reflects all the complexity of migration as a concept. And the denominator, the base population, involves either or both of two populations over the time period of the migration being measured. Cf. Thomlinson, 1962; Hamilton, 1965.

Table 8-1. Average Annual Recorded Immigration by Decades, U.S., 1819–1965

| | AVERAGE ANNUAL IMMIGRATION ( THOUSANDS ) | ANNUAL IMMIGRATION PER THOUSAND OF TOTAL POPULATION AT END OF PERIOD |
|---|---|---|
| 1819–30 | 15 | 1.2 |
| 1831–40 | 60 | 3.5 |
| 1841–50 | 171 | 7.4 |
| 1851–60 | 260 | 8.3 |
| 1861–70 | 231 | 5.8 |
| 1871–80 | 281 | 5.6 |
| 1881–90 | 525 | 8.3 |
| 1891–1900 | 369 | 4.9 |
| 1901–10 | 780 | 8.5 |
| 1911–20 | 674 | 6.4 |
| 1921–30 | 411 | 3.4 |
| 1931–40 | 53 | 0.4 |
| 1941–50 | 104 | 0.7 |
| 1951–60 | 229 | 1.3 |
| 1961–65 | 290 | 1.5 |

SOURCE: U.S. Immigration and Naturalization Service, *Reports*, summarized in U.S. Bureau of the Census, *Statistical Abstract of the United States*, various dates. For some periods the data are for fiscal rather than calendar years, but this makes no significant difference in the decennial totals, given the general level of accuracy of the records.

1850s. But the immigration of more than a million in one year was a fact that stayed in one's mind. And it was not only, not even principally, a question of numbers. Until the 1880s the "Old" Immigrants had come from Northwestern Europe, and from that date on the increasing proportion of "New" Immigrants came from Southern and Eastern Europe. Arguments for restriction of numbers were based in many instances on hostility to Italians, Poles, and Russian Jews.

The fluidity of analytical postulates on this matter can be illustrated by the several articles of Francis A. Walker, superintendent of several censuses and among post-Civil War Malthusians "probably the most influential writer on population," who molded a dozen or more important economists and demographers.[4] At the beginning of the nineteenth century one Elkanah Watson noticed that without immigration, which had been interrupted by the wars in Europe, the population of the United States had increased by about one-third during each of the two decades following the 1790 census.

[4] Joseph J. Spengler, "Population Doctrines in the United States, 2: Malthusianism," *Journal of Political Economy*, 41 ( 1933), 639–672.

His population projection at the same extraordinary rate of growth up to 1900 was widely accepted. In 1873 Walker wrote an article gently deriding Watson's thesis. When a geometrical progression is found in human affairs, "the most improbable supposition which could be formed respecting it is that it will continue." In fact, the natural increase had not been maintained at the projected rate; American fertility began to fall with the shift of the people from agriculture to manufacturing, from country to town. That nevertheless the population increase was maintained for several decades was due to "a flood of immigration unprecedented in history" (Walker, 1873).

Twenty years later the same man wrote three more articles on the relation between immigration and population growth (Walker, 1891, 1892, 1896). He used Watson's projection again, but this time as a criterion for judging the actual population growth. Immigration, he now found, "instead of constituting a net reinforcement to the population, simply resulted in a replacement of native by foreign elements," for the American "was unwilling himself to engage in the lowest kind of day labor with these new elements . . . [and] even more unwilling to bring sons and daughters into the world to enter that competition." For Walker, the essential question was how to protect "the quality of American citizenship from degradation through the tumultuous access of vast throngs of ignorant and brutalized peasantry" from the countries of Eastern and Southern Europe.

That Walker was hostile to New Immigrants is not the point, but rather that a social scientist of his high standing reversed himself on a key demographic question in an attempt to validate that sentiment. In the 1870s he found that America's fertility was falling because of the transformation into an urban-industrial society, and the only effect of immigration was to "cover from the common sight" the decline in the natural increase. In the 1890s he asserted that fertility would have remained at its projected high level but for the economic competition of immigrants. In the 1870s geometrical progressions were dismissed out of hand; in the 1890s Walker was one of the most prominent "Malthusians." The contrasts underline not only one man's inconsistencies, but also the complexity of the apparently simple question: what *is* the effect of migration on population growth?

The crucial test of Walker's thesis was to specify the date when the decline in fertility began. Using census data and the child-woman ratio, Willcox showed that, except for the single decade 1850–60, fertility had declined steadily from 1810 on. It was the rise in fertility during those ten years, probably the consequence of the heavy immigration, that had led previous investigators to conclude that the birth rate had been increasing or stationary up to the Civil War (Willcox, 1911). In short,

[Walker's] theory had its value as a challenge of the current belief that immigration regularly increased the population by an amount equal to its number.

But it is almost equally incorrect to maintain that it did not increase the population at all (Willcox, 1931, p. 103).

In summary, the relation between migration and population growth [5] can be analyzed with three components: (1) the direct movement of the migrants themselves; (2) the effect of the movement on the population structure of the two areas, which ordinarily increases the size of the transfer; and (3) the effect on social-economic conditions in the two areas, which may reduce or negate the results of the transfer. In the abstract, one can say that all three of these factors are always relevant. In the concrete, their total impact is discernible only in such extreme cases as, for example, emigration from a very densely settled country like India or immigration to a relatively empty country like the British colonies in America, which were Malthus's prime example of a population increase due to migration.

### TOTAL VS. NET MIGRATION

In the discussion thus far of how migration affects the population growth of the two areas concerned, it has been assumed that all the movement is in one direction. The official immigration figures cited in Table 8-1, for instance, are deceptive, for they list merely the numbers who came into the United States and ignore those who left. Yet during the height of the mass immigration of 1890–1910, an estimated 40 per cent of the foreign-born emigrated (Kuznets and Rubin, 1954, Table 7). Conclusions drawn from gross migration data are likely to be, indeed, grossly inaccurate with respect to not only the size of the movement but also all its other characteristics.

**Movement In vs. Out.** Most attempts to analyze migration, as we shall see, are based on the premise that in various ways one area is more attractive than the other, so that these countermovements are not explained. It is more reasonable to posit a differentiation by type of migrant: young people move out of Florida seeking better employment, whereas the old move in to one of the state's retirement settlements. One of the few attempts to develop such a broader theory was made by William Burton Hurd, a Canadian professor of political science who imported Walker's theory to that country, also in an effort to bolster his opposition to non-British immigrants. Hurd's thesis that *immigration causes emigration* follows the essence of Walker's argument: because immigrants create an economic and social

---

[5] Another attempt to sum up these diverse possibilities and the schools of thought concerning them, by the Italian demographer Corrado Gini (1946; *cf.* also Gonnard, 1927, pp. 285–286, 323–324), suggests the range of possible views. According to Gini, when the population of a country is in a state of equilibrium, neither immigration nor emigration affects the total numbers in the long run. On the other hand, if migration takes place from an overpopulated country, or to an underpopulated one, this movement does change the total population. It would be difficult to put the case less well.

environment unpalatable to native-born Canadians, these move out to the United States. Immigration thus effects not an addition to Canada's population, but only a substitution of less desirable for more desirable sectors. The hypothesis was not valid in the Canadian case, and Hurd made no effort to exemplify it with other data (*cf.* Petersen, 1955, pp. 202–210).

More generally, it can be hypothesized with respect to both internal and international movements that "for every major migration stream, a counterstream develops" (Lee, 1966). The reasons given are three: improved communication between two areas facilitates movement in both directions; the original attractions at the first destination may lessen or disappear, in part even as a consequence of the increased numbers; and some of those who moved in may always have intended to leave.

**Remigrants**—those who leave their country (or area) for a period and then return to it—typically make up a large portion of any countermovement. They ordinarily differ from the emigrants who remain abroad, but not necessarily according to any consistent pattern. Particularly during an economic depression, some immigrants leave the new country when they lose their jobs (Berthoff, 1953, p. 73). Sometimes, on the contrary, it is the relatively successful that return, either to find a wife (Borrie, 1954) or to retire. The rise of nationalism in the old country often attracts back some of the incompletely assimilated emigrants (Saloutos, 1956). Even a small percentage of the subsidized migrants to Australia and Canada return to Britain (Appleyard, 1962; Richmond, 1966).

The differences between Old and New Immigrants to the United States are far less when measured by net migration than by gross. For the period 1908 to 1923, that is, from the beginning of the record on immigration of aliens to shortly after the establishment of the national-quota system, the average remigration amounted to 35.2 per cent of the immigration. But for the different nationalities this percentage varied as follows (Ferenczi, 1929, pp. 206–207):

| | | | |
|---|---|---|---|
| Chinese | 130 | Lithuanian | 25 |
| Bulgarian, Serbian, and Montenegrin | 89 | Syrian | 24 |
| | | Scandinavian | 22 |
| Turkish | 86 | African | 22 |
| Korean | 73 | French | 21 |
| Rumanian | 66 | English | 21 |
| Hungarian | 66 | Mexican | 19 |
| Southern Italian | 60 | Dutch and Flemish | 18 |
| Cuban | 58 | Armenian | 15 |
| Slovak | 57 | Scotch and Welsh | 13 |
| Russian | 52 | Irish | 11 |
| Finnish | 29 | Jewish | 5 |

From this list it is evident that a much larger percentage of New Immigrants returned home than of Old Immigrants. (Of course, special factors influenced the remigration rate of certain of the nationalities, particularly the two extremes—the Chinese, of whom more departed than arrived, and the Jews, most of whom were undoubtedly classified elsewhere.) There is no reason to suppose that this is not true also of the period before 1908, for which direct data are not available. Indeed, one of the arguments that the advocates of restriction offered was that immigrants at the end of the century were less likely to settle permanently than those fifty years earlier. Almost by definition, the remigrants were less able to acculturate to their new environment than the immigrants who remained, but few valid generalizations can be added to that truism.

**Transmigrants,** those who move into an area for a period and then out of it, can sometimes be identified as such in the statistics of international migration, but not necessarily. For example, a person intending to immigrate to the United States but not able to get a visa may live in a neighboring country while waiting for it, and one of Hurd's complaints against immigrants to Canada was that many used that country only as a passageway. He could not substantiate this charge, for, as is usually the case, transmigrants merge into general statistics in and out, and thus by their double count artificially raise both numbers.

Similarly in internal migration, it is known from sample surveys that each year approximately one American in five moves to a new residence. However, according to a detailed analysis of one particular community (Goldstein, 1954), a sizable proportion of this large percentage is made up of persons who move more than once during a year and who are atypical also in other ways. A study of repeated migration in Denmark suggests that the phenomenon is not restricted to the United States (Goldstein, 1964).

## Migratory Selection

Even the demographic effect of a migration, not to say the economic or cultural effect, depends both on how many move and on their characteristics. In a study of migrants to Aberdeen, that is, of movement within Scotland over only a few years, it was found useful to classify respondents into a number of types. These included, among others, professionals advancing their careers, young persons seeking an education, workers taking specific jobs, casual laborers looking for employment, wives and children joining the heads of families, and remigrants (Illsley et al., 1963). The conclusions to be drawn differed to some degree for each of these categories. If it is useful to specify to this degree the types moving within a relatively homogeneous area, then manifestly it is so with respect to migration encompassing the whole world and all of history. A general analysis of migration, in other words, must begin with the various motives that determine why in any situation some leave and others stay, and since these motives cannot usually be established directly, they must be inferred from the differential migration rates.

Given a sedentary population and an inducement to leave, migrants become differentiated from nonmigrants by the fact that neither category is a random sample of the whole population. This process of migrants' self-selection according to various social characteristics is called **migratory selection** (or "selective migration"). Whether the decision is made by the migrants themselves is not a crucial distinction in a demographic context. Two centuries ago a slave-trader raiding the African coast would have chosen only young, healthy Negroes; or, more recently, various governments have established quotas by which the immigration of some classes is fostered and that of others is impeded or prohibited. Such regulations by an outside force, while quite dissimilar in some respects from a process of self-selection, are also examples of what we term migratory selection.

### AGE

With respect to age differentiation, all migration is one: in both internal and international movements, adolescents and young adults usually predominate. This is one of the most firmly established generalizations in demography. Between two-thirds and four-fifths of the immigrants to the United States in the nineteenth century were aged between fifteen and forty years (Ferenczi, 1929, pp. 212–213). The proportion in internal migration is typically just as large: for example, the median ages of persons who had moved within the United States during the year 1949/50 ranged, according to their color and the size of the 1949 place of residence, from 19.8 to 30.5 years (Duncan and Reiss, 1956, pp. 83–87). Even those inclined to doubt whether rural-urban migration is selective by other characteristics hold that it is so with respect to age and, to a lesser degree, sex (e.g., Sorokin and Zimmerman, 1929, p. 582). That young adults predominate does not mean, of course, that other persons never migrate. Families that move, particularly within a single country, may include young children (Shryock, 1964, p. 352) or, less frequently, elderly parents; and in recent years some of the migration within the United States has been the movement of retired persons.

One reason for the high proportion of young adults would seem to be that any migration involves a certain amount of adjustment at the destination, and youth connotes a better ability to adapt to new circumstances. A second reason, relevant when geographical mobility is a concomitant of job changes, is that these are more frequent among persons who have only recently started to work.

The age group of young adults is also distinguished from the rest of a population by many other characteristics, both physiological and social, and a comparison between migrants and nonmigrants is therefore misleading unless age is held constant.[6] Migrants generally enter the labor force in proportionately larger numbers than a sedentary population. In the years before World War I, it was often pointed out that immigrants to the United States had a much higher birth rate than the native population, and today some of the new suburbs appear to be mass nurseries. In both cases the real difference in fertility has been exaggerated by the atypical age structure.

## SEX

Selection by sex is also usual, but whether males or females predominate depends on the circumstances. One of Ravenstein's famous "laws" was that "females are more migratory than males," but even he noted that this was more true for short distances than for longer ones (Ravenstein, 1885–89; cf. Lee, 1966). The nineteenth-century movement into European towns from the surrounding countryside, the local movement that Ravenstein alluded to, was made up in large part of young farm girls who found work as domestic servants in the homes of the urban middle class. An international migration that does not involve great distances or the crossing of an important cultural boundary may also show a predominance of females, and for the same reason. Thus, for example, most of those who left Germany for the Netherlands in the interwar years were also domestic servants, and the sex ratio of this international immigration was therefore very low (Kirk, 1946, p. 117n). Another example is the settlement of Irish servants in England or even the United States. A nineteenth-century farm boy, on the other hand, acquired no skills useful to him in getting established in the city; if he left the farm, he would be more likely to go to a place where his youthful energy and physical strength were at a premium.

The characteristic features of any frontier town, e.g., in the white populations of the American West a century ago or of New Guinea today, derive in part from its very high sex ratio and the consequent almost total lack of family life. In Colorado in 1860, for example, only 3.2 per cent of the total population consisted of women in the reproductive age group. Similarly, males are likely to predominate during the first stages of emigration from any country, no matter what the destination. Thus, among pre-1914 migrants to the United States, the sex ratio of those from Southern and Eastern Europe was very much higher than of those from Northwestern Europe, even though at that time most newcomers of whatever nationality settled in cities. These were certainly not a frontier in the usual sense, but until a

[6] Concerning movement within the United States, "age is such an important discriminant for mobility status that we need to be sure that a difference in, for example, the migration rates of two social-economic groups is not simply attributable to differences in age composition of these groups. In many of the available statistics, however, there is no cross-classification by age, and recourse must be made to an analysis by indirect methods" (Shryock, 1964, pp. 30–31).

sizable Polish or Italian community, for example, was built up in America, there were more males among the immigrants from those countries.

Characteristically, then, internal migrants are predominantly female and international ones predominantly male, but this generalization cannot aptly be designated as a "law" that applies to non-Western societies. In both cases the reason for the sex ratio is that the social conditions at the destinations favor one or the other sex. Most who left India were contract laborers, and thus male, and only somewhat later did the more successful of overseas Indians have females brought over as brides. Those who have moved within India from village to town, however, have also been predominantly male. In the only four large cities with adequate statistics, the average sex ratio of in-migrants in 1931 was 154 (Davis, 1951, p. 135). Single girls have generally been too closely bound to traditional village roles to be able to leave independently, and when husbands have gone to the city, they very often have left their families at home and returned to them as soon as they could. The sex ratio of a city in underdeveloped areas, that is to say, is usually high, and it thus has some of the social characteristics of a frontier town.

How significant an effect international migration can have on sex ratios is indicated in Table 8-2. The great degree of consistency is particularly striking, as there is no reason to suppose that other factors influencing the ratio of males to females varied with this one. In West European countries, where immigration was at its peak around the middle of the nineteenth century, the sex ratio was well under 100 by 1900, while in the countries of East Europe and in Japan, where the high point came later, it declined from 100 in 1900 to about 90–95 in 1950. The one important exception to this pattern is Ireland, the emigration country par excellence, where the ratio actually increased; the reason presumably is the already noted sizable number of *female* domestic servants who had left. In receiving countries, on the contrary, with the influx of males to frontier areas, the sex ratio tended to be high in 1900 and to approach parity over the next half-century, as the size of the immigration decreased in many cases and the frontier was pushed back.

If the sex ratio of international migrants is high, that of remigrants, judging by the period for which American data are available, is still higher, and what is true of gross immigration must again be corrected to apply to the more meaningful group of those who came to stay. Because of the several legal provisions favoring female immigrants, they have been the predominant sex since the 1930s (Rubin, 1966), but even in this period the sex ratio of remigrants remained well above 100.

## FAMILY STATUS

Whenever their sex ratio varies markedly from 100, this means of course that many of the migrants are not married; and the usual theory is that

Table 8-2. Males per 100 Females in Various Countries, c. 1900 and c. 1950

| | c. 1900 | c. 1950 |
|---|---|---|
| EMIGRATION COUNTRIES | | |
| England and Wales | 93.6 | 93.4 |
| Ireland | 97.4 | 102.4 |
| Norway | 92.4 | 97.5 |
| Sweden | 95.3 | 99.2 |
| Denmark | 95.0 | 98.4 |
| Germany | 96.9 | 83.7 |
| Netherlands | 97.6 | 99.4 |
| Belgium | 98.7 | 97.0 |
| France | 96.8 | 92.9 |
| Spain | 95.4 | 92.2 |
| Portugal | 91.5 | 94.2 |
| Switzerland | 96.4 | 95.0 |
| Italy | 99.0 | 95.2 |
| Austria | 96.7 | 87.6 |
| | | |
| Hungary | 99.1 | 95.9 [a] |
| Rumania | 103.3 | 93.5 |
| Greece | 101.4 | 98.0 |
| Bulgaria | 104.1 | 100.5 |
| Poland } U.S.S.R. { | 98.9 | { 91.2 { 92.0 [b] |
| | | |
| Japan | 101.8 | 96.2 |
| | | |
| IMMIGRATION COUNTRIES | | |
| United States | 104.0 | 98.6 |
| Canada | 105.0 | 103.5 |
| Australia | 110.1 | 100.6 |
| New Zealand | 110.7 | 100.9 |
| Union of South Africa (Europeans) | 131.9 | 101.4 |
| Argentina | 111.9 | 105.1 |
| Brazil | 104.0 | 100.0 [c] |
| Chile | 98.7 | 98.3 |

SOURCE: Metropolitan Life Insurance Company, *Statistical Bulletin*, February 1953. [a] 1941. [b] 1939. [c] 1940.

migrants generally are *single* young adults. This is true of the two characteristic types already discussed, male pioneers and female domestic servants. It may be, however, that the contrast between unmarried transients and relatively fixed families now fits the facts less than it used to.

Urbanization was at one time predominantly a movement of single persons, but as cities grew larger and older a tendency developed to move out of the crowded centers to the suburbs. The continuing in-migration of unmarried persons was then matched by an out-migration of families.[7] In the United States today not only do married couples move about as well as single persons, but they are often motivated to do so precisely because of their family life—in order to have a larger house for an increasing number of children, in order to live in a "nicer" neighborhood or close to a better school, and so on (Rossi, 1955).

It is possible that there has been a shift in the marital status also of international migrants. In the nineteenth century the typical European who went overseas was a young unmarried adult trying to establish himself economically. The exodus of Jews from Eastern Europe during the decades before World War I, however, did not fit into this pattern. As they were induced to leave not merely for economic reasons but because of the threat of persecution or actual pogroms, Jewish migrants included a much larger proportion of females and children than other nationalities (Hersch, 1931). With the rise of totalitarian states and the consequent shift from economic to political motivations, both the stimulus to family migration and the difficulties in realizing it have increased.

### OCCUPATION

The effect of international migration on the labor force of the two countries is complex. In the Liberal economic theory of the nineteenth century, free movement was justified on the ground that those in an overcrowded occupation tended to go wherever their skill was in short supply, so that this natural functioning of the international labor market benefited everyone concerned, both the migrants and the two nations. The principle has a certain validity—or would have, if there were such a phenomenon as free movement of laborers; but in any case it must certainly be qualified: (1) It does not hold for migration that is not wholly economically motivated; and the persecution of minorities, the fear of another war, and other political considerations play a large if indeterminate role. (2) Even economic competition is weighted in favor of the area with the higher standard of living. Thus, for example, immediately after World War II, when Europe needed all its building workers for reconstruction, many of them left nevertheless, for they were wanted also for the development programs of the overseas countries, which could offer more attractive prospects. (3) The assumption in the Liberal principle that skills are fixed is not warranted. In many cases,

---

[7] One of the earliest and most careful analyses of this dual movement was made in Amsterdam; see T. van den Brink, "Vestiging en vertrek," *Statistische Mededeelingen van het Bureau van Statistiek der Gemeente Amsterdam*, No. 103 (1936), pp. 153–188; summarized in English in D. S. Thomas, 1938, pp. 70–92.

selection by occupation is less significant than the *change* of occupation that takes place as a concomitant of migration. Only a very small proportion of the villagers who flocked to the United States in the decades before 1914 became farmers, and the work that they and their sons did generally had nothing to do with what they had done in Europe. Four-fifths of the immigrants had had no previous experience in manufacturing or mining, the sectors of American industry in which most of them found jobs as unskilled laborers (Davie, 1949, p. 238). That America was a "land of opportunity" meant precisely that it was a country whose economy was expanding rapidly enough to enable a man to earn his living with aptitudes never used before.

In short, the economic factor shaping the movement of immigrants was broader than selection by occupation. According to several careful studies, if conditions in the home country were such as to build up a general desire to leave, the volume, direction, and timing of the movement were set largely by business conditions in the receiving country. The correlation between the business cycle and emigration was not negative, as might be expected, but "positive and moderately high"; for it was the pull of opportunities overseas that determined the migration rate, and in their broad trends business cycles tend to be international (D. S. Thomas, 1925, p. 148; *cf.* D. S. Thomas, 1941; Jerome, 1926).

Generalizations about business cycles do not apply, of course, to migrants impelled to escape political persecution. According to a study of refugees in the United States, their occupation in the new country was shaped by two contradictory factors (Table 8-3). Many had to accommodate to less comfortable circumstances; thus, of the females who had been

Table 8-3. Percentage of Interwar Refugees Employed in the Same Occupational Group in the United States as in Europe

|  | MALE | FEMALE |
|---|---|---|
| Professionals | 66.9 | 51.7 |
| Proprietors, managers, officials | 38.9 | 18.0 |
| Clerks and kindred workers | 46.7 | 36.7 |
| Skilled workers | 66.9 | 52.8 |
| Semiskilled workers | 62.8 | 58.4 |
| Unskilled workers | 38.7 | 38.8 |
| Housewives | — | 59.3 |
| Students | 47.9 | 33.5 |
| Unemployed and retired | 60.0 | 13.1 |

SOURCE: Maurice R. Davie, *Refugees in America: Report of the Committee for the Study of Recent Immigration from Europe,* Harper, New York, 1947, pp. 132, 135. Copyright, 1947, by Harper & Brothers.

housewives in Europe (more than half), about 40 per cent took work outside the home. Those whose livelihood had depended on facility in language (writers, teachers, etc.) obviously faced the most difficult adjustment, particularly if their profession was culture-bound also in other respects (jurists). Thus, of the refugee lawyers in the sample, only 5.8 per cent were practicing law. On the other hand, many who left for political reasons could transfer their professional and craft skills, so that in fact there was less of a shift of occupations among refugees than among the mass of economically motivated migrants.

Occupational self-selection operating in the form of the so-called "brain drain" (B.D.) has become something of an international issue (see p. 557). The term is very often loosely used; the emigration of highly qualified technicians and scientists from Britain is widely publicized, whereas that from France (*cf.* Monroe, 1966), which proportionately is almost equivalent, is barely noted. An adequate index of brain drain, thus, must control for both the size of the general emigration and the proportion in the population of persons with the skill being drained out (Grubel, in Gollin, 1966, p. 16; *cf.* Grubel and Scott, 1967; Mills, 1966). If the issue concerns physicists, thus:

$$B.D. = \frac{\text{Physicists migrating from Country } A \text{ to Country } B}{\text{Total migrants from Country } A \text{ to Country } B}$$

$$\div \frac{\text{Physicists in Country } A}{\text{Total population of Country } A}$$

If there is simply a large migration, including a large but proportionate number of the highly skilled, by this index B.D. is equal to unity. On the other hand, if there is a small general migration and a larger, though still not highly visible, migration of professionals, B.D. is greater than unity. It is true, on the other hand, that if a migration is stimulated by other factors, those with the qualifications guaranteeing successful integration may well depart in larger numbers. Thus, the roughly 300,000 Cuban refugees in the United States in the mid-1960s included nearly 2,000 physicians, plus a sizable number of medical students and nurses. This is hardly a brain drain in proportion to the total migration, but it certainly could be considered one in terms of the island's needs, a factor not included in Grubel's formula. More generally, data on the migration of high-level manpower are often too poor to substantiate reasoned argument, not to mention changes in legislation (Bayer, 1968).

The simplest case of brain drain is an unimpeded migration with no change of occupation. For example, of all those trained as nurses in Chile, about half leave the country and, of that half, most go to the United States and practice nursing (John Useem, in Gollin, 1966, p. 30; *cf.* Beijer, 1966).

Some of the 3,000 to 4,000 Italian workers at the Volkswagen factory, Wolfsburg, West Germany, who live in a nearby village that the firm built specially for them. In the early 1960s there were some 650,000 aliens employed in West Germany (*Wide World Photos*).

In many cases, however, the motivation of the migrant is at least partly to evade one or another regulation governing, for instance, the status of students. If an Israeli graduate student in science returns home immediately after receiving his American doctorate, he will begin in the civil service in grade C and be eligible for promotion to grade B after about four years, while if he remains in the United States for a year or two he will start in grade B (Paul Ritterband, in Gollin, 1966, p. 26).

Selection by occupation among internal migrants takes place to some degree, but it is difficult with the data ordinarily available to pin down motives for what has become, at least in the United States, so casual an act as moving to another home or job. Except to the degree that the motivation of migrants is implicit in the timing and direction of their movements, we know very little about it (*cf.* Shryock, 1964, Chapter 12). In the only sample survey on the subject ever conducted by the U.S. Bureau of the Census, respondents were asked their motives for having moved during the year 1945/46, and their reasons were grouped into the following classes: (*a*) to take a job, (*b*) to look for work, (*c*) housing problems, (*d*) change in marital status, (*e*) to join the head of the family, (*f*) to move with the head of the family, (*g*) health, and (*h*)"other" (of which the most frequent instances were to attend school or live in a different climate).

These reasons are obviously not all of the same order. Many studies of migratory selection are based on the assumption, usually left implicit, that all migrants choose whether or not to move and that they make their choice in response to social-economic forces. Let us designate those of whom this assumption is valid **resultant migrants,** who make up only the first three classes in the list of motives. Those with no choice in whether to move (for example, children taken by their parents) and those who decide to move for reasons not associated with social-economic forces (but rather, for example, because of their health or the climate) are termed **epiphenomenal migrants** (Hobbs, 1942, pp. 43–44). How important this differentiation can be is indicated in Table 8-4. The maxim that migration is primarily a func-

Table 8-4. Percentage Distribution of Internal Migrants, by Motive, U.S., 1945–46

|  | TOTAL | MALE | FEMALE |
|---|---|---|---|
| RESULTANT MIGRANTS | | | |
| Change of job (*a* + *b*) | 22.6 | 41.1 | 6.2 |
| Housing problems (*c*) | 6.4 | 9.8 | 3.3 |
| | | | |
| EPIPHENOMENAL MIGRANTS | | | |
| Family migration (*d* + *e* + *f*) | 61.7 | 38.1 | 82.7 |
| Health (*g*) | 1.2 | 1.8 | 0.8 |
| Other reasons (*h*) | 8.9 | 10.3 | 7.6 |

SOURCE: U. S. Bureau of the Census, *Current Population Reports*, Series P-20, No. 4, October 7, 1947, p. 9.

tion of economic and social circumstances is obviously not true in a direct sense; more than 70 per cent of the migrants were epiphenomenal. Of course, one can interpret the generalization to mean that if a man moves to take a different job, the migration of his wife and minor children is also economically motivated; but this is very evidently not quite the same thing. The sex ratio of the two types of migrants varies considerably, as indicated in the table. The age structure varies even more sharply: virtually all under 14 and over 65 are epiphenomenal migrants. The many generalizations concerning migratory selection based on the (sometimes tacit) assumption that all migrants are resultant, thus, can be valid only when family migration is insignificant.

## PSYCHOLOGICAL FACTORS

The study of psychological factors differs from that of the usual demographic variables in several respects. (1) In the definition of the characteristic: When a person tells us that he is 27 years old and married, this is information on a different level from, for instance, the results of intelligence tests. (2) In the amount of data available: Questions on age, sex, and marital status are included in all censuses and in virtually all special studies of migratory selection. Census data are lacking on factors like intelligence; and of the smaller number of specific studies that include such variables, many are based on inadequate methodology. (3) In the time of its first appearance: A statement that a person was single when he left and that he got married after he reached his destination is unambiguous. But if a migrant turns out to be a criminal or psychopathic, it is usually impossible to choose among three possible causes: (a) It may be that the home country or area has a higher incidence than the destination. This is perhaps the most common popular explanation of observed differences: thus, Italians are "prone to be criminals"; villagers are "dim-witted." (b) It may be that migratory selection takes place—that is, that persons with a predisposition to "criminality" or mental illness or whatever tend to leave in larger proportion. Or (c) it may be that the newcomers fail to adapt successfully to the strange conditions and therefore exhibit one or another form of social pathology.

A priori one can argue that either the less or the more intelligent tend to leave any particular area: (1) In the competition to achieve satisfactory living conditions, by and large the more intelligent will succeed more often, and the less so will thus be forced to seek their fortunes elsewhere. Or (2) in any population it will be the more adaptable, that is to say, the more intelligent, who will respond first to an impetus to emigrate, and the duller who will remain behind.

Whether selection by intelligence takes places in international migrations is still an open question. Indeed, many I.Q. tests have been made of the foreign stock, particularly in the United States, but it is difficult to say what these prove. Immigrants generally score lower, but one reason is certainly their less adequate knowledge of English and of the American culture generally. If this deficiency could be removed, probably the group differences would disappear with it; but the various attempts to devise a culture-free intelligence test have not been wholly successful. In any case, the testing of newcomers to the United States, whatever importance it may have for other reasons, is irrelevant to a study of migratory selection, for it is made at the wrong end of the journey. The question is not how German immigrants, for example, compare with native Americans, but rather how those Germans who leave compare with those who remain in Germany.

A large number of analyses of selectivity by intelligence has been made in internal migration. Some studies have attempted to prove, sometimes with inadequate methodology, that urbanization selected the more intelligent in the rural population; but in others this conclusion has been challenged. For example, an especially careful and important analysis of the migration of southern Negroes to the northern cities of the United States showed that there had been no selection, and that the higher intelligence ratings of Negro children in northern schools was therefore due to the more favorable social environment rather than to innate qualities (Klineberg, 1935).

It is difficult, in view of the small number of good studies and their contradictory results, to come to general conclusions. Dorothy Thomas does not believe that any generalization at all can be made: "Migration may, under given circumstances, select the intelligent; under other circumstances, the less intelligent; and under still other circumstances, be quite unselective with regard to intelligence" (D. S. Thomas, 1938, p. 125). The tentative conclusion offered by Sorokin and Zimmerman (1929, p. 571) is that "cities attract the extreme while the farms attract the mean strata in society." An essay by the Dutch sociologist Hofstee (1952) dispels some of the confusion around this question. Most of the previous discussion had centered on so-called *push* factors, that is, conditions at home that induce some persons to leave. Hofstee shifted the argument to *pull* factors, that is, conditions abroad that attract migrants. Everything that we know about selectivity by more easily defined characteristics, such as sex, indicates the greater importance of pull factors: the dominance of males or of females is generally determined less by the conditions at home than by the opportunities for one or the other at the destination. In the same way, selection by intelligence depends mainly on the level of opportunities available. Since many urban occupations both require a greater mental capacity and offer more income and status, there is a tendency for the more intelligent in a rural population, particularly if they are well educated, to migrate to the towns. On the other hand, the Negroes that Klineberg studied were moving into unskilled jobs, which did not induce any such selection. A migration from one portion of the rural area to another, similarly, is typically not selective. Thus, what has been analyzed as selection by intelligence is mainly one by actual or potential vocational skill.

Several studies on the relation between urbanization and the incidence of mental disease indicate both the possibilities of improving on the methodology of earlier analyses and the difficulties, even so, in reaching a firm conclusion. According to a monograph based on an analysis of first admissions to New York State mental institutions, in-migrants were represented in much higher proportion than those born in the state, even when migrants and nonmigrants of the same age were compared. Among whites the in-migrants' age-standardized rate was twice, among nonwhites about three times that of the native born. The admission rate of in-migrants who had lived in the state for more than five years was higher, but only slightly higher, than that of native New Yorkers (Malzberg and Lee, 1956).

These data suggest that all three of the causes noted above are relevant: (1) Since the standards of institutional care are relatively good in New York State, the incidence of mentally ill *outside* hospitals is higher in the population of many other states, particularly in the South and among Negroes. (2) In many cases admission to a mental hospital took place so soon after arrival in the state that the disease must have been well advanced prior to the migration. This implies (though only an investigation at the point of origin could prove this) that the mentally ill tend to migrate in greater proportion; but in that case some of those originally resident in New York presumably would have left. (3) The sharp contrast between recent migrants and those in the state more than five years is a clear indication that the strains of adjustment to a new environment are etiologically significant. (See also Lee, 1958, 1963.)

Two other studies on the relation between mental illness and migration supplement these findings. A comparison of first admissions in three states, New York, Ohio, and California, confirmed the datum that in-migration *per se* was "a major determinant" of admission to hospitals. "However, nonwhite natives have very much higher relative rates . . . than do corresponding classes of whites. . . . It seems, therefore, to be *not* nativity but color that determines the pattern" (Lazarus *et al.*, 1963).[8] According to a study in Jerusalem, "emotional disorder" was related to "status inconsistency" as measured by a discrepancy in either direction between an immigrant's educational level and that of his occupation (Abramson, 1966).

Even more evasive than intelligence or mental illness is the typical migrant's personality and character. In several essays, Hansen has examined the popular picture of the immigrant as pioneer, radical, innovator—and found it faulty. During the nineteenth century, he writes, the American immigrants stayed in the settled areas, following the advice of those few who had left them and generally returned: "Let the Americans start the clearing; they alone possess the specialized technique." Thus, "the first white man to pioneer in any township was not a Schultz or a Meyer, a Johnson or an Olson. He was a Robinson, a McLeod or a Boone. He was a descendant of that old Americanized stock which had learned frontiering in the difficult school that was in session from 1600 to 1800" (Hansen, 1948, pp. 66–67). The immigrant was a pioneer only in the sense that he left his

---

[8] As in other studies based on census data, "a major difficulty arose because of ambiguity in the census 'color' classification of the population. In New York and Ohio . . . 'nonwhites' were overwhelmingly Negro, . . . but in the California population this category was only 69 per cent Negro, the other 31 per cent being predominantly Japanese, Chinese, and other so-called 'minor races.' Inasmuch as the nonwhite category could not be reallocated in the denominators of rates, this ambiguous classification had to be retained in the numerators."

native country and braved the hardships of the journey, often considerable in the days of sailing ships.

Most of the immigrants were politically and culturally conservative, both in the old country and in the United States. The contrary notion grew out of the prominence of the small minority of political refugees—Carl Schurz and a few thousand like him as against the more than a million Germans who migrated to America during the 1850s. In Germany, "the areas of political disturbance did not coincide with the areas of emigration. From the cities that had witnessed bloody street fighting the emigrants were few; from the peaceful country districts the departing throngs threatened to depopulate the land" (*ibid.*, p. 80). In the American Federation of Labor, the continual re-election of Samuel Gompers, whom his opponents termed a renegade to his class, "was due largely to the support of trade organizations in which immigrant membership was strong" (*ibid.*, p. 90). The populist movement was almost wholly native. Immigrants voted against suffrage for women; "the reminiscences and reports of the suffrage missionaries agree that their opposition was perhaps the most formidable obstacle to overcome" (*ibid.*, p. 92). This strong conservatism derived principally from three sources—the immigrant's liking for the free-enterprise system and the opportunities it offered him; the influence of the immigrant churches, which were not only religious institutions but guardians of the old ways; and the newcomer's typical aspiration to be *plus royaliste que le roi*.

In Hansen's opinion, the desire for greater liberty did exist as one motive for migration, but it achieved its prominence in the public mind because other motives were depreciated. For an immigrant to speak of his material incentives would emphasize his economic competition with the natives, and to say that his sons had been growing up lazy and shiftless in a country where they could find no work would give point to the argument that foreigners were depraved and worthless.

Hence . . . the newcomer said, "I came to the United States to enjoy the blessings of your marvelous government and laws," [and] the native warmed to him and was likely to inquire whether there was not something he could do to assist him. Immigrants soon learned the magic charm of this confession of faith. They seized every opportunity to contrast the liberty of the New World with the despotism of the Old. . . . So the tradition was established, and the desire for political freedom was accounted one of the principal causes for the immigration (*ibid.*, pp. 78–79).[9]

Hansen's provocative essays do not of course prove his point, and in any case his argument is wholly negative. It discounts the love of liberty as a selective principle, but does not offer another in its place.

---

[9] According to a recent survey of British emigrants, they also tended to rationalize motives like feelings of insecurity or inadequacy into the most acceptable one, which in this instance was not love of liberty but an aspiration for economic advancement (Appleyard, 1964).

The process of migratory selection is obviously of great practical importance; to a large degree, it defines the meaning of any movement for the two areas concerned. Unfortunately, as this discussion has indicated, it is a subject about which we still know rather little. We have seen that migrants are in most respects not a random sample of the populations they leave and enter. In virtually all cases adolescents and young adults predominate. With respect to other characteristics—sex and occupation, possibly intelligence and mental health—selection usually seems to depend more on conditions at the destination than on those at the origin.

## Political Factors

Political influences on the number of migrants and their characteristics are of two broad types—inhibitions or encouragements to movement and migrations under duress or force. Examples of both could be cited from movements within the boundaries of totalitarian states (see pp. 653–660), but most of the data relate to international migration.

### IMMIGRATION RESTRICTIONS

A number of standard works on American immigration policy, using absolute freedom of migration as a standard, find that "free immigration" ended about 1830 (e.g., Garis, 1927), when some of the states along the eastern seaboard established controls, mostly ineffective. But this was before the massive flow from Europe even got under way. Just as a society can be meaningfully free though it has prisons, so to deny admission to obviously antisocial elements, as the eastern states attempted to do, is not inconsistent with the principle of free migration. The exclusion of criminals, prostitutes, and others with specific objectionable personal characteristics we will denote as the **regulation** of migration, which is to be distinguished from both **numerical restriction,** by which a certain maximum immigration is set for each year, and **qualitative restriction,** by which entry is denied to specified broad social or ethnic classes.

In the United States, restriction was enacted after World War I, following several decades of intense national debate. The exclusion of Southern and Eastern Europeans was first sought indirectly, by proposing that admission should be denied to all adults not able to read and write some language.[10] In 1917 the state was given the power to exclude or deport aliens for their political beliefs; and all immigration from the "barred zone" of Asia was banned; added to the special laws excluding Chinese and sharply limiting the immigration of Japanese, the new act all but eliminated move-

---

[10] Of the two dozen such literacy bills introduced in Congress, four were passed, to be vetoed successively by Cleveland, by Taft, and twice by Wilson. The law stipulating a literacy test that was finally passed in 1917 over Wilson's second veto kept out some Southern and Eastern Europeans, but not nearly so many as had been anticipated.

ment from that continent to the United States. The law of 1921, enacted as a stopgap measure until the problems could be studied, limited European immigration to 3 per cent of the number of foreign-born of each nationality residing in the United States at the time of the last available census figures, those of 1910. A second law, passed in 1924, set up another temporary system, more restrictive in two respects than its predecessor: the 3 per cent quota was reduced to 2 per cent, and the base population was changed from the 1910 to the 1890 census, when the proportion from Southern and Eastern Europe was smaller. In 1929 this base population was changed again to those in the total population of each "national origin" (see p. 116, n. 23). The Immigration and Nationality Act of 1952 (ordinarily known as the McCarran-Walter Act) continued to use national origins as the main criterion of eligibility, but in the ensuing period this principle was gradually eroded by a series of *ad hoc* laws that permitted refugees and others to immigrate outside the quota limitations. The national-quota system was finally abandoned in the Immigration Act of 1965, which went into effect in mid-1968.

The success of the immigration legislation in achieving the restrictionists' purpose is indicated in Table 8-5. The total immigration from Europe, 7.8 million in 1901–10 and 6.7 million in 1911–20 (the latter would have been larger if migration had not been suspended during the war), was cut down

Table 8-5. Immigration Quotas under Successive Laws, United States, 1921–64

|  | 1921 | 1924 | 1929 | 1952[a] |
|---|---|---|---|---|
| Northwest Europe [b] | 197,630 | 140,999 | 127,266 | 125,631 |
| Southern and Eastern Europe | 159,322 | 20,423 | 23,225 | 23,966 |
| Asia | 492 | 1,424 | 1,423 | 3,690 |
| All other countries | 359 | 1,821 | 1,800 | 4,874 |
| TOTAL | 357,803 | 164,667 | 153,714 | 158,161 |
|  | PER CENT | | | |
| Northwest Europe [b] | 55.2 | 85.6 | 82.8 | 79.4 |
| Southern and Eastern Europe | 44.5 | 12.4 | 15.1 | 15.2 |
| Asia | 0.1 | 0.9 | 0.9 | 2.3 |
| All other countries | 0.1 | 1.1 | 1.2 | 3.1 |
| TOTAL | 99.0 | 100.0 | 100.0 | 100.0 |

SOURCES: President's Commission on Immigration and Naturalization, *Whom We Shall Welcome*, Washington, D.C., 1953, pp. 76–77; U.S. Bureau of the Census, *Statistical Abstract of the United States, 1965*, Washington, D.C., 1965, Table 114.

[a] As amended; 1964 quotas.

[b] British Isles, Scandinavia, Germany, Low Countries, France, Switzerland.

to a decennial quota of about 1.5 million. And the Old Immigration, which made up only about a quarter of the *gross* movement during the last twenty-five years of unrestricted immigration, was assigned about 85 per cent of the European quotas, or roughly the same proportion as in the immigration around 1880. The two purposes of numerical and qualitative restriction had thus been achieved; under the 1965 law a restriction on numbers was retained but no specification of quality as defined by national origin.

The immigration policy of the United States before it was changed in 1965 has its counterpart in most of the countries to which sizable immigration might be expected. Although the formal law of Canada is different, the policy developed from it is precisely parallel (*cf.* Petersen, 1955, Chapter 7; Timlin, 1965). The "White Australia" policy and its New Zealand version have a long history (Price, 1966; Ross, 1967; Rivett, 1967). Britain imposed restrictions on the free immigration of British subjects from other members of the Commonwealth. Latin America has in general followed a similar policy. Even some of the countries of Asia have erected bars against the immigration of coolies from their Asian neighbors.

### SUBSIDIZED MIGRATION

The bar to members of certain nationalities or races has in some cases been matched by special inducements to those of other nationalities to immigrate. In Britain, after several years of preparation, the Empire Settlement Act (1922) authorized the government to pay up to half the costs of settling suitable persons in the overseas dominions. From the receiving side, the dominions have granted assistance to immigrants of British and, since 1945, of various other European nationalities. In a number of emigration countries in addition to Britain, prospective migrants have been subsidized in various ways (*cf.* Petersen, 1955, Chapter 3). Whether financial assistance greatly increases the size of migration is questionable in most instances, but it gives a country somewhat greater control over the classes of migrants to be admitted or sent out.

### REFUGEES

A far greater impetus to migration in the modern world has come from the various social catastrophes generating refugee streams. In the present age of total wars and totalitarian regimes, political motivations have set not only "Europe on the move" (Kulischer, 1948), but also, sometimes as reverberations from European disturbances, much of the rest of the world. To take a notable example, the partition of British India into the nations of India and Pakistan was accompanied by one of the largest migrations in human history, in part induced by terrorists on both sides, in part arranged under state auspices (Schechtman, 1963, Chapter 7).

In earlier ages those who fled before an invading army acquired no special status from their destination. Whole nations were dispersed in a diaspora—the Jews or the Armenians. Sectors of populations were expelled —the Jews from medieval Germany and later from Spain, the Gypsies from England, the Protestants from France. But before the twentieth century it was mostly the exiled notable individuals who captured a place in history books—the French royalists living as émigrés after 1789, or revolutionaries like Marx or Mazzini whose native countries were inhospitable.

The status of refugee, one of a mass of émigrés, developed in fact after World War I. Fridtjof Nansen, whom the League of Nations appointed High Commissioner in 1921, devoted his main effort to the succor of Armenians fleeing the Turks and of Russians fleeing the revolution; those unable to return home were eligible for the so-called "Nansen passport." Such efforts were much enhanced after the founding of the United Nations, whose activities on behalf of certain categories set administrative definitions of the major terms. "Refugees," thus, did not include those who had fled Communist regimes.[11] Those who had been "displaced" from such countries were to be sent back "as soon as possible." [12] "Stateless persons" were eligible for certain kinds of assistance, unless they were not in accord with the "purposes and principles" of the United Nations (including treatment of refugees from Communist totalitarianism?).[13] Although the blatant political bias of this period has dissipated to some degree, assistance to refugees through official agencies continues to depend, obviously, on the administrative definitions of the term.

[11] Immediately after its founding the United Nations defined *refugee* as "a person who has left, or who is outside of, his country of nationality or of former habitual residence, and who, whether or not he had retained his nationality, belongs to one of the following categories: victims of Nazi or fascist regimes or of regimes which took part on their side in the Second World War, . . . persons who were considered refugees before the outbreak of the Second World War for reasons of race, religion, nationality, or political opinion, . . . [who are] unable or unwilling to avail [themselves] of the protection of the Government of [their] country of nationality or former nationality" (*Yearbook of the United Nations, 1946–47*, New York, 1947, p. 816).

[12] A *displaced person* was defined as one who "has been deported from or has been obliged to leave his country of nationality or of former habitual residence, such as persons who were compelled to undertake forced labor or who were deported for racial, religious, or political reasons. . . . If the reasons for such displacement have ceased to exist, they should be repatriated as soon as possible" (*ibid.*). Among the two million refugees delivered to Soviet authorities by Western military officials and, later, UNRRA and IRO, there were many thousands repatriated against their will, as indicated by the high incidence of suicide among them. This policy continued until mid-1948, when the wartime alliance between the Soviet Union and Western democracies, already past its prime, was ended by the coup in Czechoslovakia and the blockade of Berlin (Kulischer, 1949).

[13] A *stateless person* was defined as one "who is not considered as a national by any state under the operation of its laws," excluding, however, criminals, those who received protection or assistance from the United Nations High Commissioner for Refugees, and those "guilty of acts contrary to the purposes and principles of the United Nations" (United Nations, Economic and Social Council, *Conference on the Status of Stateless Persons,* E/Conf. 17/5, 54-26300, 1954).

Chinese refugees in Macao, who numbered about 80,000 out of the total population of 300,000 (*United Nations*).

The principal international agency, governed by the United Nations High Commissioner for Refugees, has a narrowly restricted prime mandate: to assist persons who do not want to return to their country because of actual or feared racial, religious, or political persecution; and it may also extend its "good offices" to certain other limited categories. This definition does not include several numerically important classes of uprooted peoples: (1) Those who had fled from local political disturbances but remained within the boundaries of the same state; for example, those who fled from various outrages in Negro Africa were or were not "refugees" depending on whether they ended up on one side or the other of newly established and often artificial boundaries. (2) Those who are forcibly moved about within the boundaries of a single state; for example, the nationals of the Baltic states incorporated into the Soviet Union, who were then deported to forced-labor camps in Soviet Asia. (3) Those who had been forced to "return" to what is now defined as "their" country, after having lived "abroad" sometimes for generations; for example, the persons of French origin expelled to France from Algeria.

Some of the 60,000 refugees from Rwanda in the Congo, 1966 (*United Nations*).

As official UN definitions of *refugee* and similar categories are tied to restricted activities, the statistics issued by UN agencies understate the number of refugees more broadly defined. Data from the other main sources, the various private agencies, are not consistently compiled or equally accurate, and since the agencies generally receive funds on the basis of the number of persons aided, one can reasonably expect their figures to be on the high side. Unfortunately no demographer or other scholar has defined the term so as to lay a basis for data independent of such biases.[14] As

[14] Schechtman is in one sense an exception to this assertion. He views "refugees" in a Zionist perspective and thus excludes any "ingathering" into a counterpart of Israel. For example, almost a quarter of the West German population in 1960 was made up of some 9.3 million expellees from East Germany, 3.3 million ethnic Germans from various countries of East Europe, and 230,000 non-German refugees. The successful integration of this vast throng was something of a miracle (*cf.* Paikert, 1962), which is not obliterated by a definition of "refugee" that excludes all but the last, and smallest,

A refugee camp at Ein-Sultan, near Jericho, Jordan, 1966—one of fifty-four camps administered by the United Nations Relief and World Agency (*United Nations*).

defined by the United Nations Population and Statistical Commissions, migration "excludes population transfers, . . . deportations, refugee movements, and the movement of 'displaced persons,' " all of which fall outside "the migratory movements of normal times." [15] That an international body which includes some of the states most responsible for forced migrations should exclude them from its demographic analyses is understandable, but it is unfortunate that most independent students of migration accept this arbitrary and misleading delimitation of their subject.

---

of the three components (Schechtman, 1964).

In a different sense the late Eugene Kulischer was also an exception. If he had lived to continue his studies, the demography of war and revolution might have attained a general acceptance. Cf. A. J. Jaffe, "Notes on the Population Theory of Eugene M. Kulischer," *Milbank Memorial Fund Quarterly*, **40** (1962), 187–206.

[15] United Nations, Department of Social Affairs, *The Determinants and Consequences of Population Trends*, Population Studies, No. 17, New York, 1953, p. 98. *Cf.* p. 17.

A compilation of refugees, then, can be no more than approximate. When a person becomes one and when a refugee is considered integrated are not clearly or consistently designated. Thousands of refugees remain as "hard-core" cases from the Spanish Civil War and World War II. It was estimated that about 40 million persons became refugees in the dozen years *following* 1945 (Rees, 1959). Even if this was an inflated figure, the phenomenon it reflects is staggering in its magnitude. The implication of the datum can be better grasped when we recall that the usual estimate of the total migration from all of Europe from 1800 to 1950 is 60 million, or only one and a half times the number of refugees generated over one-twelfth of the time.

The figures in Table 8-6, compiled from a wide variety of sources, are knowledgeable estimates. The increase from 9.8 million to 11.2 million in one year may well have continued in the subsequent period, with new hundreds of thousands in Vietnam, Central Africa, and various other areas in conflict.

## Models of Migration

The various mathematical formulas that summarize migration trends omit political factors altogether. The simplest takes into account nothing but distance: within any area homogeneous with respect to all the other factors that affect the propensity to migrate, the number of migrants will be inversely related to the miles covered. One can express this relation in an equation, as follows:

$$M = \frac{aX}{D^b}$$

where $M$ stands for the number of migrants, $D$ for the distance over the shortest transportation route, and $X$ for any other factor that is thought to be relevant; $a$ and $b$ are constants, usually set at unity. In one version of this equation, the so-called $P_1P_2/D$ hypothesis, the populations of the end points of the movement are taken as the $X$ factors (Zipf, 1949). Another variation is the proposition that "the number of persons going a given distance is directly proportional to the number of [employment] opportunities at that distance and inversely proportional to the number of intervening opportunities" (Stouffer, 1940). When "opportunities" were defined operationally as the number of in-migrants, the hypothesis could be validated in a number of instances (Bright and Thomas, 1941; Isbell, 1944; Strodtbeck, 1949; see also Pihlblad and Gregory, 1957; Catton, 1965; Galle and Taeuber, 1966). According to a detailed comparison of the two, Stouffer's formulation is better than Zipf's, since in effect measuring "opportunities" corrects the total population figures for the amount of unemployment in the two areas (Anderson, 1955).

After the partition of British India, an "exchange of populations" took place. Caravans of desperate refugees crawled along the poor roads—Hindus and Sikhs south to India, Moslems north to Pakistan. They were all but defenseless against terrorists and robbers, famine and disease; thousands upon thousands died on the way (*Margaret Bourke-White—courtesy LIFE, © 1947 Time, Inc.*).

283

Table 8-6. Refugee Population of the World, by Area of Asylum and Origin, 1965–66

| REFUGEES | | ESTIMATED NUMBER | |
| --- | --- | --- | --- |
| TO | FROM | 1965 | 1966 |
| EAST ASIA | | 3,019,000 | 3,080,000 |
| Hong Kong and Macao | China | 2,019,000 | 2,080,000 |
| South Korea [a] | North Korea | 1,000,000 | 1,000,000 |
| SOUTHEAST ASIA | | 4,339,526 | 4,229,526 |
| India | Pakistan | 2,283,177 | 2,283,177 |
| Pakistan | India | 75,000 | 500,000 |
| (Intranational) | Kashmir [b] | 60,000 | — |
| Bhutan, India, Nepal, Sikkim | Tibet | 58,800 | 60,800 |
| India | Burma | 55,249 | 55,249 |
| South Vietnam | North Vietnam | 900,000 | — |
| (Intranational) | South Vietnam | 600,000 | 1,003,000 |
| Laos | (Intranational) | 250,000 | 250,000 |
| Thailand | Vietnam, Burma, China | 57,300 | 77,300 |
| MIDDLE EAST | | 1,301,879 | 1,374,714 |
| Various Arab countries | Palestine | 1,246,685 | 1,318,000 |
| Israel | Various countries | 52,000 | 52,000 |
| Iran | Various countries | 1,032 | 1,032 |
| Turkey | Various countries | 2,162 | 3,682 |
| AFRICA | | 698,520 | 1,020,038 |
| Morocco | Various countries | 2,700 | 2,700 |
| Senegal | Portuguese Guinea | 35,000 | 55,000 |
| Togo | Ghana | 5,700 | 5,700 |
| Dahomey | Various countries | 28,000 | 28,000 |
| Central African Republic | Sudan, Congo | 8,000 | 21,000 |
| Ethiopia | Sudan, Somalia, South Africa | 75,000 | 80,018 |
| Various African countries | Sudan | 100 | 70,100 |
| Tanzania | Various countries | 39,520 | 39,520 |
| Congo | Angola, Rwanda, Sudan | 290,000 | 478,000 |
| Burundi | Rwanda, Congo | 80,000 | 70,000 |
| Uganda | Various countries | 98,000 | 128,000 |

Table 8-6. Refugee Population of the World, by Area of Asylum and Origin, 1965–66 (*Continued*)

| REFUGEES | | ESTIMATED NUMBER | |
| TO | FROM | 1965 | 1966 |
| --- | --- | --- | --- |
| Zambia | Various countries | 36,000 | 41,000 |
| Various African countries | South Africa | 500 | 1,000 |
| EUROPE^c | | 170,967 | 244,314 |
| France | Various countries | 62,500 | 133,088 |
| West Germany^d | East Europe | 15,235 | 17,564 |
| Austria | Various countries | 858 | 858 |
| Italy | East Europe | 1,030 | 1,030 |
| Spain | Cuba | 13,800 | 15,000 |
| Greece | Various countries | 4,775 | 4,775 |
| Soviet Union | China | 71,500 | 71,000 |
| Various countries | Tibet | 999 | 999 |
| WESTERN HEMISPHERE | | 261,077 | 1,278,328 |
| Argentina | Chile, Bolivia, Paraguay | — | 1,000,000 |
| Bahamas, Dominican Republic | Haiti | 5,000 | 5,132 |
| Puerto Rico | Cuba, Haiti | 11,000 | 11,000 |
| United States | Cuba, Haiti | 65,036 | 97,148 |
| Latin America | Cuba | 20,000 | 35,000 |
| United States | Tibet | 41 | 48 |
| Latin America | European countries | 130,000 | 130,000 |
| TOTALS | | 9,790,699 | 11,226,920 |

SOURCE: U.S. Committee for Refugees, *World Refugee Report: Annual Survey Issue 1966–67*, New York, 1967, pp. 3–4.

^a Of the roughly 4 million who fled from North to South Korea during the Korean War, most presumably have been integrated. Yet in 1966 of all countries only India received more aid from American voluntary agencies than Korea.

^b With the cessation of fighting presumably most returned to their homes.

^c Does not include refugees in transit, e.g., some 49,000 Jewish migrants reported in 1966 to be moving toward final settlement, or the approximately 10,000 per year in transit from behind the Iron Curtain.

^d Includes 2,329 who escaped "over the wall" in 1965.

In both Stouffer's original study and several of the replications, the hypothesis leaves out not only all noneconomic factors but also some of the influences on job-hunting migrants. In a subsequent analysis, Stouffer (1960) introduced the factor of competing migrants: "Everything else being equal, the attractiveness of city Y for migrants from city X will depend, at least to some extent, on how many potential migrants are closer to Y than are the potential migrants in X." In a study of migration among Dutch provinces, the analyst extended the range of variables farther: when he included per capita income, percentage unemployed, degree of urbanization, quality of dwellings, and recreational resources, he found that the correlation between these and net migration was about 0.9 (W. H. Somermeijer, cited in Heide, 1963).

### MIGRATION STREAMS

The framework of models like Zipf's or Stouffer's is psychological: each potential migrant, operating as an individual, decides on the basis of relative gains whether or not to leave. This decision, however, is usually made in part through social contagion rather than personal calculation of pleasure versus pain. By what is called the axiom of cumulative inertia, "the longer a person remains in a given location, the lower [is] the probability that he will leave it" (Myers *et al.*, 1967). Correlatively, if migration becomes a social movement, it develops in a stream, such as—to take an example important in American history—the continuous migration to the West.

The point marking the center of the United States population has moved steadily westward along the 39th parallel at the rate of four or five miles per year, from northeastern Maryland in 1790 to southeastern Illinois in 1950. In 1960 it was just east of Salem, in Marion County, Illinois (Figure 8-1), or, including the two new states of Alaska and Hawaii, in the eastern part of Clinton County, Illinois. The movement of population that this shift denotes was continuous, though markedly affected by land grants, gold rushes, and transportation facilities, as well as by the several major geographical barriers on the way to the Pacific and beyond.

In the most recent period, after the lull in internal migration during the depression of the 1930s, the westward movement was greatly stimulated by the government's policy of establishing war plants on the Pacific Coast. Until World War II, the West had imported a substantial portion of the goods it consumed; and the cost of the long haul from the centers of manufacturing, aggravated by discriminatory freight rates, created the equivalent of a protective tariff wall behind which even marginal manufacturing plants could be set up. With the growth of the population, the consumer market is no longer too small to attract industries; once new enterprises are established, the employees who come into the area to work in one factory or office form a market for other new businesses. By such an interaction, the

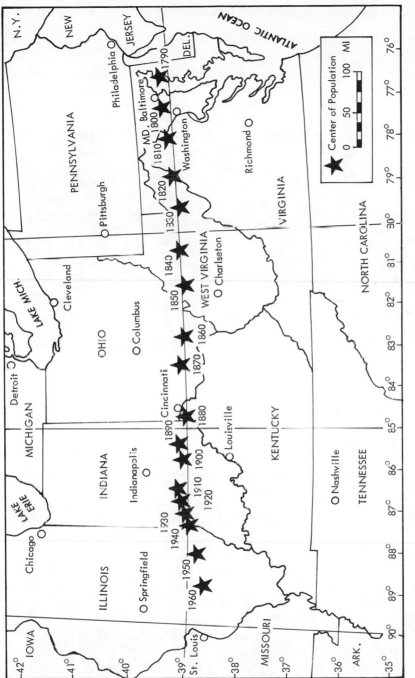

**Figure 8-1.** Center of population for conterminous United States, 1790 to 1960. Source: U.S. Bureau of the Census, *U.S. Census of Population, 1960, Vol. 1, Characteristics of the Population, Part 1, U.S. Summary*, Washington, D.C., 1964, Figure 10.

St. Paul, Minnesota, in 1857 (*Minnesota Historical Society*).

Building the St. Paul, Minneapolis, & Manitoba Railway westward through Montana Territory, 1887 (*Great Northern Railway photo*).

growth of manufacturing and of population can become cumulative, and under favorable geographic conditions it is appropriate to posit an analogy to the multiplier effect. The West now has an industrial structure ranging from the several large steel plants established during the war, through such major industries as the aerospace firms and the mammoth Ford assembly plant in California, to the literally hundreds of smaller factories established every year. California is not only the nation's leading agricultural state, with more than 200 commercial farm products, but first in the generation of power and third in the value of its mineral products. In value added by manufacturing, $17.2 billion in 1963, California was second only to New York. Processed foods, transportation equipment, wood products, petroleum, synthetic textiles, printing and publishing—California's list comprises both a more impressive and a more diversified economy than that of the West as a whole, but the same forces that have engendered California's remarkable development are apparent throughout the region. This prodigious growth has generated enormous disequilibria in both the state's institutions and in the no less prodigious growth of environmental pollution (Cook, 1966).

## A General Typology of Migration

If we try to expand these observations on the relation between migration and population growth, migratory selection, and migration models, we shall not be able to formulate valid "laws," for the empirical regularities do not always hold. The ultimate generalization in this case is a typology, in which the various conditions under which migration takes place are related to its probable effects (Heberle, 1956).

We have noted the crude first step frequently made in this direction, the contrast between "push" and "pull" factors—that is, between circumstances at home that repel and those abroad that attract. This conceptualization is inadequate, first of all, because it implies that man is everywhere sedentary, remaining fixed until he is induced to move by some force. Like most psychological universals, this can be matched by its opposite: man migrates because of wanderlust. And, like all such universals, these cannot explain differential behavior: if all men are sedentary (or migratory) "by nature," why do some migrate and some not? If a simplistic metaphor is used, it should be at least as complex as its mechanical analogue, which includes not only the concept of forces but also that of inertia.

Thus, one might better say that a social group at rest, or a social group in motion (e.g., nomads), tends to remain so unless impelled to change; for with any viable pattern of life a social structure and a value system are developed to support that pattern. To analyze the migration of Gypsies, for example, in terms of push and pull is no better than to explain modern Western migration, as Herbert Spencer did, in terms of "the restlessness inherited from ancestral nomads." [16] If the principle of inertia is accepted as valid, then the difference between gathering and nomadic peoples, on the one hand, and agricultural and industrial peoples, on the other hand, is fundamental with respect to migration. For once a people has a permanent place of residence, the relevance of push and pull factors is presumably much greater.

If wanderlust and what might be termed *sitzlust* are not useful as psychological universals, they do suggest a criterion for a significant distinction. If persons leave as a means of achieving the new, let us term such migration **innovating.** If, on the contrary, they respond to a change in conditions by trying to retain what they have had, moving geographically in order to remain where they are in all other respects, let us term such migration **conservative.** When the migrants themselves play a passive role, as in the case of African slaves being transported to the New World, the movement is termed innovating or conservative depending on how it is defined by the activating agent, in this case the slave-traders.

The fact that the familiar push-pull polarity implies a universal sedentary quality, however, is only one of its faults. The push factors alleged to "cause" emigration ordinarily comprise a heterogeneous array, ranging from agricultural crises to the spirit of adventure, from the development of shipping to overpopulation. No attempt is generally made to distinguish among underlying causes, facilitative environment, precipitants, and motives. In particular, if we fail to distinguish between personal motives and social causes—that is, if we do not take the emigrants' level of aspiration into account—our analysis must lack logical clarity.

No principled difference is usually made between what is sometimes termed "absolute overpopulation," which results in hunger and starvation, and milder degrees of "overpopulation," which reflect not physiological but cultural standards (*cf.* pp. 160–162). In the first case the aspiration of emigrants can be ignored, for it is a bare physiological minimum that can be taken as universal, but in the second case it is the level of aspiration itself that defines the "overpopulation" and sets the impetus to emigrate. Similarly, economic hardships can appropriately be termed a "cause" of emigration only if there is a positive correlation between hardship, however defined, and the propensity to leave. The mass exodus from Europe in modern times, it must be recalled, developed together with a marked *rise* in European levels of living; and this inverse relation is not exceptional. In short, it is probably true that most transatlantic migrants were economically motivated, but not that the propensity to leave was directly associated with economic conditions in the home country. As has already been noted, the correlation was rather with the business cycle in the receiving country, and even this explains fluctuations in the migration rate more than its absolute level.

[16] Herbert Spencer, *The Principles of Sociology,* 3rd Revised Ed.; Appleton, New York, 1892, 1, 566.

Nor can the class differential in the rate of emigration be ascribed simply to economic differences. Although the European bourgeoisie lived in more comfortable circumstances than the workers, for many a move to America would also have meant a definite material improvement. During the period of mass exodus, however, this was stereotyped as lower-class behavior, a bit unpatriotic for the well-to-do. For a son of a businessman to emigrate meant a break with the established group pattern, and from this class, thus, only marginal types like idealists or black sheep tended to leave the country, and these for relevant *personal* reasons. Once a migration has reached the stage of a social movement, however, such individual motivations are generally of little interest.

This kind of confusion is not limited to economic factors. Religious oppression or the infringement of political liberty was often a *motive* for leaving Europe, but before the rise of modern totalitarianism emigrants were predominantly from those countries least marked by such stigmata. An increasing propensity to emigrate spread east and south from Northwest Europe, together with democratic institutions and religious tolerance. Again, we are faced with the anomaly that those who departed "because" of the persecution tended to come from countries where there was less of it than elsewhere.

When the push-pull polarity has been refined in these two senses, by distinguishing innovating from conservative migration and by including in the analysis the migrants' level of aspiration, it can form the basis of a typology of migration. Five broad classes are defined, which are designated as primitive, forced, impelled, free, and mass. It should be noted that while these words are terms in common usage rather than neologisms, since they are here more precisely defined than in most contexts, they denote a narrower range of meaning. Free migration, thus, is *not* all migration that is not forced, for it is one of five rather than two classes.

## PRIMITIVE MIGRATION

The first class is that consequent from an ecological push, which is termed **primitive migration.** In this context, then, this does not define the wandering of primitive peoples as such, but rather a movement related to man's inability to cope with natural forces. However, since the reaction to a deterioration in the physical environment can be either remedial action or emigration, depending on the technology available to the people concerned, primitive migrations in this narrower sense are often by primitive peoples.

Many of the treks of preindustrial folk, it would seem, have been conservative as we have defined this term here. "There is often a strong tendency for [such] a migrating group to hold conservatively to the same type of environment; pastoral peoples, for example, attempt to remain on grasslands, where their accustomed life may be continued" (Dixon, 1933). The impetus to leave, the route, and the destination are set not by push and pull, but by the interplay of push and *control*. If they are indifferent about precisely where they are going, men migrate as liquids flow, along the lines of least resistance. Their way is shaped by barriers, both natural and man-made—both mountains, rivers, or rainfall or the lack of it, and the Great Wall of China or other, less monumental evidences of hostility toward aliens. Conservative migrants seek only a place where they can resume the old way of life, and when this is possible, they are content. Sometimes it is not possible, and any migration, therefore, may be associated with a fundamental change in culture.

The usual designation for treks of prehistoric primitives used to be "wandering of peoples," a translation from the German that, however inelegant, is nevertheless appropriate, for it denotes two of the characteristics that define it. It is usually a people as a whole that moves about and not merely certain families or groups, and they leave without a definite destination, as "wander" implies in English. Let us, then, term such migrations as those induced by ecological pressure **wandering of peoples.** Unintended movements over the ocean—an analogous type of primitive migrations, which can be termed **marine wanderings**—have occurred more frequently than was once supposed.

> There are countless . . . examples . . . [of] more or less accidental wanderings from island to island over oceanic expanses of water, brought about by winds and currents. The space of time and the extent of these voyages seem to play a subordinate part. Journeys covering 3,000 miles are not unusual. They may last six weeks or several months. Even without provisions the natives can get along, as they fish for their food and collect rain-water to drink (Numelin, 1937, pp. 180–181).

Contemporary primitives also often move about in a way directly related to the low level of their material culture. A food-gathering or hunting people cannot ordinarily subsist from what is available in one vicinity; it must range over a wider area, moving either haphazardly or back and forth over its traditional territory. Such movements are called **gathering.** The analogous migrations of cattle-owning peoples are called **nomadism,** from the Greek word for *graze*. Gatherers and nomads together are termed **rangers.**

The way of life of rangers is to be on the move, and their culture is adapted to this state. Their home is temporary or portable; some Australian peoples have no word for "home" in their language. Their value system adjudges the specific hardships of their life to be good. Although they are ordinarily restricted to a particular area, bounded by either physical barriers or peoples able to defend their territories, rangers are presumably more likely to migrate over longer distances (apart from differences in the means of transportation) simply because they are already in motion. Whether any particular nomad people settles down and becomes agricultural does not depend merely on geography. Geography determines only whether such a shift in their way of life is possible—it is barely feasible on the steppe, for example. But even when physical circumstances permit a change, the social pattern of ranging may be too strong to be broken down. Thus, the Soviet program of settling the Kirghiz and other nomad peoples on collective farms succeeded only because it was implemented by sufficient terror to overcome their opposition. That is to say, ranging, like wandering, is typically conservative.

A primitive migration of an agrarian population takes place when there is a disparity between the produce of the land and the number of people subsisting from it. This can come about either suddenly, as by drought or an attack of locusts, or by the steady pressure of growing numbers on land of limited area and fertility. Persons induced to migrate by such population pressure can seek another agricultural site elsewhere, but in the modern era the more usual destination has been a town. That is to say, the migration has ordinarily been innovating rather than conservative. The Irish immigrants to the United States in the decades after the Great Famine, for example, resolutely ignored the Homestead Act and other inducements to settle on the land; in overwhelming proportion, they moved to the cities and stayed there. Let us term such an innovating movement **flight from the land** (again an inelegant but useful translation from the German).

To recapitulate, primitive migration has been divided as shown in Table 8-7. These are the types set by a physical push and geographical or social controls.

Table 8-7. Types of Primitive Migration

| Primitive | Wandering | Wandering of peoples |
| | | Marine wandering |
| | Ranging | Gathering |
| | | Nomadism |
| | Flight from the land | |

### IMPELLED AND FORCED MIGRATIONS

The activating agent in migration is often not ecological pressure, but rather the state or some equivalent social institution. It is useful to distinguish **impelled migration,** when the persons involved retain some power to decide whether or not to leave, from **forced migration,** when they do not have this power. Often the boundary between the two, the point at which the choice becomes nominal, may be difficult to set. Analytically, however, the distinction is clear-cut, and historically it is often so. The difference is real, for example, between the Nazis' policy (roughly 1933–1938) of encouraging Jewish emigration by various anti-Semitic acts and laws, and the later policy (roughly 1938–1945) of herding Jews into cattle trains and transporting them to extermination camps.

A second criterion by which we can delineate types of forced or impelled migration is its function, as defined by the activating agent. If persons are induced to move simply to be gotten rid of, since this does not ordinarily bring about a change in the migrants' way of life, it is analogous to conservative migration and can be subsumed under it. Others are moved in order that their labor power can be used elsewhere, and such a migration, which constitutes a shift in behavior patterns as well as in locale, is designated as innovating. Four types are thus defined, as shown in Table 8-8. Each of these will be discussed briefly.

Table 8-8. Types of Impelled and Forced Migrations

|  | IMPELLED | FORCED |
|---|---|---|
| To be rid of migrants (conservative) | Flight | Displacement |
| To use migrants' labor (innovating) | Coolie trade | Slave trade |

In all of human history, **flight** has been an important form of migration. Whenever a stronger people move into a new territory, it may drive before it the weaker former occupants. The invasion of Europe during the early centuries of the Christian era, thus, was induced not only by the power vacuum consequent from the disintegration of the Roman Empire, but also by a series of successive pushes, originating from either the desiccation of the Central Asian steppes (Huntington, 1924) or the expansion of the Chinese empire still farther east (Teggart, 1939).

Many more recent migrations have also been primarily a flight before invading armies (Kulischer, 1948). In modern times, however, those induced to flee have often been only certain groups among the population, rather than everyone occupying a particular territory. Indeed, political dissidents had always been ousted when they became a danger to state security, but with the growth of nationalism, ethnic as well as political homogeneity has been sought. The right of national self-determination proclaimed by the Treaty of Versailles, thus, included no provision for the minorities scattered through Central Europe; and in the interwar period the League of Nations negotiated a series of population transfers designed to eliminate national minorities from adjacent countries or, more usually, to legitimate expulsions already completed (Ladas, 1932).

A forced movement intended merely to remove a dissident population is here called **displacement.** One purpose of the forced migrations under both Nazi and Soviet auspices has typically been to remove a hostile or potentially hostile group from its home. For example, after Poland was divided between Nazi Germany and Communist Russia in 1939, the more than a million Poles deported to Asiatic Russia were chosen not merely on the basis of actual or alleged opposition to their country's invasion, but more often as members of a large variety of occupational groups defined as potentially oppositionist.

Regarded as "anti-Soviet elements," and so treated, were administrative officials, police, judges, lawyers, members of Parliament, prominent members of political parties, noncommunist nonpolitical societies, clubs, and the Red Cross; civil servants not included above, retired military officers, officers in the reserve, priests, tradesmen, landowners, hotel and restaurant owners, clerks of the local Chambers of Commerce, and any class of persons engaged in trade or correspondence with foreign countries—the latter definition extending even to stamp collectors and Esperantists. . . . Many artisans, peasants, and laborers (both agricultural and industrial) were banished too, so that, in effect, no Polish element was spared.[17]

A second purpose of forced migrations has often been to furnish an unskilled labor force. During the war, for example, Nazi Germany imported workers from all occupied countries to keep its economy going. This modern variant of the **slave trade** differs in some respects from the overseas shipment of Africans during the mercantile age, but the two criteria that define the type are the same—the use of force and the supply of manpower.

The analogous form of impelled migration is termed **coolie trade.** This includes not only the movement of Asians to plantations, the most typical form, but also, for example, that of white indentured servants to the British colonies in the eighteenth century. Such migrants, while formally bound only for the period of a definite contract, very often are forced to go into debt and thus to extend their service almost indefinitely.[18] Many coolies eventually return to their homeland.

[17] Edward J. Rozek, *Allied Wartime Diplomacy: A Pattern in Poland,* Wiley, New York, 1958, p. 39.
[18] See, for example, Victor Purcell, *The Chinese in Southeast Asia,* Oxford University Press, London, 1951, p. 348.

## FREE MIGRATION

In the types discussed so far, the will of the migrants has been a relatively unimportant factor. A primitive migration results from the lack of means to satisfy basic physiological needs, and in the forced (or impelled) type the persons involved are also wholly (or partially) passive. We now consider the type in which the will of the migrants is the decisive element, or what is termed **free migration**. One of the principles established by the American and French revolutions was that, as the French constitution of 1791 put it, "the liberty of all to move about, to remain, or to leave" is a "natural and civil right." Among the founders of the United States, this tenet was axiomatic.[19]

Overseas movements from Europe during the nineteenth century can be discussed most conveniently in terms of one illustrative example, and because of the excellence of its formal analysis, Lindberg's monograph on emigration from Sweden to the United States has been chosen for this purpose. Lindberg (1930) begins by distinguishing three periods, each with a characteristic type of emigrants. During the first stage, beginning around 1840, they came principally from the two university towns of Upsala and Lund, "men with a good cultural and social background, mostly young and of a romantic disposition" (p. 3). As the risks overseas were great and impossible to calculate in a rational manner, those who left tended to be adventurers or intellectuals motivated by their ideals, especially by their alienation from European society during a period of political reaction. The significance of this **pioneer migration** was not in its size, which was never large, but in the example it set: "It was this emigration that helped to break the ice and clear the way for the later emigration, which included quite

[19] In the Declaration of Independence itself, one of the complaints voiced against George III was that, in his endeavor "to prevent the population of these States," he had obstructed the naturalization of foreigners and refused "to encourage their migration hither." Jefferson enunciated "the natural right which all men have of relinquishing the country in which birth or other accident may have thrown them, and seeking subsistence and happiness wheresoever they may be able, or may hope to find them." Or, in the words of Washington, "The bosom of America is open to receive not only the Opulent and Respectable Stranger, but the oppressed and persecuted of all Nations and Religions, whom we shall wellcome to a participation of all our rights and privileges, if by decency and propriety of conduct they appear to merit the enjoyment." This country was ordained as a haven for "the wretched refuse of [Europe's] teeming shores"—to quote Emma Lazarus's words as inscribed on the base of the Statute of Liberty.

There was, of course, also a dissident minority that challenged this basic value system, but the strength of xenophobia in American life has very often been exaggerated. If the Alien and Sedition Acts were enacted under Adams, it is no less significant that they were repealed under Jefferson, and in the aftermath were an important reason for the eclipse of the Federalist Party that had made them law. The nativist movement of the 1830s, the Know-Nothing Party of the 1850s, the American Protective Association of the early 1890s, the Ku Klux Klan reborn in 1915—all these movements indicate both the persistence of antiforeigner sentiment in America and also the fact that it has usually been limited to noisy groups of merely local importance.

different classes" (p. 7). These pioneers wrote letters home; their adventures in the New World were recounted in Swedish newspapers. Once settled, they helped finance the passage of their families or friends.

Imperceptibly, this first stage developed into the second, the period of **group migration**—the departure, for example of pietist communities under the leadership of their pastor or another person of recognized authority. Even when not associated through their adherence to a dissident sect, emigrants banded together for mutual protection during the hazardous journey and against the wilderness and the often hostile Indians at its end. The significance of this group movement also lay not in its size but in the further impulse it gave. Those leaving during the decade beginning in 1841 averaged only 400 persons annually, and during the following ten years still only 1,500.

### MASS MIGRATION

Free migration is always rather small, for individuals strongly motivated to seek novelty or improvement are not commonplace. The most significant attribute of pioneers, as in other areas of life, is that they blaze trails that others follow, and sometimes the number who do so grows into a broad stream. Migration becomes a style, an established pattern, an example of collective behavior. Once it is well begun, the growth of such a movement is semi-automatic: the principal cause of emigration is prior emigration. Other circumstances operate as deterrents or incentives, but within the attitudinal framework as already defined; all factors except population growth are important principally in terms of the established behavior.

As we have already noted, when emigration has been set as a *social* pattern, it is no longer relevant to inquire concerning *individual* motivations. For the individual is, in Lindberg's phrase, in an "unstable state of equilibrium," in which only a small impulse in either direction decides his course; thus, the motives he ascribes to his emigration are either trivial or, perhaps more likely, the generalities that he thinks are expected (*cf.* p. 274).

Migration as collective behavior can be aptly illustrated, again, by the Swedish case. The decade 1861–70, when the average number of emigrants jumped to 9,300 per year, began the transition to the third stage of **mass migration.** Transportation facilities improved. Railroads connected the interior with the port cities, and the sailing ship began to be replaced by the much faster and safer steamer. Not only was the geographical distance cut down, but also what Lindberg terms the social distance: as communities in the new country grew in size and importance, the shift from Sweden to America required less and less of a personal adjustment. Before someone left to go to a Swedish-American settlement, he started his acculturation in an American-Swedish milieu, made up of New World letters, photographs, mementoes, knick-knacks. There developed what the peasants called "America fever." In some districts there was not a farm without relatives in America, and from many all the young people had gone overseas. According to a government report that Lindberg quotes, children were "educated to emigrate," and he continues:

When they finally arrived at a decision, they merely followed a tradition which made emigration the natural thing in a certain situation. In fact, after the imagination and fantasy had, so to speak, become "charged with America," a positive decision *not* to emigrate may have been necessary if difficulties arose (pp. 56–57).

The Swedes who migrated to Minnesota became farmers or small-town craftsmen or merchants. In a more general analysis, it is useful to distinguish two types of mass movement according to the nature of the destination—**settlement,** such as Lindberg described, and **urbanization,** or mass migration to a larger town or city. No principal distinction is made here between internal and international migration; for the fundamentals of the rural-urban shift so characteristic of the modern era are usually the same whether or not the new city dwellers cross a national border.

The typology developed here is summarized in Table 8-9. These are

### Table 8-9. General Typology of Migration

| TYPE OF INTERACTION | MIGRATORY FORCE | CLASS OF MIGRATION | TYPE OF MIGRATION | |
|---|---|---|---|---|
| | | | CONSERVATIVE | INNOVATING |
| Nature and man | Ecological push | Primitive | Wandering | Flight from the land |
| | | | Ranging | |
| State (or equivalent) and man | Migration policy | Impelled | Flight | Coolie trade |
| | | Forced | Displacement | Slave trade |
| Man and his norms | Higher aspirations | Free | Group | Pioneer |
| Collective behavior | Social momentum | Mass | Settlement | Urbanization |

so-called ideal types, analytical constructs derived from historical examples but stripped of accidental, specific features in order to make them of more general significance. The most useful distinction in the typology, perhaps, is that between mass migration and all other kinds, for this emphasizes the fact that the movement of Europeans to the New World during the nineteenth century, the instance with which we are most familiar, does not constitute the whole of the phenomenon. After World War I, largely because of new political limitations imposed by both sending and receiving countries, there was a change to a different type, and this was very often interpreted as the end of significant human migration altogether. A world in which hardly anyone dies in the place where he was born, however, cannot be termed sedentary.

## Summary

Migration changes the size of population and the rate of growth of the two areas involved but usually not in the simple fashion that common sense suggests. Most migrants are young adults, and their movement changes the age structure and thus the birth and the death rates of both areas. And if the migration affects the social-economic determinants of fertility and mortality, the movement can be negated or, on the contrary, reinforced. Since remigration and transmigration are common, the net figures rather than the gross should be used to gauge the effect on population.

Given a sedentary population and a stimulus to migrate, typically some leave and some do not. There is a self-selection by age, sex, family status, and occupation, as well as possibly by intelligence, mental health, and independence of character. Such generalizations are based on migration that is predominantly economically motivated but not on the substantially larger flow of refugees.

Migration is not unitary; it differs from fertility and mortality in that it cannot be analyzed, even preliminarily, in terms of supracultural, physiological factors but must be differentiated even at the most abstract level with respect to the social conditions obtaining. This means that the most general statement that one can make concerning migration must be in the form of a typology, rather than a law. Although few today would follow Ravenstein's example and designate their statements "laws," most discussions of migratory selection still imply an almost equal degree of universality. Actually, selection ranges along a continuum, from total migration to total nonmigration, and the intermediate cases vary not only in the proportion that leave but also in the typical characteristics of those that do. The predominance of females in rural-urban migration that Ravenstein noted for England must be contrasted with male predominance in, for example, India's urbanization. In Table 8-10 a principle of selection is

Table 8-10. Migratory Selection by Type of Migration

| | TYPES | DESTINATION OF MIGRANTS | MIGRATORY SELECTION | COMMENTS; EXAMPLES |
|---|---|---|---|---|
| Wandering | Wandering of peoples | None | Survival of the fittest? | Prehistoric migrations |
| Wandering | Marine wandering | None | Survival of the fittest? | Prehistoric migrations |
| Ranging | Gathering | Greener pastures; commutation | None | Migratory way of life |
| Ranging | Nomadism | Greener pastures; commutation | None | Migratory way of life |
| | Flight from the land | More fertile land (or towns) | ? | "Malthusian" pressure |
| | Flight | Place of safety | None; or minority groups | Emigrés and refugees |
| | Coolie trade | Site of work, usually plantations | Young males | Large remigration |
| | Displacement | Any | None; or minority groups | Population exchanges |
| | Slave trade | Site of work | Young adults | Mercantile or industrial |
| | Pioneers | Frontier lands | Young males | Individually motivated |
| | Group migration | New lands | Dissident groups | Individually motivated |
| | Settlement | Rural areas | Young males predominate | Social momentum |
| | Urbanization | Towns | Young females predominate (in Europe) | Social momentum |

suggested for each type of migration. How accurate this is in each instance is an empirical question, and further research may make a revision necessary. But we know enough now to assert that migratory selection does vary considerably, and that a search for universal generalizations would be fruitless.

## Suggestions for Further Reading

Of the enormous literature on particular migrations, a few works contribute to a broader understanding of the whole subject. Shimm, 1956 is an excellent collection on American immigration policy, which is given historical perspective in Higham, 1956; Hansen, 1948; and several of the articles in Hutchinson, 1966. The chapters on migration in Kirk, 1946 are first-rate. Kulischer, 1948 and Petersen, 1955 supplement works that analyze only economic determinants. Several of the works on Australia, e.g., Borrie, 1954; Zubrzycki, 1960; and especially Price, 1966, try to use the insights from the larger American experience in analyzing the phenomenon in this different setting.

Of the monographs on internal migration, the most ambitious is Population Studies Center, 1957–63, whose first conclusions are summarized in Kuznets and Thomas, 1958. The collection of studies in Goldstein, 1961, more modest in scope, is also stimulating. Perhaps the best single analysis of internal migration is Illsley, 1963.

Isaac, 1947 on the economics of migration should be supplemented with B. Thomas, 1954, a more interesting work. The best analyses of migratory selection up to that date were collected in D. S. Thomas, 1938, and the most significant addition since then is Hofstee, 1952. Very few analysts have attempted to construct typologies similar to the one in this chapter, but see Fairchild, 1925, Chapter 1; Heberle, 1956; Gupta, 1959; Price, 1966.

The most general bibliography on international migration, B. Thomas, 1961, is heavily slanted toward economics. For sociological works, see Haskett, 1956; Lavell and Schmidt, 1956 (both on the United States); Canada, 1961 on that country; and Price, 1966 on Australia.

ABRAMSON, J. H. 1966. "Emotional Disorder, Status Inconsistency and Migration," *Milbank Memorial Fund Quarterly*, **44**, 23–48.

ANDERSON, THEODORE R. 1955. "Intermetropolitan Migration: A Comparison of The Hypotheses of Zipf and Stouffer," *American Sociological Review*, **20**, 287–292.

APPLEYARD, R. T. 1962. "The Return Movement of United Kingdom Migrants from Australia," *Population Studies*, **15**, 214–225.

° ———. 1964. *British Emigration to Australia*. University of Toronto Press and Australian National University, Toronto and Canberra.

BAYER, ALAN E. 1968. "The Effect of International Interchange of High-Level Manpower on the United States," *Social Forces*, **46**, 465–477.

BEIJER, G. 1966. "Selective Migration for and 'Brain Drain' from Latin America," *International Migration*, **4**, 28–36.

BERTHOFF, ROWLAND TAPPAN. 1953. *British Immigrants in Industrial America, 1790–1950*. Harvard University Press, Cambridge, Mass.

\* BORRIE, W. D. 1954. *Italians and Germans in Australia*. Cheshire, Melbourne.

BRIGHT, MARGARET L., and DOROTHY SWAINE THOMAS. 1941. "Interstate Migration and Intervening Opportunities," *American Sociological Review*, 6, 773–783.

CANADA. DEPARTMENT OF CITIZENSHIP AND IMMIGRATION. 1961. *Citizenship, Immigration, and Ethnic Groups in Canada: A Bibliography of Research, 1920–1958*. Ottawa.

CATTON, WILLIAM R., JR. 1965. "Intervening Opportunities: Barriers or Stepping Stones?" *Pacific Sociological Review*, 8, 75–81.

COOK, ROBERT C. 1966. "California: After 19 Million, What?" *Population Bulletin*, 22, 29–57.

DAVIE, MAURICE R. 1947. *Refugees in America: Report of the Committee for the Study of Recent Immigration from Europe*. Harper, New York.

———. 1949. *World Immigration, with Special Reference to the United States*. Macmillan, New York.

DAVIS, KINGSLEY. 1951. *The Population of India and Pakistan*. Princeton University Press, Princeton, N.J.

DIXON, ROLAND B. 1933. "Migration, Primitive," in *Encyclopedia of the Social Sciences*. Macmillan, New York, 10, 420–425.

DUNCAN, OTIS DUDLEY, and ALBERT J. REISS, JR. 1956. *Social Characteristics of Urban and Rural Communities, 1950*. Wiley, New York.

\* ELDRIDGE, HOPE T. 1964. "A Cohort Approach to the Analysis of Migration Differentials," *Demography*, 1, 212–219.

FAIRCHILD, HENRY PRATT. 1925. *Immigration: A World Movement and its American Significance*. Revised Ed. Macmillan, New York.

FERENCZI, IMRE. 1929. *International Migrations*. 1: *Statistics*. Publication 14. National Bureau of Economic Research, New York.

FOERSTER, ROBERT F. 1924. *The Italian Emigration of Our Times*. Harvard University Press, Cambridge, Mass.

GALLE, OMER R., and KARL E. TAEUBER. 1966. "Metropolitan Migration and Intervening Opportunities," *American Sociological Review*, 31, 5–13.

GARIS, ROY L. 1927. *Immigration Restriction: A Study of the Opposition to and Regulation of Immigration into the United States*. Macmillan, New York.

GINI, CORRADO. 1946. "Los efectos demográficos de las migraciones internacionales," *Revista Internacional de Sociología* (Madrid), 4, 351–388.

GOLDSTEIN, SIDNEY. 1954. "Repeated Migration as a Factor in High Mobility Rates," *American Sociological Review*, 10, 536–541.

———. 1964. "The Extent of Repeated Migration: An Analysis Based on the Danish Population Register," *Journal of the American Statistical Association*, 59, 1121–1132.

\* ———, editor. 1961. *The Norristown Study*. University of Pennsylvania Press, Philadelphia.

GOLDTHWAIT, JAMES WALTER. 1927. "A Town That Has Gone Downhill," *Geographical Review*, 17, 527–552.

GOLLIN, ALBERT E., editor. 1966. *The International Migration of Talent and Skills*. Council on International Educational and Cultural Affairs of the U.S. Government. Bureau of Social Science Research, Washington, D.C.

GONNARD, RENÉ. 1927. *Essai sur l'histoire de l'émigration*. Valois, Paris.

GRUBEL, H. G., and A. D. SCOTT. 1967. "Determinants of Migration: The Highly Skilled," *International Migration*, 5, 127–138.

GUPTA, AJIT DAS. 1959. "Types and Measures of Internal Migration," in International Union for the Scientific Study of Population, *International Population Conference*, Vienna, pp. 619–624.

HAMILTON, C. HORACE. 1965. "Practical and Mathematical Considerations in the Formulation and Selection of Migration Rates," *Demography*, 2, 429–443.

° HANSEN, MARCUS LEE. 1948. *The Immigrant in American History*. Harvard University Press, Cambridge, Mass.

HASKETT, RICHARD C. 1956. "An Introductory Bibliography for the History of American Immigration, 1607–1955," in *A Report on World Population Migrations*, edited by Stanley J. Tracy. George Washington University, Washington, D.C., pp. 85–295.

° HEBERLE, RUDOLF. 1956. "Types of Migration," Research Group for European Migration Problems *Bulletin*, 4, 1–5.

HEIDE, H. TER. 1963. "Migration Models and their Significance for Population Forecasts," *Milbank Memorial Fund Quarterly*, 41, 56–76.

HERSCH, LIEBMANN. 1931. "International Migration of the Jews," in Willcox, 1931, pp. 471–520.

HIGHAM, JOHN. 1956. "American Immigration Policy in Historical Perspective," in Shimm, 1956, pp. 213–235.

HILLERY, GEORGE A., JR., JAMES S. BROWN, and GORDON F. DEJONG. 1965. "Migration Systems of the Southern Appalachians: Some Demographic Observations," *Rural Sociology*, 30, 33–48.

HOBBS, ALBERT HOYT. 1942. *Differentials in Internal Migration*. University of Pennsylvania Press, Philadelphia.

° HOFSTEE, E. W. 1952. *Some Remarks on Selective Migration*. Research Group for European Migration Problems. Publication 7. Nijhoff, The Hague.

HUNTINGTON, ELLSWORTH. 1924. *Civilization and Climate*. 3rd Revised Ed. Yale University Press, New Haven.

HUTCHINSON, EDWARD P. 1956. *Immigrants and Their Children, 1850–1950*. Wiley, New York.

° ——, editor. 1966. "The New Immigration," *Annals of the American Academy of Political and Social Science*, Vol. 367.

° ILLSLEY, RAYMOND, ANGELA FINLAYSON, and BARBARA THOMPSON. 1963. "The Motivation and Characteristics of Internal Migrants," *Milbank Memorial Fund Quarterly*, 41, 115–143, 217–248.

ISAAC, JULIUS. 1947. *Economics of Migration*. Kegan Paul, Trench, Trubner, London.

ISBELL, ELEANOR COLLINS. 1944. "Internal Migration in Sweden and Intervening Opportunities," *American Sociological Review*, 9, 627–639.

JEROME, HARRY. 1926. *Migration and Business Cycles*. National Bureau of Economic Research, New York.

° KIRK, DUDLEY. 1946. *Europe's Population in the Interwar Years*. League of Nations. Princeton University Press, Princeton.

KLINEBERG, OTTO. 1935. *Negro Intelligence and Selective Migration*. Columbia University Press, New York.

° KULISCHER, EUGENE M. 1948. *Europe on the Move: War and Population Changes, 1917–47*. Columbia University Press, New York.

——. 1949. "Displaced Persons in the Modern World," *Annals of the American Academy of Political and Social Science*, 262, 166–177.

° KUZNETS, SIMON, and ERNEST RUBIN. 1954. *Immigration and the Foreign Born.* Occasional Paper 46. National Bureau of Economic Research, New York.

° ———, and DOROTHY SWAINE THOMAS. 1958. "Internal Migration and Economic Growth," in Milbank Memorial Fund, 1958, pp. 196–221.

LADAS, STEPHEN P. 1932. *The Exchange of Minorities: Bulgaria, Greece and Turkey.* Macmillan, New York.

LAVELL, C. B., and WILSON E. SCHMIDT. 1956. "An Annotated Bibliography on the Demographic, Economic and Sociological Aspects of Immigration," in *A Report on World Population Migrations,* edited by Stanley J. Tracy. George Washington University, Washington, D.C., pp. 296–449.

LAZARUS, JUDITH, BEN Z. LOCKE, and DOROTHY SWAINE THOMAS. 1963. "Migration Differentials in Mental Disease," *Milbank Memorial Fund Quarterly,* **41,** 25–42.

LEE, EVERETT S. 1958. "Migration and Mental Disease: New York State, 1949–1951," in Milbank Memorial Fund, 1958, pp. 141–152.

———. 1963. "Socio-Economic and Migration Differentials in Mental Disease, New York State, 1949–1951," *Milbank Memorial Fund Quarterly,* **41,** 249–268.

———. 1966. "A Theory of Migration," *Demography,* **1,** 47–57.

LINDBERG, JOHN S. 1930. *The Background of Swedish Emigration to the United States: An Economic and Sociological Study of the Dynamics of Migration.* University of Minnesota Press, Minneapolis.

LOWENTHAL, DAVID, and LAMBROS COMITAS. 1962. "Emigration and Depopulation: Some Neglected Aspects of Population Geography," *Population Review,* **6,** 83–94.

MALZBERG, BENJAMIN, and EVERETT S. LEE. 1956. *Migration and Mental Disease: A Study of First Admissions to Hospitals for Mental Disease, New York, 1939–1941.* Social Science Research Council, New York.

° MILBANK MEMORIAL FUND. 1958. *Selected Studies of Migration Since World War II.* New York.

MILLS, THOMAS J. 1966. "Scientific Personnel and the Professions," in Hutchinson, 1966, pp. 33–42.

MONROE, J. J. 1966. "Regional Variation in French Emigration Rates," *International Migration,* **4,** 186–198.

MYERS, GEORGE C., ROBERT McGINNIS, and GEORGE MASNICK. 1967. "The Duration of Residence Approach to a Dynamic Stochastic Model of Internal Migration: A Test of the Axiom of Cumulative Inertia," *Eugenics Quarterly,* **14,** 121–126.

° NUMELIN, RAGNAR. 1937. *The Wandering Spirit: A Study of Human Migration.* Macmillan, London.

PAIKERT, G. C. 1962. *The German Exodus: A Selective Study on the Post-World War II Expulsion of German Populations and Its Effects.* Research Group for European Migration Problems. Publication 12. Nijhoff, The Hague.

° PETERSEN, WILLIAM. 1955. *Planned Migration: The Social Determinants of the Dutch-Canadian Movement.* University of California Press, Berkeley.

———. 1968. "Migration: Social Aspects," in *International Encyclopedia of the Social Sciences,* Macmillan and Free Press, New York, **10,** 286–292.

PIHLBLAD, C. T., and C. L. GREGORY. 1957. "Occupation and Patterns of Migration," *Social Forces,* **36,** 56–64.

POPULATION STUDIES CENTER, University of Pennsylvania. 1957–64. *Population*

*Redistribution and Economic Growth, United States, 1870–1950.* American Philosophical Society, *Memoirs,* Vols. 45, 51, 61.

PRESIDENT'S COMMISSION ON IMMIGRATION AND NATURALIZATION. 1953. *Whom We Shall Welcome.* U.S. Government Printing Office, Washington, D.C.

° PRICE, CHARLES A., editor, 1966. *Australian Immigration: A Bibliography and Digest.* Australian National University, Canberra.

RAVENSTEIN, E. G. 1885 and 1889. "The Laws of Migration," *Journal of the Royal Statistical Society,* 48, 167–235; 52, 241–305.

REES, ELFAN. 1959. *We Strangers and Unafraid.* Carnegie Endowment for International Peace, New York.

RICHMOND, A. H. 1966. "Demographic and Family Characteristics of British Immigrants Returning from Canada," *International Migration,* 4, 21–26.

RIVETT, KENNETH. 1967. "A Proposal for Change in Australia's Immigration Policy," in *Asia's Population Problems,* edited by S. Chandrasekhar. Allen & Unwin, London, pp. 256–276.

ROSE, ARNOLD M. 1958. "Distance of Migration and Socioeconomic Status of Migrants," *American Sociological Review,* 23, 420–423.

ROSS, ANTHONY CLUNIES. 1967. "Asian Migration—An Australian Failure?" in *Asia's Population Problems,* edited by S. Chandrasekhar. Allen & Unwin, London, pp. 235–255.

ROSSI, PETER H. 1955. *Why Families Move: A Study in the Social Psychology of Urban Residential Mobility.* Free Press, Glencoe, Ill.

RUBIN, ERNEST. 1966. "The Demography of Immigration to the United States," in Hutchinson, 1966, pp. 15–22.

SALOUTOS, THEODORE. 1956. *They Remember America: The Story of the Repatriated Greek-Americans.* University of California Press, Berkeley.

SAVILLE, JOHN. 1957. *Rural Depopulation in England and Wales, 1851–1951.* Routledge & Kegan Paul, London.

SCHECHTMAN, JOSEPH B. 1963. *The Refugee in the World: Displacement and Integration.* Barnes, New York.

° SHIMM, MELVIN C., editor. 1956. "Immigration," *Law and Contemporary Problems,* Vol. 21, No. 2.

SHRYOCK, HENRY S., JR. 1964. *Population Mobility within the United States.* Community and Family Study Center, University of Chicago, Chicago.

SOROKIN, PITIRIM A., and CARLE C. ZIMMERMAN. 1929. *Principles of Rural-Urban Sociology.* Holt, New York.

STOUFFER, SAMUEL A. 1940. "Intervening Opportunities: A Theory Relating Mobility and Distance," *American Sociological Review,* 5, 845–867.

———. 1960. "Intervening Opportunities and Competing Migrants," *Journal of Regional Science,* 2, 1–26.

STRODTBECK, FRED L. 1949. "Equal Opportunity Intervals: A Contribution to the Method of Intervening Opportunity Analysis," *American Sociological Review,* 14, 490–497.

TABAH, LÉON, and ALBERTO CATALDI. 1963. "Effets d'une immigration dans quelques populations modèles," *Population,* 18, 683–696.

TEGGART, FREDERICK J. 1939. *Rome and China: A Study of Correlations in Historical Events.* University of California Press, Berkeley.

° THOMAS, BRINLEY. 1954. *Migration and Economic Growth: A Study of Great*

*Britain and the Atlantic Economy.* National Institute of Economic and Social Research. Economic and Social Study No. 12. University Press, Cambridge.

———. 1961. *International Migration and Economic Development: A Trend Report and Bibliography.* UNESCO, Paris.

THOMAS, DOROTHY SWAINE. 1925. *Social Aspects of the Business Cycle.* Dutton, New York.

———. 1941. *Social and Economic Aspects of Swedish Population Movements, 1750–1933.* Macmillan, New York.

° ———, editor. 1938. *Research Memorandum on Migration Differentials.* Social Science Research Council, New York.

THOMLINSON, RALPH. 1962. "The Determination of a Base Population for Computing Migration Rates," *Milbank Memorial Fund Quarterly,* **40,** 356–366.

TIMLIN, M. F. 1965. "Canadian Immigration Policy: An Analysis," *International Migration,* **3,** 52–70.

U.S. BUREAU OF THE CENSUS. 1963. *U.S. Census of Population: 1960.* Subject Reports. *State of Birth.* Final Report PC (2)-2A. Washington, D.C.

° ———. 1968. "Lifetime Migration Histories of the American People," *Current Population Reports,* Series P-23, No. 25.

° U.S. COMMITTEE FOR REFUGEES. 1966–67. *World Refugee Report: Annual Survey Issue.* New York.

WALKER, FRANCIS A. 1873. "Our Population in 1900," *Atlantic Monthly,* **32,** 487–495.

———. 1891. "Immigration and Degradation," *Forum,* **11,** 634–644.

———. 1892. "Immigration," *Yale Review,* **1,** 124–145.

———. 1896. "Restriction of Immigration," *Atlantic Monthly,* **77,** 822–829.

WILLCOX, WALTER F. 1906. "The Expansion of Europe in Its Influence upon Population," in *Studies in Philosophy and Psychology by Former Students of Charles Edward Garman,* edited by James Hayden Tufts *et al.* Houghton, Mifflin, Boston, pp. 41–70.

———. 1911. "The Change in the Proportion of Children in the United States and in the Birth Rate in France during the Nineteenth Century," *American Statistical Association Publications,* N.S. No. 93, March, pp. 490–499.

° ———, editor. 1931. *International Migrations.* **2:** *Interpretations.* Publication 18. National Bureau of Economic Research, New York.

ZIPF, GEORGE K. 1949. *Human Behavior and the Principle of Least Effort.* Addison-Wesley Press, Cambridge, Mass., pp. 386–409.

° ZUBRZYCKI, J. 1960. *Immigrants in Australia.* Melbourne University Press and Australian National University, Canberra, 2 Vols.

# 9 PROJECTIONS AND FORECASTS

Demographers are called on not only to furnish data about the present size and composition of the population and their past development, but also to estimate their future trend. Such a prognosis, however it is made, is likely to be incorrect, but this does not mean that it is useless. It may be compared in many respects to a weather prediction by a meteorologist. In both cases, the estimate by a competent expert will generally be more accurate than a layman's guess. Moreover, much of what we know about the weather or about the determinants of population growth has been learned by comparing false predictions with the actual events and trying to understand why the error was made. In one respect, however, there is an important difference between a meteorologist's and a demographer's forecasts. If the weather bureau predicts that it will rain on a certain day, this statement has no effect on the weather, but a population forecast, if it is made a basis for government policy, itself becomes one of the determinants of population change. One analyst speaks of a "law of forecast feedback": "If a system of forecasting achieves a significant reputation for infallibility, its forecasts tend to become part of the chain of events, affecting the outcome in an unpredictable manner" (Smith, 1964). The very predictions of incipient population decline in the 1930s, for example, may have helped reverse the trend and thus make the forecasts false. Or, on the smaller scale of urban planning, it is well known that a new road or a new school or any other new facility, constructed in accord with carefully estimated rates of in-migration and natural increase, often attracts many more families to the area than had been anticipated.

The Census Clock as of 11 A.M. on September 16, 1966. At the rate of a net increase of one person per 13½ seconds, the population passed 200 million by the end of 1967 (*U.S. Bureau of the Census*).

Analysis of how trends in fertility, mortality, and migration together set the future growth of a population sums up, in a sense, the earlier chapters of Part I. In another sense, this chapter is an introduction to the detailed discussion of the populations of various types of society in Part II. For what we extrapolate in a population projection is typically the rapid growth in numbers characteristic of the present phase of the demographic transition, the over-all topic of the rest of this work. And when we come to consider, at the end of this chapter, the future population of the world, the rationale for dividing it between developed and underdeveloped areas becomes manifest.

# Types of Population Projections

A chronological account of population projections is largely a history of developing methodology. The linear extrapolations of the nineteenth century gave way to a search for a natural law of population growth and, most recently, to attempts to analyze separately changes in fertility, mortality, and migration as these relate to population structure. It is convenient to trace this development with examples pertaining mainly to the population of the United States.

## PROJECTIONS OF TOTAL POPULATION GROWTH

The simplest type of projection is an extrapolation of the past growth of the total population. The most famous, perhaps, of the several calculations of this type made early in American history was that by Elkanah Watson, a minor figure of the revolutionary period. He noticed that the population of the United States had increased by about a third during each of the first two decades following the 1790 census, and in a two-page article he calculated the growth if this decennial rate were to continue.[1] Until 1860 this forecast proved to be extraordinarily close to the actual population growth. For 1840 the projected figure was 17,116,526 and the census count 17,069,453, representing an error of about 0.3 per cent. For 1850 the projected figure was 23,185,368 and the census count 23,191,876, representing an error of about 0.03 per cent almost forty years after the calculation was made!

An only slightly more elaborate extrapolation by Francis Bonynge also predicted actual growth over a considerable span. He divided the population into the three groups of whites, slaves, and free Negroes, and applied a rate of decennial increase to each. Watson's forecast was reasonably accurate for fifty years, Bonynge's for seventy years.[2]

In the 1840s a more thorough analysis of population growth was made by George Tucker, a professor of political economy and moral philosophy at the University of Virginia. He calculated fertility ratios from 1800 on and deduced that the family size had been decreasing since that date. This decline in fertility had begun, according to Tucker, because of "moral causes," but the decisive factor would eventually become the "difficulty of subsistence." The rate of growth would fall, therefore, unless immigration steadily increased. He predicted a population of 74 to 80 million in 1900

---

[1] Cf. Winslow C. Watson, editor, *Men and Times of the Revolution: or, Memoirs of Elkanah Watson . . .* , Dana, New York, 1856, pp. 455–456. Cf. pp. 257–258.

[2] Francis Bonynge, *The Future Wealth of America*, New York, 1852; cited in W. S. and E. S. Woytinsky, *World Population and Production: Trends and Outlook*, Twentieth Century Fund, New York, 1953, p. 245.

(the census count was 76 million) and one of 200 million in 1940 (compared with the actual 132 million).[3]

J. D. B. DeBow, superintendent of the 1850 census, believed that the most likely figure in 1900 was 100 million, but that thereafter the rate of growth would fall off sharply. He predicted the 1950 population of 150 million precisely.[4] Toward the end of the century, several efforts were made to fit the past growth to a more elaborate curve. H. S. Pritchett, who used a third-degree parabola, forecast the population of 1900 within 2 per cent and that of 1910 within less than 3 per cent; but by the year 2900, according to his series, the United States would have 40 billion inhabitants.[5]

How is it that these men, some of them wholly untrained (Bonynge was a retired China merchant), all of them using crude methods, were able to forecast the growth of the population over many decades? The astounding accuracy was a fluke; until 1860 the population counted in successive censuses increased by a regular proportion, and the formulas used by these early forecasters were usually not much more complex than this record. Most of the predictions were off by considerable amounts for the later dates, but even so they are enough of a curiosity to excite any student's wonder. None of the technically more pretentious efforts to project population growth has been nearly so successful over so long a period as the best of these early forecasts.

A well known effort to find a general growth pattern is the Pearl-Reed logistic curve, as enunciated in several books and articles and applied to the populations of various countries and times. Raymond Pearl was a zoologist, and he developed his theory from analyzing the actual multiplication of fruit flies with a given amount of food in a closed bottle. As the adult drosophilae able to propagate increased from the original pair, their number went up at an ever accelerating rate until the limiting factor of the fixed food supply became relevant. Then the S-shaped growth curve gradually flattened out, approaching but never quite reaching a maximum level fixed by the subsistence available.

The populations of a number of countries were fitted to logistic curves of various formulas, with a good deal of success in the first period.[6] For

---

[3] George Tucker, *Progress of the United States in Population and Wealth*, New York, 1843; cited in Spengler, 1936.

[4] *Compendium of the Seventh Census*, Washington, 1854, pp. 130–131; cited in Spengler, 1936.

[5] H. S. Pritchett, *A Formula for Predicting the Population of the United States*, 1890; cited in Woytinsky and Woytinsky, *op. cit.*, p. 245.

[6] It was used, for instance, by Janisch in Germany, Yule in England, and Maclean in Canada. See F. Janisch, *Das Exponentialgesetz als Grundlage einer vergleichenden Biologie*, Berlin, 1927; G. Udny Yule, "The Growth of Population and the Factors which Control It," *Journal of the Royal Statistical Society*, 88 (1925), 1–58; M. C. Maclean, "The Growth of Population in Canada," in Canada, Dominion Bureau of Statistics, *Seventh Census of Canada, 1931*, 1: *Summary*, Ottawa, 1936, 99–132. For a critical comment on the last, see William Petersen, *Planned Migration: The Social Determinants of the Dutch-Canadian Movement*, University of California Press, Berkeley, 1955, pp. 204 ff.

example, a forecast that Pearl and Reed made in 1920 predicted the 1950 population of the United States with an error of only about one per cent (Pearl and Reed, 1920). In the meantime, however, since Logistic I had predicted a population in 1940 some 3.5 per cent higher than the census count in that year, Pearl and his associates calculated Logistic II, which missed the 1950 population by 7 million rather than by 2 million.

A decisive test of his theory was to be found, according to Pearl, in the one instance of a self-contained population on which adequate statistics had been maintained over a considerable period.

> The native Algerian population . . . affords a crucial case. It is a human population which has virtually completed a cycle of growth according to the logistic curve within the period of recorded census history. One can now feel more certain that this curve is a first and tolerably close approximation to a real *law* of growth for human populations, than was possible when the completion of a cycle for a human population demanded extrapolation of the curve for many years beyond the period of the observation (Pearl, 1925, pp. 125–126).

When his first projected figure, 5,234,000 in 1931, was short of the actual population by some 300,000, Pearl fell back on the explanation that a law in 1919 had extended political rights to certain of the native Algerians and had thus changed the influences on growth. As social changes of this importance are frequent occurrences in every country, it meant that the theory, even if valid on other grounds, was far less precise than he had suggested in his first statement of it. Sometimes he combined two logistic curves of different equations into a single growth curve. In the case of Germany, for example, the shift from one equation to another was supposedly necessitated by the change from a predominantly agricultural to an industrial society; but an exactly comparable change in, for example, American society did not require a compound curve (*ibid.*, pp. 14, 21).

In retrospect, the success of the logistic curve, like that of the earlier predictions, must be regarded as coincidental. What most condemns it is the biological rationale on which it is based. The relative abundance of food, which in Pearl's basic model was the only determinant of population growth, in a country like the United States is hardly even a relevant factor— except possibly in the very long run. In Pearl's extension of this model the limit was not merely food but the total physical resources as developed by the technology of the period. While this seems reasonable enough, it is actually not a very useful theory on which to base forecasts. This is so for two, seemingly contradictory reasons: (1) In the modern period the control over the environment becomes more effective year by year. To set a maximum population (the asymptote that the logistic curve will never quite reach) in terms of present technology would be unrealistic, but to set it in terms of an extrapolation of improving technology involves a guess no less hazardous than the projection of the number of people. On the other hand, (2) the population pressure that will later develop may be felt immediately, for human decisions are made not merely in response to physical difficulties but often in anticipation of them. The ultimate limit to growth, that is to say, is not a useful guide to the future rate of increase, because that limit will change and, in any case, its effect may be significant much before the ultimate point.

The growth rate of the human population did not decline because of hunger, as with the fruit flies, but because, for various reasons possibly including hunger, parents decided to have fewer children. For a period mortality fell faster than fertility, and the population increased rapidly; then fertility fell faster and the curve began to flatten out. That is to say, the S-shaped curve, to the degree that it has actually described the growth of human populations, has done so because of the demographic transition, not because of the biological determinants that Pearl posited.

### REPRODUCTION RATES

Both the gross and the net reproduction rates, it will be recalled (see pp. 83–84), are population projections, though half-disguised as measures of fertility. A projection based on wholly unrealistic assumptions—such as that the demographic rates of any one year are a permanent fixture—is often a useful device; although we know this will not happen, let us see what the consequences would be if it did. But the synthetic cohort of the model is not the same as an actual cohort. If one forgets that these assumptions were made, the tool is less helpful than misleading (Stolnitz and Ryder, 1949). The average net reproduction rate of the United States during the 1930s was 0.98, or 2 per cent below the replacement level of 1.0. The annual age-specific birth rates during that one decade, however, were not a good indication of what the completed family size of any cohort would be. Older women, who had borne children in the 1920s, refrained in greater numbers from having more; and younger women put off having children until the 1940s. Thus, what was widely interpreted as the first step toward the impending decrease in population was in fact a temporary phenomenon.

In 1931 Dublin presented two forecasts based on the principles underlying the net reproduction rate. According to the first, which in his opinion was "altogether too optimistic," the population of the United States with no migration would reach a maximum of 154 million between 1980 and 1990 and then decline to 140 million by 2100. By the second, "more reasonable" estimate, the maximum of 148 million would be reached by 1970, followed by a decline to 140 million by 2000 and to 76 million by 2100!

These predictions are remarkable not so much for their specific numerical values as for the fact that a prominent American demographer had stated publicly that the population of the United States almost certainly would decline in the very near future. The most pessimistic of previous forecasters had assumed merely that the rate of increase would approach zero at some distant time (Dorn, 1950).

The main reason that reproduction rates are inappropriate as predictive instruments, to sum up, are that (1) they are ordinarily (though not necessarily) based on the fertility and mortality of a single year and (2) they assume that these will remain constant for a century or so after that. The rates "are analogous to the speedometer on a car in that they measure the approximate speed or force of reproduction at a given time but not necessarily the actual distance being covered or the actual time required to reach the destination. The 'speed' fluctuates too much [to be a] reliable measure of distance." [7]

## COMPONENT PROJECTIONS

In virtually all projections made today the total population is not extrapolated as such but is rather divided up first into its component parts and, as it were, reassembled at successive future dates.[8] The growth in an area during any particular period is the consequence of its natural increase and the net migration. If one analyzes separately the trend in the three components—fertility, mortality, and migration—the most important variable is the age and sex structure. Since childbearing is physiologically possible only to women between the ages, roughly, of fifteen and forty-five, the proportion of the total population in this particular age group of females is a relevant factor in judging its future fertility. Similarly, since the probability of dying within the next period is higher for infants and the old than it is for children or young adults, mortality will also vary according to the age structure. Migration, finally, is a behavior typical of young adults or, to a lesser degree, of the young children or elderly persons that they may take with them. A component projection, then, is made by applying simultaneously age-specific rates of fertility, mortality, and migration to a given population in the process of gradual change in both size and structure.

The method can be illustrated by the forecasts that Warren S. Thompson and P. K. Whelpton made in the 1930s for the Committee on Population Problems of the National Resources Committee (1938). This example is worth discussing both because of its intrinsic importance as a document that had a great impact on public opinion of the time, and because it illustrates very well the reasons why demographers in the 1930s (and also very often for a considerable period thereafter) believed that population would soon stop growing or even begin to decline.

Thompson and Whelpton tried to judge the future growth by assessing recent trends in mortality, fertility, and immigration, both in the United

---

[7] Wilson H. Grabill, Clyde V. Kiser, and Pascal K. Whelpton, *The Fertility of American Women*, Wiley, New York, 1958, p. 73; see also *ibid.*, pp. 313–314, 360.

[8] A detailed exposition of the component method for estimating the intercensal population of one particular county is given in U.S. Bureau of the Census, *Current Population Reports*, Series P-25, No. 339 (June 6, 1966). For a general manual on methods of projection, see United Nations, 1956; U.S. Bureau of the Census, 1967.

States and in other Western countries. Their appraisal is summarized in the following paragraphs.

**Death Rates.** The major advances in the past, the authors pointed out, had been made through the decline in death rates of infants and young children, especially by the greater control over infectious diseases. They believed that one important cause of death among adults, pneumonia, would decline rapidly, but others—in particular, heart disease, cancer, nephritis, and cerebral hemorrhage—were "likely to prove much more difficult to control than such former scourges as smallpox, tuberculosis, typhoid fever, and diarrhea and enteritis." They estimated, therefore, that the lowest possible mortality in 1980 could effect only a moderate decline, with expectations of life at birth at that date of 72 years for males and 74 for females. With the highest probable mortality, these figures would be 65.6 and 68.4 years, respectively, levels close to what had already been attained by New Zealand and some other countries with a Western culture. The most likely figures, in their opinion, were based on a medium assumption—68.8 years for males and 71.2 for females; and these were the ones used in most of the projections.

**Birth Rates.** "It seems far easier to judge what can be done in lowering death rates in the future than to judge what people may want to do regarding the size of their families; hence the relative difference between high and low birth rate assumptions . . . is roughly four times as great as that between the high and low death rate assumptions." "In view of the past trend in the United States, and the lower rates that prevail in certain other nations," the highest future fertility trend that seemed reasonable was that the age-specific birth rates of 1930–34 would continue unchanged until 1980. During that period the completed family size was less than 2.2 children per woman, or about 2.4 children per wife, or about 2.9 per mother. According to the probable lower limit, the decline in birth rates would continue until 1980, though at rapidly diminishing rates. In 1980, by this assumption, there would be 1.5 children per woman, or about 2 children per mother. "This is approximately the present situation in California and Washington, D.C., as well as in all of England." In the opinion of the authors, the most likely trend was a medium one, by which fertility would fall by 13 per cent over the next 50 years, ending with completed family sizes in 1980 of 1.9 children per woman, or slightly more than 2.5 per mother.

The Committee on Population Problems rejected the high estimate as too improbable to consider. In some regions of the country, it believed, fertility would continue to fall off, and "it seems extremely unlikely that this decline will be offset by increases of such magnitude, in areas where birth rates are low, as to cause fertility rates for the Nation as a whole to remain constant. Accordingly, emphasis is here placed on the estimates based on 'medium' and 'low' assumptions as regards fertility, combined with the 'medium' assumption as regards mortality."

**Immigration.** Under the quota laws in effect in the 1930s, 153,714 immigrants were permitted to enter each year from quota countries and an unlimited number from other countries. In an Executive Order of 1930 consular officers had been instructed to be especially careful in screening out aspirant immigrants likely to become public charges. Actually, in every year from 1931 to 1935 there had been a net emigration. Thompson and Whelpton chose to calculate projections with two alternative assumptions concerning migration—no immigration and the net arrival of 100,000 immigrants. The Committee seemed to lean toward the first as the more probable. New permanent restrictions were likely, it believed, in particular the extension of the quota principle to the Western Hemisphere.

With three assumptions concerning mortality, three concerning fertility, and two concerning immigration, the total number of possible projections is their product, or 18. Of these, however, only seven were worked out at all, and three were considered by the Committee to be most probable: (1) medium fertility and mortality with 100,000 immigrants per year; (2) medium fertility and mortality with no immigration; and (3) low fertility, medium mortality, and no immigration. The projected populations in 1950 and 1980 based on these three sets of assumptions were, respectively: (1) 142 and 158 million, (2) 141 and 153 million, and (3) 137 and 134 million.

Looking back at these estimates with today's perspective, one can very easily judge them too harshly. It must be emphasized that the appraisals of future trends were made in the light of what seemed to be reasonable expectations on the basis of everything that was known in the 1930s. Unlike Pearl, Thompson and Whelpton did not attempt to develop a "natural law" of population growth. And, unlike those who became so enamored of the net reproduction rate that they assumed *a priori* that the age-specific birth and death rates were fixed, Thompson and Whelpton attempted to judge this question empirically from the social and economic conditions then prevailing. So long as the depression continued the forecasts made by this method were accurate, even amazingly so. The figure for 1940 that Thompson and Whelpton had calculated in 1933 was more precise than the census count itself before this was corrected for underenumeration!

For the period after the depression, however, the forecasts made in its social-economic context were off by a wide margin. Several of the most important calculated before the census of 1950 are shown in Table 9-1 (the one dated 1935 is essentially the same as that prepared for the National Resources Committee, discussed in detail above). The succession of figures suggests what happened. The projection made in 1928, just before the onset of the depression, overstated the population of 1940 by 6.6 million and that of 1950 by almost a million, but understated that of 1960 by 16.6 million. The following projections, beginning with the one made in 1931, were adjusted to the expected population of 1940 with much greater accuracy, but they were much farther off in 1950 and thereafter. Note

Table 9-1. Some Early Component Projections, Population of the U.S. (millions)

|  | 1930 | 1940 | 1950 | 1960 | 1970 | 1980 | 1990 | 2000 |
|---|---|---|---|---|---|---|---|---|
| CENSUS POPULATION | 122.8 | 131.7 | 150.7 | 179.3 |  |  |  |  |
| Scripps Foundation: |  |  |  |  |  |  |  |  |
| 1928 | 123.6 | 138.3 | 151.6 | 162.7 | 171.5 | — | — | 186.0 |
| 1931 |  | 132.5 | 139.8 | 143.9 | 144.6 | 142.9 $a$ |  |  |
| 1933: |  |  |  |  |  |  |  |  |
| High |  | 134.5 | 148.5 | — | — | 190.0 |  |  |
| Low |  | 132.5 | 140.5 | — | 146.0 | 145.0 $a$ |  |  |
| 1935: |  |  |  |  |  |  |  |  |
| High |  | 132.6 | 146.1 | 159.5 | 172.8 | 185.8 |  |  |
| Medium |  | 132.0 | 141.6 | 149.4 | 155.0 | 158.3 $a$ |  |  |
| Low |  | 131.2 | 136.2 | 137.1 | 134.0 | 127.6 $a$ |  |  |
| 1943: |  |  |  |  |  |  |  |  |
| High |  |  | 145.0 | 156.5 | 167.9 | 179.4 | 189.4 | 198.7 |
| Medium |  |  | 144.4 | 153.4 | 160.5 | 165.4 | 167.1 | 166.6 $a$ |
| Low |  |  | 143.0 | 147.7 | 148.7 | 145.8 | 138.9 | 129.1 $a$ |
| 1947: |  |  |  |  |  |  |  |  |
| High |  |  | 148.0 | 162.0 | 177.1 $b$ |  |  |  |
| Medium |  |  | 146.0 | 155.1 | 162.0 $c$ |  |  |  |
| Low |  |  | 144.9 | 149.8 | 151.6 $a$ |  |  |  |
| Census Bureau |  |  |  |  |  |  |  |  |
| 1949 |  |  | 149.9 | 160.0 |  |  |  |  |

SOURCES: Various, as compiled in Harold F. Dorn, "Pitfalls in Population Forecasts and Projections," *Journal of the American Statistical Association,* **45** (1950), 311–344.

$a$ Declines thereafter.

$b$ Increases thereafter.

$c$ Increases until about 2000, then declines.

that not a single estimate for 1960, high, low, or medium, comes close to the actual population of 179.3 million, and only one series (the high estimate made in 1947) approaches this figure even by 1970.

The main reason these projections were so far off was the baby boom of the 1940s and the continuing high fertility of the 1950s. In the 1930s most demographers would have gone along with the Committee on Population Problems in rejecting the assumption that birth rates would remain static at the 1930–34 level, Thompson and Whelpton's highest estimate of fertility. The misjudgment concerning fertility was compounded, moreover, by errors in the same direction with respect to mortality and immigration. Death rates went down, and immigration went up, faster than was anticipated.

## Projections vs. Forecasts

In the gradual development of new techniques for extrapolating population growth, it has become usual to distinguish two types of estimates. When all of the independent variables are given in demographic terms— for example, certain age-specific birth and death rates and net migration at a given annual rate—the extrapolation of the past trend is termed a population **projection.** When at least some of the independent variables are given in social or economic terms, or the greater or lesser probability of demographic variables is posited in a social-economic framework, the same extrapolation is termed a population **forecast.** Many extrapolations are not clearly in either one class or the other. Let us consider first those that are.

Demographers often project the future population that will result from the current rate of increase not in order to make a valid forecast but, on the contrary, to demonstrate that the present growth *cannot* continue. An extreme example can be cited from the Australian demographer George Knibbs: If a population grew from a single couple at the annual rate of 1 per cent, at the end of 10,000 years it would require 248,293,000,000,000,-000,000 earths to furnish the material for the bodies of the people.[9] The actual rate of growth of the world population from 1950 to 1965 was at 1.8 per cent. With such a calculation as Knibbs made, one is struck by the fact that the current rate of increase of the human species is a temporary phenomenon, which could not have begun very long ago and cannot continue for very much longer.

On the more modest scale of extrapolations of one country's population growth over a few decades, such projections are much less useful.[10] It is quite likely that the future trends of immigration, mortality, and fertility will together favor an increase of the population of the United States. To point out that if such a process were to continue for several centuries there would be "standing room only," does not help us determine what the population will probably be a decade hence. It is only in countries where the population pressure is both already great and increasing rapidly, as in India or China, that an extrapolation over even a relatively short period helps demonstrate that present growth rates cannot continue, and may

[9] George Handley Knibbs, *The Shadow of the World's Future: Or the Earth's Population Possibilities & the Consequences of the Present Rate of Increase of the Earth's Inhabitants,* Benn, London, 1928, p. 49, n. 1.

[10] An important exception is a short-range extrapolation of particular segments of the adult population, all of whom had been born as of the date of the projection. See, for example, the analysis of the population of voting age by states up to November 1968 in U.S. Bureau of the Census, *Current Population Report,* Series P-25, No. 342, June 27, 1966.

encourage policy-makers to consider whether they would prefer a decreased fertility or an increased mortality.

At the other extreme from a projection that specifically does not forecast there is a forecast that is placed fully in the economic and social context of population change. There is no reason why a population analyst should be expected to know, for example, whether and when an economic depression will occur, or a war, or a cure for cancer, or any of the other hundred significant changes in the economy, technology, society, cultural patterns, that are relevant to population growth.[11] Even a specialist in these various fields is not only generally unable to predict their future development but also often unable to summarize their past trend accurately. For instance, the crucial error of the demographers, their failure to predict postwar fertility correctly, was based in part on the sociologists' analysis of urbanism. Since it was believed that in a Gesellschaft all social relations are atomized, it was reasonable to conclude that increasing urbanization would also transform the family from an "institution" to "companionship" (see p. 521). This too was a false prognosis.

It is within the province of the demographer to consider, however, "the determinants and consequences of population trends" (as it was put in the title of the well known United Nations publication), and these, too, cannot ordinarily be assessed with precision. The question is not whether there will be a war, or a depression, or whatever, but if there is such a break in normal development, what the demographic consequences will be. Most of the forecasts of the 1930s, for instance, were hedged with the condition

---

[11] A list compiled in 1967 of one hundred technical innovations "likely" before the end of the twentieth century (Kahn and Wiener, 1967; cf. Petersen, 1967) included the following *directly* relevant to population trends:

Mortality and health:
    Wider application of lasers to surgery.
    Major reduction in hereditary and congenital defects.
    Extensive use of mechanical aids or substitutes for human organs, senses, limbs;
        more frequent transplantation of organs.
    Effective control of appetite and weight.
    New improvements in food plants and animals.
    Human "hibernation" for short periods for medical purposes.
    Ocean "farming."
    Cheap, widely available, and extremely destructive weapons.
    Postponement of aging; limited rejuvenation.
Fertility:
    Cheap, convenient, and reliable birth control.
    Ability to designate the sex of unborn children; improved ability to change sex.
    Other genetic controls.
Population distribution:
    Some control over weather.
    Practical large-scale desalination.
Labor force:
    Automated or more mechanized housekeeping.
    Use of nuclear reactors for power, excavation, mining, etc.
    General use of automation in management and production.

that there would be no major war over the period of the projection; for the excess mortality resulting from it, together with the loss in fertility from the subsequent unbalanced population structure, would mean a faster decline in population growth. The war came, but for most of the belligerent countries the consequence was the opposite of what had been anticipated. Similarly, the effect of an economic depression on the birth rate is not really well understood. Indeed, family size fell off during the 1930s, but in part because the economic crisis came as a culmination of many other depressants on fertility. The fact that the well-to-do had the smallest families and the men on work-relief the largest should warn us against a simplistic economic interpretation of fertility trends. If there were another depression of a given severity—measured, let us say, by the precise proportion of the labor force unemployed—no demographer would be able to estimate how much, or even whether, the birth rate would fall as a result.

Forecasts, moreover, are usually based on the postulate that population growth is self-contained, with the influence of other factors merely implied in the negative assumption that no significant change in social-economic conditions will take place over the period of the projection. Occasionally alternative projections are specifically linked to various possible changes in the society or economy. But the effect of population growth on the society and thus back on itself has seldom or never been included except in such broad, generalized forecasts as the theory of the demographic transition: an improved efficiency in death-control measures increased the rate of population growth, which stimulated the need or desire for birth control. We do not know enough to discuss this kind of interaction in the framework of a specific short-term projection.

Both projections and forecasts, if these words are narrowly defined, are thus useful primarily for a rather loose analysis over a relatively long period. Most population extrapolations are a little of both, in form purely mathematical calculations of what would happen under certain demographic conditions, but in actuality with premises chosen because they seem reasonable in the given social and economic context. The difference, some critics have intimated, lies only in the temerity of the analyst. In the 1930s, when the accuracy of the extrapolations was sometimes uncanny, they were termed "forecasts," while the less successful efforts of the postwar period, though based on precisely the same type of calculations, are called "projections." And if the demographer tries to hold to the differentiation, he is put under pressure to abandon it.

Maintaining the distinction between population projections and population forecasts is not easily done. Once assumptions have been spelled out and the consequent arithmetic has been done, it seems difficult to remove the aura of predictions from the resulting numbers. Hard-pressed planners in government and business and in all other endeavors which need indications of future developments ask simply for a number. What they seem to want is a forecast, and sometimes they express impatience with the explanation that a forecast is exactly what is not available. And when confronted with several numbers and the statement that, though they differ widely, each of these is a reasonable number, there is sometimes a tendency to pick one of the numbers and treat it as though it were a forecast (Taeuber, 1957).

One way out of the dilemma would be to bring the implicit gradient of probabilities to the surface and estimate both the future population trend and the degree of uncertainty of alternative projections (Muhsam, 1956; Iklé, 1967), even though no techniques yet exist by which the relative probability of various assumptions can be reliably judged. Meteorologists now dare to put their weather predictions in the form that there is a 20, or an 80 per cent chance of rain. This puts the responsibility of choosing on the expert rather than on the laymen who must use his products.

## Forecasts of the American Population

If one follows the example of Thompson and Whelpton in their report to the National Resources Committee and attempts to appraise the relative influence of the factors that will determine the population growth of the United States over the immediate future, one must admit that this cannot be done any more reliably today than in the 1930s. The one thing demographers have learned in the interim, perhaps, is how little they really know.

### THE LESSONS OF THE 1950s

It is convenient to take as a starting point the assumptions underlying two series of Census Bureau projections made in 1955 and 1958.[12] The premises on which the 1955 projection was based were critically discussed by Whelpton (1956) and Taeuber (1957), and some of these criticisms were taken into account in the revised projection. This contrast of several points of view offers a good basis for the discussion of current practice.

**Immigration.**  In the first of the two Census Bureau projections, it was assumed that the net arrival of 1.4 million immigrants during 1950–55 would be duplicated during 1955–60, and that subsequently the figure would fall off to 1.2 million per five-year period. Over the twenty years from 1955 to 1975, this would make a total of 5 million net arrivals or, assuming the same age structure and consequently the same fertility and mortality as for those who entered during 1950–55, a total of 6.5 million

[12] U.S. Bureau of the Census, *Current Population Reports*, Series P-25, No. 123, October 20, 1955; No. 187, November 10, 1958.

persons added by immigration and the natural increase of the immigrants.

In the second projection the postulated net immigration for the entire period was 1.5 million per quinquennium, or roughly the number of net arrivals during the years 1951–56. Assuming again that the age structure, fertility, and mortality remain the same as in this base period, by 1980 a total of 10.2 million persons (rather than 6.5 million by 1975) will be added by immigration and the natural increase of the immigrants.

Presumably this revision in the assumed number of future immigrants was based primarily on the experience between the dates of the two projections. In 1956 and again in 1957 about 325,000 immigrants were admitted, or more by a considerable margin than in any previous postwar year. Immigration is more likely to rise over the period of the projections than either to fall off or to remain constant. It is true, nevertheless, that it makes up no more than a small part of the current population increase of between 2 and 3 million persons per year, and even after the change in American immigration law this continued to be so. As Taeuber pointed out, a dramatic event like the defeat of the Hungarian revolution added only some 38,000 refugees to the inflow.

**Mortality.** In the first of the two projections the Census Bureau assumed that age-specific death rates for each sex would continue to decline at the same rate as during the 1940s until 1955–60, but that after that date there would be no change up to 1970–75. This slow decline was postulated on the general premise that there would be "no disastrous war, major economic depression, epidemic, or other catastrophe" during the period of the projection. Actually, the extension of life that was anticipated over two decades was completed in one year!

According to the assumptions on which the 1958 projection was based, the crude death rate would decline from 9.5 to 8 per thousand or slightly more, depending on whether fertility is high or low.

In an important innovation, the 1958 projection was based on an attempt to forecast specific causes of death: "Hypothetical low and high age-specific death rates, by sex, for the year 2000 were arrived at by applying assumed high and low percentages of reduction between 1953 and 2000 of death rates by age, sex, and ten broad groups of causes of death, to the corresponding rates for 1953, and converting the results to age-sex-specific rates for all causes combined." Although this method may not result immediately in greater accuracy, it is certainly a step in the right direction. The future decline in mortality, if any, depends not on the past rate of decline (except indirectly) but on future advances in the control of death. That it is admittedly difficult to predict such advances accurately is irrelevant to the logical point.

In their report to the National Resources Committee in the 1930s, it will be recalled, Thompson and Whelpton pointed out that control over the major infectious diseases had become so efficient that it would be more difficult to effect further reductions in mortality. Yet a notable improvement was actually attained during the next quarter-century; the average expectation of life at birth increased considerably for all sectors of the population. Existent cures had been made available more widely, and there had also been dramatic, unexpected innovations in every relevant field—diagnosis, medicine, surgery, and public health.

It is much truer today than it was in the 1930s that the major communicable diseases have been brought under control and that further advances depend on significant medical discoveries or innovations. A layman hardly dares suggest whether, or how soon, these will be made. Will there be a conquest of fetal mortality comparable to that of infant mortality during the past fifty years? Will the considerable amount of research on cardiovascular ailments and cancers produce substantial results over the next decade or two? Will the health insurance now enjoyed through private plans or through Medicare and local counterparts spread through the rest of the population? In short, will the improvement in death control consist only in the extension of known methods to more people and to peripheral areas of infectious diseases, or will there again be new types of control?

To assume that there will be no breakthrough in medical knowledge and techniques would be rash—how rash is indicated by the 1955 projection. The assumption in the second projection, that there will be a steady progress during the rest of this century, seems decidedly more plausible. And it is also possible that significant advances will be made in combating degenerative diseases, in which case mortality might well decline faster than in the recent past. However, accidents have become proportionately more important causes of death, and public-health officials are far more cognizant of such environmental factors as air pollution or cigarette advertising. To reduce deaths from causes of this type involves skills far beyond the range conventionally defined as medical, and it would be hazardous even to guess how much success present efforts will have.

**The Crucial Question of Fertility.**  As against our uncertainty about the future trends in immigration and mortality, we are almost totally ignorant concerning future fertility. Compared with one hypothesis for immigration and one for mortality in each of the two projections, thus, the Census Bureau used four alternative assumptions about the trend of fertility. But only three years after the 1955 projection, the actual population was 360,000 greater than the projection with the highest fertility, and almost 2 million greater than that with the lowest. In the 1958 projection, therefore, the assumed fertility was increased considerably.

The range in the projected populations, as well as in the three Scripps-Michigan series (Freedman *et al.*, 1959, Table 11-1) can be suggested by citing the figures even for a single year. The various estimates of the 1975 population (in millions) are as follows:

| Census Bureau, 1955 | Census Bureau, 1958 | Scripps-Michigan, 1958 |
|---|---|---|
| AA: 228.5 | I: 243.9 | High: 239.3 |
| A: 221.5 | II: 235.2 | Medium: 222.5 |
| B: 214.6 | III: 225.6 | Low: 205.4 |
| C: 206.9 | IV: 215.8 | |

Note the increase in the range from high to low estimates; it is 21.6 million in the 1955 projection, 28.1 million in the 1958 Census Bureau projection, and 33.9 million in the Scripps-Michigan projection. All series of all three, however, indicate a substantial increase from the 1955 population of 165 million. If population extrapolations are to be believed at all, the "incipient decline" spoken of in the 1930s is indeed a thing of the past, even as a myth.

The fertility as calculated in the three Scripps-Michigan projections is shown in Table 9-2. These figures deserve special attention, not so much

Table 9-2. Completed Family Size, Actual and Projected, by Cohorts of Ever-Married Women, United States, 1920–85

| YEARS OF BIRTH | YEAR AGED 45–49 | COMPLETED FAMILY SIZE | | |
|---|---|---|---|---|
| 1871–1875 | 1920 | 4.37 | | |
| 1876–1880 | 1925 | 4.03 | | |
| 1881–1885 | 1930 | 3.73 | | |
| 1886–1890 | 1935 | 3.49 | | |
| 1891–1895 | 1940 | 3.24 | | |
| 1896–1900 | 1945 | 2.92 | | |
| 1901–1905 | 1950 | 2.63 | | |
| 1906–1910 | 1955 | 2.44 | | |
| | | HIGH | MEDIUM | LOW |
| 1911–1915 | 1960 | 2.46 | 2.46 | 2.46 |
| 1916–1920 | 1965 | 2.70 | 2.68 | 2.66 |
| 1921–1925 | 1970 | 3.05 | 2.95 | 2.85 |
| 1926–1930 | 1975 | 3.15 | 3.00 | 2.85 |
| 1931–1935 | 1980 | 3.25 | 3.05 | 2.85 |
| 1936–1940 | 1985 | 3.35 | 3.05 | 2.75 |

SOURCE: Ronald Freedman, Pascal K. Whelpton, and Arthur A. Campbell, *Family Planning, Sterility, and Population Growth*, McGraw-Hill, New York, 1959, Table 10-4.

because they are different from the Census Bureau projections (although this is true) as because the method used was superior in two important respects:

1. The calculation was based on the fertility of cohorts, which in principle is better than that based on age-specific births (see pp. 524–532). One reason for the baby boom was the lower mean age at which females married. A decline in the age at marriage affects fertility in two ways—actual, but temporary, and permanent, but only potential. The sharp increase in the number of newlyweds, and thus in the number of first and second births, raised the crude birth rate for a certain period. But earlier marriage also extended the number of years from the birth of the last *wanted* child to the woman's menopause, and thus increased the risk of *unwanted* pregnancies. The two types of influence can best be separated with a cohort analysis. As a second example, another reason for the baby boom was that many women who had postponed having children during the depression of the 1930s had them in the 1940s, relatively late in their fecund period. Once this special circumstance was no longer relevant, one could expect that the birth rates of women over 40, or perhaps even of those over 30, would fall off. That is, the age-specific birth rates of this group, and of cohorts generally, depend both on the general determinants of fertility and on the specific past experiences of each cohort.

2. The estimate of future fertility, moreover, was not simply one or another extrapolation of past trends but an interpretation of data on the expected completed family size, as gathered in a nationwide sample survey. It is true, of course, that what married women say about the number of children they expect to have is an insecure base for fertility forecasts, yet even such inaccurate and incomplete data are better than no direct contact with the presumed parents-to-be.

### POSTULATES UNDERLYING FORECASTS OF THE 1960s

During the mid-1960s the U.S. Bureau of the Census issued a series of *Current Population Reports* which revised the method of analysis, the premises underlying the figures selected, and thus the projected populations. Only one postulate was offered concerning the trend in mortality and one concerning immigration. The analysis of fertility was based on the completed family size of successive cohorts, understood as a limit of the recorded trend for those females still in the childbearing ages. Even though completed family size had risen and was expected to continue to rise— "at least" for the cohorts born in 1910–35 and ending their childbearing years in 1958–83—all of the four alternative fertility levels implied a decline from the number of children in the mid-1960s. This followed from survey data of the Michigan-Scripps study, which suggested that later cohorts "expected" smaller families on the average. However, the evidence from the same study that "many women have more children than they want" was not projected into the future (Siegel and Akers, 1964).

The range in the completed family size was as follows:

| | |
|---|---|
| Series A | 3.35 children |
| Series B | 3.10 |
| Series C | 2.78 |
| Series D | 2.48 |

From an estimated total of 193.8 million in 1965, the population of the United States would increase, according to these four series, to between 248 million and 276 million in 1985. In any case, the presumed decline in offspring per family cannot be translated into a decline in annual birth rates, for the large cohorts born in the mid-1940s will move into the principal childbearing years from the mid-1960s on. Thus, from 1964 the number of women aged 20–29 will increase by 26 per cent in 1970 and by 70 per cent in 1985, so that only a drastic decline in age-specific rates could forestall another baby boom (*ibid.*).

The rationale developed by the Census Bureau at the end of the 1960s can be indicated from its own summary of population projections.

The population of the United States is bound to grow substantially in the coming years, but how much is uncertain. . . . The projected population falls between 240 and 275 million in 1985 and between 280 and 360 million by the year 2000. This is to say that in the next 33 years or so, the country might grow by anywhere from 80 to 160 million. . . .

The increase of population of 80 million in 33 years, according to the lowest fertility assumption, is more than the total population of the country in 1900. It would be the equivalent of adding the present population of England and France to the United States. The higher figure of a 160 million increase would be equivalent to the annexation of West Germany, too. . . .

Births are the great unknown. They have fluctuated widely over the last fifty years and could well do so again. . . . The rate was low during the depression years of the 1930s, was high just after World War II, and is now falling again. . . . By 1966, it had fallen to 18.6 per 1,000, a drop of 22 per cent since 1960. It is not likely to drop below 17.0 and might return to 25.0. Even the lower rate is nearly twice the death rate and will assure a rapid rate of growth (U.S. Bureau of the Census, 1968).

Undoubtedly some of the specifics in this exposition will be revised in the years to come, but there is little chance of lessening the uncertainty and thus reducing the very wide range of projected populations for any future date.

For a country as large as the United States, a projection of the total population is almost useless for many purposes. Both government bureaus and business firms require estimates of local trends, which are far more difficult to extrapolate. Net migration into the United States is small relative to the natural increase, and both the number and the age-sex distribution of the migrants are measured with reasonable accuracy. Internal migration, on the contrary, is the dominant element of the population change of some areas, and estimates of the number and characteristics of migrants are notoriously poor. In the mid-1960s three different agencies nevertheless projected the populations of regions and states.

The Census Bureau is extrapolating past trends in birth, death, and migration rates. The National Planning Association is projecting industrial development, which is then translated into economic activity, employment, labor force, and finally, population, but with some modification to allow for noneconomic factors in growth. The projections of the Stanford Research Institute employ the relationship between the economic variables, per capita income, and the rate of net migration. The method that depends on an economic base seems more logical, but the Census Bureau method has the merit of fewer levels of assumptions relating to variables that are subject to great uncertainty (Siegel and Akers, 1964).

Table 9-3. Estimated and Projected Population (millions), by Regions, United States, 1965 and 1985

| | INTERCENSAL ESTIMATES, 1965 | PROJECTIONS, 1985 | | | |
|---|---|---|---|---|---|
| | | SERIES I-B | SERIES II-B | SERIES I-D | SERIES II-D |
| Northeast | 47.6 | 61.0 | 61.4 | 56.0 | 56.4 |
| North Central | 54.1 | 68.7 | 69.3 | 62.7 | 63.3 |
| South | 60.1 | 82.7 | 82.9 | 75.2 | 75.3 |
| West | 32.0 | 51.3 | 50.0 | 46.8 | 45.7 |
| United States | 193.8 | 263.6 | 263.6 | 240.7 | 240.7 |

SOURCE: U.S. Bureau of the Census, "Revised Projections of the Population of States: 1970 to 1985," *Current Population Reports*, Series P-25, No. 375, October 2, 1967, p. 1.

The Census Bureau used two alternative postulates: Series I—that the gross out-migration from each state in 1955–60 of each population sector, classified by sex and color into five-year age groups, would remain constant over the projection period; and Series II—that these rates for the various states would converge toward the national average. When these two series were combined with two of the four fertility series, the projected populations were as shown in Table 9-3.[13]

[13] A projection published only twenty months earlier (*Current Population Reports*, Series P-25, No. 326, February 7, 1966) had a total population in 1985 of almost 2 million less. For individual states, the percentage differences between the two projections ranged from 30.2 (Nevada) to less than 0.05 (Michigan).

## The Future Population of the World

For a country with good population data and stable institutions, as we have seen using the United States as an example, it is barely possible to construct projections that are accurate enough to be useful. One cannot pretend to the same level of precision for the whole world, and the purpose of a projection can only be to suggest the approximate dimensions of growth. However, as the world's population is both very large and growing very fast, great accuracy is not required to show that enormous numbers of people will be added over the next generations. Moreover, if countries are listed in order from the slowest to the fastest growing, most of the under-developed areas fall at the latter end. In the future increase of the world's population, that is to say, the proportion of persons living in industrial countries (most of whom are of European stock) will decline (Table 9-4).

Table 9-4. Estimated and Projected Population of the World by Social-Economic Development, 1900–2000

|  | UNDERDEVELOPED AREAS [a] | DEVELOPED AREAS [b] |
| --- | --- | --- |
| Population (millions) |  |  |
| 1900 | 1,088 | 561 |
| 1965 | 2,288 | 999 |
| 2000 | 4,204–5,478 | 1,245–1,516 |
| Average Annual Growth (per cent) |  |  |
| 1900–50 | 0.9 | 0.8 |
| 1950–65 | 2.1 | 1.2 |
| 1965–2000 | 1.8–2.5 | 0.6–1.2 |
| Share of Total Growth (per cent) |  |  |
| 1900–50 | 69 | 31 |
| 1950–65 | 78 | 22 |
| 1965–2000 | 86–89 | 11–14 |

SOURCE: John D. Durand, "A Long-Range View of World Population Growth," *Annals of the American Academy of Political and Social Science*, 369 (1967), 1–8.

[a] Asia except U.S.S.R. and Japan, Africa, and Latin America.
[b] Europe, U.S.S.R., Northern America, Oceania, and Japan.

The world's population in any year is derived from national totals whose probable accuracy ranges from high to low. For instance, when the surprising results of China's census-registration in 1953 were announced (see pp. 678–679), the world total for 1950 was raised from 2.4 to 2.5 billion, or by more than 4 per cent. There is no part of the world's population that is not increasing, but the rates vary greatly from one nation or region to another (Table 9-5).

# Table 9-5. Estimated and Projected Populations of World's Major Countries and Regions, c. 1968

| REGION AND COUNTRY | POPULATION ESTIMATES MID-1968 (MILLIONS) | CURRENT RATE OF POPULATION GROWTH (PER CENT) | NUMBER OF YEARS TO DOUBLE POPULATION [f] | BIRTHS PER 1,000 POPULATION [g] | DEATHS PER 1,000 POPULATION [g] | INFANT MORTALITY RATE [g] | LIFE EXPECTANCY FROM BIRTH (YEARS) [g] | POPULATION UNDER 15 YEARS (PER CENT) [g] | ILLITERATES 15 YEARS AND OVER (PER CENT) [g] | PER CAPITA NATIONAL INCOME (U.S. DOLLARS) [h] |
|---|---|---|---|---|---|---|---|---|---|---|
| WORLD | 3479 | 2.0 | 35 | 34 | 14 | 87 | 53 | 36 | 39 | 493 |
| AFRICA | 333 | 2.3 | 31 | 45 | 22 | 140 | 43 | 43 | 82 | 123 |
| NORTHERN AFRICA | | | | | | | | | | |
| Algeria | 12.9 | 2.8 | 25 | 46–50 | 11–14 | — | — | 44 | 75–85 | 195 |
| Libya | 1.8 | 3.0 | 24 | — | — | — | — | 44 | 80–87 | 636 |
| Morocco | 14.6 | 3.3 | 21 | 46–50 | 15–19 | 140–160 | 50–55 | 46 | 80–90 | 174 |
| Sudan | 14.8 | 2.8 | 25 | 49–55 | 22–27 | — | — | 47 | 80–88 | 90 |
| Tunisia | 4.7 | 2.8 | 25 | 45 | 17 | 140–160 | — | 41 | 75–85 | 179 |
| United Arab Republic | 31.8 | 3.0 | 24 | 44 | 15 | 110–130 | 50–55 | 43 | 75–80 | 130 |
| WESTERN AFRICA | | | | | | | | | | |
| Dahomey | 2.5 | 1.7 | 41 | 50 | 33 | 110–130 | 30–35 | 46 | 90–95 | 60 |
| Gambia | 0.4 | 2.1 | 33 | 37–42 | 19–23 | — | — | 38 | 90–95 | 75 |
| Ghana | 8.4 | 2.6 | 27 | 47–52 | 22–26 | 150–170 | 40–45 | 45 | 70–75 | 245 |
| Guinea | 3.8 | 1.1 | 63 | 50 | 38 | 210–230 | 25–35 | 42 | 80–90 | 60 |
| Ivory Coast | 4.1 | 1.9 | 37 | 52 | 33 | — | 30–35 | 43 | 85–92 | 188 |
| Liberia | 1.1 | 1.7 | 41 | — | — | — | — | 37 | 90–95 | 148 |
| Mali | 4.8 | 2.0 | 35 | 52 | 33 | 180–200 | 30–35 | 49 | 90–95 | 55 |
| Mauritania | 1.1 | 1.7 | 41 | 47–53 | 26–30 | 200–220 | 40–45 | — | 90–97 | 106 |
| Niger | 3.6 | 2.4 | 29 | 53 | 29 | — | 35–40 | 46 | 95–99 | 78 |
| Nigeria | 62.0 | 2.5 | 28 | 45–53 | 25–32 | 160–180 | — | — | 80–88 | 63 |
| Senegal | 3.8 | 2.0 | 35 | 40–45 | 23–29 | — | 35–45 | 42 | 90–95 | 149 |
| Sierra Leone | 2.5 | 2.4 | 29 | — | — | 140–160 | 30–40 | 37 | 80–90 | 123 |
| Togo | 1.8 | 2.3 | 31 | 52–58 | 27–32 | 180–200 | 30–40 | 48 | 80–90 | 82 |
| Upper Volta | 5.2 | 1.4 | 50 | 47–53 | 28–33 | — | 30–35 | 42 | 85–92 | 40 |
| EASTERN AFRICA | | | | | | | | | | |
| Burundi | 3.4 | 2.0 | 35 | 46–51 | 25–30 | 150–170 | 35–40 | 47 | 85–92 | 45 |
| Ethiopia | 23.8 | 1.8 | 39 | — | — | — | — | — | 90–95 | 42 |
| Kenya | 10.2 | 2.9 | 24 | 48–55 | 18–23 | — | 40–45 | 46 | 70–75 | 77 |
| Malagasy Republic | 6.4 | 2.1 | 33 | 42–48 | 22–26 | — | — | 46 | 60–67 | 80 |
| Malawi | 4.2 | 2.4 | 29 | — | — | — | — | 45 | 85–93 | 38 |
| Mauritius [a] | 0.8 | 2.6 | 27 | 35.3 | 8.8 | 64.2 | 58–65 | 44 | 35–40 | 215 |
| Mozambique [a] | 7.2 | 1.7 | 41 | — | — | — | — | — | 90–95 | 40 |
| Rhodesia | 4.7 | 3.2 | 22 | 44–50 | 13–16 | 100–120 | 50–55 | 47 | 70–75 | 206 |
| Rwanda | 3.4 | 2.0 | 35 | 52 | — | — | — | — | 85–90 | 45 |
| Somalia | 2.8 | 1.9 | 37 | — | — | — | — | — | 90–95 | 45 |
| Tanzania | 12.4 | 1.9 | 37 | 40–46 | 22–26 | 160–180 | 35–45 | 42 | 80–90 | 64 |
| Uganda | 8.1 | 2.5 | 28 | 42–48 | 18–23 | 160–180 | — | 41 | 65–75 | 77 |
| Zambia | 4.1 | 3.0 | 24 | 49–54 | 17–21 | — | 40–45 | 45 | 55–60 | 174 |

Table 9-5. Estimated and Projected Populations of World's Major Countries and Regions, c. 1968 (Continued)

| REGION AND COUNTRY | POPULATION ESTIMATES MID-1968 (MILLIONS) | CURRENT RATE OF POPULATION GROWTH (PER CENT) | NUMBER OF YEARS TO DOUBLE POPULATION [f] | BIRTHS PER 1,000 POPULATION [g] | DEATHS PER 1,000 POPULATION [g] | INFANT MORTALITY RATE [g] | LIFE EXPECTANCY FROM BIRTH (YEARS) [g] | POPULATION UNDER 15 YEARS (PER CENT) [g] | ILLITERATES 15 YEARS AND OVER (PER CENT) [g] | PER CAPITA NATIONAL INCOME (U.S. DOLLARS) [h] |
|---|---|---|---|---|---|---|---|---|---|---|
| **MIDDLE AFRICA** | | | | | | | | | | |
| Angola [a] | 5.5 | 1.7 | 41 | 48–52 | 25–28 | 130–150 | 40–50 | 42 | 90–97 | 55 |
| Cameroon | 5.6 | 2.2 | 32 | 46–50 | 25–31 | 170–190 | 35–40 | 39 | 80–90 | 104 |
| Central African Republic | 1.5 | 1.5 | 46 | 44–48 | 29–33 | 160–180 | 35–40 | 42 | 70–77 | 123 |
| Chad | 3.5 | 1.5 | 47 | 41–45 | 24–26 | 180–200 | 30–35 | 46 | 75–82 | 60 |
| Congo (Brazzaville) | 0.9 | 1.6 | 44 | 40–45 | 20–25 | 100–120 | 35–40 | 42 | 50–55 | 120 |
| Congo (Democratic Rep.) | 16.7 | 2.3 | 31 | 35–42 | 27–32 | 220–240 | 25–45 | 39 | 80–85 | 66 |
| Gabon | 0.5 | 0.3 | 233 | — | — | — | — | 36 | 85–90 | 333 |
| **SOUTHERN AFRICA** | | | | | | | | | | |
| Botswana | 0.6 | 2.0 | 35 | 40 | — | — | 40–50 | 43 | 70–80 | 55 |
| Lesotho | 0.9 | 2.0 | 35 | — | — | — | — | 43 | — | 50 |
| South Africa, Union of | 19.2 | 2.6 | 27 | 38–44 | 12–16 | 110–130 | 50–60 | 40 | 65–70 | 509 |
| Southern Africa [a] | 0.6 | 2.0 | 35 | — | — | — | — | 40 | 60–70 | — |
| **ASIA** | 1943 | 2.2 | 32 | 39 | 17 | 49 | 50 | 40 | 54 | 128 |
| **SOUTH WEST ASIA** | | | | | | | | | | |
| Cyprus | 0.6 | 1.3 | 47 | 24–26 | 6–8 | 27–30 | 70 | 37 | 20–25 | 623 |
| Iraq | 8.9 | 3.1 | 23 | 42–48 | 12–16 | — | — | 45 | 78–85 | 193 |
| Israel | 2.8 | 2.2 | 32 | 25.4 | 6–7 | 27–29 | 72 | 34 | 10–15 | 1067 |
| Jordan | 2.2 | 3.2 | 22 | 44–50 | 13–16 | — | — | 46 | 60–70 | 179 |
| Kuwait | 0.5 | 5.1 | 14 | 47–49 | 6–7 | 35–38 | — | 38 | 50–55 | 3184 |
| Lebanon | 2.6 | 2.5 | 28 | 32–36 | 7–11 | — | — | — | 40–50 | 335 |
| Saudi Arabia | 7.1 | 2.0 | 35 | — | — | — | — | — | 85–95 | 165 |
| Southern Yemen [b] | 1.2 | 2.8 | 31 | — | — | — | — | — | 65–70 | 156 |
| Syria | 5.8 | 3.0 | 24 | 43 | — | — | — | 46 | 60–65 | 244 |
| Turkey | 33.8 | 2.9 | 24 | — | — | — | 50–60 | 44 | 90–95 | 75 |
| Yemen | 5.2 | 1.6 | 44 | — | — | — | — | — | — | — |
| **MIDDLE SOUTH ASIA** | | | | | | | | | | |
| Afghanistan | 16.0 | 2.2 | 32 | — | — | — | — | — | 85–95 | 70 |
| Bhutan | 0.8 | 2.1 | 33 | — | — | — | — | — | — | 50 |
| Ceylon | 12.2 | 2.8 | 25 | 33 | 8 | 56 | 62 | 41 | 25–30 | 130 |
| India | 523.0 | 2.5 | 28 | 41 | 16 | 140 | 45 | 41 | 70–75 | 86 |
| Iran | 26.5 | 3.0 | 24 | 50 | 20 | — | — | 46 | 75–85 | 211 |
| Nepal | 10.7 | 2.1 | 33 | 39–43 | 18–22 | — | — | 39 | 85–95 | 66 |
| Pakistan | 126.0 | 3.1 | 23 | 50 | 20 | 140–150 | 45 | 45 | 75–85 | 89 |
| **SOUTHEAST ASIA** | | | | | | | | | | |
| Burma | 26.4 | 2.2 | 32 | 46–52 | 25–31 | — | 43–50 | 40 | 30–40 | 56 |

## Table 9-5. Estimated and Projected Populations of World's Major Countries and Regions, c. 1968 (Continued)

| REGION AND COUNTRY | POPULATION ESTIMATES MID-1968 (MILLIONS) | CURRENT RATE OF POPULATION GROWTH (PER CENT) | NUMBER OF YEARS TO DOUBLE POPULATION [f] | BIRTHS PER 1,000 POPULATION [g] | DEATHS PER 1,000 POPULATION [g] | INFANT MORTALITY RATE [g] | LIFE EXPECTANCY FROM BIRTH (YEARS) [g] | POPULATION UNDER 15 YEARS (PER CENT) [g] | ILLITERATES 15 YEARS AND OVER (PER CENT) [g] | PER CAPITA NATIONAL INCOME (U.S. DOLLARS) [h] |
|---|---|---|---|---|---|---|---|---|---|---|
| Cambodia | 6.6 | 2.4 | 29 | 40–46 | 17–22 | 120–140 | 45–50 | 44 | 60–70 | 112 |
| Indonesia | 112.8 | 2.3 | 31 | 40–45 | 18–22 | 120–130 | — | 42 | 55–60 | 85 |
| Laos | 2.8 | 2.4 | 29 | 45–49 | 22–24 | — | — | — | 70–80 | 50 |
| Malaysia [e] | 8.7 | 3.2 | 22 | 37.3 | 7.6 | 50.0 | 57–65 | 44 | 70–80 | 250 |
| Philippines | 35.9 | 3.5 | 20 | 44–50 | 10–15 | — | 50–60 | 47 | 25–30 | 219 |
| Singapore | 2.0 | 2.5 | 28 | 30 | 5.5 | 26.0 | — | 43 | 40–50 | 508 |
| Thailand | 33.7 | 3.1 | 23 | 44–48 | 13–14 | — | 65–70 | 43 | 30–35 | 105 |
| Vietnam, North | 20.8 | — | — | — | — | — | — | — | — | — |
| Vietnam, South | 17.4 | 2.6 | 27 | 35–42 | 13–18 | 35–45 | — | — | — | 113 |
| **EAST ASIA** | | | | | | | | | | |
| China (Mainland) | 728.0 [d] | 1.5 | 47 | — | — | — | — | — | 40–50 | 80 |
| China (Taiwan) | 13.5 | 2.7 | 26 | 32.5 | 5.5 | 22.2 | 65–70 | 44 | 35–45 | 185 |
| Hong Kong [a] | 3.9 | 2.7 | 26 | 24.9 | 5.0 | 24.9 | 65–75 | 40 | 25–30 | 291 |
| Japan | 101.0 | 1.1 | 63 | 13.7 [e] | 6.8 | 18.5 | 71 | 25 | 0–2 | 696 |
| Korea, North | 13.0 | 2.8 | 25 | 35–40 | 10–14 | — | — | 42 | — | 180 |
| Korea, South | 30.7 | 2.8 | 25 | 38–44 | 10–14 | — | 55–60 | 42 | — | 88 |
| Mongolia | 1.2 | 3.0 | 24 | 38–42 | 10 | — | — | 30 | 5 | 190 |
| **AMERICA** | | | | | | | | | | |
| **NORTHERN AMERICA** | 222 | 1.1 | 63 | 19 | 9 | 23 | 71 | 31 | 2 | 2793 |
| Canada | 20.7 | 1.6 | 44 | 19.4 | 7.5 | 23.6 | 72 | 33 | 0–3 | 1825 |
| United States | 201.3 | 1.1 | 63 | 18.5 | 9.5 | 22.9 | 71 | 31 | 0–3 | 2893 |
| **LATIN AMERICA** | 268 | 3.0 | 24 | 40 | 10 | 66 | 60 | 42 | 34 | 344 |
| **MIDDLE AMERICA** | | | | | | | | | | |
| Costa Rica | 1.6 | 3.5 | 20 | 44–46 | 7.7 | 75.1 | 62–65 | 48 | 10–20 | 353 |
| El Salvador | 3.3 | 3.7 | 19 | 47–49 | 9.9 | 61.4 | 57–61 | 45 | 45–50 | 236 |
| Guatemala | 4.9 | 3.1 | 23 | 46–48 | 16.6 | 91.5 | 50–60 | 46 | 60–70 | 281 |
| Honduras | 2.5 | 3.5 | 20 | 47–50 | 15–17 | 70–90 | — | 51 | 50–60 | 194 |
| Mexico | 47.3 | 3.5 | 20 | 44.1 | 9.6 | 60.7 | 58–64 | 46 | 30–35 | 412 |
| Nicaragua | 1.8 | 3.5 | 20 | 47–50 | 14–16 | 60–80 | — | 48 | 45–50 | 298 |
| Panama | 1.4 | 3.2 | 22 | 41–42 | 10–11 | 40–60 | — | 43 | 20–30 | 425 |
| **CARIBBEAN** | | | | | | | | | | |
| Barbados | 0.3 | 1.7 | 41 | 25.2 | 8.2 | 49.3 | 63–68 | 38 | 0–10 | 361 |
| Cuba | 8.2 | 2.6 | 27 | 34–36 | 8–9 | 35–45 | — | 37 | 15–25 | 310 |

Table 9-5. Estimated and Projected Populations of World's Major Countries and Regions, c. 1968 (Continued)

| REGION AND COUNTRY | POPULATION ESTIMATES MID-1968 (MILLIONS) | CURRENT RATE OF POPULATION GROWTH (PER CENT) | NUMBER OF YEARS TO DOUBLE POPULATION [f] | BIRTHS PER 1,000 POPULATION [g] | DEATHS PER 1,000 POPULATION [g] | INFANT MORTALITY RATE [g] | LIFE EXPECTANCY FROM BIRTH (YEARS) [g] | POPULATION UNDER 15 YEARS (PER CENT) [g] | ILLITERATES 15 YEARS AND OVER (PER CENT) [g] | PER CAPITA NATIONAL INCOME (U.S. DOLLARS) [h] |
|---|---|---|---|---|---|---|---|---|---|---|
| Dominican Republic | 4.0 | 3.6 | 20 | 45–48 | 14–16 | 81 | 57–60 | 47 | 40 | 212 |
| Haiti | 4.7 | 2.5 | 28 | 45–50 | 17–21 | 110–130 | 35–45 | 38 | 80–90 | 80 |
| Jamaica | 1.9 | 1.8 | 39 | 38.8 | 7.7 | 35.4 | 63–68 | 41 | 15–20 | 407 |
| Puerto Rico [a] | 2.7 | 1.5 | 47 | 28.3 | 5.9 | 42.0 | 68–73 | 39 | 15–20 | 959 |
| Trinidad and Tobago | 1.0 | 2.8 | 25 | 37–39 | 6.9 | 35.3 | 63–68 | 43 | 15–25 | 501 |
| TROPICAL SOUTH AMERICA | | | | | | | | | | |
| Bolivia | 3.9 | 2.4 | 29 | 43–45 | 20–24 | — | — | 44 | 55–65 | 144 |
| Brazil | 88.3 | 3.2 | 22 | 41–43 | 10–12 | — | — | 43 | 30–35 | 217 |
| Colombia | 19.7 | 3.2 | 22 | 40–45 | 11–13 | 82 | — | 47 | 30–40 | 237 |
| Ecuador | 5.7 | 3.4 | 21 | 45–50 | 12–14 | 93 | — | 45 | 30–35 | 183 |
| Guyana | 0.7 | 2.9 | 24 | 39.9 | 8.1 | 39.8 | 60–65 | 46 | 15–25 | 248 |
| Peru | 12.8 | 3.1 | 23 | 44–45 | 11–13 | — | 55–60 | 45 | 35–40 | 218 |
| Venezuela | 9.7 | 3.6 | 20 | 46–48 | 9–10 | — | 65–70 | 46 | 30–35 | 745 |
| TEMPERATE SOUTH AMERICA | | | | | | | | | | |
| Argentina | 23.4 | 1.5 | 47 | 21.5 | 8.2 | 60–65 | 63–70 | 29 | 5–8 | 740 |
| Chile | 9.1 | 2.2 | 32 | 32.0 | 10.7 | 107.1 | — | 40 | 13–16 | 515 |
| Paraguay | 2.2 | 3.2 | 22 | 42–45 | 12–14 | — | — | 45 | 25–25 | 186 |
| Uruguay | 2.8 | 1.2 | 58 | 23–25 | 8–9 | 40–45 | 65–70 | 28 | 8–10 | 537 |
| EUROPE | 455 | 0.7 | 100 | 18 | 10 | 31 | 70 | 25 | 5 | 1069 |
| NORTHERN EUROPE | | | | | | | | | | |
| Denmark | 4.8 | 0.3 | 88 | 18.4 | 10.3 | 18.7 | 72 | 24 | 0–1 | 1652 |
| Finland | 4.7 | 0.7 | 100 | 16.7 | 9.4 | 17.6 | 69 | 27 | 0–1 | 1399 |
| Iceland | 0.2 | 1.7 | 41 | 23.9 | 7.1 | 15.0 | 73 | 34 | 0–1 | 1870 |
| Ireland | 2.9 | 0.4 | 175 | 21.6 | 12.1 | 24.9 | 70 | 31 | 0–1 | 783 |
| Norway | 3.8 | 0.3 | 88 | 18.2 | 9.5 | 16.4 | 73 | 25 | 0–1 | 1453 |
| Sweden | 7.9 | 0.3 | 88 | 15.8 | 10.0 | 13.3 | 74 | 21 | 0–1 | 2204 |
| United Kingdom | 55.8 | 0.5 | 140 | 17.8 | 11.7 | 19.6 | 71 | 23 | 0–1 | 1451 |
| WESTERN EUROPE | | | | | | | | | | |
| Austria | 7.4 | 0.4 | 175 | 17.6 | 12.5 | 28.1 | 70 | 24 | 0–1 | 970 |
| Belgium | 9.7 | 0.6 | 117 | 15.8 | 12.0 | 25.5 | 71 | 24 | 0–3 | 1406 |
| France | 50.4 | 1.0 | 70 | 17.4 | 10.6 | 21.7 | 71 | 25 | 0–3 | 1436 |
| Germany, West | 60.3 | 0.6 | 117 | 17.6 | 11.5 | 26.4 | 71 | 23 | 0–1 | 1447 |

## Table 9-5. Estimated and Projected Populations of World's Major Countries and Regions, c. 1968 (*Continued*)

| REGION AND COUNTRY | POPULATION ESTIMATES MID-1968 (MILLIONS) | CURRENT RATE OF POPULATION GROWTH (PER CENT) | NUMBER OF YEARS TO DOUBLE POPULATION [f] | BIRTHS PER 1,000 POPULATION [g] | DEATHS PER 1,000 POPULATION [g] | INFANT MORTALITY RATE [g] | LIFE EXPECTANCY FROM BIRTH (YEARS) [g] | POPULATION UNDER 15 YEARS (PER CENT) [g] | ILLITERATES 15 YEARS AND OVER (PER CENT) [g] | PER CAPITA NATIONAL INCOME (U.S. DOLLARS) [h] |
|---|---|---|---|---|---|---|---|---|---|---|
| Luxemburg | 0.3 | 0.5 | 140 | 15.5 | 12.1 | 26.8 | 68 | 22 | 0–3 | 1498 |
| Netherlands | 12.7 | 1.1 | 63 | 19.2 | 8.1 | 14.4 | 74 | 28 | 0–1 | 1265 |
| Switzerland | 6.2 | 1.2 | 58 | 18.3 | 9.3 | 17.8 | 71 | 23 | 0–1 | 1928 |
| EASTERN EUROPE | | | | | | | | | | |
| Bulgaria | 8.4 | 0.7 | 100 | 14.9 | 8.3 | 32.2 | 70 | 24 | 10–15 | 407 |
| Czechoslovakia | 14.4 | 0.5 | 140 | 15.8 | 10.0 | 23.7 | 71 | 25 | 0–5 | 804 |
| Germany, East | 17.1 | 0.2 | 350 | 15.8 | 13.3 | 23.2 | 71 | 24 | 0–1 | 1240 |
| Hungary | 10.2 | 0.3 | 233 | 13.6 | 10.1 | 38.8 | 70 | 23 | 0–5 | 701 |
| Poland | 32.3 | 0.8 | 88 | 16.7 | 7.3 | 38.8 | 68 | 30 | 0–5 | 710 |
| Rumania | 19.4 | 0.6 | 117 | 14.3 | 8.2 | 46.5 | 68 | 27 | 5–15 | 353 |
| SOUTHERN EUROPE | | | | | | | | | | |
| Albania | 2.0 | 2.5 | 28 | 34.0 | 8.6 | 86.8 | 65 | — | 20–30 | 315 |
| Greece | 8.8 | 0.7 | 100 | 18.1 | 7.9 | 34.0 | 69 | 25 | 15–20 | 566 |
| Italy | 52.8 | 0.6 | 117 | 18.9 | 9.5 | 35.6 | 70 | 24 | 5–10 | 883 |
| Malta | 0.3 | — | — | 16.8 | 9.0 | 30.3 | 69 | 32 | 35–45 | 429 |
| Portugal | 9.5 | 0.7 | 100 | 22.3 | 10.9 | 65.0 | 64 | 29 | 35–40 | 351 |
| Spain | 32.4 | 0.8 | 88 | 20.9 | 8.6 | 34.6 | 70 | 27 | 10–20 | 594 |
| Yugoslavia | 20.2 | 1.1 | 63 | 20.2 | 8.0 | 61.3 | 65 | 30 | 15–25 | 406 |
| OCEANIA | 18.5 | 1.8 | 39 | 20 | 9 | 18 | 71 | 30 | 0–1 | 1636 |
| Australia | 12.0 | 1.8 | 39 | 19.3 | 9.0 | 18.2 | 71 | 29 | 0–1 | 1620 |
| New Zealand | 2.8 | 1.8 | 39 | 22.4 | 8.9 | 17.7 | 71 | 33 | 0–1 | 1706 |
| USSR | 239 | 1.1 | 63 | 18.2 | 7.3 | 26.5 | 70 | 32 | 0–2 | 928 |

SOURCES: Government statistical offices, United Nations, and other international agencies, as compiled by the Population Reference Bureau, Washington, D.C.

a Nonsovereign territory.
b Formerly Aden; declared independent November 30, 1967.
c Formerly West Malaysia.
d United Nations estimates; other estimates (all unofficial) range from 700 million to 950 million.
e The 1966 rate was temporarily depressed as "The Year of Fiery Horse" is inauspicious for marriages and births.
f Assuming continued growth at the current annual rate.
g Latest available year.
h Latest available year, in most cases 1965.

The figures given in Table 9-4 for the total at the end of the century, between 5.4 and 7.0 billion, are quite conservative, based on a hope for deceleration in both developed and underdeveloped areas. An earlier forecast is still realistic: "Barring either a catastrophe, or a deterioration of social conditions for progress in health, of global proportions, a world population of between 6,000 and 7,000 million by the end of the century should now be expected almost as a matter of certainty" (United Nations, 1958). It was possible to make this forecast with so much assurance because the rate of growth was rising, as it probably was still a decade later. There will have to be a considerable slowing down if the current rate of increase is merely to be maintained during the coming century.

## Summary

The need for estimates of future population growth is too great to be denied. Government agencies, both national and local; business firms; colleges, churches, and other cultural institutions—the list of those using population forecasts includes all who deal on a sizable scale with people and attempt to plan their operations some way into the future. The demand has if anything increased, in spite of the conspicuous failure of some recent projections to predict accurately. As John Hajnal once remarked, the true function of a population projection is to give an administrator the basis for action. If the forecast proves to be correct, he will continue on course; if incorrect, he will make the necessary adjustment. But in either case he will have been given the necessary stimulus to act.

So long as a population is growing at a uniform rate or is changing according to a regular pattern, one can predict its future with very simple techniques, as was done by a number of men in the nineteenth century. However, it is a useful rule of thumb in social analysis that any trend, once it goes beyond a certain point, tends to build up a resistance that eventually leads to a reversal. Merely extrapolating the decline in the rate of population growth, for example, was satisfactory for a period, but only for a period. In order to understand a change in population, one must divide it into its three components of fertility, mortality, and net migration; try to judge how these will be affected by the probable social and economic developments; and apply variable age-specific rates to a population changing in both size and structure.

The principal difficulty in making an accurate forecast is in judging the probable trend of the birth rate. In the 1930s demographers generally believed both that the incentives that had induced the middle class of Western nations to reduce its average fertility would eventually establish a one-child (or even childless) family as the norm in that class, and that this example would spread through the social structure to other classes and to other countries undergoing modernization. In the mid-1940s, however, the gradual decline in the average size of the family over the past century or more was reversed. The postwar trend in most industrial countries has been toward a relatively constant norm of a small to middle-sized family, but in all cases large enough to divert analysts from renewed speculation about "depopulation." And in underdeveloped areas *the* crucial social-economic problem is how to reduce fertility.

The probable growth of the world's population, to between 6 and 7 billion by the year 2000, will show the largest proportional gain in the underdeveloped areas. The total for Europe, the Soviet Union, the United States, Canada, Oceania, and Japan, which comprised about 30 per cent of the world's population in 1965, will be no more than 22–23 per cent at the end of the century.

## Suggestions for Further Reading

On early projections, Spengler, 1936 and Pearl, 1925 are interesting. Dorn, 1950 and Whelpton, 1956 are two of the better criticisms of projections in the 1950s. Siegel and Akers, 1964, by two Census Bureau analysts, is a more complete exposition of the rationale behind the Bureau's projections than is generally available. United Nations, 1956 explains the techniques of population projection in simple language, with examples drawn from various countries.

° DORN, HAROLD F. 1950. "Pitfalls in Population Forecasts and Projections," *Journal of the American Statistical Association,* **42,** 311–334.

DURAND, JOHN D. 1967. "A Long-Range View of World Population Growth," *Annals of the American Academy of Political and Social Science,* **369,** 1–15.

FREEDMAN, RONALD, PASCAL K. WHELPTON, and ARTHUR A. CAMPBELL. 1959. *Family Planning, Sterility, and Population.* McGraw-Hill, New York.

IKLÉ, FRED CHARLES. 1967. "Can Social Predictions Be Evaluated?" *Daedalus,* **96,** 733–758.

KAHN, HERMAN, and ANTHONY J. WIENER. 1967. "The Next Thirty-Three Years: A Framework for Speculation," *Daedalus,* **96,** 705–732.

MUHSAM, H. V. 1956. "The Utilization of Alternative Population Forecasts in Planning," *Bulletin of the Research Council of Israel,* **5c,** 133–146.

° NATIONAL RESOURCES COMMITTEE. COMMITTEE ON POPULATION PROBLEMS. 1938. *The Problems of a Changing Population.* U.S. Government Printing Office, Washington, D.C.

PEARL, RAYMOND. 1925. *The Biology of Population Growth.* Knopf, New York.
———, and LOWELL J. REED. 1920. "On the Rate of Growth of the Population of the United States since 1790 and its Mathematical Representation," *Proceedings of the National Academy of Science,* **6,** 275–288.

PETERSEN, NORMAN V. 1967. "A National Plan for Century III," *Journal of the American Institute of Planners,* **33,** 222–233.

° SIEGEL, JACOB S., and DONALD S. AKERS. 1964. "Outlook for Population at Mid-Decade," in American Statistical Association, *Proceedings 1964,* "Business and Economic Statistics Section," pp. 358–366.

SMITH, GEORGE CLINE. 1964. "The Law of Forecast Feedback," *American Statistician*, 18, 11–14.

SPENGLER, JOSEPH J. 1936. "Population Projections in Nineteenth Century America," *American Sociological Review*, 1, 905–921.

STOLNITZ, GEORGE J., and NORMAN B. RYDER. 1949. "Recent Discussion of the Net Reproduction Rate," *Population Index*, 15, 114–128.

TAEUBER, CONRAD. 1957. "The Census Bureau Projections of the Size, and the Age and Sex Composition of the Population of the United States in 1975," in *Applications of Demography: The Population Situation in the U.S. in 1975*, edited by Donald J. Bogue. Scripps Foundation for Research in Population Problems, Oxford, Ohio, pp. 53–58.

UNITED NATIONS. DEPARTMENT OF ECONOMIC AND SOCIAL AFFAIRS. 1956. *Methods for Population Projections by Sex and Age*. Population Studies, No. 25, New York.

———. ———. 1958. *The Future Growth of World Population*. Population Studies, No. 28, New York.

U.S. BUREAU OF THE CENSUS. 1967. "Projections of the Population of the United States by Age, Sex, and Color to 1990, with Extensions of Population by Age and Sex to 2015," *Current Population Reports*, Series P-25, No. 381.

———. 1968. "Summary of Demographic Projections," *Current Population Reports*, Series P-25, No. 388.

WHELPTON, PASCAL K. 1956. "Census Projections: Some Areas of Doubt," *Conference Board Business Record*, 13, 2–6.

# PART II

# FACTORS IN THE POPULATION OF VARIOUS TYPES OF SOCIETY

# 10 THE POPULATION OF PRIMITIVE SOCIETIES

Population data concerning either prehistoric or contemporary primitive societies are of a completely different order from those based on even inadequate statistics. It is not merely that population size, structure, movements, and so forth must be inferred from indirect evidence, but also that these statistics are incomplete and often biased. Information concerning present-day primitive peoples comes mainly not from themselves but from representatives of advanced societies, who usually began to record fairly reliable observations only after a considerable period of contact. Reconstructing the true primitive culture, entirely free of influence from civilized peoples, is thus almost as difficult with contemporary as with prehistoric examples.

As the population of a primitive society depends very directly on its economy, it is reasonable to combine data on the prehistoric period with those on contemporaries in the same "stage" of development. Peoples do not live in economic stages, of course; they operate economies, which are often combinations of such ideal types as collecting, hunting, fishing, cultivation, and stock-raising. However, so long as we keep in mind that these are abstractions, they can be useful in analyzing the various ways that real societies at different cultural levels acquire their food. Between the physical environment and the number of people that subsist on it, there is always an intervening variable, the cultural pattern; but the less efficient the technology, the closer the relation is between habitat and population.

Any study of primitive economics deals largely with the production and consumption of food. This is so partly because of the directness of the nutritional aim and the absence of intermediaries such as an entrepreneur and a money payment; partly because of the relatively small range of objects of economic interest; and partly because of the extensive use of food for other than purely nutritive purposes (Firth, 1950, pp. 37–38).

## Types of Primitive Economy

The geologic period that runs from about 2 million to some 10 or 15 thousand years ago is called the Pleistocene, or "most recent." Four times during this era enormous ice sheets expanded to cover substantial portions of Eurasia and North America. Forms of life suited to milder climates perished unless they adapted to the cold or migrated southward. At the beginning of the Pleistocene, or perhaps even earlier, in the Pliocene epoch, hominids began to evolve, and from these there gradually developed the new species of *Homo sapiens*. Prehistorians now recognize four phases in the probable continuum of human evolution—Australopithecine, Pithecanthropine, Neanderthal, and Modern—but these are merely the points for which there happens presently to be the most fossil evidence (Brace and Montagu, 1965, Chapter 7).

Because of the fact that each of the radioactive elements is transformed into stable counterparts (e.g., Uranium 238 into lead) at a fixed rate, it is possible to date this process approximately: by measuring the ratio of the radioactive component to its inert end-product, one can estimate the time elapsed since a fossil or artifact was deposited. For dating events within the last fifty or sixty thousand years, Carbon 14 has proved to be most successful, and it is now being supplemented with a technique using radio-active potassium and argon. However,

No two authorities can agree on the age which should be allotted to the Pleistocene. . . . Even the two laboratories . . . using the Potassium-Argon technique have differed by nearly 100 per cent. . . . It seems increasingly apparent that a two million year extent of the Pleistocene is more nearly correct [than earlier, lower figures] (*ibid.*, p. 228).

We do know that the evolution from primates through hominids to man, wherever and whenever it occurred, produced a species qualitatively different from all that had preceded it. However "wild" the first man in the fossil record may seem to us, he was much closer to present-day humans than to his animal forebears. He used tools to hunt; he kept himself warm with fire; he almost certainly spoke a language; he even had an occasional ability to represent his world on the walls of caves.

Modern archeological research, including the way that inferences are drawn from scanty data, can be exemplified by the excavation of a mesolithic site at Star Carr, near Scarborough, Yorkshire (Clark, 1954). Everything recovered from the digging was plotted on a yard-square grid, and a density of thirty-six or more fragments of flint per square yard was taken to define the area of occupation. It was assumed that, as among contemporary Eskimos, women were mainly responsible for preparing skins, so that the presence of skin-working tools "argues for the presence of women" (p. 11). "No trace was found of cultivated plants or domesticated animals and it is evident that subsistence was based entirely on such activities as plant-gathering [and] hunting" (p. 13). The nonhuman bones identified at the site were mostly of small animals—various birds, hare, wolves, hedgehogs, wild pigs, but also two species of deer, elk, and oxen (Chapter 3). Tools were found fabricated out of flint, stag antlers, and bone. Some of the antlers were cut seemingly to fit the head, and one can suppose—again following leads from contemporary primitive cultures—that they were used for stalking or for magic (p. 170).

Some of the deductions, in short, are based on the likelihood that the life of prehistoric man was not too different from that of the most primitive of peoples alive today, and that these can thus be used to fill in the details in our account of ancient man. "To modern prehistorians, concerned with reconstructing rather than with merely classifying the material traces of the past, folk culture is a vital source, but it is one which needs to be used with circumspection, since many elements . . . may represent comparatively recent emanations from urban civilization" (Clark, 1952, p. 3).

The contemporary primitives used to round out our knowledge of our earliest forebears, thus, must be a food-gathering tribe, which has not domesticated either plants or animals and which has been little influenced by more advanced cultures. The Xetá of the Brazilian interior, or the Semang, a Negrito people of the Malay peninsula, typify a class that we have termed Rangers—"peoples who (1) live very largely by gathering fruits and nuts, digging roots, collecting shellfish, and devouring reptiles, insects, and vermin; (2) have no permanent dwelling, but erect windbreaks, live in caves, or put up very slight and temporary huts of boughs or palm leaves; (3) have no spinning and weaving except in the form of plaiting, no pottery, no metal, and very poor canoes; (4) no domestic animals except the dog and possibly a few pets" (Hobhouse et al., 1930, p. 17). Because of the restricted resources of any one locality, both the Xetá and the Semang live in bands of no more than twenty or thirty persons, including children. Each one of such bands has a traditional territory of some twenty square miles over which it slowly wanders, gathering food on the way.

Temporary shelters are made of branches and leaves, and abandoned each time a move is made. From one end of his life to the other, a Semang remains with his small group, occasionally seeing other bands of similar size but total strangers only rarely. The Xetá, even more isolated, were discovered by whites only a few years ago. "This limited range of contact and stimulus is of fundamental importance in understanding the stability

Members of a primitive food-gathering people, the Xetá, who number about 100. They were discovered in 1958 in an isolated area of Paraná State in southern Brazil. Note the stone ax (*José Loureiro Fernandes—University of Paraná*).

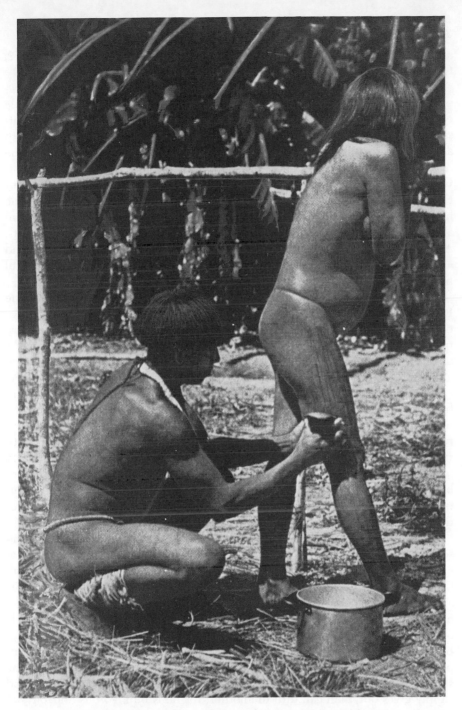

Members of the Camaiurá tribe, another primitive people of Brazil. A medicine man is scarifying the woman's leg with the teeth of a piranha fish to bleed the evil spirits from her body (*Anthony Linck—courtesy of Time, Inc.*).

and slowness of change among the simpler societies of man" (Forde, 1952, Chapter 2; Loureiro Fernandes, 1959).

The surviving Lower Hunters may be unrepresentative precisely because they have remained at this level, pushed off into an unhospitable corner by their more robust neighbors, fearful of contact with anyone outside their tiny group. The prehistoric men who shared their habitat with as many large animals of various species as were to be found, say, on the African veld a generation ago were undoubtedly more enterprising; and if Carleton Coon is correct in his interesting reconstruction, the people of that era subsisted mainly from the chase (Coon, 1955, Chapter 3). The hunting techniques of paleolithic man, the use of fire especially, made him a formidable opponent even of much more powerful and ferocious beasts. A band of five to ten men, armed with spears or bows and arrows and accompanied by dogs, could bring back a ton of meat from a successful hunt.

The economy of such primitive hunters is suggested by that of the Plains Indians before their whole culture was transformed by the acquisition of the horse. Until about 1750 the Blackfoot, for instance, were pedestrian hunters, carrying their scanty possessions on dog sledges or the backs of females. A buffalo hunt was conducted in the following fashion. Women gathered down wind from the herd and placed their sledges upright in the earth so as to form a semicircular fence. Several swift-running men up wind from the herd drove the buffalo into this enclosure. Shouting women and barking dogs confused the animals, and in the turmoil hunters were able to rush in and with lance or bow and arrow kill a number of the herd. With such a method of garnering food, the camp had to consist of ten to thirty tents, for the hunt depended on the cooperation among that many persons but did not furnish enough food for more. With only primitive means of transportation, the aged, sick, and infirm were left behind to die whenever the camp moved (Ewers, 1955).

As this example suggests, ancient man was certainly often hungry and sometimes hungry enough to die of starvation. According to a classical example in animal ecology, when rabbits increase, the foxes that live off them also multiply; then the more numerous foxes eat most of the rabbits and themselves begin to die of starvation; and when the number of foxes has been sufficiently reduced, the rabbits again increase, starting the cycle once again. Hunting peoples depend in the same way on maintaining a balance between their numbers and their food supply; many contemporary primitives that live from the chase prohibit with strong sanctions the slaughter of more animals than can be eaten. However, when one food supply gives out, man can turn to another; for he is omnivorous and physiologically adaptable to an extraordinary degree.

Among food-gatherers, fishing peoples are most likely to enjoy a regular subsistence, and they are not compelled to be on the move constantly following their food supply. Their level of culture and also their population density are typically higher than those of hunters. This observation can be exemplified by the several Indian tribes living along the Pacific coast of the United States and Canada, "whose common culture is one of the most specialized in North America and perhaps the most advanced found among any nonagricultural people." Indeed, before the white man arrived they were on the verge of developing independently the domestication of fish and plants. If the run of salmon in a particular stream began to fall off, the Nootka "restocked it, obtaining spawn from another river at the breeding season and carrying it back in moss-lined boxes to start a new generation in the depleted stream." And two of the tribes, the Tlingit and the Haida, cultivated a tobaccolike plant that was chewed for its narcotic effect. Some of the tribes carried on a primitive trade, exchanging fish for vegetable products gathered inland by neighboring groups. The houses were substantial, built in permanent settlements of thirty or more, with each village thus having a population of several hundred (Forde, 1952, Chapter 6).

For perhaps 98 per cent of his time on earth, man has lived from gathering food. Some 8,000 years ago, probably somewhere in the area between Afghanistan and Abyssinia, he learned to domesticate both plants and animals. This momentous innovation, it is believed, arose not from hunger but from leisure. "Famine-haunted folk lack the opportunity and incentive for the slow and continuing selection of domesticated forms" (Sauer, 1950). That is to say, these very first steps toward civilization depended on an economic surplus, and one wonders why this should not have been absorbed into a population increase. One reason, presumably, is that the social structure even of a food-gathering band determined the distribution of food. "Nonliterate societies everywhere, producing more goods than the minimum required for the support of life, translate their economic surpluses into the social leisure which is only afforded those members of the community who are supported by this excess wealth" (Herskovits, 1952, pp. 412–413).

The step from food-gathering to food-producing marks the transition from the paleolithic to the neolithic age. The earliest domesticated breeds of both plants and animals were, of course, indistinguishable from the wild ones. Even in areas that concentrated on them, the new modes of livelihood did not displace hunting and gathering. Early husbandry was not efficient, and the yield from hunting was not only food but also bone, antlers, hides, and even, one might suppose, sport (Clark, 1952, p. 48). Where agriculture resulted in higher density of population, thus, there was also an increased pressure on wild foods (ibid., p. 58).

The earliest cultivators established a life only slightly less mobile than hunting, Brandwirtschaft, or slash-and-burn culture. A patch of woodland was cleared and burnt, the seeds planted in the ash-strewn soil with a primitive digging stick or hoe; and then, when the soil was exhausted, the process was repeated elsewhere. Among Europeans this mode of agriculture survived longest among Finno-Ugrians, who until the 1870s obtained very large yields of grain but only for one or two seasons, and thus at an appalling cost in timber (*ibid.*, pp. 92–93, 98). If one compares the present productivity of hoe and plow culture in an area where both are used, it is found that the former takes three times as many man-hours as the latter to raise one hectare of corn (Lewis, 1949). The neolithic production with a digging stick required still more work, and the plot had to be constantly watched to protect it against predatory animals.

Specialized agriculture or stock-raising as the sole basis of food seems to have been a later development from the earlier domestication of plants *and* animals. Many of the pastoral peoples of Asia are "denuded agriculturists," induced to abandon half of their prior economy by "unsettled political conditions" (Forde, 1952, pp. 404–405). Flight to the steppe, which is difficult or impossible to cultivate, made such a specialization necessary. Nomads depend on their animals for their food, clothing, and shelter, and their culture must thus accommodate itself to the seasonal search for pasture. Such a society could subsist only in small mobile units: a Mongol camp consists ordinarily of six to ten tents of five to six persons each, or a group only about twice as large as a food-gathering band.

All the elements of the neolithic economy—hunting, hoe culture, and nomadism—implied a migratory way of life, and by 2000 b.c. the essential pattern had spread throughout Eurasia, from Ireland to China. Each local culture was specific, distinguished by its particular balance between cultivation and stock-breeding, by the plants or animals raised, by adaptations to the climate or other natural features, by accidental variations. But overlying this diversity were not only the production of food, the basic invention of neolithic man, but also tools of polished rather than chipped stone, pottery, houses.

## Population of Nonliterate Societies

For any nonliterate culture (that is, either prehistoric or contemporary primitive), the level of the economy suggests reasonable estimates concerning the maximum population density. Some deductions can be made about mortality from fossil skeletons and from the probable death rate of contemporary primitives. On fertility we must ordinarily be satisfied with the figure obtained by subtracting the presumably high mortality from the presumably low natural increase, for direct data on family size are nonexistent for prehistoric peoples and sparse for contemporary primitives.

### NATURAL INCREASE

One way of deducing prehistoric man's rate of natural increase is to show that it could not have been very great over the period since *Homo sapiens* evolved (*cf.* pp. 9–10). Starting from a single pair, man would have had to double his numbers only thirty-one times in order to reach 4.2 billion, or well over the present population of the world. Under conditions most conducive to growth each doubling takes twenty-five years, and with such a "Malthusian" projection the increase from two persons to the present world's population would have taken slightly under eight centuries. As we know that man began to evolve many hundreds of thousands of years ago, we know also that the rate of growth in the modern world is anomalous, and that during the whole of the paleolithic period man's numbers must have been close to stationary.

This conclusion is substantiated by another line of reasoning. The balance of births and deaths of hunting peoples depends a good deal on the natural environment, but under all circumstances the population densities of food-gatherers are very low. They were estimated for contemporary primitive cultures by Friedrich Ratzel, one of the great nineteenth-century pioneers of human geography, and his summary of an array of data is reproduced here in Table 10-1. Neither the peoples living in such especially

Table 10-1. The Density of Hunting Populations according to Ratzel's Estimates

|  | SQUARE MILES PER CAPITA | PERSONS PER SQUARE MILE |
|---|---|---|
| Hunting and fishing peoples in the Arctic | 75–200 | |
| Hunting peoples in semi-arid regions (Bushmen, Patagonians, Australians) | 45–200 | |
| Hunting peoples with some agriculture or trade with agricultural tribes | 0.5–2 | |
| Shepherd nomads | | 1.8–4.7 |
| Fishing peoples (North America, Polynesia) | | 4.5 |

SOURCE: Friedrich Ratzel, cited in A. B. Wolfe, "The Fecundity and Fertility of Early Man," *Human Biology*, **5** (1933), 35–60.

unfavorable habitats as the Arctic or semi-arid regions, nor those subsisting on fish or domesticated animals, are pertinent to a general discussion. The population density of typical food-gatherers, given relatively advantageous conditions, is likely to be that of the Xetá and the Semang, or on the order of one per square mile. The total land surface of the earth is about 57 million square miles, including Antarctica, the Arctic region, mountains, and deserts. The habitable portion, counting both optimum and marginal areas, is only slightly more than half this figure. If we assume one person per square mile as the average population density in the paleolithic era, then the *maximum* world population in that period was on the order of 30 million. If we restrict the area to that archeologists know to have been inhabited at that time, it could hardly have been more than 5 million.

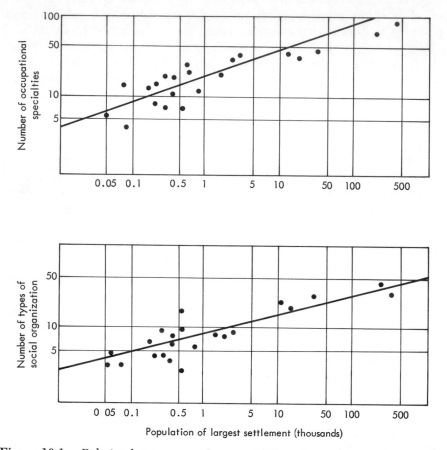

**Figure 10-1.** Relation between population growth and two other social variables in twenty-two societies. Source: Raoul Naroll, "A Preliminary Index of Social Development," *American Anthropologist,* **58** (1956), 687–715.

The domestication of plants and animals, even at the neolithic level of efficiency, increased the potential population of the earth enormously. The carrying capacity per square mile, which for hunting and fishing peoples is one to five persons, for primitive agriculture is between 26 and 64, and for more advanced agriculture ranges up to 192.[1] For example, the prehistoric population of the present area of France, as estimated from a detailed survey of archeological findings, was never more than about 20,000 so long as food-gathering furnished its subsistence. During the fourth mil-

[1] Amos H. Hawley, *Human Ecology: A Theory of Community Structure,* Ronald, New York, p. 151.

lennium B.C., when the first agricultural settlements appeared, the population grew to 500,000, and over the next thousand years to 5,000,000 (Nougier, 1954), which is also the theoretical carrying power of an area of this size with primitive agriculture. It is a reasonable inference that the spread of domestication to the rest of Europe and the world also effected an increase, though not by so large a jump as in this case.

The growth in numbers brought about by neolithic inventions was a cause as well as a result of social efficiency. Some tasks cannot even be attempted by a small group. When Robinson Crusoe was joined by Friday, the work the two could do together was much more than double what Crusoe had been able to accomplish alone, and this greater than proportionate increase in economic production with each new addition to the population continues up to a certain number. Food-gathering bands have an optimum size of about twenty-five to thirty persons, and one that grows much beyond this splits into two. Similarly, peasant agriculture can be carried on most efficiently by a village of about 500 to 1,000 persons; up to this number, the gain from new hands more than offsets the loss to new mouths. A village does not grow into a town, but rather founds daughter villages in the near distance. With conditions that favor continuous increase, the ultimate pattern is like that in sections of India or Java, with thousands and thousands of small villages making up a dense but generally nonurban population.

The precise relation between population size and the other features of a primitive society in part dependent on it has been formulated in an interesting study by Naroll. As can be seen in Figure 10-1, if the population of the largest settlement ($P$) of each of twenty-two peoples is plotted on a logarithmic grid, together with the number of occupational specialties ($S$) or the number of types of social organization ($r$) in each culture, the points tend to fall along two straight lines. The two regression lines shown have the formulas:

$$P = \left(\frac{S}{2}\right)^3 \qquad \text{and} \qquad P = \left(\frac{2r}{3}\right)^4$$

This means that if the largest settlement grew from a hamlet of 500 to a town of 10,000, say, the average number of occupational specialties in the culture would increase from 16 to 42, and the number of types of social organization from 7 to 15.

### MORTALITY AND FERTILITY

Some information on the diseases of prehistoric man is obtainable from the archeological record. The number of skeletons that have been recovered is small, of course, and we do not know to what degree they represent a typical sample. But there is no question that even before *Homo sapiens* evolved, his forebears were suffering from disease: the femur of one specimen of Java Man has marked exostoses, or knoblike protuberances, indicating a pathological condition of great severity.

Alteration of skulls due to ulcerations; scoliosis; various hyperostoses; caries of bone and teeth; atrophy of the skull; exostoses and osteomata; and many varieties of arthritides indicate to us the variety of afflictions to which early man was subject (Moodie, 1923, p. 89).[2]

Perhaps disease caused the death of primordial man less often, however, than the drownings, burns, wounds, and fractures associated with his dangerous life. Judging from the number of skeletons that show marks of heavy blows or arrow and spear points, combat was also an important cause of death. Some skeletal remains show evidence of a continued life after a serious injury and of its final healing, and these indicate at least the probability of some skill in surgery. Among 18 instances of fractures in prehistoric skeletons, one paleontologist found only three that had healed badly, and he came to the conclusion that early man was amazingly skillful at setting broken bones (ibid., p. 89). One of the more spectacular operations was trepanation, or the boring or scraping of a hole into the skull. When this is performed in modern surgery, it is usually to relieve the pressure from a brain tumor; early man, like those contemporary primitives that follow this practice, probably opened the skull also in order to release an evil spirit from the body.[3]

The triple threat of disease, violent death, and starvation made life a very precarious matter for paleolithic man. Table 10-2 shows the estimated age at death of a large sample of fossil remains. There were thirty-one additional fossils for which it was impossible to determine the age; and of these, nineteen were not yet adult and the other twelve had almost certainly not attained old age. From these and similar data, one can say that the expectation of life at birth must have been hardly twenty years, and that anyone who managed to survive to forty would be by this fact the Old Man of the band (cf. Wolfe, 1933; Cook, 1947; Vallois, 1960). Only about half of those born survived to become parents. Young humans may have been as much at a premium as they are with contemporary primitive peoples with similar high rates of infant and childhood mortality. "From one end

---

[2] The record from ancient Egypt, which provides mummies as well as skeletons for examination, is of course more complete; and it is at least probable that the diseases observable there existed also in ancient man: "Pott's disease, pneumonia, smallpox (variola?), deforming arthritides of many kinds, renal abscesses, arteriosclerosis (atheroma), many types of fractures, necroses, tumors, cirrhosis of the liver, caries, alveolar osteitis, and many other interesting lesions" (Moodie, 1923, p. 116).

[3] In a few prehistoric groups trepanation was practiced quite frequently. "In one burial mound in France yielding the bones of 120 individuals more than 40 showed the effects of trepanation. . . . A few ancient skulls reveal five cruel openings, which had all healed. The patient had survived them all" (ibid., p. 100).

Table 10-2. Estimated Age at Death of 187 Human Fossil Remains

| AGE GROUP | NEANDERTHAL | | UPPER PALEOLITHIC | | MESOLITHIC | |
| | NO. | PER CENT | NO. | PER CENT | NO. | PER CENT |
|---|---|---|---|---|---|---|
| 0–11 | 8 | 40 | 25 | 24.5 | 20 | 30.8 |
| 12–20 | 3 | 15 | 10 | 9.8 | 4 | 6.2 |
| 21–30 | 5 | 25 | 28 | 27.4 | 32 | 49.3 |
| 31–40 | 3 | 15 | 27 | 26.5 | 6 | 9.2 |
| 41–50 | 1 | 5 | 11 | 10.8 | 1 | 1.5 |
| 51+ | — | — | 1 | 1.0 | 2 | 3.0 |
| TOTAL | 20 | 100 | 102 | 100.0 | 65 | 100.0 |

SOURCE: Henri V. Vallois, "La durée de la vie chez l'homme fossile," *Anthropologie*, 47 (1937), 499–532.

of Bantu Africa to the other, there has never, until very recent times, been an unwanted child. . . . The only dispute may be as to which man has the right to claim the infant" (Goodfellow, 1939, p. 101). There is no reason to hypothesize, as some writers have done, that the natural fecundity of early man was lower than that of his present-day descendants, not only because there is no evidence on which to base this supposition but because mortality at that time was so high that, unless fecundity and fertility were high, mankind would have died out.

### PREHISTORIC MIGRATIONS

If, as prehistorians and anthropologists now generally agree, *Homo sapiens* evolved from some lower primate form only once,[4] then the existence of humans over the whole of the world indicates that a series of prehistoric migrations took place from mankind's birthplace, wherever that was. How can we imagine that ancient man was able to anticipate by many eons the extraordinary feats of the Age of Discovery, when Europeans first pushed beyond the outer frontiers of the Mediterranean basin and sailed around Africa to the South Seas and across the Atlantic to the "New" World? These primeval migrations are explicable by several of their characteristics. The passage from what is now one continent to another was made possible

[4] A notable exception is Coon, who has argued that the human species evolved by a convergence of discrete hominid stocks. See Carleton S. Coon, *The Origin of Races*, Knopf, New York, 1962.

by the fact that the succession of Pleistocene glaciations absorbed a large portion of the oceans' water into ice sheets, so that land-bridges may have been in existence across the Mediterranean, for example, and (more certainly) down through the East Indies, facilitating the movement away from the climate of the Northern Hemisphere. It must be recalled that the glaciations, which foreshortened in retrospect may seem cataclysmic, took place so slowly as to cause no perceptible fall in average temperature during the whole of a lifetime. The push to migrate, though real, was exerted so gradually as to effect a movement by stages.

Food-gatherers and hunters, because of the limitations of their economy, must be on the move; they are rangers. Herdsmen and primitive agriculturists, as we have seen, are hardly more sedentary. While today such people move over a limited area that is theirs by tradition, in a world relatively unpopulated by humans each band would follow wherever the available subsistence led it. Most prehistoric migrations, as we can imagine them, constituted movements of groups of 20 or 30 persons, walking a few miles a day, as do the Semang, in order to collect their food supply. Similarly, one can explain the wide distribution of the neolithic Danubian cultivators by their nomadic agriculture: "Assuming quite short shifts of territory every twelve years or so, it would take only a few centuries for a modest initial population to spread from say the Drave to the Harz" (Childe, 1950, p. 93). In geologic time, at the rate and with the prodigious waste of a natural process, food-gathering or agricultural bands separated by thousands of miles and became nuclei of discrete populations (*cf.* Edmonson, 1961).

It is possible, then, to state that prehistoric migrations took place, to time some of them within wide limits by carbon-dating, and to offer plausible hypotheses about routes and the rate of movement. To fill in these generalizations with details on specific migrations, however, is extraordinarily difficult. A prehistoric migration, by definition, is one of which we have no written record, and of which we must therefore reconstruct all the details from circumstantial evidence. The methodological problem to be solved—namely, to infer prior motion from static data—can be indicated by a rather farfetched analogy. Suppose that there are several species of beetles, each of which leaves a track of a different color when it walks. We have only a broken and scratched pane of glass over which various beetles, long since dead, have passed, and the task is to reconstruct their movements from the color pattern. The first step, obviously, is to classify the colors themselves: orange must be distinguished from red, green from blue, and each intermediate case must be put into one or the other category. Then all irrelevant influences must be considered and their effect taken into account: other insects may have marked the glass, portions of it may have faded in the sun, and so on. Only then, finally, can an attempt be made to reconstruct the beetles' movement over the glass.

The reconstitution of prehistoric migrations from any type of data, then, ordinarily consist of three steps: (1) classifying the data into a meaningful geographical pattern, (2) discounting the factors other than migration that might have changed the pattern, and (3) inferring migrations from the remaining systematic differences in the pattern. Whether the data have been gathered by archeologists, physical anthropologists, ethnologists, or linguists, the method is essentially this.

An attempt to reconstruct prehistoric migrations from the present distribution of human races (e.g., Taylor, 1928) does not lead to an unambiguous conclusion. (1) While human beings do differ in a number of physical traits, and while these tend to cluster into distinguishable races, where to divide adjacent clusters is an arbitrary matter on which there is little agreement among experts. (2) The hypothesis that these physical traits are wholly hereditary has been disproved with respect to some of them and is an unproved assumption with respect to some others. To the degree that racial characteristics respond to environmental influences, it is impossible to deduce a prior contact from present similarities. (3) And to the degree that physical traits are inherited, the decisive factor is the separation of gene pools, and this can be effected either by migration or by such a social pattern as caste endogamy. Migration, while it generally results in sexual isolation, is 94n., not a necessary condition to it (cf. pp. 130–132).

An attempt to reconstruct a prehistoric migration from cultural rather than physical traits must follow the same method, and thus involves the same hazards. Scientific archeology begins with the classification of artifacts, but "on many points there are two or three views that are almost equally likely. Which of them any author chooses, may depend largely on *a priori* assumptions or quite subjective prejudice" (Childe, 1950, p. 2). When a satisfactory classification has been agreed on, how shall it be interpreted? If we find two widely separated peoples with an identical or very similar item of culture, must we assume that there was a link between them at some time in the past, or can this resemblance be simply the coincidental effect of the fact that man's basic needs and the material goods with which they can be satisfied are both limited? Much of nineteenth-century anthropology was concerned with this issue. The "diffusionists" believed that invention is exceptional and that any significant similarities between two cultures indicated a prior contact between the two peoples. The "parallelists," on the other hand, postulated a natural autonomous evolution—like Morgan's progression from Savagery to Barbarism to Civilization—which needed no stimulus from the outside to reach higher cultural levels. Today these extreme positions have few if any supporters, but the dilemma remains.

Even when the probability of diffusion is accepted, one cannot reasonably infer a migration from it, or no migration from a lack of it.

Migrations . . . form the crass instances of the process, easily conceived by a simple mind. That a custom travels as a people travels carrying it along is something that a child can understand. The danger is in stopping there and invoking a national migration for every important culture diffusion, whereas it is plain that most culture changes from without have occurred through subtler and more gradual or piecemeal operations (Kroeber, 1948, p. 473).

If a prior movement *is* deduced from a similarity among the surviving artifacts, one still cannot know in every case which way the prehistoric bands went. For instance, after citing four archeologists who have reconstructed a neolithic migration from the Danube basin to what is now Macedonia, Childe suggested—"reluctantly"—that the movement had been in the opposite direction (Childe, 1950, p. 50). An analogous state of knowledge with respect to modern migration would leave us in doubt as to whether Englishmen had populated the United States, or Americans, England.

## The Depopulation of Primitive Peoples

An important limitation to the analogy that we have drawn between paleolithic populations and those of contemporary primitives results from the effect that advanced cultures have had, or may have had, on the latter. The usual contention is that food-gathering peoples, even the most isolated, have suffered a loss in numbers as compared with an earlier "natural" state; but this depopulation among primitives, though much debated, is still a subject on which there is little agreement. Forty years ago the English anthropologist Pitt-Rivers commented on this process in the Pacific Islands, and what he wrote is to a large degree true today:

During the past fifty or sixty years the dying out of the native Pacific populations has frequently been the subject of official and unofficial inquiries, and it is remarkable that there is as little agreement on the subject now as when it was first investigated. Not only does the failure in diagnosis remain as evident as before, but little or no progress has been made in methods of investigation. No satisfactory system or method has been established, and, largely in consequence of this, during the whole period few exact vital statistics are obtainable which might throw light upon the matter and establish the correctness or otherwise of diagnostic attempts (Pitt-Rivers, 1927, p. 19).

Pitt-Rivers went on to compile an amusing table, listing the "causes" of depopulation among South Sea Islanders in two columns. In the first was, for example, the allegation that the abolition of head-hunting, by depriving the natives of their chief interest in life, had brought about a despondency which eventually led to a decrease in fertility;[5] and in the second, on the

[5] In this passage the author was presumably commenting on the theorizing of a fellow anthropologist: "In the Solomon Islands the rulers stopped the special kind of war-

other hand, the fact that head-hunting still continued and contributed to a high mortality. In the first, again, were listed various types of European foods or clothing that had been condemned as unsuitable, and in the second various types of native food, clothing, housing, etc., that had been condemned as unsanitary (*ibid.*, p. 48). Analysts have found it all too easy to ascribe as the cause of depopulation any prior condition, either the continuation of elements of the native culture, or the change in these by acculturation, or whatever. *Post hoc, ergo propter hoc* has seldom been applied so freely to any problem.

Where it has taken place, depopulation can be ascribed to the following factors:

**1.** In any struggle with higher cultures, primitives have invariably lost out. The establishment of control over an area has very often been through a war in which their opponents' more effective weapons proved to be a decisive advantage. Wherever it has been introduced, slavery has probably decreased the population of the enslaved peoples. The attacks in which slaves are taken result not only in many deaths but very often in the disorganization of the native society (*cf.* Curtin, 1968). The low population density of Negro Africa, for example, is at least in part the result of over a millennium of slave-raiding, first among the African tribes themselves, then by Arabs and Europeans. In the Pacific islands, slave-raiders generally carried off young males, and the females left behind were often unable to marry and have children.

**2.** Depopulation was less the consequence of violence and servitude, however, than of disease. This is always more virulent in a fresh population, for its effect is later reduced by the natural selection of those best able to resist it, as well as often by an acquired immunity from mild childhood cases in areas where it has become endemic (see pp. 201, 222). The transfer of diseases, moreover, has usually been from advanced to primitive peoples, since the latter are relatively isolated, almost by definition, and are thus more likely to meet any infection for the first time. Europeans have transported to other parts of the world syphilis, malaria, tuberculosis, measles, whooping cough, chicken pox, dysentery, smallpox, and even the common cold; and all of these were more often fatal among the new hosts than in Europe. Venereal diseases in particular spread rapidly between a dominant

---

fare known as head-hunting, without at all appreciating the vast place it took in the religious and ceremonial lives of the people. . . . Through this unintelligent and undiscriminating action towards native institutions, the people were deprived of nearly all that gave interest to their lives. . . . Officials with the necessary knowledge of native custom and belief, and with some degree of sympathy with them, could have brought about a substitution . . . of the head of a pig for that of a human. . . . It is essential that the change should grow naturally out of native institutions and should not be forced upon the people without their consent and without any attempt to rouse their interest" (Rivers, 1922).

and a subordinate population.[6] According to one of the most careful surveys of depopulation in the Pacific islands, "the cause of native decay is largely disease" (Lambert, 1934, p. 41). "Gonorrhea alone has created enough havoc to merit a major role in the dispeoplement of the Carolines" (Lessa, 1955). In the New Hebrides, "diseases of the respiratory organs . . . are undoubtedly claiming the most victims, chiefly in the form of tuberculosis, influenza, bronchitis, and pneumonia" (Felix Speiser, in Rivers, 1922). Just smallpox was responsible for cutting the populous Mexican Indians by about a third, and the smaller Indian populations north of Mexico by substantial proportions (Stearn and Stearn, 1945; cf. Borah and Cook, 1960).

Epidemics are of course more visible, but endemic disease may disrupt a society as much. A people infected by malaria, for example, lacks energy, and anthropologists are likely to describe it as suffering from melancholia. Endemic syphilis may kill few, but it prevents the birth of many. The full effect of disease on a society is therefore not at all easy to measure, particuarly in retrospect from incomplete and inaccurate records.

3. The introduction among primitives of the elements of a more efficient culture *sometimes* has the consequence, even with no purposeful action on the part of either group, of reducing their population. It is hardly necessary to point out that steel knives and repeating rifles have made their wars more deadly. Elements of a European diet, even when wholesome if consumed together, were considerably less so after a partial transfer to other peoples. This is especially so of alcohol, which has had a deleterious effect on many primitives. According to a missionary in Melanesia,

> Of all the evil customs introduced by civilization the wearing of clothes is probably the greatest. . . . As a skirt becomes ragged another is superimposed, while the rags beneath gradually rot off. Clothes are worn till they cease to exist as recognizable garments. . . . The custom is disastrous, [particularly since] the rainfall is abnormally heavy, the average being half an inch a day all the year round. . . . Such goods as trousers, shirts, and coats should be forbidden, or so heavily taxed as to make the price prohibitive to ordinary natives (W. J. Durrad, in Rivers, 1922).

It was usually missionaries, however, who forced Pacific islanders to wear clothing unsuitable to the climate—which they might have done in any case, since European garments were the clearest mark of higher status.

4. The disruption effected by the infiltration of such alien elements can be cumulative. The social structure of a primitive people, though sometimes resilient in the face of reverses associated with traditional culture,

---

[6] "Brazil would appear to have been syphilized before it was civilized. The first Europeans . . . did not bring civilization, but there is evidence to show that they did bring the venereal plague. . . . [A] 'barbarous superstition' held that those suffering from gonorrhea would be cured if they contrived to have intercourse with a [slave] girl at the age of puberty" (Gilberto Freyre, *The Masters and the Slaves: A Study in the Development of Brazilian Civilization*, 4th Ed., Knopf, New York, 1946, pp. 71, 325).

often proves to be fragile in an encounter with a higher one. When the chief whose authority rests on his military prowess is decisively beaten, when the magic of the shaman is ridiculed and his direst spells have no effect, the whole social fabric can begin to erode. The social constraint of a non-literate society typically rests, in Durkheim's terms, on mechanical rather than organic solidarity.

Restriction of excesses was a matter of external order and not, as Christian teaching endeavors to make it, a thing of inward righteous feeling. For a time at least, Christianity tends to loosen the bonds of restraint, for it removes the terror of punishment that would have been meted out by the chiefs of former days (*ibid.*).

According to one interpretation, such a decay of the culture is transformed on the individual level into a cause of death.

The new diseases and poisons, the innovations in clothing, housing, and feeding, are only the immediate causes of mortality. It is the loss of interest in life underlying these more obvious causes which . . . allows them to work such ravages upon life and health (Rivers, 1922).

5. In a world that is falling apart, normal day-to-day activities like raising children may no longer seem to be worthwhile. All primitive cultures have the ability to limit the size of the family, and these restrictions are imposed traditionally not to maintain a balance at a subsistence level but to retain an economic surplus. "It is the demand for oysters and champagne, not for the basic bread and butter, that triggers off social conventions which hold human populations down" (Douglas, 1966). Among the Pelly Bay Eskimos, Rasmussen noted thirty-eight cases of female infanticide out of ninety-six births in eighteen families. Among the Rendille, a tribe of some 6,000 in Kenya who depend almost solely on their camel herd, population is held down by, among other measures, killing off boys born on Wednesdays. In Tikopia, the policy of maintaining the number at a steady 1,300 was exerted by contraception, abortion, and suicide.[7] Since the means of restricting population growth exist in the culture, they can be applied; and when the family declines as an institution, the consequent reduction in the birth rate may on occasion have been substantial.[8] One wonders,

[7] Such social devices do not magically come into existence whenever a population is at its optimum, as supposed in V. C. Wynne-Edwards, *Animal Dispersion in Relation to Social Behavior* (Hafner, London, 1962). (Wynne-Edwards acknowledges a debt to the early work of Carr-Saunders; *cf.* p. 163.) Rather, such patterns of regulating fertility are likely when "the whole society is under rigid social constraints, the elders have the whip hand against the juniors, their curse is feared, discipline is tight" (Douglas, 1966).

[8] A survey of three "generations" on Eddystone, one of the Solomon Islands, showed a decline in children per marriage from 2.16 to 1.28 to 0.65 (Rivers, 1922). However, as there was no attempt to control for age, the contrast was probably mainly between

however, whether the elasticity of such regulation has been in only one direction. If for certain magical reasons fertility is impeded, these taboos conceivably could be relaxed. "A rumor was current among the Yapese in 1948 that a secret meeting on the depopulation [had been] held by the chiefs and religious leaders in 1946. These men supposedly decided that most of the former taboos on coitus should be discontinued" (Hunt, 1954). More generally, if indigenous authority breaks down through European dominance, the lapse in controls might result, one would think, in the abandonment of taboos of this type.

Apart from such questions, this list of causes of depopulation is so impressive that it proves too much. How was it that primitives anywhere have survived at all? Yet although some nonliterate peoples, particularly Polynesians and American Indians, undoubtedly underwent a loss in numbers during a period, this was not the case universally. Where it took place, moreover, depopulation varied greatly in its severity. For example, among three seventeenth-century peoples in the Caribbean area, the Indians of Hispaniola (Haiti) were nearly extinct within a single generation, the Omagua were reduced by half within forty years, and the neighboring Cocama have retained about their original numbers to the present day (Steward, 1949). In the New Hebrides, the population of some islands increased—for instance, "Tanna, Malo, Paama, Merelava, and probably Tongoa" (Felix Speiser, in Rivers, 1922). The Angmagssalik Eskimos on the east coast of Greenland, who numbered 413 when Holm discovered them in 1884, increased apparently without interruption to 2,310 in 1961. Dispersal of the population into smaller settlements "became necessary because of the rise in population over the last fifty years induced by improvements in living standards and health facilities." With the addition of market products to their traditional subsistence economies, there has been a general increase in Eskimo populations and, except for the coastal villages along the Bering and Beaufort Seas, seemingly without a prior decrease (Hughes, 1965).

The range in population changes among various primitive peoples, from complete extinction to an increase, results from a complex interplay of a no less full range of factors, some of which are related to the native culture. Disease, generally the most important cause, ordinarily did not effect a permanent loss of population except in conjunction with other factors. If conditions favor growth, losses from even a calamitous epidemic can be made up in a few generations.

There is good reason to believe, moreover, that the depletion of primi-

---

the completed fertility of the older women and the partial families of the younger; cf. p. 80.

tive peoples has probably been exaggerated in many cases (McArthur, 1968). There are several reasons why this may be so, as follows:

1. Primitives, of course, keep no record of their own population, and the later estimates by anthropologists or other Westerners are seldom securely based. Table 10-3 shows, as one example, four estimates of the

Table 10-3. Estimates of Native American Population, c. 1492 (thousands)

| | SAPPER (1924) | KROEBER (1939) | ROSENBLAT (1945) | STEWARD (1949) |
|---|---|---|---|---|
| North of Mexico | 2,000– 3,500 | 1,001 | 1,000 | 1,001 |
| Mexico | 12,000–15,000 | 3,000 | 4,500 | 4,500 |
| West Indies and Central America | 8,000–10,000 | 200 [a] | 1,100 | 961 |
| South America | 15,000–20,000 | 4,300 [a] | 6,785 | 9,129 |
| TOTAL | 37,000–48,500 | 8,501 | 13,385 | 15,591 |

SOURCE: Julian H. Steward, "The Native Population of South America," in *Handbook of South American Indians*, edited by Steward. Smithsonian Institution; Bulletin 143, U.S. Bureau of American Ethnology, Washington, D.C., 1949, Vol. 5, Part 3, p. 656.
[a] Central America included with South America.

number living in the Americas at the time of Columbus's first voyage. The range in the total from 8.5 to 48.5 million is by almost six times.

The population estimates of the aboriginal population of Pacific islands, in any case of no great precision, have subsequently been mistranslated, misquoted, and otherwise garbled in later works. The principal source is Captain Cook, and we can take his estimate of the population of Tahiti as an example. On May 14, 1774, Cook projected the population of Tahiti from an enormous fleet of war canoes that he saw. A similar fleet representing all of the districts of Tahiti, he wrote, would "require Sixty eight Thousand able bodied men and as these cannot amount to One third part the number of both Sex the whole Island cannot contain less than two hundred and four thousand inhabitants."

Unfortunately, Cook's figure was immediately mistranslated in its first French edition, which rendered the crucial sentence as ". . . toute l'isle contient au moins deux cent quarante mille habitants." . . . The erroneous figure of 240,000 has been unsuspectedly quoted by [eleven authorities]. . . . Others even misquoted the mistranslation. Cook's figure was given as 140,000 by Nordmann, 130,000 by Sasportas, 100,000 by Seurat, and 30,000 by Lesson. . . .

Although Cook's 1774 estimate for Tahiti is but one of many made for the island during the 1760s and 1770s, it is virtually the only one to be either quoted or misquoted. At least seven others were reported by early visitors, and many more were offered by later authorities (Schmitt, 1965).

Cook's estimate of the number of Maori in New Zealand was 100,000, and other guesses ranged as high as five times that. From 1858, when the first census was taken, to 1896, when the downward trend was reversed, the Maori population fell from about 56,000 to about 42,000 (Borrie, 1959). Mortality was high during these thirty-eight years, probably no higher in the earlier period. If as a rough gauge we extrapolate the loss of 368 persons per year back to the time of the first substantial interaction with whites, Cook's estimate seems to be on the high side.

The first figures for any area are likely to be set by missionaries or administrators, who may exaggerate them for bureaucratic reasons; thus, those cited from Kroeber in Table 10-3 had all been reduced from the Spanish sources. There is a natural inclination, moreover, to generalize from the most horrible examples—which are also the most striking—of population decline. The deduction that a large and prosperous people flourished before the Europeans came is often given support by nativist accounts of the more or less legendary past.

2. When no figures are available at all, one common method of estimating the past numbers is to calculate the maximum population of the territory a primitive people inhabited. The figures cited from Sapper in Table 10-3, for example, were based on the assumed carrying power of various types of soil, given the level of technology and the type of land use of the various Indian peoples. He assumed that the population in each case was the greatest possible with food-gathering or primitive agriculture, and by this exclusive attention to economic factors he altogether neglected the effect of intertribal warfare or human sacrifices, to cite only the most obvious of the relevant social factors (*cf.* Cook, 1946). The population density of what is now the eastern portion of the United States, for instance, was certainly below what one could deduce with such a method. That is to say, peoples at the same technical level, even if as widely separated in time as prehistoric savages and contemporary primitives, have a population *potential* of the same general order. Whether this is realized, however, depends on more than ecological or technical or economic factors. An implicit assumption that the social-cultural milieu of primitives is optimum with respect to their numbers will generally result in an overestimate.

3. If approximations of aboriginal populations before contact with another culture tend to run too high, those of the current numbers are often too low. To the degree that racial mixture and acculturation take place, non-Europeans "disappear" not in a physical but in a statistical sense. "When is a Maori a 'Maori'?" (Pool, 1961) is a question that, appropriately specified, must be posed as the prelude to virtually every analysis of the population growth of primitives. Moreover, even those peoples that indubitably under-

went a decline in the past have in many instances experienced a more recent population growth, sometimes at a prodigious rate (e.g., Pool, 1967; Jones, 1967; Schmitt, 1968; *cf.* pp. 98–101).

## Summary

The direct evidence on paleolithic populations is so slight that it was necessary to consider ways by which it might be extended. Following the most recent trend in anthropology, certain features of the life of contemporary food-gathering primitives have been accepted as a probable close counterpart to that of pre–agricultural peoples. Combining archeological with anthropological data, we can conclude that the average density of paleolithic man was of the order of one person per square mile, and that therefore no more than about 30 million or, more probably, around 5 million lived in the entire world. Population was all but static, growing slowly in relatively favorable periods and being reduced sharply in time of distress. Expectation of life at birth was probably less than 20 years, and the maximum span not much more than double that figure. Fertility must have been high in order to offset the high mortality.

It can be assumed that the present geographical pattern of both physical and cultural traits is related in a distant way to a series of prehistoric migrations, but so many other factors have influenced it that it is not possible to trace this relation except in the most tentative fashion.

Contact with advanced cultures has often resulted in a decline of population among primitives. The factor generally most responsible was the new diseases brought by Europeans. There is good reason to believe, however, that this depopulation has often been exaggerated.

## Suggestions for Further Reading

Population analysis is not a usual topic of either prehistorians or anthropologists; and demographers, on the other hand, have generally shown little interest in building a bridge from the other side. General works on the subject of this chapter—Moodie, 1923; Krzywicki, 1934; Carr-Saunders, 1964, Chapter 20; even Kirsten, 1956—do not include the latest findings and theories. Demography is approached inferentially in works on physical anthropology (e.g., Brace and Montagu, 1965), on prehistory (e.g., Heizer and Cook, 1960; Clark, 1952), and especially on economic anthropology (Firth, 1950; Herskovits, 1952; Coon, 1955; Forde, 1952; etc.). The theory of cultural evolution (Steward, 1955) has received a classic expression in Hobhouse *et al.*, 1930. Of the various works on the population of specific primitive peoples, some of the best are Borrie *et al.*, 1957 (to be read in conjunction with Firth, 1936); Johnston, 1966; Nougier, 1954; Steward, 1949; the early chapters of Schmitt, 1968; McArthur, 1968.

Some of the readings suggested as a supplement to Chapter 4 (see pp. 138–140) are also revelant here.

BORAH, WOODROW, and S. F. COOK. 1960. *The Indian Population of Central Mexico, 1531–1610.* University of California Press, Berkeley.

BORRIE, W. D. 1959. "The Maori Population: A Microcosm of a New World," in *Anthropology in the South Seas,* edited by J. D. Freeman and W. R. Geddes. Avery, New Plymouth, N.Z., pp. 247–262.

* ———, RAYMOND FIRTH, and JAMES SPILLIUS. 1957. "The Population of Tikopia, 1929 and 1952," *Population Studies,* 10, 229–252.

BRACE, C. L., and M. F. ASHLEY MONTAGU. 1965. *Man's Evolution: An Introduction to Physical Anthropology.* Macmillan, New York.

CARR-SAUNDERS, A. M. 1964. *World Population: Past Growth and Present Trends.* Cass, London.

CHILDE, V. GORDON. 1950. *Prehistoric Migrations in Europe.* Instituttet for Sammenlignende Kulturforskning; Aschehoug, Oslo.

* CLARK, J. G. D. 1952. *Prehistoric Europe: The Economic Basis.* Methuen, London.

——— *et al.* 1954. *Excavations at Star Carr: An Early Mesolithic Site at Seamer near Scarborough, Yorkshire.* University Press, Cambridge.

COOK, SHERBURNE F. 1946. "Human Sacrifice and Warfare as Factors in the Demography of Pre-Colonial Mexico," *Human Biology,* 18, 81–100.

———. 1947. "Survivorship in Aboriginal Populations," *Human Biology,* 19, 83–89.

COON, CARLETON S. 1955. *The Story of Man: From the First Human to Primitive Culture and Beyond.* Knopf, New York.

CURTIN, PHILIP D. 1968. "Epidemiology and the Slave Trade," *Political Science Quarterly,* 83, 190–216.

* DOUGLAS, MARY. 1966. "Population Control in Primitive Groups," *British Journal of Sociology,* 17, 263–273.

EDMONSON, MUNRO S. 1961. "Neolithic Diffusion Rates," *Current Anthropology,* 2, 71–102.

EWERS, JOHN C. 1955. *The Horse in Blackfoot Indian Culture, with Comparative Material from Other Western Tribes.* Smithsonian Institution; Bulletin 159, U.S. Bureau of American Ethnology, Washington, D.C.

FIRTH, RAYMOND. 1936. *We, the Tikopia: A Sociological Study of Kinship in Primitive Polynesia.* Allen & Unwin, London.

———. 1950. *Primitive Polynesian Economy.* Humanities Press, New York.

* FORDE, C. DARYLL. 1952. *Habitat, Economy, and Society: A Geographical Introduction to Ethnology.* Dutton, New York (reprinted as a Dutton paperback, 1963).

GOODFELLOW, D. M. 1939. *Principles of Economic Sociology: The Economics of Primitive Life as Illustrated from the Bantu Peoples of South and East Africa.* Blakiston, Philadelphia.

HEIZER, ROBERT F., and SHERBURNE F. COOK, editors. 1960. *The Application of Quantitative Methods in Archaeology.* Quadrangle Books, Chicago.

HERSKOVITS, MELVILLE J. 1952. *Economic Anthropology: A Study in Comparative Economics.* Knopf, New York.

* HOBHOUSE, L. T., G. C. WHEELER, and M. GINSBERG. 1930. *The Material Culture and Social Institutions of Simpler Peoples: An Essay in Correlation.* Chapman & Hall, London.

HOWELLS, W. W. 1960. "Estimating Population Numbers through Archeological and Skeletal Remains," in Heizer and Cook, 1960, pp. 158–180.

* HUGHES, CHARLES CAMPBELL. 1965. "Under Four Flags: Recent Culture Change among the Eskimos," *Current Anthropology*, **6**, 3–69.

HUNT, EDWARD E., JR., *et al.* 1954. "The Depopulation of Yap," *Human Biology*, **26**, 21–51.

* JOHNSTON, DENIS FOSTER. 1966. *An Analysis of Sources of Information on the Population of the Navaho*. Smithsonian Institution; Bulletin 197, U.S. Bureau of American Ethnology, Washington, D.C.

JONES, L. W. 1967. "The Decline and Recovery of the Murut Tribe of Sabah," *Population Studies*, **21**, 133–157.

KIRSTEN, ERNST. 1956. *Raum und Bevölkerung in der Weltgeschichte*. 1: *Von der Vorzeit bis zum Mittelalter*. Ploetz, Würzburg.

KROEBER, A. L. 1948. *Anthropology*. Revised Ed. Harcourt, Brace, New York.

KRZYWICKI, LUDWIK. 1934. *Primitive Society and its Vital Statistics*. Macmillan, London.

LAMBERT, S. M. 1934. *The Depopulation of Pacific Races*. Special Publication 23, Bishop Museum, Honolulu.

LESSA, WILLIAM A. 1955. "Depopulation of Ulithi," *Human Biology*, **27**, 161–183.

LEWIS, OSCAR. 1949. "Plow Culture and Hoe Culture—A Study in Contrasts," *Rural Sociology*, **14**, 116–127.

LOUREIRO FERNANDES, JOSÉ. 1959. "The Xetá—A Dying People in Brazil," *Bulletin of the International Committee on Urgent Anthropological and Ethnological Research*, No. 2, pp. 22–26.

MCARTHUR, NORMA. 1959. "Fijians and Indians in Fiji," *Population Studies*, **12**, 202–213.

* ———. 1968. *Island Populations of the Pacific*, University of Hawaii Press, Honolulu.

* MOODIE, ROY L. 1923. *The Antiquity of Disease*. University of Chicago Press, Chicago.

* NAROLL, RAOUL. 1956. "A Preliminary Index of Social Development," *American Anthropologist*, **58**, 687–715.

* NOUGIER, L. R. 1954. "Essai sur le peuplement préhistorique de la France," *Population*, **9**, 241–271.

PITT-RIVERS, G. H. L. F. 1927. *The Clash of Culture and the Contact of Races*. Routledge, London.

POOL, E. I. 1961. "When Is a Maori a 'Maori'?" *Journal of the Polynesian Society*, **73**, 206–210.

———. 1967. "Post-War Trends in Maori Population Growth," *Population Studies*, **21**, 87–98.

RIVERS, W. H. R., editor. 1922. *Essays on the Depopulation of Melanesia*. University Press, Cambridge.

SAUER, CARL O. 1956. "The Agency of Man on the Earth," in *Man's Role in Changing the Face of the Earth*, edited by William L. Thomas, Jr. University of Chicago Press, Chicago, pp. 49–69.

* SCHMITT, ROBERT C. 1965. "Garbled Population Estimates of Central Polynesia," *Journal of the Polynesian Society*, **74**, 57–62.

————. 1968. *Demographic Statistics of Hawaii: 1778–1965.* University of Hawaii Press, Honolulu.

STEARN, E. WAGNER, and ALLEN E. STEARN. 1945. *The Effect of Smallpox on the Destiny of the Amerindian.* Bruce Humphries, Boston.

STEWARD, JULIAN H. 1949. "The Native Population of South America," in *Handbook of South American Indians,* edited by Steward. Smithsonian Institution; Bulletin 143, U.S. Bureau of American Ethnology, Washington, D.C., Vol. 5, Part 3.

* ————. 1955. *Theory of Culture Change: The Methodology of Multilinear Evolution.* University of Illinois Press, Urbana.

TAYLOR, GRIFFITH. 1928. *European Migrations: Past, Present and Future.* Dey, Sydney.

VALLOIS, HENRI V. 1937. "La durée de la vie chez l'homme fossile," *Anthropologie,* **47,** 499–532.

————. 1960. "Vital Statistics in Prehistoric Population as Determined from Archeological Data," in Heizer and Cook, 1960, pp. 181–222.

WOLFE, A. B. 1933. "The Fecundity and Fertility of Early Man," *Human Biology,* **5,** 35–60.

# 11 THE POPULATION OF PREINDUSTRIAL CIVILIZATIONS

The neolithic inventions of agriculture and stockherding not only gave primitive food-gathering tribes a valuable supplement to their prior means of subsistence, but also became the technical base for the urban civilizations that flourished in the Near East at the dawn of written history. By 3000 B.C., in Egypt and Mesopotamia the domesticated ox was put in front of a wooden plow, furnishing man the first source of energy apart from his own muscles. At about the same time metallurgy was developed, and coppersmiths became the first full-time craftsmen. The wheel was already in existence, and the same harness used to pull a plow could be attached to a cart. With this technical base, true agriculture (the word is from the Latin *ager*, field) could supplant the tillage of small plots.

With respect to population growth, there was no social change of comparable significance until several millennia later, when the industrial revolution transformed Western Europe in the eighteenth and nineteenth centuries. Preindustrial civilizations developed populations that, though still rather small by present standards, were tremendous when compared with the food-gathering cultures of prehistory. Urban settlements laid a base for massive technological advances. Although during peaceful, prosperous times the number of people increased, periodically it was cut back by pestilence, famine, or the breakdown of social order. Even so, the average life expectation increased from less than 20 in the neolithic era to something up to 30 years.

Great contrasts can be noted, of course, between ancient Rome and Manchu China, or Tokugawa Japan and medieval Europe. But the demographic characteristics of these and similar societies differed no more, perhaps, than those of Rangers and Fishers, and it is possible to consider the population of all preindustrial civilizations [1] as a group. One trait these societies had in common is that they maintained records, sometimes even had so-called censuses. The demographic statistics are usually just good enough to form the basis of an argument among specialists. One reason for the lack of consensus among scholars, however, is that so few have worked in this field. Most demographers have lacked the technical training to do the kind of research needed; judging the meaning of a Roman or a Chinese census is quite a different problem from analyzing modern statistics. And most historians have also shown little interest; what one of them wrote several decades ago, though fortunately less valid now, still is pertinent: "There is no subject of the first importance in ancient scholarship in which our thoughts are vaguer, in which we almost refuse to think (because the evidence is unsatisfactory), than that of population" (Gomme, 1933, p. 1). Yet the number of people in preindustrial countries is too important a subject to pass over, if only because we cannot really understand industrial societies without this perspective.

## Sources of Information

The kinds of data compiled in the several preindustrial civilizations differ considerably, and also the portion of the record that has survived from each area or period. Underlying this variation, however, there are several common features, which can be exemplified by specific instances.

The most detailed information available usually comes from the accounts of economic transactions. In this class, for instance, are the lists of grain shipments from the whole Empire to the city of Rome; but to translate these into population figures requires a rather hazardous guess as to what the per capita consumption was.

Economic and demographic data for particular localities are sometimes known in meticulous detail. In ninth-century France, for instance, abbeys maintained an estate book listing all their landed property and its produc-

---

[1] The designation *preindustrial* rather than *nonindustrial* has been chosen intentionally, in order to exclude today's underdeveloped areas. The current population development and the social and economic problems of such countries as India or China, even though they have themselves not yet become industrialized, are markedly influenced by the industrial civilizations of the West and Russia.

tion; and "we know today the name of almost every man, woman, and child who was living on these little *fiscs* [or estates] in the time of Charlemagne, and a great deal about their daily lives." [2] But one never can be certain how representative such figures are for larger areas. The most famous survey of this type, and the only one covering a considerable territory, is the Domesday Book, the inventory of his lands that William the Conqueror had made in 1086. According to the man historians know as the "Saxon chronicler," "there was not one single hide nor rood of land, nor—it is shameful to tell but he thought it no shame to do—was there an ox, cow, or swine that was not set down in the writ." [3]

Most population data were collected as part of the administration of taxes, military conscription, and similar governmental functions. Whenever it was possible, of course, people evaded such counts; and they ordinarily pertained, moreover, only to certain sectors, so that it is necessary in each case to estimate the number of inhabitants from an unknown fraction. Sometimes the enumerated portion was rather large; the Roman head-tax introduced under Diocletian, for example, apparently was imposed on the entire labor force, and thus excluded only children, the aged, the infirm, and the feeble-minded. The Roman census was narrower; originally it was a count of certain adult males primarily for military conscription. Similarly, studies based on the genealogies of nobility or the life histories of monks, two medieval classes about whom good data sometimes exist, are obviously not of universal relevance.

Even when statistics were not specific to particular portions of the population, such a limitation was often effected by their nature. One of the better sources on mortality in Rome is the life table drawn up by Ulpian, a famous jurist of the second and third centuries A.D.; since, however, this was used by courts to settle property disputes, it was presumably based on the death rates of the well-to-do classes. The inferences to be drawn from old epitaphs concerning the range in the age at death, and thus the general mortality conditions, are similarly selective. In ancient Rome, "tombstones with ages were an essentially middle-class and lower middle-class institution. The governing classes, . . . having many more interesting things to say about themselves and their relatives, generally did not give ages; and the really poor could not afford tombstones" (Burn, 1953). And these were seldom erected for infants, who constitute a very important sector in a study of mortality.

Within the social class or classes to which any set of data pertains, moreover, the unit often was not the individual but the family. A good portion of the information we have about late medieval Europe, for example, is based on the so-called hearth taxes. In order to obtain the total population

[2] Eileen Power, *Medieval People*, Doubleday-Anchor, New York, 1954, p. 17.
[3] G. M. Trevelyan, *History of England*, Doubleday-Anchor, New York, 1953, 1, 171; cf. Russell, 1948, Chapter 3.

in any area, one must multiply the given figure by a number equivalent to the size of the family, including parents, children, and others living with them. What this index should be for various countries and periods is not known precisely (*cf.* Mols, 1954, **2**, 100–109). A parallel problem is how to judge the population of a community, given certain other data about it. It is often possible from archeological research (in recent years sometimes supplemented by aerial surveys) to calculate rather exactly the area inside the walls of ancient or medieval cities, so that with a guess as to what their average density was one can estimate the number of their inhabitants.

Even within the same political unit there was seemingly little uniformity in any of the conditions surrounding the collection of statistics. Over such areas as the Roman Empire or ancient China, tax or conscription laws, or the stringency with which they were enforced, or the care with which records were kept, certainly varied greatly from one time or locality to

Two well-preserved Roman tombstones of the type from which demographic data are extracted. Note that the translations require a thorough knowledge not only of the language but of conventional abbreviations and usages (*Dr. Hilding Thylander, Stockholm*).

*Above:* "Diis Manibus [to the ancestral spirit gods]. Albia Urbica erected [this tomb] to her very sweet stepson, Marcus Octavius Aerius, who lived 10 years, 7 months, and 19 days." Marble plaque, 41 × 35 cm., attached to the wall of a tomb in Isola Sacra, Italy. Date uncertain.

*Right:* "Diis Manibus [to the ancestral spirit gods]. Ampliatus, slave of the emperors, has erected [this tomb] for Claudia Soteris, his wife, who well deserved it. She lived 19 years." Marble plaque, 24 × 35 cm., Isola Sacra, Italy. Date, second half of the second century A.D.

another. The number enumerated in the Roman census, for instance, increased abruptly from about 900,000 in 69 B.C. to 4,063,000 in 28 B.C. A jump by four and a half times in forty years obviously did not reflect only a growth in population, but scholars are not agreed on whether it represented a rapid extension of citizenship, or the inclusion of females in the count, or what (Russell, 1958, p. 48). Or, as an even more striking example, the supposed population of China increased by 78 million from 1911 to 1912 (Ho, 1959, p. 79). The obvious reason for so great a discrepancy, one can assume, is the very large underenumeration reflected in the first figure, though this was generally accepted as substantially accurate until the new one was published.

In summary, the extant statistical data on the population of various preindustrial civilizations are almost all indirect, and require a good deal of interpretation. It is ordinarily necessary to estimate the total from the number of persons, or even of families, in one particular sector. Figures on such classes as minors and females, slaves and aliens, are usually especially poor. And when the data do relate to the total population (as on grain deliveries or the areas of cities), it is nevertheless difficult to use these statistics for demographic analyses.

The estimates by different scholars, made by manipulating these unsatisfactory sources in various ways, often have a wide range. Of fourteen figures cited by Maier (1954) for the population of Rome at the time of Augustus, for instance, the low is 250,000 (Lot) and the high 1.6 million (Lugli). The population of the Roman Empire of the same period was estimated by Beloch at 50 to 60 million, by Lot at 60 to 65 million, by Stein at 70 million. The range for the third century is even wider: Delbrück suggested 90 to 100 million; Bury, 70 million; and Stein, only 50 million (Boak, 1955, pp. 5–6). Nor is it possible to assume that, because of improvements in method or in the sources available, later estimates are likely to be better. The serious study of the population of the ancient world, for instance, was initiated in the nineteenth century by Beloch, and it is generally agreed that "no one has really improved upon his work since then" (Russell, 1958, p. 7; cf. Beloch, 1886).

A much greater degree of consensus, however, is to be found on other questions. Although classical scholars differ concerning the population of the Roman Empire at any one date, they all agree that it fell off by a considerable proportion from roughly the third century on, that the density in Italy was higher than in most of the provinces, that slavery and plagues had an important influence on population trends, and so on. That is to say, one can examine the determinants, general trends, and possible effects of population growth in preindustrial civilizations even though certain data are approximate or lacking.

## Preindustrial Cities

Whatever their other characteristics, the distinguishing mark of ancient civilizations—as the etymology of the word suggests—was the development of human settlements larger and more complex than in earlier epochs. Until agriculture and stock-raising became efficient enough to provide a sizable surplus, every person had to devote himself to caring for his basic needs. In a food-gathering band, everyone is a food-gatherer. And in the late neolithic period, when hunting had been supplemented by primitive agriculture, only metal-working and magic were likely to be full-time specialties. The development of the first cities meant that the division of labor was extended beyond these few examples to become a basic principle of social structure.[4] The distinction between a village and a town or city is not primarily one of size but one of function; a village is a focal point of agriculture, a city is complementary to rural life. The very existence of a city indicates that its inhabitants live off the agricultural surplus and perform nonagricultural functions. Occupational differentiation is characteristic also within the urban sphere; there is no generalized urban "husbandry." Each urban dweller is a specialist and by this fact may also be more efficient. The urban populations in the Near East were the centers of a new level of culture and the site of a number of important inventions associated with bureaucracy (writing, accounting, censuses), religion (a solar calendar and, through astronomy, the beginnings of science), and to some degree

---

[4] Compare the formulas of Naroll, pp. 348–349.

technology (bronze and iron). These developments, and parallel ones in India and China, marked the threshold between primitive cultures and higher civilizations, and between prehistory and history.

The occupational specialization characteristic of town life, on the other hand, was often incomplete, related to a continuing osmosis between the rural and urban worlds. In Mesopotamia, "many of the townspeople worked their own fields, and the life of all was regulated by . . . the succession of the seasons" (Frankfort, 1956, p. 62). In fourteenth-century England, as a much later instance, many town dwellers cultivated their own plots just outside the walls, and grazed cattle or sheep on the common pasture.

In 1388 it was laid down by Parliamentary Statute that in harvest time journeymen and apprentices should be called on to lay aside their crafts and should be compelled "to cut, gather, and bring in the corn." . . . Even London was no exception to the rule of a half-rustic life. . . . No Englishman then was ignorant of all country things, as the great majority of Englishmen are today.[5]

Yet in an age when literacy, wealth, and political power were largely concentrated in cities, the distance along these dimensions between their upper classes and the rural mass was greater than in any developed nation today.

Archeologists generally agree that cities were first established during the fourth millennium B.C. in Mesopotamia and then Egypt, and that subsequently they appeared—whether by diffusion or independent invention is not always clear—during the third millennium in the Indus valley, the second in China, and the first in the Andes. In every case initial urbanization was a slow process, seemingly the synthesis of juxtaposed subenvironments that could be exploited symbiotically (Braidwood and Willey, 1962; Kraeling and Adams, 1960). The city's most elementary function was to furnish a haven, a place of protection. The English word *town*, like the Russian equivalent *gorod* (*cf.* Leningrad, etc.), originally meant enclosure; the German *Burg* (related to the French *bourgeois* and the English *burgher* and *borough* and hundreds of place names—Hamburg, Pittsburgh, etc.) means fortress. In medieval Europe one important criterion of a city, a feature that distinguished it from a village, was that it had a wall surrounding it. It was, in the common phrase, a "walled city."

What were the social characteristics of those living within these walls? How shall we interpret the urbanization that developed there? The answers to these questions are of more than historical pertinence. As we shall see in a later chapter, the fact that the very rapid urbanization of underdeveloped countries in recent times usually resulted in no immediate improvement of their economies has led to a debate on whether cities indeed stimulate economic advance. And if not all cities, then which type? These

[5] G. M. Trevelyan, *English Social History: A Survey of Six Centuries, Chaucer to Queen Victoria*, Longmans, Green, London, 1942, p. 28.

are in some respects the same questions that archeologists and historians have debated concerning the origin and early development of urban settlements.

### TYPES OF PREINDUSTRIAL CITIES

In their various attempts to define a city, to explain why urbanization began in certain areas, to analyze its effects on the cultural-economic level, many writers have concentrated on one major urban characteristic and passed over others. At one extreme is the interpretation that the first cities were based essentially on a new type of religious organization: "The temple community, . . . this urban form of political organization, . . . is a man-made institution overriding the natural and primordial division of society into families and clans. It asserts that habitat, not kinship, determines one's affinities" (Frankfort, 1956, pp. 76–77). Fustel (1956) developed essentially the same theme with respect to the cities of ancient Greece and Rome. At the other extreme from Frankfort-Fustel is Childe's neo-Marxist emphasis on material factors. What he terms "the urban revolution" was essentially a change "from self-sufficing food production to an economy based on specialized manufacture and external trade"; and it is "no accident" that "the beginning of writing and of mathematics and the standardization of weights and measures coincide in time" (Childe, 1951, pp. 116, 143).[6]

According to Wittfogel (1957), another technical innovation determined the characteristics of society and particularly of its administration. He divides agriculture into two types, that based on rain and that on large-scale irrigation. Rain agriculture, the usual form in all of the Western world, led to a minimum of social cohesion among a dispersed peasantry. In the great civilizations of the ancient Near East, India, China, and portions of pre-Columbian America, all based on vast irrigation and flood-control works, a leading stratum had to keep a record of available manpower, recruit it when necessary, assign it to designated jobs—both the direct construction or maintenance of dams and channels and such subsidiary tasks as assembling building materials or food for the workers. In such a **hydraulic civilization,** as Wittfogel terms it, those whose function it was to administer the complex task of maintaining the works were uniquely prepared to wield supreme political power. Once the institutional framework of bureaucratic control over the whole of the society was established for one purpose, it spread from this to military operations; a people based on rain-agriculture could flee before a stronger foe, but one that had spent generations in building irrigation works had to try to defend them. Hydraulic civilizations built Great Walls and other massive defenses, as well as highways and postal systems that provided, given the technical level,

[6] See also Davis, 1955, which rests heavily on Childe's interpretation. For a brief criticism of Childe, see Frankfort, 1956, p. 61n.

excellent communications across enormous empires. Corvée labor was also used to construct grandiose monuments—palaces, temples, tombs—to the glorification of the despotic ruler.

In Wittfogel's analysis, the keynote of West European feudalism is decentralization, the diffusion of power in many competing hands. The king, the titular head of the state, had a contractual relation with his vassals, who owed him so much allegiance but no more and were jealous of their own prerogatives. In certain periods the church was more powerful than the emperor, and in late feudalism the free cities were in some respects more powerful than either. The keynote of hydraulic civilizations, on the other hand, is centralization. All power derives from the bureaucratic apparatus, and in most cases from the person of the despot. His "vassals" owe him total and immediate obedience, and symbolize their utter degradation by such rituals as prostrating themselves before him. Religion is not an antagonistic or even an independent force, but is assimilated as the state's main ideology; in the most developed form the head of the state is also the god to be worshipped. In short, the state is stronger than the society of Oriental despotism. "The hydraulic state is a genuinely managerial state, . . . [which] prevents the nongovernmental forces of society from crystallizing into independent bodies strong enough to counterbalance and control the political machine" (p. 49).

The differentiation made by Wittfogel between two types of civilization was sharper in Max Weber's analysis. He defined the city as follows:

To constitute a full urban community a settlement must display a relative predominance of trade-commercial relations, with the settlement as a whole displaying the following features: (1) fortification; (2) a market; (3) a court of its own and at least partially autonomous law; (4) a related form of association; and (5) at least partial autonomy and [an administration by authorities that the burghers help to elect] (Weber, 1958, pp. 80–81).

Thus, "an urban 'community,' in the full meaning of the word, appears as a general phenomenon only in the Occident" (ibid.; cf. also Weber, 1950, Chapter 23), and the large human aggregates in classical China or India must be otherwise classified. The crucial difference is that "the Oriental city was unable to create or foster [the] conditions necessary for the growth of the bourgeoisie" (Murvar, 1966).[7]

---

[7] In Murvar's slight modification of the typology, Weber's differentiation between the Occidental and the Oriental city is summarized as follows: Unlike its Western counterpart, the Oriental city is juridically indistinguishable from the village (except that it might be the residence of the ruler or the site of a local administrator) in that it had no fiscal or political autonomy. Unlike even absolute monarchs of the West, the Oriental ruler had power approximating totality, often with a monopoly of military, economic, religious, and political control in the hands of one god-king; and since the sole function of the merchants and artisans who lived in an Oriental city was to serve the officialdom, they were in any case closely tied to its interests. The principle of

One can develop the differentiation further by following Pirenne's analysis of the cities of medieval and early-modern Europe, which he divided into two types. The function of the first, the center of a duchy or a diocese, was purely administrative; it was the residence of a political or religious official, together with a small class of servants and craftsmen. If the town had a market, this was only to distribute local produce, a task that required no special urban class to carry it out. As the new urban function of long-distance trade began to develop, however, a distinction arose between "burghers" (who lived in the "new burg," or mercantile quarter) and the "castellani" or "castrenses" (who lived in the "old burg," or administrative center). Merely by carrying on their trade, the merchants gradually evolved the elements of bourgeois society.

From a simple social group given over to the carrying on of commerce and industry, [the middle class] was transformed into a legal group, recognized as such by the princely power. . . . Courts whose members [were] recruited from among the burghers were able to render them a justice adequate to their desires and conforming to their aspirations (Pirenne, 1956, pp. 82–83).

Inside the city walls, whatever their differences in wealth, all men eventually were of equal civil status. A serf who fled to a city and lived there for a year and a day could not be ejected without a court trial; in the words of the German proverb, *Die Stadtluft macht frei*—the air of the city makes one free. The middle class were not consciously missionaries, but by their independent existence they challenged, and gradually eroded, the hierarchical social structure of feudalism. It was in this sense that "the" city was restricted to the Occident.

It is instructive to compare the parallel development in several civilizations other than the Western Europe that Pirenne analyzed. Classical China is especially pertinent. The unified state of feudal China began to break up around 500 B.C., and during the following several centuries of general strife there developed what one might term, by an analogy with late-medieval European history, nascent national states. In the course of the wars, much land was abandoned by its noble owners and often taken over by former serfs. Cities grew both in number and in total population, and as in Europe at a later date they were of two types: "the rectangular, planned city of the Chou conquerors, a seat of administration; and the irregularly shaped city which grew out of a market place and became only later an administrative center." The considerable independence of the latter is suggested

---

residence, the key to urban autonomy in the West, never superseded that of kinship in determining the social organization of the Oriental city. Only Western cities established their own military forces, "a brotherhood in arms for mutual aid and protection," so that eventually no Western ruler was able to overcome all of the many interdependent urban powers.

by the fact that some of them issued their own coins. Up to the eighteenth century, China's long-distance trade was as great as Europe's or greater. "An observer to whom the later Chinese history was not known," Eberhard remarks, "could have predicted the eventual development of a capitalistic society out of the apparent tendencies." The evolution of the merchant class, however, was crucially different. Merchants took over the task of collecting state taxes and thus became provincial officials, tied to the provincial (or, later, central) administrative class, and they invested their surplus money in land. In short, instead of becoming a bourgeoisie in the Western sense, the Chinese merchants contributed to the evolution of the gentry (Eberhard, 1960, pp. 51–56). The Chinese city, thus, remained "the seat of the administration, . . . the home of officials," parallel with the "old burg." There were no city charter, no municipal law, no "concept of the city as an independent unit" (Eberhard, 1956).

Islam, as another example, "was destined from the beginning to a predominantly urban history" (Benet, 1963). For Mohammed, the clearest sign that the desert tribes had accepted the new religion was their settlement in towns. (*Hegira*, literally "flight," denotes of course the Prophet's journey to Medina, but today Arab sociologists use it also to mean in-migration to cities, with spiritual overtones of human improvement.) The Bedouin nomad was not regarded as trustworthy; according to the Koran (9:98), he is strong "in unbelief and in hypocrisy and more apt not to know the limits of what Allah hath [proclaimed through] His messenger." As Islamic tradition developed, to return to the tribe from the city came to be considered a kind of apostasy. Wherever the conquering Arabs went, thus, they built new cities (Benet lists several dozen). For "only in a city, that is, a settlement harboring a central mosque fit for the Friday service and a market (and preferably a public bath), can all the requirements of the faith be properly fulfilled."[8] But those Islamic centers that did not acculturate to Western civilization often disappeared in a generation or two; "the feeble cities needed the sap of the strong tribes." During their sometimes brief life, moreover, the cities had no "community" institutions in Weber's sense. On the contrary, "the war of village against village and of quarter against quarter is eternal in the history of the oasis" (Benet, 1963). The influence of such cities on Islamic society was to civilize in the sense of spreading the faith, but certainly not to secularize. In the light of Western norms, the resultant often seems to be self-contradictory. In some respects, for instance, Mohammed raised the status of women from the general Levantine level (they were given free disposal of their property and could inherit with fewer encumbrances), but it was also the Islamic city that enforced the veil, which in Mohammed's day had apparently been limited to Meccan ladies of status.[9]

[8] Gustave E. von Grunebaum, *Medieval Islam: A Study in Cultural Orientation*, 2nd Ed., University of Chicago Press, Chicago, 1954, p. 173.

[9] *Ibid.*, p. 174.

These very brief expositions of urbanization in several diverse civilizations suggest that "the" preindustrial city is hardly less a catch-all rubric than "the" city.[10] When Sjoberg (1960) attempted to fit these variegated data into a single "constructed type," this effort was valuable, in one view, as "an implicit critique of the folk-urban typology that conditions the thinking of many social scientists," but "Sjoberg's category of preindustrial city is too broad a construct to serve as a precision tool for the purposes he envisages" (Wheatley, 1963; cf. Thrupp, 1961).

If preindustrial cities are of several different types, how shall they be classified? Without citing the analysts we have mentioned, Friedman (1961) in effect gives each of them partial credit. In his view, urban influence and power derive from the Intellectuals, who maintain and if necessary transform the "tradition of fundamental values by which men live" (Frankfort, Fustel, and Benet); from the Entrepreneurs, who express an "enterprising spirit in economic affairs" (Childe); and from the Administrators, through whom "the city comes to oppose the traditional order of communal life with the administrative order of a rationally organized society" (Wittfogel). One can classify cities according to which of these functions predominate.[11]

The main distinction—drawn in various ways by Max Weber, Wittfogel, Pirenne, Eberhard, and Redfield and Singer—is between Occidental and Oriental, mercantile and administrative, bourgeois and traditional. From the first type of city there developed both the advanced economies and the democratic institutions of Western Europe; from the second type of city, even with other circumstances as favorable as in classical China, there was no such development. The contrast is so neat one is tempted to pronounce it a law; but like so many generalizations on the prerequisites of societal development, it is upset by the instance of premodern Japan, the only non-Western country (apart from the marginal case of Russia) that has achieved a full industrial economy (see pp. 423–427).

---

[10] This impression of heterogeneity is reinforced when we include other interpretations (e.g., Mols, 1954, Vol. 1) or the cities of other preindustrial cultures (on Africa see Bascom, 1955; Schwab, 1965; Steel, 1961; Miner, 1965).

[11] Or one can distinguish types of cities in terms of "primary" and "secondary" stages (Redfield and Singer, 1954): (1) an "orthogenetic" city, or "city of the moral order," is based on an intellectual class that "carries forward" an old culture into more systematic form; (2) a "heterogenetic" city, or "city of the technical order," is based on a mercantile class that rationalizes both the production of goods and human relations. Even before cities are formed, however, the secondary phase is begun in "the institutions of travel and trade among local communities with different cultures"; thus, "even in older civilizations it is not easy to find clearcut examples of primary urbanization," through existent cities can be classified as relatively more parochial or more cosmopolitan. Neither type of city, moreover, is afforded a clear cultural role in this analysis, for "the processes of cultural innovations and 'flow' are far too complex to be handled by simple mechanical laws concerning the direction, rate, and 'flow' of cultural diffusion between 'city' and 'country.'"

## POPULATION OF PREINDUSTRIAL CITIES

In sum, there were important political and cultural differences between the free cities of Europe and the administrative centers of the Orient, but in other respects the cities in all these societies were similar. The urban population was everywhere small, in two senses: the proportion living in towns never was more than a few per cent of the total, and the size of even the large towns was modest by today's standards. The famous Ur had no more than 25,000 inhabitants, Erech about the same. Much later, around 1600 B.C., Thebes at the height of its splendor as Egypt's capital may have had as many as 225,000 by a liberal estimate (Davis, 1955). Rome was certainly the largest city of antiquity. The exact number of its inhabitants, as we have seen, is not known. After a careful consideration of the evidence, Russell has suggested 350,000 as the probable maximum in the first century A.D., equivalent to a density of about 250 persons per hectare, which would seem rather high for a city with many open squares and public buildings (Russell, 1958, pp. 63–68). From this figure, Rome declined to about half by the middle of the fourth century. Of the Holy Roman Empire's approximately 3,000 "cities" (in the sense of walled enclosures with charters) at the end of the Middle Ages, 2,800 had populations ranging between 100 and 1,000 (Dickinson, 1951, p. 290). And the others also were not large. Table 11-1 is a summary of the more detailed data that Russell has compiled from a variety of sources. All of the cities with an estimated population of 30,000 or more are included, together with a few others that might be of interest—London, with 18,000 in the eleventh century; or Nuremberg, whose medieval aspect has survived in part to today, with only 23,000 in the fifteenth century. Even if we grant that these are rough approximations and in an extravagant gesture double the number of inhabitants, these medieval towns would still be classified today as small.

The city of preindustrial civilizations was different from its modern counterpart also in its occupational structure. The various handicrafts were typically grouped together in, for example, a "street of the goldsmiths," and the in-group solidarity of such neighborhoods was strengthened by the guild, which closely regulated the conditions of work. Generally membership in a guild was a prerequisite to the practice of almost any urban occupation, and apprentices were ordinarily chosen on the basis of kinship rather than universalist standards. Not only the family but also religion (each guild had its patron saint) and even magic were interwoven with economic activities. In short, very few of what the modern Western world sees as "the" urban characteristics, as specified, for instance, in Louis Wirth's well known article (see p. 434), apply to preindustrial cities.

Table 11-1. Population Estimates of Some Large Medieval European Cities

| CITY | DATE OF ESTIMATE | POPULATION | PERSONS PER HECTARE |
|---|---|---|---|
| London | { 1086 | 18,000 | 108 |
|  | { 1377 | 35,000 | 121 |
| Milan | 13th century | 52,000 | 166 |
| Naples | 1278 | 27,000 | 133 |
| Paris | 1292 | 59,000 | 157 |
| Padua | 1320 | 41,000 | 117 |
| Bruges | 1340 | 25,000 | 58 |
| Ghent | 1356 | 60,000 | 93 |
| Venice | 1363 | 78,000 | 240 |
| Bologna | 1371 | 32,000 | 76 |
| Florence | { 1381 | 55,000 | 107 |
|  | { 1424 | 37,000 | 73 |
| Nuremberg | 1449 | 23,000 | 165 |
| Bourges | 1487 | 32,000 | 289 |
| Genoa | early 16th century | 38,000 | 129 |
| Barcelona | 1514 | 31,000 | 118 |
| Rome | 1526 | 55,000 | 40 |

SOURCE: J. C. Russell, "Late Ancient and Medieval Population," *Transactions of the American Philosophical Society*, 48, Part 3 (1958), Tables 63, 64, 65.

## Family and Fertility

Preindustrial civilizations were urban in the sense that a new type and level of culture flourished in their cities, but the large majority of the people were still rural. The depopulation in the Roman Empire, for instance, cannot reasonably be ascribed to merely the decline of fertility in the city of Rome, although the implicit assumption has sometimes been made that the urban norms, about which we know much more, were general throughout the society. It is perhaps more accurate, though also arbitrary, to posit an ideal type, the "familistic" society, or one in which the family has a range of functions far wider than those associated with the domestic unit Americans are familiar with. In societies that lack other facilities, each person depends on his kin for services rendered in the modern West by employment agencies, banks, schools, trade unions, and so on. And as the family is important in so many contexts, one can hypothesize that the pressure is great to produce a numerous progeny. Yet the fertility was markedly different in various preindustrial societies, all of which can be classified as familistic to one degree or another (*cf.* pp. 514–517, 597–603).

## ANCIENT ROME

The evidence from a sample of Roman epitaphs suggests that the average ages at marriage were 18 for females and 26 for males (Harkness, 1896). If these figures can be taken as representative, they indicate a mean duration of first marriages of eighteen years, assuming a life expectation at birth (based in large part on a very high infant mortality) of twenty-five years (Hopkins, 1965). Although under Roman law the purpose of marriage was procreation, which public officials praised as a civic duty, fertility was certainly far below what these figures would imply in a population with no controls.

That some means of controlling fertility was used does not tell us which ones. In many of the ancient Greek city-states, infanticide had not only been permitted but under some conditions prescribed; in Rome it was limited by various legal restrictions and finally, in the fourth century A.D., made a capital offense. The increasing stringency of the prohibition itself suggests that the practice was not exceptional, and the high incidence probably continued during the following centuries. Out of a list of twenty-two ancient medical writers (all whose works are extant and not on specific irrelevant topics), eleven discussed contraceptive methods and fifteen methods of inducing abortion, apart from the fact that in some texts the two were confused (*ibid.*). It is reasonable to suppose that all physicians could obtain the current knowledge on birth control, only a portion of which was efficacious. Aëtius, whose passage on contraception is relatively rational and complete, also recommended magic charms: "Wear the liver of a cat in a tube on the left foot, . . . or else wear part of the womb of a lioness in a tube of ivory. This is very effective." Even Soranus, whose work has been depicted as "the most brilliant and original account of contraceptive techniques written prior to the nineteenth century," [12] passed on the standard combination of superstition and effective practice. On the one hand, he recommended that the woman hold her breath during the sexual act or sneeze and drink something cold immediately after it; on the other hand, he prescribed spermicides that physicians were still advocating in the 1930s (*ibid.*). Several analysts assert that the most common method was *coitus interruptus*, though one cannot base this supposition on classical references.

It has been surmised that slavery constituted one important factor in reducing Rome's fertility (Landry, 1936; *cf.* Noonan, 1965, pp. 20–21). The slaves themselves had few offspring, first of all because their masters wanted it that way. So long as it was possible, their owners found it more advantageous to purchase adults than to pay for the raising of children. After the price went up (in Rome about the time of Augustus), apparently the birth

[12] Norman E. Himes, *Medical History of Contraception*, Williams & Wilkins, Baltimore, 1936, pp. 88–92.

rate still remained low, partly because the masters did not perceive their interest immediately, partly because the slaves themselves often wanted even less to reproduce. The slave population, thus, could be maintained only by continuous recruitment; when this lagged, it moved toward extinction. The number of slaves is unknown, but estimates for both Greece and Rome run as high as one-third of the free population—a large enough proportion to have a considerable effect on reproductive trends. The fertility of freed men was also very low. In Rome manumission was generally based on the condition that the slaves promised never to marry, for if they died without issue, their property reverted to their former owner. Slavery may also have been a significant depressant on the birth rate of the free population. Among the upper classes a man who owned a female was not induced to marry by either his sexual drive or his need for someone to care for his household.[13] Casual unions with slaves were generally infertile, as were, of course, the frequent homosexual ones in Greece.

One indication that the family size of Rome was effectively cut is the pronatalist sentiment expressed by various writers and officials, particularly by Augustus, emperor at the beginning of the Christian era. Three famous laws—*Lex Julia de adulteriis coercendis, Lex Julia de maritandis ordinibus,* and *Lex Papia et Poppaea*—were intended to raise the family's prestige and thus to encourage marriage and reproduction. The unmarried and childless were penalized by various legal disabilities; fathers were given preferential treatment in the allocation of public offices; "matrons" (probably the mothers of three or more children) were given the right to wear distinctive clothes. These laws were repeatedly modified, but in one form or another they remained in effect for a considerable period, finally to be rescinded by Justinian in the middle of the sixth century. Landry believes that they had a beneficial effect on family life and helped to raise the birth rate (Landry, 1934, p. 95). Their influence, however, cannot have been great, for beginning in the third century at the latest, the population of the Empire declined.[14]

The interrelation between population decline and the rise of Christianity has been analyzed in various ways. One hypothesis is that the depopulation

[13] According to the Greek historian Polybius (circa 140 B.C.), "the whole of Greece has been subject to a low birth rate and a general decrease of the population," for men have fallen into "such a state of pretentiousness, avarice, and indolence that they did not wish to marry, or if they married to rear the children born to them, or at most as a rule but one or two of them" (Polybius, *The Histories,* Vol. 4, Loeb Classical Library, London, 1927, Book 36, Para. 17.6–13).

[14] One reason for this was the out-migration from the center to the periphery. "As every Roman citizen had much better opportunities of earning a living in the provinces, Italy was constantly drained of her best men, and the gaps were filled by slaves. When an abundant supply of slaves ceased to be available, Italy began to decay in her turn, for the process of emigration never stopped, as one land after another was opened up for settlement" (M. Rostovtzeff, *The Social and Economic History of the Roman Empire,* 2nd Revised Ed.; Clarendon, Oxford, 1956, **1**, 375).

during the late-ancient and early-medieval periods brought about an economic, social, and intellectual depression, the "Dark Ages," and thus a stronger interest in religion (Russell, 1941). There may have been an influence also in the other direction. Although the Christian doctrine of the inestimable worth of every human soul, no matter how humble its vehicle, led the early Church to favor population growth, its opposition to sexuality *per se* blocked the development of an effective pronatalist policy. Church doctrine was too confused and too vacillating to become the sole ethical force even among all its own adherents.[15]

## THE JOINT FAMILY

The societies of classical India and China were both based on the **joint family,** "a group of people who generally live under one roof, who eat food cooked at one hearth, who hold property in common, and who participate in common family worship and are related to each other as some particular type of kindred" (Irawati Karve, quoted in Madan, 1963; *cf.* Lee, 1953). The strength and resilience of this institution are so great that one can discuss it in an almost timeless perspective, exemplifying its characteristics indifferently with historical or contemporary data, except of course for the family in Communist China.

The adult sons of a joint family do not leave the ancestral home when they marry but bring their wives into it, so that three or more generations live under one roof as a social, religious, and economic unit. The property and the income from it, along with the earnings of all the family members, constitute a common fund out of which the needs of all are met. Everything is formally administered by the oldest male, the patriarch, to whom all others owe absolute obedience. The larger the joint family, the greater the patriarch's realm and honor: according to legend, the head of a family of nine generations who lived during the T'ang dynasty was visited and decorated by the Emperor in person. The decision when and whom to marry does not rest with the two participants but with their elders; the Confucian classics define marriage as "a union between two persons of different families, the dual object of which is to serve the ancestors in the temple and to propagate the coming generation." The strength of the

---

[15] *Cf.* Noonan, 1965, *passim;* see pp. 491–496. Even the moral injunctions against infanticide, which were certainly less ambivalent than rules on other sexual and family matters, became effective only when they were reinforced by foundling hospitals. The first of these were established in the early Middle Ages, but their number grew very slowly; "the strong sense always evinced in the Church of the enormity of unchastity probably rendered the ecclesiastics more cautious in this than in other forms of charity" (W. E. H. Lecky, *History of European Morals from Augustus to Charlemagne,* Braziller, New York, 1955, 2, 33). As late as the seventeenth century, when St. Vincent de Paul established the order associated with his name, one impetus to his act was the continuing high incidence of infanticide.

Chinese institution, thus, was based not only on its current structure but on its intergenerational continuity, with ancestor worship reaching into the past and emphasis on a numerous progeny into the future. Although this ideal of the Chinese family was realized only among the gentry, the more numerous peasantry seemingly also accepted it as their standard and strove to imitate the upper class to the degree that their poverty permitted (Lang, 1946; Kulp, 1925).

A joint household facilitates early marriage: adolescents can undertake such roles as parenthood while they are still socially immature, for they will not bear the main responsibility of caring for their children. In classical China marriage was typically entered at an early age; in India, by an aberration from the joint-family pattern, it was, and is, still earlier, often before puberty. The betrothal at the groom's house (the *shadi*) often takes place in early childhood or even infancy, and at puberty the bride returns to the groom's home and after a second ceremony (the *gauna*) the marriage is consummated. Marriage is virtually a universal state; in India in 1961 only one female in 200 was still single at the end of the fecund period.

It is true that India's earlier tradition was changed slightly by restrictive legislation; in 1860, sexual intercourse with a wife under ten was prohibited; in 1904, the minimum age for females was raised to twelve years or, on the guardian's petition, to nine years; in the Sarda Act of 1929, the minimum ages were raised to eighteen for boys and fourteen for girls; [16] and in 1955, the minimum age for girls was raised again to fifteen (Goode, 1963, p. 234). According to the best study of the question, the average female age at marriage gradually rose from 12.77 years in 1891–1901 to 15.38 in 1941–51, or by an average of half a year per decade. The male age declined over the same period from 20.01 to 19.93 years.

On the whole the Sarda Act, which was enacted to restrict child marriages, seems to have some effect, at least among females. . . . Surprisingly enough, there seems to be a slight tendency towards increased child marriages among males (Agarwala, 1962, p. 229).

The effect of the increase in age at marriage on Indian fertility is not so simple as one would suppose. According to a sample survey of rural households near Banaras, total fertility was 730 per 1,000 females married at 14 years or less, and 680 for those married at 17 to 19 years. This is what one would expect: with a shorter period of exposure there are fewer births. However, one must consider also the factor of adolescent subfecundity: with the rise in the age at marriage, the interval to the first birth decreased appreciably. The decline in fertility from the loss of the early reproductive

---

[16] *Cf.* Agarwala, 1962, p. 74. The law resulted in a temporary *decline* in the mean age at marriage, for parents rushed their children to wed before the law went into effect. Subsequently it was never enforced very rigorously.

period, thus, was far less than one would suppose from a calculation of the years of nonexposure (Rele, 1962; *cf.* Collver, 1963).

Western sociologists often explain the rise in the marriage age, such as it was, by industrialization and urbanization, which supposedly bring about a gradual deterioration of the joint family and thus an increased age at marriage (e.g., Goode, 1963; Ross, 1961). However, with size of household as an index, the incidence of joint families did not decline, and may even have risen, from 1911 to 1951 (Orenstein, 1961; *cf.* Desai, 1964). At least among one small sample, even the attitude toward living in joint families has become more favorable (K. M. Kapadia, cited in Orenstein, 1961). Indeed, it is no longer certain that in contemporary India the family type influences fertility. According to two studies, the family was smaller, though not significantly so, in joint than in simple families (Pakrasi and Malakar, 1967). Whether the pattern one would expect from family theory has been reversed is not yet settled, if only because of the loose definition of the two types, and in any case one can assume that the theory holds for historic India, before modernizing disturbances had become significant.

### WESTERN EUROPE

The marriage pattern of most of [Western] Europe as it existed for at least two centuries up to 1940 was, so far as we can tell, unique or almost unique in the world. . . . The distinctive marks of the "European pattern" are (1) a high age at marriage and (2) a high proportion of people who never marry at all (Hajnal, 1965).

When precisely this pattern began to develop is not known. The evidence from the medieval period is fragmentary, largely imprecise (in a literary reference to "late" marriages, what is the meaning of the key word?), and in any case contradictory. On the one hand, only about 4 per cent of a sample of medieval London merchants remained bachelors; and one can surmise that the typical ages at marriage among this class were 20–24 for males and 13–14 for females.[17] On the other hand, we are told that the Middle Ages was "as familiar as our own day with the independent spinster" (Eileen Power, cited in *ibid.*). Perhaps the best evidence that the European pattern developed at an early date is etymological. The word *husband* derives from two words meaning "house" and "dwell," and its original meaning (still preserved in *husbandman* and *husbandry*) was a householder, a man who had a home. The Middle English word for an unmarried man was *anilepiman*. These two terms, one referring to the management of property and the other to marital status, gradually became associated as opposites, *anilepiman* coming to mean a man who had no living and therefore could

[17] Sylvia L. Thrupp, *The Merchant Class of Medieval London (1300–1500)*, University of Michigan Press, Ann Arbor, 1962, Chapter 5.

not marry, and *husband,* a man who was able to care for a family and therefore could get (or, eventually, was) married.[18]

Another line of argumentation relates to the family organization that developed to prevent the partition and repartition of family plots. In the **stem family** (sometimes given its French name of *famille souche,* from the usage of Frédéric LePlay, who was the first to analyze it), the entire property goes to a single heir, and his siblings either move away or do not marry. The typical household, thus, consists of a peasant, his wife and minor children, his unmarried brothers and sisters, and perhaps his aged father and mother. When this system was operative, farmhands were in some respects almost members of a farmer's family, sleeping and eating in and under no social pressure to marry early, or at all. An English report (1824) on the poor laws discussed the "old system" in the countryside by which men "did not marry until they were perhaps near thirty years of age, and until they had got a little money and a few goods about them." [19] This type of three-generation household once prevailed in much of Europe and still exists in a number of rural areas. In the towns many occupations were governed by guilds, which generally inhibited marriage until after an apprentice had finished his training period and moved up to the next level.

According to the sparse data available, then, the age at marriage in Western Europe started to rise either in the Middle Ages (if we accept merely indicative evidence) or in any case well before the eighteenth century. In Venice, to take one striking example, the ages at marriage in 1701–84 fluctuated between 29.9 and 31.7 for males and between 28.0 and 29.8 for females (Daniele Beltrami, cited in *ibid.*). The one country where this extraordinary postponement of marriage has survived is Ireland, and the more accurate and extensive data of this country can be used to analyze the demographic effect of "the European pattern" (see pp. 514–517).

## Mortality

Age-specific death rates *per 1,000 deaths* in three regions of Roman Italy, as calculated by Beloch from tombstone inscriptions, are shown in Table 11-2. The small proportion for those aged fifteen and under certainly reflects only the fact that tombstones were seldom erected for infants or young children. Note that for the relatively small number of minors represented, the sex ratio is 125, while for the major reproductive period it is 84. Childbirth apparently was dangerous to mothers, and by inference also to their children (*cf.* Russell, 1958, Tables 3 and 4; Burn, 1953). It is worth remarking also that in Beloch's more detailed table giving rates by

---

[18] *Cf.* George Casper Homans, *English Villagers of the Thirteenth Century,* Harvard University Press, Cambridge, Mass., 1941, pp. 136–137.

[19] Quoted in G. Talbot Griffith, *Population Problems of the Age of Malthus,* University Press, Cambridge, 1926, p. 109.

Table 11-2. Age-Specific Deaths per 1,000 Deaths, Roman
Italy, as Calculated from Epitaphs

| AGE GROUP | MALE | FEMALE | TOTAL |
|---|---|---|---|
| 0–15 | 315 | 252 | 289 |
| 16–30 | 331 | 428 | 370 |
| 31–45 | 171 | 169 | 170 |
| 46–60 | 81 | 71 | 76 |
| Over 60 | 102 | 80 | 95 |

SOURCE: Julius Beloch, *Die Bevölkerung der griechisch-romischen
Welt*, Duncker & Humblot, Leipzig, 1886, p. 48.

single years of age, a very definite tendency is discernible to heap at ages
ending in five and zero, exactly as in the returns from modern censuses.
Even in so personal a datum as the inscription on one's tombstone, age was
rounded off.

Median expectations of life as calculated by Beloch are given in Table
11-3. These figures have the same limitations, of course, as the "death rates"

Table 11-3. Median Expectations of Life, Roman Italy, as
Calculated from Epitaphs

| FROM AGE | MALES | FEMALES |
|---|---|---|
| 10 | 17–18 | 15–16 |
| 20 | 16–17 | 10–11 |
| 30 | 15–16 | 11–12 |
| 40 | 15–16 | 15–16 |
| 50 | 10–11 | 10–11 |
| 60 | 10–11 | 8 |

SOURCE: Julius Beloch, *Die Bevölkerung der griechisch-römischen
Welt*, Duncker & Humblot, Leipzig, 1886, p. 51.

on which they are based. In particular, it is impossible to calculate the
expectation of life from birth, for data are too poor on the mortality of
infants and young children. However, if the probability was that children
of ten would live only to their late twenties, then the expectation of life
from birth, which would take into account the certainly larger infant mortality, could not have been more than the early twenties.

The data to be gleaned concerning the leading social classes of any past
society on age at marriage or size of family are almost irrelevant to a judg-

ment of that society's general fertility, but it is reasonable to suppose that the mortality of especially favored groups was probably at the lowest level the particular culture could achieve. Among the members of all Europe's ruling houses, mortality began to fall, especially among infants, long before the development of modern medicine. Infant deaths beyond the first week, which numbered 104 per 1,000 live births in 1500–99, rose to 171 in the following century. But during 1700–99 this index dropped to 106 and then more sharply to 45 in 1800–99 and 3 in 1900–35. Between 1500 and 1849 the average life expectancy increased by some 13.5 years for males and 12 years for females (Peller, 1965). Data on the English royal house can be carried back farther than 1500. For its members born before 1348, the year that

Symbol of death with scythe, depicted in mosaic on the floor of a Pompeian villa. The motto reads: KNOW THYSELF (*The Bettmann Archive, Inc.*).

the Black Death struck England, the expectation of life at birth was generally slightly above 30 years. It fell during the plague period to 17, and then rose very slowly over the next 75 years again to something over 30. Life tables for a small sample of monks, another favored group, give about the same figures (Russell, 1948, pp. 178–193).

The causes of this high mortality cannot, of course, be specified in terms of the modern classification. We know very little about why people died in a "normal" year; but over a longer period a large proportion died as the consequence of famines, epidemics, or the breakdown of the social order (including war). Some over-all data on these three types of catastrophe are available for the whole of the historic era.

### FAMINE

Until recently most of the people in the world have suffered from a shortage of food, but in Europe—ancient, medieval, or modern—actual famines have been relatively less frequent and less severe than in Asia. That grain had to be shipped over ever growing distances to Roman Italy was a problem of increasing gravity, but so long as the state control remained intact the system never broke down. Indeed, medieval Europe suffered from severe famines, such as that in 1315–17 (Lucas, 1930), and these recurred well into the modern era. In the 1690s a succession of poor harvests created a subsistence crisis throughout most of Europe; in 1698 the death rates in two regions of Sweden rose to 90 and 160 per 1,000 population. The winter of 1708–09, long remembered in France as "*le grand hiver*," brought to that country among several others intense misery and heightened mortality (Helleiner, 1965). In the last great famine of the Western world, in Ireland in the 1840s, several hundred thousand persons died of starvation and the already large emigration was given a mighty stimulus, and on the Continent a less disastrous failure of the potato crop intensified the destitution of the poor. Yet only occasionally did these recurrent food shortages develop into a true famine, and then typically only in certain regions or countries. However disastrous they might seem to a citizen of a twentieth-century Western country, on the scale of world history Europe's food shortages have always been relatively puny.

The normal death rate of the great civilizations of Asia, on the contrary, "may be said to contain a constant famine factor." Between 108 B.C. and A.D. 1911, China withstood 1,828 famines, or nearly one per year in some of the provinces during these two millennia (Mallory, 1926, p. 1). Most of them were over only a portion of the country; the worst were nationwide. But everywhere throughout China, every district experienced a famine at least several times during each person's lifetime. And even this record understates the probable catastrophic effects of crop failures, droughts, floods, and locusts and other pests, for the information in general official works "often fails to indicate the scope and severity of a famine." A good example is provided by the province of Hupei, for which Ho calculated year by year the number of counties affected by natural calamities (including also epidemics) from 1644 to 1911. Out of this period of 267 years, there were only 27 entirely free of disaster (including those for which the record is known to be incomplete). Droughts occurred in 92 of the years, floods in 190. In the average year slightly more than one-tenth of the province was hit (Ho, 1959, pp. 228–229, 292–300).

One of the worst famines of modern China struck four northern provinces in 1877–78. Communications were so poor that almost a year passed before news of it reached the capital. Cannibalism was common, and local magistrates were ordered "to connive at the evasion of the laws prohibiting the sale of children, so as to enable parents to buy a few days' food." The dead were buried in what are still today called "ten-thousand-men holes." From 9 to 13 million, according to the estimate of the Foreign Relief Committee, perished from hunger, disease, or violence during these two years (*ibid.*, pp. 231–232).

Of course, it is not possible to measure the mortality from Asiatic famines directly. The registration of deaths, never very accurate at best, breaks down completely during such a period. One can estimate the mortality in India due to the famines during the 1890s, for example, by comparing the country's natural increase in this decade with that in the ones before and after it:

In the previous decade [the population of India] grew 9.4 per cent, and in the following decade 6.1 per cent. If the 1891–1901 decade had experienced the average rate of growth shown by these two decades, it would have grown by 7.8 per cent instead of 1 per cent. The difference is a matter of some 19 million persons, which may be taken as a rough estimate of loss due to famines. It should be borne in mind, however, that relief measures were functioning at this time and that this saved the lives of millions of persons who otherwise would have died (Davis, 1951, p. 39).

This contrast between the famine-ridden civilizations of China and India and those of medieval and early-modern Europe, relatively free of this cause of death, cannot be explained by a difference in technical skill. If anything, the Chinese peasant was a better agriculturist than his Western counterpart. (1) One reason for the difference is geographical: the uncertainty of rainfall in India is probably the biggest single factor influencing life there, and the same might be said of monsoon Asia in general. (2) In both India and China, agriculture was based to a large extent on irrigation and flood-control works, which, as we have seen, gave rise to a type of society known as Oriental despotism. Its rapacious bureaucracy, as well as the routine banditry and civil war, made it difficult to store food against times of need.[20] (3) To this day the transportation system of either China or India is poor compared with that, for example, of the Roman Empire. Most famines are local, at least in origin. If food cannot be shipped in from other areas, however, the starving people leave their homes and steal food where they can, spreading the famine and often pestilence as they go. (4) A final reason for the difference was probably the higher fertility in Asia. Although family size was controlled by means of *coitus interruptus*, abortion, and particularly infanticide, China and India probably had a higher fertility than other preindustrial civilizations. Their populations therefore may have pressed more closely on the subsistence available to them.

### PESTILENCE

With respect to diseases, the preindustrial civilizations were more or less on a par. We can illustrate their common characteristics with examples

---

[20] For a first-hand account of the "political causes of famine" in China, see Mallory, 1926, Chapter 3.

from ancient Egypt. In contrast to primitive medicine, in which the magical, the religious, and the empirico-rational are inextricably combined, in Egypt there was at least a partial segregation. In place of the single role of medicine man or shaman, three types of healer were distinguished—the physician, the priest of Sekhmet, and the sorcerer (Sigerist, 1967, p. 267). The latter two combated the evil spirits that caused disease with incantations, amulets, manipulations, and various mixtures of strange ingredients. Often the sorcerer probably had better results than the physician, for "magician and priest were able to put the sick in a frame of mind in which the healing power of the organism could do its work under the best conditions" (*ibid.*, p. 280). The rational medicine of Egypt is expounded especially in Papyrus Ebers and Papyrus Edwin Smith, both of which date from the first half of the sixteenth century B.C. and summarize a much earlier lore. Papyrus Edwin Smith is a fragment on surgery; partly because of this subject matter, its recommended practices are almost entirely free of magic. The Ebers Papyrus is a complete medical compendium,[21] which combines a magical element, a largely obsolete materia medica, and a wealth of information on related topics [22] in a more or less rational perspective. Incantations, for instance, are recommended in only twelve types of cases, most of which were defined as hopeless.

Judged by our physiology and medicine, the doctors of Egypt as of other preindustrial civilizations did not know the cause of most ailments and usually had little success in curing them. As one would expect, the best information we have concerns the most devasting—the plague, malaria, cholera, and the other major epidemic diseases.[23]

The plague appears in three forms—pneumonic, septicemic, and bubonic. A person infected with the first type, the least important of the three, is directly contagious. The other two are spread by a complex interaction among the bacillus, its host (the flea), and the flea's hosts (the rat and man). The bubonic plague was the most terrible of the epidemics of the ancient and medieval worlds. It struck in the first half of the sixth century and then again some 800 years later.

The path of the fourteenth-century epidemic, the famous Black Death, is shown in Figure 11-1. The first cases were in Constantinople in 1347; and the presumption is that the infection came from China, where it may

[21] It begins with an invocation to the gods to be recited when treating a patient and proceeds with a description of symptoms and treatment for the following types of diseases: internal, of the eyes, of the skin, of the extremities, miscellaneous, of women, of the heart and other vessels, associated with surgery (Sigerist, 1967, p. 312).

[22] "The gynecological section is followed by a number of recipes 'to expel fleas in the house, to prevent a snake from coming out of its hole, to prevent a fly from biting, to sweeten the smell of the house or the clothes,' and other similar household remedies" (*ibid.*, p. 314).

[23] For discussions in two different social contexts, see Russell, 1958, pp. 35–45, and Davis, 1951, pp. 42–61.

have been endemic. By the fall of 1347 it was reported in Sicily. During the spring of 1348 it spread throughout the Mediterranean basin to Italy, France, and Spain, reaching Paris in June, London in September. From London it went west to Dublin (1349), north to York (1349) and Scotland (1350). From Italy and France it traveled to various German cities, reaching East Prussia in 1350 and Russia in the spring of 1352. In each place it struck in epidemic form several times—in England, for example, in 1348–1350, 1360–1361, 1369, and 1375—and continued endemic for some 80 years. The mortality throughout Europe was appalling. Contemporary figures reflect the variation from one place to another and are often exaggerated, but even the more conservative estimates of present-day scholars indicate an unparalleled loss of life. One of the most careful analyses is by Russell (1948, pp. 214–232; 1958, pp. 40–45), who believes that most European nations sustained a depletion of 20 to 25 per cent in the first attack of 1348–1350, and of 40 per cent by the end of the century. Urban death rates were probably higher than the average, because of the greater contagion in congested areas, and the depopulation of cities was aggravated by a mass exodus of their terror-stricken inhabitants. Since pregnant women seem to have been particularly susceptible, the stupendous loss could not be quickly repaired. "Only one disease, the plague, seems to have been lethal enough to destroy population faster than humanity could restore it in the late ancient and medieval period (Davis, 1951, p. 45).

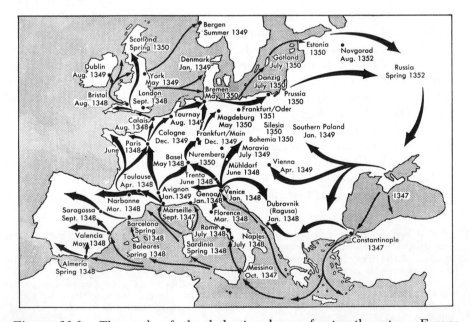

**Figure 11-1.** The path of the bubonic plague, fourteenth-century Europe.

Source: Ernst Kirsten, *Raum und Bevölkerung in der Weltgeschichte*, Ploetz, Würzburg, 1956, 1, 92. © 1956 by A. G. Ploetz-Verlag Würzburg.

A seventeenth-century woodcut of a physician during a London plague. The nose-piece filled with strong herbs purportedly protected him from the miasmas; the leather coat, leggings, and gloves were to prevent contagion (*The Bettmann Archive, Inc.*).

The total mortality from other major diseases, however, was also great. It is not possible in most cases even to suggest their rates of incidence, except to state that they were high. There is a marked difference in the relative susceptibility of various age groups. The plague strikes heaviest at the aged, which is presumably one reason why the best known personages of fourteenth-century Europe died in such an overwhelming proportion during the first attack of the Black Death. Tuberculosis, on the contrary, typically infects young children and kills at the beginning of their adult life, thus placing the burden of support on society with no economic or demographic return. The age differential for malaria is parallel to that for general mortality, very high in infancy, low in the teens, and gradually rising with adult ages.

### THE BREAKDOWN OF SOCIAL ORDER

That famine and pestilence ordinarily appear together suggests a direct relation between them, but apparently the usual reason is that both the supply of food and public health depend on—and can affect—the maintenance of social order (see pp. 215–216). People who have seen hundreds of their neighbors die of hunger or disease do not themselves continue to carry out their usual pursuits in accordance with established norms. Often they flee from their homes, carrying the blight with them.

The interaction of these three major factors in mortality can be illustrated by some pages from the history of the late Roman Empire. The process began as early as the reign of Trajan (A.D. 98–117), whose military successes, according to Rostovtzeff, brought "the empire to the verge of ruin."

The dread symptom of this decay was the depopulation of the peninsula and the concurrent decline of Italian agriculture. . . . Nerva endeavored to repopulate the country by reviving the plan of distributing land to poorer citizens. . . . Trajan forbade emigration from Italy and settled Roman veterans in the immediate vicinity of Rome; he forced senators to acquire land in the mother country; and he helped Italian landowners in general, both large and small, to improve their situation by supplying them with cheap credit.[24]

Over the following several hundred years these remedies would be applied again and again, with less and less effect (Boak, 1955, Chapter 2). The capital's disorganization was reflected in a virtual civil war in the countryside. During a fifty-year period in the third century, there were twenty-seven official emperors in Rome, plus twice that number of aspirants. Armies broke up into antagonistic units, which successively requisitioned (or stole—the distinction was not sharp) standing crops, food stores, and livestock, leaving impoverishment and starvation in their wake. At the end of the century, barbarians invaded Italy and also ravaged the countryside. The cultivators were mostly either slaves, who took the opportunity to escape, or *coloni* (tenant farmers), who also often fled from their holdings. The brigand bands that they formed in some cases constituted veritable armies, large enough in Gaul to menace cities. In the middle of the third century Italy was infested by the plague, which was rapidly spread by the movement of troops and irregulars.

Efforts to repair the damage often increased it. Much land had gone out of cultivation, and Rome was deprived both of its produce and of taxes. In the fourth century a system evolved by which these abandoned plots were assigned to adjoining estates, so that their owners would both cultivate them and pay the land tax again. Rather than accept what was often an intolerable burden, many gave up their own properties. With land out of use and drainage systems neglected, breeding places for mosquitoes multiplied, and malaria became a greater threat to the population, killing many and sapping the strength of others. Early in the fourth century the *coloni*, who had been using their contractual right to leave their farms, were bound to the soil. They became serfs. Their status was gradually imposed also on the free agricultural workers, so that by the fifth century the prior distinction between them and *coloni* had all but disappeared.

The decisive break with the civilization of antiquity came not from the German infiltration or the attendant circumstances that made it possi-

[24] Rostovtzeff, *op. cit.*, pp. 358–359.

ble,[25] but much later, in the eighth and ninth centuries, when Europe was unable to repel invasion. Moslems conquered Spain and threatened Constantinople; Norsemen plundered the coasts of the North Sea and of every river that emptied into it; the Hungarians swept in from Asia. "The devastation was so complete that, in many cases indeed, the population itself disappeared." Too weak to defend its periphery, Europe turned inward. "The Empire of Charlemagne . . . was essentially an inland one, . . . a State without foreign markets, living in a condition of almost complete isolation" (Pirenne, 1956, pp. 19, 21).

During most of the first millennium of the Christian era, then, the civilization of antiquity was in decline. It is not easy, and in this context not relevant, to distinguish such a general social disintegration, inevitably aggravated by combat, from formal warfare. Present-day Americans are likely to conceptualize war in terms of their own experience—a process in which young men are trained, sent overseas to fight, and welcomed home on their victorious return. War in the country where the battles are fought, particularly when a defeated army breaks up into small marauding bands, is much less clearly distinguished from civilian life.

Another striking example is the Taiping Rebellion of 1851–64, which Ho terms "the greatest civil war in world history." Indeed, as he writes, "in sheer brutality and destruction it has few peers." In the usual tactics against the rebels, not only were all prisoners summarily slaughtered but a scorched-earth policy was used to starve the armies into submission. In one area of some 6,000 square miles no trace of human habitation was left. The usual estimate of the number who died, 20 or 30 million, is too low in Ho's opinion. The devastation is merely suggested by the fact that in 1953 the population of three of the provinces most affected—Chekiang, Anhwei, and

---

[25] The barbarians did not so much cause the downfall of Rome as fit into a process of gradual disintegration well under way before they became a significant factor. Constantine (306–37) had forced a treaty on the Visigoths, who agreed to supply soldiers to the Roman army in return for yearly payments, and over the following period the Roman army was gradually germanized. Assigned to frontier duty, German soldiers acquired land there and in many places became the dominant element of the population. After Ulfilas (or Wulfila, 311–381), a bishop of Arian convictions, translated the Bible into Gothic, a large number of Germans were converted to Christianity and thus even more subject to Roman influence than before. In the following period the distinction between "Roman" and "barbarian" became vaguer. The relation between the two cultures was not so often a confrontation on the field of battle as a divided loyalty of marginal men—for example, Alaric, the leader of the Visigoths who sacked Rome, a romanized German, a former officer in the Roman army, a Christian; or Stilicho, the *de facto* emperor at that time, a German by descent who had reached this high post through a successful army career.

"The aim of the invaders was not to destroy the Roman Empire but to occupy and enjoy it. By and large, what they preserved far exceeded what they destroyed or what they brought that was new. . . . [The civilization of the Empire] outlived its authority. By the Church, by language, by the superiority of its institutions and law, it prevailed over the conquerors. . . . They barbarized it, but they did not consciously germanize it" (Pirenne, 1956, p. 5; *cf.* Bury, 1928).

Kiangsi—was still 19.2 million, or 14 per cent, under the estimated number in 1850 (Ho, 1959, pp. 236–246, 275).

## Population Cycles

The main emphasis in demographic analysis is usually on population growth, and this is appropriate in either of two contexts. With respect to the term of *Homo sapiens* on earth, the dominant trend has been an increase in numbers. And in the modern world, from roughly 1650 on, this increase has been at a rapid and accelerating rate. But a closer view of preindustrial civilizations reveals a striking exception to the rule: their populations typically grew and declined in a cyclical pattern.

The gradual development of classical antiquity as a unit, for example, was certainly accompanied by a substantial rise in population. The depopulation of the Roman Empire as a whole probably began in the third century and continued for several hundred years. The nadir was reached around 600, and Europe's population remained more or less static at this low level for almost 400 years. The epidemic of the bubonic plague with which this period was opened was possibly the most devastating in history. Then there came the Moslem, Norse, and Hungarian invasions (Russell, 1958, Chapter 8).

By 950 Europe had developed enough power to protect its borders, and the ensuing four centuries constitute the "medieval increase," as Russell terms it.[26] From the middle of the eleventh century to just before the Black Death, the population of England, for example, increased from 1.1 to 3.7 million, that of France (territory of 1328) from 4.0 to 13.5 million (*ibid.*, Chapter 9). A decline started with the outbreak of the plague in 1348, and continued for about 80 years. From 1430 to the present day, the population of Europe has grown steadily, though at different rates at various times.

The evidence concerning Asia also suggests a cyclical pattern.

During the two thousand years that intervened between the ancient and the modern period India's population . . . must have remained virtually stationary. . . . In "normal" times, . . . the customs governing fertility would provide a birth rate slightly higher than the usual death rate. This would build up a population surplus as a sort of demographic insurance against catastrophe. Inevitably, however, the catastrophe would come in the form of warfare, famine, or epidemic, and the increase of population would suddenly be wiped out (Davis, 1951, p. 24).

In Ho's reconstruction of China's population history, there has been an irregular increase—from 65 million in 1400, to 150 million in 1600 and still in 1700, to 313 million in 1794, 430 million in 1850, and 583 million in 1953.

---

[26] *Cf.* "The Two Ages of Feudalism," in Marc Bloch, *Feudal Society*, Routledge & Kegan Paul, London, 1961, Chapter 4 and especially pp. 60–61, 69.

Other scholars, while agreeing that growth occurred over this period, have stressed its irregularity more.[27]

What is the meaning of these long cycles? In what way are they associated with trends in economic and social life? Depopulation in the late Roman Empire coincided with the disintegration of classical society, and the low point was during the Dark Ages; from 950 to 1350 marked a new rise in population and the evolution of medieval culture to its high point; the subsequent increase from 1430 on coincided with the Renaissance and beginning of modern Europe. There certainly is a correlation here. But in which direction is the causal relation? Is population size an effect of the economic level or, on the contrary, a cause of a more general development or decline? Or is the cause-effect relation both more variable and more complex than either of these alternatives? Let us consider these questions with respect to depopulation, which is atypical in human history and therefore the most interesting feature of preindustrial civilizations.

The decline of Europe's population in the second half of the fourteenth century was indubitably caused by the Black Death. The unreliable rainfall of monsoon Asia is indeed the greatest influence on the life of its inhabitants. That is to say, sometimes a single factor is so dominant that analysts have no hesitation in designating it as the cause of demographic processes. But even in such cases, it must be emphasized, these factors operate within a certain cultural-social-economic context. India's dependence on rainfall, for example, was mitigated by irrigation systems, and increased by family-building norms that pushed the population always up to the subsistence available. And more often there is no such single factor on which all scholars agree, but a multiplicity of causes, each emphasized by a different writer. In explaining the depopulation of the ancient world, for instance, Landry (1936) singled out the fall in fertility. Others have stressed the high mortality, sometimes even that from a single disease.[28] Still others have paid greatest attention to the gradual disintegration of the state's political control, and its eventual effect on everything from family life to agricultural produce. Such separate factors can be singled out in order to examine them more thoroughly, but the most reasonable hypothesis usually is that the decline in numbers was brought about not by any single one but by the interaction of all.

Nor is it any easier to analyze the effects of depopulation on the rest of society. The first to be noted is that on military prowess. While there is not a simple one-to-one relation, it is true that states of grossly different sizes

[27] For one series of estimates for the population of China from the beginning of the Christian era, see Abbott Payson Usher, "The History of Population and Settlement in Eurasia," *Geographical Review*, **20** (1930), 110–132. See also K. W. Taylor, "Some Aspects of Population History," *Canadian Journal of Economics and Political Science*, **16** (1950), 301–313.

[28] See, for example, W. H. S. Jones, *Malaria: A Neglected Factor in the History of Greece and Rome*, Macmillan & Bowes, Cambridge, 1907.

can wield power more or less proportionate to their populations; and this was even more the case in the past, when there were not such great differences in military technology. As its title indicates, this is one principal theme of Boak's book, *Manpower Shortage and the Fall of the Roman Empire in the West*. In order to maintain the boundary of the Empire safe against incursions, Rome—as we have seen—had to recruit an increasing number of Germans into its army. A vigorous and expanding Roman population could have absorbed this barbarian element, but, as it was, the Germans not only came to dominate the ranks and officer corps but were well represented among commanding generals. Even so, the manpower shortage continued, and in the next stage treaties were signed by which nominally dependent—though actually autonomous—German tribes were paid to defend the frontiers. And the proximate cause of the fall of the city of Rome was a struggle between the Latin and German parties in the Empire.[29] Such a loss of military power, moreover, can be cumulative. One reason that Europe was unable to defend its borders against Saracens, Norsemen, or Hungarians was its lack of manpower; and, vice versa, one reason that this low population level remained characteristic of the Dark Ages is the effects, both direct and indirect, of the continued raids that Europe had to withstand.

It is a reasonable hypothesis that the transition to the rapid growth of the modern era began with a change in this cyclical pattern.

> It was the peaks rather than the plateau of mortality that were lowered. . . . The disappearance of plague above all, but also a very sensible mitigation of subsistence crises seem to have been chiefly responsible for the increase in life expectancy (Helleiner, 1965).

## Summary

The term "preindustrial civilizations" has been used to designate a class of societies based on agriculture and trade but with no industry, with an urban population and a high culture but few of the characteristics associated with urbanism in the modern West. These societies, particularly ancient Rome, medieval Europe, and classical China and India, have certain important elements in common.

It is important to distinguish, however, between the free cities of Europe and the administrative centers either there or elsewhere. The former gave rise to the new bourgeois class, and with it the origins of Europe's technological advance and democratic society. The cities of other preindustrial civilizations, though associated in their earliest stage with stu-

---

[29] See Boak, 1955, pp. 115–116. Note, however, that he concludes his discussion as follows: "I should be the last person to claim that the fall of the West Roman Empire can be explained solely in terms of a problem of shortage of recruits for the army."

pendous innovations, did not become nuclei from which the same type of society could develop.

The population of preindustrial civilizations generally grew to a maximum and then declined sharply but temporarily, as the consequence of famines, epidemics, and the breakdown of social order. This cyclical pattern was characteristic of all of them, but differences can be noted between Asia and ancient or medieval Europe. In the former, the female age at marriage was generally puberty, and virtually all adults of both sexes were married, while in Europe postponement of marriage and nonmarriage of some adults cut the fertility to well below the physiological maximum. Because of this partial control of procreation, the European population did not press so closely on its means of subsistence, with the probable consequence that it was less often devastated by famine. In Asia, on the contrary, starvation seems to have been more important even than disease as a cause of high mortality.

During the downswing of a cycle the population, economy, and culture have often declined together, and this correlation has given rise to a variety of theories. In the most general terms, the cause of the periodic depopulation was that much larger numbers survived to maturity during favorable periods than could be maintained permanently. On the other hand, though the loss of population was often an important factor in the decline in political power, economy, and culture, it cannot generally be designated as "the" cause.

## Suggestions for Further Reading

The rise of cities in the ancient Middle East is analyzed from plausible and yet quite different hypotheses in Frankfort, 1956; Childe, 1951; and Wittfogel, 1957. Braidwood and Willey, 1962 gives a range of interpretations. Perhaps the most succinct analysis of the crucial distinction between bourgeois and administrative cities is Murvar, 1966; for a more extended discussion, see Weber, 1958 or especially Pirenne, 1956.

Beloch, 1886 is still acknowledged as the best in any language on the population of ancient Greece and Rome. Russell, 1958 is a conscientious summary of a vast mass of material linking the ancient and medieval periods, and Russell, 1948 is the best over-all analysis of a medieval population. Several of the essays in Glass and Eversley, 1965, in particular the one by Hajnal, and in Revelle, 1968 are excellent. Russell, 1965, a bibliographic essay, comments on a great many new works, including some that seem to use new methods of historical research; in this respect see also Wrigley, 1966.

Ho, 1959 and Davis, 1951 are first-rate books on two high civilizations of Asia. Chiao et al., 1938 is a useful warning against a too ready acceptance of the population data of preindustrial civilizations.

\* AGARWALA, S. N. 1962. *Age at Marriage in India.* Kitab Mahal Private Ltd., Allahabad.

Bascom, William. 1955. "Urbanization among the Yoruba," *American Journal of Sociology,* **60,** 446–454.

* Beloch, Julius. 1886. *Die Bevölkerung der griechisch-römischen Welt.* Duncker & Humblot, Leipzig.

Benet, F. 1963. "The Ideology of Islamic Urbanization," *International Journal of Comparative Sociology* (Dharwar), **4,** 211–226.

Boak, Arthur E. R. 1955. *Manpower Shortage and the Fall of the Roman Empire in the West.* University of Michigan Press, Ann Arbor.

Braidwood, Robert J., and Gordon R. Willey, editors. 1962. *Courses toward Urban Life: Archeological Considerations of Some Cultural Alternates.* Viking Fund Publications in Anthropology, No. 32, New York.

Burn, A. R. 1953. "Hic Breve Vivitur: A Study of the Expectation of Life in the Roman Empire," *Past and Present,* No. 4, pp. 2–31.

Bury, J. B. 1928. *The Invasion of Europe by the Barbarians.* Macmillan, London.

Chiao, C. M., Warren S. Thompson, and D. T. Chen. 1938. *An Experiment in the Registration of Vital Statistics in China.* Scripps Foundation for Research in Population Problems, Oxford, Ohio.

Childe, V. Gordon. 1951. *Man Makes Himself.* New American Library, Mentor Books, New York.

Collver, Andrew. 1963. "The Family Cycle in India and the United States," *American Sociological Review,* **28,** 86–96.

* Davis, Kingsley. 1951. *The Population of India and Pakistan.* Princeton University Press, Princeton, N.J.

———. 1955. "The Origin and Growth of Urbanization in the World," *American Journal of Sociology,* **60,** 429–437.

Desai, I. P. 1964. *Some Aspects of Family in Mahuva.* Asia Publishing House, Bombay.

Dickinson, Robert E. 1951. *The West European City: A Geographical Interpretation.* Routledge & Kegan Paul, London.

* Eberhard, Wolfram. 1956. "Data on the Structure of the Chinese City in the Preindustrial Period," *Economic Development and Cultural Change,* **4,** 253–268.

———. 1960. *A History of China.* University of California Press, Berkeley.

Frankfort, Henri. 1956. *The Birth of Civilization in the Near East.* Doubleday-Anchor, Garden City, N.Y.

* Friedmann, John. 1961. "Cities in Social Transformation," *Comparative Studies in Society and History,* **4,** 86–103.

Fustel de Coulanges, N. D. 1956. *The Ancient City: A Study on the Religion, Laws, and Institutions of Greece and Rome.* Doubleday-Anchor, Garden City, N.Y.

Glass, D. V., and D. E. C. Eversley, editors. 1965. *Population in History.* Aldine, Chicago.

Gomme, A. W. 1933. *The Population of Athens in the Fifth and Fourth Centuries B.C.* Blackwell, Oxford.

Goode, William J. 1963. *World Revolution and Family Patterns.* Free Press of Glencoe, New York.

Goubert, Pierre. 1965. "Recent Theories and Research in French Population between 1500 and 1700," in Glass and Eversley, 1965, pp. 457–473.

° HAJNAL, J. 1965. "European Marriage Patterns in Perspective," in Glass and Eversley, 1965, pp. 101–143.

HARKNESS, ALBERT GRANGER. 1896. "Age at Marriage and at Death in the Roman Empire," *Transactions of the American Philological Association*, **27**, 35–72.

° HELLEINER, K. F. 1965. "The Vital Revolution Reconsidered," in Glass and Eversley, 1965, pp. 79–86.

° HO PING-TI. 1959. *Studies on the Population of China, 1368–1953.* Harvard University Press, Cambridge, Mass.

HOPKINS, KEITH. 1965. "Contraception in the Roman Empire," *Comparative Studies in Society and History*, **8**, 124–151.

KRAELING, CARL H., and ROBERT M. ADAMS, editors. 1960. *City Invincible: A Symposium on Urbanization and Cultural Development in the Ancient Near East.* University of Chicago Press, Chicago.

KULP, DANIEL HARRISON. 1925. *Country Life in South China: The Sociology of Familism.* Teachers College, Columbia University, New York.

LANDRY, ADOLPHE. 1934. *La révolution démographique: Études et essais sur les problèmes de la population.* Sirey, Paris.

————. 1936. "Quelques aperçus concernant la dépopulation dans l'antiquité gréco-romaine," *Revue Historique*, **61**, 1–33.

LANG, OLGA. 1946. *Chinese Family and Society.* Institute of Pacific Relations. Yale University Press, New Haven.

LEE SHU-CHING. 1953. "China's Traditional Family, Its Characteristics and Disintegration," *American Sociological Review*, **18**, 272–280.

LUCAS, HENRY S. 1930. "The Great European Famine of 1315, 1316, and 1317," *Speculum*, **5**, 343–377.

MADAN, T. N. 1963. "The Joint Family: A Terminological Clarification," in *Family and Marriage*, edited by John Mogey. Brill, Leiden, pp. 7–16.

MAIER, F. G. 1954. "Römische Bevölkerungsgeschichte und Inschriftenstatistik," *Historia*, **2**, 318–351.

MALLORY, WALTER H. 1926. *China: Land of Famine.* American Geographical Society, New York.

MINER, HORACE. 1965. *The Primitive City of Timbuctoo.* Revised Ed. Doubleday-Anchor, Garden City, N.Y.

° MOLS, ROGER, S. J. 1954–1955. *Introduction à la démographie historique des villes d'Europe du XIVe au XVIIIe siècle.* Vol. 1: *Les problèmes.* Vol. 2: *Les résultats.* Vol. 3: *Annexe.* University of Louvain. Duculot, Gembloux.

° MURVAR, VATRO. 1966. "Some Tentative Modifications of Weber's Typology: Occidental versus Oriental City," *Social Forces*, **14**, 381–389.

NOONAN, JOHN T., JR. 1965. *Contraception: A History of Its Treatment by the Catholic Theologians and Canonists.* Belknap-Harvard University Press, Cambridge, Mass.

ORENSTEIN, HENRY. 1961. "The Recent History of the Extended Family in India," *Social Problems*, **8**, 341–350.

PAKRASI, KANTI, and CHITTARANJAN MALAKAR. 1967. "The Relationship between Family Type and Fertility," *Milbank Memorial Fund Quarterly*, **45**, 451–460.

PELLER, SIGISMUND. 1965. "Births and Deaths among Europe's Ruling Families Since 1500," in Glass and Eversley, 1965, pp. 87–100.

\* PIRENNE, HENRI. 1956. *Medieval Cities: Their Origins and the Revival of Trade.* Doubleday-Anchor, Garden City, N.Y.

REDFIELD, ROBERT, and MILTON B. SINGER. 1954. "The Cultural Role of Cities," *Economic Development and Cultural Change,* 3, 53–73.

\* RELE, J. R. 1962. "Some Aspects of Family and Fertility in India," *Population Studies,* 15, 267–278.

REVELLE, ROGER, editor. 1968. "Historical Population Studies," *Daedalus,* Vol. 97, No. 2, Special Issue.

ROSS, AILEEN D. 1961. *The Hindu Family in Its Urban Setting.* University of Toronto Press, Toronto.

RUSSELL, J. C. 1941. "The Ecclesiastical Age: A Demographic Interpretation of the Period 200–900 A.D.," *Review of Religion,* 5, 137–147.

\* ———. 1948. *British Medieval Population.* University of New Mexico Press, Albuquerque.

\* ———. 1958. "Late Ancient and Medieval Population," *Transactions of the American Philosophical Society,* Vol. 48, Part 3.

———. 1965. "Recent Advances in Mediaeval Demography," *Speculum,* 40, 84–101.

———, and SYLVIA THRUPP. 1966. "Effects of Pestilence and Plague, 1315–1385," *Comparative Studies in Society and History,* 8, 464–483. (Article by Russell, comments by Thrupp.)

SCHWAB, WILLIAM B. 1965. "Oshogbo—An Urban Community?" in *Urbanization and Migration in West Africa,* edited by Hilda Kuper. University of California Press, Berkeley, pp. 85–109.

SIGERIST, HENRY E. 1967. *A History of Medicine.* 1: *Primitive and Archaic Medicine.* Galaxy-Oxford University Press, New York.

SJOBERG, GIDEON. 1960. *The Preindustrial City: Past and Present.* Free Press, Glencoe, Ill.

STEEL, R. W. 1961. "The Towns of Tropical Africa," in *Essays on African Population,* edited by K. M. Barbour and R. M. Prothero. Routledge & Kegan Paul, London, pp. 249–278.

THRUPP, SYLVIA L. 1961. "The Creativity of Cities: A Review Article," *Comparative Studies in Society and History,* 4, 53–64.

WEBER, MAX. 1950. *General Economic History.* Free Press, Glencoe, Ill.

———. 1958. *The City.* Free Press, Glencoe, Ill.

\* WHEATLEY, PAUL. 1963. "What the Greatness of a City Is Said to Be: Reflections on Sjoberg's 'Preindustrial City,'" *Pacific Viewpoint,* 4, 163–188.

\* WITTFOGEL, KARL A. 1957. *Oriental Despotism: A Comparative Study of Total Power.* Yale University Press, New Haven.

WRIGLEY, E. A., editor. 1966. *An Introduction to English Historical Demography.* Basic Books, New York.

# 12 POPULATION DURING THE INDUSTRIAL REVOLUTION

The development of industrial societies must be a recurrent theme in any work on population. It has been discussed in the most general terms as the major factor in the demographic transition, and in this chapter we shall take a closer look at two places where the immediate effect of industrialization can conveniently be studied—England from roughly 1760 to 1840 and Japan from 1868 to World War I. The major emphasis will be on the former, where an industrial society first developed. But Japan, the only wholly non-Western country to become a major industrial power, affords an opportunity to check the conclusions derived from the sparse, often dubious, sometimes contradictory data concerning the interrelation of economic and demographic trends in Britain.

## The English Model

The phrase "industrial revolution" does not define a precise period on which all agree; and its various elements, though overlapping and interacting, are also in some senses discrete. It is important, in any case, not to interpret the term too narrowly. Many present-day readers, misled by the label, would miss the point of the story about the schoolboy who began his theme on The Industrial Revolution with the sentence, "About 1760 a wave of gadgets swept over England." One must remember that while the metamorphosis was greater in manufacturing, it was also momentous in mining, transportation, and agriculture; and that while the significance of all the new machines and the technological processes together was tremendous, their impact was also "revolutionary" because they were accompanied by no less dramatic changes in the social structure. More important even than the building of factories was the creation of a factory *system*, with the gradual amalgamation of industrial entrepreneurs and urban workers into two new social classes.

Did industrialism improve urban living conditions? The controversy over this question between scholars who have come to be known as "optimists" and "pessimists" began during the industrial revolution itself and has continued intermittently ever since. In the 1830s Andrew Ure so admired the new order that he could compare factory children to "lively elves" at play, while Thomas Carlyle saw the world of the millhand as "a dingy prison-house" (Taylor, 1960). In the later decades of the century, as "the voice of the social reformer mingle[d] with that of the historian," the gloomier view came to be generally accepted, not only by liberals like Arnold Toynbee (*Lectures on the Industrial Revolution in England*, 1884), but especially by the considerable number of socialists who wrote about the period—in particular Sidney and Beatrice Webb, G. D. H. Cole, and J. L. and Barbara Hammond. Their prime inspiration was a book written by Marx's friend and collaborator, Frederick Engels (1958); and, while they did not use the whole elaborate schema developed by Marx, they, like him, explained the social history of this period principally as an opposition between "exploiting" and "exploited" classes. In the 1920s there appeared a number of works which struck a less dismal note. Several of these—by Griffith, Buer, and George—were in large part about population movements, and the most important, J. H. Clapham's *Economic History of Modern Britain* (1926), attempted to show that real wages had risen during industrialization. Even apart from the point of view expressed, this recourse to new types of statistical data opened up the dispute again.

Analysts today interpret early English industrialization in terms of an ideology somewhere along the scale from Stalin to Hayek, but typically with a more careful attention to sources than some of their nineteenth-century predecessors. Unfortunately, many of the primary data are also biased; their ambiguity reflects, at least in part, an ambivalence among the lower classes themselves toward the great changes in their life. It would be impossible here to reconcile these several points of view; a whole volume would be needed merely to spell out in full the variety of interpretations deriving from different approaches or methods of analysis. Some of the polemical areas, however, are too important to pass over altogether. The following discussion will emphasize factors in the population growth, using the rather thin statistical base to the degree that this is possible, and relating the demographic changes inferentially to those taking place in England's institutional structure.

No characteristic of the population remained unchanged in this transformation of the economy and society. The movement of laborers, even though retarded by legal impediments, became greater than ever before. Growth in numbers, which had been relatively slow from the beginning of the modern period, accelerated. Authorities agree in designating this a natural increase: the overseas emigration was about balanced in this period by immigration from Ireland. However, whether it was the consequence of a rise in births or a fall in deaths or, if both, in what proportion—has also been the subject of a learned discussion.

### SOURCES OF INFORMATION

In the second half of the eighteenth century, no one knew whether the population was increasing or decreasing. The debate on the social and demographic effects of industrialization was in full swing, with sometimes more vehemence than logic. From the fact that fewer were dying, Richard Price, for instance, argued that there were fewer to die—that the population was decreasing.[1] Even after the first censuses were taken, the dispute continued. For William Cobbett, thus, the returns of the 1821 census were "the biggest lie ever put in print, even in romance." The huge population increase they showed was fanciful: "the size of the churches alone was sufficient to convince any man of sound judgment that there had been a prodigious decrease!"[2]

At least in contrast to this confusion one can speak of an advance in knowledge. Late-medieval and early-modern England, excepting the period of the Black Death, had a population well under 4 million. At the end of the seventeenth century, according to the careful estimate that Gregory King made from hearth-tax returns, England and Wales had some 5 million inhabitants, and a hundred years later there were more than 9 million. Virtually all of this increase, moreover, was in the second half of the eighteenth century, during the first decades of quickening industrialization. This growth is summarized in Table 12-1.

The details to fill in this picture, however, are another matter. The first English census was taken only in 1801, and both it and its immediate suc-

[1] M. Dorothy George, *London Life in the XVIIIth Century*, Knopf, New York, 1925, p. 23. For Malthus's contribution to this debate, see above, pp. 149–151, 157–159.
[2] Quoted in C. R. Fay, *Life and Labour in the Nineteenth Century*, University Press, Cambridge, 1947, p. 83.

Table 12-1. Estimated Population of England and Wales, 1086–1841

| DATE | POPULATION (MILLIONS) | SOURCE OF INFORMATION |
|------|------------------------|------------------------|
| 1086 | 1.1 | Domesday Book |
| 1348 | 3.7 | Hearth tax times estimated family size |
| 1377 | 2.2 | Same, after Black Death |
| 1545 | 3.2 | Chantry lists |
| 1695 | 4.8–5.5 [a] | Gregory King's estimate |
| 1801 | 9.2 | First census (corrected) |
| 1811 | 10.2 ⎤ | |
| 1821 | 13.9 ⎥ | Census returns |
| 1831 | 12.0 ⎥ | |
| 1841 | 15.9 ⎦ | |

SOURCES: J. C. Russell, *British Medieval Population,* University of New Mexico Press, Albuquerque, 1948; D. V. Glass, "Two Papers on Gregory King," in *Population in History,* edited by Glass and D. E. C. Eversley, Aldine, Chicago, 1965, pp. 159–220.

[a] The larger figure is King's. Glass has suggested the range given, with the most probable figure above its midpoint.

cessors were less accurate and less complete than those taken later in the century.[3] National vital statistics date from 1837. For much of the key period, from 1760 to 1840, we must depend on parish records and other sources (*cf.* Krause, 1965).

John Rickman, the director of the first four censuses, compiled the basic data from which both he and several later analysts attempted to describe the population growth during the previous century. He had a questionnaire sent to every "Rector, Vicar, Curate, or Officiating Minister," asking them to extract from their parish records the numbers of baptisms and burials, distinguishing between male and female, for each decade from 1700 to 1780 and for each following single year up to 1800. How well this formidable task was performed is a question to which no definite reply can be given, though it is reasonable to suppose that there must have been great lacunae in data so collected (B. Hammond, 1928). In any case, these Anglican parish registers did not include Dissenters, some paupers, and others. To reconstruct birth and death rates, therefore, one must increase the given figures on baptisms and burials by a more or less arbitrary proportion, representing the best guess on the total size of the several deficiencies. Then, working back from the census count of 1801 (corrected for its substantial underenumeration), one can calculate the population totals and crude rates. The

[3] "There were fears that the census of 1801 was to be the basis for new taxes (the triple assessment and the income tax were fresh in people's minds) or for the levy of men for the unpopular, and at the same time, unsuccessful, war" (Krause, 1958).

method depends, thus, on three assumptions: (1) that the corrected 1801 count was accurate, (2) that the underregistration in the parish records was at the proportions given, and (3) that there was no net migration.

1. We can accept the corrected 1801 census figure as substantially accurate. At the very least, it is the best datum up to that time.

2. The disparity in the ratio of births to baptisms, and in that of deaths to registered burials, was a symptom of the transformation the country was undergoing. So long as the relatively stable agrarian society persisted, one could assume that underregistration was at a constant proportion (although even then there may have been some oscillation with the business cycle, for one factor in reducing the later registration was that many Anglicans were unwilling to pay the relatively high fees for their rites). However, as the center of population moved from the South to the new industrial regions in the North, churches and clergy were left behind. The migration from villages to towns was marked by the same lag. "The London parish of Marylebone, with 40,000 inhabitants, had church accommodations for only 200" (Krause, 1958). The war also had its effect on the record, for while soldiers died in higher proportion than equivalent civilian cohorts, they escaped ecclesiastical registration. It is more or less certain, then, that the birth/baptism and death/burial ratios varied considerably from one year or one locality to another; but this means that any average for the nation as a whole or for a decade or longer period can be only the roughest guess.[4]

3. The postulate that net migration was zero is even less well based statistically. Adequate migration data were compiled only after this transitional period was long past, and what records exist up to 1840 hardly form the basis for an informed guess. Emigrants from the United Kingdom were officially counted only from 1815 on, and the statistics were a by-product of a law, frequently evaded, introduced to compel ship masters to assign a specific minimum space to each passenger. Accuracy at a usable level begins in 1840, when the first Cunard steamships went into service and the Colonial Land and Emigration Commission was established (Thomas, 1954, p. 36). Whether the unknown number of emigrants from England and Wales was matched, as is generally assumed, by an equal number of Irish (and Scottish) immigrants also cannot be established. The English census of 1841, the first to include such data, recorded 419,000 residents of Irish birth; and this figure, even if it were wholly accurate, would represent only a portion

---

[4] Griffith (1926, p. 18) raised the recorded baptisms by 15 per cent and the burials by 10 per cent; he has been criticized—correctly, I would judge—for assuming that the two ratios remained constant. "There is . . . much reason to believe that the registration of deaths deteriorated sharply between 1781 and 1821 and improved thereafter. Farr's estimated death-burial ratios, 1.23 in 1801–10, 1.33 in 1811–20, 1.16 in 1821–30, and 1.12 in 1831–40, are plausible in so far as the trend is concerned" (Krause, 1958). For any particular parish with reasonably complete records still extant, it would be possible to improve on the national estimates. See in particular the discussion of Nottingham in Chambers, 1965a.

of the Irish who had taken up residence in England during the previous 80 years (Redford, 1926, Chapters 8 and 9). If we accept the hypothesis that the total numbers of persons entering and leaving England were the same, the age structure of the immigrants and emigrants, and consequently their fertility and mortality, presumably differed considerably.

In short, the national data concerning population growth up to 1840 have to be supplemented by analyses of parish records, and important work is being done in this respect. It would not be appropriate here, however, to summarize such monographs, bristling with difficulties of every kind, of which the first always is to what degree the locality is representative of the nation as a whole. At some time in the future it may be possible to collate these more detailed analyses and derive a better understanding of what happened to the English population during these decades. Establishing a more accurate numerical base, if it is ever possible, would still be only the preliminary step to analyzing *why* the changes in mortality and fertility occurred.

What we propose to do here is to examine the theory of the demographic transition in the context of English social history, reinforced with statistical data only when these are reasonably precise. According to this theory, it will be recalled, the population growth of an area undergoing modernization is divided into three stages: (1) a more or less static population at high levels of fertility and mortality, (2) a period of constant fertility and falling mortality, with a consequent rapid increase in population, and (3) a more or less static population at more efficient levels of birth as well as death control.

### THE TRANSFORMATION OF ENGLISH AGRICULTURE

The first step toward understanding the population developments during the industrial revolution is to survey the momentous changes that took place in the English countryside. In the first half of the eighteenth century, the agrarian system of the Middle Ages still persisted in full force over a great portion of England. All cultivation of land, whether by proprietors or by tenants, was in accord with decisions of the village council, following practices made impregnable by tradition. Arable land was divided into three strips, of which one was left fallow each year and two were planted in coarse grains. Pasture was ordinarily inadequate, and the animals fed from stubble and heath. Since there was little or no hay to store, most of the herd was killed in the autumn and eaten through the winter as salt meat. Available pasture was usually held in common, as well as woods (for both hunting and firewood) and water (which included fishing rights). Attached to most villages were a number of squatters, who were permitted to eke out a miserable living though they had no legal right to the use of the joint property.

Landlords and tenants were equally ignorant and sunken in routine, while mutual suspicion divided them; for the landlord feared that the farmer would exhaust the land by forcing a few richer crops out of his fields during the last years of his tenancy, and therefore refused to grant leases for a fixed period, preferring the unstable state of things known as tenure at will. As a result, any spirit of enterprise, any undertaking that involved a considerable period for its completion, were out of the question for the farmer, since he lived under the constant threat of instant dismissal and of the loss of a whole year's labors. Thus the effect of backwardness was to make for more backwardness (Mantoux, 1952, p. 162).

This whole mode of agriculture was transformed in the second half of the eighteenth century. In a series of individual acts of Parliament, the common land of villages was transferred to the private ownership of families with some ancient right to it. Deprived of the use of the commons, the squatters and cottagers often suffered a decline from even their modest living conditions. The more substantial cultivators, who were recompensed in land or money (the amount was set by the parliamentary commissioners, and no appeal could be made from their decision), were sometimes unable or unwilling to maintain themselves in the new circumstances, and some of them also sank into tenancy or pauperism. But if the social cost was high, it paid for an astounding advance in English agriculture. The first act of the new owner was always to enclose the open field with a hedge, in order to protect it against grazing cattle. "The age of enclosure was also the age of new methods of draining, drilling, sowing, manuring, breeding and feeding cattle, making of roads, rebuilding of farm premises and a hundred other changes, all of them requiring capital."[5] Potatoes and other root crops became staples. New breeds of farm animals were developed. Feed was grown that could be stored during the winter, the prior custom of converting the major portion of a herd into salt meat was abandoned. The improved methods were applied also to waste land, of which about two million acres were brought under cultivation during the eighteenth century.

There is hardly a question, then, that the food supply improved enormously in both quantity and variety.[6] The issue, rather, is what happened to the country people. "Enclosure was fatal to three classes: the small farmer, the cottager, and the squatter. To all of these classes their common rights were worth more than anything they received in return" (Hammond and Hammond, 1932b, p. 73). For many years it was held that these classes, ousted from the village, were the raw material out of which the industrial labor force was formed. Indeed, this "Marxist doctrine," as Chambers terms

---

[5] G. M. Trevelyan, *English Social History: A Survey of Six Centuries, Chaucer to Queen Victoria*, Longmans, Green, London, 1942, p. 376.

[6] Some analysts, it is true, have argued the contrary. From the increasing use of the potato, "the cheapest and one of the most efficient single foods man has as yet cultivated in the temperate zones," Salaman concludes that the living conditions deteriorated. See Redcliffe N. Salaman, *The History and Social Influence of the Potato*, University Press, Cambridge, 1949, Chapters 25 and 26.

it, may have been the model that the Soviet planners followed in the 1930s (see pp. 645–647). In eighteenth-century England, however, the main factor in supplying the developing urban industry with workers was not the displacement of villagers but rather the growth of the total population. While there was a good deal of migration to the towns, this did not result in the "rural depopulation" that Cobbett and others feared at the time. "The period 1780–1840 saw only a sporadic exodus . . . from the rural areas, . . . and side by side with it an actual filling up of empty spaces and a steady rise in the great majority of established centers of rural population" (Chambers, 1965b; cf. Redford, 1926, pp. 58–69; Saville, 1957). If numbers were increasing in both town and country, as was certainly the case at least for the period covered by the census records, then the supposed sharp decline in rural levels of life may well have been exaggerated.

The population grew and also the subsistence; what of the balance between them? Was the food per capita more or less plentiful, better or worse on the average? Did real wages rise or fall? It is not possible to answer such questions altogether satisfactorily, mainly because this was a period of rapid and all-encompassing change. At almost any time during these decades the situation of some in the lower classes was improving, and that of others deteriorating. For example, we can reasonably deduce from the data available that the real wages of cotton operatives went up steadily, and this may even have been so of factory workers generally. But the most important determinant of many workers' incomes was not their wage rate but how regularly they were employed. In the words of Hobsbawm (1957), "No discussion which overlooks the massive waves of destitution which swamped large sections of the laboring poor in every depression, can claim to be realistic." His view of "realism" is, on the contrary, to minimize the rise in wages of the employed workers.

And if the amount of money received by workers varied widely, what they could buy with their wages varied even more. The cost of all foodstuffs differed greatly from one part of the country to another, and in any one locality "the price of a loaf of bread or a pound of beef might double or halve within the course of a few months or even weeks" (Ashton, 1954a). Since this condition resulted from the primitive consumer market rather than specifically from food production, one can conclude that there was a similar variation in the prices of all essential commodities. For Hobsbawm (1957), "the discussion of food consumption . . . throws considerable doubt on the optimistic view." And Habakkuk (1965) also concludes: "The scantiness of the evidence makes any judgement dangerous, but the surviving examples of laborers' diets hardly suggest that any improvement in their diet can have been substantial." Another conclusion is that, "all in all, conditions of labor were becoming better, at least after 1820, and that the spread of the factory played a not inconsiderable part in the improvement" (Ashton, 1954a).

Perhaps the best evidence that diets improved during this period is the lower incidence of food-deficiency diseases, and especially their virtual disappearance as causes of death. Drummond and Wilbraham, who lean toward the pessimistic view, note that by 1830 scurvy had become so rare that a well known physician was unable to diagnose its symptoms.[7] They conclude, even if somewhat reluctantly, that the incidence of rickets also declined, possibly in part because of the beginning use of cod liver oil as a specific. This would have an important influence on fertility as well as mortality, for rickets frequently causes pelvic deformations and thus fetal and maternal deaths.

### THE REVOLUTION OF RISING EXPECTATIONS

If objective criteria like the trend in real wages are difficult to establish in themselves, this is doubly so because the subjective meaning of such measures was also undergoing a rapid change. The "standard" of living includes the norms by which conditions are judged to be better or worse. Industrialism was frequently compared with an idyllic preindustrial society. To idealize the past was characteristic of Romanticism, which flourished during these same decades; revolutionary socialists wrote prose poems celebrating the Good Old Days (Engels, 1958, pp. 10–11); and representatives of the landed gentry opposed the developing factory system in part because they saw it as a challenge to their social and political power. The last point of view especially is well represented in the parliamentary hearings. The "too liberal use of weak tea, as extremely debilitating to the stomach," was only the most frequent proof of moral degradation deduced from changes that to us would suggest economic and social advance.

Thackrah lamented the fact that children were no longer contented with "plain food" but must have "dainties." The Reverend G. S. Bull deplored the tendency of girls to buy pretty clothes "ready-made" from shops instead of making them themselves, as this practice unfitted them to become "the mothers of children." Gaskell saw decadence in tobacco. "Hundreds of men may be daily seen inhaling the fumes of this extraordinary plant." He also saw moral decline in the growth of workmen's combinations [that is, trade unions]. The men were no longer "respectful and attentive" to their "superiors" (Hutt, 1954).[8]

This last sentence suggests that the factory system was generating a new type of person, who fitted ill into the prior model of class relations.

---

[7] J. C. Drummond and Anne Wilbraham, *The Englishman's Food: A History of Five Centuries of English Diet*, Revised Ed., Cape, London, 1957, p. 392.

[8] If here tea-drinking and smoking were taken as signs of lower-class degeneration, for Hobsbawm (1957) the *slow* adoption of these new customs is proof, on the contrary, that consumption standards were lagging. The example indicates how difficult it is to distinguish what consumers wanted and could not buy from what they did not want. How many of the imprecisely recorded shifts reflected a change merely in taste?

"The ideological break with traditionalism," as Bendix terms it, was based on the proposition that "the slave must be compelled to work; but the free man should be left to his own judgment and discretion." [9] During the transition a kind of medieval paternalism was often carried over into factory management; the responsibility of the upper classes was interpreted as including the duty, and the right, to control every move the workers made. In one factory the doors were locked during working hours. It was prohibited to drink water in spite of the heat. Fines were imposed for washing oneself or for being dirty, for putting out the light too soon or not soon enough, and so on (Hammond and Hammond 1932a, pp. 19–20). Those regarded as the best of the new employers were often the most painstaking in preserving the preindustrial master-servant relation. Robert Owen, for example, who is usually cited as a prototype of the modern manager, gave his employees marks for their moral conduct—bad, denoted by black; indifferent, by blue; good, by yellow; and excellent, by white—"during every day of the week, Sundays excepted, for every year they remained in my employment." Workers in his model factory at New Lanark had to attend dancing lessons for the sake of their health, and some quit their jobs on that account.[10]

The reader is likely to sympathize with the worker who rebelled against constraints of this kind. The situation is more complex, however, when it was the workers who tried to preserve traditional patterns, and particularly such abhorrent ones—to the twentieth-century Westerner—as child labor. Although the pre-factory system of spinning and weaving varied greatly, one common element was that the family constituted an economic unit. The place of manufacture (literally, "making by hand") was the countryman's cottage, and the manufacturers were the cottager, his wife, and his children. The kinship base of this domestic system, as it is termed, survived for a while the shift to the factory.

Witnesses before the parliamentary committees from 1816 through 1819 testified consistently that masters allowed the operative spinners to hire their own assistants (piecers, scavengers, etc.) and that the spinners chose their wives, children, near relatives, or relatives of the proprietors. Many children, especially the youngest, entered the mill at the express request of their parents. . . . Most of the early trade unions' rules explicitly prohibited members from recruiting assistants outside the narrowly defined classes of children, brothers, orphan nephews, etc. (Smelser, 1959, pp. 188–189).

[9] Joseph Townsend, quoted in Reinhard Bendix, *Work and Authority in Industry: Ideologies of Management in the Course of Industrialization*, Wiley, New York, 1956, p. 74. Bendix's main theme is "the role of ideas in the management of economic enterprises," and he traces in detail the process by which the traditional master-servant relation was gradually supplanted by one between the two new urban classes, whose legitimacy evolved together with the growth in their membership.

[10] J. H. Plumb, *England in the Eighteenth Century*, Penguin, Harmondsworth, 1950, p. 145.

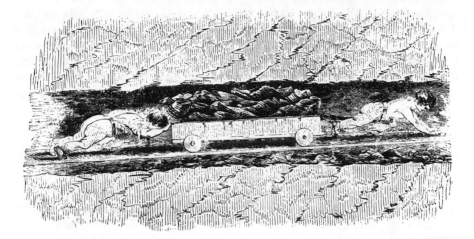

An illustration from one of the many white papers reporting governmental investigations of labor conditions in nineteenth-century England. The accompanying text reads as follows:

" 'By far the greater number of Children and persons employed in coal-mines are engaged in propelling and drawing tubs laden with coal, from the face to the pit-eye, or the main-levels in those pits where they have horses. This is done by placing the hands on the back of the waggon, and propelling it forward with as great velocity as the inclination of the mine, the state of the road, and the strength of the waggoner admit of. The mines in this district [Lancashire and Cheshire] are for the most part laid with rails, and the waggon runs on wheels. . . . There are, however, mines . . . where the old mode of drawing the baskets or wooden sledges (called in Lancashire "sleds") is still retained. The drawer is in this case harnessed by means of a chain attached to the "sled"; the other end of the chain passes between his legs, and fastens in front to a belt round the waist. When thus harnessed, and moving along on his hands and feet, the drawer drags after him the loaded basket; if he is not sufficiently strong he has a helper rather younger than himself.' . . . [The figure] represents three young Children hurrying or drawing a loaded waggon of coals. The Child in front 'is harnessed by his belt or chain to the waggon; the two boys behind are assisting in pushing it forward. Their heads, it will be observed, are brought down to a level with the waggon, and the body almost in a horizontal position. This is done partly to avoid striking the roof, and partly to gain the advantage of the muscular action, which is greatest in that position. It will be observed the boy in front goes on his hands and feet: in that manner the whole weight of his body is in fact supported by the chain attached to the waggon and his feet, and consequently his power of drawing is greater than it would be if he crawled on his knees. These boys, by constantly pushing against the waggons, occasionally rub off the hair from the crowns of their heads so much as to make them almost bald" (Great Britain, Children's Employment Commission, *First Report of the Commissioners: Mines,* H. M. Stationery Office, London, 1842, pp. 81–82).

Parents retained, thus, their traditional authority over their children, who learned their trade while contributing to the family income. "Little wonder, then, that the conditions of child labor did not offend spinners interviewed by Factory Commissioners in 1833" (*ibid.*, p. 190). But both improved technology and structural changes in the factory system led to a greater differentiation of roles, and thus both broke down the economic authority of the father-spinner over his children-assistants and in many cases reduced the composite wage that he received. *Some* of the misery of the period, as seen by those who suffered it, was due to the decline of this semi-apprenticeship system based on kinship; and the "array of threats to the family's traditional organization underlay much of the turmoil among operatives and others between 1825 and 1850" (*ibid.*, p. 199).

In short, the way that the participants in England's early industrialization defined their situation helped determine their behavior. What the members of parliamentary committees, or their witnesses, or factory operatives, saw as problems became the main content of the data collected. This "bias" is especially difficult to cope with, since it was not consistent: most of the people living through that turbulent period must have been confused concerning what it was they really wanted. And we aggravate this confusion if we assume that the common people must have demanded "progress" as a present-day liberal defines it, and that their protest *for* child labor or for a *longer* workday, because they seem to be anomalies, can best be ignored.

We have argued, then, that it is all but impossible to find conclusive evidence on the trend in living conditions during this period, and that this difficulty has typically been compounded by the fact that most data were gathered and interpreted as part of a political dispute. Many of the causal links implied in this long debate, moreover, are not necessary ones.

What happened to the standard of life of the British working classes in the late decades of the eighteenth and the early decades of the nineteenth centuries? Was the introduction of the factory system beneficial or harmful in its effect on the workers? These, though related, are distinct questions. For it is possible that employment in factories conduced to an increase of real wages but that the tendency was more than offset by other influences, such as the rapid increase of population, the immigration of Irishmen, the destruction of wealth by long years of warfare, ill devised tariffs, and misconceived measures for the relief of distress (Ashton, 1954a).

From roughly 1790 to 1815, England was at war with France; and this was "the central economic characteristic of these years." Three to five per cent of the population, and, of course, a far higher proportion of the labor force, were in military service. The rise in the real cost of many commodities, especially of imports and therefore some foodstuffs, was more the consequence of the war than of any other factor.[11]

To sum up, evidence concerning the trend in living conditions is typically ambiguous enough to permit judgments to vary considerably; and this tendency has often been compounded because of the political implications to be drawn from the conclusion that real wages were rising, or falling. Actually, the political argument is not only scientifically unfortunate but also often unwarranted, for whatever happened to the average Englishman's living conditions was not the consequence merely of "capitalism," or the factory system, or any other single factor.

### MORTALITY

There is no question that the population increased substantially from, say, 1760 to 1840. Was this growth the consequence, either wholly or mainly, of a decline in mortality, as is assumed in the model of the demographic transition? Perhaps the best answer to this question is that by two medical historians, McKeown and Brown (1965). They divided the possible causes of a reduction in mortality into three broad classes, which we consider in turn.

1. A change in the balance between the virulence of the infective organism and the resistance of the host. In specific instances—for example, the transformation of scarlet fever from a frequently fatal disease to a relatively trivial complaint—this was probably the decisive factor. The general effect of such changes on the long-term trend in the death rate, however, was slight.[12]

2. Specific preventive or curative therapy. Most treatments of the various important causes of death can be discounted for the period earlier than the middle of the nineteenth century. It is a moot question whether fever hospitals, for example, helped restrict contagion by the semiquarantine they

---

[11] W. W. Rostow, *British Economy of the Nineteenth Century*, Clarendon, Oxford, 1948, pp. 13–14. As another instance, the fact that homes in the rapidly growing cities were ramshackle, and if not worse than the hovels of the rural areas then also not much better, still does not settle the question of why this was so. The state deflected requisite materials and labor to the prior demand of military necessity, and this was an important reason for the inadequacy of the rapidly constructed homes of the new industrial towns. A new word was added to English—*jerry-built*, from the nautical word *jury* (as in "jury mast"), meaning "temporary," "emergency" (Ashton, 1954b). The shortage of houses persisted, however, and these "temporary" residences were occupied for decades.

[12] A seeming exception is the bubonic plague, which was still endemic in Eastern Europe during the eighteenth century. In 1720 an infested ship brought the disease to Marseilles, and in the furious outbreak about 40,000 of the city's 90,000 inhabitants died. It spread through Provence and a few adjoining districts with smaller losses. Inexplicably the plague stopped short, and in a bit over a year it was all over (Helleiner, 1965).

# INOCULATION

Those who are desirous to take the infection of the SMALL - POX, by inoculation, may find themselves accommodated for the purpose, by applying to.

Stephen Samuel Hawley

Fiskdale, in Sturbridge,

February 7, 1801

N. B.  A Pest-House will be opened, and accommodations provided by the first day of March next.

imposed or, on the contrary, raised the death rate by the fact that virtually all persons who entered them would be infected. So long as bleeding was the first treatment for illness, the contribution that physicians made to their patients' health was minimal; so long as something like half of surgical patients died of infection, it can be questioned whether surgeons saved more patients than they killed. "It might safely be said," McKeown and Brown conclude, "that specific medical treatment had no useful effects at all, were it not for some doubt about the results of the use of mercury in syphilis, iron in anemia, cinchona in malaria, and inoculation against smallpox."

Of the four diseases, the last was by far the most important in England of the eighteenth century, when it is estimated that one out of every five persons died from smallpox, typically in childhood. The terror it caused can be imagined. "Men would not marry until or unless the lady had had smallpox, servants were advertised for who had had it" (Griffith, 1926, p. 248). Inoculation with a small, nonfatal amount of infected liquid, it was discovered, could establish immunity. This practice was introduced in the 1720s and used intermittently through the rest of the century, but medical historians disagree on its effect. It was dangerous to the patient if not skillfully administered, and unless he was segregated he could spread the disease to others. In 1798 Edward Jenner discovered that vaccination with cowpox germs, which causes only a minor skin irritation, also effects immunity against smallpox. In part because of the ambivalent results from inoculation, there was some opposition at first also to vaccination, and we do not know how rapidly its practice spread.[13]

[13] Griffith (1926) argues that there was a sharp fall in the death rate from 1800 to 1810, largely the consequence of a reduced incidence of smallpox, and that the subse-

"The Cow Pock," a print by James Gillray, 1802, showing the alleged effects of vaccinations with cowpox serum (*The Bettmann Archive, Inc.*).

3. Improvement in living conditions, by which McKeown and Brown mean "any change which would have reduced the risk of infection, or increased the survival rate among those infected: under the first are such measures as improvements in housing, water supply, or refuse disposal; under the second influences affecting the general standard of health, of which by far the most important was probably nutrition." It is not likely that there could have been a very great improvement in living conditions in the first sense; on the contrary, the risk of infection almost certainly increased, assuming that the villagers' style of life remained essentially the same after they migrated to the towns, or even that it improved somewhat. Lower-class urban quarters were probably no more squalid than their rural counterpart, but the higher population density made of cities the graveyard of countrymen, to cite that graphic aphorism. Both in England

---

quent rise was partly due to the increased mortality from this disease until it was discovered that immunity must be periodically renewed. But the evidence is not clear on any of his allegations: We do not know whether the death rate fell in the century's first decade; many authorities believe it rose. We do not know whether Jenner's discovery was much used only two years after it was made; a widespread system of free vaccination was established only in the 1840s and there were serious outbreaks of small-pox still after that date. We do not know, finally, whether the effective control of one important disease, supposing that it took place, would have reduced substantially the death rate of a society with so few guards against epidemic diseases in general.

Compulsory vaccination during a smallpox scare, Jersey City, 1880s (*National Library of Medicine*).

and elsewhere in the Western world urban death rates were higher than rural until the last quarter of the nineteenth century, by which time public sanitation was sufficiently established to cancel the biological effect of crowded living quarters (*cf.* Rosenberg, 1966).

There was little direct incentive to control urban filth, for the theory relating it to disease was by no means universally accepted. The understandable desire to mitigate the stink of even middle-class homes was probably more relevant. In any case, public sanitation was not much improved before 1840 (*cf.* Hennock, 1957), as can be illustrated by the fact that so important a step as the separation of sewage from drinking water was taken only very gradually. During the first half of the eighteenth century excrement was dumped out of town windows on to the street, and from about 1750 on scavengers gathered the "night soil" in the better-class neighborhoods. The water closet, invented toward the end of the century, emptied into either large vaults under the houses or, later, into sewers that flowed into a river. Until 1850 one of London's drinking-water companies still had its intake within a few feet of the mouth of the Westbourne, which had become the Ranelagh common sewer! (Buer, 1926, p. 108). The cholera epidemic of 1831–32, which came just when urban sanitation was at its worst, is considered by some to have been almost a blessing, for it helped the physicians in their effort to establish minimum norms of public health.[14] As other possible factors are partly eliminated, the improvement in the food supply would seem to be a major cause of any important decline in mortality before about 1850, and McKeown and Brown believe it to be the principal reason for the population growth of the late eighteenth and early nineteenth centuries.[15]

To sum up, while it is impossible to document it statistically, there probably was a more or less continuous decline in mortality from roughly 1760 to 1840. Medical advances had little to do with this, except possibly in the single case of smallpox. The most important factor seems to have been the better food supply, and possibly the improved living conditions, in other respects, enjoyed by the lower classes. Yet the evidence for this advance is at best probable, sometimes hardly that; and the pessimistic view that there was a decline in consumption and health can also be supported with plausible data, particularly for the war years. In any case, was the decline in mortality sufficient to account for the population increase— taking only the period measured by censuses—from roughly 9.2 million in 1801 to 15.9 million in 1841? Or is there not a *prima facie* case here for the probability that fertility rose while mortality declined?

### FERTILITY

The population of early industrial England has been studied principally by economic historians, who, as one would expect, have tended to stress economic factors. While this emphasis can lead to a reasonably good understanding of mortality trends, the state of the economy is not the most important determinant of fertility. One economic historian, thus, finds the "sociological weakness" of his colleagues' studies to be "striking."

---

[14] Some changes in the environment may have brought about a fall in death rate without anyone at the time becoming aware of the relation. For example, an important factor—perhaps the decisive one—in the sharply reduced incidence of typhus was probably the shift from woolen to cotton clothing and the improved cleanliness that this facilitated. Characteristically, Engels (1958, pp. 78–79) cited this change to cotton as one further evidence of the deterioration in the living conditions of the English working class.

[15] There has been a paradoxical tendency on the part of analysts to discount the effect of the factor they studied most intensively. "Surprisingly, these medical historians [McKeown and Brown] argued that . . . medical advances, with the exception of vaccination, were demographically irrelevant, and that environmental changes, mainly economic, were at work. Their view, thus, contradicts that of T. H. Marshall, the economic historian, who held that economic factors were unimportant, and that medical factors were responsible" (Krause, 1958).

Allowing for exceptions such as Marshall and Glass, British researchers have tended to slight the analysis of the social determinants of birth rates, nuptiality, and the other components of population change. They have placed most of their emphasis on material considerations—Malthusian checks and their shifting incidence—and to such proximate relations as the immediate influence of the birth and death rate on population. And they have perhaps been too quick to assume away the significance of nonmaterial factors: witness Habakkuk's statement that "within any given social group marriage habits might be expected to be stable"; or the neglect of socially determined changes in fertility as a possible factor in population growth.[16]

As was noted in the last chapter, the growth of medieval Europe was held to well below the physiological maximum by ethical and institutional norms. The principle that a man ought to be able to support a family before he married and had children was embodied in the regulations of the major medieval institutions. In the old system, as it functioned in both town and countryside, a male assistant or apprentice, or a female domestic, generally lived in as a subordinate member of the master's family. As a consequence, the morals of adolescents were supervised; sexual dalliance meant the possible loss of one's position in a secure world. Young people were not under economic pressure to marry early, since they were meaningful members of a functioning household. At the same time, parents may have restricted the number of their children because extended kin were also included in the family economy.

Virtually all urban occupations were governed by guilds, which particularly in England prohibited their members from marrying until they had completed their apprenticeship. Guild regulations apparently were still enforced in England during the first half of the eighteenth century, but pamphleteers were finding them unnecessary and onerous. By 1775 the system was in an advanced state of decay (Griffith, 1926, pp. 114, 116), but as we have seen, it persisted for a while even in some of the new factories, where operatives retained the prerogatives of master craftsmen. As England was still predominantly rural, national population trends were set principally by what was happening in the countryside. Whatever effect the enclosure movement had on living conditions generally, it certainly tended to release the average countryman from traditional bonds, whether he stayed in the village or migrated to the towns, whether he retained his prior status or sank into pauperdom.

Indeed, the distinction between a worker and a pauper became tenuous during this period. In 1795 the magistrates of Berkshire County met at Speenhamland, a suburb of Newbury, in order to fix and enforce a minimum wage. Instead, they drew up a scale of doles to be paid on the basis of three factors—the wages earned, the price of bread, and the size of the worker's family. This so-called Speenhamland scale, which was imitated

16 David S. Landes, "Discussion," *Journal of Economic History*, 18 (1958), 531–536.

over a large portion of England, was popular with almost everyone concerned. The poor were safe from extreme want under all market conditions. Employers could find workers at almost any wage, no matter how low, for it was supplemented up to the subsistence level out of taxes. And the general public found the system good, both because it gave charity to those in need of it and because it inhibited, it was believed, the spread of revolutionary ideas from France.

In spite of its popularity, the Speenhamland system was what Malthus termed it, "a pernicious evil." [17] It is true that the alms mitigated the distress suffered by individuals, but it is no less true that in over-all terms the Berkshire scale aggravated and prolonged the misery occasioned by the rapid social change.[18] With the massive shift taking place from agrarian to industrial occupations, when a prime economic need consequently was a mobile labor force, the new poor law restricted free movement. A man who left one parish and remained for a full year in another lost his right to relief in the first and established it in the second.

For this reason parish authorities were reluctant to receive outsiders, and employers who were large ratepayers would sometimes offer work only for a period short of a full year. If before a laborer had gained a settlement in a new parish he fell on evil days, he could be moved back summarily to the parish from which he had come, and this made him think twice before leaving his native village to seek work far away (Ashton, 1948, p. 110).

The main burden of poor relief fell on the small farmer, who paid taxes but, unlike the new gentry, got no cheap labor in return.[19] The decline of the yeoman class was certainly quickened by the administration of the poor law, and undoubtedly at least some of those pushed down themselves became paupers.

In the long run the result was ghastly. Although it took some time till the self-respect of the common man sank to the low point where he preferred poor relief to wages, . . . little by little the people of the countryside were pauperized. . . . But for the protracted effects of the allowance system, it would be impossible to explain the human and social degradation of early capitalism.[20]

---

[17] See T. R. Malthus, *An Essay on the Principle of Population*, 7th Ed., Reeves and Turner, London, 1872, Book 3, Chapters 5–7; Book 4, Chapter 8.

[18] "The right solution would have been the enforcement of a legal minimum wage in agriculture. This the laborers demanded in the 1790's, appealing to the Elizabethan Statute of Artificers (1563). But the appeal was useless, for the Wages sections were by this time inoperative, and they had never been used as a lever for raising wages beyond the prevailing competitive level" (Fay, *op. cit.*, p. 92).

[19] By a wide margin, the cost of poor relief was the major item in local taxation. From 1782 to 1793, its average annual cost was £2 million, as compared with £0.2 million for all other local expenditures; in 1813 the figures were £7 million and £1.5 million (Trevelyan, *op. cit.*, pp. 353, 470).

[20] Karl Polanyi, *The Great Transformation*, Rinehart, New York, 1944, p. 80.

It is usual to conceptualize the dynamics of Western fertility patterns in terms of the changes that took place in the second half of the nineteenth century—the erosion of the preindustrial norms and the gradual evolution of the small-family system. We tend to think, following the logic of the demographic transition, that a breakdown of traditionalism always results in a lower fertility; but this is nonsense. The control of family size, no matter what means is used, demands *self*-control; and self-control is likely to prevail only in a society in which individuals have strong motives for imposing it. The smaller family of the urban middle class developed, that is to say, principally because in a mobile society a man with fewer children could advance farther (see pp. 500–503). But in the period we are discussing, and particularly for the mass of the people, there was no question of achieving self-improvement through self-control. Here the breakdown of the ethical and institutional norms, with the limitation to procreation they had set, meant only a rise in fertility.

The dissolution of village society could result in a rise in fertility because of (1) less frequent or less effective control of conception within marriage, (2) a higher incidence of illegitimacy, (3) a lower age at marriage, together with a higher proportion marrying, and (4) a change in the age structure. Let us examine each of these factors briefly, beginning with the most hypothetical.

**1. Less Effective Birth Control.** The main point to be made here is that this change was *possible*. Once again, we tend to view this period in terms of irrelevant comparisons. It is true that the mechanical and chemical contraceptives developed in the last hundred years are more efficient than prior methods, but it must not be supposed that the latter cannot reduce fertility substantially. The average family size in the United States began to fall at the beginning of the nineteenth century, and in France probably even earlier, in both cases presumably because of the more frequent practice of *coitus interruptus*. If England's marital fertility was held in check by this method in the eighteenth century, a matter on which we have no information, and if self-control was reduced during the transitional period as we have hypothesized, then——. Not a firm conclusion, but the contrary one is no firmer, and is generally believed.

**2. Illegitimacy.** Data on illegitimacy are poor. In 1830, by one estimate, 5 per cent of all births were outside marriage (Griffith, 1926, pp. 125–126), but this figure may be "far too low"; "the rate for 1851–60 was 6.5 per cent, and it had been falling" (Marshall, 1965). If we accept this view and assume that, say, 7 to 8 per cent of the births in all regions and all social classes were illegitimate, then for the particular declassed villagers evolving into the new proletariat the rate must have been, as a guess, three times that figure.

Under the law in effect from 1808 to 1834, an unmarried mother could force support from the man she claimed to be the father. Whether she married thus made little difference to her financially. It was held that under the Speenhamland system the mother of enough illegitimate children could support herself by breeding:

> There was one thing better than to marry and have a family, and that was to marry a mother of bastards. . . . As one young woman of twenty-four with four bastard children put it: "If she had one more, she should be very comfortable" (*Report on Labourers' Wages*, 1824, quoted in Redford, 1926, p. 71).

The conditions of work, particularly in the mines, afforded temptations and opportunities for extramarital intercourse, which is frequently mentioned in the reports of the period.[21] If the breakdown of village institutions meant a concomitant decline in the moral standards associated with them, as we should expect in theory, then a considerable proportion of the population must have become indifferent to the distinction between marital and illegitimate conception.

**3. Decline in the Age at Marriage.**    The reports of the period are full of complaints that young people were marrying irresponsibly as a consequence of the Speenhamland system. According to a Factory Report of 1833, thus, operatives often married before they were eighteen, and the usual age was probably not even so high in rural areas affected by enclosures. "Much of the evil [of improvident marriages] would be remedied," the *Poor Law Report* of 1831 tells us, "if the farmers would return to . . . keeping their unmarried [farmhands] as servants in the house, boarding them and lodging them and giving them pecuniary wages" (Griffith, 1926, pp. 105, 109). Malthus shared the prevalent opinion that poor relief fostered early marriages and large families, and for this reason he advocated that public relief be abolished. The one exception he would have made was families with six or more children, whose misery could be alleviated without encouraging still more procreation.[22]

Though the alleged relation between the dole and the size of the family cannot be proved statistically, there is good circumstantial evidence to support it. As the amount of the relief payment was based in part on the size of the pauper-worker's family, employers were able to pay lower wages to those with more children.

> As the farmers have under the scale system a direct inducement to employ married men rather than single, in many villages . . . they will not employ the single men at all. In others they pay them a much lower rate of wages for the same work in the hope of driving them to seek work out of the parish (*Reports on the Poor Laws*, 1834, quoted in *ibid.*, p. 263).

[21] See, e.g., Smelser, 1959, pp. 283–284. Smelser believes, however, that many of these reports were exaggerated, the product of the heated polemics on industrialism.

[22] Malthus, *op. cit.*, p. 474. As Habakkuk (1965) points out, "Malthus's views on this subject are apt to be misinterpreted. He did not argue that people had more children in order to profit from the earnings of the children in factories, or to enjoy larger poor-law benefits. His point was that the prospect of parish relief and the earning capacity of children at an early age reduced the force of the incentive to postpone marriage."

Or, as seen from the point of view of the workingmen—

Men who receive but a small pittance know that they have only to marry, and that pittance will be augmented in proportion to the number of their children. . . . An intelligent witness, who is much in the habit of employing laborers, states that when complaining of their allowance they frequently say to him: "We will marry, and you must maintain us" (*Report on Labourers' Wages*, 1824, quoted in Redford, 1926, p. 71).

In the four counties in which industry was most important, in 1821 there were 677 children under 5 per 1,000 women aged 15 to 49, as contrasted with only 580 in the rest of England. Since there is good reason to believe that infant and child mortality was greater in the first category, the higher child–woman ratio there is doubly impressive (Krause, 1958).

The implied causal relation is not proved, of course; it is just as likely that the breakdown of the traditional society increased both the average relief and fertility. In fact, it is rather unfortunate that the factual question of whether the birth rate rose has so long been associated with the policy question of whether Speenhamland was a just and efficient poor law. It is always difficult to analyze the effect of such subsidies or quasi-subsidies on the size of the family.[23] Even those instituted in the twentieth century, for which accurate fertility data are available, are not easy to separate from a dozen other factors that may have influenced family size.

4. **Change in the Age Structure.** A rise in the birth rate for any other reason may become cumulative by increasing in the next generation the proportion of persons physiologically capable of parenthood. As at this time a large proportion died in the first years of life, most of whatever decline in the death rate took place was equivalent to an additional rise in the birth rate. Even a relatively small change in each of the several factors affecting fertility or mortality, thus, could have brought about a substantial population increase over several generations.

To sum up, during this transitional period, we can hypothesize, there were three European family types in existence concurrently.[24] In the **traditional** family typical of the preindustrial period, the postponement of

---

[23] Blackmore and Mellonie, with what Marshall (1965) termed "a touching faith in the sanctity of even the shadiest figures," proved to their own temporary satisfaction that the Speenhamland system had effected a *decline* in the birth rate. Some months later, however, they offered "a second analysis" showing that there was no relation between the subsidy and fertility. See J. S. Blackmore and F. C. Mellonie, "Family Endowment and the Birth-Rate in the Early Nineteenth Century," I and II, *Economic History (Supplement to the Economic Journal)*, 1 (1927), 205–213; 1 (1928), 412–418.

[24] The following is based largely on an article by E. W. Hofstee, "Regional Differentiation in the Dutch Fertility during the Second Half of the 19th Century" (in Dutch), in Koninklijke Nederlandse Akademie van Wetenschappen, *Akademie-Dagen*, 7, Noord-Hollandsche Uitgevers, Amsterdam, 1954, 59–106. See also Petersen, 1964.

marriage, plus the nonmarriage of a considerable portion of the secular population, constituted an onerous but efficient means of reducing fertility. With the **proletarian** family, typical of the mass of either rural or urban workers who had been released from these institutional and normative restrictions, social control was barely strong enough to force a marriage even if a child had been conceived. Once the sexual urge developed, there was certainly no effective bar to marriage. In the **rational** family type, which arose first among the middle class and during the nineteenth century spread to the rest of the society, a sense of parental responsibility and, with it, a limitation of family size reappeared. The average age at marriage rose again, and the same end was also achieved with less privation by the use of contraceptives. In order to trace the change in fertility in detail, thus, we would need the statistics on completed family size by social class going back at least as far as 1750. While such data will never become available, we can be reasonably certain that the shifts in the over-all crude birth rate were largely the consequence of the gradual substitution of one of these family types for another.

## The Japanese Model

England affords one framework for analyzing population trends in a country undergoing modernization, but it is also atypical in that it was the first country to develop an industrial society. All subsequent modernization, and especially that currently under way in underdeveloped areas, has been far more rapid in some respects and thus more disruptive. And all countries that have imitated England's example have done so, to one degree or another, under the direction of the state. Among other industrial powers, Japan is most often cited as both a guide to underdeveloped Asia and a model for analysis.

Japan is a happy hunting ground for the demographer, for . . . it provides an opportunity, if not to answer, at least to add substantially to the evidence concerning one important question: how truly universal is the association of the "demographic revolution" with industrialization? Does the same configuration of trends as was observed in Western societies recur also in societies with entirely different cultural traditions? (Dore, 1959).

The Japanese case has the neatness of a laboratory experiment. The Tokugawa regime (1603–1868) cut off the country almost completely from alien influences and thus from most Western contacts; along many dimensions, therefore, the ensuing burst of modernization started from virtually zero. For much of this epoch, moreover, the population was as stable as it is supposed to be during Stage I of the demographic transition; between 1726 and 1852 the total fluctuated slightly around 25 million, with the low and the high during this century and a quarter differing by less than

10 per cent (Taeuber, 1958, p. 21). The reason for this stability was *not*, however, that unrestrained procreation was cut back by a commensurate mortality. Indeed, the death rate was high, but fertility was set (as in early-modern Europe) at well below the physiological maximum. Conscious family limitation was achieved in part through the postponement of marriage, contraception, and abortion, but in greater part apparently through infanticide, euphemistically termed *mabiki* (literally, "thinning," as of rice seedlings when some are pulled up to encourage the growth of the remainder). As in the familistic culture of classical China, so also in its adaptation to the straitened economy of the Japanese islands, the pre-eminent goal was that the family be continued through the male line. In China this was realized in principle through a numerous progeny, but in Japan by sacrificing numbers to quality (*ibid.*, p. 31).

Few analysts would have forecast from the Meiji "restoration" in 1868 anything like the subsequent remarkable rise in productivity. The country was in chaos for a decade or more, and social order was restored by the samurai, once a class of warrior knights who had become obsolescent in this traditional function. They combined old and new with a marvelous adeptness, refurbishing the imperial office and the established religion and even increasing their prior authority and, on the other hand, taking over wholesale Western technology and education, Western legal codes, details of Western political administration down to the postal system. The meteoric rise to full industrial power, in such dramatic contrast with the static misery of most underdeveloped countries, has of course stimulated much analysis: what were the crucial reasons for Japan's success?

One frequent explanation is based on the ideology of nationalism.

Nationalism is a *sine qua non* of industrialization, because it provides people with an overriding, easily acquired, secular motivation for making painful changes. National strength or prestige becomes the supreme goal, industrialization the chief means. . . . To the degree that the obstacles to industrialization are strong, nationalism must be intense to overcome them. Nationalism was a potent element in the industrialization of Japan, Germany, and Russia (Davis, 1955).

Although Japan is invariably cited as prime evidence for this argument, it is not clear that this nation's ideology was merely one instance of a universal category. The etymological meaning of *nation* (the word derives from the Latin for "to be born") suggests a people linked by common descent from a putative ancestor; and other accepted characteristics are a common territory, history, language, religion, and way of life.[25] In Japan,

---

[25] The list, compiled from various political theorists as an introduction to an analysis of newly established African states, underlines how different they are from Japan. Since "nearly all the new African nations lacked *all* these elements except a common territory, and even that has been lately and arbitrarily demarcated by alien power," whether in these instances nation-building has fostered modernization is far from clear. See Margery Perham, *The Colonial Reckoning: The End of Imperial Rule in Africa in the Light of the British Experience*, Knopf, New York, 1962, p. 26. In such cases (far

nationalism could rest securely on all of these elements. Before the advent of the Meiji regime, the country was homogeneous in ethnicity, language, and religion, and this multiple unity was reinforced not only by its geographical separation from the mainland but also by the lack of any basis for transnational loyalties similar to Pan-Africanism or Pan-Arabism. A small but crucial minority were literate, and the new regime almost immediately used the universal compulsory education it established (and, for adults, classes in the conscripted army) to breed patriotism. By 1940, the "almost total uniformity of educational experience in the first six school years of the life of every Japanese child" produced "a homogeneity of popular intellectual culture which has probably never been equaled in any society of 70 million people" (Dore, 1964). In short, Japan's nationalism could be generated largely from the natural unity of her population, and the mythical element, always a necessary supplement, was inculcated with an all but unique efficiency.

The characteristics of Japan's preindustrial civilization that made her rapid modernization feasible, however we specify them, were associated with the country's urban population. In the Tokugawa period there were three large cities—Edo, with a population variously estimated between half a million and a million, and Kyoto and Osaka, each with perhaps a third of a million—plus hundreds of castle towns, temple towns, market centers, ports, and post towns. "Japan in 1800, though an outwardly feudal land, was almost as urbanized as were the leading industrial countries at that time." [26] The urban aggregates most important for Japan's future development, surprisingly, were the castle towns, which were gradually transformed from the seats of "feudal" power into the nuclei of modern authority. Just as Edo, the capital of the Tokugawa shogun, became the capital of new Japan under the new name of Tokyo, so the shift of local authority followed. Of the forty-six prefectural capitals today, thirty-four were castle towns in Tokugawa times, and in most cases the modern prefecture is named after its capital rather than the pre-Meiji province. "The city, its life and its institutions, was in reality basically antagonistic to the type of land-centered military regime envisaged by the Tokugawa authorities. The urban environment, from its inception, was destined to have a contradictory effect upon the feudal class" (Hall, 1955).[27] If this interpretation is correct,

---

more typical than Japan in today's world), one can reasonably argue that nationalism tends to block the modernization of new nations.

[26] Edwin O. Reischauer, *The United States and Japan*, 2nd Ed., Harvard University Press, Cambridge, Mass., 1957, p. 82. If we apply Davis's thesis to that period, Japan war markedly "overurbanized" (see p. 466), and the seeming consequences of this disparity suggest that present-day policy-makers who want both to modernize and to impede the growth of cities may be trying to march in two directions.

[27] This is also the view offered in Carpenter, 1960; according to Bellah, on the contrary, "the city only to a limited extent represented a new form of social organization, that connected with the market and a differentiated economy. For many purposes it was merely a congeries of 'villages' in close geographical contiguity" (Robert N. Bellah, *Tokugawa Religion*, Free Press, Glencoe, Ill., 1957, p. 43).

Pirenne's thesis concerning the cities of early-modern Europe (see pp. 374–376) is partly true also of Japan.

From 1873, shortly after the Meiji regime was installed, to 1918, when the initial phase of rapid industrialization was over, the population of Japan went up from 35.2 to 55.0 million.[28] The rate of annual growth increased from 0.75 per cent in the 1870s and 1880s to not quite 1 per cent in the 1890s, and to almost 1.5 per cent in the first two decades of the twentieth century. This accelerating growth was *not* the consequence of a substantial decline in mortality, as one would anticipate from the transition theory. On the contrary, the death rate apparently remained almost constant at around 20 per thousand throughout these decades. The birth rate rose from about 20 to over 30 (Taeuber, 1958, p. 41), for the incidence of infanticide was much reduced: children who had no place in the village economy could now migrate to industrial jobs in the cities or to overseas posts in the colonies. This rise in fertility during the first period of industrialization, "puzzling" to one anticipating the contrary, was not a spurious artifact of improved records but a social reality (*ibid.*, p. 232; but *cf*. Morita, 1963). In short, the higher fertility that by our surmise accompanied early British industrialization (or, for that matter, the modernization of almost any Western society; for the Dutch case, *cf*. Petersen, 1964) can be established with somewhat greater certainty in the Japanese case.

In the interwar years the industrialization began to effect a decline in mortality; from 1920 to 1941, the crude death rate fell from 25.4 to 15.7, the infant death rate from 166.2 to 84.4 (Taeuber, 1958, p. 286). Fertility after World War I, on the contrary, was at an all-time high, from which it declined slowly during the following decades: from 1920 to 1941 (the same dates as above), the birth rate fell from 36.1 to 31.1, the gross reproduction rate from 2.7 to 2.2.

The population of Japan Proper (that is, excluding the Empire) increased from 56.0 million in 1920 to 73.1 million in 1940. The impact of this 17 million in two decades can hardly be communicated. The increment alone would have peopled an empty expanse of Japan's total area with 114 persons per square mile, and only 16 per cent of the land was cultivable. This period of Japan's modernization indicates another defect (at least if the virtues of modernization are seen in a liberal democratic perspective) in the policy that social-economic growth must be based on a nationalist ideology. It is certainly true that the pace was faster because the boldest of the early entrepreneurs were patriotic ex-samurai, who brought into the transitional period a traditional ethical code under which individualistic self-seeking was sacrificed to the collective good. But their willingness, and the willingness of the population generally, to subordinate personal to national interest were greatest, of course, in time of war.

[28] The first census was taken in 1920. These estimates are from Taeuber, 1958, p. 45.

The Japanese economy has thrived on war and the prospect of war. . . . [However, since] an imminent war which never comes . . . is bound to lose its psychological efficacy, Japan sustained the war atmosphere over a long period by switching the national objectives from defense to expansion (Dore, 1964).

Thus, government policy in this period was to stimulate the growth in numbers, for Japan's dominion over Eastern and Southeastern Asia in a "Co-Prosperity Sphere" demanded a continuous flow of soldiers and administrators. Although neither the prohibition of contraceptives nor various other pronatalist regulations prevented a fall in fertility, this was far slower than the population pressure warranted, or than the ultimate welfare of modern Japan demanded. The slow decline in birth rates, from an average of 36.7 in 1920–25 to 29.3 in 1935–40, was the consequence principally either of postponement of marriage or the separation of couples by the husband's military service or temporary emigration to an administrative post outside the main islands (Taeuber, 1958, p. 242). Yet the Empire, however important as an economic base, permanently absorbed only a small portion of the growing population: of the world's ethnic Japanese, 97.7 per cent lived in Japan Proper in 1920 and 95.6 per cent still in 1940.

The pressure of Japan's population, bearable so long as the main islands were the center of an expanding Empire, was less so after her defeat in World War II. Not only did the country lose its colonies, but 3.1 million soldiers and sailors, plus 3.2 million civilian administrators and former emigrants with their families, were repatriated to the war-damaged homeland (*ibid.*, p. 346). There were no houses to live in, no urban jobs, no land for sale or rent. Moreover, the natural increase went up appreciably. The birth rate, which had been as low as 26.6 in 1939, was 34.3 in 1947; this typical postwar rise, due almost entirely to the return of millions of young men from their army service, electrified public opinion. The death rate, which in the prewar years had never been below 15.7, was 14.6 in 1947 and fell rapidly in the ensuing years to about half that (*ibid.*, p. 311). Japan had been a stock example of population pressure for decades, but the situation had never been so desperate (see pp. 517–518).

## Summary

During the eighty years or so following 1760 England's economy and social structure underwent a complete transformation, commonly known as the industrial revolution. In agriculture, the medieval three-field system was supplanted by enclosed fields, resulting in both a greatly increased productivity and new social relations in the rural areas. Manufacturing, which had been scattered through the countryside, was concentrated into factories, around which new urban centers rapidly developed. The prior rural isolation ended with the construction of roads and canals, by which both men and goods could move about more easily. These economic changes constituted the first fundamental advance since the establishment of pre-industrial cities several millennia before.

All the authorities who have analyzed it agree that England's population grew at an unprecedented rate during these eighty years, and that this was primarily a natural increase, since the emigration of Englishmen was more or less balanced by the immigration of Irish and Scots. Differences arise over whether the greater numbers resulted mainly from a decline in the death rate (Griffith, McKeown and Brown, *et al.*) or from a rise in the birth rate (Malthus, Habakkuk, Krause, *et al.*). It is worth stressing that there is nothing in logic against accepting each set of arguments as partly correct, assuming the actual process was more complex than either side has pictured it. During this transitional period, in all likelihood, birth and death rates were simultaneously rising and falling in different sectors of the population. Institutional bars to early marriage still kept the birth rate low; their erosion permitted it to rise; and the small-family system, based on both the postponement of marriage and birth control, began to be established among the middle class. Death rates, similarly, certainly differed from one area or social class to another, varying with diets, styles of life, and other conditions affecting mortality. It is just this variety, compounded by the teasingly thin statistical data, that has made possible the continuous dispute over what really happened.

For England the theory of the demographic transition more or less accurately sums up the period from 1850 or even 1875 to 1945—that is, from the time when medicine and public sanitation really effected a rapid decline in mortality, particularly of infants and children, to the postwar baby boom. For earlier decades, most death-control measures were too inefficient to have been so clearly the principal factor in the demonstrable population growth. During the first three-quarters of the nineteenth century, it must be emphasized, the trend in England's birth rate was upward. The secular decline in fertility that began in the year of the Bradlaugh-Besant trial (*cf.* pp. 488, 490), that is to say, did not start from the high plateau that is assumed in the theory.

The differences between the English and the Japanese cases are manifest, but there is also a surprising similarity, some of which, but only some, seems to validate the theory of the demographic transition.

1. In both societies fertility in the preindustrial period was at well below the physiological maximum, in England mainly because of postponement of marriage and permanent secular celibacy of many adults, in Japan because of widespread infanticide. Defined by the means to achieve a relatively low fertility, the European family pattern was almost unique, as Hajnal termed it (*cf.* p. 383). But defined by a small family size irrespective of how this was achieved, the norm of Tokugawa Japan was more European than Asian.

**2.** As the new ways of life of an industrial society supplanted the older family patterns, we would therefore expect *a priori* a rise in fertility. And in both countries the poor statistical record is at least consistent with this conclusion.

**3.** In both cases whether there was an early decline in mortality is debatable and, if so, the reasons for it are not clear. That the period of rapid growth depends entirely on the fall of the death rate seems to be valid only after 1870, say, in England or 1920 in Japan—that is, not until some decades after the increase in population began.

**4.** Both England and Japan developed populations that were based, economically and in part demographically, on empires far larger than the homeland. When these overseas foundations disintegrated, the great numbers had to adjust to a comparatively straitened habitat.

## Suggestions for Further Reading

Of the considerable literature on the industrial revolution in England, perhaps the best works are Mantoux, 1952 or the shorter, more concise Ashton, 1948. The view that the mass of the people suffered as a direct result of the industrial revolution is dramatically presented in Hammond and Hammond, 1932*a*, 1932*b*, and convincingly countered in several of the essays in Hayek, 1954. No book-length discussion of England's population during the industrial revolution is wholly satisfactory. Though out of date in many respects, Griffith, 1926 and Redford, 1926 are still important. Some of the best journal articles are reprinted in Glass and Eversley, 1965, which scrimps, however, the point of view expressed in Krause, 1958, 1959. Wrigley, 1966 is partly a summary of conclusions to date about the growth of English population, partly a manual on methods of historical demography.

On the population of Japan, Taeuber, 1958 comes close to being definitive; see the interesting review-essay, Dore, 1959. Special topics are better covered in Hall, 1955 and Dore, 1964.

The demographic transition in other presently developed countries can be usefully studied in several of the essays included in Glass and Eversley, 1965 and also in Heckscher, 1950; Gille, 1949; and Petersen, 1964.

* ASHTON, T. S. 1948. *The Industrial Revolution, 1760–1830.* Oxford University Press, London.

* ———. 1954*a*. "The Standard of Life of the Workers in England, 1790–1830," in Hayek, 1954, pp. 127–159.

———. 1954*b*. "The Treatment of Capitalism by Historians," in Hayek, 1954, pp. 33–63.

BUER, M. C. 1926. *Health, Wealth, and Population in the Early Days of the Industrial Revolution.* Routledge, London.

CARPENTER, DAVID B. 1960. "Urbanization and Social Change in Japan," *Sociological Quarterly,* **1,** 155–166.

CHAMBERS, J. D. 1965*a*. "The Course of Population Change," in Glass and Eversley, 1965, pp. 327–334.

* ———. 1965b. "Enclosure and Labour Supply in the Industrial Revolution," in Glass and Eversley, 1965, pp. 308–327.

———. 1965c. "Population Change in a Provincial Town, Nottingham 1700–1800," in Glass and Eversley, 1965, pp. 334–353.

DAVIS, KINGSLEY. 1955. "Social and Demographic Aspects of Economic Development in India," in *Economic Growth: Brazil, India, Japan,* edited by Simon Kuznets *et al.* Duke University Press, Durham, N.C., pp. 263–315.

DORE, R. P. 1959. "Japan: Country of Accelerated Transition," *Population Studies,* 13, 103–111.

* ———. 1964. "Japan as a Model of Economic Development," *European Journal of Sociology,* 5, 138–154.

ENGELS, FREDERICK. 1958. *The Condition of the Working Class in England,* translated and edited by W. O. Henderson and W. H. Chaloner. Macmillan, New York.

GILLE, H. 1949. "The Demographic History of the Northern European Countries in the Eighteenth Century," *Population Studies,* 3, 1–65.

* GLASS, D. V., and D. E. C. EVERSLEY. 1965. *Population in History.* Aldine, Chicago.

GRIFFITH, C. TALBOT. 1926. *Population Problems of the Age of Malthus.* University Press, Cambridge.

* HABAKKUK, H. J. 1965. "English Population in the Eighteenth Century," in Glass and Eversley, 1965, pp. 269–284.

* HALL, JOHN W. 1955. "The Castle Town and Japan's Modern Urbanization," *Far Eastern Quarterly,* 15, 37–56.

HAMMOND, BARBARA. 1928. "Urban Death-Rates in the Early Nineteenth Century," *Economic History (Supplement to the Economic Journal),* 1, 419–428.

HAMMOND, J. L., and BARBARA HAMMOND. 1932a. *The Town Labourer, 1760–1832: The New Civilisation.* 2nd Ed. Longmans, Green, London.

———, and ———. 1932b. *The Village Labourer, 1760–1832: A Study in the Government of England before the Reform Bill.* Longmans, Green, London.

HAYEK, F. A., editor. 1954. *Capitalism and the Historians.* University of Chicago Press, Chicago.

HECKSCHER, E. F. 1950. "Swedish Population Trends before the Industrial Revolution," *Economic History Review,* 2nd Ser., 2, 226–277.

HELLEINER, K. F. 1965. "The Vital Revolution Reconsidered," in Glass and Eversley, 1965, pp. 79–86.

HENNOCK, E. P. 1957. "Urban Sanitary Reform a Generation before Chadwick?" *Economic History Review,* 2nd Ser., 10, 113–119.

HOBSBAWM, E. J. 1957. "The British Standard of Living, 1790–1850," *Economic History Review,* 2nd Ser., 10, 46–61.

HUTT, W. H. 1954. "The Factory System of the Early Nineteenth Century," in Hayek, 1954, pp. 160–188.

* KRAUSE, J. T. 1958. "Changes in English Fertility and Mortality, 1781–1850," *Economic History Review,* 2nd Ser., 11, 52–70.

——— 1959. "Some Implications of Recent Work in Historical Demography," *Comparative Studies in Society and History,* 1, 164–188.

———. 1965. "The Changing Adequacy of English Registration, 1690–1837," in Glass and Eversley, 1965, pp. 379–393.

* McKEOWN, THOMAS, and R. G. BROWN. 1965. "Medical Evidence Related to English Population Changes in the Eighteenth Century," in Glass and Eversley, 1965, pp. 285–307.

MANTOUX, PAUL. 1952. *The Industrial Revolution in the Eighteenth Century: An Outline of the Beginnings of the Modern Factory System in England.* Revised Ed. Cape, London.

MARSHALL, T. H. 1965. "The Population Problem during the Industrial Revolution," in Glass and Eversley, 1965, pp. 247–268.

MORITA, YUZO. 1963. "Estimated Birth and Death Rates in the Early Meiji Period of Japan," *Population Studies,* **17**, 33–56.

* PETERSEN, WILLIAM. 1964. "The Demographic Transition in the Netherlands," in *The Politics of Population.* Doubleday, Garden City, N.Y., pp. 166–192.

REDFORD, ARTHUR. 1926. *Labour Migration in England, 1800–50.* University of Manchester Press, Manchester.

ROSENBERG, CHARLES E. 1966. "Cholera in Nineteenth-Century Europe: A Tool for Social and Economic Analysis," *Comparative Studies in Society and History,* **8**, 452–463.

SAVILLE, JOHN. 1957. *Rural Depopulation in England and Wales, 1851–1951.* Routledge & Kegan Paul, London.

SMELSER, NEIL J. 1959. *Social Change in the Industrial Revolution: An Application of Theory to the British Cotton Industry.* University of Chicago Press, Chicago.

* TAEUBER, IRENE. 1958. *The Population of Japan.* Princeton University Press, Princeton, N.J.

* TAYLOR, A. J. 1960. "Progress and Poverty in Britain, 1780–1850: A Reappraisal," *History,* **45**, 16–31.

THOMAS, BRINLEY. 1954. *Migration and Economic Growth: A Study of Great Britain and the Atlantic Economy.* National Institute of Economic and Social Research, Economic and Social Study No. 12. University Press, Cambridge.

WRIGLEY, E. A., editor. 1966. *An Introduction to English Historical Demography.* Basic Books, New York.

# 13 THE CITIES OF INDUSTRIAL AND UNDERDEVELOPED SOCIETIES

What social characteristics do we associate with urban life, and what indexes shall we use to denote whether a place is urban? Not only is each of these questions difficult to answer in itself, but there is a strong tendency to confuse the two. A careful distinction must be made between **urbanism,** the culture of cities, the way of life of city dwellers, and **urbanization,** the process by which cities are formed or by which they come to dominate a national culture.

We tend to think of all cities as essentially one, and most of the conceptual definitions are based on this premise. It is useful, however, to divide the genus into at least three species: the cities of (1) preindustrial civilizations, which were analyzed in Chapter 10, and those of (2) modern industrial and of (3) underdeveloped nations, which are the topics of this chapter.

## Definitions of "Urban" and "Rural"

"About thirty definitions of urban population are in current use, but none of them is really satisfactory . . . in making international comparisons" (Macura, 1961). Some years ago, the United Nations Population Division conducted a detailed survey on the subject. Of the fifty-three countries with one or more censuses that were examined, only two (Costa Rica, 1927 and Thailand, 1947) did not divide the population according to urban or rural residence, though three others (Netherlands, Belgium, and Japan) were also partial exceptions. Some countries classified places as "urban" if they had a political status (e.g., "incorporated"); some, if they constituted divisions similar to townships with a certain minimum size of population, which ranged from 2,000 for Austria to 20,000 for the Netherlands; some, if they performed an administrative function (similar to that of a county seat), for example, Brazil, Colombia, Peru, Egypt, and Turkey. Among countries that defined "urban" by an aggregation of population, the minimum size ranged from 250 in Denmark to 25,000 in Mexico (United Nations, 1950). The population most commonly used to define an urban place, 2,000 persons or over, was implicitly proposed as an international standard. To adopt it as a measure would change the percentage urban in Iceland (1940) from 71.7 to 46.7, in Netherlands (1947) from 54.6 to 72.5. Yet in spite of the range in definitions, there was a correlation of 0.84 between the percentage "urban" as each country designated this sector and the percentage living in cities of 100,000 or more (United Nations, 1953).

More generally, "urban" and "rural" are defined by one or more of four criteria, which can be identified as economic, cultural, political, and demographic.

1. Economic criteria are used especially to distinguish the agriculture of the countryside from the service functions of a market town. Thus, Hawley has posited an abstraction that he terms a **community area:**

The community is comprised of two generalized unit parts, the center and the adjoining outlying area. In the one are performed the processing and service functions, and in the other are carried on the raw-material-producing functions. The two develop together, each presupposing the other (Hawley, 1950, p. 245).

But we certainly cannot mark the boundaries of a community area today by so simple an index as the source of consumer goods. The food eaten in any American city can include not only milk from the immediate locality but also (if we restrict the list to domestic products) California vegetables, Florida fruit, Wisconsin cheese, Idaho potatoes, Kansas corn and pork, and so on through all the specialized commodities of America's rationalized agriculture. On the other hand, the urban influences impinging on rural regions, while they may be transmitted through the nearest town (in the form, say, of the local newspaper or television station), are as likely as not to have originated in New York or Washington or Hollywood. The boundaries of the modern community area are "blurred, if not indeterminate," for "each index yields a different description of a community's margins" (*ibid.*, p. 249). Indeed, as we have noted, even in a preindustrial society a market town that related only to the surrounding countryside was less likely to develop full urban characteristics than either an administrative center or, especially, a depot of long-distance trade. (Sometimes "urban" and "nonagricultural" are taken to be correlative; a country is described as urban if, e.g., no more than half of its occupied males are engaged in agriculture. Yet the two factors are not necessarily complementary in this sense: the United States census classification of "rural-nonfarm" could be matched by one of manufacturing or mining nonurban; *cf.* Macura, 1961, but also Schwirian and Prehn, 1962.)

2. Cultural criteria supposedly distinguish the essential characteristics of urban life. When so defined, the city is "a state of mind, a body of customs and traditions, and of the organized attitudes and sentiments that inhere in these customs and are transmitted with this tradition" (Park, 1925).

The larger, the more densely populated, and the more heterogeneous a community, the more accentuated the characteristics associated with urbanism will be. . . . The bonds of kinship, of neighborliness, and the sentiments arising out of living together for generations under a common folk tradition are likely to be absent or, at best, relatively weak. . . . Competition and formal control mechanisms furnish the substitutes for the bonds of solidarity that are relied upon to hold a folk society together. . . . The city is characterized by secondary rather than primary contacts. The contacts of the city may indeed be face to face, but they are nevertheless impersonal, superficial, transitory, and segmental. . . . Whereas, therefore, the individual gains, on the one hand, a certain degree of emancipation or freedom from the personal and emotional controls of intimate groups, he loses, on the other hand, the spontaneous self-expression, the morale, and the sense of participation that comes with living in an integrated society (Wirth, 1938).

Sometimes the contrast with a nonurban way of life is expressed as a contrast between two polar types. In the usual formulation, rural-urban is more or less identified with Gemeinschaft-Gesellschaft, and thus with nonindustrial-industrial. Redfield, for example, designated "urban society" as the contrary of "folk society," which he defined as follows:

Such a society is small, isolated, nonliterate, and homogeneous, with a strong sense of group solidarity. The ways of living are conventionalized into that coherent system which we call "a culture." Behavior is traditional, spontaneous, uncritical, and personal; there is no legislation or habit of experiment and reflection for intellectual ends. Kinship, its relationships and institutions, are the type categories of experience and the familiar group is the unit of action. The sacred prevails over the secular; the economy is one of status rather than of the market (Redfield, 1947).

3. Political criteria distinguish an urban place by its administrative function. The centers of local or provincial control in the Chinese or Roman empires, for instance, had an urban status even though many were hardly more than hamlets. In the United States until 1874, to take a modern example, the only definition of *urban* was an incorporated place, that is, an aggregate that a state legislature had recognized as a "town."

4. Demographic criteria distinguish an urban place by the number of persons living in a town, however this is defined, or in a population conglomeration irrespective of the administrative boundaries. In the United States, as in Europe and Oceania, "underbounded" cities are common—that is, administrative urban units that constitute only part of a continuous bloc of nonagricultural population. In some other parts of the world, such as the Philippines, one finds "overbounded" cities, single administrative units made up of both an urban nucleus and a rural periphery (Gibbs, 1961, p. 17). Whether urban units are defined as actual population agglomerations or as governmental units containing a certain minimum number of persons obviously affects the denoted size of cities considerably.

Variation in the designation of "urban" is also usual in any one country's history. The gradual development of the U.S. Census Bureau's definitions, for example, illustrates the problem in assigning statistical indexes to rapidly changing social entities (Truesdell, 1949). Until 1874, as we have noted, incorporated towns were considered urban and everything else rural. In that year a *Statistical Atlas* was published showing the population density of each county in the country, and in the analysis of the data towns of 8,000 inhabitants or more were defined as urban and the rest of the population as rural. In 1880 the division that had been established almost by accident in this atlas was projected back to 1790, and eventually the series was continued until 1920. In the same census of 1880, however, a new definition was established: urban = an aggregate of 4,000 or more, rural = the balance. Even with this simple dichotomy, the division between rural and urban was complicated by the existence, particularly in New England, of large townships with low population density, and in almost all censuses some special provision has had to be made to adjust these to the national definition. In 1900 a three-way division was made between "urban" (population of 4,000 or more), "semi-urban" (incorporated places of less than 4,000), and "rural" (unincorporated places). This census, thus, introduced two novelties—a departure from the rural-urban dichotomy and the simultaneous use of two indexes.

In Willcox's supplementary analysis of the 1900 census a population of 2,500 or more was taken as the basic definition of "urban," and this has remained standard to this day. "Cities" were defined as aggregates of 25,000 or more, and this was the first step toward the later separation of metropolitan units. In a special 1920 monograph both the urban and the rural sectors were divided into farm and nonfarm, and this differentiation has been maintained for the rural one in subsequent censuses (except that in 1930 the criterion by which the "farm" population was defined was changed from occupation to residence). In 1930 the same classification was maintained with the following addition: aggregates of 10,000 or more persons with a density of 1,000 or more per square mile were defined as urban even if not so by other criteria. In 1940 the urban category was subdivided by breaking off "metropolitan districts," defined as cities of 50,000 or more together with contiguous administrative units having a population density of 150 or more per square mile.

A number of new concepts and procedures were introduced in the 1950 census. The size-of-place classification was extended to segregate two classes of villages, those of 1,000 to 2,500 inhabitants (whether incorporated or not), and those of fewer than 1,000. A new definition of "urban" was adopted, by which this population comprises all persons living in (1) incorporated places of 2,500 or more (except in New England and other states where "towns" are subdivisions of counties); (2) the urban fringe,[1] whether incorporated or not, around cities of 50,000 or more; and (3) unincorporated places of 2,500 or more outside an urban fringe. The remaining population is classified as "rural."

Two new metropolitan units were also established in 1950. An **Urbanized Area** is made up of at least one city (or a pair of contiguous twin cities) of 50,000 or more, plus the surrounding densely settled, closely spaced, urban fringe. A **Standard Metropolitan Statistical Area** (or SMSA), as it is now termed, is defined as one or more contiguous nonagricultural counties containing at least one city of 50,000 or more (or, again, a pair of contiguous twin cities of at least this joint size), and having a generally metropolitan character based on the counties' social and economic integration with the central city.[2]

Whether Urbanized Area or SMSA is the preferable unit depends on the use to which it is put. The first measures primarily the residence pattern in a city and its immediately adjoining area, the second the broader economic and social integration of whole counties. By the definition of both metropolitan units, a city's effective population is no longer counted as the number of persons who happen to live within its corporate limits. What is commonly termed the "greater" city is a much more realistic measure of the actual social aggregate, and these new census definitions approximate it in different ways. In both, formal administrative borders are ignored also in other respects: Urbanized Areas include either incorporated or unincor-

---

[1] For a discussion of the meaning of this term, see Duncan and Reiss, 1956, pp. 117–118.

[2] For the full, detailed definition, see U.S. Bureau of the Budget, *Standard Metropolitan Statistical Areas*, Washington, D.C., 1961, pp. 3–5. In New England, towns rather than counties are the units used, but the criteria of integration are the same.

porated places; both they and SMSAs extend over state lines (*cf.* Berry, 1967).

Only minor revisions were made in the 1960 classification. The name and precise definition of the SMSA were changed slightly. A new megalopolitan unit was set, the **Standard Consolidated Area,** and two such areas were delimited. The New York-Northeastern New Jersey SCA constituted the New York, Newark, Jersey City, and Paterson-Clifton-Passaic SMSAs, plus Middlesex and Somerset Counties in New Jersey—with a total population of 14.8 million (*cf.* Taeuber and Taeuber, 1964). The Chicago-Northwestern Indiana SCA was made up of the Chicago and Gary-Hammond-East Chicago SMSAs, with a total population of 6.8 million.

The development of the rural-urban differentiation is recapitulated in Table 13-1. At the beginning of the nineteenth century, residents of the *countryside* were *farmers* living in *unincorporated* places; and any one of these three elements could be taken as a sufficiently accurate measure of the composite status. Today, the "rural" isolation of that period and its concomitant social characteristics have all but disappeared; in some senses the entire population is "urban." In its continuing attempts to measure this transformation, the Census Bureau has experimented with a number of indexes, of which the most important were political status (e.g., incorporated or unincorporated), occupation (e.g., rural-farm), population density (e.g., the classification added in 1930), population size (with 2,500 becoming the dividing point between urban and rural), and social and economic integration (e.g., the number of telephone calls between the central city and the metropolitan ring, one of the criteria by which counties are included in an SMSA). For any except the roughest indication of differences, then, the simple rural-urban dichotomy is now inadequate. It is usual to break down each into at least two parts—urban into "metropolitan" and "other urban," and rural into "farm" and "nonfarm." [3]

## Systems of Cities

One reason that the definitions and analyses of "urban" vary so much from country to country is that the meaning of a human conglomeration differs according to its broader setting. Iceland, with an area of just under 40,000 square miles and a 1965 population of some 208,000, is not populous enough to have sizable cities. Reykajvik, its capital and largest settlement, had only 78,000 in 1965, and regional administrative centers were much

---

[3] It may be, however, that social analysis has actually been impeded by the increasing complexity of definitions. If we were to revert to a purely demographic measure —"urbanization is a process of population concentration" (Eldridge, 1956)—and use this as the independent variable, we would be in a much better position to analyze the social and economic characteristics, collectively known as urbanism, that depend on population size.

Table 13-1. The Definition of "Urban" and "Rural" in Successive Censuses, United States, 1874–1960

| DATE OF DEFINITION | PERIOD FOR WHICH USED | "URBAN" | | "RURAL" | |
|---|---|---|---|---|---|
| 1874 | 1790–1920 | 8,000+ | | Residue | |
| 1880 | 1880–1900 | 4,000+ | | Residue | |
| 1890 | a | | | | < 1,000 |
| 1900 | 1900 | 4,000+ | "Semi-urban": incorporated and < 4,000 | Unincorporated and < 4,000 | |
| 1906 | 1900–1910 | "Cities" 25,000+ | "Urban" 2,500+ | "Country districts" residue | |
| 1910 | 1880–1910 | | 2,500+ and incorporated | < 2,500 or unincorporated | |
| 1920 | 1920–1960 | | | Rural nonfarm | Rural farm |
| 1930 | 1930–1950 | Additional classification: population of 10,000, plus density of 1,000/sq. mi. | | | |
| 1940 | 1940 | "Metropolitan district": city of 50,000+ with contiguous areas | | | |
| 1950 | 1950–1960 | Urbanized Area b SMA c | New definition of urban b | 1,000– 2,500 | < 1,000 |
| 1960 | 1960 | Standard Consolidated Area b SMSA b | | | |

smaller; yet in the context of this nation these were economic-cultural centers of far greater importance than their size would suggest. Or, among the cities of the United States, Denver, with a population of under half a million in 1960, is a transportation, financial, and even cultural center of the Mountain West, whereas Newark, with almost the same population, is a satellite of New York. In both cases, the significance of a single urban unit can be understood fully only in relation to the whole environment.

City systems have been analyzed according to various criteria. One recurrent effort is to classify urban places by their economy—college towns, mining towns, and the like—and to try to establish some statistical regularities associated with the function. The main difficulty, of course, is that most cities and all metropolises are multifunctional, so that the analysis must depend on weighting functions by their relative importance.[4] A more rewarding effort is to analyze cities by their size, which can be done in several ways.

### THE ANALYSIS OF PRIMACY

**Primacy** is the ratio of the largest urban aggregate of a city system (for example, all the cities of one nation) to a designated portion of the remainder of the urban population. If one ranks cities by size, then according to Pareto's rule,

$$P_n = P_1 n^b$$

where $P_1$ is the population of the largest city and $P_n$ that of the city of rank $n$. In the special case when $b = -1$, an equation analyzed by Zipf,[5] for any country the $n$th-ranking city has a population equal to $1/n$th of the largest city. Using a variation of Pareto's formula, Mitra calculated the expected size distribution of Indian cities and compared it with the actual distribution; from the difference he devised an "index of differential composition," $\Delta$, shown in the last column of Table 13-2. This is the sum of either the positive or the negative percentage differences; thus, in this example, only 3.21 per cent of the total would have to be shifted between the expected

---

[4] Duncan and Reiss attempt not only to divide cities according to their functions but to correlate these with demographic variables (1956, Chapters 16–20).

[5] George K. Zipf, *Human Behavior and the Principle of Least Effort: An Introduction to Human Ecology,* Addison-Wesley, Cambridge, Mass., 1949.

---

PRINCIPAL SOURCE: Leon E. Truesdell, "The Development of the Urban-Rural Classification in the United States, 1874 to 1949," in U.S. Bureau of the Census, *Current Population Reports,* Series P-23, No. 1, August 5, 1949.

[a] In 1890 the rural population was subdivided into "compact bodies" of 1,000 or more and the remainder, but this division was not included in the census, apparently inadvertently.

[b] For definition, see text.

[c] Standard Metropolitan Area, the original designation of what is now termed SMSA.

*Above and Below:* A retirement community, Sun City, Florida (*Del E. Webb Corporation*).

Table 13-2. Comparison of Observed and Expected Distribution of Urban Places
by Size-Class, India, 1961

| SIZE-CLASS (−000) | PERCENTAGE OF URBAN POPULATION | | DIFFERENCE BETWEEN OBSERVED AND EXPECTED |
|---|---|---|---|
| | OBSERVED | EXPECTED | |
| (1) | (2) | (3) | (2) − (3) |
| 5–10 | 8.09 | 8.96 | −0.87 |
| 10–20 | 14.44 | 13.90 | 0.54 |
| 20–50 | 20.08 | 18.50 | 1.58 |
| 50–100 | 12.35 | 11.80 | 0.55 |
| 100–200 | 10.92 | 11.89 | −0.97 |
| 200–500 | 10.68 | 12.05 | −1.37 |
| 500+ | 23.44 | 22.90 | 0.54 |
| TOTAL | 100.00 | 100.00 | $\triangle = 3.21$ |

SOURCE: S. Mitra, "The Changing Pattern of Population Concentration in Indian Cities," *Eugenics Quarterly*, **12** (1965), 154–161.

and observed distributions to obtain a perfect correspondence between them.

If one is interested less in the entire rank-size distribution than in its upper segment, which for most purposes is more important, it is convenient to indicate the primacy of a city system by a simpler index, conventionally,

$$\frac{P_1}{P_2} \quad \text{or} \quad \frac{P_1}{P_2 + P_3 + P_4}$$

where these symbols represent the populations of a country's cities ranked by size (Browning and Gibbs, 1961). Which of these indices one uses is a matter almost of indifference; for eighty-two countries the coefficient of correlation between the two was 0.94 (*cf.* Table 13-3). When the second formula was used to calculate indices of primacy for the "Metropolitan Areas" [6] of the eighty-two countries, the mean primacy of each of various

[6] The most ambitious effort to establish a statistical base for international comparisons was made by a team under Kingsley Davis (International Urban Research, 1959). Following the model of the SMSA as used in the United States, they defined a "Metropolitan Area" as one with 100,000 or more inhabitants, consisting of at least one city with 50,000 or more inhabitants and contiguous areas related to the city in certain specified ways. In 1954, of the 202 countries and territories investigated, 105 had at least one "Metropolitan Area." Of the probable total of 1,046 for the world, it was possible to fix approximate boundaries for 720, omitting those for which local population data were lacking (*cf.* Gibbs and Davis, 1961; Berry, 1967).

world regions was as shown in Table 13-3. It is evident that by this index high primacy was loosely associated with low economic development, small size of country and total population, and a traditional centralization of culture and political power. In Latin America, the region with the highest primacy, the only three countries with an index below unity, Brazil,

Table 13-3. Mean Primacy for "Metropolitan Areas" of Major World Regions, 1950–55

| REGION | NUMBER OF COUNTRIES | MEAN PRIMACY OF COUNTRIES |
|---|---|---|
| Latin America | 22 | 2.94 |
| Asia (excluding Near East) | 10 | 2.35 |
| Europe (including USSR) | 22 | 1.84 |
| Near East and North Africa | 15 | 1.50 |
| Central and South Africa | 9 | 1.26 |
| Northern America and Oceania | 4 | 0.75 |
| TOTAL | 82 | 2.01 |

SOURCE: Kingsley Davis, "Las causas y efectos del fenomeno de primacía urbana, con referencia especial a América Latina," *Proceedings of the 14th Annual Congress*, Mexican Sociological Society, Hermosillo, Sonora, 1962.

Colombia, and Ecuador, have a topography (as well as, in the case of Brazil, an enormous size) that impeded the development of national unity, with a consequent rise of important regional capitals. More generally, the relatively small countries of Latin America (their average population was 7.2 million, compared with 35.6 million for the rest of the eighty-two) have concentrated their administrative, political, religious, and cultural life very heavily in one major city, the national capital in every case but Ecuador. Nor have economic forces generally fostered the growth of competing centers. A transshipment point for the raw materials that Latin America produces (ores and metals, petroleum, various agricultural products) is not likely to develop from this function, and the Latin American equivalent of a market town has typically been too much dominated by the neighboring hacienda to grow into an important regional center.

The haciendas which surround the town buy little. Their peons have no money and the hacienda grows and manufactures very nearly all that it requires. The town has no important distributing function. The hacienda sells relatively little, considering its size and the number of people living on it. What it does sell is marketed, usually, on a wholesale basis by some agent employed by the hacienda, or by a member of the family. . . . Even the mule pack carrying the hacienda goods to the city or the nearest railroad belongs to the hacienda. . . .

[Moreover,] the great family will control every local office, from the colonel of the local militia to the rural police. The tax gatherer, the mayor, the judge, the postmaster, will be related directly or through marriage or as godfathers to members of the family.[7]

A person who wants to escape from this domination, whether a peon who migrates to a big city or a young man beginning a professional career, is induced to go to the only place, if that, where the hacendado's power does not reach. This dominance by the hacienda is not, of course, a recent development (cf. Morse, 1962), and the high primacy of Latin American city systems also goes back to the sixteenth century.

Apart from such political and cultural factors, are primacy and economic development generally related? According to one study, the association of uniformly defined "Metropolitan Areas" with modernization "becomes closer as the extent of urbanization increases" (Wilkinson, 1960). Another analyst found that "different city-size distributions are in no way related to the relative economic development of countries" (Berry, 1961). Yet another concluded that the primacy of city systems "does not appear to be a function of the level of economic development, industrialization, or urbanization," but rather that high primacy is associated with "small areal and population size" (Mehta, 1964). At most, one can conclude that whatever association there may be between the two factors is loose and easily negated by other characteristics of the city system.

### SOCIAL CHARACTERISTICS BY SIZE OF PLACE

In their census monograph on the population of the United States in 1950, Duncan and Reiss divided the urban-rural continuum into eleven size-classes, which are shown here in Table 13-4. So detailed a breakdown proves its utility in their analysis, in part by differentiating those characteristics that increase (or decrease) regularly through the continuum from those whose relation to size of place is more complex. The correlation between size of place and personal income is the most striking. The median income of males (columns 7 and 8) ranged from $3,078 to $1,379 among whites and from $2,226 to $569 among nonwhites. The considerably lower incomes of females, whether considered as a unit or divided by race, were also directly correlated with size of place. For either sex the progression was in part a reflection of regional differences (the South, in particular, had the lowest median income as well as the least urbanization), but within each region income still varied together with size of place, even when educational level and type of occupation were held constant. As the money a person earns is an important determinant of a wide variety of

[7] Frank Tannenbaum, *Ten Keys to Latin America*, Random House, Vintage, New York, 1966, pp. 88–89.

## Table 13-4. Selected Social Characteristics by Size of Place, United States, 1950

| SIZE OF PLACE | SEX RATIO | MEDIAN AGE | MARRIED[a] WHITE MALE | MARRIED[a] WHITE FEMALE | CHILD-WOMAN RATIO[b] | PER CENT NON-MOBILE[c] | MEDIAN INCOME[d] WHITE | MEDIAN INCOME[d] NONWHITE |
|---|---|---|---|---|---|---|---|---|
| | (1) | (2) | (3) | (4) | (5) | (6) | (7) | (8) |
| Urbanized Areas: | | | | | | | | |
| 3,000,000 or more | 94.0 | 33.7 | −2.5 | −4.2 | 433 | 85.1 | $3,078 | $2,213 |
| 1,000,000 to 3,000,000 | 94.3 | 32.0 | −2.4 | −4.1 | 478 | 83.4 | 3,026 | 2,226 |
| 250,000 to 1,000,000 | 94.0 | 31.5 | 0.5 | −2.6 | 503 | 78.9 | 2,779 | 1,695 |
| Under 250,000 | 93.5 | 30.9 | 1.0 | −1.8 | 510 | 79.9 | 2,692 | 1,543 |
| Places outside Urbanized Areas: | | | | | | | | |
| 25,000 or more | 93.7 | 30.4 | 0.7 | −1.8 | 522 | 77.5 | 2,554 | 1,407 |
| 10,000 to 25,000 | 93.0 | 30.3 | 1.9 | −0.7 | 525 | 77.8 | 2,484 | 1,275 |
| 2,500 to 10,000 | 93.1 | 29.9 | 2.6 | 1.3 | 570 | 79.0 | 2,354 | 1,134 |
| 1,000 to 2,500 | 94.3 | 30.2 | 3.1 | 3.2 | 609 | 81.0 | 2,268 | 1,092 |
| Under 1,000 (incorporated) | 93.8 | 32.3 | 2.7 | 4.9 | 629 | 82.1 | 1,935 | 807 |
| Other rural: | | | | | | | | |
| Nonfarm | 105.7 | 26.5 | 0.5 | 6.2 | 717 | 76.5 | 2,029 | 974 |
| Farm | 109.5 | 26.1 | −0.2 | 8.4 | 766 | 85.2 | 1,379 | 569 |
| TOTAL United States | 97.6 | 30.2 | 0 | 0 | 587 | 81.1 | 2,572 | 1,341 |

SOURCE: Otis Dudley Duncan and Albert J. Reiss, Jr., *Social Characteristics of Urban and Rural Communities, 1950*, Wiley, New York, 1956, Tables 3, 4, 6, 15, 21, and 38. Copyright © 1956 by The Social Science Research Council.

[a] Deviation from per cent expected on the basis of age structure.

[b] Children under 5 years per 1,000 women aged 20 to 44.

[c] Per cent of population one year and over living in same house in 1949 and 1950.

[d] Median income of males 14 years and over with an income, 1949.

social characteristics, one would expect to find, were the data available, a gradient in style of life by size of place.

When the effect of the age structure was eliminated, the proportion of the whites married was correlated with the size of place, especially among females (columns 3 and 4). The data suggest that the age at first marriage was higher in larger places, and that the proportion of marriages dissolved was greater. Partly as a consequence of these differences in family formation, there is also the expected correlation between size of place and fertility, as measured by the number of children under 5 years per 1,000 women aged 20 to 44 (column 5). The median age (column 2), which in part reflects the fertility, varies as one would anticipate except that villages, especially small ones, deviate from the gradient.

The sex ratio (column 1), on the other hand, has a different pattern altogether: the whole population was more or less the same except "other rural," which was 10 to 15 points higher. That is to say, except in the West, the excess of females obtained in all sizes of urban places.

The relation between internal migration and size of place was different again. The percentage of the population living in the same house in 1949 and 1950 (column 6) formed a U-shaped curve. While there was a considerable variation among the four regions (the percentages nonmobile were: Northeast, 87; North Central, 83; South, 77; and West, 73), within each region the same relation with size of place held.

Several general conclusions can be drawn from the data reported in this table: (1) The conventional division between rural and urban, a population of 2,500 and over, does not mark an important break in any of the series. Nor is any alternative dividing point any better. The social world is too complicated to be analyzed any longer by a simple dichotomy, as the Census Bureau itself has in effect recognized in the growing complexity of its statistical indexes. "Rural" and "urban," at least with respect to contemporary United States, designate contrasting poles of a continuum rather than categories. (2) The "rural nonfarm" population does not fit into the size-of-place continuum. The reason, as one might suspect from its very name, is undoubtedly that it is too composite a grouping. (3) Some social characteristics vary with size of place (for example, income, marriage patterns, fertility), but this is not true of all (for example, sex ratio, mobility).

## Spatial Patterns Within the Urban Community

Just as "urban" denotes a more complicated structure than "rural," so "metropolitan" implies a still greater complexity, though the difference is generally only in degree. A farmhouse is both the center of agricultural production and the home of the farmer's family, and in a town a grocer, a physician, or a small manufacturer may live at his place of work. It is typical of the urban setting, however, that the residential neighborhood (or suburb) is separated from the business quarter. Within each type, moreover, a finer division is ordinarily discernible. Residential areas are lower or middle or upper class; they may have so high a proportion of a particular ethnic group as to become, for example, a "Little Italy" or a Harlem. Commercial enterprises, similarly, tend to be grouped into, say, a financial district, an amusement area, an industrial zone, a downtown business section, and so on. What factors influence this kind of patterning? Do they apply only to particular cities, neighborhoods, or industries, or are there also general determinants?

## CONCENTRIC ZONES IN THE UNITED STATES

One of the first serious attempts in the United States to answer questions of this kind was made in the 1920s by Ernest W. Burgess of the University of Chicago. According to his theory, all modern American cities (in the first statement he had spoken of "any town or city") are spatially divided into five concentric zones: (1) a central business district; (2) a "transitional" zone of deteriorating real property used as boarding houses; and three residential areas: (3) working-class, (4) middle-class, and (5) upper middle-class.[8] For a number of years, this hypothesis dominated both theory and research in urban sociology, particularly at Chicago. Monographs were written on the spatial distribution of crime and delinquency, family patterns, mental disorders, and other social characteristics; and all tended to validate the theory. Then, some ten or fifteen years after its initial formulation, the hypothesis of concentric-circular zones was subjected to a good deal of criticism, both theoretically and empirically based. Although the empirical studies of some cities in addition to Chicago seemed to confirm the hypothesis (St. Louis, Rochester), other cities apparently had more complex and altogether different spatial patterns (New Haven, Boston, Pittsburgh, New York, Flint). According to even a sympathetic critic, "The hypothesis of concentric zones as formulated by Burgess needs to be seriously modified if, indeed, it can be defended at all."[9]

The main reason it breaks down is that the nonresidential portion of a city is ordinarily not so unified, either functionally or spatially, as Burgess's "central business district." Remarkably, Burgess had no place in his schema for industry (cf. Davie, 1937), nor even for differentiation among several types of commercial ventures. If residential areas vary according to the distance from nonresidential centers, as is posited in the concentric-zone hypothesis, then one must first investigate the factors that determine the

[8] The theory was first offered in a paper read before the American Sociological Society in 1923. Its most mature statement is in Burgess, 1929.

[9] James A. Quinn, *Human Ecology*, Prentice-Hall, New York, 1950, p. 135. The adverse judgment by other analysts is both broader and harsher; see in particular Milla A. Alihan, *Social Ecology: A Critical Analysis*, Columbia University Press, New York, 1938.

location of commercial and industrial areas. Once the unrealistic assumption is abandoned that these are necessarily combined into a single all-encompassing unit, then the concentric circles spreading out from each one of a number of business or industrial districts overlap into the various structures to be seen in American cities.

Location theory is a branch of economics. It would not be feasible or appropriate to do more here than indicate its subject matter.[10] Each entrepreneur, when he decides where to establish a new factory or office, ideally weighs the relative advantages and disadvantages of alternative locations in terms of a large number of factors, all of which, moreover, are constantly changing.

Since the size of the market for any firm was circumscribed by high overland transport costs, our early factories and foundries had to make the best of local sources of supply and had to market their goods close to where they were made. But in the middle of the nineteenth century transport costs declined dramatically; at the same time, mass production methods gave a heavy edge in production costs to the larger firms over their smaller competitors. For a time, then, a new balance was struck. The new large-scale firms could afford to take advantage of superior materials, wherever they might be, and to ship their products for longer distances to their markets.

Then came the third stage: The relative fall of transportation costs which was so dramatic in the nineteenth century was arrested and finally reversed in the first half of the twentieth century. At the same time, many local markets grew sufficiently large to accommodate plants with most or all of the cost advantages associated with mass production. As a result, the pattern of expansion of the large firms tended more and more toward the establishment of plants closer to their local markets (Vernon, 1957).

The trend in the location of residential areas has been parallel. With the growing population density in city centers, an impetus to move to the periphery started as early as 1900. In the United States, the old family home ordinarily counted for much less than a brand new house in a "nice neighborhood," as far away as possible from the dirt and noise of the business district. Decentralization could not be realized by appreciable numbers, however, until after the full development of automobiles and good roads, electric railroads, and a telephone network. The metropolitan community is "the direct result of motor transportation and its revolutionary effect upon local spatial relations." [11] By the 1920s the same transportation system

[10] For more detailed treatments, see August Lösch, *The Economics of Location*, Yale University Press, New Haven, 1954; Walter Isard, *Location and Space-Economy: A General Theory Relating to Industrial Location, Market Areas, Land Use, Trade, and Urban Structure*, Massachusetts Institute of Technology; Wiley, New York, 1956. A good summary of the subject is given in William Alonso, "Location Theory," in Friedmann and Alonso, 1964, pp. 78–106.

[11] R. F. McKenzie, *The Metropolitan Community*, McGraw-Hill, New York, 1933, p. 69.

Congestion in central cities has increased the impetus toward decentralization.

*Above:* A four-layer crossover in Los Angeles (*J. R. Eyerman—courtesy* Life © *1953 Time, Inc.*).

*Right:* The building of the Long Island Expressway near Central Islip, 1965. Even before the road was completed, real estate developers established a new suburban community, whose residents helped crowd the highway as soon as they were permitted on it (*Drennan Photos*).

enabled the husband to commute to work daily and the wife to make periodic shopping trips to the center. Better roads or faster trains did not so much cut down the hours spent in travel as increase the distance covered. In short, the concentration into American cities up to about 1920 was countered after that date by an out-migration to the suburbs (Hawley, 1956).

In order to see the trends more clearly, some finer distinctions are required. By definition, it will be recalled, metropolitan areas include a city of 50,000 or more inhabitants; this is termed the "central city" and the remainder of the SMSA is termed the "ring." The ring is divided into **suburbs,** primarily residential areas from which many commute to their place of work in the central city, and **satellites,** which provide their residents with jobs (Schnore, 1957). The distinction cannot be a sharp one, for suburbs tend to develop their own economic life and become more like

satellites. With increasingly crowded trains and clogged roads, suburbanites paid ever more heavily in time and nervous energy for every trip to the center. A department store, a lawyer's office, or even a business firm got a competitive advantage by moving out to the consumer market. The extra floor space needed by a growing corporation, not to be bought at a reasonable cost in the downtown area, was available at the periphery. And middle-class suburbs, which initially tried to maintain their purely residential function, found that the cost of schools and other public services became very burdensome. The extra taxes that new business and industry brought became so welcome that suburban communities, far from barring them, on

Moving day in a Los Angeles housing development (*J. R. Eyerman—courtesy* Life © *1953 Time, Inc.*).

occasion sought them out. And as more and more urban conveniences became available outside the central cities, the out-migration of the middle class tended to increase.

Some of the middle-class out-migrants were replaced by in-migrants from rural areas or small towns seeking working-class jobs in the big city. On balance, however, the decentralization of metropolitan populations has accelerated in the recent period. From 1960 to 1965, while the metropolitan population increased almost three times as fast as the nonmetro-

Table 13-5. Population by Metropolitan and Nonmetropolitan Residence, United
States, 1960–65

|  | POPULATION (MILLIONS) | | AVERAGE ANNUAL INCREASE (PER CENT) | |
|---|---|---|---|---|
|  | 1960 | 1965 | 1950–60 | 1960–65 |
| 212 SMSAs | 112.3 | 123.8 | 2.3 | 1.9 |
| Central cities | 57.8 | 59.6 | 1.0 | 0.6 |
| Rings | 54.5 | 64.2 | 4.0 | 3.3 |
| Nonmetropolitan areas | 66.1 | 68.4 | 0.8 | 0.7 |
| TOTALS | 178.5 | 192.2 | 1.7 | 1.5 |

SOURCE: "Population of the United States by Metropolitan and Nonmetropolitan Residence, April 1965 and 1960," U.S. Bureau of the Census, *Current Population Reports,* Series P-20, No. 151, April 19, 1966.

politan, the growth of the rings was more than five times as fast as that of the central cities (Table 13-5).

By the decentralization of commercial and industrial enterprises, metropolitan areas have in some respects become more homogeneous. The popular view that "the" suburb is a middle-class, or even upper middle-class, dormitory is not entirely correct. On the one hand, some smaller places in SMSAs, whether suburbs or satellites, are thoroughly working-class in all their characteristics (e.g., Berger, 1960). And on the other hand, neighborhoods of older cities that have enjoyed a long period of gentility sometimes retain, or even recover if they lost them, the upper-class residents associated with that way of life (e.g., Firey, 1947). Whether the central city differs greatly in social-economic status from the suburb depends largely on how old the settlement is. In long established metropolises, the well-to-do have moved out to the suburbs, whereas in newer ones central cities often rank higher than the rings in education, occupation, and income (Schnore, 1963). As this datum suggests, suburbanization is a process.

Two fairly distinct phases of suburban development can be distinguished. The first is characterized by the efforts of individual urban families and of certain special kinds of urban social groups to take advantage of the opportunity offered by the open countryside to escape the burdens of life in the large city. . . . Individual families have simply moved out into the country on their own, settling wherever opportunity offered, along some back road, on the outskirts of old established villages or towns, or in hidden pockets of the open country where land is of such poor quality that it cannot be profitably farmed. . . . In contrast with packaged suburbs of the Park Forest type . . . there are these very different residential areas, created by the completely haphazard dispersion from the city of individual families, ranging from the very rich to the very poor, and differing as much in social values as in material possessions. . . .

Urbanization comes only with a very different type of development, in which the urban population overruns the countryside and occupies all at once great stretches of farm land. Yet it is this earlier phase of development which creates the conditions for the later. The mass movement into the suburbs comes only with the production of the kind of housing that reaches a mass market, and before this can happen the occupation of the countryside must have become great enough to support a certain level of urban services (Clark, 1963).

The Burgess model, then, can be made to fit the urban patterns of the United States only after significant modifications, and it is even less well suited to other countries. In a few West European countries there has been a redistribution of metropolitan populations somewhat in accordance with the model (on Denmark, for instance, see Goldstein, 1963, 1965). But in much of Europe government controls greatly affect the pattern. Such a suburb, for instance, as Bandhagen, nine miles out of Stockholm, is a contrived mixture of high-rise apartments and smaller dwellings; and Britain's New Towns are supposed to include a wide range of social-economic groups.

### THE CENTRAL PLAZA IN LATIN AMERICA

In some respects, the Burgess model contradicts the spatial distribution that common sense would suggest. Since commutation between home and place of work is the more onerous, the greater the daily journey between them, one might have expected the well-to-do to live in convenient proximity to their offices, while the poor had to add perhaps two hours' unpaid traveling time to their work-day. Indeed, this is the relation that developed in some countries, particularly where a strong sense of family continuity made it important to retain the same dwelling from one generation to the next.

Latin America typifies a style of urban structure reminiscent of Europe's Renaissance cities. Two Andalusian towns built shortly before Columbus's voyages, Puerto Real (1483) and Santa Fé de Granada (1491), set the rigorous form followed for hundreds of new towns in Spanish America over the following centuries.[12] This implicit model, moreover, was spelled out in

[12] George M. Foster, *Culture and Conquest: America's Spanish Heritage*, Quadrangle Books, Chicago, 1960, especially Chapter 4: "Cities, Towns, and Villages: The Grid-Plan Puzzle."

a carefully developed policy embodied first of all in the famous sixteenth-century Laws of the Indies.[13]

As a result of the standard laws, such distant cities as Bogotá, Colombia, and Concepción, Chile, and practically every city between, have exactly the same size of block, the same width of street, the same general urban pattern. . . . A uniformity of city layout has been rubber-stamped all over the face of the continent no matter what the site, hill or dale, valley or pampa (Violich, 1944, p. 28).[14]

Perhaps the most interesting physical feature is the main plaza, which though based on a European pattern is socially far more important in Spanish America than in Spain (Ricard, 1950, 1952; cf. Violich, 1962; Davis, 1960). Still today in Spanish America, the preference of the upper middle class for the environs of the plaza affects the whole city. It is generally difficult to move schools or other public buildings from their traditional central location to a presently more convenient site; business also concentrates in the center and cannot easily be dislodged. This prestige of the plaza is reflected in the land values of small Hispanic towns, but not of small Indian towns. Thus, "overcentralization is probably the most serious problem in the Latin American city." In many instances, similarly, the gridiron pattern has been followed with little or no change from the original model. For example, the design of Buenos Aires that was made in 1580 included 250 blocks, of which only 46 were built up initially. The subsequent growth of the city followed the original plan, with no subcenters,

[13] See Zelia Nuttall, "Royal Ordinances Concerning the Laying Out of New Towns," *Hispanic American Historical Review*, 4 (1921), 743–753; 5 (1922), 249–254. (The first of the two articles gives the Spanish text of the ordinances pertaining to the founding of new cities, a short commentary, and a garbled translation; a correct translation is given in the second.) By the royal will, before any new settlement was built, its plan was to be laid out with measuring cord and ruler, beginning with the main plaza, which for a medium-sized town was to be 600 by 400 feet. From the plaza the four principal streets were to diverge, one from the middle of each of its sides. "In cold climates the streets shall be wide, in hot climates narrow; however, for purposes of defense and where horses are kept the streets had better be wide." The first buildings to be erected were the church and monastery, then the royal and town houses and their administrative annexes. Meanwhile the settlers were to live in tents and "erect jointly some kind of palisade . . . around the main plaza so that the Indians cannot do them harm." "Settlers are to endeavor, as far as possible, to make all structures uniform, for the sake of the beauty of the town." Land outside the settlement was to be distributed among as many persons as there were qualified to draw lots for the plots.

[14] Kubler (1964) points out that this uniformity has sometimes been overstressed, for "a wide range of variation appears in the spatial arrangement of colonial cities." The difference, I would judge, is only in emphasis. One should note, however, that Spanish American cities were far less stable than their European counterparts, in spite of the metropolitan government's pro-urban policy. In dozens of cases, ranging in eventual importance from Buenos Aires or Havana down to much smaller places, towns were founded, abandoned, then refounded on the same or another site, and it was in part this fluidity that accounted for their great number.

either designed or other, and no functional division other than the overriding one between the center and everything else.[15]

Like the cities of other multiracial societies, those of Latin America have generally been racially zoned. Of the dozen or more case studies (*cf.* Smith, 1963), perhaps the most interesting is an analysis of Mérida, the capital of Yucatan State, Mexico, for it is one of the few that relates segregation to historical change (Hansen, 1934). The ecological pattern that the Spaniards set was "as stable as the social and cultural situation of which it was a part": the whites lived around the central plaza, the Indians in the barrios (literally, "quarters") some distance off; and as the city grew the barrios were moved farther out. The correlation was so high that one could designate social class by referring to spatial position—"the people of the center" versus "the people of the barrios" or the *"barrianos."* Each barrio was both a lower-class quarter of the city and in some respects a semi-autonomous village, with a community life, organized around its own square, under the rule of an Indian cacique. In the 1880s a man who had been to the United States tried to subdivide his land outside the city into a middle-class suburb, but both this venture and a subsequent one several years later failed completely. The traditional pattern was partially broken in the 1890s, when a sharp rise in the price of sisal, the area's main commodity, set off a real-estate boom. Though the plantation owners and substantial professionals retained their attachment to the plaza, the new rich moved to a new suburb on the far side of the barrios, reached by a new boulevard. Thus sandwiched between two parts of the growing city, the barrios were gradually transformed from more or less discrete communities into precincts.

In summary, one can distinguish some of the factors that determine the spatial distribution of city sectors, but these do not typically operate together to produce a uniform pattern in all the cities even of one culture, not to say of the world:

**1.** Industrialization (in the form of factories, lofts, office buildings, railroads, highways, airports, etc.) spreads by laws of its own, only somewhat altered by zoning regulations. Depending on the nature of his enterprise, an entrepreneur may want to locate close to raw material, skilled labor, or the consumer market; near the urban center or on cheap land at the periphery (e.g., the "industrial parks" around many American cities); near transportation facilities or away from high taxes. However industrial and commercial facilities are distributed, these determine in large part the residential pattern.

**2.** The well-to-do, who have the greatest possibility of realizing their choice of where to live, do not generally choose alike, even apart from

---

[15] Ralph A. Gakenheimer, "The Spanish King and His Continent: A Study of the Importance of the 'Laws of the Indies' for Urban Development in Spanish America" (unpublished master's thesis in regional planning, Cornell University, 1959).

individual taste. A wealthy family may want to locate near the metropolitan center or with at least a facsimile of countryside; in a home and neighborhood old enough to have a tradition or in a brand new residence; but in any case, away from industrial and commercial facilities and close to pleasant parks, good schools, and other amenities.

3. The poor flow into the interstices between industry and middle-class neighborhoods—close to railroads or factories, in areas with deteriorated property, in quarters inconveniently far from the center or, in many countries, wherever in the urban area they can establish a squatter's claim. A quarter that has developed into a slum repels the settlement of the well-to-do almost as effectively as an industrial facility, though for a generation or more contiguous areas may compete to set the tone of a city sector.

4. These three elements of urban life—industry, middle-class residences, and the homes of the poor—do not establish a fixed areal pattern but interact in a continuous and ever-changing process. Elegant neighborhoods, once the average age of their buildings is about a quarter of a century, may begin to slide down the social scale, and this slippage typically accelerates their physical deterioration. The consequent slum, on the other hand, may after some time be razed and supplanted by buildings designed to improve the tone of the quarter. Neither the constant pressure of commercial enterprises to find more suitable settings nor the counterpressure to restrict their expansion can be summarized in one all-embracing law of urban patterning. Thus, when analysts of "the" city—or of a number of cities of approximately equal age in the same culture—find a pattern, it is like one still in a reel of moving pictures.

## Cities in Economic Development

We all know, of course, that industrialization and urbanization have been related in the past. Before 1850 no society of the world was predominantly urban, and by 1900 only one, Great Britain, had become so; today all industrial nations are highly urban. In the United States, as one instance, the proportion of the population living in metropolitan areas with 100,000 or more inhabitants increased from just under one-third in 1900 to almost two-thirds in 1960. At the latter date about 70 per cent of the population of the United States was urban by the conventional cut-off point of 2,500 inhabitants, and just over half of the total population was concentrated in the 213 urbanized areas, which comprised under one per cent of the land surface. If we count metropolitan size by "urban agglomerates" (the United Nations equivalent of urbanized areas), around 1960 the world had two cities (New York and Tokyo) with populations of more than 10 million, seven more (London, Paris, Buenos Aires, Shanghai, Los Angeles, Moscow, and Chicago) with populations between 5 and 10 million, twelve more (Calcutta, Bombay, Peking, Philadelphia, Leningrad, Detroit, Cairo, Rio de

Janeiro, Tientsin, São Paulo, Osaka, and Mexico City) with populations between 3 and 5 million, and fifteen more with populations between 2 and 3 million (Davis, 1965).[16] While the very largest of these agglomerates were in industrial nations, this was by no means so of all of them.

Indeed, the city growth that was historically associated with industrialization has recently been even faster in some underdeveloped areas. For instance, Latin America, especially but not exclusively in the countries intermediate between underdeveloped and modern, is heavily urbanized (Table 13-6). Half of all Latin Americans live in cities, and more than a quarter in

Table 13-6. Estimated and Projected Population of Latin American Countries and Per Cent Urban, 1965 and 1980

| | PER CENT URBAN | | POPULATION (MILLIONS) | |
| --- | --- | --- | --- | --- |
| | 1965 | 1980[a] | 1965 | 1980[a] |
| Uruguay | 83 | 85 | 2.7 | 3.1 |
| Argentina | 69 | 72 | 22.9 | 29.3 |
| Chile | 68 | 75 | 8.6 | 12.3 |
| Venezuela | 67 | 74 | 8.7 | 14.8 |
| Mexico | 59 | 71 | 42.7 | 72.7 |
| Colombia | 50 | 62 | 17.8 | 27.7 |
| Panama | 45 | 54 | 1.2 | 1.8 |
| Brazil | 44 | 54 | 81.3 | 123.6 |
| Peru | 43 | 53 | 11.7 | 18.5 |
| Nicaragua | 36 | 46 | 1.7 | 2.9 |
| Ecuador | 36 | 44 | 5.0 | 6.1 |
| Costa Rica | 34 | 43 | 1.5 | 2.5 |
| Bolivia | 33 | 42 | 4.1 | 6.0 |
| Guatemala | 32 | 42 | 4.3 | 6.9 |
| El Salvador | 31 | 36 | 2.9 | 4.7 |
| Dominican Republic | 31 | 40 | 3.6 | 6.1 |
| Paraguay | 29 | 30 | 2.0 | 3.1 |
| Honduras | 26 | 35 | 2.3 | 3.9 |
| Haiti | 15 | 25 | 4.6 | 6.9 |
| TOTAL | 50 | 59 | 229.5 | 355.1 |

SOURCE: United Nations, Economic Commission for Latin America, *Statistical Bulletin,* August 1965.

[a] Assuming constant rates of fertility, mortality, and migration.

[16] For a perceptive description of some of these metropolises, well illustrated with photographs and maps, see Hall, 1966.

the ten metropolises with over a million inhabitants each. According to a United Nations projection to 1980, the very rapid growth of the area will be mainly in the cities: over the fifteen years from 1965 the rural population is expected to grow by over 30 million, the urban by about 340 million.

In short, while industrialization has invariably resulted in a massive shift to cities, it is not a *necessary* condition to rapid urbanization. More than half of the inhabitants of a country that by any other index would be designated as underdeveloped may live in its cities (*cf.* p. 434). Since most of the countries that lack industry would like to acquire it without the massive social cost (as they see it) of urbanization, the relation between the two processes is crucial to policy. Unfortunately, the social sciences can offer government officials no firm guides. "No systematic study has ever been made of the role of cities" in the economic development of advanced countries, and furthermore "no branch of economics yet studies the city in a comprehensive way" (Lampard, 1955). However, though it is not possible to state definitely how cities function in economic development, one can— as in the remaining sections of this chapter—approach the question from several sides and thus attain some partial insights.

## Occupational and Social Categories

It is manifest that the division between town and countryside is related to the way any population breaks down by occupation and thus by social class, but the association is seldom simple. Not only is the urban-rural division set, as we have seen, by partly arbitrary criteria, but this is true also of the classification of occupations and of the distinction between those who are and are not economically active.

Such ambiguities in the definition of the labor force are especially pertinent to any international comparisons. They are discussed in terms of four successively smaller subdivisions of a population:

1. In any population only a certain portion, designated as its **labor pool**, is capable of gainful work. The very young and the very old are dependent on the intermediate age group (*cf.* pp. 66–73), but at what ages does a person move from one category to the next? In the United States the minimum age of those in the labor pool was twice raised, from ten to fourteen years between the 1930 and the 1940 censuses, and from fourteen to sixteen as of January 1967.[17] This reflects the virtual elimination of child labor in this country, but the present dividing line is hardly relevant to the situation in many other cultures. Among the potentially active population

[17] John D. Durand, *The Labor Force in the United States, 1890–1960*, Social Science Research Council, New York, 1948, especially Chapter 2 and Appendix A; "Concepts and Methods Used in Manpower Statistics from the Current Population Survey," U.S. Bureau of the Census, *Current Population Reports*, Series P-23, No. 22, June 1967.

demarcated by age, moreover, some are insane or feeble-minded, disabled, or for other reasons not capable of performing useful work. Here again, the norms of each society partly define the limits of this category, though the total proportion of incapacitated is in any case small relative to that of dependent young and aged.

2. A greater proportion of the potential work force of any society, its labor pool, can be realized during such a national emergency as a major war, for in a normal period several categories are omitted from the labor force—those who maintain childhood roles beyond the age defining economic maturity (i.e., students) or who retire before the supposed end of their working life, and also those who work not in the labor market for wages but in their own household without remuneration (i.e., most adult females). Thus, around 1960 between 59 per cent (industrial countries) and 52 per cent (underdeveloped countries) of all males were listed as economically active, but only about a quarter of all females (Sadie, 1967). In fact, it is prudent in such international comparisons to omit females altogether, since the way their economic activity is recorded varies too much from country to country. However, this kind of ambiguity also characterizes male peasants' activities, which constitute both an extension of their domestic establishment and participation in a national economy.

The real difficulty is the impossibility of defining "labor" in any way that will refer to the same class of human activities in all societies. . . . "Production" is likely to entail esthetic, magical, or religious elements, entails kinship elements by definition, and must entail the allocation of power and responsibility (Moore, 1953).

In particular, it would be hazardous to take as an implicit model for cross-cultural analysis the situation in the United States, with its highly rationalized agriculture and the generally sharp separation between economic and other social roles.

3. The distinction between armed forces and the civilian labor force is usually clearcut (an area in which guerrillas are operating is not generally one where statistics of any kind can be collected).

4. Note that "occupied" and "employed" are not synonymous: a person not at work on a specific day is nevertheless "employed"; one unemployed but seeking a job is "occupied." As of January 1967, the slightly revised definition of an unemployed person in the United States was as follows: one who during a periodic survey is not gainfully employed, is currently available for work, and actively sought a job during the past four weeks. Those absent from a job during the survey week because of illness, a strike, bad weather, etc., are classified as employed even if they are seeking another job. In peasant countries it is still more difficult to delimit employed from unemployed, for between them there is a loosely defined category of "hidden unemployment"—comprising all those economically surplus on a job

who are retained because of family ties or other economically irrelevant considerations.

In the 1960 United States census, occupied persons were classified into 297 "occupation categories," many of which included dozens of specific occupations. If it were possible to rank occupations, or even occupation categories, by the social status associated with each, changes in the proportion of the labor force engaged in each would be a good index of social mobility. Differences over time in the still more heterogeneous "major occupational groups" give a rough indication of a significant over-all advance (Table 13–7). The greatest proportionate increase during this century was

Table 13-7. Percentage Distribution of Experienced Labor Force by Major Occupational Group, United States, 1900–65

| | 1900 | 1930 | 1960 | 1965 [a] | PER CENT CHANGE | |
|---|---|---|---|---|---|---|
| | | | | | 1900– 65 | 1960– 65 |
| Professional, technical, and kindred workers | 4.3 | 6.8 | 11.2 | 12.9 | +200 | +15 |
| Farmers and farm managers | 19.9 | 12.4 | 3.9 | 3.2 | −84 | −19 |
| Managers, officials, and proprietors, except farm | 5.8 | 7.4 | 8.4 | 10.7 | +84 | +27 |
| Clerical and kindred workers | 3.0 | 8.9 | 14.4 | 15.6 | +420 | +8 |
| Sales workers | 4.5 | 6.3 | 7.2 | 6.5 | +44 | −10 |
| Craftsmen, foremen, and kindred workers | 10.5 | 12.8 | 13.5 | 12.4 | +18 | −8 |
| Operatives and kindred workers | 12.8 | 15.8 | 18.4 | 18.7 | +46 | +0.2 |
| Private household workers | 5.4 | 4.1 | 2.7 | 3.1 | −42 | +15 |
| Service workers, except private household | 3.6 | 5.7 | 8.4 | 9.7 | +169 | +16 |
| Farm laborers and foremen | 17.7 | 8.8 | 2.2 | 2.1 | −88 | >0.05 |
| Laborers, except farm and mine | 12.5 | 11.0 | 4.8 | 5.1 | −67 | +0.6 |
| Occupation not reported | — | — | 4.9 | — | — | — |
| TOTAL | 100.0 | 100.0 | 100.0 | 100.0 | | |

SOURCES: U.S. Bureau of the Census, *U.S. Census Population: 1960, Characteristics of the Population, U.S. Summary,* U.S. Department of Commerce, Washington, D.C., 1964, p. 1–216; Donald J. Bogue, *Population of the United States,* Free Press of Glencoe, New York, 1959, p. 475; U.S. Bureau of the Census, *Statistical Abstract of the United States, 1965,* U.S. Department of Commerce, Washington, D.C., 1965, Table 313.
[a] Employed persons as of March, based on Bureau of Labor Statistics survey.

in white-collar jobs, both clerical and professional; and the categories in which there was a decline, apart from all occupations associated with agriculture,[18] were unskilled and household labor. This record, although its dimensions are related to the size, wealth, and social democracy of the United States, reflects also the shift associated anywhere with advanced industrialism—out of low-level menial jobs and to service industries and professions.

### TYPES OF RURAL-URBAN MIGRATION

Among the various reasons that internal and international migrations are distinguished conceptually, the most important is the premise that the former does, and the latter does not, constitute a movement within a single culture area. Although this postulate does not hold everywhere (*cf.* p. 41), it is often well based in modern nations. For modernization has meant, among other things, that the literacy and cultural amenities, the electricity and running water, once found almost exclusively in the towns are now close to universal. An American farmboy who moves to a large city will find much that is strange, but before he leaves home he usually will have been equipped for a rapid and relatively easy adjustment to the new environment.

In many respects, the distance between rural and urban is greater in underdeveloped than in industrial countries. The relevance of this greater disparity for the prospects of modernization was analyzed in great detail by the Dutch economist Boeke, following his considerable experience in the Netherlands East Indies. According to his concept of a **dual economy,** the European sector operated in accordance with the interrelated postulates of Western economic theory—that consumers' wants are unlimited, that the economy is based on a money exchange, that each consumer acts as an individual in the market (or actually often in both a local and an international market). But these premises did not apply, or applied only in part, to the native sector of the dual economy. In the pre-independence Indonesian village, the economic unit was not the individual but the family. Work was done to satisfy needs set by physiology and hereditary status; apart from the number of dependents, they were therefore relatively fixed. As a family grew larger, the person responsible for its care had to work harder; but if it was small, he worked only enough to maintain his charges at their appropriate level. The consequences for the operation of elementary economic "laws" were bizarre.

[18] In the United States the percentage of occupied persons employed in agriculture fell from an estimated 83 in 1820 to 53 in 1870 to a little over 30 in 1910. From the last date, the decline continued not only proportionately but also in absolute numbers. In 1960, the farm population constituted only 8.7 per cent of the total or, in absolute figures, 15.6 million, about the same number as at the time of the Civil War. By 1965, those engaged in agriculture constituted only 5.3 per cent of the labor force. With the vast improvement in agricultural labor productivity, the principal rural occupation was increasingly unable to absorb all the manpower available.

When the price of rice or coconuts is high, the chances are that less of these commodities will be offered for sale; when wages are raised, the manager of the estate risks that less work will be done; if three acres are enough to supply the needs of the household a cultivator will not till six; only when rubber prices fall does the owner of a grove begin to tap more intensively, whereas high prices mean that he will leave a larger or smaller portion of his tappable trees untapped (Boeke, 1942, pp. 29–30).[19]

A priori, if one accepts Boeke's thesis as a plausible statement of the confrontation of two economic systems, the metropolises of underdeveloped areas functioned as loci from which Western (that is, modernizing) influences disseminated. Many of these cities were the outright creation of Europeans; others grew from small towns or villages mainly as a consequence of Western influences. In Southeast Asia, for instance,

In 1800, Rangoon, Saigon, and Singapore did not yet exist in city form; Bangkok, the new capital of Thailand, was less than twenty years old; Manila and Batavia (Jakarta), though then about 200 years old, were merely small coastal towns. They began to grow rapidly after the middle of the nineteenth century [and] . . . the consolidation of Western control, direct or indirect, over most of Southeast Asia in the 1890's (Ginsburg, 1955).

So cosmopolitan are such Asian centers still that typically each can be paired with a subcenter of the native culture; thus, Shanghai-Nanking, Rangoon-Mandalay, Jakarta-Jogjakarta, Manila-Cebu, and so on. Similarly, "the modern African town did not grow out of the needs of, and in service to, its own hinterland; its primary relationship is to Europe" (McCall, 1955). The alienation of the peasant mass from such cities was based first of all on their foreignness. In the period after 1945, when many of the world's colonies achieved independence (or, as in the case of Thailand, greatly expanded its range of prior nominal independence), there was some sentiment in

---

[19] Of the several economists who have criticized Boeke, Bauer can be taken as a typical defender of academic orthodoxy. On the one hand, he admits the possibility that Western economic theorems may not apply universally: "Of course the institutional framework of the community limits and directs the operations of its economic activities; and this framework in underdeveloped countries is often very different. . . . The readiness of response varies with all sorts of factors and influences, and in stable and stratified societies with strong traditions wants may be less expansive than in other more fluid societies." On the other hand, he asserts that "those who dispute the relevance of the propositions of economics to underdeveloped countries usually base their arguments on the differences in attitudes and institutions, . . . [but] these views reflect incomplete observations or imperfect understanding of economics" (P. T. Bauer, *Economic Analysis and Policy in Underdeveloped Countries*, Routledge & Kegan Paul, London, 1965, pp. 15, 17, 23). There follow a number of anecdotes to show that in some instances non-Westerners behave as they are supposed to in Western economic theory, but in sum these add up to much less than the contrary instances cited by Boeke, not to mention works in a similar vein about India or Africa. In any case, one would expect a society in transition to exhibit psychological norms derivative both from traditional institutions and from modern ones; and which attitudes are modal in any area is an empirical question, not a doctrinal one.

the Southeast Asian nations to select as their capitals cities that had a native tradition and were located near the countries' geographical centers. In fact, almost without exception they chose cities created by Western trade and imperial rule, typically the largest urban aggregate and in some cases the only real one—Karachi, Colombo, Rangoon, Bangkok, Kuala Lumpur, Jakarta, Manila, and of course Singapore.[20] As the capitals took on the many tasks of administering these new nations, including a sizable portion of their economies, the populations of these metropolises increased even more rapidly than at Southeast Asia's generally high rate of natural increase and urbanization. In short, even if occasionally with a fresh name to recall the precolonial grandeur, the centers of new nationalism are indisputable products of the colonial rule (Murphey, 1957; cf. Fryer, 1953).

In a country whose government controls many of the factors of production—and this is the typical case, particularly among underdeveloped nations—official policy can influence the location of both public and private industry. Yet the natural attraction is to the metropolitan center, and in a country like India "any attempt to build up industrial centers of less than 100,000 to 200,000 population for sustained growth and the attraction of migrants is doomed to failure." For example, efforts to engage refugees from Pakistan in industries located in new centers forty to a hundred miles from Calcutta and Delhi were "miserable failures," while in Bangalore, a city that in the process grew to over a million, the government succeeded in establishing factories manufacturing aircraft, electronic equipment, machine tools, telephones, and porcelain. The reason for this discrepancy is that in India—which in this respect is if anything better off than most of the rest of Asia and Africa, as well as much of Latin America—the prerequisites of industrial development exist only in large cities (Harris, 1959).

The levels of training of the average Indian urban worker are very low except insofar as he may have become a member of an industrial labor pool such as exists in the larger centers. Any city of less than 100,000 population and many cities above this population will have totally inadequate public services. The streets are of mud and become running sewers during the monsoon. Water supply may be inadequate and polluted. Electrical service will be irregular. Delivery of inbound materials from the nearest rail junction may take days or weeks, and the assignment of outbound empties is uncertain. Mail and telegraph service will be regular, if slow, but telephone service will be most difficult. Visiting salesmen and customers may get there only with journeys of many hours on uncomfortable trains and will find almost no suitable accommodations. Managers and proprietors will feel . . . the pinch of inadequate schools and nonexistent cultural activities. Their contact with competitors, customers, suppliers, and the market place in general will be greatly impaired. Necessary business with government regulatory agencies will

---

[20] For India, the statement pertains more to Calcutta, which had been the capital until the British built New Delhi in 1911, in part as "a conscious effort to harmonize the alien rule with historical tradition" (Murphey, 1957).

be difficult to pursue. It is therefore evident that only the proprietors of extensive enterprises intending to build large units can afford the initial cost of overcoming all these difficulties and sacrificing the external economies of location in larger centers (*ibid.*).

In summary, since modernization means the inculcation of Western norms and behavior patterns, it is likely to proceed fastest in those sectors of underdeveloped areas most influenced by Westerners, namely, the large cities. This is particularly so since only there, if anywhere, will one probably find the technical prerequisites of new industry. With respect to economic growth, large metropolises might be termed generative, while the small towns buried in the preindustrial culture may well be parasitic.[21]

That modernization forces are so heavily concentrated in the large cities of underdeveloped areas means that, at least to some degree, what might be termed the classical model of rural-urban migration (*cf.* pp. 298–299) applies. In the development of Western nations, the urban sector has grown by its own natural increase, by the annexation of new territory, and, as the most important factor, by the massive migration of countrymen out of agriculture into city occupations. Those who have made this move are rewarded with better jobs and incomes, more diversified and comfortable living. Under these conditions, the migration to the cities of a relatively homogeneous society results in its greater diversification, which starts with the very process of the migrants' self-selection according to characteristics relevant to success in urban pursuits.

One variation of this model common in underdeveloped areas results in a markedly different urban society. In both Africa and Asia it used to be that commercial interests, in an attempt to acquire an urban labor force without paying for a city, fostered the migration of young males to industrial sites while inhibiting the development there of any normal social life. The workers' settlements once attached to African mines, for instance, were often large enough to be designated "cities," but in their truncated function, and thus in their age and sex structure, they more closely resembled enormous army camps (Mitchell, 1961; Elkan, 1960). In the past decade or two, it is true, such African firms as the Copperbelt mining companies have come to recognize that a stabilized labor force brings a substantial commercial benefit (Steel, 1961). Similarly, the European or Japanese directors of government bureaus and commercial enterprises once fostered a separa-

[21] The terms are borrowed from Hoselitz, but he draws precisely the opposite conclusion. While "it is not easy to discover actual instances in which the city has exerted a long-run parasitic influence on the economic development of the region it dominated," allegedly the "colonial capitals and other administrative centers" (Batavia is cited as a specific example) are "parasitic," if only in the short run (Hoselitz, 1960, Chapter 8). Indeed, in some contexts Hoselitz seems to designate all cities, and especially all large ones, as unfavorable for modernization. "It may well turn out that urbanization in Asia is proceeding at too rapid a rate, and that urban populations tend to be too heavily concentrated in a few primate cities. . . . At present the countries of South Asia may be regarded, on the whole, as 'overurbanized'" (Hoselitz, 1957).

A slum district of Guayaquil, Ecuador (*Paul Conklin—PIX*).

tion of their employees' lives between economic functions in many an Asian city and social ones in a nearby village, and some of this influence disappeared with national independence. Yet many reasons have remained why in Asia or Africa a countryman who wants to supplement his peasant's income migrates to a mine or city alone and temporarily, eventually to return to his village, his wife and children, his extended-family associations, his share of the tribal land. Urban housing and transportation are poor; there are no adequate substitutes, in the form of social welfare or high wages, for the communal services of the village. As Schapera (1947) pointed out in his study of Bechuanaland, a period of employment in the city where a young man can sow his wild oats came to be seen almost as a necessary prelude to full tribal manhood; once such a pattern developed, it reinforced the traditional reluctance to submit the females of one's family to the damaging entanglements, if not actual physical dangers, of the city slums. For all these reasons, in contrast to the low sex ratio of the movement into Western cities, in-migration to the cities of underdeveloped areas, and thus the urban populations themselves, have been predominantly male. Thus, even when rural-urban migration has been a response to economic opportunities in the city, it has not necessarily resulted in the separation of an advanced sector of the population from its rural base and the development of a town-based subculture.

Although the rapid urbanization of underdeveloped areas thus derives in part from the fact that better-paying industrial jobs are located in the cities, the prevalent rural stagnation is much more important. In the language of the conventional schema, the predominance of pull factors has given way to push factors. Nonindustrial countries have enjoyed a remarkable decline in rural mortality; medicines, technicians, and other death-control measures, disseminated from urbanized industrial nations through international agencies (*cf.* Chapter 15), have shattered the traditional balance between land and population. To the degree that the efforts to raise agricultural productivity succeed, the economically surplus portion of the rural population is increased. Together with the great and often growing disparity between the resources of the countryside and the number who depend on them, there has been, to use the common phrase, a revolution of rising expectations. When even the most isolated hamlet catches glimpses of metropolitan glamor, the simple life that satisfied parents or grandparents is seen as too confining; as against the village's rigid social structure, the city is even more appealing for its greater anonymity, its wider range of freedom.

One family living in a shantytown on the periphery of Brazilia, the new capital of Brazil (*Paul Conklin—PIX*).

A very large portion of this new type of in-migrants lack the most elementary urban facilities—water supply, sewerage, even a right to their hovels. Almost all large cities of underdeveloped countries are ringed by squatter settlements, shantytowns of self-constructed huts, which in Latin America, for instance, constitute a third (Caracas) or even half (Maracaibo) of the city's population. As the squatters have no legal right to the land, they invade it quickly and *en masse,* suddenly confronting authorities with the established fact of their presence. For example, on a single night of December 1954, some 5,000 persons established a new "barriada" in Lima, Peru. Previously the quasilegal promoters had organized the invasion, assigning a plot to each applicant. During the night each family rushed to throw up some kind of dwelling in order to establish squatters' rights to the land (Matos, 1961). The kind of life that a typical inhabitant of such an urban slum lives, though few details are known with any certainty, is a major element of a dispute over the social function of large cities.

### URBAN POLICY

The concept of "overurbanization," which has become a commonplace in writings on underdeveloped areas, derives originally from an article by Davis and Golden (1954); it offers a framework for analyzing the two types of rural-urban migration we have noted. As they use the concept, those countries with a greater urban population than is typical at their level of industrialization are "overurbanized." Thus, with the percentage of the country's population in cities of over 100,000 and the percentage of economically active males in agriculture as the two indices, Egypt, for example, was notably overurbanized. "The densely settled and impoverished countryside of Egypt is pushing people into the cities because they have no other alternative"; this kind of urbanization is generated by intolerable conditions at its source rather than mainly by the pull of opportunities in urban industry. The implicit confusion of statistical and ethical norms is not by design; as the authors use it, overurbanization "has only a statistical meaning, with no overtone of evaluation intended." But the word was poorly chosen to convey such a neutral meaning, and most who have adopted the concept made a policy recommendation with it.[22]

Various motives underly the very common aversion to cities, and particularly large cities. In a few instances—Gandhi or the landed upper class

[22] Two years after Davis and Golden's article appeared, thus, the summary report of a United Nations conference on the growth of cities in Asia noted that "urbanization has generally tended to move ahead of economic development" and that, since this differential development had various deleterious effects, "it is probably true to say that Asia is overurbanized in relation to its degree of economic development" and thus "consideration was given to ways in which the 'overurbanization' in many Asian countries could be combated" (Hauser, 1957). See also the quotation from Hoselitz, above, p. 463, n. 21.

of Latin America—the antipathy is to industrialism; but more usually policymakers want to acquire the benefits of modernization while preventing the growth of the "megalopolis," its typical site, and substituting a multiplicity of smaller towns. In the early 1950s, there was a reported "widespread agreement concerning the desirability of decentralization, the governments of Burma, Ceylon, Hong Kong, India, Indonesia, Pakistan, the Philippines, Singapore, and Vietnam having generally accepted this principle as one of the bases for housing and town and country planning" (ILO, 1953, p. 85).[23] Very often the separation of metropolitan centers from the rural mass is designated as one reason for such a policy; small urban centers constitute "a more effective bridge between city and country" (Wurster, 1955 p. 8). But this very fact that a small city is likely to be thoroughly embedded in its hinterland and thus markedly influenced by traditional norms suggests that the metropolis is a more effective instrument for the creation of a society that deviates from those norms. Sometimes the policy is to concentrate on agriculture and in effect to ignore the city. But the improvement of peasants' social and legal status, however desirable it may be on other grounds, need not stem the rural-urban flow. In Mexico, after forty years of vigorous land reform (supplemented in demographic terms by the absorption of some of the surplus agricultural labor into temporary jobs in the United States), cities have grown at rates high even for Latin America. Between 1951 and 1960, the population of Mexico City itself rose by 58 per cent, and that of 54 other urban centers in Mexico by 78 per cent (Haar, 1963). And technical improvements in agriculture are even less likely than social reforms to remedy the already existent surplus of agrarian labor and thus to reduce the migration to cities.

The more or less specific objections to the metropolis are strongly reinforced by general theory. In the conventional wisdom of American sociology (which has markedly influenced that in other countries), the social changes associated with the type of urbanization prevalent in underdeveloped nations (or even with urbanization altogether) are denoted as "social disorganization," or the breakdown of viable patterns of community life. "Personal disorganization, which is the subjective aspect of social disorganization, is manifest in such conditions as juvenile delinquency, crime, and vice" (Hauser, 1957). One flaw in this concept is the premise that in the countryside a viable community exists, virtually by definition, and that it is the movement to an urban setting that *dis*organizes it. The sparse data available on much of the world's present urbanization suggest that this

---

[23] As some of the countries on this list suggest, one of the problems that concerned the officials was not metropolization *per se* but the refugees who fled from Pakistan to India, from India to Pakistan, from China to Hong Kong, from North to South Korea, and so on. It is misleading to illustrate the disadvantages of large cities from conditions in such a commonly chosen example as Calcutta (e.g., Wurster, 1962; Bose, 1965), for the true comparison here is less with small towns or the countryside than with refugee camps.

In some of the worst cases of urban crowding, a flood of refugees has aggravated the normal in-migration.

*Above:* People sleeping in a Calcutta street, 1956 (*James Burke—courtesy Life © 1956 Time, Inc.*).

*Right:* Squatters' shacks built on the roofs of buildings, Kowloon, Hong Kong, 1959 (*United Nations*).

analytical framework is misleading. Typically the residents of shantytowns are not disoriented by urban life nearly so much as by the rural one they finally escaped. According to the 1956 census of 56 barriadas in Lima, most

of the migrants came seeking employment and only one per cent failed to find some remunerative job (Matos, 1961). UNESCO studies of in-migrants to a number of Asian cities found that the attraction of "city lights" was of no significance. "Economic hardship in varying degrees was the real reason for practically all migration" (UNESCO, 1956, Introduction).

Even apart from a contrast with rural circumstances, the "disorganization" of poor urban quarters is often exaggerated. From what little is known about the world's shantytowns, one can draw two quite contradictory generalizations, based in part on the varying conditions in different localities or the inconsistent responses of the inhabitants, but also in part on which over-all preconception the researcher started from. Most governmental, United Nations, and other official reports of whatever kind find the "chaos" and "festering sores" their authors expected. A number of non-establishment investigators, looking at the same "social facts" with a different set of prejudices, have been able to document another world. In an interesting survey, Mangin has contrasted these two myths—each with some, but only some, relation to objective reality.

The main rural institution of underdeveloped countries—in many the only one apart from that embodying political authority—is the family with its ramifications. According to a sizable number of reports, most in-migrants to the cities of Africa, Asia, or Latin America seek out their kin for help in adjusting to a strange and often hostile environment. Thus, in the squatter settlements of Latin America, for instance, "family and kinship relationships are strong and provide a degree of crisis insurance" (Mangin, 1967). According to the Lima census already cited, of the 21,004 squatter households enumerated, 93 per cent consisted of two parents and their children, either with or without other relatives (Matos, 1961). The shantytown birth rate is generally high, in part because of an age structure favoring fertility; the migration of both sexes in nearly equal proportion, with the immediate establishment of families at the new site, contrasts with the rule that most migrants are single and predominantly of one sex. According to a 1963 study, in Santiago de Chile each mother in the city proper had an average of 2.38 children, compared with 4.5 in the "callampas" surrounding it (Guillermo Rosenbluth, cited in Mangin, 1967). As many as half of those born in shantytowns are illegitimate (Germani, 1961); considering the prevalence of consensual unions in the Latin American culture generally, this proportion is not surprisingly high.

In sum, the concept of social disorganization is probably more misleading than helpful in analyzing squatter settlements. The very fact that people continue to pour into them reinforces the well based supposition that the average life in the villages is worse.[24] Yet it is certainly also true that, beyond quibble, the urban slums of Africa, Asia, and Latin America are unattractive places, vast conglomerations of squalor and misery. It is hardly astounding that both national governments and international agencies have continually sought ameliorative measures.

Most efforts to improve slum housing, however, have not been successful, and some have aggravated the problem. If police clear out the area of settlement, the squatters spread to other parts of the city and start again at a still lower level of hope and subsistence. If adequate housing is constructed, the result commonly is to attract still more in-migrants to the city and even to that housing project. In 1958 the Venezuelan housing agency constructed ninety-seven apartment blocks in Caracas at a total cost of some 200 million dollars, designed to house about 180,000 persons.

---

[24] Those who hold the contrary sometimes argue that there is a massive self-deception: "Only a small minority of the migrants need realize their expectations in order for the myth to survive that opportunities in the city are greater" (Tangri, 1962). There are no data to support this supposition directly, and the over-all differences in rural and urban income, health, education, and style of life, as well as the typical lack of a return migration to the villages, suggest that it is wrong.

An additional 4,000 families invaded the apartments and lived there illegally; other thousands built a shantytown on the project site. After a year unpaid rents totaled 5 million dollars, augmented by half a million per month in maintenance losses. "The accompanying social, economic, and administrative difficulties" mounted into "civil anarchy." According to an international study team called in to analyze the project's problems, it was the massive program itself that had attracted many rural migrants to the area, and the experts recommended that the government postpone the building of such residential units until it had established a "housing policy related to the economic and social development of the country and within a process of national planning and construction" (Carlson, 1959).

Sometimes it is difficult, on the contrary, to induce squatters to leave their dwellings and settle in new housing. For example, when a slum near the center of Lagos, the capital of Nigeria, was torn down and its residents were transferred to a new project on the outskirts, some were delighted by the change. For others the move was "disastrous."

They were isolated from their work, their markets, and their relatives, at the end of a long and expensive bus journey. Unable to meet the expenses of suburban life, some of the husbands sent their wives home to their families, and distributed their children among relatives. Wives, finding no opportunities for trade, left to live with their own relatives nearer the center of town; others simply deserted when their husbands could no longer support them. Old people who had lived before in a family house, where they paid no rent, and were cared for, now found themselves neglected. Craftsmen and traders who had lost their customers sold up and at last determined to go abroad out of reach of wives and children and all family responsibilities, in the hope of recovering their fortunes. For these, the kind of domestic life for which the estate was planned was a luxury they could not afford (Marris, 1960; cf. Marris, 1961).[25]

Marris's conclusion was that "many Lagos families have neither the desire nor the means to accept the social reforms which are being imposed upon them."

These reservations about slum clearance have been generalized in a vivid passage:

In a housing famine there is nothing that slum clearance can accomplish that cannot be done more efficiently by an earthquake. The worst aspects of slum life are overcrowding and excessive shelter cost. Demolition without replacement intensifies overcrowding and increases shelter cost. . . . Actually, the provision of public housing is an independent undertaking that need not be part of the clearance operation. . . . Worse than slums is a slum shortage that provides no shelter, good or bad (Abrams, 1964, pp. 126–128).

[25] Sociologists (in particular, Gans, 1962) have made similar points about rehousing programs in the United States.

In effect, Abrams is inviting the reader to accept the lower-class area as a useful and in any case irremovable fixture of the present-day city. In self-protection the local administration must try to set minimum standards of sanitation, to prevent epidemics, and of social control, to restrict crime. But for the foreseeable future it or the national government or an international agency can no more eliminate the slum than Sisyphus could finally reach the top of the hill. The possible task, and thus the proper one, is to facilitate the migration of some slum-dwellers to successively better quarters, a selective movement based on the displaced peasants' differential success in adapting to urban life. Those who leave the slum will be replaced by others; those who arrive will have at least a slum to go to. In short, "the squatter settlements represent a solution to the complex problem of rapid urbanization and migration combined with a housing shortage" (Mangin, 1967).

## THE URBANIZATION OF AMERICAN NEGROES [26]

As we have seen, the present urbanization of underdeveloped countries is in some respects different from the growth of Western cities, but it is very easy to exaggerate the contrast. In England of *c.* 1800, the reader will recall, many of the declassed peasants who swarmed into the rising industrial centers found jobs in the new factories, but over several decades the not yet established urban working class could hardly be distinguished from the lumpenproletariat of paupers and casual workers. And the present massive shift of American Negroes to the centers of American civilization has been stimulated less by the attraction of urban jobs than by the rejection of the rural South. That is, the second type of urbanization, typical of underdeveloped areas, is to be found also in industrial nations.

The demographic features of the South, whether its high fertility and mortality or the low accuracy of its statistics, have reflected its inefficient agrarian economy. So long as the antebellum society was intact, the ruling class saw its future entirely within the compass of the plantation system. This formed the industrial and social framework of government, and slavery was an important part of its legal code.[27] After the 1860s, when rapid industrialization got under way in the North, the South was devastated by the effects of the war and harassed by occupation forces; it lacked any substantial industrial base and, for decades, the incentive to establish one.

---

[26] Portions of this section derive from Daniel O. Price, "Changing Characteristics of the Negro Population: Trends in Migration, Occupation, Education, and Marital Status," an as yet unpublished monograph based mainly on the 1960 census. I am grateful to the author and to the Bureau of the Census for permission to use these data.

[27] See Rupert B. Vance, *Human Factors in Cotton Culture: A Study in the Social Geography of the American South,* University of North Carolina Press, Chapel Hill, 1929.

Until recently only a small proportion of its population has lived in cities and worked in modern industry. For a significant percentage debilitating rural poverty persisted as the regional norm.

Efforts to raise the southern economy to the national level have repeatedly foundered on the crucial racial question. After the 1880s, with caste again the fundament of its social system,[28] the South seemed to be coming to terms with the rest of the nation: after 1914–18 a reference to "the War" no longer harked back to 1865; Roosevelt's Democratic administration raised southern leaders into national prominence, and New Deal programs brought some relief to the poorest regions. And then there was "a sudden revivification of the old sectional conflict and the recrudescence of the terms 'North' and 'South,' together with special and intensified revival of the old race conflict." [29] In the 1950s, following the Supreme Court's decision outlawing segregated public schools, the resurgence of sectional feeling was even sharper. The conflict is fundamental. The white South, at least as represented by much of its political leadership, is unwilling to admit the Negro to the full political and social equality that is his right under constitutional law. On the other side, a portion of northern public opinion, white as well as Negro, is no more willing to accept the caste system as a permanent feature of American life, a permanent anomaly in American democracy.

One would expect the South, the region with the highest natural increase and the fewest economic opportunities, to be a source of out-migration, and this has generally been so. If we compare for various dates the number of persons born in the South and living in the North (that is, the Northeast and North Central regions) with those born in the North and living in the South, these census data give us a rough idea of the dimensions of the two migrations irrespective of race (Table 13-8). The total movement in both directions increased consistently from 1.8 million in 1890 to 11.1 million in 1960, and without exception a net migration to the North was shown in every census. However, Census Bureau estimates concerning the most recent period indicate a reversal of this historic trend: the South is now in a period of net in-migration, presumably mainly of whites. This affected some of the poorest states of the region: Mississippi lost an average of 3.2 per cent annually in 1950–55 but only 0.4 per cent in 1960–66; Arkansas lost 3.8 per cent annually in the first period but gained 0.2 per cent in the second.[30]

[28] For a fascinating account of this partial reversal of Negroes' emancipation, see C. Vann Woodward, *The Strange Career of Jim Crow*, Revised Ed., Galaxy-Oxford University Press, New York, 1957.

[29] Howard W. Odum, "The Way of the South," in *In Search of the Regional Balance of America*, edited by Odum and Katharine Jocher, University of North Carolina Press, Chapel Hill, 1945, pp. 16–26.

[30] U.S. Bureau of the Census, "Estimates of the Population of States: July 1, 1966," *Current Population Reports*, Series P-25, No. 380, November 24, 1967.

Table 13-8. Migration (thousands) between the North and the South according to State-of-Birth Data, United States, 1890–1960

|  | BORN IN THE SOUTH, LIVING IN THE NORTH | BORN IN THE NORTH, LIVING IN THE SOUTH | TOTAL MOVEMENT | NET GAIN OF NORTH | |
|---|---|---|---|---|---|
|  |  |  |  | ABSOLUTE | PER CENT |
| 1890 | 1,136 | 636 | 1,772 | 500 | 28.2 |
| 1900 | 1,296 | 1,021 | 2,317 | 275 | 11.9 |
| 1910 | 1,527 | 1,449 | 2,976 | 78 | 2.6 |
| 1920 | 2,152 | 1,721 | 3,873 | 431 | 11.1 |
| 1930 | 3,297 | 1,878 | 5,175 | 1,419 | 27.4 |
| 1940 | 3,457 | 2,066 | 5,523 | 1,391 | 25.2 |
| 1950 | 5,010 | 3,101 | 8,111 | 1,909 | 23.5 |
| 1960 | 6,570 | 4,546 | 11,116 | 2,024 | 18.2 |

SOURCE: U.S. Bureau of the Census, *U.S. Census of Population, 1960: Subject Reports, State of Birth*, Final Report PC(2)-2A, Washington, D.C., 1963, Table 3.

The movement of Negroes out of the southern states began very slowly in the first decade of the twentieth century. During World War I northern manufacturers, faced by a shortage of unskilled labor when the immigration from Europe was cut off, sent recruiting agents into the South to seek replacements. At that time more than nine Negroes out of every ten lived in the South, and three out of four were rural. From that time on, however, their movement to cities and especially to the North has been much larger than that of southern whites (Table 13-9). The net migrations shown in this table were estimated also by calculating for each category of the population the difference between those counted in successive censuses and those at various ages who would have survived to the dates of the census. For whites net out-migration from the South fluctuated between over a half and a quarter million per decade, while for Negroes it increased from half a million to well over a million. Among successive Negro cohorts, moreover, the proportion of net out-migrants from the rural areas of the secession states has generally risen from one decade to the next. Between 60 and 75 per cent of rural Negroes born in the Deep South now leave by age thirty, going typically to large cities in either that region or other regions; moreover, the proportion leaving has been rising and the age at which they leave has been falling. The sizable migration from rural areas to southern cities has ended the region's anomalous lack of urban and especially metropolitan centers, so characteristic before 1940. Of the 212 SMSAs in 1960, 83 were located in the South (or overlapped it and another region), and their total population was more than 26 million.

Table 13-9. Estimated Net Migration (thousands) in Urban and Rural Sectors of the South,[a] by Race, United States, 1910–60

| | WHITE | | | | | NEGRO[b] | | | | |
|---|---|---|---|---|---|---|---|---|---|---|
| | WHOLE SOUTH | URBAN | | RURAL | | WHOLE SOUTH | URBAN | | RURAL | |
| | | SECESSION | NON-SECESSION | SECESSION | NON-SECESSION | | SECESSION | NON-SECESSION | SECESSION | NON-SECESSION |
| 1910–20 | −331 | 860 | 426 | −1,139 | −478 | −425 | 528 | 60 | −958 | −55 |
| 1920–30 | −605 | 1,279 | 268 | −1,592 | −560 | −786 | 138 | 81 | −1,013 | −42 |
| 1930–40 | −294 | 747 | 158 | −824 | −375 | −347 | 412 | 87 | −793 | −53 |
| 1940–50 | −556 | 2,111 | 158 | −1,988 | −837 | −1,270 | 307 | 99 | −1,577 | −99 |
| 1950–60 | −268 | 2,874 | 168 | −2,332 | −978 | −1,171 | 289 | 91 | −1,476 | −75 |

SOURCE: Daniel O. Price, "Changing Characteristics of the Negro Population: Trends in Migration, Occupation, Education, and Marital Status," unpublished census monograph, Table 2.2.

[a] The census region of the South is divided between those states that did not secede in the Civil War (Delaware, Maryland, District of Columbia, West Virginia, Kentucky, and Oklahoma) and the rest, which did.

[b] "Nonwhite" in 1940–60.

The typical urbanization of Negroes has been to the central cities of metropolitan areas. The differentiation between center and ring in terms of color, and thus of social class, may be increasing. In almost all SMSAs and especially in the largest ones, the growing concentration of Negroes in central cities has accompanied an accelerated decentralization among whites (Figure 13-1). Only a few places deviate from this rule; in twenty

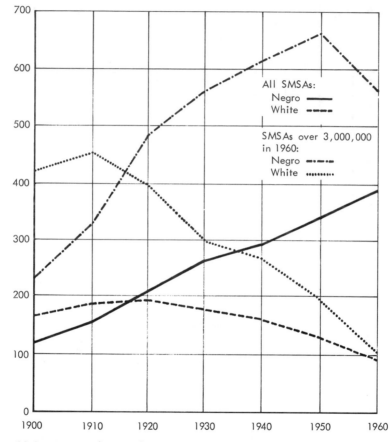

**Figure 13-1.** Ratio of central city to ring population of Standard Metropolitan Areas, Negro and white, United States, 1900–60. Source: U.S. Bureau of Labor Statistics, *The Negroes in the United States: Their Economic and Social Situation*, Bulletin 1511, Washington, D.C., 1966, Figures IA-7 and IA-9.

suburbs throughout the country the proportion of nonwhites increased from 1950 to 1960 and reached at least one-fifth by the latter date (Schnore and Sharp, 1963). A minuscule portion of this migration to the suburbs constituted middle-class Negroes fitting into integrated neighborhoods; the rest reflected a spread of the lower-class, highly segregated pattern to the metropolitan rings (*cf.* Farley and Taeuber, 1968).

In some respects the internal migration of Negroes has been analogous to the pre-1914 immigration of Southern and Eastern Europeans, in other respects to the rural-urban movements in underdeveloped countries. In all these cases the adjustment to city life has been especially difficult for transplanted peasants.[31] By any index of social or economic well-being, whether occupational distribution or family income, whether education or average length of life, Negroes are still congregated at the bottom of the scale. The changes in the Negro job structure from 1954 to 1965 are shown in Table 13-10. The greatest relative increases were in well-paying occupations (professional and clerical), the smallest in those at the bottom of the social-economic scale (laborers and domestic servants). Yet even after this differential increase, four out of every ten domestic servants were nonwhite in 1965, and one out of every four laborers. And whatever improvements there were in the job structure did not apply to the unemployed, of whom the rate was fixed for nonwhites at almost precisely double that for whites (Table 13-11). For both sexes and colors, the highest unemployment rate was among those seeking initial entry into the labor market. Even though the greatest drop in unemployment rates was for nonwhite males in the prime working years (20–44), the ratio to comparable rates for whites remained high.

As measured by almost any demographic or social index, the status of Negroes has risen tremendously in the last several decades, and it still lags significantly behind the average for whites. It is this contrast that has generated widespread social unrest; for whether at the level of revolutions or of labor-union strikes, social movements develop on an upswing, when actual improvement stimulates a demand for yet greater and faster improvement. One important reason for the disparity, to repeat, is that Negroes have not been a self-selected group especially well equipped for urban jobs and modes of life. Their migration has been primarily *out* of the rural South, and thus to cities even when there were no urban jobs available. As we are told in a popular Negro song (Beardwood, 1968),

> I'd rather be in Michigan in a rattlesnake's hole
> Than in North Carolina with a pocketful of gold.

[31] Even before 1914, it is true, a new type of Negro began to develop in northern cities. As early as the turn of the century, a small group of Negro and white intellectuals met in Niagara Falls, Canada (they had been unable to get accommodations on American soil) and laid the basis for the National Association for the Advancement of Colored People. Over the years this and other organizations have been able to enlist the power of the federal and state courts in an effort to re-establish the principle of equality in public institutions. Just as in an earlier period the various immigrant-aid societies had helped Europeans make this transition, so the Urban League was established to assist Negro "greenhorns." In both cases, the acculturation was successful, but not complete.

Table 13-10. Distribution of Nonwhite Workers by Occupational Group, United States, 1954–65

| | THOUSANDS | | PER CENT CHANGE | RELATIVE CHANGE [a] | PER CENT OF ALL WORKERS | |
|---|---|---|---|---|---|---|
| | 1954 | 1965 | 1954–65 | | 1954 | 1965 |
| Professional, technical, and kindred workers | 217 | 525 | 141.9 | 625 | 3.9 | 5.9 |
| Managers, officials, and proprietors (excluding farm) | 130 | 204 | 56.9 | 250 | 2.1 | 2.8 |
| Clerical and kindred workers | 308 | 633 | 105.5 | 465 | 3.7 | 5.7 |
| Sales workers | 89 | 146 | 64.0 | 282 | 2.3 | 3.1 |
| Craftsmen, foremen, and kindred workers | 316 | 520 | 64.6 | 285 | 3.8 | 5.6 |
| Operatives and kindred workers | 1,313 | 1,651 | 25.7 | 113 | 10.7 | 12.3 |
| Private household workers | 897 | 981 | 9.4 | 41 | 51.4 | 43.6 |
| Service workers (excluding private household) | 1,057 | 1,472 | 39.3 | 173 | 21.2 | 20.8 |
| Farmers and farm managers | 389 | 138 | 64.5 | 284 | 10.0 | 6.1 |
| Farm laborers and foremen | 589 | 491 | 16.6 | 73 | 23.6 | 24.3 |
| Laborers (excluding farm and mine) | 1,009 | 985 | 2.4 | 11 | 27.6 | 25.6 |
| TOTAL | 6,312 | 7,747 | 22.7 | 100 | 10.3 | 10.7 |

SOURCE: U.S. Bureau of Labor Statistics, *The Negroes in the United States: Their Economic and Social Situation*, Bulletin 1511, Washington, D.C., 1966, Table IIB-2.
[a] Index numbers, with the over-all increase (22.7 per cent) = 100.

## Summary

What is loosely called "urbanization" is really a combination of two phenomena—the development of large concentrated aggregates of human beings, and the rise of new culture patterns, new ways of thinking and behaving, characteristic of these cities. In order to discuss the relation between the two, one must keep the concepts separate—*urbanization*, the process or state of population concentration, and *urbanism*, the way of life

Table 13-11. Percentage Unemployed of Nonwhite Workers, by Age and Sex, United States, 1957–65

| AGE AND SEX | | PER CENT UNEMPLOYED | | RATIO OF NONWHITE RATE TO WHITE | |
| --- | --- | --- | --- | --- | --- |
| | | 1957 | 1965 | 1957 | 1965 |
| Male: | 14–19 | 17.5 | 22.6 | 1.67 | 1.92 |
| | 20–24 | 12.7 | 9.3 | 1.79 | 1.58 |
| | 25–34 | 8.5 | 6.2 | 3.15 | 2.38 |
| | 35–44 | 6.4 | 5.1 | 2.56 | 2.22 |
| | 45–54 | 6.2 | 5.1 | 2.07 | 2.22 |
| | 14 and over | 8.4 | 7.6 | 2.27 | 2.11 |
| Female: | 14–19 | 18.9 | 29.8 | 2.08 | 2.37 |
| | 20–24 | 12.2 | 13.7 | 2.39 | 2.17 |
| | 25–34 | 8.1 | 8.4 | 1.72 | 1.75 |
| | 35–44 | 4.7 | 7.6 | 1.27 | 1.85 |
| | 45–54 | 4.2 | 4.4 | 1.40 | 1.47 |
| | 14 and over | 7.4 | 9.3 | 1.72 | 1.86 |
| TOTAL, 14 and over | | 8.0 | 8.3 | 2.05 | 2.02 |

SOURCE: U.S. Bureau of Labor Statistics, *The Negroes in the United States: Their Economic and Social Situation*, Bulletin 1511; Washington, D.C., 1966, Table IIA-4.

of city dwellers. The effect of density on culture patterns is important, but not absolute; that is, the correlation between urbanization and urbanism is high, but not perfect.

In order to test this relation empirically, it is necessary to have clear and consistent definitions of the independent variable. In fact, the statistical criteria of "urban" and "rural" differ greatly from country to country and, in any one series, from one decade to the next. The simple dichotomy hardly suffices any longer; either a more complex classification (e.g., metropolis, city, village, farm) or a continuum by size of place is more useful.

Virtually every underdeveloped country of the world is endeavoring, whether effectively or not, to encourage industrialization. Judging from both the historical record of the West and the typical findings of the social disciplines, the industrialization will be associated with urbanization. In the development of mankind from its savage state, the two major advances were closely associated with urbanization, both the beginnings of civilization in the ancient Near East and the rise and spread of industrialism. In the broadest sense, then, human progress and the city have been linked for several millennia. This correlation, it is true, has not been a one-to-one relation. As we noted in Chapter 10, several of the most distinguished analysts of preindustrial cities divided them into subcategories, the free mercantile cities of Europe and the administrative centers of either Europe or other civilizations, on the ground that the first generated fundamental social change while the second, on the contrary, usually coalesced the traditions of those societies into more durable forms. In the analysis of underdeveloped countries today, somewhat similar attempts have been made to classify cities into types, according to whether they do or do not foster the development of an industrial society. It is hypothesized here that inmigrants to cities, even those motivated by nothing more than a desire to escape the destitution of the village, are potentially more suitable human resources in modernization than those who remain more fully enmeshed in traditional norms and probably less willing to risk a new way to the future. Not only has the criticism of the large city as parasitic often been based on "loose thinking and remarkably little actual research," but some of this criticism might better be diverted to the rural social structure, especially though not exclusively of Latin America (Browning, 1958).

Yet most governments attempt to impede the growth of cities, particularly of large cities; they would like to acquire the benefits of a modern industrial economy without paying the price, as they see it, of a cosmopolitan urban society. The typical attitude in underdeveloped countries toward town and country is succinctly put in two chapter headings of a United Nations work: "Programmes of Rural Development" and "Programmes and Measures for Meeting Problems of Rapid Urbanization."[32] The transformation of the villager ordinarily entails some costs, but one should always remember that high urban rates of various social pathologies are at least partly spurious, since urbanization is associated with better statistics, higher standards of efficiency, and greater visibility of social ills. Apart from the "disorganization" it supposedly generates, the city is too seldom seen as a process. The ties of American urban sociology with human ecology, of French or Dutch studies with urban geography, of American and especially British city planning with architecture, all tend to emphasize the locus of urban events rather than the social change that an urban environment fosters.

No urban place is spatially homogeneous, and its growth can be studied by analyzing the changing relationship of its several parts. Since about 1920, the rings of metropolitan areas in the United States have been increasing much faster than the central cities; and in the most recent period there has also been a decentralization of business and light industry. To

---

[32] United Nations, Bureau of Social Affairs, *International Survey of Programmes of Social Development,* New York, 1959, Chapters 11 and 13.

some degree, lower classes and especially Negroes have concentrated in the central cities and successively higher classes at greater and greater distances from it. This Burgess model is not generally true, however, of the urban or metropolitan structure in other countries, where the attraction to the center is often greater.

## Suggestions for Further Reading

A possible reading list peripheral to the subject matter of this chapter could be almost as long as one wanted to make it. Hauser and Schnore, 1965 includes chapters on the subdisciplines of history, geography, political science, sociology, and economics that pertain to urbanization. See also portions of Duncan, 1960; Reissman, 1964, perhaps the best undergraduate text in urban sociology; Friedmann and Alonso, 1964, a broadly based anthology with some excellent choices; and Gibbs, 1961, an anthology more narrowly concentrated on methodology. All of these books have bibliographies that supplement the following list.

* ABRAMS, CHARLES. 1964. *Man's Struggle for Shelter in an Urbanizing World.* M.I.T. Press, Cambridge, Mass.

BEARDWOOD, ROGER. 1968. "The Southern Roots of the Urban Crisis," *Fortune,* August, pp. 80–87, 151–156.

BERGER, BENNETT W. 1960. *Working-Class Suburb.* University of California Press, Berkeley.

BERRY, BRIAN J. L. 1961. "City Size Distributions and Economic Development," *Economic Development and Cultural Change,* 19, 573–588.

———. 1967. "Generalization of the Metropolitan Area Concept." American Statistical Association, *Proceedings, Social Statistics Section.* Washington, D.C.

BOEKE, J. H. 1942. *The Structure of Netherlands Indian Economy.* Institute of Pacific Relations, New York.

BOGUE, DONALD J. 1953. *Population Growth in Standard Metropolitan Areas, 1900–1950.* U.S. Housing and Home Finance Agency, Washington, D.C.

BOSE, NIRMAL KUMAR. 1965. "Calcutta: A Premature Metropolis," *Scientific American,* 213, 91–102.

BROWNING, HARLEY. 1958. "Recent Trends in Latin American Urbanization," *Annals of the American Academy of Political and Social Science,* 316, 111–120.

———, and JACK P. GIBBS. 1961. "Some Measures of Demographic and Spatial Relationships among Cities," in Gibbs, 1961, pp. 436–460.

BURGESS, ERNEST W. 1929. "Urban Areas," in *Chicago: An Experiment in Social Science Research,* edited by T. V. Smith and Leonard D. White. University of Chicago Press, Chicago, pp. 113–138.

CALDERÓN, LUIS, ARTURO CALLE, and JAIME DORSELAER. 1963. *Problemas de urbanización en América Latina.* Estudio Sociológico No. 13. Centro de Investigaciones Sociales de FERES, Bogotá.

CARLSON, ERIC. 1959. "High-Rise Management: Design Problems as Found in Caracas Studied by International Team," *Journal of Housing,* 16, 311–314.

* CLARK, S. D. 1963. "The Society of Suburbia," in *Social Controversy,* edited by William Petersen and David Matza. Wadsworth, Belmont, Calif., pp. 304–315.

COMHAIRE, JEAN L. 1956. "Economic Change and the Extended Family," *Annals of the American Academy of Political and Social Science*, 305, 45–52.

* DAVIE, MAURICE R. 1937. "The Pattern of Urban Growth," in *Studies in the Science of Society*, edited by George Peter Murdock. Yale University Press, New Haven, pp. 133–161.

DAVIS, KINGSLEY. 1960. "Colonial Expansion and Urban Diffusion in the Americas," *International Journal of Comparative Sociology*, 1, 43–66.

————. 1965. "The Urbanization of the Human Population," *Scientific American*, 213, 41–53.

* ————, and HILDA HERTZ GOLDEN. 1954. "Urbanization and the Development of Preindustrial Areas," *Economic Development and Cultural Change*, 3, 6–24.

DEYRUP, FELICIA J. 1967. "Social Mobility as a Major Factor in Economic Development," *Social Research*, 34, 333–346.

DORSELAER, JAIME, and ALFONSO GREGORY. 1962. *La urbanización en América Latina*. Estudio Sociológico No. 2. Centro de Investigaciones Sociales de FERES, Bogotá, 2 Vols.

* DUNCAN, OTIS DUDLEY, and ALBERT J. REISS, JR. 1956. *Social Characteristics of Urban and Rural Communities, 1950*. Wiley, New York.

———— et al. 1960. *Metropolis and Region*. Johns Hopkins Press, Baltimore.

ELDRIDGE, HOPE TISDALE. 1956. "The Process of Urbanization," in *Demographic Analysis*, edited by Joseph J. Spengler and Otis Dudley Duncan. Free Press, Glencoe, Ill., pp. 338–343.

ELKAN, WALTER. 1960. *Migrants and Proletarians: Urban Labour in the Economic Development of Uganda*. Oxford University Press, London.

* FARLEY, REYNOLDS. 1968. "The Urbanization of Negroes in the United States," *Journal of Social History*, 1, 241–258.

———— and KARL E. TAEUBER. 1968. "Population Trends and Residential Segregation since 1960," *Science*, 159, 953–956.

FIREY, WALTER. 1947. *Land Use in Central Boston*. Harvard University Press, Cambridge, Mass.

FRIEDMANN, JOHN, and WILLIAM ALONSO, editors. 1964. *Regional Development and Planning*. M.I.T. Press, Cambridge, Mass.

FRYER, D. W. 1953. "The 'Million City' in Southeast Asia," *Geographical Review*, 43, 474–494.

GANS, HERBERT J. 1962. *The Urban Villagers: Group and Class in the Life of Italian-Americans*. Free Press, New York.

GERMANI, GINO. 1961. "Inquiry into the Social Effects of Urbanization in a Working-Class Sector of Greater Buenos Aires," in Hauser, 1961, pp. 206–233.

————. 1965. "Emigración del campo a la ciudad y sus causas," in Horacio C. Giberti *et al*. *Sociedad, economía y reforma agraria*. Ediciones Libera, Buenos Aires, pp. 69–87.

* GIBBS, JACK P., editor. 1961. *Urban Research Methods*. Van Nostrand, New York.

————, and KINGSLEY DAVIS. 1961. "Conventional versus Metropolitan Data in the International Study of Urbanization," in Gibbs, 1961, pp. 419–435.

* GINSBURG, NORTON S. 1955. "The Great City in Southeast Asia," *American Journal of Sociology*, 60, 455–462.

GIST, NOEL P. 1958. "The Ecological Structure of an Asian City: An East-West Comparison," *Population Review* (Madras), 2, 17–25.

GOLDSTEIN, SIDNEY. 1963. "Some Economic Consequences of Suburbanization in the Copenhagen Metropolitan Area," *American Journal of Sociology*, **68**, 551–564.

———. 1965. "Rural-Suburban-Urban Population Redistribution in Denmark," *Rural Sociology*, **30**, 267–277.

* HAAR, CHARLES M. 1963. "Latin America's Troubled Cities," *Foreign Affairs*, **41**, 536–549.

HALL, PETER. 1966. *The World Cities*. McGraw-Hill, New York.

HANSEN, ASAEL T. 1934. "The Ecology of a Latin American City," in *Race and Culture Contacts*, edited by E. B. Reuter. McGraw-Hill, New York, pp. 124–142.

* HARRIS, BRITTEN. 1959. "Urbanization Policy in India," in Regional Science Association, *Papers and Proceedings*, **5**, 181–203.

HAUSER, PHILIP M. 1957. "Summary Report," in Joint UN/UNESCO Seminar on Urbanization in the ECAFE Region. *Urbanization in Asia and the Far East*. UNESCO, Calcutta.

———, editor. 1961. *Urbanization in Latin America*. Columbia University Press, New York.

———, and LEO F. SCHNORE, editors. 1965. *The Study of Urbanization*. Wiley, New York.

HAWLEY, AMOS H. 1950. *Human Ecology: A Theory of Community Structure*. Ronald, New York.

* ———. 1956. *The Changing Shape of Metropolitan America: Deconcentration Since 1920*. Free Press, Glencoe, Ill.

HOSELITZ, BERT F. 1957. "Urbanization and Economic Growth in Asia," *Economic Development and Cultural Change*, **6**, 42–54.

———. 1960. *Sociological Aspects of Economic Growth*. Free Press, Glencoe, Ill.

INTERNATIONAL LABOUR ORGANISATION. 1953. *Workers' Housing Problems in Asian Countries*. Geneva.

* INTERNATIONAL URBAN RESEARCH. 1959. *The World's Metropolitan Areas*. University of California Press, Berkeley.

KUBLER, GEORGE A. 1964. "Cities and Culture in the Colonial Period in Latin America," *Diogenes*, No. 47, pp. 53–62.

* LAMPARD, ERIC E. 1955. "The History of Cities in the Economically Advanced Areas," *Economic Development and Cultural Change*, **3**, 81–136.

LEWIS, OSCAR. 1952. "Urbanization without Breakdown: A Case Study," *Scientific Monthly*, **75**, 31–41.

McCALL, DANIEL F. 1955. "Dynamics of Urbanization in Africa," *Annals of the American Academy of Political and Social Science*, **298**, 151–160.

MACURA, MILOŠ. 1961. "The Influence of the Definition of the Urban Place on the Size of the Urban Population," in Gibbs, 1961, pp. 21–31.

* MANGIN, WILLIAM. 1967. "Latin American Squatter Settlements: A Problem and a Solution," *Latin American Research Review*, **2**, 65–98.

MARRIS, PETER. 1960. "Social Change and Social Class," *International Journal of Comparative Sociology*, **1**, 119–124.

* ———. 1961. *Family and Social Change in an African City: A Study of Rehousing in Lagos*. Routledge & Kegan Paul, London.

* MATOS MAR, JOSÉ. 1961. "Migration and Urbanization: The 'Barriadas' of Lima, an Example of Integration into Urban Life," in Hauser, 1961, pp. 170–190.

° MEHTA, SURINDER K. 1964. "Some Demographic and Economic Correlates of Primate Cities: A Case for Revaluation," *Demography*, 1, 136–147.

MITCHELL, J. CLYDE. 1961. "Wage Labour and African Population Movements in Central Africa," in *Essays on African Population*, edited by K. M. Barbour and R. M. Prothero. Routledge & Kegan Paul, London, pp. 193–248.

° MITRA, S. 1965. "The Changing Pattern of Population Concentration in Indian Cities," *Eugenics Quarterly*, 12, 154–161.

MOORE, WILBERT E. 1953. "The Exportability of the 'Labor Force' Concept," *American Sociological Review*, 18, 68–72.

MORSE, RICHARD M. 1962. "Latin American Cities: Aspects of Function and Structure," *Comparative Studies in Society and History*, 4, 473–493.

° MURPHEY, RHOADS. 1957. "New Capitals of Asia," *Economic Development and Cultural Change*, 5, 216–243.

PARK, ROBERT E. 1925. "The City: Suggestions for the Investigation of Human Behavior in the Urban Environment," in *The City*, edited by Park and E. W. Burgess. University of Chicago Press, Chicago, pp. 1–46.

REDFIELD, ROBERT. 1947. "The Folk Society," *American Journal of Sociology*, 52, 293–408.

REISSMAN, LEONARD. 1964. *The Urban Process: Cities in Industrial Societies*. Free Press of Glencoe, New York.

RICARD, ROBERT. 1950. "La plaza mayor en España y en América Española," *Estudios Geográficos* (Madrid), 11, 321–327.

———. 1952. "Apuntes complementarios sobre la plaza mayor española y el 'rossio' portugues," *Estudios Geográficos* (Madrid), 13, 229–237.

SADIE, JAN L. 1967. "Labor Supply and Employment in Less Developed Countries," *Annals of the American Academy of Political and Social Science*, 369, 121–130.

SCHAPERA, ISAAC. 1947. *Migrant Labour and Tribal Life: A Study of Conditions in the Bechuanaland Protectorate*. Oxford University Press, London.

° SCHNORE, LEO F. 1957. "Satellites and Suburbs," *Social Forces*, 36, 121–127.

———. 1963. "The Socio-Economic Status of Cities and Suburbs," *American Sociological Review*, 28, 76–85.

———, and HARRY SHARP. 1963. "Racial Changes in Metropolitan Areas, 1950–1960," *Social Forces*, 41, 247–253.

° SCHWIRIAN, KENT P., and JOHN W. PREHN. 1962. "An Axiomatic Theory of Urbanization," *American Sociological Review*, 27, 812–825.

SHRYOCK, HENRY S., JR. 1964. *Population Mobility within the United States*. Community and Family Study Center, University of Chicago, Chicago.

SMITH, T. LYNN. 1963. "Urbanization in Latin America," *International Journal of Comparative Sociology* (Dharwar), 4, 227–242.

STEEL, R. W. 1961. "The Towns of Tropical Africa," in *Essays on African Population*, edited by K. M. Barbour and R. M. Prothero. Routledge & Kegan Paul, London, pp. 249–278.

TAEUBER, IRENE B., and CONRAD TAEUBER. 1964. "The Great Concentration: SMSAs from Boston to Washington," *Population Index*, 30, 3–29.

TANGRI, SHANTI. 1962. "Urbanization, Political Stability, and Economic Growth," in Turner, 1962, pp. 192–212.

° TRUESDELL, LEON E. 1949. "The Development of the Urban-Rural Classification in the United States, 1874 to 1949," U.S. Bureau of the Census, *Current Population Reports,* Series P-23, No. 1, Washington, D.C.

\* TURNER, ROY, editor. 1962. *India's Urban Future.* University of California Press, Berkeley.

UNITED NATIONS. POPULATION DIVISION. 1950. "Data on Urban and Rural Populations in Recent Censuses." St/SOA/Series A. Population Studies, No. 8. Reprinted in part in Gibbs, 1961, pp. 472–489.

———. 1953. *Demographic Yearbook, 1952.* New York, Chapter 1.

———. Bureau of Social Affairs. 1961. "Some Policy Implications of Urbanization," in Hauser, 1961, pp. 294–321.

UNESCO. 1956. *The Social Implications of Industrialization and Urbanization: Five Studies in Asia.* Calcutta.

\* U.S. BUREAU OF LABOR STATISTICS. 1968. *Recent Trends in the Social and Economic Conditions of Negroes in the United States.* BLS Report No. 347, Washington, D.C.

VERNON, RAYMOND. 1957. "Production and Distribution in the Large Metropolis," *Annals of the American Academy of Political and Social Science,* 314, 15–29.

VIOLICH, FRANCIS. 1944. *Cities of Latin America: Housing and Planning to the South.* Reinhold, New York.

\* ———. 1962. "Evolution of the Spanish City: Issues Basic to Planning Today," *Journal of the American Institute of Planners,* 28, 170–179.

WILKINSON, THOMAS O. 1960. "Urban Structure and Industrialization," *American Sociological Review,* 25, 356–363.

WIRTH, LOUIS. 1938. "Urbanism as a Way of Life," *American Journal of Sociology,* 44, 1–24.

WURSTER, CATHERINE BAUER. 1955. "The Optimum Pattern of Urbanization: Does Asia Need a New Type of Regional Planning?" in United Nations. *Seminar on Regional Planning.* Tokyo.

———. 1962. "Urban Living Conditions, Overhead Costs, and the Development Pattern," in Turner, 1962, pp. 277–298.

# 14 THE TREND OF FERTILITY IN INDUSTRIAL COUNTRIES

Mortality and fertility change for three kinds of reasons: (1) technical advances in medicine and contraception; (2) differences in social groups' access to the more advanced techniques and (3) in their attitudes toward using them. The third factor is occasionally significant with respect to mortality (as in the opposition to vaccination or the persistence of folk medicine), but the high value placed on good health and long life generally transcends social boundaries. With respect to fertility, however, attitudes are decidedly more relevant. Because the number of children desired differs among social groups, a couple with knowledge of contraceptives, physical access to them, and no moral inhibitions about their use still may or may not exercise birth control. The analysis of fertility, which now includes this third factor as an important element, is therefore more complex than the analysis of mortality.

It is convenient to divide the discussion of fertility by societal types—industrial countries in this chapter and underdeveloped ones in Chapter 16. The present analysis, thus, picks up themes that were discussed earlier. The section on Malthus leads, even if by a route that he did not mark, into the rise of the neo-Malthusian movement; the discussion of the physiology of reproduction as this relates to contraception is a necessary introduction to the analysis here of differential attitudes toward birth control. Such links are obvious, but the reader should also note that the rise of urban-industrial society, the over-all background to Part II of this book, is the main dimension along which birth rates can be meaningfully differentiated.

## The Birth-Control Movement and Its Opponents

The battle for what Himes termed the democratization of birth control constitutes one of the most interesting episodes in the history of ideas. Neo-Malthusianism was no less an invention of the nineteenth century than, say, the vulcanization of rubber, which made possible the development of efficacious contraceptive devices. From one country or period to another, one can distinguish differences in dogma; and occasionally the same country had several competing birth-control leagues, which opposed each other with all the vehemence of political or religious sects. Underlying the variation, however, a fundamental agreement on several key doctrines evolved from the works of the English and American pioneers (Himes, 1936, Chapters 9–10): [1] (1) Control of family size is both physically possible and morally desirable. (2) The ultimate decision whether and when to have children should be made by parents, rather than by fate, or tradition, or church, or state. (3) A relatively small number of children is a social good, both because of favorable effects within the family and because a too rapid population growth is a serious danger to social welfare.

The first book to recommend contraceptive measures as a substitute for Malthus's moral restraint appeared in England in 1822—*Illustrations and Proofs of the Principle of Population,* by Francis Place.[2] Though derivative from a number of predecessors (among them Benjamin Franklin), Place was original in that he gave the birth-control movement its first systematic social theory and ethical rationale. The postponement of marriage that Malthus advocated, he argued, is too onerous a means of limiting population growth ever to be widely adopted. Marriages between young people, in his view, are generally happier ones, for older persons cannot adjust to each other so readily. If one accepts Malthus's thesis that too rapid a population growth leads inevitably to social and economic distress—and Place repeated it in a simplified version—then "to avoid these miseries, the answer is short and plain": the use of contraceptives.

On the other side of the Atlantic, the first book on birth control, *Moral Physiology* (1830), was written by Robert Dale Owen (the oldest son of Robert Owen), shortly to be followed by Charles Knowlton's *Fruits of Philosophy* (1832). Unlike Place and Owen, Knowlton was a physician,

---

[1] See also Field, 1931; Micklewright, 1961. On the birth-control movement of Denmark, see Mangin, 1962; of Sweden, Sutter, 1960; of France, Bergues, 1960.

[2] See the edition that Himes edited: Houghton Mifflin, Boston, 1930.

and in medical terms his pamphlet was an improvement over its predecessors. "Perhaps it is no exaggeration to say that Knowlton's treatment
of contraceptive technique is the first really important account after those
of Soranos and Aëtios two millennia earlier" (Himes, 1936, p. 227). Place
and his associates had recommended a sponge, and Owen *coitus interruptus;*
Knowlton's chief method was a douche with an astringent solution.

In England, neo-Malthusianism was beginning to attract some of the
best minds of the period, in particular, Jeremy Bentham and John Stuart
Mill. The most important figure in the middle of the century was George
Drysdale, author of *The Elements of Social Science* (1854), a book of some
600 finely printed pages. In medical terms, the author was less accurate
than Knowlton or even Place, but by his extensive and sympathetic exposition of classical economic theory, he established a firmer link between it
and neo-Malthusian doctrine than had existed previously. During half a
century *The Elements* appeared in thirty-five English editions and was
translated into at least ten languages.

After fifty years of obscurity, in 1876–77 the birth-control movement
was suddenly given wide publicity by the prosecution of two of its advocates, Charles Bradlaugh and Annie Besant. They had organized a firm for
the express purpose of publishing and distributing Knowlton's *Fruits of
Philosophy,* and thus testing a court decision banning it. Arrested and tried,
for four days the defendants argued their case in social as well as legal
terms. It was desirable, they held, that the poor should be informed on
contraceptive means. The trial was reported in both the national and the
local press, often with long verbatim passages from their testimony and
even quotations from Knowlton's book itself. The sale of *Fruits of Philosophy,* which had been only 700 copies a year, jumped to some 125,000 in
three months, not including a flood of imitations and pirated editions. The
defendants were convicted and sentenced to six months' imprisonment and
a fine of £200; they appealed and a year later were acquitted on a techni-
cality. As a direct consequence of the publicity furnished by the Bradlaugh-
Besant trial and a number of other prosecutions of birth-control proponents,
a new Malthusian League was founded, with Charles R. Drysdale (brother
of George) as president and Mrs. Besant as secretary. The League grew
rapidly, receiving a sympathetic reception from a portion of the population
not only in large cities but in remote villages (Himes, 1936, Chapter 10;
Banks and Banks, 1954; Glass, 1940, p. 38).

The United States went through a similar cycle a generation later. In
1913 Mrs. Margaret Sanger, then a visiting nurse in New York's East Side
slum, went to England, Holland, and France in search of information on
reliable contraceptive methods. On her return she opened a clinic and
served thirty days in prison for maintaining a "public nuisance." She started
*The Birth Control Review,* a propaganda organization, another clinic, and
a research bureau, the National Committee on Maternal Health. As early

as 1922, she helped set up birth-control movements in Hawaii, Japan, and China (Sanger, 1931; 1938). That contraceptives are legal today in most of the United States is due in considerable degree to the courage and perseverance of this one woman.

Admirers welcome Margaret Sanger after she is released from jail (*Planned Parenthood/World Population*).

## TRADITIONAL OPPOSITION

In all countries the birth-control movement has been shaped to a considerable degree by the opposition to it.[3] In the traditional view children come as gifts of God, and should be accepted gratefully, unquestioningly. To subject the process of reproduction to man's will is "unnatural." One difficulty with this view is that it makes no allowance for the no less unnatural death control that has been achieved in the modern world. An inefficient check to fertility, combined with modern medicine, public sanitation, insecticides, and so on, results in a population growth so great that, indeed, the balance with nature is endangered.

The notion that parents should be permitted to determine the size of their family began everywhere as the point of view of an embattled mi-

[3] Concerning opposition by nationalists and socialists, see pp. 586–588, 634–637.

nority, the sort of people who held and expressed unpopular opinions of all kinds. Bradlaugh, for instance, was a militant atheist; Mrs. Besant was an ardent feminist, later a theosophist. More generally, the advocacy of birth control tended to overlap with support of other sectarian views—pacifism, temperance, vegetarianism, and especially secularism; when the link did not exist in substance, it was often created in form by the libertarians who defended anyone whose freedom of speech had been infringed (but see Banks and Banks, 1964, which analyzes the disjunction between the birth-control movement and feminism). Like any other social reform, then, neo-Malthusianism was opposed first of all because of its novelty, its affront to conventionality. And in this case the automatic rejection was strengthened by the specific proposal, particularly in so prurient a nation as Victorian England. One of the worst offenses of Bradlaugh and Besant was their plain speaking, their threat to what *The Times* termed "certain reserves and proprieties surrounding the first law of Nature and the domestic hearth" (Banks and Banks, 1954).

The principal institution that preserves the cultural tradition concerning family norms is the church, and religious thought throughout the world is generally favorable to family life and thus to procreation. Yet the opposition to birth control that some see as implicit in this normative stance is often lacking either from sacred works or from recent exegeses. Even a brief review of the major religions suggests that the range is wide—from strong and explicit condemnation, through a frequent ambivalence that depends on interpretation to give it concrete meaning, to a positive endorsement of contraception. Of the three important sources of religious thought in the West—Judaism, Protestantism, and Roman Catholicism—the first two have gradually moved away from an earlier traditionalist opposition to birth control, so that the Catholic doctrine is now anomalous and, if only for that reason, of especial interest.

**Judaism.** Relevant passages in the Old Testament, as also in Christian thought, have been subjected to various interpretations. According to modern exegesis, the sin of Onan (Genesis 38:9) was not *coitus interruptus*, but rather the refusal to beget offspring by his deceased brother's wife, as required under the law of the levirate. A more pertinent imperative is "Be fruitful and multiply" (Genesis 1:28), which the orthodox interpret as a prohibition of both contraception and celibacy and, above all, as an abhorrence of childlessness (Patai, 1959, Chapter 5). But according to certain commentators, the Talmud permitted contraception and even made it mandatory if the health of the mother or the welfare of previous children so indicated. "The Jewish attitude never considered the function of intercourse to be for procreation only" (Glasner, 1961). In 1959, the parent body of American Reform Judaism passed a resolution against all legal barriers to contraception and in favor of its wider public dissemination through both public and private agencies (General Assembly, Union of American Hebrew Congregations, November, 1959). This more or less represents the present stance, apart from the most orthodox, of Jews throughout the world.

**Protestantism,** while it hardly constitutes a single entity on this question, has followed a path parallel to that of Judaism. Opposition to birth control was general at the time of the Reformation. For Calvin *coitus interruptus* was "doubly monstrous," for "it is to extinguish the hope of the race and to kill before he is born the son who was hoped for." Luther, while less specific on contraception, condemned it by implication (Noonan, 1965, p. 353). Such views were all but universal in world Protestantism up to the nineteenth century. The change since then can be illustrated by the successive statements of Anglican bishops at the Lambeth conferences.

In 1908 they spoke out unambiguously against the use of contraceptives. In 1920 they were still opposed, but Bishop Kirk, the leading Anglican authority on moral theology, sensed the beginnings of permissiveness on the subject. The Lambeth Conference gave clear permission for the conscientious use of contraceptives in 1930, and was even more forthright in 1958 in presenting the case for birth control. This development is significant, partly because Anglican bishops . . . look for guidance to a considerable extent to the Catholic tradition of moral theology and are often cautious about taking any action that widens the separation between their Church and the Roman Church (Bennett, 1959).

In the United States, the Federal Council of the Churches of Christ in America published a report in 1931 approving contraception in principle; and more recently a number of Protestant denominations have taken the stand that "responsible family planning is today a clear moral duty" (this is the wording of one such statement, by the Council for Christian Social Action, United Church of Christ, January 30, 1960).

### THE CATHOLIC POSITIONS ON BIRTH CONTROL

Roman Catholicism is the one important world religion that still upholds its opposition to contraception, though here too the doctrine is in disarray. The present position, as one priest has put it, "may appear as metaphysical hair-splitting" (Gibbons, 1956); and strong pressure to resolve the contradictions is being exerted not only by non-Catholics (who resent the Church's influence on the general society's law and public policy) and Catholic laity, but by a considerable section of the hierarchy itself. No account of this ongoing debate in a book not devoted exclusively to that subject can be complete or, probably by the time this is read, up to date.

Of the flood of printed matter on Catholics and birth control, the best by a wide margin is *Contraception,* by John T. Noonan, Jr., at the time professor in the Notre Dame Law School and director of its Natural Law Institute. Neither the punishment of Onan nor any other passage, in his opinion, establishes Biblical authority for the prohibition of birth control. Given the Jewish laws against homosexuality, against bestiality, against temple prostitution, against marital intercourse during menstruation, "it is surely strange that . . . the illegality of contraception should be left to inference, if the compilers of the Pentateuch believed contraception to be unlawful" (Noonan, 1965, p. 35). As the early Church lacked a clear guide from either Testament, it gradually worked out a position in opposition to competing movements. On the "left" were the Gnostics, who regarded themselves as "royal sons" of the Lord and thus bound by no law; they scorned marriage and lived as libertines. On the "right" were the Manichees and various other neo-Platonist groups, who believed that sexuality is evil and only absolute continence is wholly good.[4]

The most important figure in the early development of Catholic doctrine, Augustine, was of course a Manichee for some decades before his conversion, and these imprints were "never effaced from his mind; his concern with evil, his concern with sexuality, were Manichean" (ibid., p. 119). Augustine purged himself of his background by denouncing Manichean morals, including in particular contraception by the method the Manichees had taken over from Greek medicine, the fallacious use of the sterile period.[5] The Augustinian doctrine was given a more definite form in early medieval penitentials, which classified the criteria by which confessors were to judge the relative gravity of sins. These were concerned to an overwhelming degree with sexuality;[6] during the same period there evolved also the rule on priestly celibacy and the cult of virginity (cf. May, 1931). Contraception was condemned as a form of homicide, a ruling preserved in Catholic law until 1917 (Noonan, 1965, pp. 168–169, 232–237).

---

[4] Compare: "In a fully populated world a substantial proportion of men and women should lead celibate lives, . . . [which] would hardly be possible at all except in a Catholic community. . . . The only real answer is that the whole world should become Christian in the course of the next century or so" (Russell, 1958).

[5] It is indeed "piquant that the first pronouncement on contraception by the most influential theologian teaching on such matters should be a vigorous attack on the one method of avoiding procreation accepted by twentieth-century Catholic theologians as morally lawful" (Noonan 1965, p. 120). Augustine held also that it was sinful for spouses to have intercourse during pregnancy, and generations of theologians followed him. Two centuries later Pope Gregory the Great held that if any pleasure was "mixed" with the act of intercourse undertaken for the licit purpose of procreation, the spouses were guilty of "befouling" their intercourse and thus "transgressed the law of marriage"; and generations of theologians followed him (ibid., p. 159).

[6] It is interesting to compare the schedule in traditional China, where transgressors are assigned to one of the eight hells according to the gravity of their sins. Apart from homosexuality, sodomy, incest, and adultery only "if the adulterer talks about it," all other sexual acts are sinful only if they are related to religion. Thus, "the worst sin is a sexual act with a Buddhist saint" (Wolfam Eberhard, Guilt and Sin in Traditional China, University of California Press, Berkeley, 1967, pp. 61–63).

A numerous progeny was recommended for its own sake, for "the more offspring, the bigger the population of heaven" (*ibid.*, pp. 275–276).[7]

"The most independent critique of the Christian sexual ethic undertaken by an orthodox critic" was made by Martin LeMaistre (1432–1481), who was the first (!) to "establish the general lawfulness of the marital act" (*ibid.*, pp. 306–312). "Between 1450 and 1750 there was a substantial rejection of the Augustinian view that intercourse may be initiated only for procreation" (*ibid.*, p. 339). Contraception was still banned mainly because, following Aquinas, it was seen as "unnatural," but various statements in the 1820s and 1830s "encouraged a belief that the Church was about to modify its position on contraception" (*ibid.*, p. 403). The change came only in 1930, with the papal encyclical *Casti connubii*, a small section of which was interpreted, against much ecclesiastical opposition, to sanction the rhythm method if there is a "serious motive" for avoiding childbearing (*ibid.*, pp. 438–447; Sulloway, 1959, Chapter 7).

How shall this "serious motive" be defined? In present-day Catholic doctrine, as expressed in the Code of Canon Law, "The primary end of marriage is the procreation and education of offspring; the secondary end, mutual aid and the remedying of concupiscence" (quoted in Gibbons, 1956). Under some circumstances, Catholic doctrine defines it as licit to serve the secondary ends (mitigating the sex drive and mutual aid, which is interpreted to include increasing the bond of marital affection) even when conception is impossible; for example, persons known to be sterile may enjoy marital relations without sin. It might seem that intercourse during a wife's sterile period is free from sin in the same way, and indeed the Catholic Church's stand has seemingly moved toward this interpretation. According to Pius XII (1951), it is legitimate for a Catholic couple to restrict intercourse to the sterile period "always and deliberately" under a wide array of loosely specified conditions:

---

[7] How important this last theme became can be illustrated by the writings on birth control in the Jesuit journal *America* from its first issue in 1909 to the 1960s (Reiterman, 1965). The overwhelming emphasis up to 1930, when *Casti connubii* was promulgated, was on the simple value of procreation, the moral worth of large families irrespective of any contrary considerations. "Suppose a child is born deaf, dumb, blind, idiotic, in utter poverty, and that its parents know beforehand that such would be its condition." Suppose, in another example, that there is a "tubercular father with no prospects of supporting his family." Suppose, in a third example, that a wife is told by "a very modern physician" that "she could not give birth to her child without imperiling her own life." In all these cases, *America*'s answer was the biblical injunction to "increase and multiply." "To be born, even with a strong probability of future infirmity, is better than not to be born." Similarly: "We must make every effort to accommodate the increased numbers which God, in His wisdom, sees fit to place upon the earth through men" (Kelly, 1960, p. 75). "The family which courageously and even heroically rears a large number of children in an overpopulated area merits special praise for its virtue" (Zimmerman, 1957, p. 103). In contrast, *America* more recently (September 30, 1967) spoke editorially of the "necessity of some use of contraception in the life of the genuinely Catholic family."

There are serious motives, such as those often mentioned in the so-called medical, eugenic, economic, and social "indications," that can exempt for a long time, perhaps even the whole duration of the marriage, from the positive and obligatory carrying out of the act [of procreation]. From this it follows that observing the nonfertile periods alone can be lawful only under a moral aspect. Under the conditions mentioned it really is so.[8]

From "every attempt to hinder procreation is immoral" (*Casti connubii*, 1930) to the "so-called medical, eugenic, economic, and social" exceptions to this dictum (1951), a considerable distance was covered. Unlike most moral injunctions, whether of the Catholic or of other Christian churches, the emphasis here is neither on the motive of the person nor on the effect of his behavior, but simply on the means used to bring about a desired end.

The argumentation for the exclusive legitimacy of periodic abstinence has been openly attacked by respected members of the hierarchy throughout the world. According to Father John A. O'Brien, Professor of Theology at the University of Notre Dame, the primary end of marriage is not mere procreation but also the education of offspring, and this means responsible parenthood (O'Brien, 1963). Father Stanislas de Lestapis, S.J., professor at the Catholic Institute of Paris, argues that "there is in principle a right or, better, a duty to practice a form of birth limitation based on careful thought. . . . There is an optimum number for each family and each family alone can judge what it is" (quoted in Cook, 1965). In the introduction to the book that he edited,[9] Archbishop Thomas D. Roberts, S.J., asked the Vatican Council to consider whether voluntary sterilization is not licit. "Schema for a Document on Responsible Parenthood," the position paper submitted in 1966 by a *majority* of the papal birth-control commission, marks the high point of this line of criticism.[10] The text condemned abortion and declared that sterilization "is generally to be excluded," but

[8] Quoted in Edgar Schmiedeler, O.S.B., editor, *Moral Questions Affecting Married Life*, National Catholic Welfare Conference, Washington, D.C., 1952, pp. 3–23.

[9] The refreshing tone of this work is suggested by this passage: "When primitive man was trying to press northward from the tropics and was worrying about how his naked body would stand the winter cold, it is fortunate he had no witch doctors to limit him to three choices: 1. Don't go north (complete abstinence); 2. Go north only in the summer time (periodic abstinence); or 3. Go north as you are and trust in the spirits of your clan (accept all the biological consequences of your action). But man found a fourth choice, 'instant fur,' and became thereby the most adaptable mammal" (Julian Pleasants, "The Lessons of Biology," in Roberts, 1964, pp. 92–108).

[10] This was written by the Rev. Joseph Fuchs, a German Jesuit teaching at the Gregorian University in Rome; the Rev. Raymond Sigmond, a Hungarian Dominican, president of the Institute of Social Science of the Pontifical University of St. Thomas Aquinas; the Rev. Paul Anciaux, a professor at the seminary of Malines-Brussels, Belgium; the Rev. A. Auer, a specialist in sexual questions, Würzburg, Germany; the Rev. Michel Labourdette, O.P., a theologian from Toulouse, France; and the Rev. Pierre de Locht of the National Family Pastoral Center, Brussels. Thirteen other theologians and several experts from other fields also signed the document. It and the minority statement were printed in a full English translation in the *National Catholic Reporter*, April 19, 1967.

made no other specification of a licit method of contraception. The means should be selected by "the couple" on the basis of the following criteria: (1) "The whole meaning of the mutual giving and of human procreation [shall be] kept in a context of true love," and extramarital contraception is barred. (2) The method used shall have an appropriate "effectiveness." (3) There shall be the "least possible" number of negative side-effects, whether biological, hygienic, or psychological. (4) No absolute rules shall apply, for the best means may depend on the situation of "a certain couple."

The commission submitted its two reports to Pope Paul VI on June 28, 1966, and for two years the world wondered whether the Catholic Church would accept the majority's recommendation and abandon its opposition to "artificial" birth control. In an encyclical issued in March 1967, *Populorum progressio* ("Development of Peoples"), the Pope pointed out the population problem of underdeveloped areas and the need for family planning—though by what means was left indefinite. But in another encyclical, *Humanae vitae* ("Of Human Life"), issued on July 29, 1968, the traditional doctrine was reaffirmed:

Marriage and conjugal love are by their nature ordained toward the begetting and education of children. Children are really the supreme gift of marriage and contribute very substantially to the welfare of their parents. . . . In the task of transmitting life, therefore, [the parents] are not free to proceed completely at will, as if they could determine in a wholly autonomous way the honest path to follow; but they must conform their activity to the creative intention of God. . . . Each and every marriage act must remain open to the transmission of life. . . . Abortion, even if for therapeutic reasons, [is] absolutely excluded, . . . [as is also] sterilization, whether perpetual or temporary, whether of the man or of the woman. Similarly excluded is every action which, either in anticipation of the conjugal act, or in its accomplishment, or in the development of the natural consequences, proposes, whether as an end or as a means, to render procreation impossible.

The sanctioning of the rhythm method was affirmed, provided its use is "for just motives," not further specified.

"It can be foreseen," one sentence of the encyclical reads, "that this teaching will perhaps not be easily received by all." Indeed, the anticipated opposition was great enough to induce Paul not merely to argue the case against contraception but, amazingly, also to urge that he had the right to do so.[10a] And in one Catholic country after another, large numbers of Catholic laity,

10a "No believer will wish to deny that the teaching authority of the Church is competent to interpret even the natural law. It is, in fact, indisputable. . . . The Church has always provided—and even more amply in recent times—a coherent teaching concerning both the nature of marriage and the correct use of conjugal rights and the duties of husband and wife." For a translation of the full text, see *National Catholic Reporter*, August 7, 1968.

priests, and higher prelates have openly challenged both the wisdom of the ban and this application of the Church's magisterium, or teaching authority.

That it is possible to speak realistically of Roman Catholic *positions* on contraception is the most dramatic fact that can be adduced in any discussion of this subject. Doctrine is in flux, and today authoritative statements can be quoted to support a wide range of mutually contradictory stands. Many of the best educated spokesmen for the Church advocate a new interpretation of "responsible parenthood." The manuals used to teach the laity Catholic family norms, as one might expect, are a generation behind these pioneers. In these texts, not only is the licit use of rhythm highly restricted but the small family is denigrated as an incomplete social institution, the large one eulogized as most blest by God (Blake, 1966a).

## Class Differences in Fertility

The social analysis of a nation's population is made by comparing the rates of relatively homogeneous categories. How should they be delimited? Differential rates have been calculated by region or urban-rural residence (suggesting the impact of urbanization on demographic trends), by social class (as measured by education, occupation, income, or some combination of such factors), and by religion or ethnic group (indicating a vestigial element of traditional culture). The comparison of such groups, even if at a single point in time, is often implicitly dynamic. For the demographic rates of any sector suggest that its way of life affects fertility and mortality, and if others seem to be imitating that way of life, then the trend of one segment may indicate the future of the whole population. The lower birth and death rates of the urban middle classes, to take the most obvious example, have often been seen as a kind of forecast of the levels to which rural or working-class rates would fall some time later. By the rationale of the demographic transition, thus, social groups are roughly of two types, those that introduce and help disseminate modernizing attitudes and behavior patterns and those that, for whatever reasons, lag behind.

### RURAL-URBAN DIFFERENCES

Irrespective of other variations, urban fertility in the West has almost always been lower than rural. Very often the decline in the birth rate was greatest in the largest cities. From the last decades of the nineteenth century to the 1930s, completed family size in Norway and the Netherlands, to take two disparate examples, fell steadily; but the earliest and most rapid declines were in Oslo and Amsterdam and the latest and slowest in the rural areas, while the smaller towns stayed between the two extremes (Johnson, 1960).

What is the meaning of this rural-urban contrast? It has often been pointed out that urban living conditions favor smaller families in a number of ways. City apartments permit expansion less comfortably than the one-family houses typical of villages and farms. Children are more expensive to rear when everything has to be bought than when at least a portion of the food is home-produced. On a farm minors help earn their keep by doing chores from a very young age on, whereas under urban conditions parents get no financial return, as it were, on their investment in offspring. In towns women are more likely to find alternative roles to being a housewife and thus to postpone procreation or even to put it off altogether. In judging the probable weight of these factors, it is useful to distinguish the physical constraints of rural and urban life from the city's ideas and culture patterns—that is, urbanization from urbanism.

Since the United States lacks adequate registration data for the nineteenth century, particularly for the early decades, the only measure available is the child-woman ratio (sometimes called the fertility ratio), or the number of children under 5 per 1,000 women in the child-bearing period, however this is specified.[11] For well over a century the urban child-woman ratio fluctuated at under two-thirds of the rural one. The factors underlying the long-term decline in fertility from 1810, when it began, to 1940, when at least temporarily it ended, can be allocated as follows: 24 per cent because of the continuing decline in the size of town families, 20 per cent because of rural-urban migration, and 56 per cent because of the decreased fertility in the countryside (Grabill et al., 1958, Tables 7–8; cf. Okun, 1958, pp. 99–101). That is to say, the small-family system spread much more by the diffusion of what we term urban norms to rural areas than by the migration of rural persons to urban places. At least for a nation like the United States, where one can hardly speak of a peasantry, one should not stress too much the direct influence of habitat on family size. A country population that is literate and in close touch with the city-based culture assimilates, even if partially and more slowly, the behavior patterns that originate there. But if the city is seen less as an ecological unit than as a center from which innovations and new attitudes flow, then rural-urban contrasts are in large part an index of the differences by social class.

## INVERSE CORRELATION BETWEEN CLASS AND FERTILITY

In traditional societies the class differentiation is more or less the same with respect to both mortality and fertility. For where long life and a numerous progeny are seen as good, the classes with the greatest control

---

[11] It is well known that underenumeration is particularly serious in the youngest age groups, not so much apparently because infants and children are passed over altogether as because their ages are often given as of their next rather than their last birthday (Grabill et al., 1958, pp. 406–413). If mothers were consistent in this respect, no infants under one year would be counted; in any case the error is less for the first five years than for the first year. The fertility ratio, moreover, measures what might be termed effective fertility—not the number of births per se but that figure reduced by the often substantial mortality during infancy.

over their destiny ordinarily live longer and also have larger families. The pattern is well illustrated by a study of twenty villages of present-day Poland. Among two successive peasant generations, the wealthier the couple was, the more children they had. "Rich peasant girls, being much sought after as marriage partners, marry earlier than poorer girls, begin to bear children sooner, and bear them more frequently and up to a later age." Even among the present generation, where the contrast was less because a few women were practicing contraception, the average number of children born ranged from about three in families with one hectare or less of land up to more than nine in those with 15 to 20 hectares (Stys, 1957).

In modern Western societies, on the contrary, the typical pattern has been that the better a family is able to afford children, the fewer children it has. The details differ according to the index used, but the general conclusion in the United States, for instance, is the same as far back as our information will take us. Using whatever data were available for the first several decades of the nineteenth century, Jaffe divided the inhabitants of New York, Boston, and Providence by the taxes they paid; those of the rural counties of New York State by their per capita ownership of agricultural property; and those of the counties of several southern states by the number of slaves owned. In each case he found an inverse relation between wealth and family size, largest in the cities but significant also in the rural areas (Jaffe, 1940).

In several United States censuses, women were asked how many children they had ever borne. For a female past her fecund years, this figure is known as the **completed family size,** a remarkably simple and direct measure of natality. Table 14-1 shows the completed family size of women aged forty-five to forty-nine years according to the major occupation group of their husbands. The contrast between urban and rural is sharp for each occupation group at all three dates, especially when (as in the table) the sponge class of "rural nonfarm" is eliminated. It should be kept in mind that the women had had most of their children when they were in their twenties and early thirties—thus, some twenty years before the census dates given. At the end of the nineteenth century (1910 census) a tendency was discernible within each residence class toward an inverse correlation of occupation and fertility, but after World War I (1940 census) there was some convergence. During the 1930s (1950 census), however, a clear progression in family size by occupational group was re-established, especially among the urban population. More than any other datum, these figures on family-building during the 1930s rule out a simple economic interpretation of fertility. During a major depression, when economic burdens weighed heavily on all groups but most on those at the bottom of the social scale, the inverse relation between social class and fertility not only did not disappear but was more firmly established than in prior decades.

Differentials by the education of the wife, as shown in Table 14-2, are

Table 14-1. Completed Family Size,[a] White Population, by Major Occupation Group of Husband and Residence, United States, 1910, 1940, 1950

|  | 1910 | | 1940 | | 1950 | |
|  | URBAN | RURAL-FARM | URBAN | RURAL-FARM | URBAN | RURAL-FARM |
|---|---|---|---|---|---|---|
| Professional, technical, and kindred workers | 2.8 | 4.3 | 2.0 | 2.9 | 1.7 | 3.0 |
| Managers, officials, and proprietors, except farm | 3.3 | 4.8 | 2.1 | 3.4 | 1.9 | 2.7 |
| Clerical, sales, and kindred workers | 3.1 | 4.7 | 2.0 | 3.0 | 1.9 | 2.8 |
| Craftsmen, foremen, and kindred workers | 4.0 | 5.2 | 2.6 | 4.0 | 2.3 | 3.5 |
| Operatives and kindred workers | 4.1 | 5.6 | 2.7 | 4.4 | 2.5 | 4.2 |
| Service workers, including private household | 3.9 | — | 2.5 | — | 2.3 | 3.5 |
| Laborers, except farm and mine | 4.8 | 5.5 | 3.2 | 4.4 | 3.1 | 4.4 |
| Farmers and farm managers | 4.2 | 5.6 | 2.7 | 4.1 | 3.1 | 3.6 |
| Farm laborers and foremen | 4.4 | 5.1 | — | 4.4 | 3.6 | 4.2 |

SOURCE: Wilson H. Grabill, Clyde V. Kiser, and Pascal K. Whelpton, *The Fertility of American Women*, Wiley, New York, 1958, Table 54.

[a] Children ever born to women aged 45–49 years, married once, whose husbands were still living with them at the time of the census. Data are for white women in 1950, for native white women in 1910 and 1940. Rates are not shown when there were fewer than 1,200 women in 1910 or 3,000 in 1940.

parallel to those by the occupation of the husband, except that the contrasts stand out even more clearly. Education has several advantages over occupation as an index of social class. There is no question about ordering: under all circumstances, college can be ranked above high school, but the same cannot be said of a professional, for example, as compared with a managerial position. Also, comparisons by husband's occupation often reflect the fact that young men start in low-level jobs and rise during their lifetime. Since in any one year their wives will usually have more children while they are younger, an annual rate (such as the birth rate, though not a cumulative rate, like the completed family size) will generally exaggerate class differences in fertility. Education, however, is ordinarily completed as a unit and then becomes a fixed attribute of adults for the rest of their lives.

Table 14-2. Completed Family Size,[a] White Population, by Education of Wife
and Residence, United States, 1940 and 1950

| | PER WOMAN | | | | PER WIFE | | | |
| --- | --- | --- | --- | --- | --- | --- | --- | --- |
| | 1940 | | 1950 | | 1940 | | 1950 | |
| | URBAN | RURAL-FARM | URBAN | RURAL-FARM | URBAN | RURAL-FARM | URBAN | RURAL-FARM |
| College: | | | | | | | | |
| 4 years or more | 1.1 | 1.8 | 1.0 | 1.6 | 1.8 | 2.2 | 1.4 | 1.8 |
| 1–3 years | 1.5 | 2.5 | 1.4 | 2.1 | 1.9 | 2.8 | 1.6 | 2.2 |
| High school: | | | | | | | | |
| 4 years | 1.6 | 2.6 | 1.5 | 2.5 | 1.8 | 2.8 | 1.7 | 2.6 |
| 1–3 years | 2.0 | 3.4 | 1.9 | 3.1 | 2.2 | 3.6 | 2.1 | 3.3 |
| Elementary or none | 2.5 | 4.2 | 2.4 | 3.9 | 2.8 | 4.4 | 2.6 | 4.1 |

SOURCE: Wilson H. Grabill, Clyde V. Kiser, and Pascal K. Whelpton, *The Fertility of American Women,* Wiley, New York, 1958, Tables 75 and 76.

[a] Number of children ever born to women aged 45–49 years. Data are for white women in 1950, for native white women in 1940.

Another advantage of education as an index is that it applies to all women and not, like the occupation of the husband, only to those who are married. Thus, Table 14-2 indicates the significant effect on fertility of women who do not marry or marry at a relatively advanced age: the gradients for completed family size are somewhat steeper per woman than per wife. Among white women aged forty-five to forty-nine years in 1950, for example, a quarter of the college graduates had never married, as compared with less than 6 per cent of those with eight years or less of schooling (Grabill et al., 1958, Table 67). According to a later study, however, the higher education of a sample of college-trained women made very little difference in their fertility values and expectations (Westoff and Potvin, 1967).

### THE DUMONT-BANKS MODEL

These differences by social class in the United States were parallel with those in England (Innes, 1938; Glass and Grebenik, 1954), France, the Low Countries, Scandinavia, and Western nations generally. The contrast was usually especially marked in each country when its birth rate began to fall.

"As national birth rates turned downward, class fertility differentials increased greatly" (Wrong, 1958). The pattern strongly suggests that the decline in fertility was started by the middle classes, whose smaller families were gradually imitated by the rest of Western populations.

In the theory of the demographic transition, it is assumed that mortality fell first and that the subsequent decline in fertility was largely a response to the resultant increase in population. In the West, there is more validity to the converse of this thesis. The norm proscribing reproduction before a suitable place was available for the wife and children, which had been embedded in preindustrial institutions, was shattered with the advent of the industrial society. Thus, among some social classes the incidence of marriage rose and the average age at which it occurred went down, resulting in a rise in fertility and a sharp increase of population. Together with other analysts of that day, Malthus proposed a return to the practice by which marriage was postponed until a living had been established for the future family. In what is sometimes termed "the" Malthusian doctrine, he warned that if prudence did not govern sexual passion, the population would be cut back instead by food shortages and other "positive" factors. In a second thesis more applicable to Western countries, Malthus held that those with an opportunity to advance themselves would reduce the family obligations they incurred in order to improve their chances of success. Not malnutrition but the best possibility of moving to a higher social rung induced the middle classes to adopt the norm of small families.

Any man tends to rise from inferior positions in society to higher ones. This tendency can be blocked by the material or other obstacles that immobilize him, but the tendency itself is beyond question. . . . —to climb unceasingly, as oil rises in a lamp wick, toward a marvelous ideal which attracts and seduces [him]. . . . For one who starts at the bottom to arrive at the top, it is necessary to run fast and not to be encumbered with baggage. Thus, while an ambitious man can be served by a good marriage, either because of the wealth or the contacts it brings him, his own children, particularly if they are numerous, almost inevitably slow him down (Dumont, 1890, pp. 106, 110).

The best study of this process of "social capillarity" is a work titled *Prosperity and Parenthood: A Study of Family Planning among the Victorian Middle Classes* (Banks, 1954). During the nineteenth century, Britain became the world's wealthiest nation and the urban middle classes her wealthiest social stratum. To move into that favored position was possible for many, but aspirants had to set and maintain an appropriate pattern of expenditures. One full-time servant, the minimum index of social respectability, constituted only the opening wedge. "With three servants—cook, parlormaid, and housemaid, or cook, housemaid, and nursemaid—a household was considered complete in all its functions. Further extensions were merely variations on this theme" (p. 76). The paraphernalia of gentility at the next step up included a carriage, of which the endless varieties provided a ladder of social status, from a humble pony and gig to a luxurious coach with three powdered footmen in elegant livery. An annual holiday away from home, which had been reserved for the wealthiest, came to be seen as a necessary part of middle-class life. The cost of children, particularly of the upbringing that would fit them for a suitable career, increased steadily. While at the beginning of the century seven boarding schools had sufficed to educate the sons of the aristocracy and upper gentry, thirty-five to forty new public schools were established between 1840 and 1870 for the far more numerous progeny of the advancing middle class. During this period a university degree became useful, if not indispensable, in more career lines. In short, during "the twenty years leading up to the Great Depression [that began in 1873] . . . there took place a striking expansion in the numbers of the English middle classes, in their wealth, and in their level and standard of living" (p. 113). The depression, far from reversing the trend among the nouveaux bourgeois, intensified the competition for the fewer opportunities for social advancement. There was thus a greater incentive to cut down on some expenditures, "especially those not directly relevant to their appearing affluent to the eyes of the world" (p. 133).

The limitation in family burdens was effected first of all by a postponement of marriage. Among the clergymen, doctors, lawyers, members of the aristocracy, merchants, bankers, manufacturers, and others of the gentlemen class who married between 1840 and 1870, the average age was a shade under 30 years (p. 48). So long as the industrial expansion continued unabated, late marriage was for most in the middle classes a sufficient check on reproduction, though undoubtedly some practiced birth control as well. By 1876–77, the dates of the Bradlaugh-Besant trials, many were finding it "increasingly difficult to preserve the kind of differential standard to which they had become accustomed," and the trials acted as a catalyst to the earlier partial and surreptitious spread of contraception (pp. 167–168). "Anthony Trollope's advice to a young lady: 'Fall in love, marry the man, have two children, and live happily ever afterwards,' seems neatly to sum up the outlook of this later period" (pp. 166–167).

What general prerequisites to a decline in fertility can be deduced from Banks's study? (1) Reproduction must be perceived not in a "natural" but in a "rational" perspective, that is, as legitimately subject to human control.[12] When this view became general among the English middle classes depends on how one phrases the question. To behave responsibly and postpone marriage to the "proper" age was a norm in part taken over from European tradition, while limiting family size by contraception was undoubtedly adopted in practice long before it was publicly accepted in

_____

[12] For this reason, one author terms it the "Weber-Banks hypothesis"; see James M. Beshers, *Population Processes in Social Systems*, Free Press, New York, 1967, Chapter 4,

respectable circles. (2) The social structure must be open, with social advance possible for those who curtail their family responsibilities. "The widespread desire for self-advancement economically, which is such an outstanding characteristic of capitalistic civilization, is fundamental" (Himes, cited in Banks, 1954, p. 8). As we have noted, the upper classes of static societies typically reflect their favored position in high fertility, the correlative of their low mortality. Similarly, the lower classes respond to their poorer chances for social advancement with a lesser control over their reproductive capacity. (3) The crucial element is the social class's aspirations: as its income level goes up, its hope for greater wealth goes up faster. When a middle-class woman says she cannot "afford" another child while women with much lower incomes can and do, the difference obviously does not lie in the cost of subsistence or even of comforts. (4) The propaganda for family limitation and even the increased efficacy of contraceptives are relevant mainly as catalysts, reinforcing motivations that derive from the social structure.

### DISSEMINATION OF THE SMALL-FAMILY SYSTEM

During the first decade of this century, more or less, the pioneering upper middle classes passed on the leadership to groups lower on the social scale. The route by which the small-family norm was disseminated varied, of course, from one country to another, but typically it was the lower middle and the upper working classes that next adopted it. In England just before World War I, the birth rate of members of a sickness-benefit society (mostly small shopkeepers and skilled workers) fell more than twice as fast as that of the general population. "The birth rate was falling most conspicuously, if not exclusively, not among the wealthy or the middle class as such, but among those sections of every class in which there is most prudence, foresight, and self-control" (Webb, 1913). As another instance, among French civil servants above a certain income, this was positively correlated with family size as early as 1906 (Wrong, 1958). In short, "before 1910 the upper classes led the decline in fertility, but after 1910 the intermediate groups assumed the lead" (ibid.). In a number of instances, thus, the relation between social class and fertility formed a J-shaped curve: among families of successively lower incomes, the number of children decreased slightly and then, from the upper-middle bracket down, increased steadily.

In a more general restatement of the Dumont-Banks model, several economists have suggested the means by which the negative correlation between social class and fertility may eventually be reversed. The original formulation of the Dumont-Banks thesis, that persons with high material aspirations and a genuine possibility of realizing them would forgo a numerous progeny, can be restated as the postulate that potential parents define the children themselves as consumption goods. Among the consumer durables that they might choose, then, Becker holds that they might decide either for more offspring or for fewer of "higher quality," just as a person might buy one Cadillac or two Volkswagens.[13] According to this hypothesis, "a rise in income would increase both the quality and quantity of children desired" (Becker, 1960; but *cf.* Blake, 1968). In short, the well-to-do of an affluent society could opt for *both* a middle-sized family *and* greater material welfare. The first realization of this possibility, apparently, was in Sweden in the 1930s. Among a considerable sample of Stockholm families, the correlation between social class and fertility was positive throughout the income range, and this association was strengthened when class was defined jointly by income and education (Edin and Hutchinson, 1935). In the sizable number of tests of the Dumont-Banks hypothesis since 1945, the results have generally depended on how wealthy the country was and how open its social structure. Most of the studies in the United States and one in Australia (Tien, 1961) showed no relation between mobility and family size, while research in France, Belgium, Denmark, and Brazil supported the hypothesis.

The American findings may indicate what happens in a society when mobility becomes so predictable and routine as to minimize its social and monetary costs and when the goal of mobility is a life style which includes a moderate number of children. . . . In a society with high mobility even the nonmobile may limit family size simply to maintain their place in the social order. They must run in order to stand still (R. Freedman, 1961–62, p. 60).

That mobility into the small and highly restricted upper class of the United States, rather than into the well-to-do middle class, *is* negatively correlated with family size (Baltzell, 1953) would seem to validate Freedman's explanation.

In Victorian England, the reference group of the rising middle class—the benchmark against which it measured its own welfare—was still higher in the social scale. But for many in the United States today the reference group constitutes persons of equivalent age and occupation. Thus, "an income above the average for one's status is associated with more children, but being in a higher absolute income class means fewer children if the higher income is only what is usual for the husband's age and occupation" (D. S. Freedman, 1963; *cf.* Kunz, 1965). In other words, the inverse correlation between class and fertility, which was instituted by the social ambitions of the upwardly mobile, tends to disappear among those who measure their well-being by that of their own kind.

---

[13] One could challenge the utility of extrapolating to a social institution like the family the notion that all choices are possible to all men. As James S. Duesenberry remarked in a "Comment" on Becker's paper, "Economics is all about how people make choices. Sociology is all about why they don't have any choices to make." It is hardly conceivable that a middle-class American would choose to have six children who could go only to high school rather than three that he could send to college, or that persons anywhere could evade similar constraints imposed by their social status.

To summarize: The modern small-family system originated among persons rising in the social scale. Not only can one move farther and faster with fewer dependents, but in an upwardly mobile family aspirations are typically higher than any income can satisfy, so that, however paradoxical it may be in simple economic terms, persons of middle incomes are often under heavier financial pressure than those who earn less. Implicit in this Dumont-Banks hypothesis is the corollary that among the upper class, as distinguished from those moving up into it, the rule might be large families, which often constitute one exception to the negative correlation. As the small-family norm spread down the social structure, the first consequence was an over-all reduction in fertility, with smaller class differences in family size than before. In rich societies, particularly where the upper middle class is in fact the highest stratum, those who reached the top were able to set their own family norm, which often included a moderate number of offspring. With such a decline of differentials by social class, those by residual factors like religion and ethnicity became more prominent.

## Variations on the Dumont-Banks Model

Banks's analysis manifestly describes not only the behavior of middle classes in Victorian England but that of sectors of various Western populations at some phase in the historic decline of family size. But whether the model fits France and the United States, the two countries where fertility fell first, depends on how specifically one defines the various factors. Dumont held that the breakdown of social barriers in the French Revolution accelerated interclass mobility, but according to a subsequent analysis his thesis applied even better to eighteenth-century France: "Social promotion was not so difficult that all ambition was stifled; it was not so easy that unlimited fertility did not constitute a serious handicap in the struggle to rise in the social scale" (Blacker, 1957). The contraction of family size in France was associated, however, not with a dynamic social class attempting to establish an industrial society, but with the contrary.

There was in the economy of the old regime a distinct configuration of wealth, noncapitalist in function, that may be called "proprietary." It embodied investments in land, urban property, venal office, and annuities. The returns it yielded were modest, ranging between one and five per cent, but they were fairly constant and varied little from year to year. They were realized not by entrepreneurial effort, which was degrading, but by mere ownership and the passage of calendar intervals. Risk was negligible. . . .

Both before and after the Revolution, the social values of the old elite dominated the status-conscious men and women of the wealthy Third Estate. Avid for standing, they had little choice but to pursue it as the aristocracy defined it, and the result was a massive prejudice that diverted . . . wealth into comparatively sterile proprietary investments (Taylor, 1967).

Those who sacrificed to acquire these various types of noncapitalist wealth preferred rent to profit, security to risk, tradition to innovation, gentility to skill. France displayed nearly all the traits of a traditional society as Rostow defined it,[14] yet this unlikely population constituted another source from which the small-family system spread. The most striking overlap with the Dumont-Banks model is that the French *propriétaire* limited the size of his family in order to acquire status as defined by another class. The relative insignificance of contraceptives is also apparent. The reason French fertility declined farther than in the rest of the Western world, one might hypothesize, is that the two contexts of a small-family system, the proprietary and the industrial-bourgeois, eventually reinforced each other.

### THE DECLINE OF AMERICAN FERTILITY

The very high fertility of the American colonies in the eighteenth century was noted by a number of contemporaries—Malthus, Benjamin Franklin, and Jefferson, among others; and it is also the conclusion of modern analysts using several techniques to manipulate various kinds of inadequate data. According to the consensus of these estimates, both contemporary and modern, around the end of the eighteenth century each married woman bore an average of almost eight children (e.g., Lotka, 1927). The decline in white fertility began in 1810 and continued steadily until 1940 (Table 14-3).[15] During this period the child–woman ratio of the white population fell off by 939 units (1,358 − 419)—about one-third by 1850, about three-quarters by 1900, and the remainder in the twentieth century. The rate for Negroes began at a higher point in 1850 but decreased more rapidly, reaching parity with the whites in 1920.

When women who have passed their childbearing period are divided into successively older categories, the number of children they report gives an approximate indication of the decline in family size over a considerable time, as shown in Table 14-4.[16] In any analysis of fertility, it is important

[14] W. W. Rostow, *The Stages of Economic Growth: A Non-Communist Manifesto*, University Press, Cambridge, 1960, Chapter 2.

[15] It has been estimated that about 78 per cent of white infants born around 1800 survived to the age of 2.5 years, the midpoint of "under 5." For 1900 the comparable figure is 84 per cent; for 1950 or later, about 97 per cent. Corresponding estimates for Negro infants are 72 per cent in 1900, 95 per cent in 1950 or later. As these last figures suggest, both underenumeration and infant mortality have generally varied considerably from one social group to another. In Table 14-3, thus, the number of white children has been increased by 5 per cent and that of Negro children by 13 per cent, these factors representing one estimate of the underenumeration for each race. *Cf.* Coale and Zelnik, 1963, Chapter 3, for another estimate.

[16] The main sources of error in such a measure derive from the facts that underreporting probably increases with age, particularly for the higher ages, and that there is some relation (though not a simple one) between longevity and completed family size (Grabill *et al.*, 1958, pp. 400–404). In Table 14-4, the rows for women aged 45–49 and 55–59 at successive censuses indicate that the discrepancy to be found in these age

Table 14-3. Adjusted[a] Number of Children under 5 per 1,000 Women Aged 20 to 44, by Race, United States, 1800–1960

|      | WHITE | NEGRO |
|------|-------|-------|
| 1800 | 1,342 | [b] |
| 1810 | 1,358 | [b] |
| 1820 | 1,295 | [b] |
| 1830 | 1,145 | [b] |
| 1840 | 1,085 | [b] |
| 1850 | 892 | 1,087 |
| 1860 | 905 | 1,072 |
| 1870 | 814 | 997 |
| 1880 | 780 | 1,090 |
| 1890 | 685 | 930 |
| 1900 | 666 | 845 |
| 1910 | 631 | 736 |
| 1920 | 604 | 608 |
| 1930 | 506 | 554 |
| 1940 | 419 | 513 |
| 1950 | 587 | 706 |
| 1960 | 667 | 860 [c] |

SOURCES: Wilson H. Grabill, Clyde V. Kiser, and Pascal K. Whelpton, *The Fertility of American Women*, Wiley, New York, 1958, Table 6. Copyright © 1958 by The Social Science Research Council. U.S. Bureau of the Census, *Statistical Abstract of the United States, 1965*, Washington, D.C., 1965, Table 18.

[a] The number of white children enumerated in each census except the last has been increased by 5 per cent, that of Negro children by 13 per cent, "these being factors obtained from a study of data for 1925 to 1930." All data from 1830 to 1950 have been standardized indirectly to the age distribution of American women in 1930.

[b] Data not available.

[c] Based on sample.

to include marriage trends. We know virtually nothing about the age at marriage in the nineteenth century even for the whole population of the United States, not to speak of its various sectors. The proportion of the females who never married, as shown in column 6 of Table 14-4 forms a

---

groups is not serious. On the other hand, the jump over only five years between two successive rows, women aged 45–49 in 1910 and those aged 70–74 in 1940, is probably based in part on the fact that the latter—that is, very much older—age group is less representative of their complete cohort.

## Table 14-4. Completed Family Size, United States, 1910–60

| AGE OF WOMEN AT GIVEN DATE | | | | MAIN CHILD-BEARING PERIOD [b] | PER CENT NEVER MARRIED | OF EVER MARRIED, PER CENT CHILDLESS | CHILDREN EVER BORN [c] | | |
| 1910 | 1940 [a] | 1950 [a] | 1960 [a] | | | | PER WOMAN | PER WIFE | PER MOTHER |
|---|---|---|---|---|---|---|---|---|---|
| (1) | (2) | (3) | (4) | (5) | (6) | (7) | (8) | (9) | (10) |
| 70–74 | | | | 1858–1882 | 6.5 | 7.7 | 5.0 | 5.4 | 5.8 |
| 65–69 | | | | 1863–1887 | 6.5 | 7.9 | 5.0 | 5.4 | 5.8 |
| 60–64 | | | | 1868–1892 | 7.3 | 8.2 | 4.8 | 5.3 | 5.7 |
| 55–59 | | | | 1873–1897 | 7.2 | 8.3 | 4.8 | 5.2 | 5.7 |
| 50–54 | | | | 1878–1902 | 8.4 | 8.9 | 4.5 | 5.0 | 5.5 |
| 45–49 | | | | 1883–1907 | 9.0 | 9.5 | 4.3 | 4.7 | 5.2 |
| | 70–74 | | | 1888–1912 | 10.0 | 12.5 | 3.4 | 3.8 | 4.4 |
| | 65–69 | | | 1893–1917 | 10.0 | 14.0 | 3.2 | 3.6 | 4.2 |
| | 60–64 | | | 1898–1922 | 9.5 | 15.0 | 3.0 | 3.4 | 4.0 |
| | 55–59 | | | 1903–1927 | 9.0 | 16.5 | 3.0 | 3.3 | 3.9 |
| | 50–54 | | | 1908–1932 | 9.1 | 16.3 | 2.8 | 3.1 | 3.7 |
| | 45–49 | 55–59 | | 1913–1937 | 8.9–8.0 | 16.1–16.9 | 2.7–2.7 | 3.0–2.9 | 3.5–3.5 |
| | | 50–54 | | 1918–1942 | 8.0 | 18.0 | 2.5 | 2.7 | 3.3 |
| | | 45–49 | 55–59 | 1923–1947 | 8.4–8.4 | 19.5–20.0 | 2.3–2.2 | 2.5–2.5 | 3.1–3.1 |
| | | | 50–54 | 1928–1952 | 7.8 | 20.0 | 2.1 | 2.3 | 2.9 |
| | | | 45–49 | 1933–1957 | 6.6 | 17.1 | 2.2 | 2.4 | 2.8 |

SOURCES: Wilson H. Grabill, Clyde V. Kiser, and Pascal K. Whelpton, *The Fertility of American Women*, Wiley, New York, 1958, Tables 9 and 16. Copyright © 1958 by The Social Science Research Council. U.S. Bureau of the Census, *U.S. Census of Population, 1960*, Vol. I, *Characteristics of the Population*; Part I, *U.S. Summary*, Washington, D.C., 1964, Table 190.

[a] Whites only.

[b] Dates over which the middle cohort (aged 72 in 1910, etc.) was 20 to 44 years old.

[c] Children ever born "per 1,000 women," "per thousand women ever married," and "per 1,000 women who bore at least one child."

∩-curve, with low points among cohorts having their children in the quarter of the nineteenth century and the second quarter of the twentie century, and an intermediate high point among those having their children just before World War I. As at least nine out of ten married during all periods in the past century, the loss to fertility by nonmarriage was probably never greater than one-tenth.

Childless couples, equivalent so far as fertility trends are concerned to persons who remain single, are a class particularly difficult to analyze, for they are made up of two quite different categories—sterile marriages and those in which the forces toward smaller families have reached the ultimate point. Some authorities hold that on the average one marriage in ten is naturally sterile (see p. 180). The figures at the top of column 7 suggest both that this estimate is too high and that deliberate childlessness was all but nonexistent in the middle of the nineteenth century. A large part of the decline in fertility can be accounted for by the rise in the number of childless couples, which constituted one out of every five in the period just preceding World War II.

Note that there was also a steady but gradual decline in the completed size of families with at least one child (column 10). The average number of children per mother, estimated at more than eight in 1800, was less than six in the third quarter of the century, just four in the first quarter of the twentieth century, and less than three in the second quarter. Even ignoring the women who remained single and the increasing proportion of married women who were childless, the completed family size decreased by almost one child per generation.

It is worth emphasizing the date when this transformation started. The decline began when the United States was a relatively empty country with a wide open frontier, when it was still overwhelmingly rural and agricultural (although the rural sector was becoming increasingly involved in the town-oriented market economy), when the very term *birth control* had not yet been coined and contraceptive means were more or less limited to *coitus interruptus*—when almost all of the factors cited in the later studies as causes of the decline were still in the future. Does the United States fit the Dumont-Banks model? Certainly the new industrialists that transformed the country after the Civil War were the provincial cousins of their English counterparts. But whether the opportunity of social mobility alone brought about the decline in family size two generations earlier could be answered only by a study in depth—in fact, a replication of Banks's volume using American data.

### THE FERTILITY OF AMERICAN NEGROES

Differentiation by race is largely an index of the effects of social class on fertility. The Negroes' considerably higher child-woman ratio in 1850

ntration in the rural South, the region and the economic children per family. But the sharp decline from that ng before the movement of some Negroes out of rural h, and out of the lowest economic level (Table 14-3). riod the rise in Negro fertility has been both sharper oom and from a higher level (Figure 14-1). "Negro

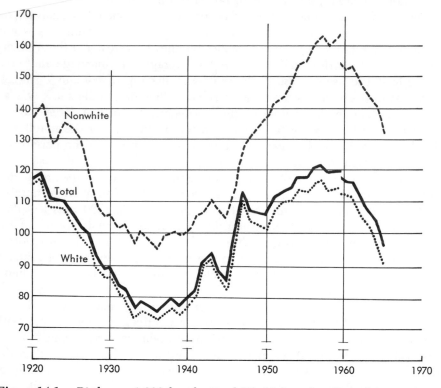

**Figure 14-1.** Births per 1,000 females aged 15–44, by color, United States, 1920–65. Rates from 1920 to 1959 adjusted for estimated underenumeration; rates for 1960 to 1963 based on registered live births. Sources: Anders S. Lunde, "White-Nonwhite Fertility Differentials in the United States," *Health, Education, and Welfare Indicators,* September 1965; National Center for Health Statistics, Monthly Vital Statistics Report, Vol. 15, No. 11, February 10, 1967.

fertility rates present the paradox of falling when demographic-transition theory would predict the maintenance of high rates and then rising when a decline would be expected" (Farley, 1966).

In Chapter 13 (pp. 472–478), a parallel was drawn between the current urbanization of underdeveloped nations and the migration of Negroes to American cities. In both cases the movement has been less of self-selected persons qualified to succeed in urban pursuits than the push from the countryside of poverty-stricken declassed peasants. That under such conditions urbanization is not accompanied by an immediate decline in fertility may be regarded as a negative confirmation of the Dumont-Banks hypothesis. Birth control by any method is based fundamentally on self-control, which socially mobile persons exercise because their restraint is rewarded with an improvement in social-economic status. But those ill prepared for urban-industrial jobs (or blocked from them by race prejudice —the demographic effect is the same) lack such an incentive. Indeed, those with little hope of economic stability may not have the personal prerequisites of family stability. During the early period of English industrialization, it will be recalled, the urban paupers and new industrial workers, raw from the deteriorating village culture, probably had more children, legitimate and illegitimate, than their immediate forebears.[17]

The traditional Negro family in the United States, a residue of slavery, was highly matricentric, with barely enough cohesion to retain the husband-father in the household. With the shift of lower-class Negroes to a new metropolitan environment, this weak institution disintegrated further. One important index is the absent father who "haunts the Negro family" (Lincoln, 1965). In spite of a decline in widowhood, the proportion of Negro women who state that they have ever been married and are now living alone is between a fifth and a quarter at the youngest ages, rising to almost a third in middle age (Table 14-5).[18]

The Negro women who in so many cases must carry unaided the full financial burden and moral responsibility for their children would have,

Table 14-5. Percentage of Ever Married Negro Women with Spouses Absent, United States, 1910–64

| AGE OF WOMEN | 1910 | 1940 | 1960 | 1964 |
|---|---|---|---|---|
| 14–19 | 15.0 | 14.6 | 28.3 | 19.8 |
| 20–24 | 17.4 | 14.2 | 26.4 | 23.5 |
| 25–34 | 20.0 | 15.4 | 28.8 | 29.6 |
| 35–44 | 29.9 | 15.1 | 31.9 | 32.7 |

SOURCES: Census data and Current Population Survey, compiled in Reynolds Farley, "Recent Changes in Negro Fertility," Demography, 3 (1966), 188–203.

[17] See the section on the "proletarian" type of family, pp. 422–423. The high rate of illegitimacy in the squatter settlements of Latin America (p. 470) is only partly of this type, as it also reflects the general lower-class norm.
[18] Obviously such data are less accurate than those on morally neutral questions. In reply to the census questions, women may state that they were married even if they were not, that their absent husbands died even if this was not the case, or that their husbands are presently living with them even if they are alone. As such evasions are possible, the figures may understate actual proportions, though it is impossible to guess by how much.

one would think, the maximum incentive to exercise birth control. But it is the Negroes with higher education, stable families, and middle-class aspirations who have small families. "The excess of nonwhite over white fertility is concentrated among couples with . . . children in addition to the number desired (Whelpton *et al.*, 1966, p. 349). Lower-class Negro women sometimes have moral objections to contraception, and many are ignorant of the most effective means, but the crucial factor is apathy. "They seem to regard the burden of numerous children with the same fatalism (and, perhaps, despair) with which they 'accept' their extreme poverty" (*ibid.*, p. 356). One consequence is an extraordinarily high proportion of illegitimate births, well over one-quarter in the 1960s and rising (Table 14-6).[19]

Table 14-6. Illegitimate Births, by Color, United States, 1940–66

| | NUMBER (THOUSANDS) | | PER CENT ILLEGITIMATE OF ALL LIVE BIRTHS | |
|---|---|---|---|---|
| | WHITE | NONWHITE | WHITE | NONWHITE |
| 1940 | 40 | 49 | 2.0 | 16.8 |
| 1945 | 56 | 61 | 2.4 | 17.9 |
| 1950 | 54 | 88 | 1.8 | 18.0 |
| 1955 | 64 | 119 | 1.9 | 20.2 |
| 1960 | 83 | 142 | 2.3 | 21.6 |
| 1965 | 124 | 168 | 4.0 | 26.3 |
| 1966 | 133 | 170 | 4.4 | 27.7 |

SOURCE: U.S. Bureau of Labor Statistics, *Recent Trends in Social and Economic Conditions of Negroes in the United States,* BLS Report No. 347, Washington, D.C., 1968, p. 23.

The rapid cultural change that the nonwhite population is undergoing has left its mark on fertility differences between whites and nonwhites. We find that nonwhite couples have had and expect more births than white couples, and that this difference is brought about partly by the unusually high fertility of a minority of nonwhite couples who live in the rural South, and partly by the moderately high fertility of the many nonwhite couples who have Southern farm origins. Nonwhite couples with no Southern farm background have and expect about the same number of births as similar white couples. These differentials suggest that as the influence of Southern rural patterns of mating and childbearing diminishes, the fertility differences between whites and nonwhites will decline (*ibid.*, p. 369).

[19] One of the values that money can buy is privacy, and many illegitimate births to middle-class women are not recorded as such. According to one important study, unwed mothers in the middle class do not differ greatly from a random sample of other white middle-class females (Vincent, 1961). However, even if the white rate in Table 14-6 is raised substantially in order to include an approximation of such hidden births out of wedlock, the rate for nonwhites will still be several times larger.

## WORKING WIVES

In its original formulation the Dumont-Banks thesis applied exclusively to males. It was the men with an opportunity to rise who decided to have fewer children; their wives, who bore the children, fitted passively into the background. This was an accurate enough representation of at least the outward forms of family life in Victorian England, but most students of stratification have continued to define the status of couples exclusively by the husband's occupation, ignoring the increasing proportion of married women who work outside the home and the effect of this trend on family life (Day, 1961). The possibility of rapid social mobility is far greater, of course, if a young husband and wife both work, postponing reproduction until the man is established at a higher level. We should expect the inverse correlation with fertility to be higher than with the social mobility of the male alone, for it is especially burdensome for the female to combine child-rearing with employment outside the home. The cause-effect relation, moreover, can work in both directions: a woman with no children is more likely to seek a job, and a woman who is earning a wage is more likely to prevent conceptions.

Work for females outside the home, which is relatively rare in under-developed countries, has increased appreciably in almost all Western countries (Leser, 1958). The main reason is that the trend of advanced economies is toward a greater concentration of the labor force in occupations in which females had been traditionally dominant—middle-level, service-oriented professions (nursing, social work, teaching, librarianship), as well as office or factory jobs of a relatively low skill that can easily be shifted from one part of a bureaucratic structure to another (stenographers and typists, textile workers).[20] Within this general context, motivations vary greatly. Most studies cite economic deprivation as an important reason that married women work, and this applies in an absolute sense to a minority, particularly those with husband absent or dead. The fact, however, that the employment of married women has increased greatly during a period of economic prosperity indicates that the "deprivation" is often measured against a rising standard of expectations.

The question has an answer that borders on the cliché: "Why do you work?" "For money." . . . Somewhere between 55 and 90 per cent of the answers will be in terms of money, depending on the particular sample of women being questioned, the phrasing of the question, etc. . . . A young professional woman said to her secretary, "It's all right for you to have a baby; it only costs you $4,000 to

---

[20] This is an inadequate summary of the major theme of an as yet unpublished doctoral dissertation, from which I have taken some of the data and interpretations for this section: Valerie Kincade Oppenheimer, "The Female Labor Force in the United States: Factors Governing Its Growth and Changing Composition," Department of Sociology, University of California, Berkeley, 1966. See Oppenheimer, 1967, 1968.

quit your job. But it would cost me $9,500, so I can't afford it" (Nye and Hoffman, 1963, pp. 22–25).

It is useful to exemplify the recent international findings with a more detailed discussion of the trend in one advanced country. In the United States, the proportion of females in the labor force remained static at about one-quarter of those aged fourteen and over from 1910 to 1940. Then, with the labor shortage during World War II, it rose to 29 per cent in 1950 and, surprisingly, continued to rise to 34.5 in 1960. Of this growing number of females in the labor force, the percentage married and with husband present —only 13.8 in 1940—rose to 21.6 in 1950 and 30.6 in 1960. Typically females used to work as long as they were single, then leave the labor force when they married and bore children. This pattern has continued, especially during the "motherhood mania" of 1946–57 (Bernard, 1968), but an increasing proportion now return to work after the children are old enough to attend school. In 1965, some 9.7 million mothers with children under 18, or about one-third of all mothers with children of this age, were in the labor force. Almost 40 per cent of these working mothers had children under six years (U.S. Bureau of Labor Statistics, 1966). Not only has it become conventionally acceptable to hire married women, but under the Civil Rights Act of 1964 it is unlawful to discriminate on the basis of sex in hiring, job retention, and promotion. Thus, it is now legal to forbid the hiring of married women only if the ruling applies also to married men. It is likely that the proportion of females in the labor force will continue to rise and that make-shift adjustments between occupational and familial duties will be institutionalized, thus facilitating the combination of an outside job with a moderate number of children.[21]

## THE IRISH PATTERN OF LATE MARRIAGE [22]

In common with the rest of Western Europe, Ireland in the eighteenth century lived by the tradition that a young man ought not to marry until he had a patch of land to cultivate, so that in general he had to wait for his inheritance. By 1780 several factors together increased the amount of free land available; under the impetus of mercantilist encouragements to the cultivation of grain, pastureland was converted to agriculture; much swampland was drained; the potato, introduced from America, increased greatly

[21] Note that competition with *any* other role is not a reason to have smaller families. According to an interesting study based on the "Growth of American Families" data (Freedman *et al.,* 1959), among both Protestants and Catholics, while club activities had no effect on expected family size, this varied inversely with the number of years worked (Ridley, 1959).

[22] Some of the data and interpretations are from an as yet unpublished doctoral dissertation: Robert E. Kennedy, Jr., "Irish Emigration, Marriage and Fertility," Department of Sociology, University of California, Berkeley, 1967.

the food value per unit of tilled land. An adolescent boy with a small holding could now build a hut and grow enough potatoes to raise a family. Girls were typically mothers by their early teens, and in a country with no birth control this decrease in the age at marriage had a decisive effect. In sixty years the population of Ireland more than doubled, increasing from 4.0 million in 1781 to 8.2 million in 1841.[23] This growth stimulated a large emigration, which became a mass exodus after the failure of the potato crop and the great famine of the 1840s. At mid-1965 the estimated population of Eire and Northern Ireland together was 4.3 million, or only slightly more than it was in 1781, at the start of the tremendous increase. This massive depopulation, unique among modern Western countries, was effected only in part by emigration. The age at marriage in Ireland has generally been the highest in the world, and the proportion that never marry the greatest, so that in spite of a high rate of marital fertility, the natural increase was only moderate.

An analysis of the long-term trend in age at marriage cannot be made from vital statistics. Until about a decade ago the exact age was not recorded, and the data from which it can be estimated are not available for every census. The proportions reported single in each census, which are an alternative index of family formation, are shown in Table 14-7. In recent decades between half and three-quarters of the males, and between a third and half of the females, were still single at about thirty years, and more than a quarter did not marry while they still could have children. Since many single persons emigrated, the extraordinary proportions of the population in Ireland counted as single at the time of each census in fact understate the reluctance of the Irish to accept family responsibilities.

In their aspiration for a better life, the Irish did not differ from other peoples of Western Europe, and that they sought to reduce the size of their families by an extended postponement of marriage was also in accord with general European norms. The Irish pattern differs in degree. The discrepancy between actual conditions and those aspired to was probably especially great in Ireland, whose poor inhabitants received regular reports from relatives and friends on the comparative affluence in America and England. While other populations gradually shifted to contraception, the clergy, the law, and the pressure of public opinion made this adaptation difficult in this strictly Roman Catholic country.[24] The negative attitude toward sexuality in the Augustinian tradition, which has remained espe-

---

[23] The first census was in 1821; the estimate for the earlier period is that in K. H. Connell, *The Population of Ireland, 1750–1845*, Clarendon, Oxford, 1950.

[24] It is illegal to advocate, advertise, import, or sell contraceptives, on pain of a fine up to £50 and/or imprisonment up to six months. Manifestly, it is difficult to gauge how efficiently the law proscribing contraceptives is enforced; circumstantial evidence suggests that it can be evaded but that few attempt to do so. The marital fertility particularly but not exclusively of non-Catholics has fallen in recent years, indicating that some Irish control conception. The commonest means used, Kennedy believes, may be prolonged continence.

Table 14-7. Percentage Single of the Population, by Age Group
and Sex, Ireland, 1841–1961

| | MALES | | FEMALES | |
|---|---|---|---|---|
| | 25–34 | 45–54 | 25–34 | 45–54 |
| 1841[a] | 43 | 10 | 28 | 12 |
| 1851 | 61 | 12 | 39 | 11 |
| 1861 | 57 | 14 | 39 | 14 |
| 1871 | 57 | 16 | 38 | 15 |
| 1881 | 62 | 16 | 41 | 16 |
| 1891 | 67 | 20 | 48 | 17 |
| 1901 | 72 | 24 | 53 | 20 |
| 1911 | 74 | 29 | 56 | 24 |
| 1921 | b | b | b | b |
| 1926 | 72 | 31 | 53 | 24 |
| 1931 | b | b | b | b |
| 1936 | 74 | 34 | 55 | 25 |
| 1946 | 70 | 32 | 48 | 26 |
| 1951 | 67 | 31 | 46 | 26 |
| 1961 | 58 | 30 | 37 | 23 |

SOURCE: Ireland, *Censuses of Population,* 1946 and 1951: "General Report," Table 32, p. 51; 1961: Vol. II, Table 2, p. 4.

[a] Age groups were 26–35 and 46–55 years.

[b] Data not available.

cially strong in Irish Catholicism, may also have induced some young people to postpone marriage out of a fear or disgust even of licit sex between husband and wife.[25]

With the rise in life expectancy during the second half of the nineteenth century, sons had to wait longer to inherit their fathers' holdings, and some that put off marriage eventually decided not to marry at all. With many unmarried males, institutions developed that catered to their special wants; celibacy was not so lonely a state with so many to share it. As bachelors, most men can count on their mothers to keep house for them—or those unmarried sisters who remain in this man's land rather than emigrating.

[25] "Most of us," one Irishwoman recalls, "remember with a shiver those three-day retreats at school, [after which] . . . the confessor put questions to us concerning sex habits of which in our genuine innocence we had never dreamed in the worst nightmare and which so shocked and sickened us that we remained sex-frightened for years" (Maura Laverty in O'Brien, 1953).

In the opinion of some Irish women, "the men are cagey, spiritless, selfish, and spoiled by their mothers." One of them said:

[Ireland] is a paradise for the male. It is not that the young man in modern Ireland cannot afford to get married. It is that he cannot get married and still afford his car, his club, his betting, his poker, his golf, and his holidays (Seán O'Faolain in O'Brien, 1953).

### THE CONTROL OF FERTILITY IN POSTWAR JAPAN

As we noted in the chapter on the industrial revolution, Japan's rapid population increase—the consequence of a rise in fertility, a decline in mortality, and the remigration from the lost empire of administrators and settlers—had become intolerable by the end of World War II (see p. 427). The response was equally dramatic. Japan's birth rate fell from 34.3 in 1947 to 17.2 in 1957, or by almost exactly half in a decade, and this remarkable record has been widely cited as a goal for such countries as India.

It can hardly be said that the Japanese government guided the people into adopting a program of planned parenthood. The measure under which the subsequent population policy developed did not have this overt intention: the stated purpose of the Eugenic Protection Law of 1948 was "to prevent the increase of the inferior descendants from the standpoint of eugenic protection and to protect the life and health of the mother as well." [26] Under the law, the state provided voluntary and in some cases compulsory sterilization, abortion facilities, and "practical guidance in adjustment of conception" when there were eugenic or medical reasons for preventing births. In an amendment the following year, economic factors were added, and the program quickly developed into a mass state-subsidized effort to reduce natality, as its liberal sponsors had originally intended. The official fees for an abortion are from 1,000 to 2,000 yen, but the actual amount paid under insurance plans and health services is usually about 300 yen (or less than $1), and in at least one place the cost to the woman is only 15 yen. By 1953 there were 692 public clinics, as well as 55 private ones. The number of abortions performed under the law rose from 320,000 in 1950 to 1,128,000 in 1958 (or from 137 to 682 per 1,000 live births). After 1958 efforts were made to encourage contraception, and the number of abortions declined slightly from this high point. According to one estimate for the year 1955, the number of births would have been 1.4 to 2.1 million larger (depending on varying estimates of fecundity) if there had been no legal abortions (Muramatsu, 1960).

[26] Quoted in Taeuber, 1958, p. 269. Taeuber does not believe that the law was "a devious route by which the government could sponsor abortions as a means of 'solving' the population problem," but she does point out that "its major advocates were those who favored the diffusion of contraception" (pp. 269, 372).

Japan's record is the only one that affords an opportunity to test the common notion that abortions are intrinsically injurious to the women's health—that is, apart from the conditions prevailing in countries where they are illegal. In Japan trained physicians perform aseptic operations and prescribe penicillin for every patient. On the other hand, while the program was being set up, there were some unskilled practitioners, and operations were permitted up to the seventh month of pregnancy rather than only before the end of the third month, as medical opinion generally considers mandatory. The inconclusive evidence to date suggests that one or two abortions under optimum medical conditions are not typically harmful, but repeated abortions may be, as are also repeated deliveries in many cases. For this reason, the sentiment has grown in Japan to shift the major emphasis in the state clinics from abortion to contraception or sterilization, or both. A representative view was expressed in a 1967 book by Tenrei Ota, a socialist gynecologist and the inventor of the intra–uterine contraceptive device that bears his name.[27] His basic aim, to protect the health of mothers especially in the poorer classes, would in his opinion be best served if the physician could at his own discretion prescribe the most effective contraceptive or induced abortion or sterilization, depending on the circumstances. In a three-year program to introduce contraception among a large sample of railroad workers, the birth rate was cut from 40.8 to 19.4, with a small and decreasing proportion of unwanted pregnancies ended by abortion (Koya, 1962). In other words, since postwar Japan is not hampered by tradition, religion, or any other ideology from responding rationally to population pressure, any efficacious means of reducing fertility can work fast.[28]

## "Depopulation" and the Baby Boom

Changes in the class differentials in fertility, which have been analyzed in this chapter to exemplify a historic era, were typically seen during that process as a medium of the degeneration of Western societies. The inverse correlation between education and family size, and thus implicitly between innate intelligence and family size, was widely interpreted as the means by which the genetic quality of Western populations was being reduced. This theory is especially associated with right-wing politics, but it was shared, for instance, by Sidney Webb, one of Britain's best known socialist intellectuals.

[27] "The Prohibition of Induced Abortion and the Eugenic Protection Law" (in Japanese); see the book review by John Y. Takeshita in *Milbank Memorial Fund Quarterly*, 45 (1967), 467–471.

[28] In 1968, the Demographic Research Institute of the Japanese Welfare Ministry issued a warning that the low rate of population growth, one per cent or less per year, would result in continued labor shortages. It recommended higher wages and better housing conditions as stimuli to the birth rate (*The New York Times*, February 23, 1968).

It is the differential character of the decline in the birth rate, rather than the actual extent of the decline, which is of the gravest import. . . . In Great Britain at this moment [1913], when half, or perhaps two-thirds, of all the married people are regulating their families, children are being freely born to the Irish Roman Catholics and the Polish, Russian, and German Jews, on the one hand, and to the thriftless and irresponsible, . . . on the other. . . . This can hardly result in anything but national deterioration; or, as an alternative, in this country gradually falling to the Irish and the Jews (Webb, 1913).

As the norm of small families spread down through the social structure and the fertility of whole societies declined, concern shifted from the comparative quality of new cohorts to their small size. The advantages that accrued to married couples from reducing the number of their offspring, whether in less expense or in more convenience, were the greater the smaller the number of children; and once persons saw family formation in this perspective and had the means of limiting births, the trend seemed to be toward one-child or no-child families (cf. Rossi, 1968). Even liberals came to see the fact that potential parents were able to control conception as what Carr-Saunders termed "the small-family problem."

If for any reason, however remote, trivial, selfish, or unsubstantial, parents do not want a child, the child does not come. Consequently there is no assurance whatever that children will come in sufficient numbers to prevent a decline of population and ultimate extinction.[29]

Indeed, in all Western countries demographers spelled out the gloomy implications of this analysis. For instance, Enid Charles projected the population of England and Wales on the basis of three postulates with respect to fertility and mortality: (1) that fertility and mortality would continue at the 1933 rate; (2) that fertility and mortality would continue to fall as they had in recent years; and (3) that fertility would rise to the 1931 level, or to about 10 per cent higher than in 1933, while mortality would continue to fall. In a volume published three years later, the substance of the memorandum was republished but the estimate based on the third assumption, the one closest to what turned out to be the actual trend, was omitted altogether.[30] A summary of this "classic study" was incorporated in Reddaway's exposition of Keynesian theory, called The Economics of a Declining Population. The "more reasonable forecast" was taken

[29] A. M. Carr-Saunders, World Population: Past Growth and Present Trends, Cass, London, 1964 (reprint of the 1936 edition), p. 244.

[30] Enid Charles, The Effect of Present Trends in Fertility and Mortality upon the Future Population of England and Wales and upon Its Age Composition, Royal Economics Society, London, Memorandum No. 55, December, 1935; "The Effect of Present Trends in Fertility and Mortality upon the Future Population of Great Britain and upon Its Age Composition," in Political Arithmetic: A Symposium of Population Studies, edited by Lancelot Hogben, Macmillan, New York, 1938, pp. 73–105.

to be that the population of England and Wales would start to decline in 1939 and would be reduced by nine-tenths over the following century. Yet Reddaway's book was published in 1939, four years after the low point of British fertility, when the actual population was larger than the upper limit in Charles's projection.[31] According to a forecast that Louis I. Dublin presented in 1931, with no migration the population of the United States would reach a maximum of 154 million between 1980 and 1990 and then decline to 140 million by 2100. Since in his opinion this prognosis was "altogether too optimistic," he offered a second, "more reasonable" estimate, by which the maximum of 148 million would be reached by 1970, followed by a decline to 140 million by 2000 and to 76 million by 2100 (cited in Dorn, 1950; cf. above, pp. 312–313).

Curiously, one reason that professional demographers went so far astray is that, unlike the general public, they knew that a portion of even the low fertility of the 1930s was the consequence of a relatively favorable age structure. In most Western countries large numbers had been born in the pre-1914 decade, and the proportion of potential parents in the 1930s, therefore, was far greater than it would be when the later, much smaller cohorts grew to maturity. This important qualification to any understanding of the current birth rate was incorporated in the reproduction rates, which became very popular during the 1930s.[32] Properly understood, these rates have their uses. Unfortunately demographers sometimes forgot that reproduction rates are in fact population projections, half-disguised as measures of fertility or natural increase. Charles categorically asserted the contrary: "In parts of Europe and America the population has already ceased to be capable of maintaining its numbers. It cannot be too clearly emphasized that this statement is not a prediction of future events . . . but a description of what is actually happening at the moment."[33] The comment of Carr-Saunders that England's "reproduction rate is about 25 per cent below replacement rate"[34] was also subject to misunderstanding. Net reproduction rates, it must be stressed, do *not* show that populations are increasing or decreasing. A rate of more than unity does *not* mean that a population is increasing or that it will necessarily increase in the future. A net repro-

[31] W. B. Reddaway, *The Economics of a Declining Population,* Allen & Unwin, London, 1939.

[32] It will be recalled (see pp. 82–83) that a gross reproduction rate is the ratio of female births in two successive generations, assuming no change in the age-specific birth rates and no deaths before the end of the childbearing period, and a net reproduction rate is the ratio of female births in two successive generations, assuming no change in the age-specific birth and death rates. That is, the gross rate measures fertility only, the net rate the natural increase. Both rates are related to the stable population—that is, the population of fixed age and sex distribution that would develop if the present age-specific fertility and mortality were to continue without change for about a century.

[33] Enid Charles, *The Menace of Under-Population: A Biological Study of the Decline of Population Growth,* Watts, London, 1936, p. 104.

[34] Carr-Saunders, *op. cit.,* p. 258.

duction rate of 0.75 means not that the growth of population *is* 25 per cent under replacement, but that it *would* decline if the current age-specific fertility and mortality continued without change for several generations.

That demographers' population forecasts were wrong is indisputable, but one must recall also that their view of future trends fitted in with what was being predicted in other social sciences as well. The notion that the family was being transformed from an institution to "companionship," to quote the title of a very widely used college text,[35] prevailed; and even after the rise in fertility was well under way it took years before commentators revised their analyses. In 1946, Talcott Parsons, whom many regard as the country's foremost sociological theorist, explained the decline in fertility in the most general terms. The growing girl, he wrote, discovers that "she must compete for masculine favor and cannot stand on her own feet," and this discovery cannot but be a source of insecurity and hence aggression. The aggression, in turn, "underlies the widespread ambivalence among women toward the role of motherhood, which is a primary factor in the declining birth rate." [36] In 1950, a full five years after the upturn in the birth rate, David Riesman (now also a Harvard sociologist) based his whole analysis of the American "character structure" on a presumed "incipient decline" in the country's population.[37] It would be possible to add to these prominent examples a full array of economists, sociologists, journalists, and others, virtually all of whom held that Oswald Spengler's "decline of the West" was being enacted in literal fact.

### PRONATALIST MEASURES

According to one view of the decline in fertility, it was a "birth strike," a refusal of potential parents to reproduce until their onerous economic burdens were reduced—that is, borne in part by nonparents. The countries that initiated such programs ranged politically from Nazi Germany or the

---

[35] Ernest W. Burgess and Harvey J. Locke, *The Family: From Institution to Companionship*, American Book Co., New York, 1945. In this 800-page book on "the family," what the authors term "birth folkways" is covered on pages 491–501. *Cf.* above, pp. 318–320.

[36] Talcott Parsons, "Certain Primary Sources and Patterns of Aggression in the Social Structure of the Western World," reprinted in his *Essays in Sociological Theory, Pure and Applied*, Free Press, Glencoe, Ill., 1949, pp. 251–274.

[37] David Riesman *et al.*, *The Lonely Crowd: A Study in the Changing American Character*, Yale University Press, New Haven, 1950. An abridged edition published three years later (Doubleday-Anchor, 1953) still retained the same fallacious demography as the fundamental structure. In 1960, Riesman recalled that ten years earlier critics had pointed out the faults in the theory of the demographic transition, but that "the nice analogy between the three stages posited by such demographers as Notestein and our own hypothetical stages proved too tempting to resist." (Riesman, *"The Lonely Crowd: A Reconsideration in 1960,"* in *Culture and Social Character: The Work of David Riesman Reviewed*, edited by Seymour Martin Lipset and Leo Lowenthal, Free Press of Glencoe, New York, 1961, pp. 419–458.)

Soviet Union to Britain or Sweden, and the philosophies underlying pro-natalist policies were similarly diverse:

1. Catholic doctrine: The natural unit of society is not the individual but the family, and wages should therefore be paid at least in part according to family needs, rather than individual economic worth.

2. Egalitarianism: Since in general there is a negative correlation between income and family size, family subsidies help effect a more equitable distribution of income.

3. Social welfare: The children of large families are often those who most need assistance.

4. Nationalism: To the extent that the secular decline in the birth rate has been caused by economic factors, it can be checked by family subsidies, thus increasing the manpower and military prowess of the nation.

These four principles are ranked in order of decreasing importance, from a fundamental norm to a contingent expedient of unproved value. In general, therefore, the earliest strongest advocates of family subsidies were Catholics, especially in countries (such as France) with very low natality. Fascist countries (and, since the middle 1930s, the Soviet Union) also uni-formly adopted some mode of family endowment, particularly because of the assumed value to the nation of a rapidly growing population (see pp. 586–588). Socialists and liberals, on the other hand, were less consistent. In Anglo-Saxon countries, they were sometimes among the most vigorous pro-ponents of a family wage (for example, Eleanor Rathbone in Britain, Paul Douglas in the United States); but the historic role of Continental socialist parties and their affiliated trade unions was forthright opposition, petering down to acquiescence. In line with the trade-union slogan, "Equal pay for equal work," members of the French trade-union federation went so far in the 1920s as to refuse to accept family benefits after the system had been established; members of the metalworkers union in Berlin threatened to leave the organization unless the system was effectively opposed. However, it became increasingly difficult, particularly during the depression of the 1930s, to align this stand with fundamental socialist principles; for one could hardly find a more direct translation into social action of "To each according to his needs" than a law regulating workers' pay according to the number of minor children they had to support. Fundamental opposi-tion to family subsidies, therefore, tended to give way to differences over administration and other details.

Some pronatalist means were repressive, such as taxes on bachelors in Italy or more stringent prohibition of contraception and abortion in Ger-many. Other measures constituted positive attempts to induce young per-sons to marry or couples to have more children, in return for cash grants (or their converse, reduced taxes) or for preference in acquiring housing, government posts, or other values in short supply. In general, to the degree that one can separate the governments' efforts from other determinants of fertility, the pronatalist policies were a failure. "In one case only—Germany since 1933—does there appear to have been any marked success, and even in that case the reasons for success are not clear" (Glass, 1940, p. 370). One determinant there may have been the "psychic rebirth" afforded by Nazi Germany's bloodless victories over Western Europe in the 1930s. Glass held, however, that "material measures [were] more important than 'psychic' changes and that, in particular, the suppression of illegal abortion [was] a major factor" (*ibid.*, p. 312).

The reasons for the usual failure of pronatalist measures vary from case to case. In some instances the policy was administered blindly, with little regard for the underlying causes of the decline in fertility, but the time and intelligence that Sweden devoted to a full and painstaking analysis proved to be of no avail. Repressive measures failed because, except in Germany, they were not well enforced. Monetary inducements and, *a fortiori*, allowances in kind, were "not large enough to cover the additional costs of family life. . . . However urgently governments may have declared their desire to increase the supply of births, they have nevertheless persistently tried to buy babies at bargain prices" (*ibid.*, p. 371). But it was utopian to expect that any government could afford to pay enough to cover the additional costs of family life, as Davis demonstrated with the example of middle-class Americans around 1930:

Parents spent between $9,180 and $10,485 in rearing a child through the age of eighteen. Dividing this figure (say $10,000) by 18, and multiplying by the number of children in the country, we can calculate the total annual amount a nation would need to spend to cover cash expenditures made on children. For the United States it would be around $23,990,079,540, or more than six times the total governmental expenditures in 1930. . . . *At least* this amount would be required if genuine economic rewards for having children were given (Davis, 1937).[38]

In fact, the effort to buy children, whether at bargain prices or any other, failed for more fundamental reasons. (1) It was particularly the low fertility of the middle and upper-working classes that governments hoped to raise, but these prudent parents, anxious to get ahead, would expend monetary relief on higher quality rather than more quantity. "As incomes increase from class to class, so do opportunities of spending money upon what is in effect buying openings for children; therefore relief from taxation will result in the long run, not in making money available for more children,

[38] The heavy expenditures by parents, which have risen markedly since the 1930s, do not mean that the community contributions to the costs of child-rearing are small. In the state of North Carolina around 1965, the sum of federal, state, and local expenditures over the 25 first years of life for relevant health, education, and welfare budgets amounted to $3,187 per birth. See J. William Leasure, "Some Economic Benefits of Birth Prevention," *Milbank Memorial Fund Quarterly*, 45 (1967), 417–425.

but in the expenditure of more money upon the placing of each child." [39] (2) In any case, Becker to the contrary notwithstanding, parents do not regard children merely as one "consumer durable"; parenthood is not undertaken only rationally or, if rationally, not only for possible monetary gain or minimum monetary loss. Indeed, pronatalist measures may boomerang among the more traditional-minded sectors of a population, who thus may come to view parenthood as a *quid pro quo* and join in the "birth strike" unless the remuneration for reproduction is generous. It is only among the lowest classes, who are not motivated to exercise self-control in order to advance themselves and their children, that monetary rewards may increase the birth rate, usually already on the high side.

### POSTWAR RISE IN FERTILITY

In most countries of the Western world, after various kinds of pronatalist policies had failed, the birth rate increased during and immediately after World War II, when Europe suffered from shortages of housing and even of food and all of these countries lacked some of the material comforts that their affluent classes had come to expect. Europe's fertility rose enough to make nonsense of the dire forecasts of depopulation, as well as of the theory underlying most family-subsidy programs, yet on a global scale the increase was to only a modest figure. For the five years 1956–60 Europe's average annual rate was 19 births per 1,000 population (contrasted with 36 for the whole world), and the crude rates of natural increase for that quinquennium were, respectively, 8 and 18 per 1,000. In the United States, five-year averages of the crude birth rate went down steadily from 46.5 (white) in 1855–59 to 18.0 in 1935–39, then rose dramatically and declined again (Figure 14-2), reaching 17.9 in 1967 (compared with 18.4 in 1933 and 1936, the low points during the interwar depression).

The crude birth rate, of course, gives only a first impression of the trend. Because the base population for the most recent period includes all the boom babies, the very increase in fertility was, paradoxically, one reason why the rising rate decelerated and then fell off. Like the reproduction rate, crude rates generally relate to the data of a single year and thus exaggerate minor fluctuations. For a long-term analysis, the only adequate index is completed family size—the average number of children that women bear during the whole of their lifetime—but it has the obvious disadvantage that it cannot be used to measure current trends. A partial answer to this question can be made with cohort analysis (Grabill *et al.*, 1958, Chapter 9). A birth cohort, it will be recalled, is a group of persons all born at the same time, who are analyzed as a unit through their lifetime. For example, those born during the twelve months centering on January 1, 1900, constitute the cohort of 1900. Table 14-8 illustrates how useful this method is in

[39] Carr-Saunders, *op. cit.*, p. 251.

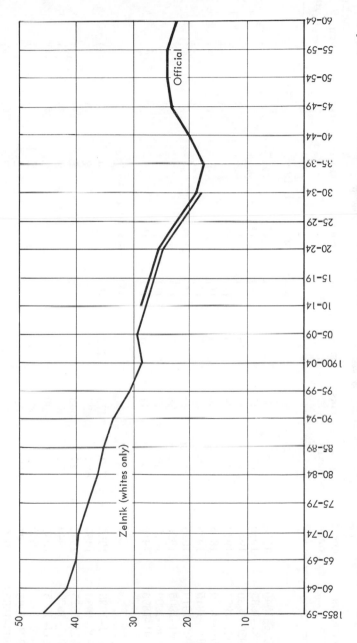

**Figure 14-2.** Quinquennial averages of crude birth rates, United States, 1855–59 to 1960–64. Sources: Melvin Zelnik, "Estimates of Annual Birth and Birth Rates for the White Population of the United States from 1855 to 1934" (unpublished doctoral dissertation, Princeton University, October 1958); U.S. Bureau of the Census, *Statistical Abstract of the United States*, various dates.

Table 14-8. Cumulative Birth Rates, by Order of Birth, for Cohorts of Native White Women, United States, 1910–55

| COHORTS OF— | JAN. 1 OF— | ALL BIRTHS | FIRST | SECOND | THIRD | FOURTH | FIFTH | SIXTH | SEVENTH | EIGHTH AND HIGHER |
|---|---|---|---|---|---|---|---|---|---|---|
| | | | | | ORDER OF BIRTH | | | | | |
| | | | | EXACT AGES 15 TO 19 [a] | | | | | | |
| 1936–1940 | 1955 | 77 | 65 | 11 | 1 | (b) | ... | ... | ... | ... |
| 1931–1935 | 1950 | 67 | 57 | 9 | 1 | (b) | ... | ... | ... | ... |
| 1926–1930 | 1945 | 44 | 39 | 5 | 1 | (b) | ... | ... | ... | ... |
| 1921–1925 | 1940 | 44 | 39 | 5 | (b) | (b) | ... | ... | ... | ... |
| 1916–1920 | 1935 | 41 | 36 | 4 | (b) | (b) | ... | ... | ... | ... |
| 1911–1915 | 1930 | 49 | 43 | 5 | (b) | (b) | ... | ... | ... | ... |
| 1906–1910 | 1925 | 51 | 45 | 5 | (b) | (b) | ... | ... | ... | ... |
| 1901–1905 | 1920 | 43 | 38 | 5 | (b) | (b) | ... | ... | ... | ... |
| 1896–1900 [c] | 1915 | 49 | 43 | 5 | (b) | (b) | ... | ... | ... | ... |
| 1891–1895 [c] | 1910 | 50 | 44 | 6 | (b) | (b) | ... | ... | ... | ... |
| | | | | EXACT AGES 20 TO 24 [a] | | | | | | |
| 1931–1935 | 1955 | 789 | 479 | 222 | 67 | 17 | 4 | 1 | (b) | (b) |
| 1926–1930 | 1950 | 636 | 427 | 159 | 39 | 9 | 2 | (b) | (b) | (b) |
| 1921–1925 | 1945 | 520 | 348 | 125 | 36 | 9 | 2 | (b) | (b) | (b) |
| 1916–1920 | 1940 | 453 | 308 | 108 | 29 | 7 | 1 | (b) | (b) | (b) |
| 1911–1915 | 1935 | 454 | 300 | 112 | 32 | 8 | 2 | (b) | (b) | (b) |
| 1906–1910 | 1930 | 526 | 340 | 133 | 40 | 10 | 2 | 1 | (b) | (b) |
| 1901–1905 | 1925 | 560 | 358 | 144 | 44 | 11 | 2 | 1 | (b) | (b) |
| 1896–1900 [c] | 1920 | 533 | 339 | 138 | 44 | 10 | 2 | (b) | (b) | (b) |
| 1891–1895 [c] | 1915 | 557 | 349 | 146 | 48 | 12 | 2 | (b) | (b) | (b) |
| 1886–1890 [c] | 1910 | 568 | 349 | 151 | 50 | 14 | 3 | (b) | (b) | (b) |

Table 14-8. Cumulative Birth Rates, by Order of Birth, for Cohorts of Native White Women, United States, 1910–55 (Continued)

| COHORTS OF— | JAN. 1 OF— | ALL BIRTHS | ORDER OF BIRTH | | | | | | | |
| --- | --- | --- | --- | --- | --- | --- | --- | --- | --- | --- |
| | | | FIRST | SECOND | THIRD | FOURTH | FIFTH | SIXTH | SEVENTH | EIGHTH AND HIGHER |
| | | | EXACT AGES 25 TO 29 [a] | | | | | | | |
| 1926–1930 | 1955 | 1,642 | 757 | 519 | 233 | 87 | 30 | 10 | 3 | 2 |
| 1921–1925 | 1950 | 1,389 | 715 | 415 | 163 | 60 | 22 | 8 | 3 | 1 |
| 1916–1920 | 1945 | 1,158 | 621 | 337 | 140 | 57 | 22 | 8 | 3 | 1 |
| 1911–1915 | 1940 | 1,054 | 555 | 293 | 127 | 55 | 22 | 8 | 3 | 1 |
| 1906–1910 | 1935 | 1,149 | 567 | 320 | 151 | 69 | 28 | 10 | 3 | 2 |
| 1901–1905 | 1930 | 1,275 | 604 | 357 | 178 | 83 | 34 | 13 | 4 | 2 |
| 1896–1900 c | 1925 | 1,331 | 618 | 373 | 191 | 91 | 37 | 14 | 5 | 2 |
| 1891–1895 c | 1920 | 1,335 | 619 | 372 | 194 | 91 | 37 | 15 | 5 | 2 |
| 1886–1890 c | 1915 | 1,417 | 629 | 389 | 220 | 109 | 46 | 17 | 5 | 2 |
| 1881–1885 c | 1910 | 1,453 | 632 | 394 | 228 | 119 | 52 | 19 | 6 | 3 |
| | | | EXACT AGES 30 TO 34 [z] | | | | | | | |
| 1921–1925 | 1955 | 2,126 | 845 | 648 | 346 | 158 | 69 | 32 | 15 | 12 |
| 1916–1920 | 1950 | 1,857 | 789 | 554 | 274 | 126 | 60 | 29 | 14 | 11 |
| 1911–1915 | 1945 | 1,638 | 715 | 462 | 230 | 115 | 59 | 30 | 15 | 12 |
| 1906–1910 | 1940 | 1,639 | 689 | 445 | 238 | 129 | 69 | 37 | 18 | 14 |
| 1901–1905 | 1935 | 1,795 | 704 | 478 | 277 | 159 | 88 | 48 | 23 | 17 |
| 1896–1900 c | 1930 | 1,938 | 724 | 510 | 310 | 183 | 105 | 57 | 29 | 20 |
| 1891–1895 c | 1925 | 2,016 | 742 | 521 | 326 | 198 | 113 | 62 | 31 | 23 |
| 1886–1890 c | 1920 | 2,076 | 747 | 533 | 340 | 209 | 118 | 68 | 35 | 26 |
| 1881–1885 c | 1915 | 2,175 | 757 | 544 | 362 | 230 | 135 | 76 | 40 | 30 |
| 1876–1880 c | 1910 | 2,282 | 759 | 545 | 380 | 256 | 163 | 95 | 48 | 36 |

Table 14-8. Cumulative Birth Rates, by Order of Birth, for Cohorts of Native White Women, United States, 1910–55 (*Continued*)

| COHORTS OF— | JAN. 1 OF— | ALL BIRTHS | ORDER OF BIRTH | | | | | | | |
|---|---|---|---|---|---|---|---|---|---|---|
| | | | FIRST | SECOND | THIRD | FOURTH | FIFTH | SIXTH | SEVENTH | EIGHTH AND HIGHER |
| | | | EXACT AGES 35 TO 39 [a] | | | | | | | |
| 1916–1920 | 1955 | 2,278 | 839 | 653 | 376 | 195 | 99 | 53 | 29 | 35 |
| 1911–1915 | 1950 | 2,046 | 782 | 567 | 316 | 168 | 91 | 53 | 30 | 38 |
| 1906–1910 | 1945 | 1,987 | 748 | 524 | 299 | 172 | 100 | 61 | 36 | 46 |
| 1901–1905 | 1940 | 2,112 | 745 | 533 | 327 | 201 | 123 | 78 | 47 | 58 |
| 1896–1900 [c] | 1935 | 2,300 | 760 | 563 | 366 | 234 | 149 | 97 | 60 | 71 |
| 1891–1895 [c] | 1930 | 2,448 | 780 | 581 | 393 | 260 | 168 | 111 | 69 | 86 |
| 1886–1890 [c] | 1925 | 2,567 | 791 | 597 | 414 | 280 | 184 | 125 | 79 | 98 |
| 1881–1885 [c] | 1920 | 2,707 | 802 | 615 | 438 | 305 | 204 | 140 | 90 | 112 |
| 1876–1880 [c] | 1915 | 2,873 | 809 | 630 | 464 | 335 | 235 | 162 | 103 | 135 |
| 1871–1875 [c] | 1910 | 3,051 | 812 | 632 | 486 | 367 | 270 | 192 | 125 | 167 |
| | | | EXACT AGES 40 TO 44 [a] | | | | | | | |
| 1911–1915 | 1955 | 2,224 | 799 | 597 | 350 | 196 | 111 | 66 | 40 | 64 |
| 1906–1910 | 1950 | 2,174 | 770 | 557 | 331 | 196 | 118 | 75 | 47 | 79 |
| 1901–1905 | 1945 | 2,274 | 761 | 554 | 348 | 219 | 140 | 93 | 60 | 100 |
| 1896–1900 [c] | 1940 | 2,473 | 770 | 579 | 384 | 254 | 168 | 115 | 76 | 125 |
| 1891–1895 [c] | 1935 | 2,656 | 791 | 597 | 414 | 283 | 191 | 133 | 91 | 156 |
| 1886–1890 [c] | 1930 | 2,828 | 803 | 616 | 440 | 309 | 213 | 154 | 106 | 186 |
| 1881–1885 [c] | 1925 | 3,010 | 816 | 636 | 467 | 337 | 238 | 174 | 123 | 218 |
| 1876–1880 [c] | 1920 | 3,206 | 824 | 654 | 494 | 367 | 265 | 199 | 144 | 260 |
| 1871–1875 [c] | 1915 | 3,424 | 828 | 662 | 521 | 399 | 300 | 231 | 171 | 312 |

Table 14-8. Cumulative Birth Rates, by Order of Birth, for Cohorts of Native White Women, United States, 1910–55 (Continued)

| COHORTS OF— | JAN. 1 OF— | ALL BIRTHS | ORDER OF BIRTH | | | | | | | |
|---|---|---|---|---|---|---|---|---|---|---|
| | | | FIRST | SECOND | THIRD | FOURTH | FIFTH | SIXTH | SEVENTH | EIGHTH AND HIGHER |
| | | | | | EXACT AGES 45 TO 49 [a] | | | | | |
| 1906–1910 | 1955 | 2,209 | 773 | 561 | 335 | 200 | 122 | 78 | 50 | 89 |
| 1901–1905 | 1950 | 2,313 | 764 | 557 | 352 | 223 | 143 | 96 | 63 | 114 |
| 1896–1900 [c] | 1945 | 2,510 | 772 | 581 | 387 | 257 | 172 | 119 | 81 | 143 |
| 1891–1895 [c] | 1940 | 2,703 | 792 | 599 | 417 | 286 | 195 | 138 | 96 | 180 |
| 1886–1890 [c] | 1935 | 2,887 | 805 | 618 | 443 | 313 | 218 | 159 | 113 | 217 |
| 1881–1885 [c] | 1930 | 3,084 | 817 | 639 | 471 | 342 | 244 | 182 | 131 | 258 |
| 1876–1880 [c] | 1925 | 3,292 | 826 | 657 | 498 | 372 | 273 | 207 | 153 | 307 |
| 1871–1875 [c] | 1920 | 3,515 | 830 | 666 | 526 | 405 | 308 | 239 | 181 | 360 |
| | | | | | EXACT AGES 50 TO 54 [a] | | | | | |
| 1901–1905 | 1955 | 2,315 | 764 | 557 | 352 | 224 | 144 | 96 | 63 | 115 |
| 1896–1900 [c] | 1950 | 2,512 | 772 | 581 | 387 | 257 | 172 | 119 | 81 | 144 |
| 1891–1895 [c] | 1945 | 2,705 | 792 | 599 | 417 | 286 | 195 | 138 | 96 | 182 |
| 1886–1890 [c] | 1940 | 2,891 | 805 | 618 | 443 | 313 | 218 | 160 | 113 | 221 |
| 1881–1885 [c] | 1935 | 3,088 | 817 | 639 | 471 | 342 | 244 | 182 | 132 | 261 |
| 1876–1880 [c] | 1930 | 3,299 | 826 | 657 | 498 | 372 | 273 | 207 | 153 | 312 |
| 1871–1875 [c] | 1925 | 3,521 | 830 | 666 | 526 | 405 | 308 | 240 | 181 | 365 |

SOURCE: Scripps Foundation for Research in Population Problems, cited in Wilson H. Grabill, Clyde V. Kiser, and Pascal K. Whelpton, The Fertility of American Women, Wiley, New York, 1958, Table 114.

[a] The year in which these ages were reached is given in the second column from the left. For example, the cohorts of 1936–1940 reached ages 15 to 19 at the beginning of 1955; i.e., on January 1, 1955, the average age of the women in the cohort of 1940 was exactly 15 years; for those in the cohort of 1939 it was exactly 16 years; etc.

[b] 0.5 or less.

[c] The rates for the cohorts of 1896–1900 and earlier are preliminary estimates, subject to minor changes.

breaking down the several factors in any fertility rate.[40] The first row concerns girls who were born during 1936–40 and were aged 15 to 19 years at the beginning of 1955; that is, on January 1, 1955, the average age of the girls in the cohort of 1940 was exactly 15 years, for those in the cohort of 1939 it was exactly 16 years, and so on. The next column gives the cumulative birth rate; this means that the five cohorts had had a total of 77 births per 1,000, of which 65 were first births, and so on.

It is evident that a large part of the baby boom was due to the higher fertility of young women, reflecting the decline in the age at marriage (Table 14-9). For females the median age fluctuated between 1890 and

Table 14-9. Age at Marriage and Proportion Married, United States, 1890–1960

| YEARS | MEDIAN AGE AT FIRST MARRIAGE | | PERCENTAGE MARRIED OF PERSONS AGED 14 AND OVER | |
|---|---|---|---|---|
| | MALES | FEMALES | MALES | FEMALES |
| 1890 | 26.1 | 22.0 | 52.1 | 54.8 |
| 1900 | 25.9 | 21.9 | 52.8 | 55.2 |
| 1910 | 25.1 | 21.6 | 54.2 | 57.1 |
| 1920 | 24.6 | 21.2 | 57.6 | 58.9 |
| 1930 | 24.3 | 21.3 | 58.4 | 59.5 |
| 1940 | 24.3 | 21.5 | 59.7 | 59.5 |
| 1950 | 22.8 | 20.1 | 68.2 | 66.1 |
| 1960 | 22.8 | 20.3 | 69.3 | 68.0 |

SOURCES: U.S. Bureau of the Census, U.S. Census of Population: 1950, Vol. 2, Characteristics of the Population, Part 1, U.S. Summary, Washington, D.C., 1953, p. 1–97; Current Population Reports, Series P-20, No. 105, November 2, 1960; U.S. National Office of Vital Statistics, Vital Statistics of the United States, 1953, Washington, D.C., 1955, 1, xxxiii.

1940 and then in the following two decades fell off by 1.2 years. For males, similarly, there was a decline by 3.3 years from 1890 to 1960. In part as a reflection of this lower age, the proportion married of those aged fourteen and over increased from somewhat more than half in 1890 to over two-thirds in 1960. The decline in age at marriage was greatest among those with most education, so that the class differential along this dimension fell off appreciably (Tietze and Lauriat, 1955; Lauriat, 1959). The interval

[40] A similar table for all women (rather than only native white women) and brought up to 1958 is given in U.S. National Office of Vital Statistics, "Fertility Tables for Birth Cohorts of American Women, Part 1," Vital Statistics—Special Reports, Vol. 51, No. 1, Washington, D.C., 1960.

between marriage and the birth of the first child is usually short, and "more young wives than formerly are having their second child relatively soon after their first, and their third relatively soon after their second" (Grabill *et al.*, 1958, p. 330). The trend toward earlier marriage, in other words, was generally linked to the increase in fertility, even though effective contraceptives might have broken this relation.

Marriage at young ages is surprising, as over the same period the amount of preparatory training needed to begin remunerative work has certainly increased on the average, and in particular the proportion of adolescents attending college has gone up sharply. But the pattern of social maturation has changed. Sons of the middle class, who used to make up the larger part of the college population, had a regular progression prescribed for them: earn a degree, find a job, and get established in it, marry, then, and not before, have children. This postponement of family formation until his late twenties or early thirties was the price a young man paid to start in a good position. Whether the pattern would have survived the spread of college education to greater numbers and different social classes can perhaps be questioned. In any case, it was shattered by World War II. Veterans going to college were four or five years older than the standard student body, and in other respects still more mature. They could live, single or married, on their income under the so-called G.I. Bill and its supplements. In 1947, thus, an estimated 200,000 college students were married; and once the pattern was set, it continued without the impetus of veterans' benefits. By the fall of 1956, one out of every four college students was married; among students in the typical college age, eighteen to twenty-four, one out of every six.

The consequences for fertility of the lower age at marriage can be seen in Table 14-8. The cumulative birth rate of cohorts aged 15–19 years increased from 50 in 1910 to 77 in 1955, that of those aged 20–24 from 568 to 789, that of those aged 25–29 from 1,453 to 1,642. Note that the percentage increase declines for higher ages. The 1955 cumulative birth rates for cohorts aged 30–34 years, while higher than for the immediately preceding period, are lower than for 1910; and those for cohorts aged 45 and over are lower in 1955 than at any preceding date.

What of the order of births? Of course, most of the teen-age girls giving birth were having their first baby; but in 1955, 11 per 1,000 births to mothers aged 15–19 were second births, and one per 1,000 was a third one. Compare the women aged 20–24 in 1955 with those aged 20–24 in 1940, the last group before the baby boom started. That there should have been more first and second births one expects, but the rate went up from 29 to 67 for third births (an increase of 130 per cent in 15 years), from 7 to 17 for fourth births (140 per cent), from 1 to 4 for fifth births (300 per cent), from less than 0.5 to 1 for sixth births (at least 100 per cent). It is true that these increases are calculated from the period of lowest fertility, but note that for the women aged 20–24 the cumulative birth rates in 1955 are also higher than those in 1910 for every order of births up to the sixth!

Another reason for the baby boom was that women who postponed having children during the depression of the 1930s often had them after 1945, relatively late in their fecund period. This can also be illustrated from Table 14-8. Note the cohorts born in 1911–15 in the third deck: their cumulative birth rate at ages 25–29 was 1,064 per thousand, or the lowest of any group of cohorts of this age. In 1955, when the 1911–15 cohorts were aged 40–44, their cumulative birth rate was 2,224. Of the increase, 244 (799 — 555) units represented first births to women aged 30–44 years.

The annual average number of births to native white women increased from 1.90 million in 1930–39 to 3.01 million in 1945–54, or by 58.7 per cent. These are the dimensions of the baby boom. What caused this unprecedented and wholly unanticipated rise in natality? Four factors are relevant: (1) The population increased, so that there were more people to have children. (2) The age at marriage went down, and a larger proportion married. (3) Of those who married, a larger proportion had children. (4) The average number of children per family increased (Grabill *et al.*, 1958, pp. 365–371).

In an especially interesting paper, Frank Notestein has made a *post factum* analysis of why demographers in the 1930s, he himself included, had been mistaken in their expectations with respect to fertility. His thesis is that they had been wrong in their timing but not fundamentally. Notestein cited three main reasons for the belief generally held during the interwar period that the decline in the birth rate would continue:

In the first place, the downward trend got under way in a differential fashion, spreading from the upper urban classes of the population down through the social-economic structure and outward from the city to the rural region. By the end of the interwar period the highest rates were the ones that were declining most rapidly, the lowest were declining least rapidly, and no evidence of a real upturn was in sight. In the second place, the differences in fertility were closely correlated with differences in the prevalence and effectiveness of contraceptive practice, and there was every indication that contraceptive materials were becoming more abundant, and that the knowledge of their use was spreading. In the third place, the middle-class standards, which had been such a strong factor in the motivation for small families, appeared to be spreading throughout the mass of the population. Thus the nature of the trends, the means by which they were brought about, and the nature of the pressures and incentives motivating restrictionist practices all suggested a pattern of decline that had not run its course (Notestein, 1950).

Each of these points calls for some comment.

Certainly the wider distribution of contraceptive knowledge and means facilitated the decline in fertility, but it was never decisive, even in the nineteenth century. As we have seen, the child-woman ratio began to fall off in the United States from 1810 on, and its decline was substantial before a method of control more reliable than *coitus interruptus* became available. In the Western world generally the trend in fertility depended less on the manner of controlling conception than on the will to control it. In Ireland, where the Catholic Church blocked the general sale of contraceptives, the demand for smaller families found alternative expression in the postponement of marriage; and in the Netherlands, which had had a fairly successful birth-control movement, fertility never declined to the general Northwest European level. In other words, the statement that "differences in fertility were closely correlated with differences in the prevalence and effectiveness of contraceptive practices" is true only with important qualifications.

One can also question the extrapolation of a past trend to its completion. It is true that most Americans try to plan the size of their families, but even today many do so inefficiently. With the wider dissemination of contraception, some of the fervor of the pioneers of the movement evaporated. Advocates of birth control, in order to emphasize that they favored the *control* rather than the limitation of births, began using the term "planned parenthood," and their clinics started to devote a good deal of time and effort to treating sterility ( *cf.* pp. 588–589).

Similarly, the assertion that "no evidence of a real upturn was in sight" in the 1930s is subject to challenge. The first studies in differential fertility had shown a negative correlation between social class and size of family, but this uniform pattern was broken, possibly first in Sweden but also in other Western countries, especially if the length of marriage was held contant.[41] Particularly when one uses income as the index of social class, the typical pattern seemed to be a J-curve rather than a linear relation. The average family size of upper classes in the cities, precisely those who had led the revolt against procreation up to the physiological limit, was in some cases no longer declining in the 1930s. Middle-class standards were indeed spreading throughout the mass of the population, but they were not unambiguously "such a strong factor in the motivation for small families" as they had once been.

Finally, the point that "the highest rates were the ones that were declining most rapidly, and the lowest were declining least rapidly," could also have been offered as evidence that the downward trend was leveling off. In the United States, if not in Europe, the immediate postwar trend seemed indeed to be toward stabilization at a middle-sized family, with the social classes below this fertility level moving up to it and those above it moving down.

[41] Frank W. Notestein, "The Relation of Social Status to the Fertility of Native-Born Married Women in the United States," in *Problems of Population*, International Union for the Scientific Investigation of Population Problems, *Proceedings,* London, 1931, edited by G. H. L. F. Pitt-Rivers, Allen & Unwin, London, 1932, pp. 147–169.

Table 14-10. Live Births per 1,000 Women Aged 15–49 Years, Western Europe, Selected Years

|  | APPROXIMATE PERIODS | | | |
|  | 1935–39 | 1950–54 | 1955–59 | 1960–64 |
|---|---|---|---|---|
| Eire | 84 [a] | 94 [a] | 96 | 103 |
| England and Wales | 54 | 62 | 67 | 77 |
| Norway | 55 | 76 | 78 | 76 |
| Sweden | 54 | 64 | 61 | 62 |
| Finland | 74 | 88 | 80 | 74 |
| Denmark | 66 | 73 | 71 | 72 |
| West Germany | 68 [a,b] | 60 [a] | 64 [a] | 75 [a] |
| Netherlands | 77 | 90 | 90 | 89 |
| Belgium | 60 | 68 | 72 | 76 |
| France [c] | 60 | 80 | 82 | 82 |
| Switzerland | 55 | 68 | 70 | 76 |
| Austria | — | 58 | 67 | 80 |
| Italy | 90 | 70 | — | 73 |
| Spain [d] | 90 | 72 | — | 84 |
| Portugal | 105 | 90 | 91 | 94 |

SOURCES: Various, as compiled in D. V. Glass, "Fertility Trends in Europe since the Second World War," *Population Studies*, 22 (1968), 103–146, Table 4.

[a] Single-year rates for the second year of each period.
[b] Prewar territory of Germany, 1937.
[c] It is not clear whether live-born children who died before registration are included.
[d] Single-year rates for 1940, 1950, and 1960.

The recent trend in Western Europe, though with important differences among the various countries, is generally quite similar to the postwar pattern of American fertility (Table 14-10). In Italy, Spain, and Portugal, there has been a decline from the relatively high rates of the 1930s, but in every other country the fertility of the most recent period is higher than during the depression. True, there is no evidence of a return to very large families. The proportions of married women with four or more children have generally continued to fall, but also the proportions of childless or one-child families. Somewhat as in the United States, the family size is leveling off at two to three children, with usually a convergence along all the structural lines of European societies.

We ought to have learned one thing from the postwar baby boom: that parents can rationally choose to have children, as against alternative ways of life. In the 1930s it was believed that the most probable choice for a couple, once contraception was made available in both physical and moral terms, was to help establish a norm of childless marriages. For all the reasons that potential parents had for preventing the conception of a fifth or sixth child seemed to apply *a fortiori* to the first child, which cost them the most in money, time, effort, and loss of freedom. The conceptual framework in which population extrapolations were made was a simple equation: middle-class rationality added to access to contraceptives ultimately will effect an average family too small to maintain the population. But potential parents' decisions on whether to have children are determined not only by their "selfish" desire for "comfort" but also by "pride in progeny." Now that birth control is all but universal in Western countries, it is the relation between these conflicting goals of parents that principally determines the size of the family—and the accuracy of population projections. The forces that impelled the decline in American fertility from the beginning of the nineteenth century on did not suddenly disappear in 1940; some of the value and styles of living in modern America still push toward a decline in the birth rate. On the other hand, the counter forces that resulted in the baby boom are also a reality, not merely an aberration from the downward trend.

## Attitudes and Family Size

The analysis of familial events by such broad categories as social classes is based on the premise, validated by the small range of differentiation within any one of them, that by and large persons in the same place in the social structure, subject to the same pressures, will usually make more or less the same decisions. But children are born to a single pair of parents, and it is really their decisions, if they make any, that help determine the size of their family and the spacing of their children. In some ways, then, it makes sense to shift the focus of research from social groups to individuals, from sociological to social-psychological concepts, from demographic to public-opinion data. The new trend developed in part because the convergence of class fertility rates induced analysts to look for finer distinctions, but attitude research had become so important a preoccupation in sociology generally that in any case one could have expected its use in demographic analysis.

Against the important gains that this new type of research brings to the discipline, one must mark certain limitations. Standard demographic data are perhaps the best in any social science, collected at government expense by highly qualified experts; attitude polls, typically made from small samples by either commercial firms or research teams, are ordinarily of a lower quality. Stated preferences concerning family size undoubtedly relate to actual fertility, but not necessarily closely. In perhaps the best study ever made of the matter, the correlation between the stated preference and the actual number of children twenty years later was only 0.30, or separately 0.45 for those who did and 0.19 for those who did not plan every pregnancy (Westoff *et al.*, 1957; *cf.* Westoff *et al.*, 1963; Freedman *et al.*, 1965). Even when the preferred and the actual number of children coincide, it is difficult to say which is the independent variable; for instance, Catholic mothers who refuse to use efficient contraceptives and therefore expect to have large families may also say that this is what they desire.

According to thirteen public-opinion polls in the United States between 1936 and 1961, the mean family size considered ideal ranged from 2.8 to 3.5 children (men) and from 2.7 to 3.6 (women). During the depression of the 1930s, World War II, and the years of postwar prosperity, reported shifts were within a range of less than one child (Blake, 1966*b*). That the changes in actual fertility were greater may mean that couples were unable to realize their ideal families, that responses to poll questionnaires merely approximate the actual decisions concerning family size, or that a significant proportion of fertility was not subject to rational control.

### THE INDIANAPOLIS STUDY

Of the various analyses in the United States that concentrated on psychological factors, the first sizable one was the Indianapolis study, "Social and Psychological Factors Affecting Fertility." This was published in thirty-three articles in the *Milbank Memorial Fund Quarterly*, and later bound in five volumes.[42] It was in many respects a pioneer effort, with the virtues and also the faults one might expect from any attempt to break new ground, particularly concerning psychological motivation. A rather miscellaneous list of twenty-three hypotheses on the factors possibly affecting either planned or actual family size were tested. Of these, three pertained to the effect of economic security, five to the family background and health of the potential parents, five to their expressed interest in children and their home, eight to their personality characteristics (feelings of inadequacy, fear of pregnancy, general tendency to plan, conformity to group patterns, etc.), and two to the relations between husband and wife. One of the hypotheses, for instance, was the following paraphrase of the Dumont-Banks thesis: "The greater the difference between the actual level of living and

---

[42] See in particular the final article, Kiser and Whelpton, 1958. This includes references to previous articles in the series and to various discussions of the study. After a preliminary household survey of most of Indianapolis (from which it was possible to compare the fertility of religious denominations), couples were divided into "relatively fecund" and "relatively sterile" classes, depending on whether there had been any considerable periods during which intercourse without birth control had not resulted in conception. A more detailed analysis was restricted to a sample of 1,444 relatively fecund native white Protestant couples, who had been married during 1927–29 and had lived in a large city most of the time since then. Of this group, 98 per cent reported some experience with contraception; 14 per cent had planned the number, and an additional 28 per cent both the number and spacing of all pregnancies.

the standard of living desired, the higher the proportion of couples practicing contraception effectively and the smaller the planned families." To test this, respondents were asked what they would like in order to live in a satisfactory manner, and their reply was compared with their actual mode of living. Very often a person with a second-hand car, for instance, expressed the desire for a new one, whereas someone who owned a new Cadillac, say, indicated his satisfaction with it. Economic tension decreased with greater incomes, rather than the contrary, as it should have to validate the hypothesis. Yet probably no demographer doubts the at least partial validity of the thesis as stated; indeed, when it was negated, the analysts rejected their own findings. We cannot measure levels of aspiration nearly so accurately as the behavior patterns associated with them, so that if respondents say one thing but do another, we accept the latter as the more meaningful.

Another of the hypotheses tested in the Indianapolis study was the following: "The stronger the interest in and liking for children, the lower the proportion of couples practicing contraception effectively and the larger the planned families." If one grants that it is possible to measure "liking" for children with reasonable accuracy from what people say, and if this proves to be positively correlated with the size of the family, then it would seem to be just as likely (as the analysts themselves point out) that couples who have children have learned to like them as *vice versa*. A still more probable cause-effect relation, both in this instance and generally, is that the independent variables cited in the twenty-three hypotheses and the supposed effects of planned and actual family size were both consequences of the relatively undifferentiated culture pattern of this white Protestant sample of a midwestern city. As the authors put it: "Our measures of psychological characteristics probably were too crude to afford precise differentiations, [and] it may be little wonder that the Study failed to indicate strong and consistent relations of fertility behavior to psychological characteristics" among so homogeneous a sample.[43] "The chief lesson" to be learned from the Indianapolis study, according to the men who directed it, is that fertility is generally more closely related to "broad social factors (including the economic)" than to psychological. Both family planning and actual fertility were clearly correlated with social-economic status; but when this variable was held constant, "the observed relation of fertility behavior to most of the psychological characteristics considered was generally much less pronounced or less regular." [44]

### RELIGIOUS DIFFERENCES IN FERTILITY

In most Western countries, Jews and irreligious have the smallest families, Protestants of various denominations are in the intermediate range,

[43] *Ibid.*, p. 323.
[44] *Ibid.*, pp. 318–319.

and Catholics have the largest. According to public-opinion polls in the United States, the three groups generally fall in the same order with respect to the number of children (1) desired and (2) expected, and the (3) approval and (4) use of contraception (Freedman *et al.*, 1961). The significance of these findings depends to some degree on the interpretation of the researcher. In an analysis of Western fertility concentrated on over-all long-term trends, differences in religion and similar culturally defined characteristics can be regarded as minor, residual to the differentiation by social class. In the process of modernization that the growth of cities and of urban-based social classes effects, one typical consequence is secularization, the tendency of religious-cultural differences to become smaller. Thus, the effect of religion *per se* on the reproductive behavior of most persons in the West is now probably close to nil. What may seem to be a religious influence often reflects the fact that the members of any denomination are typically concentrated in a very few places in the social structure as defined by occupation, education, income, or any other of the usual indices.

American Jews, for example, are not merely a religious-cultural ethnic stock, but also a sector of the population that moved up with great speed into metropolitan upper middle-class positions. Their generally very low fertility can be explained most plausibly as a prime instance of the Dumont-Banks thesis. That some orthodox rabbis condemn contraception seems to have little effect on family size. According to data from a random sample of 1,603 Jewish households in the Providence metropolitan area, the mean size of completed families among three generations of Orthodox, Conservative, and Reform Jews ranged only from 3.2 to 1.8, and variations in Jewish doctrine had virtually no effect on family size when social class was held constant (Goldscheider, 1965). Similarly, family size varies among the major Protestant denominations as one would expect from the typical social class of their membership and can be denoted a specific effect of the group's religious doctrines only in a few minor sects.

The one numerically significant faith that has an important effect would seem to be Catholicism, and even here the data are not consistent. France, at least nominally a Catholic country, was the first in the West to establish the small-family system. The fertility of Italy's northern, more industrial provinces is almost as low as anywhere in the world (birth rates between ten and fourteen in 1959), and that of the southern, agrarian provinces (birth rates between twenty-two and twenty-four) was only intermediate on a world scale (Seppilli, 1960). Manifestly, the doctrinal prohibition of effective contraceptives is not a sufficient explanation. Van Heek's perceptive analysis of Dutch Catholics, whose fertility has been extremely high by Western standards, is applicable more generally. Oppressed by Protestants in the seventeenth and eighteenth centuries, the substantial bloc of Catholics acquired a fighting spirit that persisted long after their full emancipation. This religious élan has been expressed in their stricter discipline, their more rigid adherence to dogma, and thus their larger families (Van Heek,

1956 [45] ). Other Catholic populations with a similar grievance about past persecutions include the French Canadians and the Irish, and in both cases the fertility has been very high (in the Irish case, because of the late age at marriage, this applies to marital fertility rather than the birth rate).

American Catholics reflect a number of influences. As peasant immigrants they carried old-country norms with them, and they typically fitted in the American occupational structure at a low level, with a correspondingly high fertility. In the 1930s the birth rate of Catholics was higher than that of non-Catholics but declining faster, and the general prognosis was that the difference would eventually disappear. "It is quite clear that the main reason why Catholic fertility is falling more rapidly arises from the fact that it has farther to fall; because there has been, in fact, a cultural lag" (Himes, 1936, p. 413). In the postwar period several analysts have challenged this prognosis (e.g., Kirk, 1955), and others have confirmed it (e.g., Brooks and Henry, 1958). According to the so-called Princeton study, Catholics desire larger families than other Americans, but in part because "the more fundamentalist Protestant sects found in the southern and rural parts of the country" were omitted from the sample (Westoff et al., 1961, p. 179). Even so, the range in the mean number of children desired, unchanged in a later study, was very small—from 3.6 by two Catholic parents to 2.7 by two Jewish parents (ibid., p. 180; Westoff et al., 1963, p. 89). When a Catholic had been married to a non-Catholic by a priest, the wife wanted 3.3 children on the average; when not by a priest, she wanted 3.0 children. The stated preference among the eight Protestant denominations surveyed ranged between 2.8 and 3.1 children. Among Catholics the mean number of children desired was highest in the professional class (4.0) and lowest in the unskilled (3.4). From those data the authors concluded that "religion exerts a strong influence on fertility" and that "the comparative influence of class appears negligible" (Westoff et al., 1961, p. 191). But when differentials along all dimensions contract to so narrow a range, it is a more or less arbitrary decision whether to stress one or another among the remaining differences. Yet the small difference by religion presumably means that Catholicism per se tends to induce a high fertility. This would be so even if the average family size were the same; for Catholics, like Jews, are predominantly urban, so that if the weight of other factors were equal their fertility ought to be lower than that of the Protestants, who are distributed between the rural and urban sectors. Middle-class Catholics in particular have a higher fertility than others in the middle class, presumably because they fit in best with Van Heek's hypothesis: "the minority status has developed a sect type of mentality in its most committed membership" (Hunt, 1967).

[45] This English summary is of course not so well documented as the full argument: Het geboorte-niveau der Nederlandse Rooms-Katholieken, Stenfert Kroese, Leiden, 1954. See also William Petersen, "Fertility Trends and Population Policy: Some Comments on the Van Heek-Hofstee Debate," Sociologica Neerlandica (Leiden), 3 (1966), 2–13; Day, 1968.

## Summary

The birth-control movement that arose in Europe and the United States during the nineteenth century gradually legitimized the small-family norm. The route by which this norm was disseminated to the various sectors of Western populations was class differentiation in fertility. The secular decline began in the urban middle classes, and from them spread to the urban working classes and the rural population. It seems that the small family became established more by the diffusion of urban ideas to rural areas than by the migration of rural persons to urban places. It is necessary to look for causes, thus, not so much in the living conditions in cities as in the ideas and aspirations of city people. The greater rationality (in Max Weber's sense of the word) of town life presumably induced a larger and larger proportion of the population to weigh the advantages and disadvantages to be derived from each child and to adjust the size of the family accordingly. In the 1930s almost every demographer thought in terms of such a stylized picture of Rational Man and believed that the downward trend in fertility would continue. Once it became general to adjust family size according to the loss in money and convenience incurred from having children, it was thought that many couples, perhaps eventually most, would have none at all.

In the postwar decade, however, there was a wholly unexpected revival of births. In general, this was most marked among the social classes that previously had shown the greatest decline, so that the present trend seems to be toward a greater convergence in fertility, with both social-economic extremes moving toward a central norm of a middle-sized family (or, according to the trend in the late 1960s, one on the slightly smaller side), with possibly a *positive* correlation between social class and family size over a very small range. Analysts of the most recent period, therefore, have generally concentrated on religious-cultural differences in fertility and turned to a new source of data, public-opinion polls on attitudes that relate the desired to the actual family size.

## Suggestions for Further Reading

The bibliography on the fertility of Western nations is tremendous, and growing rapidly. Some of the supplementary readings listed at the end of Chapter 6 (pp. 195–198) are relevant here, and the general bibliographic guide cited here, Freedman 1961–62, is also useful.

The definitive history of the birth-control movement is still to be written. Himes, 1936, originally intended as the first of two volumes, remains the best book-length analysis, but it can be usefully supplemented by various articles, such as Micklewright, 1961; Banks and Banks, 1954.

Banks, 1954 is indispensable in understanding the social background of the secular decline in fertility, and Wrong, 1958 is an excellent summary of the demographic trends. The several large-scale studies in the United States, which in this chapter have been discussed only partially in connection with designated topics, deserve a fuller analysis from a student particularly interested in fertility. For over-all critical reviews, see Goldberg, 1960; Westoff *et al.*, 1963, Chapter 2. Of all the works that combine demographic analysis with attitude studies, Freedman *et al.*, 1959 is still the best.

BALTZELL, E. DIGBY. 1953. "Social Mobility and Fertility within an Elite Group," *Milbank Memorial Fund Quarterly*, 31, 411–420.

° BANKS, J. A. 1954. *Prosperity and Parenthood: A Study of Family Planning among the Victorian Middle Classes.* Routledge & Kegan Paul, London.

————, and OLIVE BANKS. 1954. "The Bradlaugh-Besant Trial and the English Newspapers," *Population Studies*, 8, 22–34.

————, and ————. 1964. *Feminism and Family Planning in Victorian England.* Liverpool University Press, Liverpool.

BECKER, GARY S. 1960. "An Economic Analysis of Fertility," in National Bureau of Economic Research, 1960, pp. 209–231.

BENNETT, JOHN C. 1959. "Protestant Ethics and Population Control," *Daedalus*, 88, 454–459.

BERGUES, HÉLÈNE, et al. 1960. *La prévention des naissances dans la famille: Ses origines dans les temps modernes.* Presses Universitaires de France, Paris.

BERNARD, JESSIE. 1968. "The Status of Women in Modern Patterns of Culture," *Annals of the American Academy of Political and Social Science*, 375, 3–14.

BLACKER, J. G. C. 1957. "Social Ambitions of the Bourgeoisie in 18th Century France, and their Relation to Family Limitation," *Population Studies*, 11, 46–63.

BLAKE, JUDITH. 1966a. "The Americanization of Catholic Reproductive Ideals," *Population Studies*, 20, 27–43.

————. 1966b. "Ideal Family Size among White Americans: A Quarter Century's Evidence," *Demography*, 1, 154–173.

° ————. 1968. "Are Babies Consumer Durables? A Critique of the Economic Theory of Reproductive Motivation," *Population Studies*, 22, 5–25.

BROOKS, HUGH E., and FRANKLIN J. HENRY. 1958. "An Empirical Study of the Relationships of Catholic Practice and Occupational Mobility to Fertility," *Milbank Memorial Fund Quarterly*, 36, 222–277.

CAMPBELL, ARTHUR A. 1965. "Fertility and Family Planning among Nonwhite Married Couples in the United States," *Eugenics Quarterly*, 12, 124–131.

COALE, ANSLEY J., and MELVIN ZELNIK. 1963. *New Estimates of Fertility and Population in the United States.* Princeton University Press, Princeton.

COOK, ROBERT C., editor. 1965. "The Vatican and the Population Crisis," *Population Bulletin*, 21, 1–15.

DAVIS, KINGSLEY. 1937. "Reproductive Institutions and the Pressure for Population," *Sociological Review*, 29, 289–306.

DAY, LINCOLN. 1961. "Status Implications of the Employment of Married Women in the United States," *American Journal of Economics and Sociology*, 20, 390–398.

° ————. 1968. "Natality and Ethnocentrism: Some Relationships Suggested by an Analysis of Catholic-Protestant Differentials," *Population Studies*, 22, 27–50.

* DORN, HAROLD F. 1950. "Pitfalls in Population Forecasts and Projections," *Journal of the American Statistical Association*, 42, 311–334.

DUMONT, ARSÈNE. 1890. *Dépopulation et civilisation: Études démographiques.* Lecrosnier et Babé, Paris.

EASTERLIN, RICHARD A. 1961. "The American Baby Boom in Historical Perspective," *American Economic Review*, 51, 869–911.

* ———. 1966. "On the Relation of Economic Factors to Recent and Projected Fertility Changes," *Demography*, 3, 131–153.

EDIN, KARL A., and EDWARD P. HUTCHINSON. 1935. *Studies of Differential Fertility in Sweden.* King, London.

* FARLEY, REYNOLDS. 1966. "Recent Changes in Negro Fertility," *Demography*, 3, 188–203.

FIELD, JAMES ALFRED. 1931. *Essays in Population and Other Papers.* University of Chicago Press, Chicago.

FREEDMAN, DEBORAH S. 1963. "The Relation of Economic Status to Fertility," *American Economic Review*, 53, 414–426.

* FREEDMAN, RONALD. 1961–62. "The Sociology of Human Fertility: A Trend Report and Bibliography," *Current Sociology*, 10–11, No. 2.

* ———, PASCAL K. WHELPTON, and ARTHUR A. CAMPBELL. 1959. *Family Planning, Sterility, and Population Growth.* McGraw-Hill, New York.

———, ———, and JOHN W. SMIT. 1961. "Socio-Economic Factors in Religious Differentials in Fertility," *American Sociological Review*, 26, 608–614.

———, LOLAGENE C. COOMBS, and LARRY BUMPASS. 1965. "Stability and Change in Expectations about Family Size," *Demography*, 2, 250–275.

GIBBONS, WILLIAM J., S.J. 1956. "Fertility Control in the Light of Some Recent Catholic Statements," *Eugenics Quarterly*, 3, 9–15 and 82–87.

GLASNER, SAMUEL. 1961. "Judaism and Sex," in *The Encyclopedia of Sexual Behavior*, edited by Albert Ellis and Albert Abarnel. Hawthorn, New York, 2, 575–584.

* GLASS, D. V. 1940. *Population Policies and Movements in Europe.* Clarendon, Oxford.

* ———. 1968. "Fertility Trends in Europe since the Second World War," *Population Studies*, 22, 103–146.

———, and E. GREBENIK. 1954. *The Trend and Pattern of Fertility in Great Britain: A Report on the Family Census.* H. M. Stationery Office, London.

GOLDBERG, DAVID. 1960. "Some Recent Developments in American Fertility Research," in National Bureau of Economic Research, 1960, pp. 137–151.

GOLDSCHEIDER, CALVIN. 1965. "Ideological Factors in Jewish Fertility Differentials," *Jewish Journal of Sociology*, 7, 92–105.

GRABILL, WILSON H., CLYDE V. KISER, and PASCAL K. WHELPTON. 1958. *The Fertility of American Women.* Wiley, New York.

* HIMES, NORMAN E. 1936. *Medical History of Contraception.* Williams & Wilkins, Baltimore.

HUNT, CHESTER L. 1967. "Catholicism and the Birthrate," *Review of Religious Research*, 8, 67–80.

INNES, J. W. 1938. *Class Fertility Trends in England and Wales, 1876–1934.* Princeton University Press, Princeton, N.J.

JAFFE, A. J. 1940. "Differential Fertility in the White Population in Early America," *Journal of Heredity*, 31, 407–411.

JOHNSON, GWENDOLYN Z. 1960. "Differential Fertility in European Countries," in National Bureau of Economic Research, 1960, pp. 36–72.

KELLY, GEORGE A. 1960. *Overpopulation: A Catholic View*. Paulist Press (Paulist Fathers), New York.

KIRK, DUDLEY. 1955. "Recent Trends in Catholic Fertility in the United States," in Milbank Memorial Fund, *Current Research in Human Fertility*. New York, pp. 93–105.

KISER, CLYDE V., and P. K. WHELPTON. 1958. "Summary of Chief Findings and Implications for Future Studies," *Milbank Memorial Fund Quarterly*, 36, 282–329.

KOYA, YOSHIO. 1962. "A Family Planning Program in a Large Population Group," *Milbank Memorial Fund Quarterly*, 40, 319–327.

* KUNZ, PHILLIP R. 1965. "The Relation of Income and Fertility," *Journal of Marriage and Family*, 27, 509–513.

LAURIAT, PATIENCE. 1959. "Marriage and Fertility Patterns of College Graduates," *Eugenics Quarterly*, 6, 171–179.

LESER, C. E. V. 1958. "Trends in Women's Work Participation," *Population Studies*, 12, 100–110.

LINCOLN, C. ERIC. 1965. "The Absent Father Haunts the Negro Family," *New York Times Magazine*, November 28.

LOTKA, ALFRED J. 1927. "The Size of American Families in the Eighteenth Century," *Journal of the American Statistical Association*, 22, 154–170.

MANGIN, MARIE-REINE. 1962. "La politique néo-malthusienne au Danemark," *Population*, 17, 75–96.

* MAY, GEOFFREY. 1931. *Social Control of Sex Expression*. Morrow, New York.

* MICKLEWRIGHT, F. H. AMPHLETT. 1961. "The Rise and Decline of English Neo-Malthusianism," *Population Studies*, 15, 32–51.

MURAMATSU, MINORU. 1960. "Effect of Induced Abortion on the Reduction of Births in Japan," *Milbank Memorial Fund Quarterly*, 38, 153–166.

* NATIONAL BUREAU OF ECONOMIC RESEARCH. 1960. *Demographic and Economic Change in Developed Countries*. Princeton University Press, Princeton.

* NOONAN, JOHN T., JR. 1965. *Contraception: A History of Its Treatment by the Catholic Theologians and Canonists*. Belknap-Harvard University Press, Cambridge, Mass.

NOTESTEIN, FRANK W. 1950. "The Population of the World in the Year 2000," *Journal of the American Statistical Association*, 45, 335–349.

NYE, F. IVAN, and LOIS WLADIS HOFFMAN. 1963. *The Employed Mother in America*. Rand McNally, Chicago.

O'BRIEN, JOHN A. 1963. "Family Planning in an Exploding Population," *Christian Century*, 80, 1050–1052.

* ———, editor. 1953. *The Vanishing Irish: The Enigma of the Modern World*. McGraw-Hill, New York.

OKUN, BERNARD. 1958. *Trends in Birth Rates in the United States since 1870*. Johns Hopkins Press, Baltimore.

* OPPENHEIMER, VALERIE K. 1967. "The Interaction of Demand and Supply and

Its Effect on the Female Labour Force in the United States," *Population Studies,* **21,** 239–259.

———. 1968. "The Sex-Labeling of Jobs," *Industrial Relations,* **7,** 219–234.

PATAI, RAPHAEL. 1959. *Sex and Family in the Bible and the Middle East.* Doubleday, Garden City, N.Y.

\* REITERMAN, CARL. 1965. "Birth Control and Catholics," *Journal for the Scientific Study of Religion,* **4,** 213–233.

RIDLEY, JEANNE CLARE. 1959. "Number of Children Expected in Relation to Non-Familial Activities of the Wife," *Milbank Memorial Fund Quarterly,* **37,** 277–296.

ROBERTS, THOMAS D., editor. 1964. *Contraception and Holiness: The Catholic Predicament.* Herder and Herder, New York.

\* ROSSI, ALICE S. 1968. "Transition to Parenthood," *Journal of Marriage and the Family,* **30,** 26–39.

RUSSELL, JOHN L. 1958. "Christian Theology and the Population Problem," *The Month* (London), **19,** 197–208.

SANGER, MARGARET. 1931. *My Fight for Birth Control.* Farrar & Rinehart, New York.

———. 1938. *Margaret Sanger—An Autobiography.* Norton, New York.

SEPPILLI, TULLIO. 1960. "Social Conditions of Fertility in a Rural Community in Transition in Central Italy," *Annals of the New York Academy of Sciences,* **84,** Article 17.

STYS, W. 1957. "The Influence of Economic Conditions on the Fertility of Peasant Women," *Population Studies,* **11,** 136–148.

SULLOWAY, ALVAH W. 1959. *Birth Control and Catholic Doctrine.* Beacon, Boston.

SUTTER, JEAN. 1960. "Bilan de la politique néo-malthusienne en Suède (1939–1957)," *Population,* **15,** 677–702.

TAEUBER, IRENE B. 1958. *The Population of Japan.* Princeton University Press, Princeton, N.J.

TAYLOR, GEORGE V. 1967. "Noncapitalist Wealth and the Origins of the French Revolution," *American Historical Review,* **72,** 469–496.

TIEN, H. YUAN. 1961. "The Social Mobility/Fertility Hypothesis Reconsidered: An Empirical Study," *American Sociological Review,* **26,** 247–257.

TIETZE, CHRISTOPHER, and PATIENCE LAURIAT. 1955. "Age at Marriage and Educational Attainment in the United States," *Population Studies,* **9,** 159–166.

U.S. BUREAU OF LABOR STATISTICS. 1966. *Marital and Family Characteristics of Workers.* Special Labor Force Report, No. 64. Washington, D.C.

VAN HEEK, F. 1956. "Roman-Catholicism and Fertility in the Netherlands: Demographic Aspects of Minority Status," *Population Studies,* **10,** 125–138.

VINCENT, CLARK E. 1961. *Unmarried Mothers.* Free Press of Glencoe, New York.

WEBB, SIDNEY. 1913. *The Decline in the Birth-Rate.* Fabian Tract No. 131. Fabian Society, London.

WESTOFF, CHARLES F., ELLIOT G. MISHLER, and E. LOWELL KELLY. 1957. "Preferences in Size of Family and Eventual Fertility Twenty Years After," *American Journal of Sociology,* **62,** 491–497.

———, and RAYMOND H. POTVIN. 1967. *College Women and Fertility Values.* Princeton University Press, Princeton, N.J.

———, ROBERT G. POTTER, JR., PHILIP C. SAGI, and ELLIOT G. MISHLER. 1961.

*Family Growth in Metropolitan America.* Princeton University Press, Princeton, N.J.

———, ———, and ———. 1963. *The Third Child: A Study in the Prediction of Fertility.* Princeton University Press, Princeton, N.J.

WHELPTON, PASCAL K., ARTHUR A. CAMPBELL, and JOHN E. PATTERSON. 1966. *Fertility and Family Planning in the United States.* Princeton University Press, Princeton, N.J.

* WRONG, DENNIS H. 1958. "Trends in Class Fertility in Western Nations," *Canadian Journal of Economics and Political Science,* 24, 216–229.

ZIMMERMAN, ANTHONY F. 1957. *Overpopulation.* Catholic University of America Press, Washington, D.C.

# 15 MORTALITY IN THE MODERN WORLD

Differences in the level of fertility have grown smaller among Western nations and the social classes within them, but the over-all contrast between the fertility of advanced and that of underdeveloped countries has become more pronounced. With respect to mortality, on the contrary, the world-wide range has narrowed. The reason, obviously, is that the control over the number of children that is exercised inside each family varies greatly from one culture to another, whereas the control of early death has become in great part independent of the will of the persons affected. Thus, it is convenient to discuss in this one chapter the mortality of all the world, while the analysis of fertility has been divided into two parts. The arrangement is designed to emphasize the chronology: (1) the fall of birth rates in the West, which began before the substantial decline in Western death rates; (2) the decline in mortality throughout the world (this chapter); and (3) the attempts to bring the fertility of underdeveloped countries under control, following the sizable decline in mortality. This is not to suggest, however, that the effect of life-saving techniques has been the same in the rest of the world as in the historic West. Over the decades, as new medicines, surgical practices, and medical institutions were invented in Europe or its overseas extensions, these improvements were used to bring about a gradual reduction in mortality; but in many underdeveloped areas the control of early death went from witchcraft to antibiotics in one fantastic leap.

546

## Decline of Mortality in the West

The most remarkable fact about modern death control is how recently it began. As we noted in Chapter 11, the probable decline in English mortality around 1800 is difficult to explain. Only toward the middle of the nineteenth century was a serious attempt made to separate sewage from drinking water, and most of the specifics against various infections did not become available until several decades later.

From the middle of the nineteenth century on, it is possible to trace international mortality trends with life tables, of which about 250 were available by the mid-1950s (Stolnitz, 1955-56). The gains in life chances of West Europeans from the 1840s to the 1940s—or, more precisely, mainly in the second half of that century—were probably greater than those over the previous two millennia (Table 15-1). Just before World War I, the pat-

Table 15-1. Proportion Surviving in Five West European Countries, by Sex, 1840s and 1940s

|  | 1840s | | | | 1940s | | | |
|---|---|---|---|---|---|---|---|---|
|  | $l_1{}^a$ | | $l_{15}{}^a$ | | $l_1{}^a$ | | $l_{60}{}^a$ | |
|  | MALE | FEMALE | MALE | FEMALE | MALE | FEMALE | MALE | FEMALE |
| Netherlands | 776 | 814 | 615 | 644 | 967 | 973 | 805 | 839 |
| Sweden | 835 | 859 | 710 | 741 | 966 | 974 | 759 | 802 |
| England and Wales | 836 | 865 | 673 | 697 | 952 | 963 | 722 | 799 |
| France | 822 | 847 | 659 | 676 | 943 | 957 | 684 | 776 |
| Belgium | 836 | 864 | 655 | 670 | 936 | 951 | 673 | 772 |

SOURCE: George J. Stolnitz, "A Century of International Mortality Trends: I," *Population Studies*, 9 (1955), 24–54.

[a] The symbol $l_x$ denotes the number of an original 1,000 live births that survive to age $x$ (see pp. 210–211). Early values for France cover the period 1840–59, for England and Wales 1838–54. Later values for all countries except Sweden are for postwar years.

tern of Europe's mortality followed that of its economic development. In Northwest Europe—that is, the British Isles, the Low Countries, Germany, Switzerland, and Scandinavia—only 15 persons died each year per thousand of the population; in France, Italy, and the western portion of Austria-Hungary this death rate was about 20; and in Spain and the Balkans it was about 25 (Kirk, 1946, Chapter 4). Since that time death rates have fallen steadily—apart from the two world wars—throughout Europe, and this regional variation all but disappeared. The very acquisition of an urban-industrial culture, once the major travail of the transition was past, was invariably accompanied by a substantial decline in mortality.

Direct information on mortality in the United States before 1900 is limited to surmises from local figures (Taeuber and Taeuber, 1958, pp. 269–272). These indicate that expectation of life at birth at the beginning of the nineteenth century was probably not much higher than 35 years, or about half of what it is today. Data on deaths on a national scale go back only to 1933, when the last state was admitted to the Death-Registration Area (see pp. 39, 52), and rates for earlier dates are based on the assumption that the death-registration states were typical. As there is every reason to believe, on the contrary, that greater control over death developed together with better statistics concerning it, such a series probably understates the decline in mortality that has taken place in the twentieth cenury, great as this has been according to the record. In Massachusetts, the first state to collect vital statistics systematically, the expectation of life at birth went up from 38.3 years in 1850 to 46.1 in 1900–02 for males, and from 40.5 to 49.4 for females (Dublin *et al.*, 1949, p. 48).

The most remarkable improvements were in the control of deaths at the earliest ages. The fall in infant mortality can be illustrated by the example of Sweden, which has both the longest historical series of accurate statistics and, at the present time, one of the world's best records for effective control. From 1750 to about 1810 infant mortality in Sweden fluctuated around 200 per 1,000 live births; that is, at that time one child out of every five born died before its first birthday. During the rest of the nineteenth century the rate fell slowly but consistently, reaching 100 by 1900 and, after a much faster decline, 21 by 1950 and slightly more than 15 in 1962. The reduction in infant mortality over 150 years, thus, was by about 90 per cent. For the most recent decades, death rates are available by shorter periods than the whole of the first year, and these are suggestive. From 1915 to 1945 the proportion of deaths under the age of one week remained essentially constant at about 16 per 1,000 live births, while deaths from age one week to one year fell off by about 70 per cent (United Nations, 1954, pp. 29–35; *cf.* Anderson and Rosen, 1960).

By 1950 Sweden had the lowest infant mortality rate in the world, having cut it by enough to pass the Netherlands and Norway, which fifteen years earlier ranked first and second (Table 15-2). In the United States the infant mortality rate fell from 95.7 in 1915–19 to almost precisely half that, 47.0, in 1940 (Table 15-3). Again, this decline can be taken as a minimum, for until 1933 the figures excluded some of the states with the highest mortality. To a considerable degree this improved control was stimulated by the work of vital statisticians. The American Association for the Prevention of Infant Mortality, organized in 1909, devoted its main effort during the first years to campaigning for the extension and improvement of birth

Table 15-2. Infant Mortality Rates, Selected Western Countries, 1935, 1950, 1962

| | INFANT MORTALITY RATE AND RANK AMONG COUNTRIES | | | PER CENT DECLINE | |
| --- | --- | --- | --- | --- | --- |
| | 1935 | 1950 | 1962 | 1935–62 | 1950–62 |
| Sweden | 45.9 (3) | 21.0 (1) | 15.3 (1) | 67 | 27 |
| Netherlands | 40.0 (1) | 26.7 (2) | 17.0 (2) | 57 | 36 |
| Norway | 44.2 (2) | 28.2 (3) | 17.7 (3) | 60 | 37 |
| Denmark | 71.0 (6) | 30.7 (6) | 20.0 (4) | 72 | 35 |
| England and Wales | 56.9 (5) | 29.9 (5) | 21.7 (5) | 62 | 27 |
| United States | 55.7 (4) | 29.2 (4) | 25.3 (6) | 55 | 13 |
| Scotland | 77.8 (7) | 38.6 (7) | 26.5 (7) | 65 | 31 |

SOURCE: Helen C. Chase, *International Comparison of Perinatal and Infant Mortality: The United States and Six West European Countries*, U.S. National Center for Health Statistics, Series 3, No. 6; Washington, D.C., 1967, p. 23.

and death registrations. As more accurate statistics on infant mortality became available, these denoted both the seriousness of the problem and the causes of death that most urgently required medical attention. The rate has continued to fall in the most recent period, from 55.7 in 1935 to 22.1, or less than half, in 1967. The rate of decline, however, has been much slower than in comparable Western countries. Among all the Scandinavian nations and white British dominions, only Scotland and Canada had rates higher than the United States. Infant mortality among nonwhite Americans actually rose slightly from a low in 1961, after a very slow decline during the 1950s. The reasons are that registration improved and that Negroes are concentrated in the South and in the low-income classes, which have high rates for both colors (see Hunt and Huyck, 1966; Stockwell, 1962). This inverse correlation between social class and infant mortality does not depend merely on access to medical services. In Great Britain, full antepartum, partum, and postpartum care became available to the whole childbearing population when the National Health Service was initiated, but in the subsequent period the gap between social classes has apparently widened (Chase, 1967, p. 67). By one interpretation the higher death rate of infants is due not to lack of money *per se* but to such related factors as less healthful housing and the parents' poorer physique, health, and education (Morris, 1963).

In the abstract, it should be possible to analyze the endogenous factors in infant mortality by comparing it with the incidence of fetal deaths. In

Table 15-3. Infant and Neonatal Mortality Rates per 1,000 Live Births, by Color, Birth-Registration Area of the United States, 1915–63

| YEAR | INFANT MORTALITY RATE | | | NEONATAL MORTALITY RATE | | |
|---|---|---|---|---|---|---|
| | TOTAL | WHITE | NONWHITE | TOTAL | WHITE | NONWHITE |
| 1915–19 | 95.7 | 92.8 | 149.7 | 43.4 | 42.3 | 58.1 |
| 1920–24 | 76.7 | 73.3 | 115.3 | 39.7 | 38.7 | 51.1 |
| 1925–29 | 69.0 | 65.0 | 105.4 | 37.2 | 36.0 | 47.9 |
| 1930–34 [a] | 60.4 | 55.7 | 92.9 | 34.4 | 32.8 | 45.5 |
| 1935–39 | 53.2 | 49.2 | 81.3 | 31.0 | 29.5 | 41.4 |
| 1940 | 47.0 | 43.2 | 73.8 | 28.8 | 27.2 | 39.7 |
| 1941 | 45.3 | 41.2 | 74.8 | 27.7 | 26.1 | 39.0 |
| 1942 | 40.4 | 37.3 | 64.6 | 25.7 | 24.5 | 34.6 |
| 1943 | 40.4 | 37.5 | 62.5 | 24.7 | 23.7 | 32.9 |
| 1944 | 39.8 | 36.9 | 60.3 | 24.7 | 23.6 | 32.5 |
| 1945 | 38.3 | 35.6 | 57.0 | 24.3 | 23.3 | 32.0 |
| 1946 | 33.8 | 31.8 | 49.5 | 24.0 | 23.1 | 31.5 |
| 1947 | 32.2 | 30.1 | 48.5 | 22.8 | 21.7 | 31.0 |
| 1948 | 32.0 | 29.9 | 46.5 | 22.2 | 21.2 | 29.1 |
| 1949 | 31.3 | 28.9 | 47.3 | 21.4 | 20.3 | 28.6 |
| 1950 | 29.2 | 26.8 | 44.5 | 20.5 | 19.4 | 27.5 |
| 1951 | 28.4 | 25.8 | 44.8 | 20.0 | 18.9 | 27.3 |
| 1952 | 28.4 | 25.5 | 47.0 | 19.8 | 18.5 | 28.0 |
| 1953 | 27.8 | 25.0 | 44.7 | 19.6 | 18.3 | 27.4 |
| 1954 | 26.6 | 23.9 | 42.9 | 19.1 | 17.8 | 27.0 |
| 1955 | 26.4 | 23.6 | 42.8 | 19.1 | 17.7 | 27.2 |
| 1956 | 26.0 | 23.2 | 42.1 | 18.9 | 17.5 | 27.0 |
| 1957 | 26.3 | 23.3 | 43.7 | 19.1 | 17.5 | 27.8 |
| 1958 | 27.1 | 23.8 | 45.7 | 19.5 | 17.8 | 29.0 |
| 1959 | 26.4 | 23.2 | 44.0 | 19.0 | 17.5 | 27.7 |
| 1960 | 26.0 | 22.9 | 43.2 | 18.7 | 17.2 | 26.9 |
| 1961 | 25.3 | 22.4 | 40.7 | 18.4 | 16.9 | 26.2 |
| 1962 [b] | 25.3 | 22.3 | 41.4 | 18.3 | 16.9 | 26.1 |
| 1963 [b] | 25.2 | 22.2 | 41.5 | 18.2 | 16.7 | 26.1 |
| 1964 | 24.8 | 21.6 | 41.1 | 17.9 | 16.2 | 26.5 |
| 1965 | 24.7 | 21.5 | 40.3 | 17.7 | 16.1 | 26.4 |
| 1966 | 23.7 | 20.6 | 38.8 | 17.2 | 15.6 | 24.8 |
| 1967 | 22.1 [c] | [d] | [d] | 16.2 [c] | [d] | [d] |

SOURCE: Mary A. McCarthy, *Infant, Fetal, and Maternal Mortality, United States, 1963*, National Center for Health Statistics, Series 20, No. 3; U.S. Public Health Service,

fact, however, underregistration is so considerable that statistics on still-births are difficult to interpret. New York City is the only political unit in the United States that has required the registration of *all* fetal deaths for a period of some years. In contrast to the 80,000 fetal deaths reported nation-ally c. 1950, the total may have been as high as half a million (Yerushalmy and Bierman, 1952). In the mid-1960s the number of fetal deaths registered was still under 100,000 (Chase, 1966). For the entire postwar period the recorded rate of fetal deaths of 28 or more weeks' gestation was lowest in the United States among all the countries listed in Table 15-2, but this was mainly the consequence of poor data (Chase, 1967, p. 27). As in many cases the cause of fetal mortality can be determined only by a postmortem exami-nation, which is seldom made, we know even less about how to classify it than about its incidence.

### DIFFERENTIALS BY RESIDENCE AND SOCIAL CLASS

The relation of urban and rural life to mortality is a complex question. A century or two ago towns were termed "the graveyard of countrymen," and this widely held folk belief has the implicit support of much sociological theory.[1] In American cities during an epidemic year perhaps as many as one person out of twenty died; but what urban death rates were in other periods we do not know. Contemporary opinion held not only that urban mortality was higher than rural but that it was increasing. Indeed, so long as sanitation and public health were relatively primitive, the greater con-centration of population increased the dangers of infection. A part of the recorded difference, however, is often spurious: one reason for the higher death rate of the towns of the past is that a better count is made there than in the countryside.

In the twentieth century public-health measures and new medicines have cut down the importance of infectious diseases as causes of death, and eliminated altogether the epidemics that used to decimate town popula-tions. Air pollution, traffic, overcrowding, and the stress of urban life still present special hazards, but the medical care available to city dwellers of

---

Washington, D.C., 1966, Table 1; U.S. Bureau of the Census, *Statistical Abstract of the United States, 1968*, Washington, D.C., 1968, Table 68.

   [a] In 1932–34, Mexicans were included with "Nonwhites."

   [b] Figures by color exclude data for residents of New Jersey.

   [c] Provisional.

   [d] Data not available.

[1] According to a "census of opinion" from ancient times to a generation ago, 95 per cent of those who expressed a view believed that rural life is more healthful than urban; see Pitirim A. Sorokin, Carle C. Zimmerman, and Charles J. Galpin, *A Sys-tematic Source Book in Rural Sociology*, University of Minnesota Press, Minneapolis, 1930, 1, 143.

all classes has become better than that in rural areas, which in the United States, for instance, have generally been supplied with proportionately smaller numbers of physicians, dentists, nurses, technicians, and every other class of medical personnel except untrained midwives and possibly chiropractors. The interaction of these two factors—the greater hazards of city life and the better medical care available there—has resulted in a complicated pattern. In some regions of the United States and for some age groups, age-specific death rates have been higher in urban environments, but in other regions and for other age groups they have been lower (Wiehl, 1948). The over-all trend has been toward convergence, particularly in the most recent years. As measured by white males' expectation of life at birth, the rural advantage amounted to 10.0 years in 1900, 7.7 years in 1910, 5.4 years in 1930. By 1950, with the continuation of this trend, the contrast had disappeared.

One would expect differences in mortality by social class to show a clearly marked inverse correlation. Those at the upper level have less dangerous occupations, live under more healthful conditions, and can more easily afford medical attention whenever it is necessary. But with mass control of infectious disease, the influence of living conditions on mortality is not so great and direct as it once was; and the development of free clinics, group health insurance, and similar institutions has made adequate medical care much more widely available than it once was. The evidence from various recent studies is not wholly consistent, probably because of both the inadequacy of the primary data and marked variation from one area to another during a period of rapid change.

In one study, all American men aged twenty to sixty-four were divided into six broad occupational groups, and the age-adjusted mortality of each in 1950 was calculated as a percentage of that of all males in this age group. The resultant **standardized mortality ratios** were as follows:

|   |   |   |
|---|---|---|
| I. | Professionals | 84 |
| II. | Technicians, administrators, and managers | 87 |
| III. | Proprietors, clerks, sales persons, and skilled workers | 96 |
| IV. | Semiskilled workers | 100 |
| V. | Laborers, except farm and mine | 165 |
| VI. | Agricultural workers | 88 |
|   | All U.S. males aged 20–64 | 100 |

Among the five urban classes there was a definite tendency for the curves of the age-specific ratios of the first four to cluster and overlap. The sharpest difference at all ages was in the higher ratios for laborers (V). The expected inverse correlation between social class and mortality, that is to say, is somewhat blurred for occupational groups apart from the definite contrast between unskilled workers and all others (Moriyama and Guralnick, 1956). More detailed studies in Cincinnati, Chicago, and rural Ohio have shown similar inverse relations between social class and mortality, with a substantial convergence over time (Taeuber and Taeuber, 1958, pp. 275–276; cf. Ellis, 1957). Two other studies indicated no consistent relation between social class and morbidity (Graham, 1957; Laughton et al., 1958).

The differentiation in the United States was similar to that in England and Wales, though with a greater range in every age group (Table 15-4).

Table 15-4. Standardized Mortality Ratios, by Occupational Level, Males Aged 20 to 64, United States and England and Wales, 1950

| AGE GROUP | I–VI[a] | | 1[a] | | II, III, IV[a] | | V[a] | | VI[a] | |
|---|---|---|---|---|---|---|---|---|---|---|
| | OCCUPATIONAL LEVEL | | | | | | | | | |
| | US | E-W | US | E-W | US | E-W | US | E-W | US | E-W |
| 20–24 | 100 | 100 | 49 | 102 | 80 | 94 | 190 | 122 | 132 | 139 |
| 25–34 | 100 | 100 | 53 | 90 | 84 | 95 | 232 | 138 | 125 | 104 |
| 35–44 | 100 | 100 | 66 | 83 | 91 | 96 | 219 | 143 | 92 | 87 |
| 45–54 | 100 | 100 | 87 | 98 | 96 | 97 | 178 | 129 | 84 | 75 |
| 55–59 | 100 | 100 | 94 | 99 | 99 | 99 | 146 | 115 | 84 | 75 |
| 60–64 | 100 | 100 | 97 | 100 | 101 | 101 | 128 | 106 | 85 | 72 |

SOURCE: I. M. Moriyama and L. Guralnick, "Occupational and Social Class Differences in Mortality," in Milbank Memorial Fund, Trends and Differentials in Mortality, New York, 1956, pp. 61–73.

[a] I—Professionals; II, III, IV—managers, white-collar, skilled, and semi-skilled workers; V—laborers, except farm and mine; VI—agricultural workers.

American professionals had a greater relative advantage than their English peers, American workers a greater relative disadvantage, but in both countries the disparity among social groups decreased with increasing age. Since 1950 the occupational differences were reduced in England, though the inverse relation between social class and especially infant mortality persisted or even, as we have noted, increased.

That the higher mortality of lower classes is partly the consequence of noneconomic factors contradicts conventional attitudes, and it may be worthwhile to exemplify the relation with another set of data. In a traditional agrarian society, a peasant is typically thin and a member of the upper classes often shows in his physique that he has access to more food. What is the situation in advanced countries? We know that being overweight is often a factor in cardiovascular ailments and that these have become a major cause of death. We have very few data, however, on the class distribution of weight. According to one study based on a sample of 605 white, elderly couples in Providence, the relation of obesity and social class is the opposite of what it would be in a peasant society (Table 15-5).

Table 15-5. Percentage Distribution of Comparative Weights in a Sample of White Elderly Couples, by Social-Economic Status and Sex, Providence, R.I., 1962

|  | THIN | NORMAL | OVERWEIGHT | OBESE |
|---|---|---|---|---|
| **Males** |  |  |  |  |
| High SES | 0.8 | 55.7 | 29.8 | 13.7 |
| Medium SES | 6.1 | 40.5 | 35.5 | 17.9 |
| Low SES | 5.9 | 39.6 | 31.7 | 22.8 |
| **Females** |  |  |  |  |
| High SES | 1.6 | 46.4 | 39.8 | 12.2 |
| Medium SES | 1.1 | 28.5 | 31.4 | 39.0 |
| Low SES | 0.5 | 23.4 | 30.3 | 45.8 |

SOURCE: Robert G. Burnight and Parker G. Marden, "Social Correlates of Weight in an Aging Population," *Milbank Memorial Fund Quarterly*, **45** (1967), 75–92.

"Normal" was defined as the average weight of persons aged twenty to twenty-four of each sex and height category. Those more than fifteen pounds under this norm were defined as "thin," those sixteen to thirty-five pounds over the norm as "overweight," and those more than thirty-five pounds over as "obese." Particularly among females, the inverse correlation between social class and obesity was marked. In order to control for the effect of subcultural cuisines, the sample was divided into Italian, Irish, other Catholic, Protestant, and Jewish. Among all these religious-ethnic groups, a high proportion of lower-class women were overweight or, among the three Catholic groups, obese.

Differentials by color can be interpreted as mainly a reflection of the contrast between the lowest social-economic group and the rest of the population. The mortality of American Negroes has been higher than that of whites for as far back as there are data, but it has been falling faster. In 1900, the death rate of the white population of the death-registration states was 17 per 1,000, that of nonwhites 25. By 1966, the rates had declined to 9.5 and 9.7, respectively. At the beginning of the century, thus, the nonwhite rate was 47 per cent higher; in 1963 it was 6 per cent higher. Most of this improvement was independent of the different age structures of the two populations: life expectancy at birth, 33.0 years for nonwhites and 47.6 years for whites in 1900, was 63.6 and 70.8 years in 1963, respectively. The added life expectancy was by 30.6 years for nonwhites, 23.2 years for whites (Chase, 1965; *cf.* Tomasson, 1960, 1961).

Negro mortality in the mid-1960s was above that of whites at all ages up to 75 years, but varied considerably from one age category to another. Why this was so can be plausibly explained in some cases. One reason for the higher rates of infants (Table 15-3) and young females, for example, is the family-building pattern. Negro women bear more children on the average, have them both earlier and later than the optimum childbearing period, receive less prenatal and postnatal care even when this is available at no cost, and give birth in a hospital only three-fourths as often as whites. As a consequence of such social, economic, and medical factors, in 1966 the neonatal mortality rate for nonwhites was more than one and a half that of whites, the death rate of infants aged 28 days to one year almost three times as high, and the maternal death rate almost four times as high. Other factors in the high Negro mortality are also more the consequence of a slum culture than of medical or even economic causes. Homicides were proportionately ten times more numerous than in the white population. The rate of fatal accidents was also higher, and the gap between white and nonwhite rates has been increasing. Such differences, tied in with the way of life of the two races, will not be eliminated as easily as the earlier higher mortality from communicable diseases. In short,

The highest ratios of nonwhite to white mortality are found for maternal and postneonatal mortality, tuberculosis, influenza and pneumonia, vascular lesions affecting the central nervous system, and homicides. For each of these, the ratios are 2 :1 or higher. Only for suicides is the rate for the white population more than double the rate for the nonwhite counterpart.

The differentials in mortality between the white and nonwhite populations are the end-product of a multidimensional problem. The many facets include hereditary factors, the distribution and availability of medical facilities and services, socio-economic factors which affect the utilization of available medical services, and the personal motivation to achieve a state of positive health (Chase, 1965, p. 36).

### DIFFERENTIALS BY MEDICAL SERVICES

Differences in mortality among the various Western countries, significant as they are, overlie a basic similarity in past trend and present level. The major decline was effected by the control of the important infectious diseases (*cf.* Table 7-3, p. 223). As these diseases became relatively less significant as causes of death, the sharp fall in mortality decelerated, and in the most recent period the death rates of subpopulations in various countries became stationary or even increased. For medical science has no truly effective cure for chronic malignancies, and social science none for accidents and other types of violence (*cf.* U.S. National Center for Health Statistics, 1964).

Improvements beyond the death control associated with a fully developed urban-industrial society depend on how effectively the benefits of industrialization are distributed among the whole population. Of the countries of Northwestern Europe, thus, those with the fullest and most efficient social services have achieved the most effective death control. In Sweden, for example, all residents are provided with a full range of general social security and medical care under an insurance plan paid by employers, employees, and the government. Insured persons also receive cash benefits to compensate for losses from sickness, injury, or childbirth (U.S. Social Security Administration, 1964, pp. 184–185; *cf.* Uhr, 1966).

In his work on the population of Europe, Kirk found a way of dramatizing the superior death control practiced in Holland, whose recent record is comparable to Sweden's. He contrasted the number of deaths in each country with the number there would have been if Holland's age-specific rates in 1939 had obtained, and then he calculated the difference as a percentage of the total and labeled this "excess deaths." On this basis, in that year excess mortality for Europe as a whole amounted to 35 per cent, and for Northwestern and Central Europe alone it was 23 per cent (Kirk, 1946, pp. 180–182; *cf.* Guralnick and Jackson, 1967; Burgess *et al.*, 1966). Since this variation in mortality was not based on a difference in medical techniques, which were more or less identical all over Western Europe, the reasons for it must be sought in the country's social history.

The rise of Dutch industry and the development of social-welfare legislation in Holland were almost simultaneous. There were only thirty years of uncontrolled urbanization—from about 1870, when industrialization really got under way, to 1900, when the first housing act was passed. The evils associated with the factory system of England, to take a classic example, existed in the Netherlands, but on a proportionately much smaller scale and for a much shorter period. The impetus to develop this social-welfare program, moreover, came in large part from such traditionalist institutions as the churches, which thus established for themselves a significant function in relation to the new society. As one consequence, the best of modern medical science is now made available to the people through institutions connected with religious or other groups to which they are bound by strong sentiments. The Dutch equivalent of the Red Cross, for example, is three "Cross Societies," associated respectively with the Catholic, the Protestant, and the secularist sectors of the population. Similarly, the Dutch medical profession itself established a health-insurance plan, which has remained private in the sense that the physicians and the member-patients control it, but health insurance is now compulsory for all wage and salary earners, with half of the premiums paid by the employers (*cf.* U.S. Social Security Administration, 1964, pp. 140–141). The age-adjusted death rates of six occupational groups in Amsterdam in 1947–52 showed a marked lack of variation by social class: the ratio of worst to best (117:100) was barely above the level of statistical significance. In contrast with a number of studies made in other countries, the rates for unskilled and skilled workers were the same. Only the clerical group had relatively high death rates, presumably because of their poor physiques (Antonovsky, 1967).

Under Britain's National Health Service, medical care is available to all residents, together with sickness or maternity benefits to those enrolled in insurance plans. The family doctor has more or less disappeared into the bureaucratic system. "Only two-thirds of nuclear families are registered as whole families with one doctor. More than half of the National Health Service patients are on lists of doctors with more than 2,500 patients" (Benjamin, 1964). Certainly the program furnishes far better medical service to low-income groups than any prior system in Britain, but it is alleged that the middle classes have paid in a reduced quality of care as well as in money (e.g., Eckstein, 1956). Nor are British physicians well satisfied with their "capitation fee" for each patient. When the service was instituted in 1948, it was opposed by a substantial portion of the medical profession (as later also in Saskatchewan; see Badgley and Wolfe, 1965), and the physicians now contribute substantially to Britain's "brain drain." Each year between one-fifth and one-third of the graduates of her medical schools emigrate, stimulating the Health Minister to complain that "Britain simply cannot afford to train doctors for the purpose of swelling the membership of the American Medical Association." The system continues to function only because of the drain to Britain of Indians and Pakistanis, who constitute almost half of the country's junior medical staff, and the partly successful effort to induce some of the emigrants to return.[2]

The institutional framework of medical care is more complex in the United States. Its fundament is still **private practice,** under which the physician and the patient come together as individuals, based solely on the patient's desire for care and his ability to pay for it. Dr. Milford O. Rouse, who became president of the American Medical Association in 1967, strongly espoused this system in his inaugural address. In his view, health care is not a right but a privilege; thus, the medical profession should attack Medicare, Medicaid, and other "social concepts" in medicine.[3] The advantages of private practice, in the view of its proponents, is that the consumer's free choice of medical care, like free enterprise generally, effects the maximum quality of the product or service; that patient-doctor relations are at their best; and that physicians are more efficient because their income is commensurate with their long training and high level of skill. Disadvantages are that it is probably more cumbersome than in alternative systems to organize the teamwork among various specialists on which

[2] *The New York Times,* September 16, 1966; January 7, 1968.
[3] *Ibid.,* June 26, 1967.

diagnosis and therapy often depend, that adequate care depends on private income rather than medical need. In fact, to be workable the system must be linked to complementary charitable services, organized through churches, municipalities, or the state.

In the United States, **health insurance** began in the 1930s, initiated for the employees of various large corporations or the members of trade unions, and then through such organizations as Blue Cross and Blue Shield. In the middle 1960s, it was estimated by the health-insurance association that almost 80 per cent of the civilian population was covered by some form of hospital or health insurance (Reed, 1965b; cf. 1965a). Such insurance spreads the costs of medical care over periods of health and sickness and between well and sick, thus rendering the burden easier to carry for middle-income groups. Under many schemes, such advantages of private practice as the free choice of a physician are retained. However, the sector of a population least able to pay for medical care (the bottom fifth) is typically also excluded from insurance plans.

In 1965 two amendments to the Social Security Act brought Medicare into existence: all those aged sixty-five years and over and entitled to old-age, survivors', or disability insurance (OASDI), totaling initially some 19 million persons, were enrolled free in a hospital-insurance plan and permitted to participate in a low-cost supplementary medical-insurance plan (cf. Myers, 1966). The program is supported out of separate taxes, paid at the same rate by employers, employees, and the self-employed (West, 1967; Forgotson, 1967). Only one year after it went into effect, it was obvious that Medicare would have a number of probably unanticipated side-effects. Since the aged now constitute a source of considerable income, nonaccredited hospitals and medical laboratories had a strong incentive to improve their services sufficiently to meet the conditions for participation in the program. One such condition, specified in Title VI of the Civil Rights Act of 1964, was that hospital care must be offered without discrimination, and Medicare became a basis for enforcing this guarantee more effectively (Stewart, 1967).

The most important side-effect, however, was to help accelerate the rise in medical costs, which in any case had been going up faster than other consumer prices (Table 15-6). From 1946 to 1960, when prices of the entire "market basket" of goods and services increased by an average of 3 per cent per year, the increase of every item in medical care was greater. One reason, it was alleged, was that the quality of medical services had improved over this period. In 1964, in order to remove the consequent bias in the index, a revised list of medical items was priced, and the difference between the over-all inflation and medical costs became greater, especially in the year following institution of nationally guaranteed medical fees for the aged. With the advent of Medicare and reimbursement on the basis of reasonable costs, hospitals throughout the country have raised particularly

Table 15-6. Consumer Price Index for Specified Goods and Services, United States, 1946–66

| GOODS AND SERVICES | INDEX NUMBERS (1957–59 = 100) | | | | PER CENT AVERAGE ANNUAL INCREASE | | |
|---|---|---|---|---|---|---|---|
| | 1946 | 1957–59 | 1965 | 1966 | 1946–60 | 1960–65 | 1965–66 |
| All items | 68.0 | 100 | 109.9 | 113.1 | 3.0 | 1.3 | 2.9 |
| All services | 62.7 | 100 | 117.8 | 122.3 | 3.9 | 2.0 | 3.8 |
| Medical care, total | 00.7 | 100 | 122.3 | 127.7 | 4.2 | 2.5 | 4.4 |
| Medical services, total | 58.4 | 100 | 127.1 | 133.9 | 4.6 | 3.1 | 5.4 |
| Daily hospital service charges | 37.0 | 100 | 153.3 | 168.0 | 8.3 | 6.3 | 9.6 |
| Physicians' fees | 66.4 | 100 | 121.5 | 128.5 | 3.4 | 2.8 | 5.8 |

SOURCE: Dorothy P. Price and Loucele A. Horowitz, "Trends in Medical Care Prices," *Social Security Bulletin,* 30 (1967), 13–28.

the notoriously low salaries of employees below professional level. Also as a consequence of Medicare, physicians' incomes rose by more even than the rise in customary charges indicated in Table 15-6, since presumably they no longer applied a sliding scale of fees to low-income aged clients (Price and Horowitz, 1967).

In spite of the seeming predominance in the United States of private or quasi-private medical care, in fact **public-health services** account for a sizable portion of the country's medical bill. The care of public health has been an element of urban civilization almost from its beginning, and in the West it has developed fastest since the rise of industrial metropolises (Rosen, 1958). The concept overlaps what is now termed **preventive medicine,** which is "not so much *preventive* as *social* medicine—concerned with interacting *social* variables." According to one survey, the physicians in this field are generalists rather than specialists, interested not only in the full range of medical topics but also in biostatistics and the organization of health services. Practitioners try to synthesize their skills with insights from social disciplines in order to achieve control of diseases on a broad basis, rather than patient by patient (Backett, 1964).

The relative worth of the various medical systems is not a subject often discussed in an objective fashion. To the degree that various statistical systems are commensurable, one can compare the value received per unit of expenditure. In 1964 the United States spent for health an estimated $36.8 billion, or $191 per capita (Reed and Hanft, 1966). Compared with two of the Western European countries we have discussed, this is the greatest outlay, yet by various criteria the amount of medical value received in the United States was the least of the three (Table 15-7). On the face of it, it would seem that fewer physicians per unit of population can perform more efficiently if they work in a country with more hospitals than in the United States, as in England and Sweden.

## Decline of Mortality in Underdeveloped Countries

The death rate, the number of deaths per 1,000 population, requires both vital statistics and a census count. Even for those underdeveloped areas with a reasonably accurate census, therefore, it is often impossible to calculate it directly, since underregistration is still generally too great. The mortality of such countries can be estimated, however, from the age structure in successive census years. Using this method, Davis concluded that India's death rate before 1920 fluctuated between 40 and 50 and that after that date it fell off to an average of 36.3 in 1921–31, and 31.2 in 1931–41 (Davis, 1951, p. 36). The precise reasons for this decline are difficult to establish, since any explanation must embrace medical, economic, political, and social factors. Some of the causes that Davis suggests seem to be relevant mainly to an earlier period: the elimination of war and banditry, which was completed long before the decline began; improvement of the food supply, which was undertaken on a large scale from the middle of the nineteenth century on and was efficient enough by 1900 to prevent nationwide famines. The trend in diseases is difficult to analyze; up to 1945, 60 per cent of all registered deaths in British India were ascribed simply to "fever" and over 25 per cent to a catch-all, "other causes." Nevertheless, it is reasonable to suppose that three of the most important epidemic diseases —plague, smallpox, and cholera—became less important as causes of death.

The experience of British India is typical of a fairly large number of underdeveloped areas. At the beginning of usable records, crude death rates were generally around 45 or 50; and one can assume that still earlier, before the social order permitting the collection of statistics was established, even higher rates sometimes prevailed. During the several decades prior to World War II, mortality in various nonindustrial countries underwent a gradual decline, the consequence of a no less gradual improvement in the level of living (Bourgeois-Pichat and Pan, 1956). Progress was often faster than it had been in Western countries, for of course it was not necessary to duplicate the slow process by which each medical or technological innovation had been developed.

### CEYLON

The most startling instance of a new pattern was in Ceylon, where the estimated expectation of life at birth increased from 43 years in 1946 to 52

Table 15-7. Relative Position of the United States, England and Wales, and Sweden by Selected Measures of Medical Care

| | UNITED STATES | ENGLAND AND WALES | SWEDEN |
|---|---|---|---|
| Percentage of Gross National Product for medical expenditures | 5.2 (1957)<br>5.8 (1964) | 4.7 (1956) | 4.7 (1960) |
| Physicians per 100,000 population | 136.9 (1962) | 127.0 (1961) | 105.5 (1963) |
| Number of doctor's visits per patient per year | 5.3 (1957–59) | 4.7 (1955–56) | 2.6–2.8 (1963) |
| Hospital beds per 1,000 population<br>All hospitals<br>Omitting psychiatry | 9.0 } (1963)<br>4.9 } | 10.1 } (1962)<br>5.6 } | 14.0 } (1963)<br>9.3 } |
| Life expectancy at birth<br>Males<br>Females | 66.6 } (1963)<br>73.4 } | 68.0 } (1962)<br>73.9 } | 71.3 } (1961–63)<br>75.4 } |

SOURCE: Osler L. Peterson et al., "What Is Value for Money in Medical Care?," Lancet, April 8, 1967, pp. 771–776.

in 1947. The gain achieved in this one year had taken half a century in most Western countries. This amazing decline in mortality seemed to derive essentially from one factor—DDT, an insecticide that had been developed during World War II, which when sprayed from airplanes over low-lying areas all but eliminated malaria, the principal cause of death, by killing the mosquitoes that carry it. "The antimalaria campaign is estimated to have contributed 60 per cent of the rise in the rate of [Ceylon's] population growth since the war, resulting in a population size that by the end of 1960 was a million larger than it otherwise would have been" (Newman, 1965, p. 69). But this interpretation has been challenged by a number of other analysts (Frederiksen, 1960, 1961; Meegama, 1967). The differences among them are interesting, for they highlight the difficulties in interpreting what at first appeared to be a simple cause-effect relation.

Malaria was virtually eliminated, all three agree, as a cause of death. However, since before the war and after it almost three-quarters of the population lived in nonmalarial areas, this direct effect was not in itself sufficient to explain the extraordinary decline in mortality. In view of the primitive reporting of diseases in Ceylon,[4] it was hardly possible to specify the changes in mortality by cause of death. Newman stressed the indirect effects of the spraying—the reduced incidence of other insect-borne diseases (pp. 78–79) and especially the mitigation of the debility that malaria brings to those it does not kill. Frederiksen and Meegama emphasized that the food shortages during the war were suddenly eased at its end; for example, the importation of milk and milk products almost doubled from 1945 to 1946. The number of hospitals on the island increased from an average of 146 in 1941–46 to an average of 247 in 1947–50, the number of maternity homes from 26 to 79, the number of midwives from 492 to 951, the number of health centers from 476 to 634, the number of pregnant women under care in centers from 126,125 to 288,646 (Meegama). The crucial test, it would seem, is to determine what would have been the course of Ceylon's death rate if only malaria had been brought under control without these other measures. According to Newman, the control by spraying was just as effective in reducing mortality in British Guiana, where the high incidence of the disease had been the consequence of agricultural practices rather than natural conditions. But according to Meegama, in Guatemala the contrary was true: from 1958 to 1959, the number of deaths reported as due to malaria fell sharply from 6,238 to 124, but the general death rate was cut only from 21.3 to 17.3, and it remained more or less constant at that level for the subsequent decade.

[4] In Ceylon two frequently cited causes of death are *rathe* (literally, "redness"), loosely applied to a variety of symptoms that may or may not be related to the fatal disease, and *mandama* (literally, "wasting"), under which are subsumed food-deficiency states. "'Grahaniya,' which . . . was at one time the name of a she-demon who pursued the lives of young children, now appears to be a synonym for 'mandama' and is coded as such" (Padley, 1959).

Coupled with the decline in mortality, however one analyzes its causes, there was an appreciable increase in Ceylon's fertility, due in part to the in-migration of young couples into previously malarial areas, in part to a change in the age structure. Newman (p. 39) speculated that there may also have been a more direct relation, because of the decline in the number of malaria-related miscarriages; and one can plausibly argue as well that there may have been a higher incidence of marital coitus in a population no longer weakened by endemic malaria. Certainly the population grew at an alarming pace. "If the sequence of events in Ceylon," Frederiksen wrote (1961), "had demonstrated that economic development is no longer a prerequisite for a decline in the death rate, it might have seemed plausible to postulate that modern public health measures would tend to reduce per capita income as well as mortality." Yet that conclusion, however unwelcome it may be to a conscientious practitioner of public health, seems to follow from the record no matter how one interprets its background.[5]

### THE GENERAL PATTERN

That the decline in Ceylon's death rate had nothing to do specifically with the country's culture, its social structure, or its economy is shown by the fact that the stupendous success achieved there was repeated elsewhere. In India, as another example, the incidence of malaria fell from more than 100,000,000 cases annually before the war to fewer than 50,000 in 1966. In Mauritius the remarkable government campaign to combat malaria resulted in a "spectacular drop in mortality within a year [that] almost precisely duplicated the pattern of postwar mortality control . . . in Ceylon" (Titmuss and Abel-Smith, 1961, p. 49).

In the United States, a National Malaria Eradication Program was set up in 1946, and within a few years mortality from this cause, which had ranged between 200,000 and 400,000 annually, was eliminated completely. In 1955 the World Health Organization undertook to eradicate malaria altogether, and during the following decade almost $1 billion was spent in this momentous task. Of the total world population (excluding Communist China) of some 2.5 billion at the end of 1964, almost 1.6 billion lived in areas that were or had been malarious. According to WHO estimates, 28.5 per cent of this latter population now enjoy a completely malaria-free environment and 46.3 per cent can observe eradication in progress. Only 25.2 per cent were in areas where such programs had not yet been started (Hinman, 1966, p. 102).

[5] Ceylon's work force, thus, will increase from 3.4 million in 1956 to an estimated 7.1 million in 1981, and unemployment was rising already in the early 1960s. According to an official of Ceylon's Department of National Planning, "the high rate of population growth observed recently in Ceylon imposes serious strains on the economy and restricts its capacity to expand rapidly" (Selvaratnam, 1961).

An Indian eradication team spraying insecticide in a malarial area (*P. N. Sharma—WHO*).

The effort to eliminate malaria, which before World War II had been the world's most potent single cause of sickness and death, has not been without reverses. Spraying insecticides from airplanes, by far the cheapest means of mass control, was found to be less effective than hand spraying in and around homes. Of the roughly sixty species of Anopheles that transmit most of the world's malaria, some seventeen became highly resistant to both DDT and other insecticides that were substituted for it. Yet one researcher regards this as no more than "annoying," for the development of still more

A swarm of locusts on the Kenya-Uganda border. A recent infestation in this area destroyed $7 million worth of crops, and several hundred cattle died of starvation (*British Information Services*).

deadly insecticides is under way (*ibid.*, p. 90). The spraying program worked best when supplemented with some new medicaments, especially chloroquine. In British Guiana, eight weeks after a law was passed requiring the admixture of some chloroquine into all salt sold in the country, no new cases of the disease appeared. But this miracle was also short-lived; a strain of malaria evolved that proved to be resistant to this new specific, and the

RAF planes spraying poison dust on a locust breeding area in Tanganyika (*British Information Services*).

American servicemen in Vietnam down with malaria were treated with that old standby, quinine. It was also found that man is susceptible to monkey malaria, so that even if the disease is eradicated in the entire world population of humans, reservoirs of infection would remain among their simian cousins (Gilmore, 1966).

In spite of such setbacks, the mass attack on human disease with insecticides is as significant an innovation as the development of Western public sanitation a century ago. It is true that the wholesale destruction of insect life inevitably disturbs the ecology of any area, often to the detriment of man, but in this war the odds are that scientific ingenuity will outwit the blind adaptations of nature. Malaria control can be started with a mass assault, but to be completely successful this must be followed up with a continuous, careful check of the infected areas and populations—the kind of program likely to succeed fully only in a country with a stable and effective government. Yet it is also true that, since antimalarial campaigns have been carried out largely through such international agencies as WHO, they are independent of whether any particular country has the personnel, equipment, funds, and drive to exert these efforts itself.

A second postwar development, potentially no less important than insecticides, is the use of sulfa compounds and antibiotics to combat still
other diseases on a mass scale. Trachoma, endemic syphilis, yaws (Hinman,
1966, Chapters 11–12), as well as infections better known to the West,
yield to such treatment readily. Peasants all over the world who know
nothing of modern medicine in any other sense have become quite familiar
with penicillin. These preparations are rather expensive, but the cost of
both supplying and dispensing them is generally borne in large part by
advanced countries, acting through the dozen international agencies helping
to reduce mortality in underdeveloped areas.

One of the first major diseases that modern nations were able to control
completely among their own populations was smallpox. With the present
worldwide vaccination campaign the estimated number of cases had been
cut from 500,000 in 1951 to 50,000 in 1965. An extended program adopted
by the WHO Assembly in 1966 had as its objective the acceleration of past
efforts and the complete elimination of the disease in one more decade
(Cockburn, 1966).

As recently as 1942, the very idea was strange that the worldwide eradication of infectious diseases was feasible.

Many workers in the control of mosquito-borne disease have been reluctant
to accept the idea that man has it in his power to eradicate any mosquito anywhere.
. . . Psychologically, it is apparently much easier to visualize the geometric increase of a species from a single gravid female to the millions of *gambiae* existing
at one time in Northeast Brazil than it is to picture the reverse process, as all
possible breeding places in a region are treated week after week with [insecticides].
. . . The traditional ingrained philosophy that species eradication is impossible,
. . . and that when species disappear they do so only in response to "cosmic" or
"biological" rather than man-made factors, is most persistent (F. L. Soper and
D. B. Wilson, cited in Hinman, 1966, p. 40).

Eradication goes beyond control. In practical terms, it means that a regularly tested area can be considered clear of a disease when no new case
appears for three years. In its literal sense, "pulling out by the roots,"
eradication implies action on a world scale, and while no disease has been
totally defeated in this sense, the notion may no longer be utopian.

The consequences of such campaigns are illustrated in Table 15-8. For
comparison the table lists mortality measures of three Western countries
with the best controls (Sweden, the Netherlands, and New Zealand), as
well as the United States and Japan. The underdeveloped countries are
those on three continents with readily available data for 1960 or later. When
Western nations were at a social-economic level comparable to these latter
countries, the infant mortality was of the order of 200, rather than 24 to 119.
Because, without exception, the populations of underdeveloped areas in-

Table 15-8. Measures of Mortality, Selected Countries at Recent Dates

| | CRUDE DEATH RATE | INFANT MORTALITY RATE | LIFE EXPECTATION AT BIRTH | | |
|---|---|---|---|---|---|
| | | | MALE | FEMALE | |
| Sweden | 10.0 (1964) | 13.6 (1964) | 71.49 | 75.45 | (1960–64) |
| Netherlands | 7.7 (1964) | 15.8 (1964) | 71.1 | 75.7 | (1962) |
| New Zealand | 8.7 (1965) | 20 (1965) | 68.44 | 73.75 | (1960–62) |
| United States | 9.4 (1964) | 25.2 (1965) | 66.9 | 73.7 | (1964) |
| Japan | 6.9 (1964) | 20.4 (1964) | 67.21 | 72.34 | (1963) |
| Mexico | 10.3 (1964) | 64 (1964) | 56.90 | 60.37 | (1960) |
| Trinidad and Tobago | 6.1 (1964) | 42 (1963) | 62.15 | 66.33 | (1959–61) |
| Venezuela | 7.2 (1964) | 49 (1964) | 61.2 | 65.6 | (1960) |
| Mauritius | 8.6 (1965) | 64 (1965) | 58.66 | 61.86 | (1961–63) |
| Egypt | 14.8 (1965) | 119 (1963) | 51.6 | 53.8 | (1960) |
| Taiwan | 5.5 (1965) | 24 (1964) | 61.33 | 65.60 | (1959–60) |
| India | 12.9 (1963–64) / 8.6[a] (1963) | 78[a] (1963) | 47.00 | 46.33 | (1961) |

SOURCES: National data as collated by the U.N. Statistical Office; *Population Index,* Vol. **32** (1966), No. 3–4.
[a] Registration area.

clude a very high percentage of children and young adults, there are proportionately few who die of old age. Thus, once the major causes of early death have been brought under control, the death rates are lower in many cases than in advanced industrial countries with excellent social-security systems. The life-expectation figures, which are independent of age structure, are comparatively lower, yet often hardly more than ten years less than those in advanced industrial countries.

### THE SOCIAL-ECONOMIC CONTEXT OF MORTALITY CONTROL

Before 1940 the effective operation of most death-control measures depended on a rise in the general welfare, which, when it occurred, took place slowly. The crucial difference in the postwar period is that this prior link between a rise in the level of living and a decline in mortality has been broken to some degree. How permanent are these declines in mortality likely to be (*cf.* Balfour, 1956)? One way of getting an approximate answer to this question is by dividing diseases according to the mode of control that is feasible (Table 15-9).

Table 15-9. Measures of Control or Eradication of Specified Diseases

| CONTROL OR ERADICATION OF INSECT VECTORS | VACCINATION OR IMMUNIZATION | CLINICAL TREATMENT | CONTROL OF HUMAN WASTES |
|---|---|---|---|
| Malaria | Smallpox | Yaws | Hookworm |
| Typhus | Typhus | Malaria | Bilharziasis |
| Plague | Whooping cough | Leprosy | Roundworm |
| Encephalitis | Poliomyelitis | Tuberculosis | Cholera |
| Onchocerciasis | Typhoid fever | Syphilis | Amebiasis |
| Filariasis | Tuberculosis | Bejel | Dysentery |
| Yellow fever | Influenza | Pinta | |
| | Cholera | Trachoma | |
| | Plague | | |
| | Yellow fever | | |

SOURCE: U.S. Senate, *Report of the Committee on Government Operations: The Status of World Health,* 86th Congress, 1st Session, Senate Report 161, April 10, 1959, p. 58; cited in Stephen Enke, *Economics for Development,* Prentice-Hall, Englewood Cliffs, N.J., 1963, p. 399.

1. Control or eradication of insect vectors depends almost wholly on the availability of funds to use appropriate technical facilities. When an insecticide is sprayed over a whole area from the air, the people affected are not involved at all, and when it is sprayed over the walls of each house, the occupants generally still have no voice in the matter. The skills involved are generally slight enough so that the personnel needed for eradication campaigns can be recruited from the local work force. This is a type of control, in short, that can be exercised without any prior change in the cultural-economic level.

2. Immunization campaigns are also organized on a mass scale, and each person's decision whether or not to participate may be no more than nominal. If the preventive means is wholly effective (e.g., vaccination against smallpox), the eradication campaign can succeed with hardly any more direct involvement of the general population than in an effort to wipe out a species of insects. Some of the diseases listed, which require early diagnosis for effective treatment, come closer to the third category of clinical treatment.

3. Some cures are so simple and effective (e.g., quinine for malarial symptoms) that no medical facilities are required. More generally, if diseases are to be controlled through clinical treatment, a sufficient number of highly trained professionals and quite elaborate facilities must be available to a widely dispersed population. Thus, any treatment that depends on a

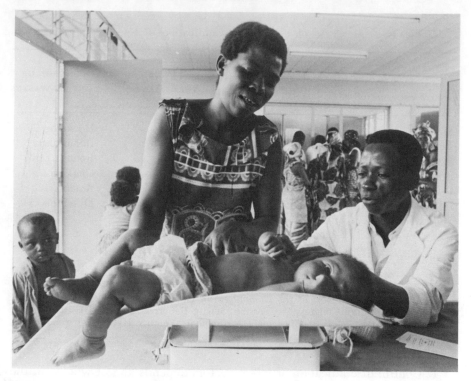

One of the seventy children a day who are examined and treated at the N'Djili Health Center, Leopoldville, Congo. The Center was opened in 1963 with technical experts and medical specialists from UNICEF and WHO (*United Nations*).

physician's direct diagnosis and care is linked to the shortage of physicians typical of underdeveloped countries. In Mauritius, to take one of the best studied small areas, there was one doctor per 4,500 persons—a relatively favorable ratio. There were more students in medical schools abroad than practicing physicians, but from past experience it was known that a large proportion would not return to the island after their graduation (Titmuss and Abel-Smith, 1961, pp. 178–181). In Africa generally, according to the regional director of WHO, the ratio is one doctor per 25,000 to 50,000 people. In twenty-six African countries that WHO surveyed, the total number of physicians *fell* from 4,700 in 1962 to 4,400 in 1965. In one country there were no doctors at all; in another the ratio was one to a million persons.[6]

4. The control of human waste is likely to conflict with cultural patterns. Promiscuous defecation, with the subsequent transmission of pathogens to a new host via water, food, flies and other insects, or dust, is an important channel by which diseases are spread in most underdeveloped countries.

[6] *The New York Times*, April 4, 1967.

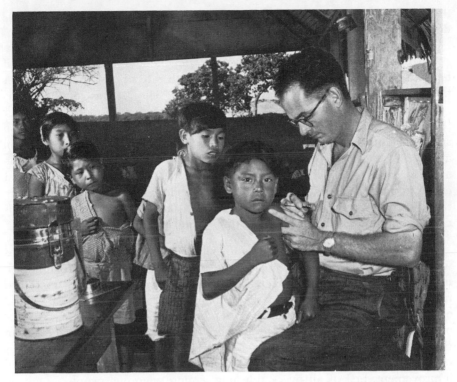

Children in British Guiana being vaccinated against tuberculosis (*British Information Services*).

In the West the chain was broken by public action—the construction of sewerage systems, the enactment of pure-food laws, and so on. To duplicate the physical equipment would be vastly more expensive than anti-malarial campaigns, for instance, and not necessarily effective. "Mere provision of sanitary latrines is no solution to this problem, as field experience [in India] has shown. For latrines to be used, traditional behavior and attitudes must change as well" (Yankauer, 1959).

In Ethiopia, a relatively favored country by African or even worldwide standards, some 300 physicians of about fifteen different nationalities operate one of "the best public health programs in Africa." The ratio of doctors to population is 1:10,000, or precisely the worldwide goal that WHO has set, and training facilities promise an increase in professional medical personnel. Yet the level of health is low, mainly because virtually all water supplies are contaminated.

People who do not know about germs and disease transmission are not concerned with wells and latrines. Even the capital city of almost half a million people has no sewerage system. . . . Probably the most efficient sanitation corps in the country is in the town of Harar, where each night large numbers of hyenas roam the streets and pick them clean. . . . Teachers are probably as important to the development of health in Ethiopia as are doctors (Torrey, 1967).

In 1873, when the pioneer Max von Pettenkofer wrote on "the value of health to a city," he compared the crude death rate of his Munich, 33 per thousand, with the 22 per thousand in London. The reasons for the difference, he said, were that the Londoners lived better, with more and better food per capita, better housing, and warm clothing, all organized under a spirit of *noblesse oblige*. Each of Munich's 170,000 inhabitants was sick an average of twenty days per year, and the total annual cost (taking the average earnings at one florin per day) was 3.4 million florins. This first crude attempt at a benefit/cost study of public health set a precedent in the West; how relevant is it to presently underdeveloped countries? This critical question is discussed under three main points.

1. "Benefit/cost analysis for health studies . . . [is] ill adapted for areas where underemployment of labor is the critical characteristic. To diminish mortality and morbidity in such instances . . . serves markedly to retard rates of general economic growth" (Perlman, 1966). This is the most general criticism: does it serve economic or humanitarian ends if the consequence of health programs is not an improvement of the level of life but merely an increase in the number who survive at subsistence or starve? One reply is that an effective public-health program may lay the basis for continued improvement, first of all by establishing a more vigorous people. Someone determined to retain "optimism and some faith" may even hold that "with encouragement and independence the people will resist a lowering of their standard of living" and therefore limit the size of their families (Balfour, 1956).[7] The eradication of malaria from Venezuela more than doubled the portion of that country that is habitable by humans (Arnaldo Gabaldón, quoted in Rubel, 1966), and thus in effect may have doubled the potential food supply, space, and other values that a rapid population increase threatens.

To the question often asked, "Is malaria eradication a good thing, bearing in mind its contribution to the population explosion?" I would reply that this question cannot be answered scientifically, since it depends on one's judgment regarding the value of human life. My own feeling is that no one should take it on himself to withhold such effective, and marvelously cheap, methods of improving the general health of a people and, indeed, that the campaigns should be pressed with considerable vigor, since we now know that the indirect effects can be very great. But those embarking on such campaigns should be fully aware, and should make

---

[7] Whether population growth can be substantially reduced by contraception and, if not, what effects the increase in numbers has on hopes for development—these issues are too important to analyze in passing. They are the main topic of the following chapter.

their governments aware, of the enormous demographic effects in several endemic countries, and should be prepared to push even harder for economic development in the decade or so following eradication (Newman, 1965, p. 6).

2. If one accepts the moral stance that to save lives is good even if the consequent population increase creates problems that may be insoluble, the question remains, which lives shall be saved? In other words, given a certain amount of money, a certain number of personnel, to be used in health programs, how shall they be allocated in a country rife with preventable or curable diseases? If most of the effort is expended on the easiest "marvelously cheap" means, are the quick returns likely to be permanent, or will the masses saved from death by malaria succumb to malnutrition and cholera? As the list of diseases in Table 15-9 suggests, a reduction in mortality that is effected by eradication of only some infectious diseases may mean not a permanent fall but a shift in the usual cause of death. This would be analogous to the shift to cancers and heart diseases that has taken place in advanced countries, but with potentially much more disastrous consequences.

3. Allocations can be made not only among different ways of spending money for public health but also between public health and such other benefits as, particularly, education. Like individual parents in the Dumont-Banks model, governments may choose quality rather than quantity. Under some circumstances an expenditure for education will result in a greater productive capacity than the same expenditure for public health (Enke, 1963, pp. 410–413). The direct benefits to mortality control may be greater from education once health projects advance to the point where the government requires the informed, intelligent participation of the general population. As we have seen, even a physician believes that in a country like Ethiopia the improvement of health depends as much on teachers as on doctors.

### TAIWAN

It is perhaps easier to understand the generalizations concerning the control of mortality if they are put in the context of one country's development. One might choose any underdeveloped area to illustrate various points, but perhaps the most remarkable record of effective death control, documented by excellent data, has taken place in Taiwan (*cf.* Petersen, 1967). To duplicate this achievement is the best that any underdeveloped country could hope to do.

The Taiwan that Japan took over in 1895 was notorious as a malarial deathtrap, with more rainfall than any part of Mainland China and in the lowlands a subtropical climate throughout the year. The island was poor in agriculture and almost without other economic activities, truly an inauspicious first colony in Japan's new empire. The crude death rate, not recorded, was certainly well above 40, possibly closer to 50. The conditions in the nineteenth century can be suggested by the record of the Japanese expeditionary forces. Of an army that landed on Taiwan in the spring of 1895, four out of five were either sick or dead of cholera, malaria, dysentery, typhus, pneumonia, or beri-beri by the end of September.

In 1896, the plague spread to Taiwan from Hong Kong, and over the next twenty-two years 30,000 persons were stricken and 24,000 died of it. It was wiped out largely by harsh but effective police power, through the isolation of patients, burning of contaminated houses, extermination of rats, and quarantine at ports. Serious outbreaks of cholera occurred in 1902, 1912, 1913, and 1920, but by the last of these years, the public-health system was sufficiently developed to prevent a recurrence. Compulsory vaccination, initiated in 1903, reduced the incidence of smallpox, of which the last serious outbreak was in 1918–20. By 1920, thus, three major epidemic diseases—the plague, cholera, and smallpox—were under effective control. In that year also the growing number of Western-style physicians exceeded for the first time the declining number of Chinese herbalists.

The most troublesome remaining problem was malaria, which had ranked as the first or second cause of death each year from the beginning of the century to 1916, after which date the Japanese measures began to pay off. They eventually set up as many as 200 antimalaria stations equipped to analyze the blood of local populations, and persons found to be infected were given free a compulsory treatment with quinine and mepacrine. When this costly program broke down during World War II, malaria epidemics again swept the island. Beginning in 1951, the new government has undertaken a continuous antimalaria program using the pesticides developed during the war and concentrating its efforts in areas that periodic checks of the school population indicate as the most seriously affected. The incidence of malaria has been reduced to a few dozen cases, and it has all but disappeared as a cause of death. As elsewhere in the world, the control of this disease has contributed also to the improvement in general health and the reduction of mortality from other causes.

In 1965, Taiwan's crude death rate was 5.5, the lowest in the world (Table 15-8). How accurate is this astounding datum? Apart from the war period, registration has in general been reasonably complete and accurate, but the reporting of infant deaths has been deficient, in part because of the effect of folk beliefs that persist in rural areas. To speak of a dead child is a bad omen for the living ones. Parents should not grieve for a child that dies before the age of twelve, for whom neither a coffin nor a funeral service is appropriate by traditional usage. According to field studies in three townships, in the late 1950s the corrected infant mortality rate was of the order of 50 per 1,000 live births, and up to 30 per cent of the infant deaths may not have been registered (Chow and Hsu, 1960). If one assumes that the 1964 infant mortality rate of 24 was deficient in the same proportion, this would raise it only to about 31. And in that case the corrected crude death rate would be about one-tenth higher than the official one, or still an extremely low figure. Based on life tables for several recent years, the expectation of life from birth has gone up remarkably, from 38.8 (male) and 43.1 (female) in 1926–31 to 61.3 (male) and 65.6 (female) in 1959–60. The latter figures are slightly higher than the comparable ones in the United States for 1930–39.

To have transformed a notorious death trap into a nation with the world's lowest death rate in about 70 years is a unique achievement. What generalizations does this experience suggest? (1) The prewar controls laid a broad base for effective utilization of postwar techniques. The precipitous decline in mortality that we have noted in Ceylon and elsewhere was not duplicated in Taiwan; there was rather a continuation of the earlier advances, which the war and Japan's defeat had interrupted. (2) Mortality control was based as much on political and social factors as on purely medical ones. The Japanese administrators established what an American analyst has termed "one of the most successful colonial programs in the world" (Barclay, 1954, p. 7), and one important consequence was the institutionalization of effective public health. (3) The increase of population has become a serious problem, which may be mitigated by a family-planning program that has shown some initial success. (4) Even so, the island has enjoyed an enormous economic progress, based in part on monetary and technical assistance from the United States but more fundamentally on the ability of the Taiwanese to put this to good use. In mid-1965, since the economy was adjudged able to continue under its own momentum, American economic aid was discontinued after a "graduation" ceremony.

## Summary

According to the scattered data available from the beginning of the nineteenth century, the average expectation of life at birth in Western Europe and its overseas extensions was 35 to 40 years. In the most favored nations the present figure is about double that. The major causes of the declines in the early and middle decades of the century were general rather than specific—public sanitation, better personal hygiene, the over-all rise in the level of living, as well as vaccination against smallpox. In the next period there was a great improvement in cures of most infectious diseases, a process that reached its climax with the development of antibiotics and other "wonder drugs." Recent medical advances have also included progress in surgical techniques, particularly in obstetrics; in diagnosis and medicaments; and in institutional forms of care—blood banks, medical teams, group health insurance, and so on. The recent advances in death control have been almost equivalent to the elimination of all mortality before the age of 40.

Now that infectious diseases are relatively unimportant in mortality, they have been replaced by cancers, diseases of the heart, and fatal crimes and accidents. This shift in the causes of death has meant that differentials by age, sex, and social group have also changed markedly. The sharpest decline was in the mortality of infants and young children, whereas for the advanced ages improvement in control of death has been slow and moderate. The difference in death rates between the sexes is large and can be expected to increase still more. All social differentials—by urban-rural residence, by social class or occupational group, by race—are converging. In the United States, that between whites and Negroes is still significant, in part because Negro mortality is tied in with the lower-class culture.

In the years since 1945 insecticides and antibiotics have made possible enormous advances in the mass control of mortality in underdeveloped countries. A major portion of the cost of these measures is ordinarily borne by Western countries, acting through international agencies. The death rate can fall, though of course not inevitably, to around ten per thousand population irrespective of the culture, the economy, or the government. Until fairly recently a people did not achieve a higher average life expectation until this was earned, as it were, through better food, more healthful living conditions, and an economy able to carry more people. Now the very fact that people are kept alive so easily makes it more difficult to realize these other goals.

## Suggestions for Further Reading

Some of the references cited at the end of Chapter 7 (see pp. 246–251) can be recommended again, in particular Dublin et al., 1949, which remains the best general discussion of the factors that determined life expectancy in the United States. Stolnitz, 1955–56 is an especially conscientious compilation of international trends. Differentials by social class are well analyzed in Antonovsky, 1967; Moriyama and Guralnick, 1956.

The recent record of mortality control in underdeveloped countries has not really been analyzed yet in sociological terms. One of the few commentaries that gets beyond the techniques of death control and the economic problems of population increase to "the cultural base" of mortality is Yankauer, 1959. On the sociology of illness, see Jaco, 1958; Gordon, 1966.

ANDERSON, ODIN W., and GEORGE ROSEN. 1960. *An Examination of the Concept of Preventive Medicine*. Series 12. Health Information Foundation, New York.

* ANTONOVSKY, AARON. 1967. "Social Class, Life Expectancy and Overall Mortality," *Milbank Memorial Fund Quarterly*, **45**, 31–73.

BACKETT, E. MAURICE. 1964. "The Teaching of Preventive Medicine in Europe and in the United States," *Milbank Memorial Fund Quarterly*, **42**, 22–44.

BADGLEY, ROBIN F., and SAMUEL WOLFE. 1965. "Medical Care and Conflict in Saskatchewan," *Milbank Memorial Fund Quarterly*, **43**, 463–479.

BALFOUR, MARSHALL C. 1956. "Some Considerations Regarding the Permanence of Recent Declines in Mortality in Underdeveloped Areas," in Milbank Memorial Fund, 1956, pp. 35–43.

BARCLAY, GEORGE W. 1954. *A Report on Taiwan's Population*. Office of Population Research, Princeton, N.J.

BENJAMIN, B. 1964. "The Urban Background to Public Health Changes in England and Wales, 1900–50," *Population Studies*, 17, 225–248.

BOURGEOIS-PICHAT, JEAN, and CHIA-LIN PAN. 1956. "Trends and Determinants of Mortality in Underdeveloped Areas," in Milbank Memorial Fund, 1956, pp. 11–25.

BURGESS, ALEX M., JR., THEODORE COLTON, and OSLER L. PETERSON. 1966. "Avoidable Mortality: Some Practical Aims for Regional Medical Programs," *Archives of Environmental Health*, 13, 794–798.

BURNIGHT, ROBERT G., and PARKER G. MARDEN. 1967. "Social Correlates of Weight in an Aging Population," *Milbank Memorial Fund Quarterly*, 45, 75–92.

CHANDRASEKHAR, S., editor. 1967. *Asia's Population Problems*. Allen & Unwin, London.

CHASE, HELEN C. 1965. "White-Nonwhite Mortality Differentials in the United States," *Health, Education, and Welfare Indicators*, June.

————. 1966. "The Current Status of Fetal Death Registration in the United States," *American Journal of Public Health*, 56, 1734–1744.

* ————. 1967. *International Comparison of Perinatal and Infant Mortality: The United States and Six West European Countries*. U.S. National Center for Health Statistics, Series 3, No. 6, Washington, D.C.

CHOW LIEN-PIN, and HSU SHIH-CHU. 1960. "Statistical Studies on Mortality in Taiwan during the Last Decade," *Industry of Free China* (Taipei), 14, 7–34.

COCKBURN, W. CHARLES. 1966. "Progress in International Smallpox Eradication," *American Journal of Public Health*, 56, 1628–1633.

DAVIS, KINGSLEY. 1951. *The Population of India and Pakistan*. Princeton University Press, Princeton, N.J.

DUBLIN, LOUIS I., ALFRED J. LOTKA, and MORTIMER SPIEGELMAN. 1949. *Length of Life: A Study of the Life Table*. Revised Ed. Ronald, New York.

ECKSTEIN, HARRY. 1956. "Planning: A Case Study," *Political Studies*, 4, 46–60.

ELLIS, JOHN M. 1957. "Socio-Economic Differentials in Mortality from Chronic Diseases," *Social Problems*, 5, 30–36.

ENKE, STEPHEN. 1963. *Economics for Development*. Prentice-Hall, Englewood Cliffs, N.J.

FORGOTSON, EDWARD H. 1967. "1965: The Turning Point in Health Law—1966 Reflections," *American Journal of Public Health*, 57, 934–946.

FREDERIKSEN, HARALD. 1960. "Malaria Control and Population Pressure in Ceylon," *Public Health Reports*, 75, 865–868.

————. 1961. "Determinants and Consequences of Mortality Trends in Ceylon," *Public Health Reports*, 76, 659–663.

GILMORE, C. P. 1966. "Malaria Wins Round 2," *New York Times Sunday Magazine*, September 25.

GORDON, GERALD. 1966. *Role Theory and Illness: A Sociological Perspective*. College and University Press, New Haven, Conn.

GRAHAM, SAXON. 1957. "Socio-Economic Status, Illness, and the Use of Medical Services," *Milbank Memorial Fund Quarterly*, 35, 58–66.

* GURALNICK, LILLIAN, and ANN JACKSON. 1967. "An Index of Unnecessary Deaths," *Public Health Reports*, 82, 180–182.

HINMAN, E. HAROLD. 1966. *World Eradication of Infectious Diseases*. Thomas, Springfield, Ill.

HUNT, ELEANOR P., and EARL E. HUYCK. 1966. "Mortality of White and Nonwhite Infants in Major U.S. Cities," *Health, Education, and Welfare Indicators*, January, pp. 1–19.

JACO, E. G., editor. 1958. *Patients, Physicians, and Illness*. Free Press, Glencoe, Ill.

KIRK, DUDLEY. 1946. *Europe's Population in the Interwar Years*. League of Nations. Princeton University Press, Princeton, N.J.

LAUGHTON, KATHERINE B., CAROL W. BUCK, and G. E. HOBBS. 1958. "Socio-Economic Status and Illness," *Milbank Memorial Fund Quarterly*, 36, 46–56.

* MEEGAMA, S. A. 1967. "Malaria Eradication and Its Effect on Mortality Levels," *Population Studies*, 21, 207–237.

* MILBANK MEMORIAL FUND. 1956. *Trends and Differentials in Mortality*. New York.

* MORIYAMA, I. M., and L. GURALNICK. 1956. "Occupational and Social Class Differences in Mortality," in Milbank Memorial Fund, 1956, pp. 61–73.

MORRIS, J. N. 1963. "Some Current Trends in Public Health," *Proceedings of the Royal Society*, 159B, 65–86.

MYERS, ROBERT J. 1966. "The Impact of Medicare on Demography," *Demography*, 3, 545–547.

NEWMAN, PETER. 1965. *Malaria Eradication and Population Growth, with Special Reference to Ceylon and British Guiana*. Bureau of Public Health Economics, Research Series, No. 10. University of Michigan School of Public Health, Ann Arbor, Mich.

PADLEY, RICHARD. 1959. "Cause-of-Death Statements in Ceylon: A Study in Levels of Diagnostic Reporting," *Bulletin of the World Health Organization*, 20, 677–695.

PERLMAN, MARK. 1966. "On Health and Economic Development: Some Problems, Methods, and Conclusions Reviewed in a Perusal of the Literature," *Comparative Studies in Society and History*, 8, 433–448.

PETERSEN, WILLIAM. 1967. "Taiwan's Population Problem," in Chandrasekhar, 1967, pp. 189–210.

PRICE, DOROTHY P., and LOUCELE A. HOROWITZ. 1967. "Trends in Medical Care Prices," *Social Security Bulletin*, 30, 13–28.

REED, LOUIS S. 1965a. *The Extent of Health Insurance Coverage in the United States*. Research Report No. 10. Social Security Administration. U.S. Department of Health, Education, and Welfare, Washington, D.C.

———. 1965b. "Private Health Insurance in the United States: An Overview," *Social Security Bulletin*, 28, 3–20, 47–48.

———, and RUTH S. HANFT. 1966. "National Health Expenditures, 1950–64," *Social Security Bulletin*, 29, 3–19.

ROSEN, GEORGE. 1958. *A History of Public Health*. M.D. Publications, New York.

RUBEL, ARTHUR J. 1966. "The Role of Social Science Research in Recent Health Programs in Latin America," *Latin American Research Review*, 2, 37–56.

SARKAR, N. K. 1956. "Population Trends and Population Policy in Ceylon," *Population Studies*, 9, 195–216.

° SELVARATNAM, S. 1961. "Some Implications of Population Growth in Ceylon," *Ceylon Journal of Historical and Social Studies* (Colombo), 4, 33–49.

STEWART, WILLIAM H. 1967. "The Positive Impact of Medicare on the Nation's Health Care Systems," *Social Security Bulletin*, 30, 9–12, 50–51.

STOCKWELL, EDWARD G. 1962. "Infant Mortality and Socio-Economic Status: A Changing Relationship," *Milbank Memorial Fund Quarterly*, 40, 101–111.

° STOLNITZ, GEORGE J. 1955 and 1956. "A Century of International Mortality Trends," *Population Studies*, 9, 24–55; 10, 17–42.

TAEUBER, CONRAD, and IRENE B. TAEUBER. 1958. *The Changing Population of the United States*. Wiley, New York.

TITMUSS, RICHARD M., and BRIAN ABEL-SMITH. 1961. *Social Policies and Population Growth in Mauritius*. Methuen, London.

TOMASSON, RICHARD F. 1960. "Patterns in Negro-White Differential Mortality, 1930–1957," *Milbank Memorial Fund Quarterly*, 38, 362–386.

———. 1961. "Bias in Estimates of the U.S. Nonwhite Population as Indicated by Trends in Death Rates," *Journal of the American Statistical Association*, 56, 44–51.

TORREY, E. FULLER. 1967. "Health Services in Ethiopia," *Milbank Memorial Fund Quarterly*, 45, 275–285.

UHR, CARL G. 1966. *Sweden's Social Security System: An Appraisal of its Economic Impact in the Postwar Period*. Social Security Administration, Research Report No. 14. U.S. Department of Health, Education, and Welfare, Washington, D.C.

UNITED NATIONS, DEPARTMENT OF SOCIAL AFFAIRS, POPULATION DIVISION. 1954. *Foetal, Infant and Early Childhood Mortality. 1: The Statistics*. Population Studies, No. 13, New York.

U.S. NATIONAL CENTER FOR HEALTH STATISTICS. 1964. *The Change in Mortality Trend in the United States*. Vital and Health Statistics, Series 3, No. 1. Public Health Service, Washington, D.C.

U.S. SOCIAL SECURITY ADMINISTRATION. 1964. *Social Security Programs Throughout the World*. Washington, D.C.

WEST, HOWARD. 1967. "Health Insurance for the Aged: The Statistical Program," *Social Security Bulletin*, 30, 3–16.

WIEHL, DOROTHY G. 1948. "Mortality and Socio-Environmental Factors," *Milbank Memorial Fund Quarterly*, 26, 335–365.

° YANKAUER, ALFRED. 1959. "An Approach to the Cultural Base of Infant Mortality in India," *Population Review*, 3, 39–51.

YERUSHALMY, J., and JESSIE M. BIERMAN. 1952. "Major Problems in Fetal Mortality," *Obstetrical and Gynecological Survey*, 7, 1–34.

# 16

## FERTILITY, POPULATION INCREASE, AND ECONOMIC STAGNATION IN THE UNDERDEVELOPED WORLD

What is termed *industrialization* or *economic development* is never merely a change in techniques of production. Although an underdeveloped country that lacks basic scientific knowledge and ability can assimilate much so-called know-how, even minor technical innovations, if they are alien to a society, eventually disrupt the institutional structure. In the long run, industrialization is possible only as part of a much deeper social change, and in the shorter run, the industrializing country acquires benefits but also the burdens of a painful transition. To appraise the social effects of industrialization, then, we cannot merely compare the birth rates, for example, of advanced and underdeveloped countries. Such a comparison implies that the transitional phase, which is the only one that the present generation will know, is too short and insignificant to be analyzed *per se*, and that once it is passed, the social concomitants of the advanced economy will necessarily be the same as can be observed in presently developed countries. Neither assumption is well based.

That the fertility of underdeveloped countries has not fallen nearly so fast as their mortality is what we should expect from both the population history of the West and our knowledge of social behavior. Indeed, it would have been *more* amazing if the decline in Ceylon's death rate by one-third within one year, to cite that example again, had been matched by a comparable decline in the birth rate. For no matter how underdeveloped areas vary in their cultural values, these generally include a hatred and fear of early death and thus a more or less willing acceptance of any life-saving technique that has proved its efficacy. Moreover, the acquiescence of each person is neither asked for nor required in the mass spraying of insecticides or often even mass inoculations. The control of fertility, on the contrary, must operate by influencing the personal behavior of the individual parents. It is a crucial question, then, what values underlie decisions concerning family size, and whether and how fast those values are changing.

We can try to come to grips with these matters with three quite different sets of data, on: (1) ideologies, (2) attitudes, and (3) social structure, each interpreted in terms of (4) demographic theory.

1. People's behavior is governed to some degree by religions, nationalist myths, or superstitions; and concerning these broad determinants there is a mass of written evidence available. But which of such norms actually influence behavior, and which are as effective as the Sermon on the Mount is in setting the pattern of life in Christian countries?

2. From survey data we can get attitudes of the actual participants in procreation toward immediately relevant issues like the number of children desired and the relative acceptance of various means of contraception. But are replies to such questionnaires frank and complete enough to give the analyst a reliable indicator of subsequent behavior?

3. Any constraint on individuals' acts generally derives less from an ideology than from their place in a social structure, and the differential analysis of fertility has therefore constituted the mainstay of research in advanced countries. But it is seldom possible merely to use the same categories (e.g., "urban" versus "rural") in an analysis of quite different cultures, and the sociological analysis of the fertility of underdeveloped countries is just beginning.

4. That fertility has seemingly risen in a number of underdeveloped countries contradicts the expectation from conventional theory, which must also be amended. Birth rates are changing in response to impersonal social-economic forces, as before, but in part also to governments' efforts to control family size; and this shift means that some of the postulates underlying earlier demographic theories are no longer valid.

In other words, the four types of data can each contribute to our understanding, but each has specific limitations. The high birth rates typical of nonindustrial societies constitute not only a massive social problem but one to which we have no assured answer. Programs designed to reduce fertility have occasionally been successful, but only in small, homogeneous countries with stable governments and advancing economies.

## Traditional Ideologies and Modernizing Movements

When a Brahmin bride bows to her elders, the traditional blessing is, "Be the mother of eight sons and may your husband live long." In Pakistan, children are referred to as "blessings of God." In Latin America the cult of *machismo* (literally, "maleness") induces men to prove their virility with a large progeny (Stycos, 1955, pp. 34–36). How relevant are such ceremonies, symbols, and myths to actual attitudes and behavior? Until recently most Western demographers assumed that, indeed, the world's peasant masses saw reproduction in a traditional perspective (e.g., Notestein, 1945). So long as out of every four infants born one died in its first year and a considerable additional proportion before maturity, the society could continue to exist only with a value system and institutional structure that effectively encouraged a generous procreation. Children were said to be economic assets: set to work at an early age, each offspring later helped provide for his parents in their declining years. "The head of a large family gains social importance in the rural setting of India and the prospect of children to look after him in his old age adds to his feeling of security both economically and emotionally" (Mathen, 1962; *cf.* Sadik, 1965). Thus, the weight of traditionalist thought and the logic of functionalist theory together supported the notion that parents wanted the large families characteristic of peasant societies.

Yet both the premises leading to this conclusion are subject to reasonable challenge. According to the same analyst of Indian data, just because of the high incidence of infant and child mortality—"the household survey showed that at least fifty per cent lost one or more children"—persons were said to be more favorably disposed to a family-planning program (Mathen, 1962). And while the norms taught by the great religions of Asia reinforce, as do their European counterparts, the high valuation of family life and a numerous progeny, there is typically a far greater ambiguity on the key issue of contraception than in Christian fundamentalism of whatever denomination. We need only look at the content of traditions and of the ideologies that counter them to recognize that modernization is not so simple a transformation as was once supposed.

### RELIGION

The frank sexuality in **Hinduism** is matched by the call to *dama*, or self-restraint. "We should reduce our wants and be prepared to suffer in the interest of truth. Austerity, chastity, solitude and silence are the way to attain self-control." [1] Among the most orthodox, marital coitus is a semi-

---

[1] S. Radhakrishnan, editor, *The Principal Upanisads*, Harper, New York, 1953, p. 109.

religious rite, often associated with the recital of hymns and prayers, the wearing of talismans and charms. "Sexual contact in wedlock is only permissible specifically for procreation of the species, coitus otherwise being considered vulgar, if not sinful." [2] Accepting this Hindu heritage, a secularist like Gandhi—once he was too old to be driven by the sexual urge himself—stipulated absolute continence as the only permissible means of limiting births.[3]

Yet compare this passage from the Upanishads themselves:

Now the woman whom one desires [with the thought] "may she not conceive," after inserting the member in her, joining mouth to mouth, he should first inhale and then exhale and say, "with power, with semen I reclaim the semen from you." Thus she comes to be without semen. . . .

Now the woman whom one desires [with the thought] "may she conceive," after inserting the member in her, joining mouth to mouth, he should first exhale and then inhale and say "with power, with semen I deposit semen in you." Thus she becomes pregnant.[4]

Manifestly, the desire of the man either to ensure conception or to prevent it is seen as licit, though the efficacy of the method may be questioned.

**Buddhism** can be represented by the denomination dominant in Ceylon, Burma, Thailand, and Cambodia (Hinayana, or Theravada).

Buddhist texts say nothing directly upon the subject of contraception, nor do they even provide such injunctions as "Be fruitful and multiply." . . . Villagers [in Ceylon] generally look upon any conscious attempt to prevent conception other than through restraint as being "unnatural," "sinful," . . . [but] Buddhist priests [have not] concerned themselves (Ryan, 1954).

A questionnaire on the subject was administered to a sample of eighty-six monks and priests, who split sharply according to how much schooling they had had. Not one of the best educated found in Buddhism any opposition to contraception, but 41 per cent of a middle group and 90 per cent of the least educated disagreed, asserting usually that willfully to prevent birth is tantamount to killing (*ibid.*).

**Confucianism** was in China the principal ethical underpinning of what is ordinarily termed a familistic culture. Under the traditional Chinese sys-

---

[2] Lelal M. Shah, "Sex Life in India and Pakistan," in *The Encyclopedia of Sexual Behavior,* edited by Albert Ellis and Albert Abarnel, Hawthorn, New York, 1961, 1, 528–537.

[3] In a discussion of how to cope with India's population pressure, Gandhi once remarked that "perhaps we need some good epidemics." He laughed as he said this, for a professed democrat cannot offer such a proposal seriously; but he *was* serious in holding to his absolute opposition to contraceptives, no matter what the demographic consequences. See Louis Fischer, *A Week with Gandhi,* Duell, New York, 1942, p. 89, and, for a compilation of his various writings on the subject, Gandhi, 1959.

[4] Radhakrishnan, *op. cit.,* p. 324.

tem, it is often stated, "whenever economic circumstances permit, the family membership will continue to grow" (Lee, 1953). As we have noted already (pp. 185–186), noneconomic factors cannot be entirely dismissed, and the economic pressure that reduced normative obligations was a constant of Chinese society. It is true that Confucian scholars condemned abortion and infanticide (the modes of population control of, respectively, the urban gentry and the peasantry), but to little effect. The transformation of Chinese familism in traditional Japan (see pp. 423–424) indicates how susceptible the system is to a new environment.

**Islam** also emphasizes that offspring, especially sons, are essential to a marriage. A barren wife is a hapless creature, who to this day may induce her husband to take a second spouse, either in the superstitious hope that the first wife will then become fruitful, or with the simple desire to bring children into her home.[5] That the family line must be continued does not necessarily imply, however, a ban on contraception. "The stand of the Koran on methods of fertility control is not specific and . . . is subject to various interpretations" (Yaukey, 1961, p. 7). *Azal,* a man's desire that his wife shall not conceive, is permitted in one saying ascribed to the Prophet, forbidden in another; the two rules are said to relate to different situations. One verse of the Koran reads, "And do not slay your children for fear of poverty. We give them sustenance and yourselves, too." Some authorities interpret this ban to include prospective children as well as infants already born (Lorimer, 1954, pp. 186–187). On the other hand, one authoritative Islamic stance was given in a reply to a physician's question by His Excellency Ayatollah (a title of the highest ecclesiastical order) Hajji (one who has made a pilgrimage to Mecca) Sheikh Bahaedin Mahallati. The exchange, in 1964, was as follows: [6]

I request that you send me a formal answer to the following question: Would you permit a physician temporarily to prescribe drugs or contraceptive devices [in order to prevent] excessive human reproduction, and is this religiously licit?—Dr. Mohammad Sarram.

In the name of God: From the standpoint of the divine law, the use of drugs or contraceptive devices, especially if it is temporary, to control human fertility does not seem to be illicit if this practice does not damage the female's fecundity and make her barren.—Bahaedin Mahallati.

The great non-Western religions, in short, are ambivalent on the question of whether contraception is permissible, so that typically their moral teachings become explicit only by exegesis. The influence of the West in reinforcing modernist ideas might have resolved the ambiguity, but the most direct transmission of Europe's ethical dicta was through missionaries,

[5] Raphael Patai, *Sex and Family in the Bible and the Middle East,* Doubleday, Garden City, N.Y., 1959, p. 79.
[6] I am indebted to Dr. Ali A. Paydarfar for a translation from the Arabic original.

typically even less receptive to new ideas than their counterparts at home. In any case, Christian pretensions to a monopoly of religious truth often emerged as partisan support of the imperial power or the white race, and each denomination's proselytizing was undercut by its Christian competitors, so that the long-term religious effects of Asian and African missionaries may be close to nil.[7]

Table 16-1. Percentage of Married Catholic Women Who Have Used Contraceptives Forbidden by the Church, Three Latin American Cities, 1960s

| FREQUENCY OF CHURCH ATTENDANCE | PANAMA CITY | RIO DE JANEIRO | SAN JOSE, COSTA RICA |
|---|---|---|---|
| Once a week or more | 59 | 58 | 65 |
| Once or twice a month | 64 | 47 | 54 |
| Several times a year | — | 51 | 53 |
| Once a year | 58 | 60 | 62 |
| Once in years | — | 64 | 78 |
| Never | 50 | 58 | 72 |

SOURCE: Carmen A. Miró and Ferdinand Rath, "Preliminary Findings of Comparative Fertility Surveys in Three Latin American Countries," *Milbank Memorial Fund Quarterly*, Vol. 43, No. 4, Part 2 (1965), 36–62.

The only Western religion with a significant hold in underdeveloped areas is the Roman Catholicism of Latin America. The faith espoused in the Spanish colonies had been that of the Counter-Reformation—fervently orthodox, crusading, resourceful. In the revolutions that established the republics, the Church was indifferent or, more often, hostile to nationalist aspirations; Leo XII distributed an encyclical in support of "our dearly beloved son Ferdinand, the Catholic King of the Spains." Until very recently, this history set a pattern in Latin America, with the Church the defender of reaction and all who hoped for a better world pushed to an anticlerical stance.[8] With the disintegration of Catholic orthodoxy on the question of birth control (see pp. 491–496), the Church in Latin America has begun to reflect all the positions in the continuing dispute. According to surveys in three large cities, a majority of Catholic women, whether or not they were actively involved in their religion, used contraceptive means condemned by the Church (Table 16-1). In three cities of Chile, just under one woman in four interviewed had had at least one induced abortion; 42 per cent of admissions to hospital emergency services were abortion

[7] *Cf.* K. M. Panikkar, *Asia and Western Dominance*, Day, New York, n.d., Part VII.

[8] *Cf.* Germán Arciniegas, *Latin America: A Cultural History*, Knopf, New York, 1967.

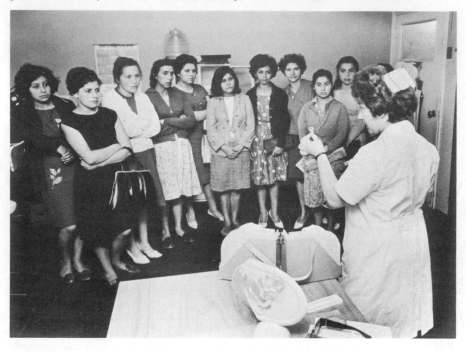

A nurse explains the principle of intra-uterine devices to a group of Chilean women (*Bernard Cole, Planned Parenthood/World Population*).

cases. When these data were revealed in 1962, they prompted parallel studies in a number of other Latin American countries, which uncovered abortion rates ranging from 75 per cent of all pregnancies in Uruguay to 15 per cent in Guatemala (Stycos, 1966). As a Colombian priest noted, the difficulties of "millions of well intentioned couples" in reconciling the licit ends of marriage "are leading to conflict, perversion of conscience, abandonment of the Church, and a loss of harmony between the spouses" (Pérez, 1966).

### NATIONALISM

While the general mass of the population has continued to follow a folk or religious tradition, most of the leaders of the underdeveloped countries have been driven by a secularist faith in nationalist aspirations. In the view of many analysts, nationalism is a *sine qua non* of industrialization, even though it works both ways (Davis, 1955; *cf*. pp. 424–425). In the new nations it tends to block modernization because: (1) it reinforces the already existent hostility to the West, the prime source of modernizing institutions; (2) it is often based on an exaggerated reaffirmation of ancient preindustrial models; and (3) the large element of myth in protestations of superiority and reconstructions from a prehistoric past block the ready development of rational solutions to the problems of societal transition ( e.g., Stycos, 1963*b* ). And, in particular, ( 4 ) the shift of fervor from religion to a new credo does not dispel the ambiguity concerning contraception.

India, for instance, has now established a courageous and expensive birth-control program, but it took some time for it to get under way. In the first years after independence, most national leaders were either opposed to contraception on moral grounds (especially Gandhi and his followers) or, at best, indifferent to family planning as a social program.

In the first flush of national awakening, Indian leaders became acutely conscious of the poverty of the masses and they believed that it was increasing year after year and that its main cause was economic exploitation by Britain. To this accusation the British reply was that the growing poverty of the people of India was a result of population growth and the people of India were themselves responsible for it. This gave the cue to the nationalist leaders to argue that . . . India was a land of infinite and rich natural resources which could support a much larger population at a considerably higher standard of living than that obtaining in recent times. . . . This [dispute] prevented for a very long time an objective appraisal of the population situation (Sovani, 1952).

Reflecting this point of view, Nehru in 1948 termed India "an underpopulated country": "If we increase our production, agricultural and other, if this population is put to work for production, then we are not overpopulated" (quoted in *ibid.*). Only three years later was a population policy held to be "essential to planning" (Indian Planning Commission, *Report*, 1951, quoted in *ibid.*). Apparently some remnant of the earlier position remains. China's invasion of India in 1962, thus, made Indians less willing to accept the government's birth-control program. "With 700 million marching on the northern frontier, people began wondering why they should reduce their population" (Dr. K. N. Rao, in Muramatsu and Harper, 1965, p. 62).

Not merely in India but in almost all the new nations, the ruling elite is to some degree motivated by what has been termed a kind of ideological *machismo*—"the feeling on the part of the intellectual classes that to reduce or to slow down the rate of population growth or the fertility of a nation is a kind of cultural castration," which offends all who believe that because the nation is good, therefore it must grow (J. M. Stycos, in *ibid.*, p. 180). In a statement summarizing a survey of Mexican males, population growth was equated with power and prestige:

Mexico was once weak, divided and helpless, her people were dominated by alien conquerors, and she was underpopulated, her lands were taken by foreign invaders. But Mexico is growing. There is strength in numbers. True, numbers bring problems, but we are forging these numbers into a great nation (Stycos, 1965*b*).

To N. Viera Altamirano, the influential editor of San Salvador's *El Diario de Hoy,* population is an almost mystical force in promoting Latin American grandeur. "To populate America is to civilize America. To oppose population is to oppose civilization" (quoted in *ibid.*). When nationalism is tinged with socialism, as it so often is in underdeveloped countries, the Marxist hostility to any planning applied to fertility [9] reinforces this kind of sentiment. Both in Latin America and more generally,

It is not the poor and the ignorant who are [mainly responsible for] blocking the use of birth control. It is the educated elite who still think in nineteenth-century terms and therefore fail to organize programs for utilizing government public-health services to reduce fertility (Kahl and Stycos, 1965).

### PLANNED PARENTHOOD

In the West traditional and religious opposition to the use of contraceptives had been confronted by a counter movement, neo-Malthusianism, which evolved its own rationale for the ethics it advocated. The birth-control associations established in many underdeveloped countries have serviced a minority of urban professionals and the middle class, but in many cases there was no time to go beyond this beginning. In Pakistan, for instance, from the founding of the first private family-planning group (in Lahore in 1952) to the institution of a government program (Rs. 30.5 million allocated in the Second Five-Year Plan, 1961–65) was less than a decade. More generally, the birth-control movement is not equipped to cope with the problems of underdeveloped areas.

Even in the West, wherever the use of contraceptives became general enough to dissipate conventional opposition, the transition was accompanied by a change in the character of the movement itself. In Britain the early emphasis on the economic effects of population growth gave way to a narrower concentration on family budgets or the health of the mother; political economists were supplanted by social workers or physicians; and in 1927 the role of the Malthusian League, which disbanded itself at a celebration dinner, was taken over by the Society for Constructive Birth Control, headed by Marie Stopes, a physician. A similar shift of emphasis, even if not accompanied by a change in organization, took place also in other countries, with the new value orientation indicated by the substitution of "planned parenthood" or "child spacing" for "neo-Malthusianism" or "birth control." [10] Today the international planned-parenthood movement

---

[9] *Cf.* pp. 634–637, 668–672. The Catholic-Communist coalition opposing efforts of United Nations agencies to help reduce fertility has been something of an embarrassment to both these strange allies, and if either position is liberalized, one effect may be to harden the opposition to birth control from the other camp.

[10] It was an honorable task, well performed, to have provided the legal and medical system by which individuals in Western middle classes could space their three to

"views itself as a medical program, directed by medical personnel, dealing with medical problems" (Stycos, 1962). In underdeveloped areas this conventional approach can help a tiny westernized elite to control its reproduction, but it is almost irrelevant to the staggering problem of population growth on a scale unimagined in the nineteenth century. Among peasant masses of underdeveloped areas, one measures advances not by the hundreds of individuals who attend a clinic but by the pregnancy rate per century of exposure. No limitation of means is admissible in order to satisfy standards of middle-class prejudice or archaic ethics; the methods that these criteria would exclude are historically the most successful on a mass scale.[11] Moreover, merely to make contraceptives available, even if gratis, does not ensure that those who lack Western middle-class values will thereby reduce their fertility. Birth control is in fact a type of planned social change, brought about by revising people's attitudes or social institutions and by organizing the most efficient system of distributing the contraceptive means available.

## Survey Data on Fertility Determinants

What are the attitudes of the peasant masses concerning the use of contraceptives, the size of the ideal family, and other matters that help determine the trend in fertility? A reply to such a question based on deductions from ideologies or from actual family size is not sufficient. As we have seen, neither religions nor modernist ethical systems have been consistent in their stance toward fertility determinants; thus, how could an analyst guess which of several leads, if any, the people were following, or whether large families were the consequence of ignorance or apathy, rather than of the acceptance of pronatalist doctrines? Manifestly, direct data on people's attitudes, if they were of reasonable quality, would constitute an important addition to our knowledge.

---

four children and, surreptitiously, could be assured of almost absolute contraception in their premarital or extramarital sex. But in advanced countries where contraceptives are legally available to the affluent through private physicians and to the poor through free public clinics, a private organization has few residual functions today. In the United States, for instance, the greatest successes of the Planned Parenthood Association in the past were in smaller cities, and it is ill prepared to cope with metropolitan populations (Rein, 1964). It has shown little interest and less imagination in breaking through slum residents' reluctance to control births efficiently. In an effort not to affront the conservative among its members and allies, it has generally avoided the advocacy of abortion, sterilization, or even contraception for unmarried adolescents. Under the slogan of "maternal health," it has concentrated on the individual female as patient, denigrating an efficient contraceptive like the condom because it is used by the male.

[11] "*Coitus interruptus* and condom have been largely responsible for fertility declines in Western modernized societies; abortion is primarily responsible for fertility declines in [Japan], and sterilization may be of crucial importance in fertility decline in [Puerto Rico]" (Stycos, 1962; cf. Gopalaswami, 1962).

Polling is fraught with methodological difficulties even in Western countries and even with questionnaires that do not touch on questions as private as coitus and birth control. What kind of response should one anticipate from a peasant population that anywhere in the world is likely to follow the Chinese proverb, "Before a stranger it is better to express only a third of your opinion"?

In a traditional folk society [like Taiwan] it is almost impossible to get a clear individual opinion on many problems. What are problems for the modern are not considered problems by these people, because they are connected with unquestionable mores. Some of our queries were considered just too foolish to answer. Other questions were looked on as impolite or of bad omen (Chen et al., 1963).

In Pakistan a question on the number of years of cohabitation elicited only a comment to the interviewer, "You are shameless" (Choldin et al., 1967). Another example, from an analysis of fertility in Uganda:

Complete refusals to answer questions were very rare, although it was some-times necessary to visit a house three times in order to get cooperation. . . . A more common form of refusal was a civil greeting, followed either by reluctance to give any information or by quite obvious misstatements . . . or frivolous answers. For instance, a man who had refused to give any information to the first two investigators finally gave the names of two children to the third investi-gator. . . . [He] later admitted to ten children, [while] he still concealed a second wife living in another village (Richards and Reining, 1954).

If the study is so designed, it is possible to check survey data for **reliability,** or their consistency with a variation in conditions that should have no effect on the response. Whether the husband or the wife informs the researcher concerning their marital practices, for instance, should make no difference, but in a Calcutta study in which both were separately asked questions about birth control, only 22 per cent completely agreed when the husbands were professionals or executives, only 14 per cent when they were manual laborers (Poti et al., 1962). Or, as another example, the age that adult Ceylonese gave in a first visit was "often" inconsistent with that declared in a second visit (Kinch, 1962; cf. Choldin et al., 1967 on Pakistan). In a survey in Tanganyika the age given to a doctor and that computed by a sociologist were the same in only 35 per cent of the cases (Richards and Reining, 1954).

Even if data are completely reliable, this affords no guarantee concern-ing their **validity,** or their agreement with objective reality. For example, in the Calcutta study both husbands and wives often stated that an acci-dental pregnancy had actually been planned. "Errors of these types are systematic in nature and extremely difficult to eliminate, no matter what efforts the interviewers make" (Poti *et al.*, 1962). It is often insignificant or peripheral questions that are easiest to validate. "The most important misstatements were with respect to the number of children, as was expected" (Richards and Reining, 1954).

An early study, which WHO organized at the request of the Indian government, was conducted by Dr. Abraham Stone, for many years the national director of the Planned Parenthood Association in the United States. He was restricted to investigating the feasibility of using the rhythm method, the only one, in the opinion of the Indian Minister of Health at that time, that would not come into conflict with India's "traditions, culture, or mores." [12] About three-quarters of the couples interviewed wanted information on how to control conception, but of these only 4 per cent were still using rhythm at the end of the observation period of almost two years. The method was therefore declared to be "scarcely favorable" (C. P. Blacker, 1955), yet this enormous gap between the proportion that express initial interest and the very much smaller proportion that effectively practice contraception does not depend on the method advocated. "It is somewhat depressing, but not exactly surprising, to find that though 92 per cent of the women [surveyed in Madras] were definitely desirous of limiting their families, only 4 per cent did anything about it" (Gopalaswami, 1962). Of a rural sample in India (Ramanagran), three out of four expressed interest in learning a method of controlling births but only 14 per cent of these actually learned it (Mauldin, 1965).

In spite of their lacks, what information can be gained from fertility surveys? In the mid-1960s they were completed or in process in a remarkably large number of both advanced and underdeveloped countries in addition to the United States (*ibid*):

[12] The difficulties of teaching the rhythm method to an illiterate population posed special problems, which Dr. Stone overcame with great ingenuity. "I constructed a special necklace containing twenty-eight beads, one bead for each day of an average cycle. There are orange beads to indicate the days of the menstrual flow, green beads to indicate the days of the cycle which are safe from conception, and red beads for the fertile days. The beads could be strung for the individual woman on the basis of the duration of her cycles by the physician or health worker, and the woman could then be instructed to move one bead daily from one side of the string to the other, beginning with the first day of her menstrual flow. During the time that the green beads appear, she will be in her safe period; but when the red ones come around, sexual relations should be avoided" (Stone, 1953).

"No one anticipated how many snags there were going to be in translating this apparently simple device into effective action. After a week the women came to the clinic with the complaint that they could not distinguish the color of the beads in the middle of the night. An improvement was effected in retaining the color but changing the shape of the beads into round and square ones: round red beads were unsafe, square green beads were safe. . . . Some women simply forgot to push the beads. Some decided not to wear the necklaces because they didn't want the whole village to know that they were practicing family planning. And some mistook the beads for charmed amulets distributed through the courtesy of the Government of India. They thought it was enough to simply push the beads to space or limit their families" (Chandrasekhar, 1967a).

| EAST ASIA | AFRICA AND MIDDLE EAST | EUROPE | LATIN AMERICA |
|---|---|---|---|
| Ceylon | Egypt | Czechoslovakia | Argentina |
| India | Ghana | Greece | Brazil |
| Indonesia | Israel | Hungary | Chile |
| Japan | Lebanon | Italy | Colombia |
| Korea | Tunisia | United Kingdom | Costa Rica |
| Pakistan | Turkey | | Jamaica |
| Taiwan | | | Mexico |
| | | | Panama |
| | | | Peru |
| | | | Puerto Rico |
| | | | Venezuela |

Most of these studies were technically inferior to the few administered with full attention to methodological difficulties, and it is likely that their biases are consistently on the optimistic side, reflecting the patent wishes of the researchers that fertility would soon decline. But even if we accept the data at face value, polls on the ideal size of family give little basis for optimism. According to most of the surveys in India, the mass of the people want an average of close to four children. In Santiago de Chile and in Taiwan, in underdeveloped countries generally, more than half of the respondents held four *or more* children to be ideal. Only in Jamaica and Puerto Rico are smaller families becoming the ideal (Blake, 1965; Mauldin, 1965).

The assumption is made that high birth rates in developing countries are today primarily a result of unwanted births. . . . In fact, because the family size desired [is] so substantial in these countries, primary reliance on inhibiting the births in excess of these desires may have little effect on birth rates under conditions of relatively high mortality, and no effect on present population growth rates if mortality declines (Blake, 1965).

## The Fertility of Underdeveloped Areas

The analysis of quantitative data so far in this chapter has been based on the results of surveys, typically undertaken in order to achieve a better understanding of the reasons for the generally high fertility and thus of means by which it can be controlled. But how high really is the fertility, and what has its trend been over the past several decades? Paradoxically, these are questions on which the data in many cases are so inadequate that some analysts have preferred to shift from the "hard" empirical fact of a birth to the relatively "soft" one of an attitude concerning it. Yet the more important datum, both in itself and as a check on the validity of opinion polls, pertains to family size, its present level and its probable trend in the countries seeking to establish an industrial base for their economies.

## QUALITY OF THE DATA

The statistical data of underdeveloped nations are generally scanty and of poor quality, but also steadily improving. When we try to assess any of the social transformations these countries are undergoing, we must keep in mind that our measuring rods are in all probability changing as rapidly as anything else in the society. Some types of statistics are today fairly satisfactory for some countries, but in almost every case this level of accuracy is too recent to permit equally firm comparisons with those of even several decades earlier.

The best past data were collected in a number of European colonies, and we can take British India as an example of an underdeveloped country with an exceptionally good statistical record. The directors of the nineteenth-century censuses included great scholars of Indian civilization—historians, anthropologists, and linguists as well as, later, statisticians. From 1870 on, the censuses they supervised represent "the most fruitful single source of information about the country, . . . an accomplishment of which India may be justly proud" (Davis, 1951, p. 5). This judgment should not be interpreted to mean, however, that the censuses were accurate by modern Western standards. For example, when the population count of British India in 1871 was corrected for underenumeration and areas not included, the number was raised from 203.4 to 236 million, and by Davis's estimate the actual population was 255.2 million (ibid., pp. 26–27). Similar though smaller corrections must be made for each of the subsequent counts at least through that for 1901. These figures of gross population are, of course, only the most basic demographic data, and breakdowns by any classification are typically less rather than more accurate.

A uniform system of vital statistics was established in British India in 1864, but a reasonable level of completeness was never achieved. For the first four decades of the twentieth century, the underregistration of births and deaths certainly exceeded 30 per cent at all times and was probably nearer to half (ibid., pp. 34, 67). In independent India, the roughly half-million village headmen are required by law to register vital events, and the record is still very poor (Chandrasekhar, 1960).

A more general appreciation of the population statistics of underdeveloped areas in the recent past can be had by browsing through the *Demographic Survey of the British Colonial Empire*, to which Kuczynski devoted the last ten years of his life.[13] It is hardly possible to summarize this massive

[13] Robert R. Kuczynski, *Demographic Survey of the British Colonial Empire*, Vol. 1: *West Africa;* Vol. 2: *South Africa High Commission Territories, East Africa, Mauritius and Seychelles;* Vol. 3: *West Indian and American Territories,* Oxford University Press,

work except to say that no generalization is valid, not even the obvious one that all the statistics analyzed in it are poor. British colonial officers were long required to give basic demographic information in their regular reports, and when they lacked statistics, they furnished the results of their limited observations and general impressions. Thus,

> Thousands of reports . . . submit as facts what are actually reasoned guesses. [The demographer] finds over and over again a consensus of opinion without any real evidence to support this opinion. . . . A considerable portion of this Survey had, therefore, to be devoted to reinterpretation of the statistical data. . . . [But] to appraise fertility, morbidity, mortality, or migration is about as difficult in most African Dependencies as to appraise the frequency of adultery in [Great Britain].[14]

Kuczynski rigorously judges "censuses," "counts," poll-tax estimates, and vital statistics, and the authority with which he dismisses many of them makes this work much livelier reading than its subject matter would suggest.

At least in quantity, and generally also in quality, the period since 1945 has seen a considerable improvement in the demographic statistics collected in underdeveloped areas. As early as the decade centering on 1950 about four-fifths of the world's population was enumerated in some kind of census, a larger proportion than had ever been counted previously. The United Nations has been pushing for an expansion of this program, as well as for an improvement in the accuracy of the data collected.[15] The statistics available are published annually by the United Nations in its *Demographic Yearbook*, a uniquely valuable compilation. Laymen must learn to use it with care, however, and to pay very close attention to the comments on the estimated adequacy of the data. In general, statistics are printed as they are received from the various national governments and coded as "C," meaning that the coverage was judged to be reasonably complete; "U," meaning that this was not so; or ". . . .," meaning that no judgment was possible. The alternative procedure, to apply different correction factors to various sets of data, would require not only detailed knowledge of each country's statistical procedures, but also the willingness to offer affront in assessing the degree to which official figures are probably incorrect. By their very nature, the anonymous teams working for international agencies do not qualify on either count.

How divergent some of the census data are from presumed reality is

---

New York, 1948–53. When he died in 1947, he had completed the first two volumes, as well as drafts of two more; the third, edited by his daughter, has since appeared. *Cf.* Robert Blanc and Gérard Théodore, "Les populations d'Afrique noire et de Madagascar," *Population*, 15 (1960), 407–432.

14 Kuczynski, *op. cit.*, 1, v–vi.

15 United Nations, Statistical Office, *Principles and Recommendations for National Population Censuses*, Statistical Papers, Series M, No. 27, New York, 1958.

suggested by a review of the recent counts in Latin America. When under-enumeration is estimated to be high, the total figures were increased by 4.6 per cent (Chile, 1952), 7.5 per cent (Peru, 1940), 8.4 per cent (Bolivia, 1950), or even 10 per cent (Honduras, 1950). Sometimes such augmentations are "due to fraudulent adulterations" (Guatemala, 1940). "In some cases, local census officials with misconceived motives of prestige, introduce fantastic additions; . . . in other cases, census takers, paid proportionally by the number of persons enumerated, add nonexistent individuals or households." The accuracy of data on subpopulations is especially doubtful. In Brazil in 1950, for instance, an estimated half million women aged thirty to sixty-nine declared their ages as fifteen to twenty-nine (Mortara, 1964).

Because censuses are carried out in one concentrated effort of the central government, their results are generally better than registration data, which depend on a nationwide administrative system that operates continuously. As of the early 1960s birth registrations were reasonably accurate and complete in only twenty-three underdeveloped countries, plus the Colored and Asian populations of the Union of South Africa:

| EAST AND CENTRAL ASIA | AFRICA AND MIDDLE EAST | LATIN AMERICA | |
|---|---|---|---|
| Ceylon | Mauritius | Argentina | Martinique |
| Malaya | Tunisia | British Guiana | Mexico |
| Réunion | Union of South Africa | Chile | Panama |
| Ryukyu Islands | Colored | Costa Rica | Puerto Rico |
| Singapore | Asian | El Salvador | Surinam |
| Taiwan | | Guadeloupe | Trinidad and Tobago |
| | | Guatemala | Venezuela |
| | | Jamaica | |

Even among these twenty-five populations, few had adequate registration systems as recently as 1945, so that a direct establishment of trends is usually impossible. As can be seen from the list, these populations are hardly representative of underdeveloped countries.[16] "The achievement of adequate birth registration may in fact be viewed as an indicator of a country's modernization" (Ridley, 1965; cf. Gaete-Darbó, 1964).

Also in the past history of many Western countries, census data were of acceptable quality long before the registration system became adequate. One adjustment to this situation was to substitute the child-woman ratio for other measures of fertility (see pp. 258–259). For lack of anything better,

[16] Note, too, the large overlap with the underdeveloped countries in which survey data have been collected (p. 592). With the notable exceptions of India and, more recently, several countries of South America, most of the demographic polls have been taken in countries with the best conventional population statistics.

this is still used in analyzing the natality of underdeveloped countries, but it is an especially defective index for temporal or cross-cultural analyses. (1) The age data on which the ratios are based are quite poor, and the errors are greater in the number of children than of women. This constitutes a hindrance to comparative analysis especially when the censuses of some countries, or of some sectors of populations, are improving much faster than others. (2) The undercount of children, as we have noted from an African survey, may vary greatly. (3) Wherever infant mortality used to be high and has since fallen dramatically, the relative level of the child-woman ratio rose very fast. In such instances there has been an increase in what could be termed effective fertility but not necessarily in the number of births.

With a statistical base that is often so insecure, the reader may ask, how is it possible to discuss in detail and with assurance the population trends of underdeveloped areas? If any data exist at all, even if quite faulty, a demographer can often derive better estimates with various techniques. At the most elementary level, these are the ones already discussed under the heading, "Correction of Errors," in Chapter 2. For example, when the results of a 1953–54 sample census in the Indian state of Uttar Pradesh were compared with the registration records, it was found that about 30 per cent of births had been omitted and an additional 20 per cent had been lost in the transmission of the records to the central office for compilation (Gupta, 1958). Census data can be used to estimate fertility not only with the child-woman ratio but also by calculating back from the number of survivors at specified ages, given certain assumptions about mortality, to the fertility rates that must have obtained (Table 16-2). In this example,

Table 16-2. Index Numbers (Crude Birth Rate of 40 = 100) of Birth Rates as Estimated from Various Data, India, 1891–1951

| CENSUS YEAR | OFFICIAL REGISTRATION STATISTICS | REVERSE-SURVIVAL CALCULATED FROM COHORTS AGED | |
|---|---|---|---|
| | | 0–4 | 0–9 |
| 1891 | — | 111 | 122 |
| 1901 | 87 | 98 | 115 |
| 1911 | 94 | 108 | 120 |
| 1921 | 92 | 100 | 123 |
| 1931 | 83 | 112 | 116 |
| 1941 | 85 | 97 | 113 |
| 1951 | 68 | 90 | 98 |

SOURCE: Ajit Das Gupta, "Determination of Fertility Level and Trend in Defective Registration Areas," *Bulletin de l'Institut International de Statistique*, 36 (1958), 127–136.

however, not only are the two sets of data calculated from the census significantly different but even their trends are not the same over the six decades. A periodic National Sample Survey, which the federal Indian government has made about twice a year since 1950–51, indicated a birth rate of 34 in the mid-1950s, or still about 20 per cent under the estimated correct level. Indeed, this was a considerable improvement over figures derived from registration or censuses, but the level of accuracy was hardly satisfactory (*cf.* Sabagh and Scott, 1967; Romaniuk, 1967).

Incomplete and inaccurate data can be rounded out also by checking the consistency among fertility, mortality, natural increase (if migration is a significant factor), and a stable population structure—or the one, it will be recalled, that would result from the prolonged continuation of unchanged age-specific birth and death rates (Rele, 1967). Recorded gross reproduction rates have ranged between 0.80 (Austria, 1933) and 4.17 (Cocos-Keeling Islands, 1928–32). Mortality as measured by the expectation of life at birth has ranged from about 20 (in areas before accurate records were taken) to above 70 (in various advanced countries; *cf.* Table 15-8, p. 568). These two schedules, thus, designate the possible combinations of fertility and mortality, and each pair is associated with a particular stable population structure. The relation is illustrated with the proportions of young and aged females in Table 16-3. The approximate nature of a rule of thumb used by some demographers, that in underdeveloped countries the sector aged 0–14 constitutes 40 per cent of the total (e.g., Naraghi, 1960, pp. 101–107), is suggested in this table.

The postulate in the stable-population model that age-specific birth rates remain unchanged approximates the actual situation in many underdeveloped areas, while that pertaining to fixed age-specific death rates, of course, does not. A quasi-stable model, or the age structure that would result from unchanging age-specific birth rates and age-specific death rates falling in a specified pattern, can also be a useful tool (Rele, 1967; Coale, 1963; Demeny, 1965).

### THE TREND IN FERTILITY

By making use of this interrelation among fertility, mortality, and population structure, Collver (1965) has calculated crude birth rates for twenty **Latin American** countries as far back as the incomplete and inaccurate data permit. At the earliest date (Chile in 1850–54) the estimated crude birth rate was 46.6, and in no country except Uruguay did it fall below 40 until after World War I. For the most recent period it is useful to compare Collver's estimates with those of the United Nations (Table 16-4). Apart from the most advanced countries (Uruguay, Argentina, Chile, and Cuba), all had birth rates of 40 or over. More disturbingly, over this decade Collver's figures generally show a slight *upward* trend, which the more approxi-

Table 16-3. Parameters of a Stable Female Population with Various Expectations of Life at Birth and Gross Reproduction Rates

| EXPECTATION OF LIFE AT BIRTH, YEARS | GROSS REPRODUCTION RATE | | | | | | |
|---|---|---|---|---|---|---|---|
| | 0.80 | 1.00 | 1.50 | 2.00 | 2.50 | 3.00 | 4.00 |
| | PROPORTION AT AGES 0–14 | | | | | | |
| 20 | 0.099 | 0.129 | 0.198 | 0.257 | 0.308 | 0.351 | 0.420 |
| 30 | 0.117 | 0.152 | 0.230 | 0.294 | 0.348 | 0.393 | 0.464 |
| 40 | 0.129 | 0.167 | 0.251 | 0.319 | 0.374 | 0.420 | 0.491 |
| 50 | 0.138 | 0.178 | 0.266 | 0.336 | 0.393 | 0.439 | 0.510 |
| 60 | 0.144 | 0.186 | 0.277 | 0.349 | 0.407 | 0.453 | 0.524 |
| 70 | 0.148 | 0.192 | 0.286 | 0.359 | 0.417 | 0.464 | 0.534 |
| | PROPORTION AT AGES 65 AND OVER | | | | | | |
| 20 | 0.168 | 0.135 | 0.086 | 0.059 | 0.042 | 0.032 | 0.020 |
| 30 | 0.180 | 0.143 | 0.088 | 0.058 | 0.041 | 0.031 | 0.018 |
| 40 | 0.189 | 0.149 | 0.090 | 0.059 | 0.041 | 0.030 | 0.018 |
| 50 | 0.198 | 0.155 | 0.091 | 0.059 | 0.041 | 0.030 | 0.017 |
| 60 | 0.206 | 0.160 | 0.093 | 0.060 | 0.041 | 0.029 | 0.017 |
| 70 | 0.215 | 0.166 | 0.096 | 0.061 | 0.042 | 0.030 | 0.017 |

SOURCE: Ansley J. Coale, "Birth Rates, Death Rates, and Rates of Growth in Human Population," in *Public Health and Population Change*, edited by Mindel C. Sheps and Jeanne Clare Ridley, University of Pittsburgh Press, Pittsburgh, 1965, pp. 242–265.

mate UN estimates confirm in a few cases (Costa Rica, Venezuela). To speak of a sustained high fertility would seem to be overoptimistic for most of Latin America.

Apart from Egypt, **Arab countries** have few reliable data on fertility, and births in Egypt are underregistered in those rural areas lacking health bureaus. The crude birth rate corrected for this deficiency, which fluctuated just under 50 in 1934–41, fell to 44.8 in 1959. The uncorrected rate of 42.6 in 1959 compares with an average uncorrected figure of 42.8 in 1960–64 and 41.6 in 1965 (El-Badry, 1965). Jordan's "birth registration is officially recognized to be deficient and to vary in extent from one year to the next." Palestinian refugees, who constitute a sizable portion of the population, have maintained a birth rate of 50 in other countries, where more accurate records are kept. According to the 1961 census of Jordan's Maan District, the completed family size of ever-married women was 7.8 children (*ibid.*). The Syrian birth rates published in the United Nations *Demo-*

Table 16-4. Crude Birth Rates in Latin America According to Two Estimates, 1945–60

| | COLLVER 1945–49 | ECLA 1945–50 | COLLVER 1955–59 | ECLA 1955–60 |
|---|---|---|---|---|
| **Middle America** | | | | |
| Mexico | 44.5 | 44–48 | 45.8 | 44–47 |
| Guatemala | 49.1 | 48–52 | 49.0 | 48–52 |
| Honduras | 44.5 | 45–50 | 46.0 | 45–50 |
| El Salvador | 44.8 | 44–48 | 47.9 | 44–48 |
| Nicaragua | | 45–52 | — | 45–52 |
| Costa Rica | 42.7 | 44–48 | 45.3 | 45–50 |
| Panama | 38.3 | 38–42 | 40.5 | 39–42 |
| **Caribbean** | | | | |
| Cuba | 30.0 | 32–36 | — | 30–34 |
| Haiti | — | 42–50 | — | 42–50 |
| Dominican Republic | — | 48–54 | — | 48–54 |
| **Tropical South America** | | | | |
| Colombia | 43.4 | 44–47 | 45.1 | 43–46 |
| Venezuela | 43.6 | 44–48 | 44.3 | 45–50 |
| Ecuador | 45.9 | 45–50 | 46.5 | 45–50 |
| Peru | 44.9 | 42–48 | 46.2 | 42–48 |
| Brazil | — | 43–47 | — | 43–47 |
| Bolivia | 47.0 | 41–45 | — | 41–45 |
| **Temperate South America** | | | | |
| Paraguay | — | 45–50 | — | 45–50 |
| Argentina | 25.2 | 25–26 | 24.1 | 23–24 |
| Chile | 37.0 | 34–37 | 37.6 | 35–38 |
| Uruguay | — | 20–23 | — | 19–22 |

SOURCES: O. Andrew Collver, *Birth Rates in Latin America: New Estimates of Historical Trends and Fluctuations,* Institute of International Studies, University of California, Berkeley, Calif., 1965; United Nations, Economic Commission for Latin America, *Boletín Económico de América Latina,* Vol. 7 (1962), Table 4.

*graphic Yearbook,* ranging around 25 in the 1950s, are based on perhaps half the actual number of births. The annual population increase of 3.5 per cent estimated for the 1950s may be under the actual rate, for instead of the shortage of land typical of the Middle East, "there exist vast fertile areas in the Northeast which have adequate water supply and which are still inadequately exploited" (*ibid.*). Between 1951 and 1960, Lebanon's reported birth rate fluctuated erratically between 24 and 41, presumably reflecting temporary improvements in registration (*ibid.*). According to a sample survey, completed family size in Lebanon ranged from 8.09 children among Shiite Moslems down to 6.56 among Maronite and other Catholics; and for those still in their reproductive years the total fertility rate per woman ranged from 7.65 among Shiites to 4.08 among Orthodox Christians (Yaukey, 1961, p. 29).

In **Tropical Africa** crude birth rates as calculated in particular studies have generally ranged upward from about 40 to well above 50 (T. E. Smith, 1963). According to an attempt to estimate fertility from all of the population data available (some twenty-four censuses or surveys since 1950), "the birth rate for all of the populations analyzed combined is about 49 per 1,000 and [the completed family size] is probably about 6.5 children." [17] While the fertility of westernized sectors of African populations is lower, the relative size of these subpopulations is too small to affect national rates (e.g., Caldwell, 1967). Low natality is sometimes due to venereal disease; for example, a survey in the former Belgian Congo in 1956–57 found that the areas with birth rates under 40 had the highest rates of syphilis, and in these localities some 20 to 30 per cent of the women of 45 years and over had borne no children (T. E. Smith, 1963). According to another study made in the 1950s, however, the relatively low fertility in one area of northeast Tanganyika had resulted from the breakdown of tribal controls on marriage patterns, with a consequent high proportion of unmarried adults and particularly women (Roberts and Tanner, 1959). The fertility of the settled population of Sudan has been rising from very high levels (Henin, 1968).

In terms of sheer numbers, the enormous populations of **Asia** are more significant than the generally much smaller ones noted thus far. Communist China, the most populous nation of the world, is discussed in the following chapter. In the mid-1960s, the other three giants' estimated populations and annual rates of growth were as follows:

|  | *Millions* | *Per Cent* |
| --- | --- | --- |
| India | 472 | 2.3 |
| Pakistan | 101 | 2.1 |
| Indonesia | 100 | 2.3 |

[17] "A ridge of high fertility in East Africa extends from southeastern Sudan through parts of Uganda and Kenya, through Rwanda and Burundi and parts of Tanzania, and through the southern and eastern provinces of the Congo into Zambia, Southern Rhodesia, and the southern province of Mozambique. The provinces in this strip show a [completed family size] of 6.5 or higher. . . . The lowest fertility in Tropical Africa is in a region extending, apparently, from the West Coast in Gabon through north central and northwestern provinces of the Congo into the Southwestern region of the Sudan . . . [and with a gap for which no estimate is available] the northern part of Cameroon. . . . Another strip of exceptionally high fertility is found . . . in West Africa from coastal Nigeria to the Ivory Coast, with a branch extending up through the western part of Nigeria into parts of Niger and Upper Volta" (Coale, 1966).

At the present rate of growth, during each five-year period India, for instance, must accommodate an *additional* number about equal to Great Britain's population or almost three times that of California.

India's birth rate fell during this century from close to 50 to around 40, as shown in Table 16-5 (but see also Table 16-2). The estimates cited from

Table 16-5. Crude Birth Rates, According to Registration Figures and Two Revised Estimates, India, 1881–1960

|  | REGISTERED | SOM, 1961 | INDIA, DEPT. OF STATISTICS, 1963 |
|---|---|---|---|
| 1881–90 | — | 48.9 | — |
| 1891–1900 | 34 | 45.8 | — |
| 1901–10 | 37 | 48.1 | 52.4 |
| 1911–20 | 37 | 49.2 | 48.1 |
| 1921–30 | 34.6 | 46.4 | 46.4 |
| 1931–40 | 34.2 | 45.2 | 45.2 |
| 1941–50 | 27.3 | 39.9 | 43.0 |
| 1951–60 | 29.8 | — | 40.0 |

SOURCES: R. K. Som *et al.*, *Preliminary Estimates of Birth and Death Rates and of the Rate of Growth of Population*, National Sample Survey, No. 48, Government of India, Delhi, 1961; S. Chandrasekhar, "India's Population: Fact, Problem, and Policy," in *Asia's Population Problems*, edited by Chandrasekhar, Allen & Unwin, London, 1967, pp. 72–99.

the government's Department of Statistics, which show a somewhat steeper and more consistent decline, may be the better of the two series; they were calculated on the basis of a quasi-stable population model except for the 1911–20 figure, which was based on the reverse-survival method. However, by either of the estimates there has been little or no decline from 1960 on; the estimated rate for the mid-1960s was still around 40. It was in this most recent period that the government's program to institute family planning might have begun to show nationwide results.

Pakistan's demographic statistics are poor even compared with those of other major underdeveloped countries.

Vital statistics in Pakistan are extremely meager and highly understated. In urban areas they are maintained by the extremely uninterested municipal authority; in rural areas they depend on reports made by illiterate and uninterested *chawkidars* (village watchmen) who, having as a rule to travel on foot considerable distances to make their reports, are inclined to neglect a very troublesome duty even today (Ahmed, 1966).

Pakistan's birth rate as estimated from a stable-population model was 60.3 in 1951 (62.2 among Moslems, 50.7 among non-Moslems), or close to the

Wheat from the United States is sucked through a pipe from a ship's hold into a Bombay warehouse. Workers are weighing and packing it (*Wide World Photos*).

highest ever observed anywhere in the world. If a family-planning program did not take effect quickly, it was anticipated that fertility would remain constant or even undergo a short-term increase "because of the peculiar responses of reproduction to changes in various socio-economic factors" (*ibid.*). Between 1951 and 1961 the population increased by an estimated 2.16 per cent per year, since the latter date by 2.6 to 2.8 per cent or more (Querishi, 1967).

The estimated birth rate of Indonesia, 43 in the early 1960s, was about the same as in the 1930s. In the interim, with World War II and the Japanese occupation, the rate may have been as low as 20 (or if much higher, then negated by an increase in infant mortality). The consequent strange population structure in 1961 will greatly affect the proportion of new parents in the years to come:

| Aged | | |
|---|---|---|
| 0–9 | 33.6 per cent |
| 10–19 | 16.5 |
| 20–34 | 24.6 |
| 35–44 | 11.5 |
| 45 and over | 13.8 |

"There are no signs yet as to probable changes in the future course of the over-all level of fertility" (Hawkins, 1967).

In summary, the birth rate of the major underdeveloped areas of the world, to the degree that imprecise data can tell us, is 40 or above. Where it is possible to indicate a trend, sometimes there has been a probable decline (India), sometimes a probable rise (most of Latin America).

### DIFFERENTIAL ANALYSIS

A decline in family size, should it come about, would of course not take place evenly throughout any society. As earlier in the West, so also in underdeveloped countries today, the inducements to control fertility vary according to one's place in the particular social structure. The best indication of probable future trends, therefore, could be derived from a differential analysis, though of course in areas where even the over-all fertility is known only approximately, that of sectors of the population must be estimated very cautiously.

In the history of the West cities constituted the main driving wedge of the new social order, but the role of cities in underdeveloped areas, as we have seen, is more complex (see pp. 460–466). Thus, some evidence suggests that cities in underdeveloped areas, like their earlier Western counterparts, are leading the population toward a smaller family. According to one analysis, in Latin America as of 1950 "the lower the general rate of reproduction in a country, the greater the rural-urban differentiation" (T. Lynn Smith, 1958). With urbanization proceeding apace, this conclusion implies a certain optimism: "as the urban population becomes a more significant proportion of the total population, national birth rates are likely to fall, perhaps sharply" (ibid.). It is now manifest that this conclusion does not apply to all countries undergoing development. In his analysis of pre-independence Indian data, Davis found a sizable gap between cities and countryside, but he did not feel that this indicated a future decline in fertility. "The rural-urban differentials are certainly present, and are correlated with size of city, but they have not increased in fifty years" (Davis, 1951, p. 81). This distinction between rural and urban natality, according to a number of more detailed studies of local areas, has since disappeared (Table 16-6). In Egypt, as a third example, the estimated levels of fertility in the cities and countryside are substantially the same after the differential underregistration has been taken into account. Urban mortality, on the other hand, is much lower: the installation of a sewerage system in Cairo during World War I resulted in an almost immediate decline in the city's death rate by five units, and between 1945 and 1947 Cairo's death rate fell again from about 33 to about 25. With fertility equal to that in rural areas and a substantially lower mortality (estimated in the mid-1950s to be 16 per thousand as against 22–24), Egypt's cities are now growing largely by their natural increase, contrary to the conventional doctrine that in-

Table 16-6. Completed Family Size by Rural-Urban Residence, India, c. 1951

|  | CHILDREN EVER BORN TO MARRIED WOMEN AGED 45 AND OVER | |
| --- | --- | --- |
|  | RURAL | URBAN |
| Travancore-Cochin | 6.6 | 6.4 |
| Madhya-Pradesh | | |
| Eastern | 6.1 | 6.3 |
| Other | 6.6 | 6.4 |
| Mysore State | 5.8 | 5.9 |

SOURCES: Various, as compiled in Ansley J. Coale and Edgar M. Hoover, *Population Growth and Economic Development in Low-Income Countries: A Case Study of India's Prospects,* Princeton University Press, Princeton, N.J., 1958, pp. 47–48.

migration is always the main source of urban growth (Abu-Lughod, 1964).

In short, the lower urban fertility that has been routine in the West is only one of several patterns in underdeveloped areas. "Instead of uniformity, there is a spectrum" (Robinson, 1963). For various dates from 1950 to 1960, the child-woman ratios of urban populations ranged from barely more than half the rural up to two-thirds larger than the rural (Table 16-7).

The first question that these figures pose is whether the relation is spurious. Not only is the child-woman ratio a deceptive measure for cross-

Table 16-7. Urban Child-Woman Ratios as a Percentage of Rural, Selected Underdeveloped Countries, 1950–60

| | | | |
| --- | --- | --- | --- |
| Nigeria | 165.4 | Sudan | 88.7 |
| British North Borneo | 121.9 | Libya | 85.7 |
| Burma | 107.0 | Ceylon | 81.7 |
| Algeria | 105.8 | Union of South Africa, | |
| Malaya | 105.5 | "Natives" | 69.3 |
| Pakistan | 97.8 | Morocco | 64.2 |
| Nepal | 96.1 | Chile | 63.6 |
| India | 96.0 | Jamaica | 58.8 |
| Iran | 91.0 | Brazil | 55.3 |
| Mauritius | 90.3 | Cuba | 51.4 |

SOURCE: Warren C. Robinson, "Urbanization and Fertility: The Non-Western Experience," *Milbank Memorial Fund Quarterly,* 41 (1963), 291–308:

cultural analysis, as we have noted, but any international comparison can be thrown off by the fact that the rural-urban distinction is not based on uniform criteria. In Mexico, for instance, data are collected according to *municipios* (essentially equivalent to townships), and an analysis of differential fertility has to be based on an elaborate manipulation of the census figures (Burnight *et al.*, 1956). In some cases, however, the lack of a rural-urban difference in fertility cannot be explained as merely an artifact of the data.

In the main, urban-rural differentials derive not from the direct effect of the urban or rural physical environments but from the fact that social influences on family size are associated with the size of the community, at least in the West. But a society in transition has two overlapping class structures, one more or less equivalent to that in Western societies and the other vestigial from the earlier hierarchy of social classes. In the former structure we should anticipate an inverse correlation between an index of social class and fertility, in the latter case possibly a positive one. Moreover, in plural societies the class structure and the hierarchy of ethnic minorities often overlap, so that it may be difficult to distinguish the social from the cultural differences in fertility determinants (*cf.* J. G. C. Blacker, 1959).

1. The simplest situation to understand, obviously, is the one closest to the pattern that one would anticipate from Western antecedents. Thus, judging from studies in Santiago de Chile, Rio de Janeiro, and Lima, the cities of Latin America show the standard progression of family size inversely correlated with social class (Miró, 1964). However, if the small-family sector is a westernized elite, in most underdeveloped countries it will constitute a very small segment of the whole population. In one Indian study, for instance, C. Chandrasekaran found that completed family size ranged from more than six children for women with no more than primary schooling, to five for women with high school, down to two for women with a college education, but the number of women with more than primary schooling was too tiny to have a measurable effect on national rates (cited in Coale and Hoover, 1958, p. 48).

2. For some of the in-migrants to cities, the geographical move is not associated with one toward the social situation that induces smaller families. According to a study in Brazil, migrants to cities who advanced in social class underwent the expected fall in fertility. But nearly a quarter of the in-migrants who had been born into a nonmanual status moved down to lower positions, and among this sample the mean family size increased by 8 per cent from one generation to the next (Hutchinson, 1961).

3. Some of the variations both over time and between cities, thus, depend on the degree to which "urban" populations consist in fact of recent in-migrants who have not yet been able either to absorb the city's cultural

norms or take advantage of its broader opportunities for social advancement. The changes in India between 1921 and 1951 "probably tended to favor modest increases in the urban fertility ratios," for Indian cities are "clusters of villages full of recent migrants from the rural areas, quite unlike the stable cities of a few decades ago" (Robinson, 1961). Since rural-urban migration in India has been predominantly of males who leave wives and children in their home villages, elsewhere the effect of migration on the fertility potential could be greater than this cautious conclusion suggests. For example, the urban populations of Africa are said to differ according to whether they are "country-rooted" or "town-rooted" (Mayer, 1961). And the sizable migration to the world's shantytowns, so far as data exist, seems not to be strongly selective by sex (cf. pp. 468–472).

One of the best studies illuminating this relation between in-migration and fertility is a survey of a large sample of adult males in Monterrey, Mexico (Zarate, 1967a).[18] The Monterrey metropolitan area, with a population in 1965 of just under one million, is an important center of heavy industry; in 1960, 43 per cent of the economically active males were employed in manufacturing. In this urban-industrial center, however, the mean number of live births to the wives of men aged 51 to 60 was 6.03, about one child more than the highest completed family size in other Latin American studies. An inverse correlation was found between fertility and education, occupational level, or income. The most interesting datum is that the mean number of live births was also significantly related to the size of the respondent's birthplace, obtained from the census closest to his date of birth, as shown in Table 16-8 (cf. Zarate, 1967b).

4. The most complex pattern is to be found in a country where the correlation between social class and family size is both positive (among the traditionalist sector) and negative (among the modernist one). In either sector higher status is marked by some of the same indices (wealth, education, etc.), and many inhabitants of a society in transition are not so much in *either* sector as partially in *both;* thus, one should not expect clear indications of class differentials. Several studies of fertility in Egypt suggest such a dual pattern. Urban fertility was negatively correlated with education, one index of social class, but in the countryside women of the lowest class, as designated by either their own education or that of their husbands, had fewer children than the barely literate (Table 16-9). In each of three villages that Rizk analyzed, there was the same positive correlation of fertility and class as indicated by occupational status (cf. also A. M. Zikry, cited in Roberts, 1967):

---

[18] That males rather than females were interviewed constitutes an interesting departure from the conventions of fertility research. One of the most careful checks on survey results reached the conclusion that "the reports of husbands are more dependable than those of the wives" (Poti et al., 1962).

Table 16-8. Fertility by Size of Birthplace Among a Sample of Ever-Married, Urban, Native Mexican Males, 1960s

| | NO. OF CASES | MEAN NUMBER OF LIVE BIRTHS | |
| SIZE OF BIRTHPLACE | | REPORTED | STANDARDIZED FOR AGE |
| --- | --- | --- | --- |
| Under 5,000 | 1,166 | 4.64 | 4.42 |
| 5,000–19,999 | 417 | 4.17 | 4.14 |
| 20,000–99,999 | 291 | 4.30 | 4.28 |
| 100,000 or more | 52 | 3.06 | 3.13 |
| Totals | | | |
| Born outside Monterrey | 1,926 | 4.44 | 4.31 |
| Born in Monterrey | 755 | 3.74 | 3.98 |

SOURCE: Alvan O. Zarate, "Differential Fertility in Monterrey, Mexico: Prelude to Transition?" *Milbank Memorial Fund Quarterly*, 45 (1967), 93–108.

Table 16-9. Average Number of Children per Married Woman, Standardized for Length of Marriage, by Years of Schooling and Urban-Rural Residence, Egypt, 1960

| SCHOOLING | URBAN GOVERNORATES | RURAL GOVERNORATES |
| --- | --- | --- |
| Wives | | |
| None | 4.51 | 4.13 |
| 1–2 years | 3.94 | 4.68 |
| 3 years | 3.68 | 4.42 |
| 4–5 years | 3.86 | 3.76 |
| 6+ years | 2.39 | — |
| Husbands | | |
| None | 4.45 | 4.31 |
| Elementary | 4.71 | 4.54 |
| Secondary | 3.95 | — |
| University | 2.78 | — |

SOURCE: Hanna Rizk, reported in M. A. El-Badry, "Trends in the Components of Population Growth in the Arab Countries of the Middle East: A Survey of Present Information," *Demography*, 2 (1965), 140–186.

Agriculturists      4.04 children
Unskilled laborers    4.18
Skilled laborers      4.47

El-Badry suggests that the association may be due to differential under-reporting or to the higher incidence of miscarriages among the lower-class women. It may also be, however, that the higher social levels of the rural sector (and in most underdeveloped countries, of course, this sector con-stitutes the greater portion of the population) use their greater wealth to realize the goal of a larger family. According to an earlier study of differ-ential reproduction by occupational level, thus, the highest fertility rates in Egypt were among those most imbued with traditional values (religious employees, teachers, and merchants, in that order) and the lowest among Western-type professionals, while those of agricultural and nonagricultural laborers fell in between (El-Badry, 1956).

### HAS FERTILITY INCREASED?

Demographers typically assume that social-economic development re-sults in a sizable decline in natality. The evidence for this is overwhelming if we compare the fertility levels of economically advanced and under-developed countries. In the long run, it is certainly true, modernization is associated with a smaller average family, but in this case Keynes's quip that in the long run we are all dead is almost too apt. The crucial question is what happens during the transitional stage, which in the best cases must be measured in decades. The dogma handed down in the transition theory is that fertility declines, and the data to challenge this are typically too poor to make an indisputable case. All of the indices are approximate; the proportion of births measured by any index generally increases with suc-cessful modernization, and any upward movement that is accepted as valid may be merely a short-term fluctuation (e.g., Davis, 1964). In Taiwan, one of the few areas with reasonably accurate statistics over the whole period of early economic development, the birth rate rose from the low 40's to above 45 before it began to decline, and this was not a spurious trend based on improved registration (Petersen, 1967). Is Taiwan an anomaly in this respect; and, if not, what modernizing forces can result in a higher fertility?

**1.** Improved health leads to higher fecundity. Most strikingly, the efforts to bring venereal disease under control in Tropical Africa will reduce the widespread sterility that we have noted exists there and, *ceteris paribus,* will result in a sizable rise of the birth rate (A. Romaniuk, cited in Heer, 1966). Any improvement in health, as from antimalaria projects or improved nutrition (e.g., M. and R. G. Kamat, cited in Mauldin, 1965) is likely to stimulate greater reproduction; and this applies to the health of both sexes.

Of females in the fecund age group in one rural township of Taiwan, the percentage of widows fell by about half from 1905 to 1935. By the prolongation of *males'* life expectancy, thus, women's effective reproductive period was extended almost three years, and their completed family size by about one more child (Tuan, 1958).

2. Whatever means the traditional society used deliberately to reduce population growth may not survive modernization. In Japan of the late Tokugawa period, for instance, infanticide was practiced in all classes of the population in all regions of the country. While the practice persisted in a few backward communities, the official effort to prohibit it was almost completely successful within several decades after the institution of the new regime in 1867. The fertility of the Meiji period, according to a reconstruction from defective data, rose until the 1880s or 1890s, then remained at a high plateau until after the turn of the century; the child-woman ratio increased from 490 in 1888 and 497 in 1898 to 559 in 1913.[19]

3. If in the traditional society the usual age at marriage is well past puberty, the transition to an urban-industrial society may break down the social controls by which this pattern is maintained. The classic case is Western Europe, which almost alone among preindustrial civilizations had established a high average age at marriage as the general norm (see pp. 383–384). Elsewhere in the world other kinds of changes in marital patterns can also effect a rise in reproduction.

4. Village taboos and religious practices unintentionally inhibiting fertility may break down; "the loosening of bonds of tradition . . . can also lead to the abandonment of practices that kept Indian fertility rates from being even higher" (Coale and Hoover, 1958, p. 60). For example, among four social classes of rural India fertility was more or less equal for the first fifteen years of marriage, but the completed family size of upper-class Hindus was "substantially lower" because fewer were willing to tolerate the remarriage of widows (Rele, 1963). Similarly, the modernization of Moslem countries is likely to reduce the incidence of polygamy, and thus to increase the fertility per woman.

5. To the degree that traditional norms favoring a large family persist, moreover, an improved economy may push fertility upward. It has been known for many decades that marriage rates (and thus, after a certain lag, birth rates) fluctuate with good or poor harvests, the business cycle, or other indices of relative economic prosperity (see pp. 150, 344, and for other analyses also those cited in Heer, 1966). If efforts to improve the economy succeed, then, those who had refrained from marrying or, if married, from having children solely because of economic pressures may respond to their improved situation with a more numerous progeny.

[19] Irene B. Taeuber, *The Population of Japan,* Princeton University Press, Princeton, N.J., 1958, pp. 29, 52, 272. *Cf.* above, pp. 423–427.

In short,

The direct effect of economic development is to increase rather than decrease the level of fertility. If this hypothesis is true, the historical fact that fertility over the long run has declined in all present-day industrial societies as their income advanced must then be explained by an inverse association between fertility and other social factors which tend to be positively associated with income (Heer, 1966).

Among the most important of such factors are education, which opens up a wider range of possible living styles and thus affords both the incentive to reduce family size and the knowledge of how this can be done; lower infant and child mortality, which by increasing effective fertility reinforces all the pressures to reduce the number of children born; and social mobility, the mechanism by which society both offers potential parents other values in exchange for forgoing some reproduction and, as they move up the social ladder, changes the concept of suitable care so as to increase the cost per child (ibid.).

## Government Programs to Reduce Fertility

That the rapid population growth in underdeveloped areas is a serious block to modernization has become a commonplace. Apart from an occasional Catholic like Colin Clark, virtually all economists outside the Communist bloc now accept this truism.[20] It is not merely the issue of whether people or food will increase faster. Coale and Hoover's *Population Growth and Economic Development in Low-Income Countries* (1958), for example, goes well beyond the issue of subsistence. This interesting and important work attempts to give a specific answer to the question, how would India's over-all economic development have been affected if its birth rate, instead of remaining constant, had fallen by half during the next generation? The population of the country was projected from 1956 to 1986, assuming that the probable sharp fall in mortality will take place, together with one of three alternative hypothetical courses in fertility: (1) no change or (2) a decline by half between 1966 and 1981 or (3) between 1956 and 1981. The population of 357 million in 1951 will increase, depend-

[20] Almost any statement challenging the damage that population growth does to development programs is likely to depend on Colin Clark or Peter Bauer for its economic expertise. That "population is growing faster in Latin America than anywhere else in the world," and that rapid growth "shows the increase of the per capita gross product," should not, it is alleged by one group following the lead of these two economists, be used to argue for birth control. "Many valid arguments, not only economic but moral and religious ones, can be used against such a proposal" (Inter-American Council for Commerce and Production, *Economic Development of Latin America*, Committee for Economic Development, New York, 1966, pp. 44–46.

ing on the trend in the birth rate, to 775, 634, or 590 million in 1986, respectively, and the rate of continued growth in that year will be 2.6, 1.0, or 1.0 per cent per annum. Growth is cumulative; the failure to control fertility early will present the next generation with the same problem of population pressure in much aggravated form.

In a country like India economic development depends very largely on how much of the national income can be invested. A rapidly increasing population diverts income, instead, to current consumption of food, housing, education, and general "social overhead." Cutting the birth rate, the authors show, would raise total production, which would have to be divided, more-over, among a smaller number. The real income per consumer of the low-fertility population thus would be *at least* 38 per cent higher in 1986, and growing much faster than with the alternative projections. If a rise in real income is possible with a rapidly increasing population, that is to say, it would be substantially greater if births were controlled.

Economists can demonstrate that *if* population growth is not curtailed, economic development is hindered or, in the worst cases, blocked. But the influence operates also in the other direction. The principal lesson to be learned from the historical decline of family size in the West, which we have summarized in the Dumont-Banks model, indicates that the economy and thus the social structure must be flexible enough to motivate some, and then others, and finally virtually all to exercise self-control over procreation in exchange for improved chances to climb the social ladder. But if the economy is stagnant (in part because of rapid population growth), then for most this avenue to the small-family system is not available. The countries outside the Western core where the birth rate has fallen well below 40 are generally economically developed (Japan, Israel) or marginal to the category of "underdeveloped" (Argentina, Chile); those at an early stage of development afford no clear indication of what level of fertility should be expected in the "normal" course of change. Nor is an analysis of such a "natural" trend necessarily a good guide to the probable future.

In the years since World War II, more and more nations and inter-national agencies have come to see population growth, and thus also fer-tility, in a new light. At one time nontotalitarian governments viewed an increase in numbers as a social good or, if not, as outside the range of legitimate intervention. Still in the mid-1960s, official concern about popu-lation in most of Latin America was expressed only by sponsoring confer-ences or research centers to study the problem, while private groups attempted to institute birth-control programs (Delgado, 1966).[21] In the

---

[21] North American criticism of such procrastination is hardly appropriate, for the shift in orientation came very late in the United States. The new official policy begun under President Kennedy flowered under the administration of President Johnson into what one enthusiastic official called "the most startling reversal of federal policy I've ever seen" (Jonathan Spivak in the *Wall Street Journal*, October 21, 1965). Domestic

present perspective of some other underdeveloped countries, population is not merely a dependent variable but one element in the complex interrelation of economy, social structure, and culture. A society attempting to plan its transition to a modern industrial level cannot leave this crucial factor to "nature," while policy decisions control every other one.

### SMALL-COUNTRY PROGRAMS

Among American demographers and sociologists, a good deal of attention has been paid to a number of small areas, mainly in Asia, where family planning was introduced under joint government-private auspices. Often this effort was a by-product of research, for many of the so-called attitude surveys in fact constituted "a relatively noncontroversial way of initiating activity in population control in countries where direct efforts are not possible" (Stycos, 1965b). Some who have worked out standardized formulas for changing attitudes through propaganda (e.g., Bogue and Heiskanen, 1963) view their efforts as eminently successful.

The years 1963–64 very probably will go down in demographic history as one of the great landmarks of social-science research progress. In twelve months from June 1963 to June 1964 researchers in fertility control began to get a string of successes that left no doubt that by planned intervention they had induced a downward change in the birth rate in high-fertility populations. . . . Six ingredients are the necessary and sufficient conditions for intervention . . . : (1) awareness of the possibility and benefits of family planning; (2) knowledge of how to implement family planning; (3) impersonalization, desexualization, and public discussion of family planning, primarily through private, informal personal interaction; (5) self-involvement in family planning; (6) supplies through convenient and nonpunitive channels (Bogue, 1964).[22]

By a somewhat more realistic appraisal, such programs can indeed do several useful things. They correct misinformation and tell a public about efficient contraceptives, how to use them and where they are available;

---

programs were under way in the mid-1960s through the Children's Bureau, the Public Health Service, the National Institutes of Health, and, more cautiously and partially, the Office of Economic Opportunity and the Federal Welfare Administration. As formulated on January 24, 1966, for the first time the policy of the U.S. Department of Health, Education, and Welfare is "to conduct and support programs of basic and applied research on [population dynamics, fertility, sterility, and family planning]; to conduct and support training programs; to collect and make available such data as may be necessary; to support, on request, health programs making family-planning information and services available, and to provide family-planning information and services, on request, to individuals who receive health services from operating agencies of the Department" (U.S. Department of Health, Education, and Welfare, Report on Family Planning, Washington, D.C., 1966, p. iv).

[22] Projecting this kind of self-gratification, Frank Notestein stated that "within two decades the rate of population growth may well be brought to 1 per cent or 1.5 per cent throughout the major sectors of the newly developing world" (Berelson et al., 1966, p. 829). See also "The End of the Population Explosion" (Bogue, 1967).

and they may "change attitudes" in the sense of resolving existing conflicts of values. Thus they may help some persons overcome aversion to birth control and reduce the number of their children to the family size they desire, which, as has been noted, is about four in most underdeveloped areas (but see also Hyrenius and Åhs, 1968).

Some of the most enthusiastic reports pertain to Taiwan, and it may be useful to analyze their general import. A significant decline was effected during the decade beginning around 1955, when the birth rate was 45 per thousand. In 1964 the rate was 34.5; in 1965, 32.7; in 1966, 32.4; and in 1967 something under 30. It was among women aged 30 and over, and especially 40 and over, that the birth rate fell. In many cases interest in family planning started when there were already more than four children and even when many mothers were close to the end of their child-bearing period. If one extrapolates this achievement into the future, it means reducing the average completed family size from about six to about four children, but even this limited achievement is not certain. The success achieved to date has been mainly among social classes most favorably disposed toward family planning, and to continue even among the same age group of the remaining population may be more difficult. There will be many more young women whose fertility has not fallen at all: between 1966 and 1975 the number aged 20–24 will increase by 87 per cent, and that aged 25–29 by 29 per cent. With the age-specific birth rates prevailing in 1966, by 1975 this change in the number of mothers will raise the crude birth rate by 11 per cent and the number of births by 45 per cent (Petersen, 1967; Keeny, 1967).

Even if we accept the most optimistic guesses about the future of family-planning campaigns, there is little warrant for extending this euphoria to the whole of the underdeveloped world. Those areas where efforts to reduce fertility have attained at least a modicum of success—Puerto Rico, Jamaica, Taiwan, Singapore, South Korea, Thailand—have a number of characteristics in common. They are relatively small, stable, and generally well administered, so that the substantial financial grants from advanced countries could be put to good use, affording new opportunities to those equipped to take advantage of them. A realistic prognosis for the populations of all underdeveloped countries must be based on the fact that in many (e.g., in Africa and Latin America) government programs to cut natality have not yet started, and in others (e.g., the larger countries of Asia) the official efforts have had no discernible effect on their birth rates. In size, in complexity, in receptivity to any modernizing influence, Taiwan is not India, Puerto Rico is not Brazil.

## FAMILY-PLANNING PROJECTS IN INDIA

The Indian government's efforts to reduce fertility were initially opposed, as we have seen, by Gandhi, Nehru, and his Minister of Health,

According to the advertisements of a sexologist in the old section of Delhi, he can either control births or increase fertility (*Baldev—PIX*).

but by now the family-planning program is the most important, with the possible exception of China, in a sizable underdeveloped country. It evolved slowly. In the progress reports on the First Five-Year Plan (1951–56) the program was described as of "supreme" importance, but as late as 1955 the Deputy Minister of Health, when asked whether it would be accelerated, replied, "The question is still under consideration." With the Rs. 6.5 million allocated, 147 clinics were established in all of India, 126 in cities and 21 in rural areas (Samuel, 1966). The allotment in the Second Plan (1956–61) was also small, and a large part was not spent. Three months after the start of the plan period, Nehru asserted that family planning was being assisted "not in a major way but in experimentation." The emphasis was medical, to promote the "health and happiness" of the family. A bureaucratic structure was set up both in the federal government and in each of the states, and by the end of the Second Plan the government had

established over 4,000 clinics, where contraceptives were issued at subsidized rates or gratis. After three years, of the 75 to 80 million families
in India, contact had been made with 7 million, and of these only 1.4 million
had been given advice. "It is evident that the pace of progress is slow"
(Gopalaswami, 1962).

One reason for this fact was that, in imitation of private planned-
parenthood associations, the work was organized through clinics, which
by their very nature reached only a fraction of the population. For the
first year the only contraceptives available were those conventionally distributed through such agencies. These required the couple to exercise regular and responsible control each time they had intercourse; to clean and
store the pessary in a home with no running water and little privacy; to
return periodically to the clinic for new supplies (Israel, 1966). An acceptable contraceptive method, Chand had stated in 1956, should be fully
effective, completely harmless, cheap, suited to the conditions of the particular community, and esthetically satisfactory; he concluded that "a contraceptive meeting these requirements and adapted to the needs of India
does not exist at present" (Chand, 1956, p. 98). At the end of the Second
Plan,

India has not achieved any reduction of its birth rate, . . . and there is no
sign that a downturn will occur in the next few years. . . . So far we have been
engaged only on what may be regarded as pilot experimentation (Gopalaswami,
1962).

The year 1961, according to one analyst, marked "the beginning of the
policy of population control" (Samuel, 1966). An additional impetus was
the result of the 1961 census, after which the government evinced a greater
concern with population increase and its economic and social consequences.
In the Third Plan (1962–67) the family-planning program was decen-
tralized, with federal allocations spent through state projects, and a greater
effort was made to evaluate the results. The search for an appropriate
means of contraception continued. The so-called "natural" methods (rhythm
and *coitus interruptus*) were still advocated by some on moral grounds, by
others (e.g., Gopalaswami, 1962) because of the low cost of a campaign
to the government. Diaphragm and spermicide were inappropriate for the
reasons already cited. Oral contraceptives have never become popular in
India. "Twenty pills a month for months on end is expensive. And, expense
apart, there will always be women who will forget to take their daily dose"
(Chandrasekhar, 1967a).

Some saw intra-uterine devices as the ideal means, but the experience
in India has not warranted this confidence (Table 16-10). Very few of the
women who retained the IUD—according to a number of Indian studies,
less than one per cent—became pregnant, but as many as one-tenth of the

Table 16-10. Failure Rates of Intra-uterine Devices According to Various Studies, India, 1960s

| PLACE OF STUDY | SAMPLE | RATES PER 100 IUD USERS | | | |
| --- | --- | --- | --- | --- | --- |
| | | EXPULSIONS | REMOVALS | PREG-NANCIES | TOTAL FAILURES |
| Ajmer | 1,850 | 3.5 | 14.4 | 0.6 | 18.5 |
| Ambala (1) | 144 | 11.1 | 34.0 | 0.7 | 45.8 |
| Ambala (2) | 100 | 8.0 | 24.0 | 0 | 32.0 |
| Bareilly | 1,581 | 4.3 | 14.3 | 0.9 | 19.5 |
| Bombay [a] | 775 | 10.9 | 21.9 | 0.9 | 34.0 |
| Hooghly | 200 | 4.5 | 7.0 | 0.5 | 12.0 |
| Poona | 265 | 3.7 | 18.5 | 0.4 | 22.6 |
| Trivandrun (1) | 86 | 6.0 | 6.0 | 0 | 12.0 |
| Trivandrun (2) | 80 | — | — | — | 37.5 |

SOURCE: S. N. Agarwala, "The Progress of IUCD in India," in International Union for the Scientific Study of Population, *Proceedings, 1967*, Sydney, 1967, pp. 424–430.
[a] Based on life-table method; *cf.* p. 213, n. 7.

users automatically expelled the device and as many as one-third removed it because of excessive bleeding, pain or discomfort, or the fear generated by the bleeding of others. Failure rates were higher among young women and among those above the lowest income bracket. During the first year (1965–66), after a slow start, 800,000 IUDs were inserted, but in the following year only about 790,000, or 19 per cent of the target of six million (Murty, 1967).

In 1967, Sripati Chandrasekhar became Minister of Health and Family Planning. A world-renowned demographer, he had spent much of his professional life advocating that India control her population growth. With his appointment, there came a new emphasis on sterilization, "of all the methods tried so far the only [one that] has yielded significant results" (Chandrasekhar, 1967a). As early as 1957, Madras State (of whose Family-Planning Board Gopalaswami was a prominent member) had started a program of subsidized sterilization. Subsequently three other states—Mysore, Kerala, and Maharashtra—instituted similar projects. A central-government program was started on a small scale in 1958, and from 1966 on New Delhi reimbursed state governments at the rate of Rs. 11 for each IUD insertion, Rs. 30 for each vasectomy, and Rs. 40 for each salpingectomy. The enthusiasm for sterilization has been great.

Effective, inexpensive and entirely harmless methods are already available, by which every married couple can stop their career of child-bearing at that stage of their married life when they decide they have had enough children. What is

In a demonstration section restricted to men, a doctor explains how a pessary works. National Family Planning Exhibit, New Delhi (*Peter Schmid—PIX*).

Street scene in India (*Baldev—PIX*).

required to be done immediately is for the leaders of the people to acquire the conviction that this is so and to transmit that conviction to the people. The next step is for every State Government to organize the provision of necessary surgical facilities free of all expense to the people. There is no doubt whatever that India's birth rate can be halved if such facilities are organized and used on a scale sufficient to perform five operations every year in every local community of one thousand people. The solution of the population problem of India, which seems so intractable today, is really as simple as that (Gopalaswami, 1959).

The calculation has been cited often, but it is somewhat misleading. The laws under which doctors perform the operation, whether vasectomy or salpingectomy, vary from one Indian state to another; but they all prescribe a written agreement from both spouses, a minimum number of living children, a minimum age of the patient (e.g., Gopalaswami, 1962). The consequence—which is of course reinforced by the usual characteristics of those who volunteer to undergo a generally irreversible end to fecundity—is that only the top of India's excess fertility can be removed. According to a four-year study of vasectomy in Maharashtra, the average age of the 3,465 men sterilized was 39 to 40 (the ages of 102 of the patients ranged from 53 to 68+), and they were fathers of an average of 5.33 living children. "There appears . . . to be no possibility of vasectomy camps having a significant effect on the birth rate, . . . [but] they have no doubt helped to create a climate favorable for popularizing family planning" (Dandekar, 1963; cf. Kurup and Mathen, 1966).

If . . . calculations are made on the basis of the projected population as given by the Expert Committee on Population, it is found that 28 million operations performed in ten years will bring down the birth rate by only 5.5 points [from an estimated 42 per thousand]. . . . If the birth rate is to be reduced from 40 to 25 in a period of ten years, roughly 6 million sterilization operations will have to be performed each year (Agarwala, 1966a).

The total number of operations actually performed from 1956 to March 1967 was 2.27 million (Murty, 1967), or about 3.5 per cent of the annual rate required according to this calculation.

With any method of contraception, a prime factor in determining its success is the strength of the people's motivation, and in India some efforts have been made to generate this. In one of the volumes of the 1951 census, Gopalaswami, writing officially as the Registrar General, defined all childbirths above the third order as "improvident maternity."

The task before the nation is first of all to bring about such a change in the climate of public opinion that every married couple will accept it as their duty (to themselves, to their family, and to that larger family—the nation) that they should avoid improvident maternity. The occurrence of improvident maternity should evoke social disapproval, as any other form of anti-social self-indulgence.[23]

[23] R. A. Gopalaswami, *Census of India, 1951*, Vol. 1, *India*, Part 1-A, *Report*, New Delhi, 1953, pp. 218–219.

In this opinion, the incidence of improvident maternity, between 40 and 45 per cent in 1951, had to be reduced to under 5 per cent within fifteen years. Whether such appeals, however reasonable, have any effect on the fertility of potential parents can be doubted. Even those who become aware of the argument and accept it in over-all terms may not apply it to themselves. Among a sample of rural high-school teachers, while 60 per cent believed that India is overpopulated, more than 40 per cent were opposed in principle to birth control and three-quarters did not practice it themselves (Reeder and Krishnamurty, 1964).

Since a decline in fertility in underdeveloped countries would help accelerate economic growth, it would be worthwhile for these nations to invest, as it were, in nonbirths. The American economist Stephen Enke has calculated that in India today the value of permanently preventing a birth is roughly $125, and that a considerable percentage of this sum might advantageously be offered as a bonus to young, married, fecund men who volunteer to have themselves sterilized (Enke, 1960; cf. Enke, 1963, pp. 377–384; Krueger and Sjaastad, with reply by Enke, 1962). A partial approach to this rationale has been in operation in certain areas of India. As Madras State set it up in mid-1958, the allowance was limited to lower civil servants in Madras City; fathers who underwent an operation were paid 14 rupees (one rupee = approximately U.S. 20¢) and mothers 25 rupees. A year and a half later, the scheme was extended to include the 35 million people of Madras State, and the bonus was increased to 30 rupees. In Maharashtra a sterilization campaign was started on "All-India Family-Planning Day," December 18, 1950, and during the next three weeks the more than 7,000 men who underwent a vasectomy were each paid 20 rupees for their loss of working time. As a member of Parliament, Chandrasekhar suggested that India request permission of the U.S. Government to use counterpart funds accumulated in India to pay a cash bonus of, say, 100 rupees to each man undergoing a vasectomy. That would still be only about $20 rather than the $125 Enke proposed, but for nine-tenths of the sample studied in Maharashtra it would have been more than a month's income (Dandekar, 1963). However, nothing came of the proposal; "both Governments are extremely sensitive in this area" (Chandrasekhar, 1967a).

In a few small areas of India where an intensive effort to reduce fertility was made, the estimated birth rates fell appreciably up to the mid-1960s. But "it is doubtful if the national birth rate has shown any decline" (Murty, 1967; cf. Chandrasekhar, 1967a). According to twenty-seven studies of family-planning practices in India, not more than 2 per cent of currently married rural females of reproductive age were practicing birth control of any kind (Agarwala, 1966b).

## SOCIAL STRUCTURE

Modernization, as we have seen, exerts pressures to increase fertility as well as to reduce it, and countries already suffering from overpopulation cannot wait for these countervailing forces to resolve themselves into an eventual desire for a small family. The major portion of the effort to reduce fertility in underdeveloped areas, however, has concentrated on: (1) furnishing contraceptives and, as part of this process, combating (2) ignorance about the physiology of fertility or the effects of birth control and changing (3) attitudes concerning the legitimacy of contraception or the ideal number of children. A program so defined has its own limits. If it worked perfectly, it would reduce family size to the preferred average of four children and depend on propaganda to move farther. Only in India have such exhortations been reinforced with meager cash bonuses.

Nothing in the decline of Western fertility suggests that this heavy emphasis on the technical, instrumental elements of controlling births is appropriate. When a people, or a social class, felt itself to be suffering from population pressure, it used whatever means were available to reduce it (Davis, 1963). It adopted this perception of its state not from the message of a social movement or the government, but because shifts in the institutional and class structure brought about changes in modal expectations and attitudes. All nontotalitarian methods of birth control depend on generating a serious motivation to reduce family size among potential parents; this is truly possible, so far as we know, only by altering the conditions of their life so as to make small families more attractive. From the point of view of a sociologist, rather than of a public-health administrator or social psychologist, the overwhelming lack in planned efforts to reduce fertility is that they have ignored the social framework.

Many policies adopted for other reasons, it is true, also affect fertility; for example, as a consequence of the successful campaigns to reduce infant and child mortality, the strong desire for one male heir, which once could be satisfied only with a numerous initial progeny, can realistically be gratified with an average of, say, three children. And many other policies that governments favor but cannot implement because of their cost also would influence the birth rate if once they became feasible; for example, if the care that each man expects his children to give him in his old age were supplanted by social welfare, the rational basis of the desire for many offspring would be undercut. Actual and potential modernization programs, then, generally affect the institutional structure and thus the country's fertility, but direct intervention to this end is unusual, if only because an interference in family functions is likely to be politically dangerous. In any case, there are few programs that a conscientious administrator could adopt. The relation between the size and structure of family types is an issue in current scholarly polemics (e.g. Burch, 1967). The matricentric quasi-families common in parts of Latin America and especially the West Indies, for instance, pose a dilemma to officials. The quality of socialization is generally poor in a family that lacks a stable two-adult team to bring up the children; thus, responsible policy would seem to be to reinforce formal marriage as a universal norm. However, in Jamaica in the mid-1940s (as generally in the West Indies, also for later dates), the average number of children per mother aged over 45 was 6.6 among married women, 5.6 among those in common-law unions, and 4.7 among single women (Roberts, 1957, p. 297; cf. Blake, 1961). As Stycos (1963a) noted in the case of Peru, if the somewhat random sexuality of the lower class is channeled into a regular marital pattern, one can expect a consequent rise in fertility.

There is one induced institutional change that would entail no hindrance to over-all modernization, namely, a program to provide work training and jobs for females, who would thus acquire useful and attractive alternatives to purely domestic roles as housekeepers and recurrent mothers, as well, however, as competing with the usually superabundant male work force. There is a high correlation between countries' level of economic development and the proportion of females working outside the home, particularly if domestic service is excluded (Collver and Langlois, 1962). According to both such an international comparison and studies in individual countries, fertility is the lower, the larger the proportion of women (especially of married women, when data are available to make the distinction) who work outside the home. Of course, the causal relation operates in both directions. Women who have few children because of subfecundity or some other socially irrelevant reason are more likely to engage in nondomestic activities (e.g., Stycos, 1965a). And women for whom another child means sacrificing their actual or potential income and career are motivated to have fewer children (e.g., Blake, 1965). Yet in India, for instance, from 1911 to 1951 there was a decline of about 2.3 million working females as against an increase of 23.5 million in the female population (Government of India studies, cited in ibid.).

The generally low rates of economic activity among women in Latin American countries remained low throughout the 1950s. There may have been a considerable increase in Mexico and Nicaragua, [but] in most of the other countries there was apparently little or no change. . . . Divorced women had the highest activity rates in all but two of the nine countries [for which there were data]. . . . The lowest rates were for women reported as living in consensual unions or married women. . . .

The prevailing high levels of fertility may not by themselves be hindering many mothers from taking outside employment. The view that mothers belong at home and, in some cases, the higher labor costs which labor regulations concerning mothers bring about may be more important obstacles to higher activity rates for wives and mothers (Gendell and Rossel, 1967; *cf.* Gendell, 1965; Weller, 1968).

## Summary

So far as we can tell from various types of data, none of them fully adequate, the crude birth rate of major underdeveloped areas is 40 or above, in some countries perhaps even as high as 60. Combined with a death rate sometimes around 10, or if substantially higher still falling, this natality results in a population growth so rapid that plans to modernize the economy are endangered. It is not feasible to wait for the decline in average family size that will presumably accompany full social-economic development, for during the period of transition it would seem that fertility is as likely to rise as to fall. In an era when no other element of the society operates according to laissez-faire principles, the "natural" functioning of reproduction can result in disaster.

The conflict between traditional ideologies and modernizing movements,

Concrete conveyors, 1957. Female workers at Durgapur, in eastern India, helping in the construction of a bridge (*Wide World Photos*).

a conventional framework for studying trends in underdeveloped countries, is a misleading guide to the analysis of their fertility. The major religions of the non-Western world, it is true, reinforce the family and prescribe parental responsibilities, but their stands on such a key question as the legitimacy of contraception are generally ambivalent or self-contradictory. The weight of left-wing nationalism, on the contrary, has usually been to stress the moral and economic worth of a large and rapidly growing population and thus, until the pressure becomes acute, to oppose family planning. And the planned-parenthood movement, whatever its value in the West, is almost irrevelant to problems on the massive new scale of present-day Asia, Africa, and Latin America.

Government programs to reduce the birth rate have had a certain success in a number of small, stable countries, typically transitional to a developed economy rather than truly "underdeveloped." In the large, populous countries (apart from Communist China, which is discussed in the following chapter), official efforts have not yet begun or, as in India, have not yet succeeded in reducing the country's fertility at all. One reason is the erroneous premise that people want small families, so that their numerous progeny results from ignorance and loosely based attitudes, both of which can be changed by propaganda. Actually, polls in various countries give the average number of children desired as four. Propaganda cannot affect the apathy that derives from entrenched poverty, which for individual couples can be undercut by fostering institutional changes that give parents a genuine choice between children and other values. In general,

Current programs will not enable a government to control population size. . . . The unthinking identification of family planning with population control is an ostrich-like approach in that it permits people to hide from themselves the enormity and unconventionality of the task (Davis, 1967).

Modernization takes place not by any regular, precise process, but by a complex interaction among a typical range of key institutions in a manner that reflects both the interrelation among them (e.g., modern industry demands a literate population; literacy opens up new potentials in culture and politics) and the tie of each culture to its specific past. Those analysts in each social discipline who have attempted to transgress the bounds of a single case have very often erred on the side of too facile generalization, and repeatedly we have been put to the task of freeing our thought from one or another monistic bond—in earlier generations racist or geographic determinism, and more recently their economic or demographic analogues. How much of a guide is the past development of advanced countries for mapping the future modernization of presently backward areas? In some over-all sense, obviously, the world is becoming more homogeneous, and it is just this metamorphosis that we mean by modernization. But to assume that details of the process must follow a known course, or that the homogenization must eventually eliminate all fundamental differences, is to commit the egregious error of comparative analysis.

## Suggestions for Further Reading

A good selection of the enormous literature on fertility in underdeveloped areas is available in several collections of generally excellent papers—Sheps and Ridley, 1965; Muramatsu and Harper, 1965; Kiser, 1962; and Milbank Memorial Fund, 1952. Good summaries of trends in particular countries or areas are given in Chandrasekhar, 1967b; Stycos and Arias, 1966; El-Badry, 1965; and T. E. Smith, 1963. For stimulating discussions of the ambivalent effects of modernization on fertility, see Robinson, 1961; Abu-Lughod, 1964; Heer, 1966; Zarate, 1967a. Two books on India, though out of date, are well worth reading—Davis, 1951; Coale and Hoover, 1958.

\* ABU-LUGHOD, JANET. 1964. "Urban-Rural Differences as a Function of the Demographic Transition: Egyptian Data and an Analytical Model," *American Journal of Sociology,* 69, 476–490.

————. 1965. "The Emergence of Differential Fertility in Urban Egypt," *Milbank Memorial Fund Quarterly,* 43, 235–253.

AGARWALA, S. N. 1966a. "The Arithmetic of Sterilization in India," *Eugenics Quarterly,* 13, 209–213.

————. 1966b. *Some Problems of India's Population.* Vora & Co., Bombay.

————. 1967. "The Progress of IUCD in India," in International Union for the Scientific Study of Population. *Proceedings, 1967.* Sydney, pp. 424–430.

AHMED, MOHIUDDIN. 1966. "Rates and Levels of Mortality and Fertility in Pakistan," *Population Review,* 10, 44–60.

\* ARMIJO, RONALDO, and TEGUALDA MONREAL. 1965. "Epidemiology of Provoked Abortion in Santiago, Chile," in Muramatsu and Harper, 1965, pp. 137–160.

BERELSON, BERNARD, *et al.,* editors. 1966. *Family Planning and Population Programs: A Review of World Developments.* University of Chicago Press, Chicago.

BLACKER, C. P. 1955. "The Rhythm Method: Two Indian Experiments," *Eugenics Review,* 47, 93–105, 163–172.

BLACKER, J. G. C. 1959. "Fertility Trends of the Asian Population of Tanganyika," *Population Studies,* 13, 46–60.

BLAKE, JUDITH. 1961. *Family Structure in Jamaica: The Social Context of Reproduction.* Free Press of Glencoe, New York.

\* ————. 1965. "Demographic Science and the Redirection of Population Policy," in Sheps and Ridley, 1965, pp. 41–69.

BOGUE, DONALD J. 1964. "The Demographic Breakthrough: From Projection to Control," *Population Index,* 30, 449–454.

————. 1967. "The End of the Population Explosion," *Public Interest,* No. 7, pp. 11–20.

————, and VERONICA STOLTE HEISKANEN. 1963. *How to Improve Written*

*Communication for Birth Control.* Community and Family Study Center, University of Chicago, Chicago.

BURCH, THOMAS K. 1967. "The Size and Structure of Families: A Comparative Analysis of Census Data," *American Sociological Review,* 32, 347–363.

BURNIGHT, ROBERT G., NATHAN L. WHETTEN, and BRUCE D. WAXMAN. 1956. "Differential Rural-Urban Fertility in Mexico," *American Sociological Review,* 21, 3–8.

CALDWELL, J. C. 1967. "Fertility Differentials as Evidence of Incipient Fertility Decline in a Developing Country," *Population Studies,* 21, 5–21.

CHAND, GYAN. 1956. *Some Aspects of the Population Problem of India.* Patna University Press, Bihar, India.

CHANDRASEKHAR, S. 1960. "A Note on Demographic Statistics in India," *Population Review,* 4, 40–45.

———. 1967a. "India's Population: Fact, Problem and Policy," in Chandrasekhar, 1967b, pp. 72–99.

———, editor. 1967b. *Asia's Population Problems.* Allen & Unwin, London.

CHEN SHAO-HSING, WANG YAO-TUNG, and FREDERIC J. FOLEY. 1963. "Pattern of Fertility in Taiwan," *Journal of Social Science* (Taipei), 13, 209–294.

CHOLDIN, HARVEY M., A. MAJEED KAHN, and B. HOSNE ARA. 1967. "Cultural Complications in Fertility Interviewing," *Demography,* 4, 244–252.

COALE, ANSLEY J. 1963. "Estimates of Various Demographic Measures through the Quasi-Stable Age Distribution," in Milbank Memorial Fund, *Emerging Techniques in Population Research.* New York, pp. 175–193.

———. 1966. "Estimates of Fertility and Mortality in Tropical Africa," *Population Index,* 32, 173–181.

* ———, and EDGAR M. HOOVER. 1958. *Population Growth and Economic Development in Low-Income Countries: A Case Study of India's Prospects.* Princeton University Press, Princeton, N.J.

COLLVER, O. ANDREW. 1965. *Birth Rates in Latin America: New Estimates of Historical Trends and Fluctuations.* Institute of International Studies, University of California, Berkeley.

———, and ELEANOR LANGLOIS. 1962. "The Female Labor Force in Metropolitan Areas: An International Comparison," *Economic Development and Cultural Change,* 10, 367–385.

DANDEKAR, KUMUDINI. 1963. "Vasectomy Camps in Maharashtra," *Population Studies,* 17, 147–154.

* DAVIS, KINGSLEY. 1951. *The Population of India and Pakistan.* Princeton University Press, Princeton, N.J.

———. 1955. "Social and Demographic Aspects of Economic Development in India," in *Economic Growth: Brazil, India, Japan,* edited by Simon Kuznets, Wilbert E. Moore, and Joseph J. Spengler. Duke University Press, Durham, N.C., pp. 263–315.

———. 1963. "The Theory of Change and Response in Modern Demographic History," *Population Index,* 29, 345–366.

———. 1964. "The Place of Latin America in World Demographic History," *Milbank Memorial Fund Quarterly,* 42, 19–47.

* ———. 1967. "Population Policy: Will Current Programs Succeed?" *Science,* 158, 730–739.

DELGADO GARCÍA, RAMIRO. 1966. "Perspectives of Family Planning Programs in Latin America," in Stycos and Arias, 1966, pp. 214–227.

DEMENY, PAUL. 1965. "Estimation of Vital Rates for Populations in the Process of Destabilization," *Demography*, 2, 516–530.

EL-BADRY, M. A. 1956. "Some Aspects of Fertility in Egypt," *Milbank Memorial Fund Quarterly*, 34, 22–43.

———. 1965. "Trends in the Components of Population Growth in the Arab Countries of the Middle East: A Survey of Present Information," *Demography*, 2, 140–186.

* ENKE, STEPHEN. 1960. "Government Bonuses for Smaller Families," *Population Review*, 4, 47–50.

———. 1962. "Some Misconceptions of Krueger and Sjaastad Regarding the Vasectomy-Bonus Plan to Reduce Births in Overpopulated and Poor Countries," *Economic Development and Cultural Change*, 10, 427–431.

———. 1963. *Economics for Development*. Prentice-Hall, Englewood Cliffs, N.J.

GAETE-DARBÓ, ADOLFO. 1964. "Appraisal of Vital Statistics in Latin America," *Milbank Memorial Fund Quarterly*, 42, 86–103.

GANDHI, M. K. 1959. *Birth-Control: The Right Way and the Wrong Way*. Navajivan, Ahmedabad.

GENDELL, MURRAY. 1967. "The Influence of Family-Building Activity on Women's Rate of Economic Activity." United Nations World Population Conference, Belgrade, *Proceedings*, New York, 4, 283–287.

———, and GUILLERMO ROSSEL U. 1967. "The Economic Activity of Women in Latin America," Inter-American Commission of Women, Fourteenth Annual Assembly, Montevideo. Pan American Union, Washington, D.C.

GOPALASWAMI, R. A. 1959. "How Japan Halved Her Birth Rate in Ten Years: The Lessons for India," *Population Review*, 3, 52–57.

———. 1962. "Family Planning: Outlook for Government Action in India," in Kiser, 1962, pp. 67–81.

GUPTA, AJIT DAS. 1958. "Determination of Fertility Level and Trend in Defective Registration Areas," *Bulletin de l'Institut International de Statistique*, 36, 127–136.

HAWKINS, EVERETT. 1967. "Indonesia's Population Problems," in Chandrasekhar, 1967b, pp. 119–145.

* HEER, DAVID M. 1966. "Economic Development and Fertility," *Demography*, 3, 423–444.

HENIN, R. A. 1968. "Fertility Differentials in the Sudan," *Population Studies*, 22, 147–164.

HUTCHINSON, BERTRAM. 1961. "Fertility, Social Mobility, and Urban Migration in Brazil," *Population Studies*, 14, 182–189.

* HYRENIUS, HANNES, and ULLA ÅHS. 1968. *The Sweden-Ceylon Family Planning Pilot Project*. Demographic Institute, University of Göteborg, Göteborg, Sweden.

ISRAEL, SARAH. 1966. "Contraceptive Testing in India," *Population Review*, 10, 51–60.

KAHL, JOSEPH A., and J. MAYONE STYCOS. 1965. "The Philosophy of Demographic Policy in Latin America," *Studies in Comparative International Development*, Vol. 1, No. 2.

KEENY, S. M. 1967. "Korea and Taiwan: The Score for 1966," *Studies in Family Planning*, No. 19, pp. 1–7.

KINCH, ARNE. 1962. "A Preliminary Report from the Sweden-Ceylon Family Planning Pilot Project," in Kiser, 1962, pp. 85–102.

* KISER, CLYDE V., editor. 1962. *Research in Family Planning.* Princeton University Press, Princeton, N.J.

KRUEGER, ANNE O., and LARRY A. SJAASTAD. 1962. "Some Limitations of Enke's Economics of Population," *Economic Development and Cultural Change*, 10, 423–426.

KURUP, R. S., and T. K. MATHEN. 1966. "Sterilization as a Method of Family Limitation in Kerala State," *Population Review*, 10, 61–68.

LEE SHU-CHING. 1953. "China's Traditional Family, Its Characteristics and Disintegration," *American Sociological Review*, 18, 272–280.

LORIMER, FRANK, et al. 1954. *Culture and Human Fertility: A Study of the Relation of Cultural Conditions to Fertility in Non-Industrial and Transitional Societies.* UNESCO, Zurich.

MATHEN, K. K. 1962. "Preliminary Lessons Learned from the Rural Population Control Study of Singur," in Kiser, 1962, pp. 33–49.

* MAULDIN, W. PARKER. 1965. "Application of Survey Techniques to Fertility Studies," in Sheps and Ridley, 1965, pp. 93–118.

MAYER, PHILIP. 1961. *Townsmen or Tribesmen.* Oxford University Press, Cape Town.

MILBANK MEMORIAL FUND. 1952. *Approaches to Problems of High Fertility in Agrarian Societies.* New York.

MIRÓ, CARMEN A. 1964. "The Population of Latin America," *Demography*, 1, 15–41.

———, and FERDINAND RATH. 1965. "Preliminary Findings of Comparative Fertility Surveys in Three Latin American Countries," *Milbank Memorial Fund Quarterly*, Vol. 43, No. 4, Part 2, pp. 36–62.

MORTARA, GIORGIO. 1964. "Appraisal of Census Data for Latin America," *Milbank Memorial Fund Quarterly*, 42, 57–71.

* MURAMATSU, MINORU, and PAUL A. HARPER, editors. 1965. *Population Dynamics: International Action and Training Programs.* Johns Hopkins Press, Baltimore, Md.

MURTY, D. V. R. 1967. "Evaluation of Family Planning Programme in India," in International Union for the Scientific Study of Population, *Proceedings, 1967.* Sydney, pp. 468–475.

NARAGHI, EHSAN. 1960. *L'étude des populations dans les pays à statistique incomplète.* Mouton, Paris.

NOTESTEIN, FRANK W. 1945. "Population—The Long View," in *Food for the World*, edited by Theodore W. Schultz. University of Chicago Press, Chicago, pp. 35–57.

PÉREZ RAMÍREZ, GUSTAVO. 1966. "The Catholic Church and Family Planning—Current Perspectives," in Stycos and Arias, 1966, pp. 196–213.

PETERSEN, WILLIAM. 1967. "Taiwan's Population Problem," in Chandrasekhar, 1967*b*, pp. 189–210.

* POTI, S. J., B. CHAKRABORTI, and C. R. MALAKAR. 1962. "Reliability of Data Relating to Contraceptive Practices," in Kiser, 1962, pp. 51–65.

QUERISHI, ANWAR IQBAL. 1967. "Pakistan's Population Problem," in Chandrasekhar, 1967b, pp. 146–164.

REEDER, LEO G., and GOTETI B. KRISHNAMURTY. 1964. "Family Planning in Rural India: A Problem in Social Change," *Social Problems*, 12, 212–223.

REIN, MARTIN. 1964. "Organization for Social Change," *Social Work*, Vol. 9, No. 2, pp. 32–41.

° RELE, J. R. 1963. "Fertility Differentials in India: Evidence from a Rural Background," *Milbank Memorial Fund Quarterly*, 41, 183–199.

———. 1967. *Fertility Analysis through Extension of Stable Population Concepts*. University of California, Berkeley, Calif.

RICHARDS, AUDREY I., and PRISCILLA REINING. 1954. "Report on Fertility Surveys in Buganda and Buhaya, 1952," in Lorimer, 1954, pp. 353–403.

RIDLEY, JEANNE CLARE. 1965. "Recent Natality Trends in Underdeveloped Countries," in Sheps and Ridley, 1965, pp. 143–173.

ROBERTS, D. F., and R. E. S. TANNER. 1959. "A Demographic Study in an Area of Low Fertility in North-East Tanganyika," *Population Studies*, 13, 61–80.

ROBERTS, GEORGE W. 1957. *The Population of Jamaica*. University Press, Cambridge.

———. 1967. "Reproductive Performance and Reproductive Capacity in Less Industrialized Societies," *Annals of the American Academy of Political and Social Science*, 369, 37–47.

° ROBINSON, WARREN C. 1961. "Urban-Rural Differences in Indian Fertility," *Population Studies*, 14, 218–234.

———. 1963. "Urbanization and Fertility: The Non-Western Experience," *Milbank Memorial Fund Quarterly*, 41, 291–308.

———, and ELIZABETH H. ROBINSON. 1960. "Rural-Urban Fertility Differentials in Mexico," *American Sociological Review*, 25, 77–81.

ROMANIUK, A. 1967. "Estimation of the Birth Rate for the Congo through Nonconventional Techniques," *Demography*, 4, 688–709.

RYAN, BRYCE. 1954. "Hinayana Buddhism and Family Planning in Ceylon," in Milbank Memorial Fund, *The Interrelations of Demographic, Economic, and Social Problems in Selected Underdeveloped Areas*. New York, pp. 90–102.

SABAGH, GEORGES, and CHRISTOPHER SCOTT. 1967. "A Comparison of Different Survey Techniques for Obtaining Vital Data in a Developing Country," *Demography*, 4, 759–772.

SADIK, NAFIS. 1965. "Population Problems in Pakistan: Programs and Policies," in Muramatsu and Harper, 1965, pp. 27–34.

° SAMUEL, T. J. 1966. "The Development of India's Policy of Population Control," *Milbank Memorial Fund Quarterly*, 44, 49–67.

° SHEPS, MINDEL C., and JEANNE CLARE RIDLEY, editors. 1965. *Public Health and Population Change: Current Research Issues*. University of Pittsburgh Press, Pittsburgh.

SMITH, T. E. 1963. "A General Survey of Current Population Trends in the Commonwealth Countries of Tropical Africa," in *Population Characteristics of the Commonwealth Countries of Tropical Africa*, edited by Smith and J. G. C. Blacker. Commonwealth Papers, No. 9. Athlone Press, London, pp. 9–53.

SMITH, T. LYNN. 1958. "The Reproduction Rate in Latin America: Levels, Differentials and Trends," *Population Studies*, 12, 4–16.

SOVANI, N. V. 1952. "The Problems of Fertility Control in India: Cultural Factors and Development of Policy," in Milbank Memorial Fund, 1952, pp. 62–73.

STONE, ABRAHAM. 1953. "Fertility Problems in India," *Fertility and Sterility*, 4, 210–217.

STYCOS, J. MAYONE. 1955. *Family and Fertility in Puerto Rico: A Study of the Lower Income Group*. Columbia University Press, New York.

* ———. 1962. "A Critique of the Traditional Planned Parenthood Approach in Underdeveloped Areas," in Kiser, 1962, pp. 477–501.

———. 1963a. "Culture and Differential Fertility in Peru," *Population Studies*, 16, 257–270.

———. 1963b. "Obstacles to Programs of Population Control—Facts and Fancies," *Marriage and Family Living*, 25, 5–13.

———. 1965a. "Female Employment and Fertility in Lima, Peru," *Milbank Memorial Fund Quarterly*, 43, 42–54.

* ———. 1965b. "Opinions of Latin-American Intellectuals on Population Problems and Birth Control," *Annals of the American Academy of Political and Social Science*, 360, 11–26.

———. 1966. "Demography and the Study of Population Problems in Latin America," in Stycos and Arias, 1966, pp. 228–244.

———, and JORGE ARIAS, editors. 1966. *Population Dilemma in Latin America*. American Assembly. Potomac Books, Washington, D.C.

TUAN CHI-HSIEN. 1958. "Reproductive Histories of Chinese Women in Rural Taiwan," *Population Studies*, 12, 40–50.

WELLER, ROBERT H. 1968. "The Employment of Wives, Dominance, and Fertility," *Journal of Marriage and the Family*, 30, 437–442.

YAUKEY, DAVID. 1961. *Fertility Differences in a Modernizing Country: A Survey of Lebanese Couples*. Princeton University Press, Princeton, N.J.

* ZARATE, ALVAN O. 1967a. "Differential Fertility in Monterrey, Mexico: Prelude to Transition?" *Milbank Memorial Fund Quarterly*, 45, 93–108.

———. 1967b. "Some Factors Associated with Urban-Rural Fertility Differentials in Mexico," *Population Studies*, 21, 283–293.

# 17 THE POPULATION OF TOTALITARIAN SOCIETIES

The distinction between democracy and totalitarianism is the most important one of twentieth-century life, and it is necessary to make it precisely. In a simplistic view, all societies that are not "democratic" are "totalitarian," and *vice versa*. As I use the term, a totalitarian society is one dominated by a single minority Party, which, in order to realize its particular vision of a perfect community, attempts to achieve total control over the major workings of all significant institutions. The several components of the definition are all essential. Rule by a minority over a country with important loci of competing power is not totalitarian; in the Ghana of Nkrumah, for instance, the rule of his supporters could be challenged by traditionalist chiefs, the urban middle class, and the army; in Franco's Spain, by the army, the Church, and the monarchist clique. And even if a group holds complete political power, it is not totalitarian (but "authoritarian" or "autocratic") if it does not also penetrate the social institutions in order to move them toward its utopian goal; the military dictatorship of a Latin American country or of a province of pre-Communist China is not totalitarian. No society, indeed, is completely totalitarian (just as none is completely democratic). The three that come closest to the pure type are the Soviet Union,

Nazi Germany, and Communist China, and this chapter has a section on each.

These three countries differ in much more than the national cultures, diverse as they are. Yet whatever the context, totalitarian population phenomena differ systematically from those in a nontotalitarian country. In order to specify this contrast in concrete terms, to discuss the type of controls that totalitarian states impose on fertility, mortality, and migration and the effect of these controls on population structure and composition, we shall focus on the Soviet Union. The reasons for this choice are that (as contrasted with Communist China) there are enough data to analyze over several decades and that (as contrasted with Nazi Germany) the Soviet system is of more than historical interest. The following, less exhaustive analyses of China and Germany help lay a basis for generalizing about population in the whole class of totalitarian societies.

## The Population of the Soviet Union

In this discussion of the half century since the 1917 revolution, greater emphasis will be laid on three out of those five decades—from the death of Lenin in 1924 to that of Stalin in 1953—during which the latter was either in ascendancy or in full control. For the Stalinist phenomenon, of considerable historical importance in itself, is also a key to understanding a wider range of political, economic, and population trends. And no one can yet be certain whether the post-Stalin revisions, however significant in some respects, are indications of a continuing democratization or merely "within-system changes" that leave the totalitarian essence intact.[1]

### SOURCES OF INFORMATION

Soviet statistics differ from those available for any Western country first of all in sheer quantity. If a planned economy is feasible, it must be by relating a record of past production to future goals; and as in principle virtually everything in the society is planned, a huge, complex system of reporting, record-keeping, and accounting embraces almost every activity and every person in the country. Whether even primary data are accurate, however, is often dubious. A statistical count is likely to be most accurate if it is independent of any other administrative function, but in a planned economy *all* data are compiled as one element of State control. A person asked a question by the representative of a totalitarian regime may answer falsely either because of fear or, on the contrary, as a mild form of sabotage. How often hospital clerks and registration officers tamper with the original

[1] For characteristic arguments on either side, see the contributions, respectively, of Isaac Deutscher and Bertram D. Wolfe in *Soviet Society*, edited by Alex Inkeles and Kent Geiger, Houghton Mifflin, Boston, 1961.

compilations of births and deaths, for example, we do not know, but "there are many reports of such cases in the Soviet press and in the pages of *Vestnik Statistiki,* the organ of the Central Statistical Administration of the USSR" (Gordon, 1957; *cf.* Schattman, 1956).

Whatever the accuracy of the data, only some of them are made available outside the country, and those that Westerners can work with are often the least reliable.[2] Specifically, those responsible for compiling demographic statistics know that these reflect in part the welfare that the economy affords the common man, and that the discrepancy between Soviet propaganda on this subject and Soviet reality has been great. The vital statistics issued to the public, for instance, are grossly incomplete.

Publishing the statistics only for favorable factors or periods is certainly very much akin to falsification. For example, the birth rate in 1938 was made known in due time (38.3 per 1,000), but not for 1939 and 1940. Western analysts realized that, due to the change in age composition and other factors, the birth rate in 1940 must have been lower than in 1938, but nobody seems to have thought of as low a figure as 31.7 per 1,000, now, after all those years, disclosed in the *Handbook* (Jasny, 1957, p. 13).

Our main source of Soviet population data is the censuses, but these also are not very satisfactory. The first census taken under Soviet auspices was in 1920, only three years after the Bolsheviks took power and while their rule was still being fought in parts of the country. Scores of enumerators were beaten up as representatives of the government, and thirty-three were murdered by the people they were attempting to count. The 1920 census is not regarded as accurate.

[2] In 1956 the Soviet government issued an official statistical *Handbook,* translated a year later into English (USSR Council of Ministers, Central Statistical Board, *National Economy of the USSR: Statistical Returns,* Foreign Language Publishing House, Moscow, 1957). This was reviewed by Naum Jasny, an outstanding Western sovietologist. His criticisms of this particular volume apply to Soviet statistics generally, and represent an excellent introduction to this difficult terrain. Many important data, which we know from other sources are collected in the Soviet Union, were omitted from the *Handbook*—for instance, all statistics on family budgets or the consumption of various goods. As in this case, the reason for the concealment is usually patent.

The figures available abroad are full of traps for nonspecialists. For example, the territory of the Soviet Union is now appreciably larger than before the war, but time series have in general not been redone to take this difference into account. Some series are calculated as percentages of the figures for 1940, a year when several territorial changes occurred, without informing the reader which area is taken as the base. Or, as another example, the crop "yields" reported until 1954 were estimates made in the field, before harvesting; for the years 1950–53 these "biological" crops ranged between 121 and 131 million tons, while the actual annual yields as now officially reported for these same years were between 76 and 89 million tons (Jasny, 1957, pp. 94–95). In short, "Soviet statistics are an amalgam of elements varying from trustworthy data (mostly pertaining to physical units or details) through ambiguities to obviously distorted estimates (mostly data for aggregates)" (*ibid.,* p. 14).

The next Soviet census was taken in 1926, after the country had been pacified. In order to insure an accurate return, special directives were issued to the public promising, on the one hand, to treat all information received as confidential and, on the other hand, threatening with reprisals and indictments those who gave false information. No enumerators were killed, but the response of the people in many areas was not friendly (Selegen and Petrov, 1959). In spite of these limitations, the 1926 count was relatively good.

Censuses were ordered in 1933 and 1935, but they did not take place (Holubnychy, 1958). A census was taken in 1937, but the results were suppressed in their entirety because, according to the official report, inaccuracies and ideological errors were discovered in the formulation of questions and the development of the data (Lorimer, 1946, p. 222n.). The actual reason, it can be surmised, is that the population figure would have suggested how many millions had been killed in the enforced collectivization of agriculture during the First Five-Year Plan (cf. pp. 645–647, 662–668).

The next attempt was made two years later in 1939. Both "unconscientious" respondents and irresponsible enumerators were threatened with official reprisals (Selegen and Petrov, 1959). Only a small portion of the data collected in this census was published in the original volume. Some of the unpublished parts were found in German-occupied areas during the war, and these formed the basis for a new analysis of population trends during the 1930s (Martschenko, 1953). Two decades later, as part of the 1959 census, a substantial portion of the 1939 data was finally issued by the Soviet government.

According to rumors, a sample survey of the population was taken shortly after World War II, but the numbers of survivors indicated such devastating losses that the data were suppressed (Gordon, 1957).

The last population census was taken in 1959, after two years of careful preparation. The detailed results, published in sixteen volumes, constitute the most important source of demographic information on the Soviet Union to date (cf. Perevedentsev, 1967).

In summary, Soviet statistics available abroad include distortions and inaccuracies of a number of types, apart from the errors that result simply from human fallibility or inefficiency. (1) The pressure to maintain production norms is so great that the response to it sometimes is to tamper with one's reports. Original data include deliberate falsifications in a literal sense; a manager of a factory or a collective farm changes 5,000 to 6,000. Whether adulteration of this kind takes place at the level of the Central Statistical Administration is a moot point among Western sovietologists. (2) A more appropriate term to describe the usual practices of the Moscow bureaus is contextual distortion. For example, two percentages are compared without informing the reader that they were calculated on different bases, or a standard word like *harvest* is used in a very special sense. The intent is to give the foreign public a wrong impression, but this intent can sometimes be defeated (as it cannot be with falsification of the first type) by the application of careful and informed scholarship. (3) The omission of crucial data can be considered another type of distortion. For example, figures are published for good years, none for poor years. Or statistical aggregates are calculated with no hint as to which of several alternative formulas was used.

There has been a considerable improvement in the amount and somewhat less in the quality of the data available during the most recent years. Important gaps still persist, however, and any discussion of trends must be based in part on earlier, less reliable statistics.

### COMMUNIST IDEOLOGY AND POPULATION THEORY

Why should Communists, whose first principle is a planned society, object to family planning? This hostility continues the dispute that Malthus started in his attack on utopians like Condorcet and Godwin. In Marx's writings, "the contemptible Malthus" is rejected as a "plagiarist," "a shameless sycophant of the ruling classes," who perpetrated a "sin against science," "this libel on the human race." Apart from such vituperations, Marx's main objection to the principle of population can be stated in a single sentence: "Every special historic mode of production has its own special laws of population, historically valid within its limits alone." [3] Marx himself, however, had nothing to say about what governed growth of numbers in primitive, feudal, or socialist societies; and he took the rapid population increase of nineteenth-century Europe as a permanent feature and built his system around it, without even so imperfect a theory as Malthus's principle to account for it. If the population declined at the same rate at which machines displaced workers (a contingency that many demographers of the 1930s considered not only possible but even likely), then there would be no industrial reserve army, no "immiseration," no Marxian model altogether. Marx could reject Malthus only by taking vulgar Malthusianism for granted.

Both socialism and neo-Malthusianism sometimes appealed to the same rebellious individuals, but the usual pattern, and the all but invariable one for organizations rather than individuals, was contravention. Socialists and neo-Malthusians dealt in competing utopias. For the "Malthusian" true believer, the one social problem was population; to solve that was to solve all. An orthodox Marxist, on the contrary, believed that when the capitalist system was supplanted by a planned economy, population pressure would disappear, and that before such a fundamental transformation took place, the limitation of family size could not improve matters substantially.

[3] Karl Marx, *Capital*, Kerr, Chicago, 1906, 1, 693.

The variation of this theme in the Soviet Union can be exemplified by a typical attack on Malthusianism, "the man-hating ideology of imperialists" (Popov, 1953). It began with the basic Marxist dictum that each type of society—slave-owning, feudal, capitalist, socialist—has its own law of population. But under all circumstances population growth is good. "There is no absolute overpopulation under any social order. Even under capitalism, the level of productive forces is entirely adequate to feed the people." Indeed, a population increase in a country that has not yet achieved socialism is progressive in that it can help the transition from one stage to the next higher. "For example, the considerable population growth in the United States during the nineteenth century (due primarily to immigration) undoubtedly contributed to the rapid development of its capitalist economy." At any stage before the final one, it is true, society may suffer from a "relative" surplus of population, or unemployment. But,

Socialism does not know crises, poverty, and unemployment. Relative overpopulation, therefore, does not exist and cannot exist under socialism. The growth of population accelerates the development of a socialist society, increases its power and strength.

By the standards of Communist orthodoxy, the advantages derived from a growing population have no limit.

I would consider it barbaric for the [U.N. Population] Commission to contemplate a limitation of marriages or of legitimate births, and this for any country whatsoever, at any period whatsoever. With an adequate social organization it is possible to face any increase in population.[4]

The population doctrine of the Stalinist period, thus, consisted of a number of theses:

1. The Party is omnipotent. It can cope with any increase in population. The idea that the resources at the command of society are not only unlimited but "clearly" so, that man's ability to shape his environment to his

---

[4] The Soviet delegate to the Commission, speaking at its first meeting, in 1947; quoted in Alfred Sauvy, *Théorie générale de la population*, 1: *Économie et population*, Presses Universitaires de France, Paris, 1952, 174. In subsequent sessions, although continuing to reject the concept of an optimum population even as a theoretical abstraction, the Soviet delegates eventually accepted, "reluctantly," one of an optimum *rate* of population growth, thus compromising their utopian stand very little, for even in a socialist society a population can hardly grow at an infinite rate (Sauvy, 1948). See also Bronislaw Minc, speaking for the Soviet delegation, as paraphrased in the official preliminary report of the Rome population congress (U.N. Population Commission, "World Population Conference," E/CN.9/115, January 18, 1955, pp. 33–34); T. Ryabushkin, "On the World Population Conference" (translated in full from *Vestnik Statistiki*, No. 1, 1955), *Soviet Studies*, 7 (1955), 220–230.

needs is manifestly infinite, is the fundamental faith. "The notion of optimum is bourgeois because it sets a limit" (Sauvy, 1948).[5]

2. Population theory has the same purpose as any other science: to bolster the power of the Party within Soviet society, and that of the Soviet State in the international arena.

3. Control of fertility is associated with neo-Malthusianism and is thus anathema. "Raving fascists," "bestial imperialists," "lackeys of American monopolies who openly advocate cannibalism," "racist lynchers in Himmler's footsteps"—these are some of the designations of planned-parenthood advocates culled from the Soviet press of the 1950s.[6]

4. The welfare of the proletariat can be enhanced, however, by improving maternal health through birth-control measures that are ruled out on social-political grounds.

In one branch of international socialism, the utopianism of Marx and Engels was eventually relinquished: the Revisionists in Germany, the labor parties elsewhere, became more reasonable—that is, both more moderate and more rational. In the Soviet Union such Revisionist views began to be expressed openly only in the mid-1960s, mainly in a series of articles in *Literaturnaya Gazeta* (*cf.* Brackett, 1967). Within a few weeks at the end of 1965, several junior economists moved from a cautious recognition of population pressure elsewhere, to an admission that it exists also in the Soviet Union, to a proposed change in Marxist dogma. Orthodoxy was defended by, among others, Strumilin, who suggested that the spread of socialism may cause birth rates to fall so much as to cause underpopulation.[7] The final voice in this dialogue up to mid-1966 was an article by the

---

[5] In this sense, totalitarian rulers are the direct descendants of pre-Marxian socialists like Godwin and Condorcet. For both, the only limitations on man's control over nature are those imposed artificially, and thus remediably, by his inadequate institutions. The early utopians were idealists in both senses of the word: they based their acts on a humanitarian ideal of the future, and they refused to accept the limitations of the material world. As they remained ineffectual, they are remembered for their humanitarian values, but when their view of the world is combined with state power, it leads directly to mass terror. For one of man's principal limitations is his own physical nature, and in a state where human frailties are not admitted, weakness must be defined as malingering and error as sabotage. For a totalitarian state to grant that any task is physically impossible would be to forgo the total control over its people to which it aspires. To the Party, nothing is impossible: "there is no fortress," said Stalin, "that Bolsheviks cannot take by storm."

[6] *Cf.* William Petersen, "The Evolution of Soviet Family Policy," in *The Politics of Population,* Doubleday, Garden City, N. Y., 1964, pp. 103–124.

[7] Compare the suggestion (cited, p. 492, n. 4) that the way to bring population growth under control is to foster the spread of Catholicism. Stanislav G. Strumilin speaks with the greatest authority among the older generation of Soviet economists and statisticians. Born in 1877, he had professional and revolutionary careers well under way by 1917, and through all the subsequent shifts of policy he stayed in some post of authority and high honor. One is reminded of Abbé Sieyès, who, when asked what he had done in monarchist, revolutionary, Napoleonic, and republican France, replied, "I survived."

demographer, E. Arab-Ogly (June 11, 1966). This is a rounded statement of the new rationale.

The capital investment which any society can afford every year is not arbitrary; the amount is limited by annual accumulations. Every accumulation is a deduction from current consumption. Depending upon how they are earmarked, these capital investments can in turn be directed toward . . . doubling the prosperity of a constant population, say every twenty years, or doubling the population while maintaining the same level of living in approximately the same period. One and the same pudding cannot be eaten twice under two different names. . . . The state, of course, is not entitled to decide for people who should have children and how many. But it can, on the basis of the current and long-term demands of society as well as of a judicious combination of personal and social interests, bring to light the optimal rate of population growth. And it is entitled to influence the wishes of people to have more or less children, to help free them from prejudices in order to realize their objective interests, as well as to place at their disposal the most perfected and harmless means by which the actual number of children in the family may be made to correspond to the number desired. . . .

Malthus's notorious geometric progression should not make us despair, but the formula establishing the inverse correlation of birth rate and prosperity is a highly problematic basis for optimism. Genuine optimism stems from confidence that mankind is able to prevail over spontaneous social processes, including demographic ones, and that in the last analysis it will be able, as Engels noted, "to control the production of people just as it will by that time control the production of things" (Arab-Ogly, 1966).

Only a few symbols of orthodoxy remain—the attack on Malthus, the respectful quotation from Engels. In the main, this statement differs remarkably little from what non-Catholic Western demographers have been arguing for years. Those aberrant Soviet voices are like the Catholic ones that have attacked the Church's stand on birth control. In both cases it is a new departure that the attack was made openly and without immediate and overt punishment for the dissidents. But in neither instance can we expect the institution, the Soviet State or the Catholic Church, to divest itself completely of its considerable investment in traditional dogma. Although those arguing for a new position try to base themselves on new interpretations of sacred texts, it is not possible in either context to disguise the fact that what they want resembles very closely, in fact, what has heretofore been condemned as the kernel of heterodox thinking.

### NATIONALITIES IN THE USSR

Population theory, narrowly defined as the specification of how the number of undifferentiated persons can and should relate to the economy, is in flux in the Soviet Union. Communist doctrine on the rights of ethnic minorities was never consistent, and it has also contributed to wide fluctuations in policies concerning the diverse units of the Russian empire.

The fate of the minority peoples in the Soviet Union (and, with the extension of its influence, in Eastern Europe) has been based on three doctrines: (1) the Marxist and particularly the Bolshevik opposition to nationalism, (2) the Communist slogan of national self-determination, and (3) the growth of Russian patriotism from the First Five-Year Plan on. National self-determination has been consistently followed only at the propagandistic level of folk dancing and the like. With respect to more significant elements of minority cultures, the Party has vacillated, sometimes encouraging minority-language schools, newspapers, and theaters, sometimes banning them (cf. Kucera, 1954). Over the whole period of Soviet rule the dominant trend has been toward russification; for example, the program adopted at the 22nd Party Congress (1961) called for the "voluntary" adoption of the Russian language as "the common medium of intercourse and cooperation" (Vardys, 1965). Another policy, an internal version of the Pan-Slav movement, has been to consolidate "the Russians as first-class citizens, the Ukrainians as second-class, and the remainder as third-class" (Conquest, 1960, pp. 125–126).[8]

Party policy is ubiquitous. Even the simplest statistical fact—how many ethnic groups exist—has marked political overtones. National self-determination of a kind has been encouraged for small minorities, in order to prevent them from coalescing into more meaningful but also more powerful units. The Bashkir Republic is one instance of this policy of divide and rule: "the task of Bashkir nationalism from the Soviet point of view was to render impossible the emergence of a Moslem State on the borders of Europe and Asia, which might have covered over 150,000 square miles with a population of over 5,000,000" (Kolarz, 1955, p. 41). Some 180 nationalities, the figure often cited in Soviet statistics, is double the number of peoples with even a minimum cultural or linguistic self-expression; and only 30 to 45 of the nationalities are generally represented in formal institutions.

The Soviet population has been classified by nationality in each of the three major censuses, as shown in Table 17-1. These figures are difficult to interpret, however, for a recorded intercensal growth or decline can be the consequence of any of three factors:

[8] The increase in Slav, as contrasted with Russian, control can be shown most graphically by comparing the proportions of various nationalities in the population with those in the Party and especially its leadership. Under Stalin a number of Caucasian nationalities had been favored, especially Georgians (Stalin, Yezhov, and Beria were all of Georgian stock) and Armenians. From 1939 to 1961, while the Russians remained the dominant group, the percentages of both full and alternate members of the Party's Central Committee changed as follows: Georgians, 4.3 to 0.7; Armenians, 3.6 to 1.7; Jews, 10.8 to 0.3; Ukrainians, 7.9 to 18.5; Byelorussians, 0.7 to 3.4 (Bialer, 1964).

Table 17-1. Nationalities in the USSR, 1926, 1939, and 1959

| | POPULATION (THOUSANDS) | | | PERCENTAGE CHANGE | |
| | 1926 | 1939 | 1959 | 1926 TO 1939 | 1939 TO 1959 |
|---|---|---|---|---|---|
| U.S.S.R. | 147,028 | 170,467 | 208,827 | +16 | +22 |
| Major nationalities[a] | | | | | |
| Russian | 77,791 | 99,020 | 114,588 | +27 | +16 |
| Ukrainian | 31,195 | 28.070 | 36,981 | −10 | +32[b] |
| Byelorussian | 4,739 | 5,267 | 7,829 | +11 | +49[b] |
| Uzbek | 3,955 | 4,844 | 6,004 | +22 | +24 |
| Tatar | 3,478 | 4,300 | 4,969 | +24 | +16 |
| Kazakh | 3,968 | 3,099 | 3,581 | −22 | +16 |
| Azerbaidzhanian | 1,707 | 2,275 | 2,929 | +33 | +29 |
| Armenian | 1,568 | 2,152 | 2,787 | +37 | +30 |
| Georgian | 1,821 | 2,249 | 2,650 | +24 | +18 |
| Lithuanian | 43 | 32 | 2,326 | −24 | b |
| Jewish | 2,072 | 3,020 | 2,268 | +13 | −25 |
| Moldavian | 279 | 260 | 2,214 | −7 | b |
| Displaced nationalities | | | | | |
| German | 1,247 | 1,424 | 1,619 | +14 | +14 |
| Kirghiz | 763 | 884 | 974 | +16 | +10 |
| Chechen | 319 | 408 | 418 | +28 | +2 |
| Ingush | 74 | 92 | 106 | +24 | +15 |
| Balkar | 33 | 43 | 42 | +28 | −2 |
| Karachay | 55 | 76 | 81 | +37 | +7 |
| Kalmyk | 129 | 134 | 106 | +4 | −21 |

SOURCES: Frank Lorimer, *The Population of the Soviet Union: History and Prospects*, League of Nations, Princeton University Press, Princeton, N.J., 1946, Table 55; *Pravda*, February 4, 1960, translated in *Current Digest of the Soviet Press*, March 2, 1960.

[a] Those with more than 2 million in 1959, in order of size at that date.

[b] Increase due to annexation of new territory.

**1. Statistical reclassification.** The counts in the three censuses, it must be emphasized, are not wholly comparable. Even the Russian word translated as "nationality" was different (*narodnost* in 1926, *natsionalnost* in 1939 and 1959), and the returns in 1939 and 1959 were far less complete than in 1926. Supposedly, some of these adjustments were made to disguise the size of the depletion of the peoples that had suffered especially from one or another policy.

**2. Assimilation.** Between 1926 and 1939, there was an absolute decrease in most of the minorities not then identified with a USSR republic or district—Poles, Estonians, Latvians, Lithuanians, Bulgarians, Kurds, Iranians, and Chinese—presumably because these scattered groups assimilated to one of the major Soviet nationalities, particularly the Russian. Although in previous censuses persons were required to prove their nationality from their internal passports, in 1959 they were permitted to state the nationality with which they chose to be identified. This was an opportunity for members of ethnic minorities to "pass" as Russians, and some took advantage of it. Thus, the number of enumerated Ukrainians living outside the Ukraine fell from 8.0 million in 1926 to 5.1 million in 1959; and most of this loss may have been through a change in self-identification.[9]

**3. Differential Growth.** Since the Ukraine bore the brunt of the enforced collectivization of agriculture and the consequent famine, another portion of the decline in the number of Ukrainians represents the price they paid for the social transformation. The demographic effect of the parallel policy of forcing nomads to settle on the land, similarly, can probably be measured by the figures given for some of the nomadic peoples. The reported number of Kazakhs, for instance, decreased by 869,000 between 1926 and 1939, and as this is a group whose age structure and social norms favored rapid procreation, we should have expected an *increase* at least at the average rate for the whole country, or by 635,000 persons. Thus, some 1.5 million out of 4.0 million disappeared during the enforced "denomadization," when the Kazakhs' herds were depleted by about four-fifths. The virtually stationary Kalmyk population presumably reflects the somewhat less devastating effects of the policy on *this* nomadic people. The nationalities subjected to special terror during the 1930s, in short, included those at both ends of the cultural spectrum—large minorities with a cultural level comparable to the Russians', such as the Ukrainians and the ethnic Germans, and the more primitive, smaller peoples, many of which had a long and often bloody prerevolutionary history of opposition to russification.

During and immediately following World War II the government dissolved four Autonomous Republics of the USSR and expunged four major and several minor peoples from the ethnographic list, banishing their populations *en masse* (see Table 17-1). In his speech in 1956 to the 20th Party Congress, Khrushchev characterized these deportations as "monstrous." The policy of the Soviet government, in his words, had been "to make whole nations responsible for inimical activity, including women, children, old people, Communists and Komsomol; to use mass repression against them; and to expose them to misery and suffering for the hostile acts of individual persons or groups of persons" (Khrushchev, 1956, pp. 44–45). In 1957, some twelve or more years after the banishment, the list of "autonomous" republics and territories was expanded to include again some of those who had been expunged, and some of the deported people—of those

[9] Solomon M. Schwarz, "K natsional'nomu voprosu v SSSR," *Sotsialisticheskii Vestnik,* April 1960, pp. 63–64. See also Lorimer, 1946, p. 139.

who had survived—were permitted to return.[10] The re-established Chechen-Ingush Republic does not have the old boundaries: some of the Ingush territory was not regained, and in its place the inhabitants were compensated with an area marked "sand" on the official map (Conquest, 1960, p. 173). In 1967 the exoneration was extended to the Tatars, whose banishment was then also condemned as unjust. Nevertheless a return to their traditional home land was not envisaged; the Tatars "will be encouraged to remain in their present homes." [11]

Soviet policy toward the Jews deserves special examination for, from the 1917 revolution on, propaganda has contrasted it with tsarist or Nazi programs. Actually, Soviet policy has never been entirely free of anti-Semitism. Many Jews of tsarist Russia were socialists, but few were Bolsheviks. The Bolshevik victory meant that Jews were persecuted as members of a religious faith, as businessmen, as nationalists, and as socialists, but for a time the pogroms that had been endemic in tsarist Russia disappeared. Specific opposition to Jews as Jews developed during the 1930s, was strongly reinforced by the Nazi-Soviet Friendship Pact of 1939–41, and survived the German invasion of Russia. In the postwar period, in both Russia and its East European satellites, the campaign against Jews developed from opposition to "cosmopolitans" or "Zionist bourgeois nationalists" to virulent, undisguised persecution of Jews.[12]

Some of the major events or trends have been:

**The "Doctors' Plot" (1953).** Nine Jewish physicians were to be unmasked as agents of an American-Zionist conspiracy, allegedly masterminded by the Joint Distribution Committee (a relief agency active in Eastern Europe but not in the Soviet Union). Only Stalin's death saved them and—considering the fate of other minorities—perhaps the entire Jewish community.

**Judaism as a religion** is subjected to far greater hostility than other reli-

---

[10] *The New York Times,* February 12 and May 5, 1957.

[11] *Ibid.,* September 12, 1967.

[12] Among the most informative accounts are a number of articles in *Commentary,* published by the American Jewish Committee—for example, Peter Meyer, "Soviet Anti-Semitism in High Gear," February 1953, pp. 115–120; Franz Borkenau, "Was Malenkov Behind the Anti-Semitic Plot?," May 1953, pp. 438–466; Walter Z. Laqueur, "Soviet Policy and Jewish Fate," October 1956, pp. 303–312; A. Wiseman and O. Pick, "Soviet Jews under Khrushchev," February 1959, pp. 127–132; Maurice Friedberg, "The State of Soviet Jewry," January 1965, pp. 38–43. See also, as among the best of a sizable literature, Schwarz, 1951; Erich Goldhagen, "Communism and Anti-Semitism," *Problems of Communism,* 9 (1960), 35–43; Decter, 1963; Moshe Decter, "Silence and Yearning," the whole of a special issue of *Congress Bi-Weekly,* December 5, 1966; Maurice Friedberg, "On Reading Recent Soviet Judaica," *Survey* (London), No. 62 (1967), 167–178. In England a regular periodical was established to report on "events affecting Jews in the Soviet bloc": *Jews in Eastern Europe* (London). Patterns of anti-Semitism in satellite countries are variations on the Russian theme; for a detailed account up to the death of Stalin, see Peter Meyer *et al., The Jews in the Soviet Satellites,* Syracuse University Press, Syracuse, N.Y., 1953.

gions. Prayerbooks, hymnals, and other sacred works are available to all other denominations; no Hebrew Bible has been published since 1917. The study of Hebrew was long banned. Until after Stalin's death the Soviet Union had no yeshiva (rabbinical seminary); up to 1963, the one established in 1957 graduated two men, neither of whom functioned as a synagogue leader.

**Yiddish culture** has been all but obliterated. In 1932 (the high point since 1917) 668 Yiddish books were published; in 1940, still 359; from 1949 to 1958, none; from 1959 to 1966, a total of eleven, mostly classics by authors no longer living. There is one periodical, *Sovietish Heimland* (Soviet Fatherland), a bimonthly founded in 1961; among probably all the world's Jewish periodicals, it had the dubious distinction of being the only one to ignore *Babii Yar*, Yevgenii Yevtushenko's poem indicting Soviet anti-Semitism.

**Official anti-Semitism**, especially virulent in the provincial press, uses all of the conventional Russian stereotypes—Jews as money-worshippers, drunks, cosmopolitans who are potentially or actually subversive, and so on. In 1963 the Ukrainian Academy of Sciences officially sponsored a book, *Judaism without Embellishment*, by Trofim K. Kichko, illustrated by caricatures hauntingly reminiscent of Julius Streicher's *Der Stürmer*, the most vicious of the Nazis' anti-Jewish publications.[13]

**Jews are barred from social advancement.** The two main roads, the upper positions in the Party and university study, once had as many Jews as one would expect from their concentration in urban centers and their frequent professional qualifications for administrative posts. The percentage of Jews in the student bodies of "higher education" (which includes normal schools, music conservatories, and journalism institutes) fell from 13.5 in 1935 to 3.1 in 1962; in universities alone, the decline was even sharper. The increasing dominance of Slavic peoples in the leading ranks of the Party (see p. 638, n. 8) has reduced the status especially of the Jews.

**Jews as embezzlers and speculators** have been featured in the campaign against economic crimes. During the first two years after a 1961 law establishing the death penalty for such acts, thirty-six trials were reported in twenty-six different cities. Not only were there forty-two Jews among the seventy condemned to death, but they were so identified and depicted as typical of a cunning and unscrupulous people.

In sum, Soviet policy places the Jews in an inextricable vise. They are allowed neither to assimilate, nor live a full Jewish life, nor to emigrate (as many would

---

13 One cartoon, for example, shows a hook-nosed man bowing obsequiously to an enormous boot emblazened with a swastika; the caption reads, "During the years of the Hitlerite occupation, the Zionist leaders served the Fascists." These drawings were reproduced in the *New Leader*, March 16, 1964. See also Moshe Decter, editor, *Israel and the Jews in the Soviet Mirror: Soviet Cartoons on the Middle East Crisis*, Conference on the Status of Soviet Jews, New York, 1967.

wish) to Israel or any other place where they might live freely as Jews (Decter, 1963).

### WAR AND REVOLUTION

Thus far we have reviewed the sources of information on the Soviet population available to Western scholars and the Communist theories that, at least in principle, guide the demographic policies of the Soviet State. How in fact have these theories worked out, so far as one can tell from the partial and deficient record?

Under the new regime that the Bolsheviks established in November 1917, the sale or purchase of commodities was prohibited, but no alternative system of distribution could be established. Industry was disorganized, the transportation system damaged and worn out, the government administration disrupted by widespread strikes. Cities could be fed only by sending armies out into the countryside to confiscate the peasants' food. The state printing presses deprived paper rubles of all value: from 1913 to 1917, prices increased by three times, but by 1921 they were some 16,800 times the 1913 figure (Vernadsky, 1961, p. 316). A serious strike wave in Petrograd, which quickly developed from economic to political goals, was broken with lockouts and military force.

The seven years of war, aggravated by tsarist and Bolshevik bureaucratic inefficiency, had a fearful impact on the population. Thousands were killed by terror and counterterror, hundreds of thousands in the civil strife, but these were by far not the major component of the extraordinary mortality. With the constant movement of hungry hordes, epidemics spread through the country. Typhus alone killed more than 1.5 million in 1919–20. In the winter of 1921–22, after years of food shortages and a serious drought, Russia suffered a devastating famine (Fisher, 1927).

The depletion in the population during this whole period is not at all easy to calculate. Tsarist Russia's only census had been in 1897, and, as we have noted, the first reliable Soviet census was in 1926. Over this interval, adjusting for changes in Russia's territory, the population increased from 106 to 147 million, or by 38.6 per cent in slightly less than 30 years. The losses between 1914 and 1923 can be estimated if we postulate that the "normal" rate of natural increase was constant from 1897 on. Such an assumption would seem to be reasonable. In the 39 provinces of European Russia that remained Russian after the revolution, the average birth rate fell from 50.4 in 1899–1901 to 47.6 in 1911–13, and the average death rate from 33.1 to 29.6. The rate of natural increase varied, thus, only between 17.3 and 18.0 per thousand. If, to be conservative, we take 17.15 as the average annual increase per thousand from 1897 on, this would have resulted in a population of 175 million in 1926. The actual census count was 28 million short of this (or 16 per cent); and this difference can be taken as the total deficit (Lorimer, 1946, Chapter 3). The factors responsible for this population loss from 1914 to 1926, as estimated by Lorimer from various more or less satisfactory data, are as follows:

| | |
|---|---|
| Military deaths | 2 million |
| Civilian deaths | 14 |
| Net emigration | 2 |
| Birth deficit [14] | 10 |
| | |
| TOTAL | 28 million |

These figures are not precise, of course, but they are probably correct to the nearest million, as shown. "During the years 1915–23 the Russian people underwent the most cataclysmic changes since the Mongol invasion in the early thirteenth century" (*ibid.*, p. 42).

The Bolshevik revolution was a *political* coup; its main purpose was to take power. The Bolshevik *social* revolution began on October 1, 1928, when the First Five-Year Plan went into effect. The principal purpose of the planned economy as a whole has been to develop heavy industry, but in the first plan the emphasis was on the collectivization of agriculture, which could be realized only through mass terror. This momentous process not only converted the peasantry into a landless proletariat, peons of the State, but also shaped every element of Soviet society. In particular, it had a tremendous effect on the population both directly by the millions who were killed and indirectly by the fact that the Soviet Union has to this day not been able to establish an efficient agriculture.

The Russian peasantry was essentially a single class, unified by both its miserable living conditions and its hostility to the regime. In Soviet law and in Party practice, however, the class was divided into three: the "wealthy" kulaks, the "middle" peasants, and the "poor" peasants.[15] The Party's program of "dekulakization" was to be achieved, if possible, by engaging the poor and middle peasants against the kulaks. In Stalin's words,

We have recently passed from the policy of *restricting* the exploiting proclivities of the kulaks to the policy of *eliminating the kulaks as a class*. . . . The expropriation of the kulaks is an integral part of the formation and development of the

---

[14] That is, the difference between the actual number of births and the number that would have occurred if the "normal" rate of natural increase had continued during this period.

[15] The word *kulak* means "fist"; the implication is a greedy, grasping person who closes his hand around anything he can get hold of. The designations of the three peasant classes are not to be interpreted in Western terms; in 1926 their average per capita *annual* income was, respectively, $88, $46, and $39 (data presented at the 15th Party Conference, cited in Vernadsky, 1951 edition, p. 328n.).

collective farms. That is why it is ridiculous and fatuous to expatiate today on the expropriation of the kulaks. You do not lament the loss of the hair of one who has been beheaded.

There is another question which seems no less ridiculous: whether the kulak should be permitted to join the collective farms. Of course not, for he is a sworn enemy of the collective farm movement. Clear, one would think.[16]

As the collectivization proceeded, the legal criteria defining kulaks were changed repeatedly; the precise boundary became more and more elusive as the Party approached its goal. Eventually all those who tried to fight the Party programs were defined as kulaks or, if this was too preposterous, as kulak-followers (*podkulachniki*).[17]

By reinforcing the jealousies and hatreds in the village, by recreating the mood of the civil war, the tiny Party was able to manipulate the overwhelming majority of the population and expropriate the peasants' property *in toto* almost before they knew what was happening. At first some of the "middle" and "poor" peasants probably really believed that the Party organizer had intervened in their interest. All through the year 1929 collectivization was pushed forward with quasi-legal methods—through extra tax levies, quotas, attachments, auctions, trials before special traveling courts, and so on. As a consequence, "a million families suddenly found themselves pariahs, without any rights which need be respected, and without any knowledge as to what they might do to be saved" (Strong, 1931, p. 81). This newly created class of outcasts was expropriated of its means of subsistence, disfranchised, deprived of ration cards and of the right to purchase in the cooperative stores; their children were expelled from school, and their sick were excluded from medical treatment. By the beginning of 1930, when still less than a quarter of the peasant households were collectivized, the Party dropped its pretense that it was intervening to support the poor peasants against their class enemies and opened up a mass offensive against the Soviet peoples. The world was justifiably horrified when the Nazis punished the activities of the Czech underground by completely destroying one village, Lidice; but we have no record of how many Russian Lidices were obliterated by their own state police. For example,

Sixteen villages in the Ukraine failed to produce the grain required from them, and their failure was attributed by the authorities to deliberate sabotage. A decree was published in the local papers announcing that all grain hoarded in the offending villages was to be confiscated, the cooperative stores in the villages were to be closed, and no State distributing authority was to arrange to send food to them—in

---

[16] Joseph Stalin, "Problems of Agrarian Policy in the USSR" (1929), *Leninism: Selected Writings*, International Publishers, New York, 1942, pp. 145–164; italics in the original. Compare Hitler on Jews: "One must not show mercy to people whom fate has determined will perish" (Hilberg, 1967, p. 662).

[17] See pp. 688–689 on the ambiguities in the Nazis' definition of "Jews."

other words, sixteen villages were condemned to starve or secretly flee from their homes (Monkhouse, 1934, p. 207).

With such methods, Stalin's "solid collectivization" developed rapidly. From January 20 to March 1, 1930, the number of peasant homesteads collectivized increased from 4.4 to 14.3 million, or from 21.6 to 55.0 per cent of the total.[18] After these forty days of terror, Stalin condemned the "feverish pursuit of inflated collectivization figures" he had previously decreed. His famous speech, "Dizziness from Success," was promptly published and distributed by the millions. "The Bolsheviks had pursued their typical tactics—they had driven through with greater strength than needed, and could retire to consolidate position" (Strong, 1931, p. 93).

The collectives formed by these methods were hardly model farms. Rather than deliver their property to the State, the peasants burned the seed grain and killed the livestock. Two-fifths of the cattle disappeared, two-thirds of the sheep and goats, more than half of the swine and of the horses (Lorimer, 1946, p. 109). In 1930 all Russia had only 72,000 tractors, and this was the mechanical base of the collectivization. And on such a base a large farm without draft animals was a contradiction in terms. There was a comparable depletion in human labor power. After the most skillful and diligent peasants had been ousted, their place as rural leaders was taken by 25,000 city men and youths,[19] anxious only for the Party career they could establish by successfully corraling the peasant mass.

The chaos in agriculture had as its inevitable consequence an increasing food shortage, culminating in another famine. In the number of deaths it brought about, this was comparable to the one twelve years before, but the regime's attitude was different. In 1921–22, the Soviet Union had appealed for and received substantial aid from abroad; in 1932–33, the government denied the very fact of the famine. Dr. Ewald Ammende, who had worked in Russia a decade earlier as a representative of the Red Cross, in 1933 became secretary of another international relief organization; but he was not permitted to do more than send in a few food parcels, some of which were returned (Ammende, 1936; cf. Chamberlin, 1934).

In general, city dwellers fared better, but their life was not easy. Housing was incredibly poor, and for a period got worse. To enforce labor discipline, the government reintroduced from tsarist days the internal passport and instituted a wide range of measures designed to quicken the country's industrialization. Food cards were abolished, and class distinctions were established in the amount of food given out.

[18] *Izvestia*, March 9, 1930, cited in Alexander Baykov, *The Development of the Soviet Economic System*, University Press, Cambridge, 1946, p. 196.

[19] See the report of Kaganovich to the 16th Party Congress, "Organizational Report of the Central Committee," *International Press Correspondence*, **10** (July 25, 1930), 638–649.

Street scenes in Kharkov, USSR, Summer 1933. *Top:* Familiarity breeds indifference: pedestrians pass by several who had died of hunger with hardly a glance. *Bottom:* Collecting corpses for burial.

SOURCE: Ewald Ammende, *Human Life in Russia*, London: Allen & Unwin, 1936.

### POLITICAL-ECONOMIC TERROR AND FORCED LABOR

Under such conditions the control of the population was possible only by a considerable increase in the size and power of the terror apparatus.[20] Forced labor was of several types, ranging from lesser to greater severity:

1. Work performed by those detained in ordinary prisons. This differs from the system in other countries mainly in that under a planned economy there is no pressure from trade unions or private entrepreneurs to restrict the unfair competition of prison labor.

2. "Corrective" labor performed by a person at his usual place of work, usually as a punishment for a minor infraction of labor discipline.

3. The corvée, or the sixth day's work without pay, required of all able-bodied male and female members of collective farms.

4. Forced resettlement, or deportation to a prescribed place of exile where persons lived in the general community but under Chekists' supervision.

5. "Labor colonies," which combined deportation, forced labor during working hours, and residence outside camps.

6. Forced labor *per se*, under which persons were sent to forced-labor camps where they worked and lived entirely under control of the NKVD.

Which elements constitute characteristic features of a totalitarian regime —where in this list to draw the line—is to some degree a matter of opinion. This discussion is restricted mainly to the last type, the ultimate degradation of laborers to the status of industrial slaves. By now we have hundreds of detailed descriptions of Soviet forced labor. From such accounts—by former inmates, by NKVD officials who defected, by Western analyses of the half-hidden information in official records—we know how many camps there were, where they were situated, and what camp life was like.

[20] A few weeks after they took power, the Bolsheviks had established the Cheka, or the Extraordinary Commission for Combating Counterrevolution, Sabotage, and Speculation. Over the years, the designation of the security police has been changed repeatedly— from Cheka to GPU (State Political Administration) to OGPU (United GPU) to NKVD to MVD (the People's Commissariat—or, later, Ministry—of Internal Affairs)—reflecting a continual enlargement of its function, reorganization based on Party-State jealousies, and possibly the attempt to keep some of its activities secret. As the NKVD or MVD, it became an outlandish combination of routine civil administration and terror apparatus. Its duties ranged from tasks like the registration of vital events or fire-fighting to the resettlement of populations and the control of forced-labor camps and other penal institutions. In 1941, a portion of the NKVD was separated off as the NKGB (People's Commissariat of State Security), and it was this unit that carried out the postwar purges. Its successor, the MGB, was transformed after Stalin's death into the KGB (Committee of State Security), headed initially by General Ivan A. Serov, a veteran of the system who had been responsible for some of its greatest terror. The partial continuity throughout the term of the Soviet regime is suggested by the fact that members of the security police have always retained their original designation—"Chekists."

The one point on which there is substantial disagreement among Western scholars is also one of the most important—what was the slave-labor population?

Up until 1928 the figures were relatively negligible; at the beginning of that year there were only 30,000 men detained in the camps. Thereafter the figure rose to many millions, but how many? The variation in estimates is due in part, of course, to the inherent blocks to interpreting the incomplete and defective data. But a portion of the range reflects the cyclical growth in the total camp population from one period to another. To borrow the terminology of the economists, slave labor was a commodity with a rapid turnover, so that it is important to distinguish between stock and flow.

The death rate in the camps was extremely high. Many of them were situated in the far North, where even under the best conditions life is dangerous. A camp inmate worked ten to fourteen hours a day at heavy, exhausting labor—removing earth, felling and chopping trees, mining, fishing. He was driven to work hard both by guards and by a differential food ration, which ranged from grossly inadequate for those who completed their quota of work to a starvation diet for those who did not. The clothing of the prisoners was unsuitable, and when they took sick they had to depend on a poorly staffed dispensary that lacked essential equipment and drugs. According to one estimate, during a six-month period 30 per cent of the inmates of one camp died; and something like this rate must have been typical until the middle-aged and less sturdy portions of a new group of prisoners were killed off. The general mortality of the camp population, estimated at about 10 per cent in 1933, probably rose to about 20 per cent by 1938 (Swianiewicz, 1965, p. 17).

Therefore the number of slaves, whatever it was at any time, could hardly have been maintained by the routine terror of normal Stalinism. It must have depended on the extraordinary spurts that recurred every several years. We can distinguish three periods of major recruitment: (1) 1929–32, when the principal source of slaves was the disaffected peasantry; (2) 1936–38, when Yezhov, starting in the Party and its periphery, was eventually able to uncover traitors in every sector of the society; and (3) 1941–45, when the camp population was renewed from substantial percentages of conquered nations, Soviet ethnic minorities, enemy prisoners of war, and former Soviet prisoners of war, who were presumed to have been contaminated. At the height of these drives the total was at a maximum, and during the intervening periods of relaxed terror, at a minimum. Depending on where in this cycle estimates happened to fall, they could be quite precise and yet vary by a factor, say, of one to three.

1. During the transformation of the Soviet countryside, 70 to 80 per cent of the labor-camp population—or some 3.5 million persons—were peasants. Perhaps as many were deported to forced settlements, where limits in the

type of work usually available generally also meant a shift out of agriculture, and as many again died from privation or were executed. The surplus
agricultural population, which had resulted in the underemployment of
peasants and their families, was thus reduced by some 10 million—the figure
that, according to Churchill's memoirs, Stalin gave him as the number of
peasants processed during the four-year collectivization campaign.

2. Once the rational economic purpose of the terror had been achieved,
a sizable number of the Party were for a relaxation. The leading advocate
of this position was Sergei M. Kirov, whose murder started a new and
greater cycle of terror.[21] In 1936 Nikolai I. Yezhov, who had been Stalin's
liaison between the Politburo and the security police, was appointed chief
of the NKVD. During the two years he held the post he administered a
wave of terror that has been named after its director—the Yezhovshchina.
The first victims were those in the Party and its affiliates who had opposed
Stalin, and from these nuclei the purge spread throughout Soviet society.

The vicious practice was condoned of having the NKVD prepare lists of persons
whose cases were under the jurisdiction of the Military Collegium and whose
sentences were prepared in advance. Yezhov would send these lists to Stalin personally for his approval of the proposed punishment. In 1937–38, 383 such lists
containing the names of many thousands of Party, Soviet, Komsomol, Army, and
economic workers were sent to Stalin. He approved these lists (Khrushchev, 1956,
p. 32).

The number of forced laborers on the eve of World War II, consisting
of the remnants of dissident peasants and the victims of Yezhov's policy,
was probably some 6.9 million (Swianiewicz, 1965, p. 31; cf. Lorimer, 1946,
p. 229).[22]

3. During the war and its aftermath, non-Russians comprised the new
stock from which forced laborers were selected. In addition to the ethnic
minorities expunged from Russia's polyglot empire (see pp. 638–641), these
new sources were occupied Poland; the roughly 23 million persons in-

[21] His assassin was one Nikolaev, a former member of the Komsomol (Communist
Youth) and of the Cheka, but behind him in all likelihood stood Stalin and his faction
in the Party, whose imminent defeat was thus circumvented. See Boris I. Nicolaevsky,
*Power and the Soviet Elite*, Praeger, New York, 1965, especially pp. 26–65.

[22] The lowest responsible estimate, 2.3 million in 1937, was by Professor Nicholas S.
Timasheff of Fordham University; the figure was based on electoral statistics and thus
on the probably fallacious assumption that, during the appalling confusion of the
Yezhovshchina, the names of persons sent to camps were immediately deleted from
voters' lists. Naum Jasny, working from a captured reprint of the 1941 plan, arrived at
a total of 3.5 million; but a number of regular forced-labor activities were not included
in the edition of the 1941 plan that had fallen into American hands, and he also omitted
the sizable number of laborers contracted from the NKVD by other units of the Soviet
economy (cf. Swianiewicz, 1965, pp. 30–31). The estimate of Dallin and Nicolaevsky
(1947, p. 86) was 7 to 12 million. Other approximations, presumably including forced
settlers as well as forced laborers, go as high as 20 million (Swianiewicz, 1965, p. 85).

habiting annexed territories (Table 17-2); some 5 million prisoners of war; former Soviet prisoners of war and so-called *Ostarbeiter* (Slavs sent from German-occupied territories to forced labor in Germany), both of whom were regarded as suspect. Out of the total new stock of some 14.7 million (Table 17-3), the proportion subjected to forced labor or forced settlement differed among the various categories—virtually all of the 400,000 Volga Germans or 200,000 Crimean Tatars, a relatively small percentage of the returned Soviet prisoners of war. "The total war-time influx of compulsory labor from [non-Russian] external and internal sources . . . was probably between 7 and 8 million, not counting the Poles released in 1941–42" (Swianiewicz, 1965, p. 43). The estimate of 6.9 million in 1941 included about a million alien deportees; and if this overlap is excluded and mortality

Table 17-2. Annexations to the USSR, 1939–45

| DATE | REGION | SIZE (SQ. KM.) | POPULATION (THOUSANDS) |
|---|---|---|---|
| November, 1939 | Polish provinces (excluding Vilna) | 194,800 | 12,500 [a] |
| March, 1940 | Finnish provinces | 35,100 | 420 [a] |
| August, 1940 | Rumanian provinces (Bessarabia and North Bukovina) | 50,400 | 3,700 |
| August, 1940 | Lithuania (including Vilna) | 59,800 | 2,925 |
| August, 1940 | Latvia | 65,800 | 1,951 |
| August, 1940 | Estonia | 47,500 | 1,122 |
| September, 1944 | Petchenga Raion (Murmansk) | 10,480 | 5 |
| September, 1944 | Tuva Autonomous Oblast | 150,000 | 70 |
| October, 1944 | Memel territory | 2,850 | 150 |
| August, 1945 | Kaliningrad Oblast (Koenigsberg area) | 9,000 | 400 |
| August, 1945 | Byalistock-Suwalki and Przemysl areas—lost to Poland | −14,200 | −850 |
| September, 1945 | Transcarpathian area | 12,620 | 800 |
| September, 1945 | Karafuto (South Sakhalin) | 36,090 | 420 |
| September, 1945 | Kurile Islands | 10,100 | 5 |
| Net gain, November, 1939–September, 1945 | | 670,340 | 23,618 |

SOURCE: Abram Bergson and Hans Heymann, Jr., *Soviet National Income and Product, 1940–48*, Columbia University Press, New York, 1954, Table 1, p. 6. Copyright 1954, The RAND Corporation.

[a] The cited figures do not take into account concomitant losses. Following the partition of Poland, an exchange of populations between Germany and the USSR resulted in a net loss of 260,000 persons from the Soviet-annexed Polish provinces; similarly, from the Soviet-incorporated Finnish areas some 415,000 Karelians were evacuated to Finland.

Table 17-3. Estimated Numbers Deported to the Soviet Union from Annexed or Occupied Territories, Including Soviet Minorities Transported within the USSR, 1939 to c. 1948

| | | |
|---|---|---|
| Alien Deportees | | 2,044,000 |
| Polish | 880,000 [a] | |
| Lithuanian | 38,000 | |
| Latvian | 34,000 | |
| Estonian | 97,000 | |
| German and Volksdeutsche [b] | 700,000 | |
| Hungarian | 295,000 | |
| Rumanian | (?) | |
| | | |
| Prisoners of War | | 4,889,000 |
| German | 3,740,000 | |
| Japanese | 594,000 | |
| Hungarian | 325,000 | |
| Rumanian | 230,000 | |
| Italian, Spanish, French, Finnish, Slovak | (?) | |
| | | |
| Soviet Subjects Returned to USSR | | 4,500,000 |
| Prisoners of War | 2,000,000 | |
| Civilians | 2,500,000 | |
| | | |
| Soviet "Unpeoples" [c] | | 3,261,000 |
| Germans | 1,424,000 [d] | |
| Kirghiz | 884,000 | |
| Chechens | 408,000 | |
| Tatars | 200,000 | |
| Ingushi | 92,000 | |
| Balkars | 43,000 | |
| Karachay | 76,000 | |
| Kalmyks | 134,000 | |
| | | |
| TOTAL | | 14,694,000 |

SOURCE: Various estimates, as compiled in S. Swianiewicz, *Forced Labour and Economic Development: An Enquiry into the Experience of Soviet Industrialisation,* published by Oxford University Press for the Royal Institute of International Affairs, London, 1965, pp. 42–45.

[a] This may be too conservative an estimate. According to figures compiled by the Polish Embassy in Moscow from the testimony of some 18,000 witnesses, from September 17, 1939, to June 14, 1941 (that is, during the period of the Soviet-Nazi Friendship Pact), 1,692,000 Poles, Jews, Ukrainians, and Byelorussians, including 160,000 children and adolescents, were forcibly taken from their homes and deported to the Soviet Union. Included were 230,000 soldiers and officers of the Polish Army; 990,000 civilians with a "nationalistic bourgeois background"; 250,000 "class enemies"; 210,000 Poles conscripted into the Red Army and then sent deep into the Soviet Union; and 12,000 other Poles

during the period is ignored, the postwar total comes to some 13 million. In 1948 the British Government concluded that the number of forced laborers was more than 10 million (*ibid.*, p. 44), and this is perhaps as good a guess as one can make of the total when the post-Stalin relaxation got under way.

### INTERNAL MIGRATION SINCE 1953

In a free economy one factor determining the location of industry is an available supply of workers; but if not enough are in the area to start with, an effort is made to attract more with higher wages. Soviet industry has been developed mainly in areas chosen by national or specifically military criteria, and the system by which consumer goods are supplied and distributed has never been efficient enough to afford attractions to in-migrants. Public-opinion surveys have been taken over from the United States in the hope that, by pinpointing the main reasons for dissatisfaction, the State will be able to achieve labor's compliance as cheaply as possible. However, according to a large manpower survey conducted by a Novosibirsk institute, higher wages would not be enough to get people to settle in Siberia, for the main discontent was with inadequate housing and public services. During the Seven-Year Plan (1959–65), probably more people left Siberia than could be induced to come to it.[23] In any case, the continued push to disperse the Soviet population could be effected by a differential income only to the degree that the supply of commodities permits. Agriculture has remained the prime headache of the economy, but after decades of a narrow concentration on capital accumulation, the recurrent crisis in food production is only one block to the repeatedly proclaimed intention to shift to a greater stress on consumer goods. Each manager in charge of manufacturing them knows that his professional reputation and income depend on whether he meets or overfulfills the factory's output quota, as defined in terms of weight or price or, in plants operating under the newly implemented Liberman system, profit—but hardly ever quality (*cf.* Shaffer, 1963). Soviet distribution services are notoriously inefficient: in each shop each customer must line up three times, once to price the merchandise, once to pay for it, and once to pick it up.

---

gathered from the Baltic area. See Edward J. Rozek, *Allied Wartime Diplomacy: A Pattern in Poland,* Wiley, New York, 1958, pp. 46, 66n.

*b* The "Volksdeutsche" were persons of German stock and culture living in German-speaking enclaves in various East European countries.

*c* The figures given are the totals in the 1939 census.

*d* The Volga Germans, those most immediately affected, numbered about 400,000. However, persons of German culture living in other parts of the Soviet Union were probably also subject to deportation (*cf.* Frederick C. Barghoorn, *Soviet Russian Nationalism,* Oxford University Press, New York, 1956, p. 80).

[23] *The New York Times,* October 31, 1967.

Apart from the quality of the goods and the consumer's convenience, how much can he acquire? The minimum wage for Soviet nonagricultural workers is 40–45 rubles a month, but until the mid-1960s collective farmers were not covered. Very roughly, one ruble is equivalent to one dollar in

Table 17-4. Approximate Work Time Required to Buy Selected Commodities in Moscow and New York City, January 15, 1966

| COMMODITY | MOSCOW | NEW YORK | MOSCOW AS PER CENT OF NEW YORK |
|---|---|---|---|
| **Food** | | | |
| White bread (half kilogram) | 28 min. | 6.6 min. | 400 |
| Potatoes (kilogram) | 10 min. | 3.3 min. | 300 |
| Rib roast (kilogram) | 160 min. | 44 min. | 350 |
| Salted butter (kilogram)[a] | 360 min. | 37 min. | 1,000 |
| Sugar (kilogram) | 104 min. | 6 min. | 1,500 |
| Milk (liter) | 30 min. | 6.2 min. | 500 |
| Eggs (per 10)[b] | 90 min. | 11.7 min. | 800 |
| Tea (50 grams) | 38 min. | 3.2 min. | 1,200 |
| **Clothing** | | | |
| Men's cotton shirt, low-priced (each) | 13 hrs. | 1.7 hr. | 750 |
| Men's suit, wool, single-breasted, medium-priced (each) | 183 hrs. | 23.6 hrs. | 800 |
| Men's leather shoes (pair) | 41 hrs. | 6.6 hrs. | 600 |
| Women's street dress, rayon (each) | 49 hrs. | 5 hrs. | 1,000 |
| Women's leather shoes, medium-priced (pair) | 38 hrs. | 5.5 hrs. | 700 |
| Nylon stockings (pair) | 5 hrs. | 0.51 hr. | 1,000 |
| **Other** | | | |
| Toilet soap (100-gram cake) | 21 min. | 2.7 min. | 800 |
| Cigarettes (package of 20) | 20 min. | 8 min. | 250 |
| Vodka (half liter) | 5 hrs. | 1.25 hr. | 400 |

SOURCE: Edmund Nash, "Recent Changes in Labor Controls in the Soviet Union," in Congress of the United States, Joint Economic Commitee, *New Directions in the Soviet Economy,* Part III: *The Human Resources,* 89th Congress, 2nd Session, Washington, D.C., 1966, pp. 849–870.

[a] First quality in New York; quality not specified in Moscow.

[b] Large, Grade A, in New York; second grade in Moscow, though eggs at this price were usually not available.

purchasing power. In the Soviet Union, medical services are free and rent is cheap, but the costs of other consumer goods and services are much higher than in the West (*cf.* Chapman, 1964). The relative costs of various consumer goods in hours of working time indicate how much the Soviet consumer lags behind, for example, his American counterpart (Table 17-4). Wages were the averages earned by workers in manufacturing, 0.60 rubles per hour in Moscow and $2.70 per hour in New York. Moscow prices were those in State stores, and since these are lower than those in private trade, the indicated purchasing power of Soviet workers may be somewhat inflated.

As the economy does not furnish sufficient means to stimulate the redistribution of population called for in plans, this is effected also through a number of programs, which are briefly described in the following paragraphs, beginning with the most voluntarist and ending with current examples of forced migrations.

1. **The family-resettlement program,** intended mainly to facilitate the migration of peasants to thinly populated rural areas, operates as a truly voluntary system. Under certain conditions, the head of a family is permitted to investigate the proposed resettlement site and to return home before making his decision. Inducements to move may include, in addition to assurance of work in the new place, exemption from taxation for a specified period, financial assistance in building a home and getting settled, free transportation of the whole family and in some cases also of household possessions and personally owned livestock (Roof, 1960).

2. **"Volunteer" programs,** ordinarily organized through the Komsomol, are designed mainly to recruit young people for unskilled construction or agricultural work. Recent graduates from the ten-year general school, who often have difficulties in finding a job, sometimes welcome a chance to work elsewhere, but local youth organizations may be assigned "quotas," or may "pledge" a certain number of "volunteers" in advance of any solicitation. Volunteers have the theoretical right to return home if they so choose, but they must accumulate their own return fare by saving a portion of their meager pay. Those who cooperate willingly are publicly commended as "patriots" and given various honorific insignia. In short, the program is a kind of labor draft mitigated by voluntarist features (*ibid.*).

3. **Graduates of institutions of higher learning** are dispersed according to the type of school. Assignments to universities and technical schools are sought after. In order to ensure a sufficient supply of semiskilled workers, the State used to draft from each collective farm a quota of lower-class boys and girls aged fourteen to eighteen to be sent to labor-reserve schools; in 1955 this recruitment was put on a voluntary basis. Graduates of labor-reserve schools are assigned to a specific job for four years and those of the other institutions for three years. As many of the schools are in European Russia and most of the vacancies for trained personnel in the trans-Urals

region, the assignment often involves a removal from a large or middle-sized city with temperate seasons to a raw provincial area with a harsh climate. Graduates sometimes connive with administrative officials to be excused from their three or four years of service, or to be assigned to a large city even if not in a post requiring their skill (*ibid.*).

**4. Organized recruitment** of labor was instituted in 1931, and from 1932 to 1940 some 2.5 to 3 million workers were drafted annually. The system was set up to settle workers permanently in the new areas, and under a 1940 decree they were bound to the job all their life. This industrial serfdom lapsed after the war and was formally abolished in 1956. Presently workers and employees are required to sign contracts for a number of years (varying according to the type of work, location, etc.), and if they then leave their jobs, they forfeit the substantial monetary and social-security benefits that can accrue with seniority. Allocation of laborers is based on local needs as specified by the economic councils. Only about one-third of the recruits begin with definite vocational skills, and most of even these undergo retraining when at their new place of work. According to one Soviet report, "almost four-fifths" of those drafted under the system had been fired from previous jobs, some of them because of "infractions of labor discipline" (M. Y. Sonin, cited in *ibid.*). When skilled workers are recruited into the system, administrators have the right to use them in any job, irrespective of their training and qualifications.

**5.** By 1957, according to Soviet sources, 70 per cent of the inmates of **forced-labor camps** had been released (Roof and Leedy, 1959). At the 21st Party Congress in 1959, Khrushchev declared categorically that there were "no political prisoners in our country's prisons at present." The reform, while significant, was less wholesale than this assertion implies. It is not clear, first of all, what proportion were permitted to return home and how many became forced settlers, still restricted to the general region of the camps. "In important respects, the freedom . . . to migrate internally has not improved. A forced-labor 'colony' system has replaced the former forced-labor 'camps' " (Roof, 1960). And for the general rubric "political prisoners" there has been substituted such more specific designations as "enemies of the state," "traitors," "saboteurs," "counterrevolutionaries," all as defined anew in the 1958 criminal code (Gsovski, 1959). Two Soviet studies published in 1960—one a manual for law students, the other a study on "the purpose of the corrective-labor law"—have added much to what is known about this change of policy. But for the 1960s it is "impossible to say whether the present camp population should be counted in millions or in hundreds of thousands" (Barton, 1962).

**6.** Forced labor, moreover, has been replenished through the operation of the **"anti-parasites decrees"** of most of the Soviet republics. "Parasites," variously defined, are subject to arrest, exile, and forced labor for various periods. According to "the shortest, mildest, and least comprehensive" version, decreed in Georgia in September 1960, adult, able-bodied, urban citizens who avoid "socially useful" work and lead an "antisocial and parasitic life" may be deported for six months to two years, with forced labor at the place of exile. In the Ukrainian decree the definition of "parasites" includes alcoholics, those who "manifestly live beyond their earned income," "persons with an unconscientious attitude toward their work," and those who accept employment "only to divert attention" from their parasitism. Both in the Ukraine and in the Russian Republic, "parasites" are subject to punishment either by People's Courts or by vigilante meetings of workers or collective farmers (Beerman, 1961; cf. Nash, 1966). Like the traditional forced labor of the 1930s, such decrees apparently are intended to serve a double purpose—to transfer "antisocial" types to areas where they must produce for the socialist economy, and to frighten the rest of the population into working harder.

From this review of practices current in the mid-1960s, it is apparent that the post-Stalin relaxation, significant as it was, had important limits. The recurrent cycle of more or less terror has never resulted in full substitution of Soviet legality for control by security police. The anti-parasites decrees (as well as the more stringent control of the arts and the invasion of Czechoslovakia in 1968) suggest that the high point of relative liberalization is passed.

### URBANIZATION

In most countries of the world the population is becoming increasingly urban, for people are moving from the periphery to the centers of national culture. In the Soviet Union urbanization under State auspices has meant, on the contrary, a predominant shift from the center to the periphery.

The tsarist government tried repeatedly to entice a larger portion of the Russian population across the Urals into Siberia, but these efforts were unsuccessful. In even the most inhospitable areas the Soviet government has been able to establish large cities—in the sense of population settlements of a certain minimum size. Between the 1926 and the 1939 censuses, net in-migration to towns and cities totaled some 23 million. Urbanization was still at a relatively low rate in 1927–28, but from 1929 on, with deportations getting under way, it rose rapidly. 1931 marks the high point of both dekulakization and urbanization, with a net in-migration to cities of 4.1 million persons in that year (Lorimer, 1946, p. 150). The impression given by this chronology is reinforced when we look at the new urban sites. Lorimer lists 49 "boom cities"—that is, those with 50,000 or more inhabitants in 1939 that had increased by three times or more during the intercensal period. The one heading the list, which did not exist in 1926 and in 1939 had a population of 166,000, was Karaganda (ibid., p. 148), the center of a particularly notorious forced-labor complex. A number of other Soviet "cities" grew in the same way. Similarly, among the country's regions Karelo-Murmansk underwent the largest intercensal urban increase—by 5.6 times; and this growth was concentrated in the extreme northern districts, the site of a number of large forced-labor mining complexes. The intercensal increase in urban population in Central Siberia was by 3.1 times, in East Siberia by 3.8 times, in the Soviet Far East by 3.3 times (*ibid.*, p. 152). In large part these figures reflect mining, logging, and construction camps, all peopled by forced laborers.

After 1938–40, when the Soviet Union instituted the controls already mentioned (internal passports, labor books, and labor conscription for youths of 14 to 19), migration was "almost totally an expression of government plans and programs" (Shimkin, 1960). Between 1939 and 1959 inmigrants to the cities totaled between 24 and 25 million, and in the ensuing period up to 1965 the urban population increased by another 21 to 22 million. In the intercensal decades, except for the environs of Moscow and Leningrad and the region bordering the Black Sea, European Russia underwent a population loss or, at most, a slight gain, while most of the vast trans-Urals reaches increased by 30 per cent, and after 1959 the over-all direction of the migration was still generally to the East (*ibid.;* Brackett and DePauw 1966; see Figure 17-1).

The 1939–65 period overlaps the war, the prewar and postwar terror, and the relaxation after 1953. While there were important differences in some respects, in others the Stalinist pattern has been continued with a remarkable consistency. The stream of reports announcing new industrial cities being built in the Soviet wilderness are highly reminiscent of the socialist State's earlier conquests of hostile nature.

A regional Party secretary, V. Uvachan, could write in *Kommunist,* No. 14, 1967: "The North contains virtually all the diamond resources of the country, nearly half the gold and tin, and a large part of the nickel, mica, and apatites." This alone justifies . . . the construction of many towns: Norilsk (over 120,000 in 1964), Vorkuta (200,000, with its neighbors in the coalfield, in 1965), Kirovsk (40,000 in 1959), Apatity (20,000 in 1959), Mirny (20,000 in 1965), and numbers of smaller places (Armstrong, 1968; *cf.* Ways, 1968).[24]

How many persons does the Soviet state still want to move to industrial cities? Over the next ten or fifteen years, Strumilin stated in 1960, "we must,

---

[24] "In the new heart of the taiga," the swampy forest south of Lake Baikal, the new city of Baikalsk was constructed, the site of a cellulose plant scheduled to go into operation in 1965, conveniently close to the timber camps (*Pravda,* April 25, 1961). New cities are springing up in the mining areas of West Siberia; "some of them already have names, such as Nikitinsky" (*Trud,* January 25, 1962)—presumably after Khrushchev. In "Far Siberia," the new town of Shelekhov was being built as the center of the aluminum industry (*Pravda,* February 16, 1962). Mirny, the "diamond center of the country," was "hewn out of wilderness" in temperatures of 50 to 60 degrees below zero; the first in-migrants lived in tents while building "a beautiful and modern city" (*Pravda,* December 29, 1961).

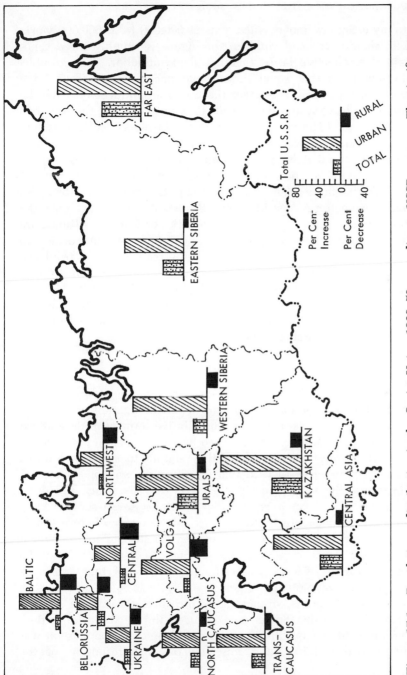

**Figure 17-1.** Population redistribution in the Soviet Union, 1939–59, according to USSR censuses. The significant population shift during this period was to the cities of the East, while the rural population of the East remained virtually constant. In the West (European Russia), the population remained more or less stable, with urban gains approximately rural losses. Population Reference Bureau, Inc., *Population Bulletin*, Vol. **17** (October 1961), No. 6.

according to my estimates, move as many as 20,000,000 to 30,000,000 workers—and with their wives and children this figure is roughly three times greater—from the collective farms to other fields of labor." The trouble, as Strumilin saw it, is that some farms have become prosperous: "the wealthier the collective farm, the fewer the economic inducements for the collective farmer to leave it in order to shift to other work and the less they are inclined to do so. [The well-to-do collective farmers] feel themselves to be 'bosses' . . . and not workers." [25] This can be regarded as a Stalinist diagnosis (down to the definition of agriculturists as class enemies), pointing toward the Stalinist solution of forced migration.

Resistance to the State plans for dispersing the population has also affected migration patterns considerably. Persistent efforts to limit the growth of Moscow and some of the other large cities of European Russia are successfully circumvented by both industry and in-migrants. According to a Soviet city planner, "measures to stem the flow—restrictions on residence registration, the drawing of hard city boundaries, and the creation of such barriers as green belts—have proved futile." [26] "Tens of thousands of skilled specialists for whose knowledge and experience Moscow has no use . . . do not leave Moscow because this would mean they would not return" (*Literaturnaya Gazeta*, March 10, 1966).

### DEMOGRAPHIC EFFECTS OF SOVIET TOTALITARIANISM

Soviet policies and practices have affected fertility and mortality, age structure, population distribution and composition. Although it is not possible to specify any of these effects in precise quantitative terms, the data afford the basis for some reasonable estimates. It so happens that the dates of the three censuses fall almost exactly where they should to separate internal terror from international war. In 1926 War Communism was long over and, two years later, the five-year plans would start. In 1939, when the drive to collectivize agriculture was over and that to purge Soviet society of its "treasonable" elements was interrupted, it was only two years before Russia was to enter the war. The losses in the war were so stupendous that for a period demographic facts were guarded as State secrets, but from the count of age groups in 1959 we can estimate the size of that enormous blood-letting and thus of postwar purges.

A male deficit in a census count roughly measures the cost in lives of some of the special risks that Soviet men incurred during the prior period, not only war and civil war but also forced labor (the camp population was overwhelmingly male), terror, and miscellaneous manifestations of the

[25] Stanislav G. Strumilin, "On Differential Ground Rent under Socialism," *Voprosy Ekonomiki*, No. 7 (1960), pp. 81–97; excerpted in *Current Digest of the Soviet Press*, 12 (September 14, 1960), 3–4.

[26] Boris Y. Svetlichny, quoted in *The New York Times*, November 13, 1966. *Cf.* Theodore Shabad, "Expansion of Moscow City Limits," *Soviet Geography*, 1 (1960), 92–93.

regime's ill will. Not all types of extraordinary mortality, one should emphasize, are reflected in a distorted sex ratio. Famine, for example, generally
affects the two sexes equally, and in each of the two famines the Soviet
regime brought about (1921–22 and 1933–34), millions died of hunger or
accompanying diseases. Some of the other acts against whole populations,
such as the deportation of minorities, also must have killed off males and
females in more or less equal proportion. The female surplus, thus, can be
taken as an index of the minimum cost of wars and the Bolshevik regime.

The male deficit has grown steadily in the Soviet Union (Table 17-5).

Table 17-5. Population by Sex, the Soviet Union at Each Census, 1897 to 1959

|  | MILLIONS OF PERSONS | | | MALES PER 100 FEMALES |
|---|---|---|---|---|
|  | MALE | FEMALE | FEMALE EXCESS | |
| 1897 (Russia) | 62.5 | 63.2 | 0.7 | 98.9 |
| 1926 | 71.0 | 76.0 | 5.0 | 93.4 |
| 1939 | 81.7 | 88.8 | 7.1 | 92.0 |
| 1959 | 94.0 | 114.8 | 20.8 | 81.9 |

SOURCE: Yury P. Miromenko, "The Ratio between Men and Women in the Population
of the USSR," *Analysis of Current Developments in the Soviet Union,* Institute for the
Study of the USSR, Munich, May 19, 1959.

Even in prerevolutionary Russia there was a slight female surplus, probably
due more to emigration than to differential rates of natural increase. In 1926
the excess of females amounted to 5 million. As we have noted (p. 645),
military deaths for this period are estimated at about 2 million; thus, the
remaining male deficit of about 3 million must be ascribed to extraordinary
mortality among the civilian males. During the more than twelve years
between the censuses, the imbalance should have been reduced by the
twelve new cohorts, each with a sex ratio of approximately 104. The excess
of females, on the contrary, amounted to 2.1 million more in 1939 than in
1926; one can estimate that during this period perhaps 4 million more
males than females died. By 1959 the depletion of males amounted to
20.8 million, the population of a middle-sized country.

From this datum alone it is not yet possible to distinguish between the
portion due to military casualties and that resulting from other elements of
Stalinism. With the age structure as well as the sex ratio, however, one can
estimate the timing of losses more precisely.[27] If we relate the age groups

[27] This may be why publication of these data for the 1939 census was held up so
long. Lorimer's analysis in 1946 had to be based on a fitting together of fragments from
scattered sources, and an article published ten years later still lacked a full schedule of
age groups (Kulischer and Roof, 1956). This basic information became available only
in 1957, 18 years after the census count (Roof, 1957; Biraben, 1960).

Table 17-6. Population by Sex and Age Group, Soviet Union, 1959

| AGE GROUP | THOUSANDS OF PERSONS | | | MALES PER 100 FEMALES |
| | MALE | FEMALE | FEMALE EXCESS | |
| --- | --- | --- | --- | --- |
| 0–4 | 12,100 | 11,650 | −450 | 103.9 |
| 5–9 | 11,508 | 11,105 | −403 | 103.6 |
| 10–14 | 7,516 | 7,325 | −191 | 102.6 |
| 15–19 | 8,550 | 8,417 | −133 | 101.6 |
| 20–24 | 10,056 | 10,287 | 231 | 97.8 |
| 25–29 | 8,917 | 9,273 | 356 | 96.2 |
| 30–34 | 8,611 | 10,388 | 1,777 | 82.9 |
| 35–39 | 4,528 | 7,062 | 2,534 | 64.1 |
| 40–44 | 3,998 | 6,410 | 2,412 | 62.4 |
| 45–49 | 4,706 | 7,558 | 2,852 | 62.3 |
| 50–54 | 4,010 | 6,437 | 2,427 | 62.3 |
| 55–59 | 2,906 | 5,793 | 2,887 | 50.2 |
| 60–64 | 2,335 | 4,550 | 2,215 | 51.3 |
| 65–69 | 1,764 | 3,087 | 1,323 | 57.1 |
| 70–74 | 1,210 | 2,300 | 1,090 | 52.6 |
| 75–79 | 760 | 1,640 | 880 | 46.3 |
| 80–84 | 400 | 1,025 | 625 | 39.0 |
| 85–89 | 150 | 350 | 200 | 42.9 |
| 90+ | 25 | 120 | 95 | 20.8 |
| TOTAL | 94,050 | 114,777 | 20,727 | 81.9 |

SOURCE: 1959 Census of the Soviet Union.

counted in 1959 (Table 17-6), with the cohorts that bore the brunt of successive disasters, we can estimate the effect of each on mortality. The most interesting datum pertains to the various age groups' sex ratios, since these give us, as before, a basis for estimating the cost in lives of events especially dangerous to males. The following list refers to successive rows of Table 17-7.

1. Males born in 1900 or before were old enough to be soldiers in World War I and to die from any of the later social catastrophes, including World War II for a portion of the cohort. If we ignore the effect of females' naturally greater longevity, this age group suffered the greatest losses, with only one male surviving to 1959 for every two females.

2. However, the males just too young to be soldiers in World War I, whose extraordinary mortality thus began with the period of War Communism, had no relative advantage. In fact, those aged 55–59 in 1959 had

Table 17-7. Basis for Analyzing Extraordinary Male Mortality in the Soviet Union, 1917–59

| BORN | AGE IN DESIGNATED YEAR | | | | |
|---|---|---|---|---|---|
| | 1917[a] | 1921[b] | 1928[c] | 1941[d] | 1959[e] |
| (1) 1900 or before | 17+ | 21+ | 28+ | 41+ | 59+ |
| (2) 1901–04 | 13–16 | 17–20 | 24–27 | 37–40 | 55–58 |
| (3) 1905–24 | 12 or under | 16 or under | 4–23 | 17–36 | 35–54 |
| (4) 1925–29 | — | — | 3 or under | 12–16 | 30–34 |
| (5) 1930–39 | — | — | — | 2–11 | 20–29 |
| (6) 1940–59 | — | — | — | 1 | 0–19 |

[a] End of World War I, beginning of civil war.
[b] End of War Communism, beginning of NEP.
[c] End of NEP, beginning of First Five-Year Plan.
[d] The Soviet Union became a belligerent in World War II.
[e] Date of last Soviet census.

a sex ratio slightly lower than those five or ten years older. The human losses in World War I, great as they were, were less than those in the establishment of Bolshevik power.

3. Persons aged 35–54 in 1959 had a sex ratio of 62 to 64. These had been children during the founding of the Soviet Union, and they grew up during a low point in the terror cycle. Only a portion of the males were old enough at the beginning of forced collectivization to suffer differentially from that. All of this age group were of military age during World War II, and it can be regarded as the prime source of the army's manpower. Remarkably, its sex ratio, though low enough by normal standards, was yet significantly higher than the cohorts that suffered more of the prewar terror. The number of men reported to have served in the Soviet army during the war was about 20 million. If we assume that half were killed (even considering conditions on the eastern front, this is probably an overestimate, and hence conservative for our argument), this still leaves an unexplained deficit of males of almost 11 million in 1959 (Eason, 1959b). The reason cannot have been the bombing of cities or other civilian hardships, for deaths from such causes, just because of the concentration of males at the front, would have had a higher incidence among females, if there was any difference by sex at all.

4. Persons born in 1925–29 were all still children when the war started, and most of the males of this group who fought as soldiers started after the bloodiest battles were past. Probably the male deficit of 1.8 million was

mainly the consequence of the postwar terror, from 1945 to after Stalin's death.

**5.** The interpretation that the postwar terror killed some millions is reinforced when we look at those born too late to serve in the army during the war but who were aged 14–23 in 1953, when Stalin died. The male deficit of something over half a million is suggestive.

**6.** Only among those born in 1940 or after, all of whom were children during the postwar terror, is the sex ratio normal.

From the male deficit of 20.8 million in 1959, then, we should subtract the 12 million military casualties in the two world wars, leaving a balance of some 9 million. These nonmilitary male deaths, to repeat, represent only those elements of extraordinary mortality to which males were especially susceptible. And in order to get the full demographic effect of the periodic social cataclysms, we must add extraordinary deaths of both sexes and the birth deficit; the latter is estimated at 10 million for World War I and the civil war (*cf.* p. 645) and, including extraordinary infant mortality, at 20 million for the 1940–50 decade (Eason, 1959*b*). The total depletion during the whole of the Bolshevik era has been 80 million, probably correct to the nearest 10 million—about 25 million extraordinary deaths and nonbirths during the civil war and the establishment of the Communist dictatorship, at least 10 million during the social revolution of the 1930s, and some 45 million during and immediately after World War II.

However correct these assertions are about the past, the distortion of the population structure revealed in the 1959 census will affect every element of Soviet life for as long as the depleted cohorts live. The U.S. Bureau of the Census has projected the future growth assuming constant fertility and found that the abnormal structure will persist well into the next century. In 1980 there will be a male deficit of 14 million, in 1990 one of 9.4 million, in 2000 still one of 5.2 million. Not until the year 2020 will the sex ratio again be over 100 (Brackett and DePauw, 1966).

The depletions in the population structure have affected the economy most directly through the shrunken and malformed labor force. Young people in the Soviet Union generally start work at sixteen; and sixteen years after each major disaster there is a shortage in the number of workers to be recruited into the work force. Up to 1920, according to an estimate by Strumilin, the male labor potential was cut by more than a tenth, and for both sexes by almost 15 per cent (Strumilin, 1961). From admittedly poor data, Eason estimated the size of the Soviet labor force from 1930 through 1975 (Table 17-8). Whether the figures are precise or not, the trend is accurate, reflecting the end of the collectivization and famine in the mid-1930s, the relative prosperity of the late 1930s, and the war beginning in 1941 and quickly developing into a national calamity, the postwar terror and relaxation.

Table 17-8. Soviet Labor Force, Estimated and Projected, 1900–75

| | LABOR FORCE (THOUSANDS) | | | | | | PER CENT FEMALE OF TOTAL LABOR FORCE |
|---|---|---|---|---|---|---|---|
| | TOTAL | AVERAGE ANNUAL INCREMENT | MALES | AVERAGE ANNUAL INCREMENT | FEMALES | AVERAGE ANNUAL INCREMENT | |
| 1900 | 64,400 | — | 35,400 | — | 29,000 | — | 45.0 |
| 1930 | 88,500 | 803.3 | 47,400 | 400 | 41,100 | 403.3 | 46.4 |
| 1940 | 105,300 | 1,680 | 58,400 | 1,100 | 46,900 | 580 | 44.5 |
| 1950 | 105,300 | — | 51,900 | −650 | 53,400 | 650 | 50.7 |
| 1955 | 111,600 | 1,260 | 58,000 | 1,220 | 53,600 | 40 | 48.0 |
| 1960 | 114,800 | 640 | 62,100 | 820 | 52,700 | −180 | 45.9 |
| 1965 | 117,100 | 460 | 65,800 | 740 | 51,300 | −280 | 43.8 |
| 1970 | 123,100 | 1,200 | 72,000 | 1,240 | 51,100 | −40 | 41.5 |
| 1975 | 130,600 | 1,500 | 79,400 | 1,480 | 51,200 | 20 | 39.2 |

SOURCE: Warren W. Eason, "Comparisons of the United States and Soviet Economies: The Labor Force," in Joint Economic Committee, Congress of the United States, *Comparisons of the United States and Soviet Economies*, Part 1, 80th Congress, 1st Session, Washington, D.C., 1959, Table 1.

Labor shortages, an important reason that the Sixth Five-Year Plan aborted after two years (1959–60), were perhaps the most critical factors also in the Seven-Year Plan (1959–65),[28] during which the population of working age increased by only half of the 11.5 million additional employed persons that the Plan had called for. Nevertheless the net increment in the work force reported at the end of the seven years was by almost double the number planned. The difference of 17 million (22.3 — 5.3) was squeezed out of various other categories—students, armed forces, females, "volunteers," pensioners. New entrants into the work force for the 1966–70 Plan, based on the large cohorts born in the postwar years, will on the contrary total some 15.3 million. How widely the shift in the population structure ramified through Soviet society is indicated by a number of reforms in several institutions, seemingly designed first to alleviate the labor shortage and, later, to absorb the vast inflow of young persons (Feshbach, 1966).

### NORMAL MORTALITY

The demographic feature most distinctive of a totalitarian regime is the massive extraordinary mortality it inflicts on the population. These deaths are ordinarily not included in the standard statistics, which measure the

[28] There was not originally a seven-year plan, of course, but in order to give the impression of continuity in the planned economy, the two completed years of the Sixth Plan were lumped together with a new five-year period.

types of mortality registered in any country. The contrast in normal mortality between totalitarian and other types of states, while of course much smaller than in other characteristics, is yet significant. To the primary goals of the Soviet regime—collectivization of agriculture, rapid industrialization, and military prowess—all other purposes have been subordinated, including specifically the welfare of the population. Allocation of resources to medicine and public health, thus, have been "the minimum consistent with a certain level of functioning of the system as defined by the regime" (Mark Field, 1957, p. 12). In the most recent period this minimum has been raised, but there has been no change in the State's rationale.

The doctor's role, similarly, is to balance his professional duties with his job as a State official. "The Soviet physician often saw his best efforts frustrated by political and economic organs, with disastrous results in morbidity and accident rates," for which the physician himself was often held responsible (*ibid.*, p. 22). Medical services are available according to one's place in the class hierarchy. In what Field terms the "closed network," reserved to members of the Party and associated elites, everything from care to food is superior. The "open network" available to the general population differs greatly among various regions of the country and, over-all, between cities and rural areas. In the early 1960s, the physician-population ratio ranged between 54 per 100,000 in rural institutions and 276 in those serving urban centers. For a physician as for most specialists, "an assignment to the countryside is regarded as a kind of exile from the urban cultural amenities, to be avoided if at all possible." Many rural areas are serviced only by *feldshers,* ostensibly semiprofessional physicians' assistants but in fact often the dispensers of second-class medicine (Mark Field, 1966). The Soviet Union's relatively high ratio of physicians to population, 202 per 100,000 in 1965, cannot be taken as unambiguous evidence of excellent medical service, for this is poorly distributed and in part at least of low quality.[29]

Crude death rates have been lower in the Soviet Union than, for example, in the United States, and Soviet publicists were not receptive to the comment that one reason (as in underdeveloped countries—*cf.* p. 568) was the relative paucity of elderly persons. According to the first Soviet life table published in several decades, in 1958–59 the average life expectancy at birth was 64.4 years (male) and 71.2 (female), or only slightly less than in advanced Western countries (Pressat, 1963*b*; Myers, 1964). Is this an accurate measure of Soviet mortality; and, if so, does it reflect, as Soviet propaganda assures us that it does, the superiority of the Communist social system?

That something is wrong with the record is suggested by the schedule

[29] On the quality of regular medical training and service, expert Western testimony differs. See for example the exchange between Mark Field and F. J. L. Blasingame, *The New York Times,* December 13, 1960 and January 7, 1961; Roemer, 1962.

of age-specific death rates, which compared with that for most countries (the United States is used as an example) is relatively high for ages up to forty-four and relatively low thereafter (Table 17-9). The reasons for this

Table 17.9. Age-Specific Death Rates, the Soviet Union, 1958–59, and the United States, 1959

| | SOVIET UNION 1958–59 | UNITED STATES 1959 | SOVIET UNION AS PER CENT OF THE US |
|---|---|---|---|
| All ages | 7.4 | 9.4 | 78.7 |
| Under 1 year | 40.6 | 29.5 | 137.6 |
| 1–4 years | 4.0 | 1.1 | 363.6 |
| 5–9 | 1.1 | 0.5 | 220.0 |
| 10–14 | 0.8 | 0.5 | 160.0 |
| 15–19 | 1.3 | 0.9 | 144.4 |
| 20–24 | 1.8 | 1.1 | 163.6 |
| 25–29 | 2.2 | 1.2 | 183.3 |
| 30–34 | 2.6 | 1.7 | 152.9 |
| 35–39 | 3.1 | 2.2 | 140.9 |
| 40–44 | 4.0 | 3.6 | 111.1 |
| 45–49 | 5.4 | 5.7 | 94.7 |
| 50–54 | 7.9 | 9.2 | 85.9 |
| 55–59 | 11.2 | 14.0 | 80.0 |
| 60–64 | 17.1 | 20.8 | 82.2 |
| 65–69 | 25.2 | 33.3 | 75.7 |
| 70 years and over | 63.8 | 80.8 | 79.0 |
| 75 years and over | 87.0 | 105.1 | 82.8 |

SOURCE: James W. Brackett, "Demographic Trends and Population Policy in the Soviet Union," in Congress of the United States, Joint Economic Committee, *Dimensions of Soviet Power,* Part VII, Washington, D.C., 1962, p. 499.

anomaly suggested by Soviet demographers include the high incidence of pneumonia as a cause of death (but there is no reason why only in the Soviet Union the elderly should not be susceptible to this disease) and the high mortality of the weak during an earlier period of war and famine, leaving many who are resistant to all infections (but the effect of social disasters has always been to kill off some of the population and weaken most of the rest).

Two seemingly valid explanations can be offered for the low death rates for advanced ages. (1) As longevity is especially prized in both Russian folk culture and Soviet medicine, one can assume that once past the middle years more persons exaggerate their age than elsewhere. The consequence would be artificially low age-specific death rates for the elderly. (2) According to the supposition of some Soviet statisticians, "the lower death rates are the results of defects in the registration." Underregistration is admittedly greater in rural areas, which have a greater proportion of older persons, and throughout the country among those not presently part of the work force, including especially those who have retired (Brackett, 1962).

It may be that not only at higher but at all ages there is considerable underregistration. Age-standardized death rates, computed from officially registered crude death rates for 1960 and the 1959 age distribution, are lowest in Central Asia, the part of the USSR where medical facilities are at their poorest (Heer, 1968). If the interpretation is correct that the lower rates for ages 45 and over are spurious, then the higher rates at ages 0–44 denote something closer to the overall mortality. If all age-specific rates are understated, then the Soviet Union's mortality is higher than that of the United States or Western Europe.

### FAMILY AND FERTILITY

In any society the family has three main functions: to perpetuate the population, to maintain cultural continuity from one generation to the next, and to determine the place of each newborn infant in the social structure. The family policy of totalitarian societies often reflects a conflict among these functions. On the one hand, the State denies the legitimacy of the society it has supplanted, and it cannot tolerate the strong emotional bond between the old and the new inherent in the father-son relation. Nor can such a regime accept the principle that the son shall inherit, even as a base from which to rise, his father's place in society, for ultimately each person's status must be determined solely by his relation to the Party. On the other hand, a totalitarian regime finds the family something of a necessary evil, for the State's expansionist aims demand a rapidly growing population. The only way out of this contradiction would be to devise an alternative procreative institution, but all attempts to do this have failed.

In the Soviet Union the Party has responded to the dilemma by a gradual shift of emphasis in its family policy. During the first fifteen years or so of Soviet rule a generally consistent and complete policy was gradually developed (Schlesinger, 1949, pp. 33–41). All legal inequalities between the sexes were abolished. Bigamy, adultery, even incest were dropped from the statutory list of crimes. Religious marriage was no longer recognized by law, and even a civil ceremony was legally unnecessary and socially unimportant. There were perhaps a quarter-million "nonregistered marriages" by 1936, when the law was changed. Divorce could be had simply and cheaply at the wish of either partner, and at least among the small minority directly influenced by the Party line, it was frequent. That these early decrees were predominantly negative reflects their principal purpose: to hasten the disintegration of the patriarchal family of tsarist Russia, the most pervasive and therefore, perhaps, the most powerful brake on the forward course of the revolution. This early phase is now often passed over lightly in Communist accounts, which propagate the myth that "concern for children and mothers and for strengthening the family has always been a major task of the Soviet State" (*Pravda*, May 10, 1959).

And in spite of another assiduously propagated legend to the contrary, the right of parents to decide for themselves the spacing and number of their children was not a Soviet norm. Opinion on the matter within the Party was divided, and policy therefore ambivalent, but in the dominant official view "birth control [was] . . . a bourgeois panacea for social ills which could have no place in a socialist society" (Smith, 1928, p. 186). As contraceptives were not generally available, even in the cities, abortion was the usual means for limiting family size. The official policy toward abortions was unambiguously hostile: they were legalized only in order to facilitate their rigid control. A woman desiring an operation was required to go before an official committee, which tried to convince her that it was her duty to society to give birth to her child. In cases of first pregnancy, requests were denied except when supported by urgent medical considerations (Alice Field, 1932, p. 89). According to the official in charge of Moscow's clinics, the Soviet Union of this period was "the country in which abortion is least practiced" (Halle, 1934, p. 144). This was hardly the case in Moscow itself during the worst years of the dekulakization and famine. The rate in that city is not known for the early 1930s, but in 1934 there were 2.71 recorded abortions for every birth (Lorimer, 1946, p. 127).

While combating the traditional family, the State also tried to institute various alternatives to it. During the middle 1920s an attempt was made in Party circles to develop "socialist" marriage and other family ceremonies, and the regime also began to establish State-run nurseries and kindergartens as substitutes for the parents. Progress was slow, however, in translating these visions into actuality, and all these early efforts to make over the family were more important as indications of future Soviet policy than for their immediate effect.

Beginning in the mid-1930s the line shifted toward tightening family bonds again. Marriages were stimulated by an official approval of romantic love of the old-fashioned bourgeois variety. Divorce was discouraged by a succession of increasingly restrictive measures, which ultimately removed all but political reasons as absolute grounds. These changes in policy culminated in a decree issued in 1944 (Schlesinger, 1949, pp. 367ff.), which re-established the distinction between civil and unregistered marriages, and hence between legitimate and illegitimate children. The restrictions on abortion were replaced by a flat prohibition except when it was necessary to save the woman's life. Unmarried persons and parents of only one or two children were subjected to special taxes, while especially fertile mothers received progressively larger subsidies according to their procreation. A woman who had borne and raised ten or more children was entitled to the highest award—the title of "Heroine Mother," carrying a lump payment of 5,000 rubles plus 300 rubles monthly for four years.

The Soviet Union was not, of course, the only state to pay family subsidies (see pp. 521–524). The political range of countries that have instituted such a policy suggests that various ends can be sought by this means, and it is necessary to estimate their purpose if family endowments are to be judged accurately. The most succinct way of doing this is to ask, *cui bono*—the individual, the family, or the state? In the Soviet Union the device of progressive premiums was, as Schlesinger has pointed out, primarily intended as "an incentive to the production of enormous numbers of children." By his estimate, a mother of six or more children, but not of a smaller number, could acquire an income sufficient to live modestly during her childbearing years (*ibid.*, pp. 368, 372, 397; *cf.* Heer and Bryden, 1966).

The usual explanation of the shift in Soviet family policy after the early 1930s has been that "conservatism, in the sense of respect for the acceptable heritage of the past as well as for the fruitful achievements of the present, was edging radicalism out of the picture." [30] But this explanation seems somewhat wide of the mark. While it is difficult to find a single adjective to describe the Soviet society of the Stalinist period, "conservative" scarcely characterizes the stupendous goals of the five-year plans, the collectivization of the peasants at the rate of one million a day (with 5 or 6 million discards), the Moscow show-trials, the *Gleichschaltung* of the arts and sciences, the territorial expansion in Europe and Asia.

Two factors underlay the decision to revitalize the family. The first was the huge population loss resulting from the collectivization program, the Yezhovshchina, and World War II. The second was the need to restore stability to Soviet society, which the social revolution of the first two five-year plans had broken down into a dangerously fluid mass. [31] In both phases the Soviet family was different from its Western counterpart. When

---

[30] Maurice Hindus, "The Family in Russia," in *The Family, Its Function and Destiny*, edited by Ruth Nanda Anshen, Harper, New York 1949, pp. 111–124. This has been the dominant interpretation offered not only by Soviet apologists but also by anti-Communist writers like the Catholic sovietologist Nicholas S. Timasheff, in *The Great Retreat: The Growth and Decline of Communism in Russia*, Dutton, New York, 1946.

[31] The trend in Soviet education policy was parallel. The first period was dominated by a calculated chaos, instituted "consciously and purposely in order to eliminate the power of the old school and undermine the domination of the pre-Revolution intellectuals." Then, when the system had been reduced to a malleable pulp, it was restructured as a prop to Soviet authority. See Fred M. Hechinger, *The Big Red Schoolhouse*, Doubleday, New York, 1959.

the policy was ostensibly "liberal," individuals were not given the right freely to determine what size family they would have. When it became "conservative," religious and other traditional norms did not set the pattern of family life. During the whole of the Stalinist regime, that is to say, the Party set family policy by what it interpreted the State's interests to be.

In the post-Stalin period the two earlier, partly contradictory policies have both persisted. The fundamental thesis of the earlier years—that the prime purpose of the family is to serve the State—is retained, but the Party is now not sure about precisely what it wants or how to achieve it. As we have seen (pp. 634–637), Soviet economists and demographers no longer adhere unanimously to the dogma that population growth is an unmitigated blessing. After the large postwar cohorts started to flood the labor market, earlier doubts about population theory were expressed more and more openly. In any case, it has become obvious that fertility is far less subject to State control than migration or mortality. In spite of the pronatalist decrees, the crude birth rate fell from 31.3 in 1940 to 25–27 in the 1950s and to 18.2 in 1966. The urban-rural differential increased as the decline accelerated (Pressat, 1963a), and, amazingly, religion seems still to be a major factor (Mazur, 1967). Soviet officials have taken pains to explain away the fall in the birth rate as merely a consequence of the combat losses in World War II, but it continued after the larger cohorts born in the postwar years began to reach the usual age at marriage. The trend in family size independent of the distorted age structure and sex ratio is best shown by the paternal gross reproduction rate (the number of sons born per father, assuming constant age-specific fertility and no mortality), which was estimated at 2.25 in 1950 and 20 per cent lower in 1965 (Pressat, 1963a).

In the main, a high fertility is interpreted as a symptom of social health, and most of the policies are either clearly or ambiguously pronatalist.

1. The family is seen as an institution to be encouraged. The State's effort to glamorize marriage is suggested by Leningrad's "Palace of the Happy," where weddings are performed in blue or gold rooms with costly rugs, crystal chandeliers, and radios playing Tschaikovsky marches. Champagne is served in the restaurant; a souvenir shop is available on the premises (Komsomolskaya Pravda, October 24, 1959). In 1961 two similar palaces were opened in Moscow. The decree of 1944, designed to make divorce both expensive and difficult, remains in effect, but nevertheless some 300,000 divorce cases go through the courts annually, plus many thousands of de facto separations. There is much discussion of whether the law should be changed in order to strengthen family ties (Juviler, 1963).

2. Births continue to be subsidized. During the late 1950s the number of women receiving family allowances for four or more children remained constant as a proportion both of fecund women and of children born (Kantner, 1960).

3. Abortion has been legal again since 1955, ostensibly for the pro-natalist purpose of discouraging the large number of illegal operations. Although no statistics are published, presumably the incidence of abortion is high. Among 26,000 abortion patients surveyed in the Russian Republic in 1958–59, almost all were married and the median numbers of children they had borne were only 2.06 (rural) and 1.47 (urban).[32]

4. According to slight indications, there is some interest in making contraceptives more generally available to the mass of the Soviet population. In 1958, at the first official meeting of Soviet gynecologists convened in twenty-two years, the delegates discussed the advantages of birth control; by official invitation, Dr. Abraham Stone attended from the United States. In the early 1960s Soviet journals were frequently arguing that contraception should be improved in order to reduce the incidence of abortion (Heer, 1965). As with other proposed policy changes that seemingly favored smaller families, one cannot assume that this one implied an antinatalist intention.

## The Population of Communist China

No one familiar with the development of social-economic policy in the Soviet Union can overlook the parallels in Communist China. As in Russia, so also in China, the Party came to power in part because the peasantry was won over by a land reform, which some years later was obliterated in a mass collectivization of agriculture. The forced-labor camps, the Yezhovshchina, the manmade famines, and so on through the list of Soviet terror—all have their Chinese counterparts. It is an oversimplification, however, to assume that Communism in China is a replica of the other version, or even that it is Russian totalitarianism filtered through the remnants of traditional Chinese culture and society. One quite important difference is in the economic level from which the two regimes started. Another is in scale. In 1967, when the Soviet Union celebrated the fiftieth anniversary of the 1917 revolution, Communist China had been in existence only eighteen years. Crowding a half-century into two decades, Mao was both Lenin and Stalin.[33] China's rulers, even if they no more than reproduced

[32] From this survey, Heer (1965) extrapolated to a national abortion rate somewhat higher than the birth rate—it "may be as high as any in the world." East European satellites, where statistics on the number of legal abortions *are* published, have indeed shown a decline in fertility, particularly marked in Hungary. See Christopher Tietze, "Legal Abortion in Eastern Europe," *Journal of the American Medical Association,* **175** (1961), 1149–1154; Tietze, "The Demographic Significance of Legal Abortion in Eastern Europe," *Demography,* **1** (1964), 119–125; Dorothy Good, "Some Aspects of Fertility Change in Hungary," *Population Index,* **30** (1964), 137–171.

[33] Mao Tse-tung, born in 1893 to a "middle" peasant of Hunan province, joined the Party when it was founded in 1921. After some years spent organizing the peasants of his native province, he broke with Marxist orthodoxy and declared that the peasantry, rather than the urban proletariat, constituted China's revolutionary potential. In 1933,

the Soviet pattern, would have wreaked a far greater havoc on the quarter of the world's population under their control, and their demand for a yet speedier pace of social transformation multiplied the toll in human suffering and life.

### PERIODS OF POLITICAL-ECONOMIC DEVELOPMENT

As all of the demographic topics to be discussed—measurement, number of people, population policy—followed the violent shifts in the economic line, it is useful to begin with a brief review of China's over-all development. The swing of the pendulum from maximum terror to relative relaxation is more clearly marked there than in the Soviet Union. Five periods are quite precisely delineated: 1949–52, 1953–57, 1958–60, 1961–65, and 1966 and after (Ashbrook, 1967).

**Establishment of Power** (1949–52). In about three years from the taking of power, the Party extended its rule over the whole country, restored the rail system and irrigation dikes, established nationwide tax and rationing systems, and generally laid a basis for continued rule and economic advance. A portion of China's 5 million soldiers fought in the Korean War (1950–53), with casualties estimated as high as a million men. Far larger numbers of "bandits," "landlords," "warlords," "reactionaries," "counterrevolutionaries," and other "enemies of the people" lost their lives.

According to an official figure, the number of landlords executed for "various crimes" was about 2.5 million. And in 1951 Lo Jui-ch'ing, then Minister for Public Security, claimed that his Ministry alone had "liquidated 15 million counterrevolutionaries," although it was not made clear what the term "liquidation" in this context meant. In 1952 Po I-p'o, then Minister for Finance, publicly admitted that the People's Government had liquidated 2 million "bandits" in the preceding three years. The term "bandit" was not defined [apart from the fact that] the regime applies the word to anyone who is against the present Communist Government (Chandrasekhar, 1959a, p. 58).

"The objectives of this period—the establishment of economic law and order, the seizure of the commanding heights of the economy, and the restoration of existing productive facilities—were all achieved" (Ashbrook, 1967).

**First Five-Year Plan** (1953–57). Under a series of agreements, the Soviet Union committed itself to transfer to China over the next fifteen

---

after the Communist-Nationalist alliance had changed into civil war, Mao led the hard-pressed Party cadres on the legendary 6,000-mile march to a new base in Yenan. Some fifteen years later the regrouped Communists emerged from this remote retreat and took power, with Mao as Party Chairman.

years (1953–67) some 300 industrial plants worth a total of $3 billion, plus the cost of training and equipment needed for further advance. This enormous assistance laid the base for the notable progress in industrialization. From very small starts, the production of major industrial materials increased several fold, and some thousands of workers acquired industrial skills (Li, 1960).

More than a decade passed from the distribution of land to Russian peasants to the reversal; in China it was less than half that time. Collectivization began in 1953, reached a high tide after the 1955 harvest, and according to official reports was successfully completed by the end of the following year. In a nationwide "liquidation of counterrevolutionaries," huge numbers of "upper" or "middle" peasants were executed or shipped to labor camps. The consequence was a rapid deterioration in agriculture. "Slaughter of farm animals and destruction of farm implements were widespread" (*ibid.*). "As late as the end of 1957, official statements admitted that agricultural production could be increased by 20 or 30 per cent if the collectives could raise their yield to the level of the remaining individual peasants" (Lindsay, 1960). The increase in agricultural production over the five years was far less than the population growth.

**The Great Leap Forward (1958–60).** Sweeping aside the targets sketched out for a Second Five-Year Plan (1958–62), the Party greatly quickened the hyperrapid pace it had set. The theories underlying the "Great Leap Forward" were three: (1) China's vast population was an economic asset; "man should be viewed as a producer rather than a consumer" (Liu Shao-chi, at the 8th Party Congress, 1958, quoted in Ashbrook, 1967). (2) Chinese agriculture was dragged down by a vast, wasteful underemployment, since for much of the year no farm work was possible (actually the peasants used these intervals for all the other activities necessary to sustain the almost self-sufficient village economy). (3) Material incentives could be dispensed with; the whole population could be imbued with the same fervor that had inspired the Party during its struggle for power. Production was at a frenzied rate, with little or no regard for the reduction in quality, the exhaustion of workers, or the depletion of machinery and other capital stock.

Agricultural collectives were converted into "people's communes." Each comprised some 25,000 people rather than the several hundred in the largest of the collectives. All remaining private property was taken over by the State; and the peasant, no longer entitled to a share of the crop, was paid a wage of usually 100 yuan (or $40) *per year*, half in money and half in kind (the figure is from an article by Finance Minister Li Hsien-nien, quoted in Rousset, 1959). The commune was not merely an agricultural unit but a general work force: labor armies sowed and harvested in season, and during unproductive periods they were shuttled about the country digging canals and wells, dragging rivers, draining swamps, building levees, carrying fertile soil onto naked rock, reforesting. After a slight pause to consolidate the Party's gains, a new leap was taken—communes in the cities. According to an official statement, by the spring of 1960 communal living had been imposed on not only 400 million Chinese peasants but also 20 million town dwellers, a majority of those living in the three populous northern provinces of Heilungkiang, Honan, and Hopei.

The commune was intended as a complete substitute for the home. In order to "emancipate" women from domestic chores so that they could also produce for the State, communes established great mess halls, nurseries and kindergartens, and tailor shops. According to the description of one commune in a nationally distributed Party magazine, "The frames of individual families which had existed for thousands of years have been completely smashed."

In the more advanced communes, children see their parents twice a month. [During the day] wives see their husbands only at mealtimes, which are given only half to eating and half to participating in discussion in vast communal mess halls—unless, of course, their husbands are "camping out" at work projects from 60 to 100 miles away from their commune base. Grandparents are isolated in "Happiness Homes" where they will serve the "big family" by tilling communal vegetable plots, weaving communal baskets or feeding communal chickens. . . . A group of Young Pioneers (7- to 14-year olds) in Canton recently smelted their first heat of medium-carbon steel (Rich, 1959).

The commune was controlled by naked terror. Part of what Rousset terms China's "universalization of forced labor" was the creation, also in August 1958, of a new "people's militia." These were armed units of young activists, both male and female, organized as integral parts of the labor armies.

As in Russia, the transformation of the countryside was carried out by young men anxious for a Party career. Following a decision at the highest level, they insisted that furrows be dug six feet deep rather than one, that rice seedlings be planted two inches apart rather than the traditional five to six inches. Triumphantly the regime announced an increase in the crop from 185 million tons in 1957 to 375 million in 1958; plans for 1959 reduced the acreage of food crops. But this "harvest," estimated while the rice was still growing, proved to be a mirage. The stalks grew, but the heads were mostly empty. This momentous error, when compounded by the drought and floods two years running, developed into what was finally admitted to be the worst famine in a century. But the Party was too thoroughly inculpated to be able to react quickly. Still in 1959 more than $1 billion in exports, mostly agricultural products, were shipped out, and even in 1961 the regime rejected an offer of help from the International Red Cross. Three emergency measures were taken: (1) "Bad elements" in the State bureaucracy, estimated at one-tenth of the total, were blamed for the catastrophe and purged. (2) Members of communes were permitted to have small private plots and to work them two to four days a month. Since twice before the Party had sanctioned such a modest return to private ownership and then commandeered the produce, the peasants may well have been mistrustful. (3) Food, too little and too late, was purchased from the capitalist world. Each year from 1961 on, China paid $300 million to $400 million out of its meager stock of foreign exchange to import 5–6 million tons of grain (Ashbrook, 1967).

As part of its manic euphoria, China mounted an increasingly acerbic attack on Russia, which it claimed had not moved so far toward full Communism as Mao's State. In the mid-1960s the Soviet technicians were summarily withdrawn, and those plants built with Russian aid, lacking expert managers and spare parts, sometimes could not continue operating. Much of the capital stock built up with eight years of iron rations suddenly became useless. "A revolution," as we know from one of Chairman Mao's famous aphorisms, "is not an invitation to a banquet."

**The Great Retreat (1961–65).** The famine of 1959–61 was manmade, and the name of the man was Mao Tse-tung. In 1961, Po I-p'o, then chairman of the National Economic Council, warned that there had to be a slowdown in industrial production, so that not only all surplus manpower but millions of factory workers could be diverted to agriculture. Even two of the most publicized achievements of the earlier period, the Wuhan steel works and the Anshan industrial complex, were cut back. Only the chemical industry, manufacturing fertilizers and insecticides to foster food production, was exempted from the over-all industrial retreat. Peasants were once again encouraged to tend tiny private plots, and private enterprise was permitted to reappear in the form of petty traders and craftsmen.

In the only significant advance during this period, China set off its first nuclear device.

**Proletarian Cultural Revolution (1966–?).** In five years some—certainly not all—of the damage incurred in the Great Leap was repaired, and the Party shifted again to reckless activism. The country's children and youth were organized into Red Guards, who attacked, verbally and physically, all who deviated from absolute adherence to absolute orthodoxy. All schools were dismissed in order to fill the ranks of these frenetic guardians of revolutionary purity. By the autumn of 1966, ten million were engaged in a struggle against "bourgeois" and "revisionist" elements in the Party and affiliated elites. Thirty per cent of the country's transport was placed at their disposal, and they swarmed like locusts on the meager resources of the overcrowded cities.[34] Children at the age of three began

[34] "Hundreds of cesspools have been dug in the central streets as temporary toilets. They are screened off from the crowds only by strips of canvas on which are traced on huge red hieroglyphs the words: 'Raise higher the banner of Chairman Mao's ideas'" (Andronov, 1966).

The Red Guard use a truck to convey "counterrevolutionaries" wearing dunce caps through the streets of Peking (*Wide World Photos*).

their training in blind loyalty to Chairman Mao, canonized as the font of all wisdom, the inspiration that solves all problems.[35]

How much damage this new manic phase inflicted on the economy cannot be assessed precisely. Any hope of a Soviet-Chinese rapprochement, and thus of a renewal of Soviet aid, was quashed.[36] With the revived em-

[35] In fact, the struggle was over who would succeed Mao, aged 73 in 1966. Of all sectors of the Chinese population, none was less capable of understanding than those disseminating ideological cant through the Red Guards' wall posters. Clearly they were being used: their seemingly anarchic antics were directed by the army; until mid-1962 they had their headquarters in the Peking public-security building; during their mass demonstrations, they traveled in army trucks, with two or three soldiers in each. And the heir apparent to Mao became Lin Piao, Minister of Defense (*cf.* Ravenholt, 1967).

[36] Virtually the whole of the April 1967 issue of *Survey* is devoted to translations from a variety of Soviet periodicals on China. The articles typically display a detailed knowledge of the manifestations that they condemn. Some of these have an unconscious humor. Thus, *Komsomolskaya Pravda* (September 27, 1966) finds it "amazing" that "in the seventeenth year of the Chinese People's Republic's existence," laconic accusations against "counterrevolutionary, rightist elements" are heard everywhere. The seventeenth year of the Soviet Union's existence was the winter of 1934–35.

phasis on "spiritual" incentives, those who would pay for efficient and conscientious work with good wages were guilty of "economism." Whether the vague allusions to a Third Five-Year Plan (1966–70) have any substance was not apparent, but none of the elements of a nationally planned economy were being fostered.

### SOURCES OF INFORMATION

With the cycle of manic-depressive politics, there was a fluctuation also in the amount and accuracy of the quantitative data available. In preparation for the First Five-Year Plan, a State Statistical Bureau was established in 1952, and by the middle of that period data were as reliable as at any time during the Communist regime. With the Great Leap into wishful thinking, all realistic appraisals of actual achievements were dispensed with,[37] and with the debacle came an end even to such misleading figures as had been available.

The overwhelming problem that faces all students of the contemporary Chinese economic scene is the blackout of economic statistics imposed by the Chinese authorities in 1960, and continued ever since. . . . The Chinese have gone far beyond the Russians. . . . Visitors have been given an odd figure or two, but there is nothing of a systematic character, not even plan figures (Galenson, 1967).

A crucial misrepresentation was in agricultural statistics. The National Agricultural Research Bureau of the Republic of China had estimated the production on about three-quarters of the cultivated land. For the base figure from which they started in 1949, the Communists took this estimated production and divided it by the *total* number of cultivated acres. Beginning from too low a figure in 1949, they exaggerated each year's increase up to 1958, the year of the paper harvest (Buck, 1966, p. 48). According to the best analysis possible from the available data, the calories per capita from all food, adjusted for imports or exports of food grains, decreased from an average of 2,410 in 1929–33 to 2,017 in 1949–58—what the Communists term "the great ten years" (*ibid.*, p. 11). "After seventeen years of Communist rule, the economy of Mainland China . . . does not yet provide a tolerable living standard for the exploding population, let alone a margin necessary for sustained growth" (Larsen, 1967).

The demographic data are no better than any other. For more than a century before the Communists took power, we have only unreliable estimates of the total population. The new regime also has not collected much information, and a portion of that has not been released. The one important

[37] The "harvest" of 1958, already noted, is but one example of recurrent exaggeration or falsification. For example, as proof of the allegation that the level of living increased from 1950 to 1955, the regime cited the rise in retail sales in State-operated stores (which merely took over the business previously done by private merchants).

exception is the 1953 census-registration, which constitutes the only relatively firm set of data.

According to that count, the population of Mainland China in mid-1953 was almost 583 million. Understandably, the first reaction in the West to this stupendous figure was disbelief. Previously even the Communists themselves had generally estimated the population of the country at about 100 million less than this. The jubilant tone of the announcement, the fact that it was used to make political capital (*cf.* Kirby, 1958), also argued against accepting it. And the further statement that a check on the enumeration had uncovered a net undercount of only 0.116 per cent, thus making this the most accurate large-scale census in world history, was "both preposterous and foolish" (Aird, 1967*b*). Western scholars, however, soon began to accept as a fact the claim that China represents one-quarter of the human race. The census administrators had expert Soviet advisors, who probably kept the census's faults within limits. According to the most comprehensive Western analysis of the enumeration and processing, the claimed total may even have reflected a considerable undercount (Krader and Aird, 1959; Aird 1960; U.S. Bureau of the Census, 1961).

For the period since 1953, the further growth of population was supposedly recorded through a continuous registration. In fact, this was not begun for several years, and then it was conducted as a police check on the population. According to Party newspapers, the household registration was used to lay the basis for grain expropriations and to expose "counter-revolutionaries and other bad elements," who "assume false identities, fake evidence, and make false reports to the registration authorities." The records so collected are two or three times removed from their source when they reach the county (*hsien*) administrative center where they are compiled (Orleans, 1965). "With the appearance late in 1959 of the registration figure of 647 million for year-end 1957, publication of official population totals came to an end" (Aird, 1967*a*).

For a half-dozen years the announced population of China remained static at 650 million, and by all indications the country's leaders had no better data themselves.[38] The full 1953 schedule of ages by sex was never released to the public, and the partial schedule only through papers of individual Chinese demographers (Ch'en, 1958). The sex ratio was high, 107.7 males per 100 females, presumably reflecting the female infanticide practiced during these cohorts' entire lifetime. Various other anomalies in

[38] There has been a distinct reluctance to admit the existence of a larger number. The official estimate of grain requirements of 220 million tons, divided by the conventional standard of 300 kilograms per capita, indicated a population of 733 million at the end of 1964. When Edgar Snow cited these figures, Mao responded that, as deaths were concealed in rural areas in order to augment the grain rations, the registration data were inflated (Jones, 1967). It is a telling commentary on Asian socialism, whether or not Mao was lying. In 1966, however, Mao himself referred to "the 700 million Chinese people."

the population structure—in particular, the lack of a male deficit in the cohorts most affected by war casualties—cannot be explained without better primary data.

Aird has constructed several models of China's population, assuming that mortality changed with the political-economic cycle, that crude birth rates were 40 or 45 per thousand, and that the enumeration in the 1953 census was up to 15 per cent under the actual number. The various combinations of these assumptions yield sixteen series, with populations ranging between 583 and 678 million in 1953 and between 859 and 1,298 million in 1985. The crude rates of natural increase in 1965, similarly, range between 1.9 and 2.2 per cent (Aird, 1967b). According to the U.S. Bureau of the Census, the best estimate for China's population as of January 1, 1966, was 760 million. If one rejects the postulate that the 1953 count was accurate and adjusts for underenumeration, the number of Mainland Chinese in 1966 would be between 800 and 894 million.

### MORTALITY

How many have been killed in China by terror and manmade famine we have no way of estimating, though the figure is certainly in the tens of millions. The Party was more reckless with its human charges than in Russia, and a depletion by even the same proportion would have meant a considerably greater mortality.

Nor is there any reliable basis for gauging the rate of normal mortality,[39] though some intimations are available from the changes in medical institutions. The slight basis from which the Communist State started is suggested by a single datum: the number of physicians in the whole country in 1950 was 41,400, increased to 70,500 by 1955 (Davidoff, 1957). Whether the quality remained constant, however, is doubtful. In 1956, when Mao invited criticism with his famous speech, "A Hundred Flowers Must Bloom and One Hundred Schools of Thought Contend," intellectuals—with doctors among them—denounced the rigid Party control that had hampered their professional work. The following year a "rectification movement" was initiated to rid the country of these nonconformists. Modern medicine had derived from the West, very often by way of Christian missionaries, and physicians were more suspect than members of some other professions. Those professors of medical schools who were Christians were denounced in student-faculty assemblies, and with the depleted training staffs the course of medical study was cut from seven to five years.

---

[39] According to a survey conducted by the Ministry of the Interior in 1953 (the most important of several such), for a sizable sample of the population the birth rate was 37, the death rate 17 (Chen, 1967, p. 6). The information given to Chandrasekhar (1959a, p. 50) was that by 1957 these rates had fallen to 34 and 11, respectively. No subsequent figures are available.

Nevertheless during the First Five-Year Plan much was accomplished in a vigorous all-out attack on China's major epidemic diseases. The experiences of a young parasitologist, who fled to Hong Kong in 1962 after having worked as a physician in six different provinces, are indicative. He practised in Fukien province, for example, where the director of public health was an energetic woman who had been a nurse with the Communist forces in Yenan. Under the system that she set up, a hospital was established in each of the 60-odd *hsien*, usually staffed by two doctors and ten "assistant doctors." "This entire health organization was energized by vigorous support and ample funds from above, such as had never been available during the pre-Communist era. . . . Vaccines [were] available in abundance from the new factories established for their production." The effort concentrated on eliminating major epidemic diseases. Peasants were vaccinated against cholera, forcibly if necessary; school children were required to kill flies and to deliver a daily quota of dead rats to their teachers. The incidence of cholera and the plague, as well as of smallpox and typhoid, was brought under substantial control, and there was some success in the attack on other diseases (Ravenholt, 1962).

With the chronic malnutrition brought on by the Great Leap Forward, much of this progress was negated. For example, in 1962 Fukien's per capita ration of bean curd, the country's protein staple, was one small block per month. The refugee doctor estimated that 40 per cent of the province suffered from nutritional hepatitis; there and elsewhere in China, edema, another disease of malnutrition, was common (*ibid.*).

As Chinese Communism became increasingly xenophobic, the Party laid greater emphasis on traditional Chinese medical lore. In 1959 the Central Committee ordered all geographical units of the country to establish two-year courses through which Western-style physicians could learn Chung-i, or Chinese medicine and pharmacy. In this system much diagnosis is by a complicated procedure for feeling the pulse. A sixteenth-century herbal, with 1,892 remedies and 10,000 prescriptions, lays the basis for the present pharmacopeia, which includes such exotic items as crickets, deer musk, toad tears, tiger bones, the preserved Adam's apple of an elderly monkey. Apart from such drugs, the best known treatment is acupuncture, or the insertion of needles some inches into various portions of the body. For acute appendicitis, for example, a needle is inserted into the right leg. In six-month cram courses thousands of practitioners of this ancient art are trained in, among other places, the former Peiping Union Medical College, American-founded and once American-supported, and in the pre-Communist era famous throughout Asia (Durdin, 1960). In 1967, a French television team that recorded Chung-i practitioners on film reported that the "coexistence" between it and Western medicine was breaking down, that doctors were "abandoning modern medicine altogether." [40]

[40] *The New York Times*, January 24, 1967.

### FERTILITY AND FAMILY POLICY

During the first years of the Communist regime, the policy was to encourage China's traditionally high fertility. Not only infanticide but also birth control were condemned, the latter as "a means of killing off the Chinese people without shedding blood" (quoted in Kirby, 1958). The Party repeatedly boasted of the high rate of population growth, which reflected, it claimed, the improved living conditions. Its "hundreds of millions of people" were constantly referred to as China's most treasured asset. By this view, "overpopulation is not the cause of China's impoverishment, but merely a reflection of that deterioration in Chinese society which began under the rule of the alien Manchus." With the new Communist regime, this deterioration had been reversed and all difficulties now would vanish as though by magic (Chang, 1949; Barclay, 1950).

A convincing argument for the position that the 1953 census was either correct or an undercount is that the Chinese Communists themselves re-

One of the hundreds of thousands of New York cards inculcating the then current Party line—in this case a bumper crop in both children and agricultural produce (*New York Times Magazine*).

acted to it. After the census the naive approbation of large numbers disappeared, to be replaced by what might be called a "soft" and a "hard" population policy. The soft line has been to reduce fertility, the hard one to risk measures demanding a sizable increase in mortality in a frenetic Leap Forward. The two have run parallel courses, but over the following two decades the effort to reduce fertility apparently increased.

In 1953, it would seem, some tentative plans for controlling population existed, and in August of that year the Ministry of Health was quietly instructed to foster both abortion and contraception (Tien, 1963). Two years later *Study,* the Party's principal ideological journal, came out for the new line—to retain Marx, repudiate Malthus, hurl invectives at neo-Malthusians, and advocate the limitation of births. According to this article, no "conceivable" rates of population growth could approach the increase in production envisioned in the First Five-Year Plan. The advocacy of family planning was not in the interest of society but only of individual families (Taeuber, 1956).

A somewhat more direct support of family planning was made by Ma Yin-chu, an economist trained at Yale and Columbia and then president of Peking University. Although subjected to a widespread and virulent attack, he was permitted to voice his still deviant position, perhaps because of his age (he was in his seventies), more likely because of the protection of someone high in the Party. His "New Principle of Population," made public in 1957, offered the following argument. China's population growth, which he believed to be higher than the assumed 2 per cent per year, impedes the economic development. Of her low national income, 79 per cent must be used for current consumption (compared with 75 in the Soviet Union). "Our population is too large; it drags down the speed of industrialization" (quoted in Chandrasekhar, 1959*b*).

A no less direct connection between population increase and economic difficulties was made by Premier Chou En-lai [41] in an official report to the National People's Congress in 1957: 10 to 15 per cent of China's population—that is, some 60 to 90 million persons—"are short of food and clothes and need aid from the State or the agricultural producers' cooperatives" (quoted in Sarker, 1958). Another speaker, without mentioning Malthus by name, repeated the essence of his principle: "The proverb, 'Two in the first generation means a thousand in ten generations' (1, 2, 4, 8, 16, 32, 64, 128, 256, 512, 1024), is not without foundation" (quoted in Tien, 1963). During the term of the First Five-Year Plan, thus, the Party's hostility to family planning was opposed at first indirectly and finally in open recogni-

[41] Chou En-lai, born in Huaian, Kiangsu, in 1898 of an old Mandarin family, was educated in Chinese universities and in Japan and France. He joined the Communist movement while in France and became a founding member of the Chinese Party in 1921. For three years, 1928–31, he was trained in Moscow. After serving in several local Party posts, he participated in the Long March to Yenan, acted as the chief liaison officer between the Communist Party and the Nationalist Government.

tion of the social-economic consequences of rapid increase in numbers. "Maternal health" became "population control."

All methods of birth control were considered. Abortion specifically for medical reasons was legalized in 1954, and in the following years the conditions were liberalized. The at first severe restrictions on sterilization were gradually eased. The main emphasis throughout the campaign, however, was on contraception. The Minister of Health was reportedly collecting the centuries-old Chung-i formulas as part of a search for contraceptives. One herbalist seriously offered the following prescription to a National People's Congress:

Fresh tadpoles coming out in the spring should be washed clean in cold well water, and swallowed whole three or four days after menstruation. If a woman swallows fourteen live tadpoles on the first day and ten more on the following day, she will not conceive for five years. If contraception is still required after that, she can repeat the formula twice, and be forever sterile. . . . This formula is good in that it is effective, safe, and not expensive. The defect is that it can be used only in the spring (quoted in Taeuber, 1956).

When he was in China at the end of 1958, Chandrasekhar was permitted to visit two contraceptive factories, a small one in Shanghai manufacturing 500,000 diaphragms and 5 million condoms annually, and a larger one in Canton, only two years old, with a productive capacity of 120 million condoms but an actual output in that year (after the propaganda for family planning had ceased) of only half that. Condoms cost 4 cents to produce and were sold in the villages for 2 cents. During the height of the campaign, from 1955 to 1958, birth control was advertised in newspapers, magazines, and special pamphlets; with posters and billboards; at exhibitions and meetings, with lantern slides and lectures. At a Birth Control Exhibition in Peking, "the authorities were not leaving anything to chance. Even the most illiterate peasant and the least intelligent worker went away from the exhibition knowing exactly what to do to prevent conception" (Chandrasekhar, 1959b).

With the Great Leap Forward, the line on birth control changed abruptly; part of the manic phase was the certainty that economic development would be fast enough to absorb any growth in numbers (but see Aird, 1962). Six persons who had been members of the State Council when it initiated the new policy in 1953 were accused of being "anti-Party, anti-people, anti-socialist, and anti-democratic dictatorship, and of harboring political ambitions" (Tien, 1963). Several who had earlier advocated population control saved themselves by joining in the denunciations.

In the bitter aftermath of the Great Retreat, contraception again became the Party line. In the spring of 1962 an exhibition in Canton, a counterpart to the earlier one in Peking, displayed charts, models, and specimens. Contraceptives were imported duty-free. The principal Party newspaper advertised publications like *China's Women* in which methods of birth control were described and advocated.

A vigorous birth-control program has been waged in the cities since early 1963, employing rather stringent social pressures and evidently achieving significant results. Its extension to the rural areas is as yet limited, and possibly experimental, and few successes have been noted. However, a recent hardening of pressures in some rural areas, such as denying rations to fourth and subsequent births, may be effective (Jones, 1967).

If all other means of controlling population fail—and if the Party line does not shift again—this reversion to China's tradition of infanticide should help induce the peasants to reduce their family burdens.

### INTERNAL MIGRATION AND URBANIZATION

China is a vast land, but a large portion of its 3.7 million square miles is economically useless and hardly habitable. About 60 per cent of the country is a mile or more above sea level, the greater part of the Tibetan highlands more than two miles. "Over about eight-ninths of China, the terrain limits or completely excludes human endeavors" (Pearcy, 1966). The present territory is the same as that traditionally known as Greater China, except that the former Outer Mongolia is now the People's Republic of Mongolia. Greater China comprised five major regions—China Proper, Manchuria, Mongolia, Sinkiang, and Tibet—and the main drift of migrations over all of history was from the periphery to the first of these, in the southeast corner. Beginning in the seventeenth century the Manchus raided China for laborers, who were used to develop their land; by 1850 Chinese colonization, first forced and later surreptitious, had virtually obliterated the indigenous culture of Manchuria, now China's northeast province.

The consequence of China's geography and migratory streams is a great concentration of population in the East and extremely low densities inland. A straight line drawn from Ai-hui on the border of Manchuria and Soviet Siberia to T'eng-chung near the border of Burma divides the country into two unequal parts—to the east 40 per cent of the land with 96 per cent of the population in 1953 and to the west the remaining 4 per cent scattered over 60 per cent of the land (Orleans, 1960). The densities in the settled areas are among the highest in the world. In 1967 the number of persons per square mile of cultivated land was about 1,100 in India, 1,400 in Pakistan, and 1,800 to 2,200 in China, depending on what assumptions are made concerning the size of China's population (Aird, 1967b).

Until very recently geographers believed that China's interior was as empty of resources as of people. According to present estimates, "China is one of the richest coal nations in the world"; its iron ore totals between a conservative 12 billion and a probably too extravagant 100 billion tons;

sizable deposits exist of other industrial metals and of petroleum (Pearcy, 1966; *cf.* Wang, 1967). Some of these finds were on the border of the settled area, others as far away as Urumchi, Sinkiang, deep in the Asian heartland. Rail lines have been built to outlying areas, but a rail network exists only in the eastern region, and even there no highway system exists for fast vehicles. Travel that used to be reckoned in weeks or months sometimes can be completed now in days, or in hours if an airline has been established (Pearcy, 1966).

Migration since 1949 has been on the same scale as the country's size and population. The millions moving or being moved in various directions can be classified into three main types:

**1.** The Soviet policy of fostering a population movement eastward into the Siberian steppes has had a Chinese counterpart. The exploitation of the new mineral discoveries; the construction of factories, transportation lines, cities, dams, and hydro-electric plants—all this demanded new reserves of labor. A program for the reclamation of wasteland was cast on even more ambitious dimensions. According to government estimates, the 1.6 billion mou (one mou = 0.1647 acre) under cultivation, amounting to only slightly more than a tenth of China's total area, could be matched by another 1.5 billion mou of potentially arable land, almost a third of which was reported to be of good quality. During the First Five-Year Plan some 40 million mou were to be reclaimed; and if one assumes an average of 3 mou per settler, or slightly more than the average in China Proper, some 13 million persons could be established per five-year period, or about one-fifth of the estimated natural increase (Tien, 1964).

**2.** Spontaneous migrations, what official reports term "blind" movements, continued the shift from west to east and especially from countryside to cities. If one postulates that the rural population of some 500 million increased at 2 per cent per year and that only half of this increment left, the demand for new urban jobs and homes would be at the rate of 5 million annually. In fact, once collectivization got under way and hunger was reinforced by terror, in many areas the proportion fleeing the land was undoubtedly much greater. In the first years the regime exulted in the large rural-urban migration as a sign of industrial progress, but from 1952 on this was seen as excessive.

**3.** The government not only restricted movement to cities but organized return migrations from the cities. The numbers involved, according to Aird's compilation of the few official data, were large but, considering the fact that many did not stay put, far too small to relieve urban population pressure or that on the densely settled agricultural land. By 1957, after five years of effort to control the movement, a survey of fifteen cities showed that 60 per cent of their inhabitants were "nonproductive," that is, mostly in-migrants unable to find work. In that year the planned redistribution of population was extended to sectors of the established urban population. By a decentralization of government and Party offices, some 1.3 million administrative personnel were moved from urban centers in one year, and many graduates of primary and middle schools were assigned to rural or frontier areas. When the Five-Year Plan ended in 1958, the official record showed an increase in urban population of 8 million, aggravated each year by a natural increment of some 2 million. During the Great Leap, the peasants being herded into communes fled when and where they could: over the three years, some 20 million additional in-migrants went to the cities or mining areas. The Leap failed not only in its central purpose but also in such corollary goals as preventing the unproductive growth of China's cities (Aird, 1967b).

## A Note on Nazi Germany

Nazi (that is, National Socialist) Germany lasted only twelve years, from the taking of power in 1933 to the final defeat in 1945, and during half of that period the country was at war. In many cases, thus, totalitarian institutions were either never fully developed or were linked to the military machine. Some parallels with the Soviet Union or Communist China are nevertheless manifest—the ubiquitous control by the Party, the deaths imposed by the terror apparatus, the forced labor and forced migrations. Many of the data from Nazi Germany are far more accurate—though not, of course, the record of specifically totalitarian practices. The excellence of "normal" statistics, moreover, can be regarded as a probably temporary residue from the pre-Nazi period; if the regime had persisted long enough, its corrupting influence would undoubtedly have spread to economic and demographic records, for every administrator responsible for collecting, collating, and publishing data had to see that they reinforced the officially sponsored faith in the social system's superiority.

Two topics only are discussed here—the partial and preliminary attempts to make over the family, and the annihilation of Jews.

Like Soviet and Chinese officials, those in Nazi Germany tried to break down the family, and more than in the other two states they wanted to increase fertility. One avowed purpose of the Hitler Youth, for instance, was to reduce parental influence, whereas on the other hand such anti-feminist slogans as *Kinder, Kirche, Küche* (Children, Church, Kitchen) were given substance by decrees granting subsidies to parents of large families. One of Heinrich Himmler's titles was Reich Commissar for Strengthening German Folkdom,[42] and he and his assistants proposed a number of

[42] His main function, of course, was to head the *Schutzstaffel*, or SS ("Security Guard"), but in fact Himmler was more important than any formal designation would suggest: he was the main liaison between Party and State (*cf.* Hilberg, 1967, p. 134).

means of improving—from the Nazi point of view—Europe's racial composition (Koehl, 1957). SS-men were given weekend leaves in order to impregnate women that the Party had selected for their racial characteristics, and this effort to bypass the family, though not successful, is important as an indication of the regime's intent. In the words of Martin Bormann, second only to Hitler in the Party structure, "After the war, those women who have lost husbands, or who do not get husbands, should enter a marriage-like relationship with preferably one man, from which should result as many children as possible." [43]

The most notorious expression of the Nazis' demographic policies was their campaign to exterminate the Jews. In what ways was this specific, in what ways part of the general totalitarian pattern?

That anti-Semitism was not restricted to National Socialism everyone knows,[44] and the conventional attacks on Jews, which in the 1920s the Party had used to rouse revolutionary passions, were rationalized very soon after the Nazis came to power. There were to be "no more beerhouse brawling and indiscriminate parading of uniforms and banners" (Reitlinger, 1953, p. 7). As late as 1938, Hermann Göring (Deputy to Hitler and Commander of the Air Force) was protesting that random demonstrations against Jewish businessmen "don't harm the Jew, but me, because I am responsible for the coordination of the German economy" (Hilberg, 1967, p. 26). Nazism was distinguished from other versions of anti-Semitism, in short, by the Party's insistence that Jews be degraded in an orderly fashion, and that this degradation was carried to the "final solution" of organized mass murder.

The first step in this process was **to define** Jews.[45] In the Reichstag of the 1890s the anti-Semitic faction had been unable to identify the group they wanted to attack precisely enough to write discriminatory laws. The Nazis found a way to link the long Christian tradition against Judaism with an attack on Jews who had become irreligious or been converted to Christianity. By the original proposal, all persons with at least one (religiously)

[43] The stipulation "after the war" was made, of course, only to prevent a drastic decline in morale: if the plan had been made public immediately, "not every soldier forthwith would desire that in event of his death his wife or his betrothed should beget children with another man" (Hale, 1957). The whole of Bormann's memorandum is a fascinating admixture of Nazi ideology, opportunist checks on its immediate application, and such progressive ideas as, for instance, that the legal distinction between legitimate and illegitimate births must be abolished.

[44] Hilberg (1967, Chapter 1) gives in parallel columns items from the canon law of the Catholic Church or from the secular laws of pre-Nazi Germany and those decreed under Hitler. The overlap in many instances in startling.

[45] According to one school of thought this was not only unnecessary, but silly. Karl Lueger, an anti-Semitic mayor of nineteenth-century Vienna, was famous for his aphorism, "Wer Jude ist, bestimme ich!" (*I decide who is a Jew*). And later Himmler wrote to one of his underlings, "Do not publish the decree defining Jews. Such foolish precision ties our hands."

Jewish grandparent would be categorized as a (racial) Jew. But this was not sufficient to draw a rigorous line between "Aryan" and "non-Aryan." [46] Party experts and the Ministry of the Interior disagreed on how to differentiate the two castes being established (Hilberg, 1967, p. 46), and the problem was not wholly solved by the Nuremberg decree that in 1935 set suitable relations between Jews and Gentiles. (1) Those Jewish by "race" but Christian by religion were repeatedly granted certain concessions; as one example out of many, when their deportation from Holland was postponed, some few were saved from destruction (*ibid.*, p. 375). (2) The *"Mischlinge,"* of part Jewish and part non-Jewish family background, were categorized by the proportion of Jewish "blood," their religion, the "race" of their spouse, etc. Still in 1941 the *Mischlinge* were "unfinished business." The Party wanted to exterminate them, the State ministries to sterilize them, and the civil service to leave them alone (*ibid.*, p. 269). In the Nazi-occupied countries with their own tradition of anti-Semitism, the confusion was compounded (e.g., on Hungary, *ibid.*, p. 513).

Until the outbreak of the war, the denigration of Jews was by legal or quasi-legal methods—ousting them from the civil service, professions, and business; subjecting them to special taxes, wage regulations, and rationing; fining them a billion marks to pay for the damage in anti-Semitic riots. All of these Hilberg classifies as the second stage—**expropriation.**

Various attempts were made to free Germany of Jews through forcible **emigration**—for example, to induce the Western powers to ransom Jews by assisting them to move to Madagascar or some other equivalent of Siberia. When this plan failed, "the most fanatical" of the racists, as Reitlinger terms Reinhardt Heydrich,[47] believed that small nations might be used as compulsory dumping grounds for German Jews, and this policy continued for the first year and a half of the war. Some thousands of Jews were bundled into freight trains and transported to Vichy France; many more were pushed into Poland, to join there the two million Jews who had fallen into the Gestapo's hands when the Nazi-Soviet Friendship Pact was signed. Subsequently thousands more were shipped still farther east, particularly to the area of Riga and Minsk.

Preparatory to these moves, both German and Polish Jews were con-

---

[46] In Sanskrit, "Aryan" meant "noble" or "a nobleman"; thus, like many of the locutions that people use to designate themselves, it had overtones of greatness or superiority. Properly used, *Aryan* now refers to the Indo-European group of languages or to the language from which they all hypothetically derived; but long before Hitler, many believed the racially heterogeneous peoples who spoke these related languages to be biologically one. As the great nineteenth-century linguist Max Müller put it, "To me an ethnologist who speaks of Aryan race, Aryan blood, Aryan eyes and hair, is as great a sinner as a linguist who speaks of a dolichocephalic dictionary or a brachycephalic grammar."

[47] Chief of the Reichssicherheitshauptamt, which controlled the Gestapo (Secret State Police) and the Criminal Police.

centrated into ghettos. In the fall of 1940 authorities closed off the Warsaw ghetto, for example; 360,000 Jews were congregated in an area that normally housed 160,000 people. It was left to the Jewish welfare organization to provide food, mainly a weak brew. "By the end of 1941 there were 100,000 people living on this soup which had sometimes to be made of hay" (Reitlinger, 1953, pp. 58–59). The conditions were murderous, and many died. When the deaths in the Warsaw ghetto hovered around 5,000 per month, a government official reported laconically, "The first case of hunger-cannibalism was recorded" (Hilberg, 1967, p. 172).

But was this mass murder in the full sense? "It does not seem," in Reitlinger's opinion, "that at this period systematic extermination of the Jews was considered" (p. 59; cf. Poliakov, 1954, p. 2). Indeed, in 1939 two SS-men had been courtmartialed for murdering fifty Jews and sentenced to nine and three years of imprisonment, respectively (Reitlinger, 1953, p. 33). Seemingly, the Nazis' Endlösung—final solution—of the Jewish problem meant total emigration until July 31, 1941. This was some six weeks after the Nazi invasion of the Soviet Union had started, and shortly before the United States and Japan entered the war. In short, around the time that the European combat developed into World War II, "a new policy of annihilation was inaugurated" (Hilberg, 1967, p. 262). However, in none of the subsequent voluminous correspondence directing the slaughter was the policy openly stated. Killing centers were referred to collectively as "the East," individually as "labor camps," "concentration camps," "PW camps," even "transit camps"; killing was usually called by the same term used in the Soviet Union, "special treatment" (ibid., p. 619). In the West these efforts to conceal the operation were aided by the fact that rumors about killing centers were mixed with false statements borrowed from propaganda that the Allies had used against Germany in World War I, for instance, that humans were boiled down to make soap (ibid., p. 624).

As the German armies moved east into Russia, they were followed by four Einsatzgruppen, or Action Groups, which operated in the field. Action Group A was assigned to the Baltic countries, up to the outskirts of Leningrad; Action Group B to the area of White Russia between Warsaw and Moscow; Action Group C to the major portion of the Ukraine, including Kiev and Kharkov; and Action Group D to Crimea and the Caucasus. Their function was to check the conduct of German military commanders, and to supervise the murder of Jews, Gypsies, and Communist commissars.

Basically, the procedure of "Resettlement" was the same everywhere. Jews who could produce no sort of protection certificate were collected in market places or large buildings, herded into trains, buses, lorries, or sledge carts and taken to the woods or moors, where the burial pits had been prepared. . . . A Semitic appearance or a neighborly denunciation was enough. Thus numerous Tatars, Gypsies, and people of Oriental appearance were often included (Reitlinger, 1953, pp. 203–204).

The main death camp was four kilometers from Auschwitz (in Polish, Oswiecim), a small town in Upper Silesia. It was adjacent to several rail lines, close to forced-labor camps, and yet in a relatively isolated site. Its director, Rudolf Höss, a former convict, told the Allied judges at the Nuremberg trial that under his administration 2.5 million persons were killed at the camp. According to the estimates of both Hilberg and Reitlinger, the actual total of those killed was about a million. It is significant that Höss, the ambitious Nazi bureaucrat, chose a higher figure. His SS service file commended him as "a true pioneer in this field." At the railroad siding, two SS-physicians divided newcomers between able-bodied workers and victims by pointing their canes right or left. Their rule of thumb depended mostly on age and sex, and the percentage denoted fit for labor varied greatly from one shipment to another. Höss used hydrogen cyanide crystals for killing his charges, rather than the less efficient carbon monoxide from internal-combustion engines. He initiated a routine deception that saved time and trouble: candidates for gassing were informed that they were to take a shower, so that they undressed themselves and walked into the gas chamber. The conditions of the forced laborers at Auschwitz, on the other hand, were no different from those in other Nazi camps.

How many Jews *did* the Nazis kill? In the Nuremberg indictment in 1945 the figure 5,721,800 was given, and in most subsequent accounts this has been rounded up to 6 million. This total was derived by subtracting the number of survivors from the prewar Jewish population, which for many countries is highly conjectural. The difficulty in establishing a more precise figure derives not only from the paucity of accurate data but from the ambiguity of the question. As we have noted, the delimitation of "Jews" caused the German authorities almost as much trouble as that of "kulaks" or "saboteurs" to the Soviet officials. And what is meant by "kill"? At Theresienstadt, the relatively indulgent concentration camp set up especially for the elderly and for severely wounded war veterans, a quarter of the inmates (about 33,000 out of 140,000) died from the conditions they were subjected to (Hilberg, 1967, p. 283). More generally,

That prisoners should be cheated of their food and forced to "organize" in order to live, that they should be beaten to death at their work in order to give their guards exercise, that they should drop from exhaustion at evening *Appell* because of the inability of these guards to count, were inevitable things, given the nature of their masters (Reitlinger, 1953, p. 121).

The process of destruction in the labor camps and ghettos differed from that in the killing centers, but genocide, as defined by the United Nations, includes both. If we are to use the term at all precisely, we cannot define it broadly with respect to Nazi operations but narrowly with respect to counterparts in other totalitarian States.

From SS records, which he believes are fairly accurate and err, if at all,

Door to a gas chamber at the Dachau concentration camp. The words under the skull read: "Caution, gas. Mortal danger. Do not open." The sign above gives time when door may be opened again (*Documentation Française*).

in exaggerating the extraordinary mortality, Reitlinger estimated the total number of Jews killed between 4,194,200 and 4,581,200 (p. 501). More than a third of the missing European Jews, and of German Jews perhaps as many as four-fifths, died from overwork, disease, hunger, and neglect. Two-thirds, or roughly 3 million, were exterminated directly. Hilberg also gives 3 million as the number annihilated in the killing centers, and to this he adds 1.4 million in the area of operations of the *Einsatzgruppen* (900,000 authenticated plus a more approximate 500,000 not tabulated) and 700,000 "aggravated deaths" in ghettos and elsewhere. His total, thus, is 5.1 million. Even these figures, monstrous as they are, understate the number of Nazi victims, as both pertain only to Jews, who constituted the major component. The total is considerably larger, for it includes also other "inferior" "races"

British troops clearing the Belsen concentration camp (*Imperial War Museum, London*).

(Gypsies, Slavs, Soviet ethnic minorities), political opponents (democrats, socialists, Catholics, Communists), and bystanders.

## Summary

Ever since Yugoslavia broke with Moscow in 1948, more and more of the conflicts within the Communist world, which Stalin half-succeeded in suppressing or at least hiding, have come out into the open. Western observers, many of whom once overstressed the oneness of the Communist "monolith," have sometimes swung over to an exaggeration of the multiplicity of Communism. To insist on the fact that there are important differences between the Soviet Union and China, or between East Germany and Rumania, or between all of them and Nazi Germany, should not mean that we overlook the common characteristics that distinguish these societies from all others. Even between Nazism and Communism, distinct species of the totalitarian genus, the differences are less striking than the parallels.

With respect specifically to population, we have noted similiarities in family and migration policies and practices. But the key point is mortality, the demographic feature that most clearly distinguishes totalitarianism. Just as the death rates of the great civilizations of Asia contained, in Mallory's words, "a constant famine factor," so the vital statistics of totalitarian states include a constant terror factor. For not only has the population been depleted periodically by mass purges, but these have a marked effect on the age structure and sex ratio, and thus on the birth and death rates during the whole of the subsequent generation. Causes of death have included not only diseases, accidents, and old age, but also war and civil war, purges, forced labor, and man-made famines. These are not accidental features but reflect the essence of totalitarian systems, the "constant balance between oppression and relaxation." [48]

In the Soviet Union the total population deficit up to 1959 from both extraordinary deaths and nonbirths is of the order of 80 million or more: 25 million during the taking of power and the wrecking of the capitalist economy; another 10 million during the collectivization, denomadization, purge of the Party, and russification of the 1930s; and 45 million during World War II and its aftermath. In this category political rather than economic or social factors have dominated.

These depletions in the population have not been randomly distributed in any sense. The totalitarian system has been a decisive factor in determining the population composition by nationality, by religion, by social class, by rural or urban residence. Among cohorts aged 32 and over in 1959, there were only six males to every ten females, and the consequences for postwar marital and fertility patterns hardly need to be specified. Efforts to encourage a high fertility, though they undoubtedly have had some influence, have not been successful. One reason is the Party's initial hostility to the family, but more important is the fact, as Martin Bormann put it concerning Nazi Germany, that the Party "cannot order the women and girls to beget children." The effort to increase family size was frustrated also by the necessity of bringing as many females as possible into the Soviet labor force. Males had been killed off in monstrous numbers, and the new cohorts that were to replace them were initially extremely small. In 1955, by Eason's estimate, more than half of the labor force was female, and more than two-thirds of women aged 16 and over were gainfully employed. But in the 1960s, when the larger cohorts born in the postwar years began to seek jobs, the economy suffered from what is esoterically termed a relative surplus population—or, more prosaically, mass unemployment.

In short, the population trends of a totalitarian state, like all other social phenomena, are shaped by the Party's drive for total power. The word *shaped* is used advisedly: most social events are in response to policy decisions, but not necessarily the response that the Party planned. Yet the terror has also been functional, as some sociologists would say, in maintaining the

[48] Zbigniew K. Brzezinski, *The Permanent Purge: Politics in Soviet Totalitarianism*, Harvard University Press, Cambridge, Mass., 1956, p. 168.

regime, and not merely in the obvious sense that actual or potential oppositionists were obliterated. If we accept an estimate of 50 million as the total extraordinary mortality in the rural sector, what effect did this have on the economy?

With 50 (or 40, or 30) million more people in the village after the War, could the rate of extraction of agricultural "surplus" have been as high as it was? If not: Could recovery in urban living standards from the postwar low in 1946 have been as fast as it was? Could there have been as large an urban population, and hence as rapid reconstruction and further economic growth, as there was in the late 'forties and the 'fifties? . . .

If both the total and the rural population of the USSR were now, say, 50 million larger than they are, the urban population would comprise not about 45 per cent of the total population as it does [48 per cent in the 1959 census], but about 35 per cent (Grossman, 1958).

The period since the mid-1950s constitutes a new era in the Soviet Union, but the new was linked to the old by the continuity of the country's institutions. Should one stress that the forced-labor population is much smaller than at its postwar peak—or that forced labor continues as one element of the economic-punitive system; that the Chechen-Ingush minority has been permitted to return to its homeland—or that the Volga Germans have not; that the rule of the Party is less harsh—or that it remains the implacable rule of a tiny minority? Since the early 1920s Western statesmen, experts, and intellectuals have seen each turn in Soviet policy as a mellowing, and their prognoses were usually wrong.[49] In a demographic analysis, moreover, the continuity is inescapable: even if Stalin had been succeeded by a democrat, the trends in the economy and the society would still have been determined in part by the gaps he had made in the population.

The differences and parallels between the extraordinary mortality under Nazi and Communist auspices can be summed up as follows:

1. The Nazis lost the war. Their own statements, their own records, were used to make a legal case against them at Nuremberg. Otherwise we would have had to depend mainly on the testimony of former camp inmates, the often biased source on which we must rely for much of our information about labor camps in Communist countries. Until almost the end of the war, a false death certificate was in principle prepared for each person the Nazis exterminated, and this fabrication might have withstood any but minute scrutiny. For even when the evidence became overwhelming, the ordinary man in the West found it difficult to believe that death-camps were part of the world he thought he knew.

[49] For a fascinating review of some of these overoptimistic appraisals, see Bertram D. Wolfe, "Communist Ideology and Soviet Foreign Policy," in *The Realities of World Communism*, edited by William Petersen, Prentice-Hall, Englewood Cliffs, N.J., 1963, pp. 19–40.

**2.** The Nazi ideology was *racist;* the Communists oppose *class* enemies.[50] The difference is important but not fundamental, for a person is no more responsible for his "class origin" than for his blood type. Moreover, terror generates a momentum of its own. Both the Nazis and the Communists have used hardened criminals under the supervision of self-hardened zealots, and under these circumstances the careful discrimination between the "guilty"—however defined—and the innocent is impossible. The slaughter begins in different sectors of the population and is concentrated there, but in both cases spreads to the whole society.

**3.** The Soviet terror is more rational, or less rational, than the Nazi. Both points have been made by various writers, and both have an element of truth. The Soviet regime never erected gas chambers and crematoriums, but it has not hesitated to exterminate large numbers of persons by other means. The massacre of some 14,000 Polish army officers in Katyn Woods is a well known example.[51] Moreover, large areas of the Soviet Union constitute, under the conditions of life imposed on camp dwellers, natural killing centers. Forced labor was apparently more important in Soviet than in Nazi camps (Reitlinger, 1953, p. 115). The Soviet rationalization of forced labor is that it "reforges" the criminals, whereas the dominant purpose of Nazi camps was to punish. Nazi prisoners were poorly fed, but until shortages developed throughout Germany, probably the food was better than in Soviet camps, where differential hunger was used as a spur to harder work.[52]

How Chinese forced labor compares with its two counterparts we do not know in detail. At least in intention, as manifested during the Great Leap Forward, China goes beyond the prior dimensions of terror, with forced labor generalized to virtually the whole of the population. Especially in China the manic-depressive cycle has constituted the opposite of rational

[50] However, the tendency toward xenophobia in the Marxist tradition is greater than most persons realize. Frederick Engels wrote two pamphlets on the national question so devoid of socialist feeling that many believed they had been composed by a Prussian general; and Marx, his good friend and collaborator, wrote to congratulate him on his "exceedingly clever" analysis. The key point was to classify European nationalities into two types—one, Germany, Poland, and Hungary, which are destined to triumph, and the other comprising "ruins of peoples, leftovers . . . subject to the nation which had become the bearer of historical development" (see Bertram D. Wolfe, *Marxism: One Hundred Years in the Life of a Doctrine*, Dial Press, New York, 1965, Chapter 2). The Russian nationalism of Soviet Communism and the Han nationalism of Chinese, while contradicting the whole spirit of Western social democracy, yet derive from one important element of the Marxist tradition.

[51] For a survey of the evidence, see Rozek, *op. cit.*, Chapters 4–5.

[52] A number of persons who survived both Nazi and Soviet camps have written interesting comparative reports; see in particular Margarete Buber, *Under Two Dictators*, Gollancz, London, 1949. Mrs. Buber, a German oppositionist Communist, was arrested in Moscow in 1938 and sent to Siberia. During the Nazi-Soviet Friendship Pact, she and a number of other former German Communists were handed over to the Gestapo, and she spent another five years in the Ravensbrück camp.

planning: what is accomplished in one phase is ruthlessly destroyed in the next.

Totalitarian ideology is based on what in German is called a *Stufenlehre*, a doctrine of stages. All analysis, all planning, begin not from the empirical present but from the inevitable, perfect future. This last stage in mankind's forward development is typically not clearly depicted, except that it is homogenized into a "classless" (or *Judenfrei*, "Jewless") sameness, with rural-urban and other structural distinctions reduced to the minimum. The road to this inescapable paradise is clearly seen only by the Party, whose function it is to move the rest of the population toward its destiny. The drive for industrialization, as Barrington Moore remarked of the Soviet Union, thus "comes almost wholly from the top," which must substitute its impetus for "the adventurous spirit that has built the great industrial and financial empires of the Western world." A built-in stagnation lies just beneath the surface, and whenever the elite's drive is slackened, the apathy of the population becomes apparent.[53] In all totalitarian countries the problem of squaring military-economic advance with political cohesion continually invites a terrorist solution, and this generic feature overrides the specifics of this or that example.

## Suggestions for Further Reading

Elsewhere I have collaborated with a political scientist in compiling a general bibliography on Communism.[54] This introductory note is restricted to books and articles on population. Lorimer, 1946, the standard work on the prewar population, has no full counterpart concerning the last several decades. Several collections of articles can be recommended, especially U.S. Congress, 1966, but also Milbank Memorial Fund, 1960 and a special issue of *Population*, "L'U.R.S.S. et sa population," Vol. 13:2-*bis*, June 1958. These can be usefully supplemented by more specific works on famines (Fisher, 1927; Ammende, 1936; Dalrymple, 1964–65); forced labor (Gorky, 1935; Dallin and Nicolaevsky, 1947; Swianiewicz, 1965; Barton, 1962); medical institutions (Mark Field, 1957); fertility (Schlesinger, 1949; Heer, 1965); ethnic minorities (Kolarz, 1955; Conquest, 1960; Decter, 1963; Vardys, 1965); internal migration (Roof, 1960); statistics (Jasny, 1957; Gordon, 1957; Holubnychy, 1958; Eason, 1963); population ideology (Sauvy, 1948; Brackett, 1967).

The first period of Chinese Communism is well documented; Walker, 1955*a* is excellent on politics, Li, 1959 on economics. For the later period U.S. Congress 1967 (including many of the articles not otherwise cited) affords the best symposium on social-economic development. Specifically, Aird, 1967*b* is the most com-

---

[53] Barrington Moore, Jr., *Terror and Progress—U.S.S.R.* Harvard University Press, Cambridge, Mass., 1954, p. 71.

[54] William Petersen and Paul E. Zinner, "World Communism: A Reading List for Nonspecialists," in Petersen, *Realities of World Communism*, pp. 202–220.

plete and up-to-date analysis of population trends, Galenson, 1967 an interesting discussion of statistical sources. On population data see also Orleans, 1960; Aird, 1960. Yang, 1965, the standard work on the Chinese family under Communism, should be supplemented by Tien, 1963. On population redistribution, Orleans, 1960; Tien, 1964; and Aird, 1967*b* are informative.

Three works on Nazi population practices are excellent. Koehl, 1957 concentrates on resettlement; Hilberg, 1961 and Reitlinger, 1953 are parallel analyses of the annihilation of Europe's Jews.

AIRD, JOHN S. 1960. "The Present and Prospective Population of Mainland China," in Milbank Memorial Fund, 1960, pp. 95–140.

———. 1962. "Population Policy in Mainland China," *Population Studies,* **16,** 38–57.

———. 1967*a.* "Estimating China's Population," *Annals of the American Academy of Political and Social Science,* **369,** 61–72.

° ———. 1967*b.* "Population Growth and Distribution in Mainland China," in U.S. Congress, 1967, pp. 341–401.

AMMENDE, EWALD. 1936. *Human Life in Russia.* Allen & Unwin, London.

ANDRONOV, L. 1966. "China This Autumn," *New Times* (Moscow), November 30 and December 14.

ARAB-OGLY, E. 1966. "Scientific Calculation or Reliance on Spontaneity?" *Literaturnaya Gazeta,* June 11, translated in *Atlas,* September, pp. 24–26.

ARMSTRONG, TERENCE. 1968. "The Soviet North," *Survey,* No. 67, pp. 116–121.

° ASHBROOK, ARTHUR G., JR. 1967. "Main Lines of Communist Economic Policy," in U.S. Congress, 1967, pp. 15–44.

BARCLAY, GEORGE W. 1950. "China's Population Problem: A Closer View," *Pacific Affairs,* **23,** 184–192.

° BARTON, PAUL. 1962. "An End to Concentration Camps?" *Problems of Communism,* **11,** 38–46.

BEERMANN, R. 1961. "The Parasites Law," *Soviet Studies,* **13,** 191–205.

BIALER, SEWERYN. 1964. "How Russians Rule Russia," *Problems of Communism,* **13,** 45–52.

B[IRABEN], J[EAN-] N[OEL]. 1960. "La structure par âge de la population de l'U.R.S.S.," *Population,* **15,** 894–898.

BRACKETT, JAMES W. 1962. "Demographic Trends and Population Policy in the Soviet Union," in U.S. Congress, Joint Economic Committee. *Dimensions of Soviet Economic Power,* Part VII. Washington, D.C., pp. 487–589.

° ———. 1967. "The Evolution of Marxist Theories on Population: Marxism Recognizes the Population Problem." Paper prepared for the annual meeting of the Population Association of America, 1967.

———, and JOHN W. DEPAUW. 1966. "Population Policy and Demographic Trends in the Soviet Union," in U.S. Congress, 1966, pp. 593–702.

BUCK, JOHN LOSSING. 1966. "Food Grain Production in Mainland China before and during the Communist Regime," in Buck, Owen L. Dawson, and Yuan-li Wu. *Food and Agriculture in Communist China.* Hoover Institution on War, Revolution, and Peace. Praeger, New York, pp. 3–72.

° CHAMBERLIN, WILLIAM HENRY. 1934. *Russia's Iron Age.* Little, Brown, Boston.

CHANDRASEKHAR, S. 1959a. *China's Population: Census and Vital Statistics.* Hong Kong University Press, Hong Kong.

———. 1959b. "China's Population Problems: A Report," *Population Review,* 3, 17–38.

CHANG CHIH-YI. 1949. "China's Population Problem—A Chinese View," *Pacific Affairs,* 22, 339–356.

CHAPMAN, JANET. 1964. "The Minimum Wage in the USSR," *Problems of Communism,* 13, 76–79.

CHEN NAI-RUENN. 1967. *Chinese Economic Statistics: A Handbook for Mainland China.* Aldine, Chicago.

CH'EN TA. 1958. "New China's Population Census of 1953 and Its Relations to National Reconstruction and Demographic Research," *Bulletin de l'Institut International de Statistique,* 36, 255–271.

° CONQUEST, ROBERT. 1960. *The Soviet Deportation of Nationalities.* Macmillan, London.

° DALLIN, DAVID J., and BORIS I. NICOLAEVSKY. 1947. *Forced Labor in Soviet Russia.* Yale University Press, New Haven.

DALRYMPLE, DANA G. 1964. "The Soviet Famine of 1932–1934," *Soviet Studies,* 15, 250–284.

———. 1965. "The Soviet Famine of 1932–34: Some Further References," *Soviet Studies,* 16, 471–474.

DAVIDOFF, GEORGES. 1957. "De la médecine et de la sécurité sociale en Chine," *Population,* 12, 679–694.

° DECTER, MOSHE. 1963. "The Status of the Jews in the Soviet Union," *Foreign Affairs,* 41, 420–430.

DURDIN, PEGGY. 1960. "Medicine in China: A Revealing Story," *New York Times Magazine,* February 28.

° EASON, WARREN W. 1959a. "Comparisons of the United States and Soviet Economies: The Labor Force," in U.S. Congress, Joint Economic Committee, *Comparisons of the United States and Soviet Economies,* Part 1. 86th Congress, 1st Session, Washington, D.C., pp. 73–93.

———. 1959b. "The Soviet Population Today: An Analysis of the First Results of the 1959 Census," *Foreign Affairs,* 37, 598–606.

———. 1963. "The 1959 Census of Population of the U.S.S.R.," *Population Index,* 29, 117–120.

FESHBACH, MURRAY. 1966. "Manpower in the USSR: A Survey of Recent Trends and Prospects," in U.S. Congress, 1966, pp. 703–788.

FIELD, ALICE W. 1932. *Protection of Women and Children in Soviet Russia.* Dutton, New York.

° FIELD, MARK G. 1957. *Doctor and Patient in Soviet Russia.* Harvard University Press, Cambridge, Mass.

———. 1966. "Health Personnel in the Soviet Union: Achievements and Problems," *American Journal of Public Health,* 56, 1904–1920.

FISHER, H. H. 1927. *The Famine in Soviet Russia, 1919–1923.* Macmillan, New York.

° GALENSON, WALTER. 1967. "The Current State of Chinese Economic Studies," in U.S. Congress, 1967, pp. 1–13.

GORDON, MYRON K. 1957. "Notes on Recent Soviet Population Statistics and Research," *Population Index,* **23,** 2–16.

* GORKY, MAXIM, *et al.* 1935. *Belomor: An Account of the Construction of the New Canal between the White Sea and the Baltic Sea.* Smith and Haas, New York.

* GROSSMAN, GREGORY. 1958. "Thirty Years of Soviet Industrialization," *Soviet Survey,* **26,** 15–21.

GSOVSKI, VLADIMIR. 1959. "The Soviet Union's Revised Criminal Code," *New Leader,* April 27, pp. 10–13.

HALE, ORON J. 1957. "Adolf Hitler and the Post-War German Birthrate: An Unpublished Memorandum," *Journal of Central European Affairs,* **17,** 166–173.

HALLE, FANNINA W. 1934. *Woman in Soviet Russia.* Routledge, London.

* HEER, DAVID M. 1965. "Abortion, Contraception, and Population Policy in the Soviet Union," *Demography,* **2,** 531–539.

———. 1968. "The Demographic Transition in the Russian Empire and the Soviet Union," *Journal of Social History,* **1,** 193–240.

———, and JUDITH G. BRYDEN. 1966. "Family Allowances and Fertility in the Soviet Union," *Soviet Studies,* **18,** 153–163.

* HILBERG, RAUL. 1961. *The Destruction of the European Jews.* Quadrangle Paperbacks, Chicago.

HOLUBNYCHY, VSEVOLOD. 1958. "Organization of Statistical Observation in the U.S.S.R.," *American Statistician,* **12,** 13–17.

JASNY, NAUM. 1957. *The Soviet 1956 Statistical Handbook: A Commentary.* Michigan State University Press, East Lansing, Michigan.

JONES, EDWIN F. 1967. "The Emerging Pattern of China's Economic Revolution," in U.S. Congress, 1967, pp. 77–96.

JUVILER, PETER. 1963. "Marriage and Divorce," *Survey,* No. 48, pp. 104–117.

KANTNER, JOHN F. 1959. "The Population of the Soviet Union," in U.S. Congress, Joint Economic Committee. *Comparisons of the United States and Soviet Economies,* Part 1. 80th Congress, 1st Session, Washington, D.C., pp. 31–71.

———. 1960. "Recent Demographic Trends in the USSR," in Milbank Memorial Fund, 1960, pp. 35–63.

* KHRUSHCHEV, NIKITA S. 1956. "The Crimes of the Stalin Era: Special Report to the 20th Congress of the Communist Party of the Soviet Union, Closed Session, February 24–25, 1956," *New Leader,* Section 2, July 16.

KIRBY, E. STUART. 1958. "Peiping's Growing Dilemma—Population," *Problems of Communism,* **7,** 36–41.

KOEHL, ROBERT L. 1957. *RKFDV: German Resettlement and Population Policy, 1939–1945.* Harvard University Press, Cambridge, Mass.

* KOLARZ, WALTER. 1955. *Russia and Her Colonies.* 3rd Ed. Praeger, New York.

KRADER, LAWRENCE, and JOHN AIRD. 1959. "Sources of Demographic Data on Mainland China," *American Sociological Review,* **24,** 623–630.

KUCERA, JINDRICH. 1954. "Soviet Nationality Policy: The Linguistic Controversy," *Problems of Communism,* **3,** 24–29.

KULISCHER, EUGENE M., and MICHAEL K. ROOF. 1956. "A New Look at the Soviet Population Structure of 1939," *American Sociological Review,* **21,** 280–290.

LARSEN, MARION R. 1967. "China's Agriculture under Communism," in U.S. Congress, 1967, pp. 197–267.

LI CHOH-MING. 1959. *Economic Development of Communist China: An Appraisal of the First Five Years of Industrialization.* University of California Press, Berkeley.

———. 1960. "Economic Development," *China Quarterly,* No. 1, pp. 35–50.

LINDSAY, MICHAEL. 1960. "Agrarian Policy and Communist Motivation," *China Quarterly,* No. 1, pp. 15–17.

* LORIMER, FRANK. 1946. *The Population of the Soviet Union: History and Prospects.* League of Nations. Princeton University Press, Princeton, N.J.

MARTSCHENKO, BASILIUS. 1953. "Soviet Population Trends, 1926–1939" (in Russian with an English summary). Research Program on the USSR, New York.

MAZUR, D. PETER. 1967. "Fertility among Ethnic Groups in the USSR," *Demography,* 4, 172–195.

MILBANK MEMORIAL FUND. 1960. *Population Trends in Eastern Europe, the USSR and Mainland China.* New York.

* MONKHOUSE, ALLAN. 1934. *Moscow, 1911–1933.* Little, Brown, Boston.

MYERS, ROBERT J. 1964. "Analysis of Mortality in the Soviet Union According to 1958–59 Life Tables," *Transactions of the Society of Actuaries,* 16, 309–317.

NASH, EDMUND. 1966. "Recent Changes in Labor Controls in the Soviet Union," in U.S. Congress, 1966, pp. 849–870.

ORLEANS, LEO A. 1959. "The Recent Growth of China's Urban Population," *Geographical Review,* 49, 43–57.

* ———. 1960. "Population Redistribution in Communist China," in Milbank Memorial Fund, 1960, pp. 141–156.

———. 1965. "Population Statistics: An Illusion," *China Quarterly,* No 21, pp. 168–178.

* PEARCY, G. ETZEL. 1966. "Mainland China: Geographic Strengths and Weaknesses," *U.S. Department of State Bulletin,* August 29.

PEREVEDENTSEV, V. 1967. "Controversy about the Census," *Literaturnaya Gazeta,* January 11; translated in *Current Digest of the Soviet Press,* 19 (February 1), 15–16.

POLIAKOV, LÉON. 1954. *Harvest of Hate: The Nazi Program for the Destruction of the Jews of Europe.* Syracuse University Press, Syracuse, N.Y.

POPOV, A. Y. 1953. *Sovremennoe Mal'tusianstvo—Chelovekonenavistnichevskaya ideologiia imperialistov.* Gosudarstvennoe Izdatel'stvo Politicheskoe Literatur, Moscow.

PRESSAT, ROLAND. 1963a. "La natalité et la nuptialité en Union Soviétique," *Population,* 18, 777–786.

———. 1963b. "Les premières tables de mortalité de l'Union Soviétique, 1958–1959," *Population,* 18, 65–92.

RAVENHOLT, ALBERT. 1962. "The Human Price of China's Disastrous Food Shortage: A Refugee Doctor Describes His Patients," in American Universities Field Staff, *Reports,* East Asia Series. Vol. 10, No. 4.

———. 1967. "The Red Guards," in American Universities Field Staff, *Reports,* East Asia Series, Vol. 14, No. 3.

REITLINGER, GERALD. 1953. *The Final Solution: The Attempt to Exterminate the Jews of Europe, 1939–1945.* Beechhurst, New York.

RICH, STANLEY. 1959. "The Communes—Mao's 'Big Family,'" *Problems of Communism,* 8, 1–5.

ROEMER, MILTON I. 1962. "Highlights of Soviet Health Services," *Milbank Memorial Fund Quarterly*, **40**, 373–406.

ROOF, MICHAEL F. 1957. "Supplementary Note Concerning the Soviet Population Structure of 1939," *American Sociological Review*, **22**, 581–582.

* ———. 1960. "Recent Trends in Soviet Internal Migration Policies," Research Group for European Migration Problems, *Bulletin*, **8**, 1–18.

———, and FREDERICK A. LEEDY. 1959. "Population Redistribution in the Soviet Union, 1939–1956," *Geographical Review*, **49**, 208–221.

* ROUSSET, DAVID. 1959. "The New Tyranny in the Countryside," *Problems of Communism*, **8**, 5–13.

SARKER, SUBHASH CHANDRA. 1958. "Population Planning in China," *Population Review*, **2**, 49–58.

SAUVY, ALFRED. 1948. "Doctrine soviétique en matière de population," *Rivista Italiana de Demografia e Statistica*, **2**, 475–484.

SCHATTMAN, STEPHAN E. 1956. "Dogma vs. Science in Soviet Statistics," *Problems of Communism*, **5**, 30–36.

SCHLESINGER, RUDOLF. 1949. *Changing Attitudes in Soviet Russia: The Family in the U.S.S.R.* Routledge & Kegan Paul, London.

SCHWARZ, SOLOMON M. 1951. *The Jews in the Soviet Union.* Syracuse University Press, Syracuse, N.Y.

SELEGEN, GALINA V., and VICTOR P. PETROV. 1959. "Soviet People versus Population Census," *American Statistician*, **13**, 14–15.

SHAFFER, HARRY G. 1963. "A New Incentive for Soviet Managers," *Russian Review*, **22**, 410–416.

* SHIMKIN, DEMITRI B. 1960. "Demographic Changes and Socio-Economic Forces within the Soviet Union, 1939–59," in Milbank Memorial Fund, 1960, pp. 224–246.

SKINNER, G. WILLIAM. 1951. "A Study in Miniature of Chinese Population," *Population Studies*, **5**, 91–103.

SMITH, JESSICA. 1928. *Woman in Soviet Russia.* Vanguard, New York.

* STRONG, ANNA LOUISE. 1931. *The Soviets Conquer Wheat: The Drama of Collective Farming.* Holt, New York.

STRUMILIN, STANISLAV G. 1961. "Nos ressources de main-d'oeuvre et les perspectives: Une étude d'un économiste soviétique en 1922," *Population*, **16**, 249–258.

* SWIANIEWICZ, S. 1965. *Forced Labour and Economic Development: An Enquiry into the Experience of Soviet Industrialisation.* Royal Institute of International Affairs. Oxford University Press, London.

TAEUBER, IRENE B. 1956. "Population Policies in Communist China," *Population Index*, **22**, 261–274.

———. 1965. "Policies, Programs, and Decline of Birth Rates: China and the Chinese Populations of East Asia," in *Population Dynamics: International Action and Training Programs*, edited by Minoru Muramatsu and Paul A. Harper. Johns Hopkins Press, Baltimore, Md., pp. 99–104.

* TIEN, H. YUAN. 1963. "Birth Control in Mainland China: Ideology and Politics," *Milbank Memorial Fund Quarterly*, **41**, 269–290.

———. 1964. "The Demographic Significance of Organized Population Transfers in Communist China," *Demography*, **1**, 220–226.

U.S. Bureau of the Census. 1961. "The Size, Composition, and Growth of the Population of Mainland China," *International Population Statistics Report,* Series P–90, No. 15.

* U.S. Congress. Joint Economic Committee. 1966. *New Directions in the Soviet Economy.* Part III: *The Human Resources.* 89th Congress, 2nd Session, Washington, D.C.

* ———. ———. 1967. *An Economic Profile of Mainland China.* 2 Vols. Washington, D.C.

Vardys, V. Stanley. 1965. "Soviet Nationality Policy Since the XXII Party Congress," *Russian Review,* **24,** 323–340.

* Vernadsky, George 1961. *A History of Russia.* 5th Rev. Ed. Yale University Press, New Haven.

* Walker, Richard L. 1955a. *China Under Communism: The First Five Years.* Yale University Press, New Haven.

———. 1955b. "Collectivization in China: A Story of Betrayal," *Problems of Communism,* **4,** 1–12.

Wang, K. P. 1967. "The Mineral Resource Base of Communist China," in U.S. Congress, 1967, pp. 167–195.

Ways, Max. 1968. "The 'House of the Dead' Is Now the Liveliest Part of the U.S.S.R.," *Fortune,* August, pp. 112–115, 182–192.

Yang, C. K. 1965. *Chinese Communist Society: The Family and the Village.* MIT Press Paperback Edition, Cambridge, Mass.

# INDEX

Abarnel, Albert, 583n
Abel-Smith, Brian, 563, 570, 579
abortion, see birth control, methods
Abrams, Charles, 471–472, 481
Abramson, Harold J., 129, 134
Abramson, J. H., 273, 301
Abu-Lughod, Janet, 14n, 19, 604, 624
accidents, see mortality, causes of
acculturation, 115
  See also assimilation
Adams, John, 296n
Adams, Robert M., 371, 399
adolescent subfecundity, 176
Aetios, 379, 488
Afghanistan, 329t
Africa (-ns), Sub-Sahara
  culture, 102, 178n, 228, 247t, 424n, 590
  fertility, 350–351, 590, 600, 608, 613
  migration, 279, 280p, 282, 284–285, 295
  mortality, 570
  population, 31, 40, 63, 64, 103, 260, 327t, 328–329t, 347t, 351, 355, 357, 376n
  population data, 36–37, 593–594
  social-economic conditions, 176, 217, 221, 565p, 566p
  urban population 461, 463–465, 471, 606
  See also individual countries
Agarwala, S. N., 382, 397, 616t, 618–619, 624
age
  biologic vs. chronologic, 205

age (Cont.)
  classification of, 29, 61, 66–76
  errors in reporting, 60–63, 185, 590
  fertility and, 175–176, 178–180
  groups, 66–76, 662t
  heaping, 61–62, 385
  labor force by, 72–74, 262–263, 457
  median, 66–67, 443–445
  at menarche, 175–176
  at menopause, 176
  migration and, 262–264
  mortality and, 206–213, 224–226, 666–667
  sex ratio, 63–66
  See also marriage, age at; population structure
aged, the
  in China, 70
  dependent, 68–71
  health of, 70, 205–206
  problems of definition of, 29
  in U.S., 69–71
aging, 68–69, 204–205
agriculture
  advances in, 219–221
  British, 406–409
  Chinese, 388, 673–676, 678, 686
  hoe culture, 346
  origins of, 345–346, 365
  plantation, 132n
  rain vs. irrigation, 372–373, 388
  Soviet, 408, 632n, 640, 645–647, 649–650, 658–660, 695

NOTE: f stands for figure, n for footnote, p for photograph, and t for table.